# INDIANS, NRIs & THE LAW

# INDIANS, NRIs & THE LAW

**ANIL MALHOTRA**
**RANJIT MALHOTRA**

*Foreword by*

Soli J. Sorabjee

Former Attorney General for India

Universal
Law Publishing Co. Pvt. Ltd.
NEW DELHI - INDIA

2012 Edition

ISBN: 978-93-5035-124-6



*Published by*
**UNIVERSAL LAW PUBLISHING CO. PVT. LTD.**
C-FF-1A, Dilkhush Industrial Estate,
(Near Azadpur Metro Station) G.T. Karnal Road,
Delhi-110 033
Tel.: 011-27438103, 27215334, 42381334
Fax : 011-27458529
E-mail *(For sales inquiries)* : sales@unilawbooks.com
E-mail *(For editorial inquiries)* : edit@unilawbooks.com
*Website* : www.unilawbooks.com

Recommended citation: Anil Malhotra & Ranjit Malhotra, *Indians, NRIs & the Law*, (New Delhi: Universal Law Publishing Co. Pvt. Ltd., 2012).



*Computer Typeset* at Aesthetic and *Printed* at Nice Printing Press, Sahibabad (U.P.)

*To our parents*

Justice, justice you shall pursue (deut. 16:20)

*Soli J. Sorabjee*

Senior Advocate, Supreme Court of India
Former Attorney General for India

# FOREWORD

Indians, NRIs and the Law, as the title of the book reveals, is a commendable compilation of articles written by the authors on problems and legal issues which pertain to Non-Resident Indians and all those persons who may be closely or remotely associated with them. With large number of Indians migrating abroad and the nomenclature of Non-Resident Indian (NRI), Person of Indian Origin (PIO) and Overseas Citizen of India (OCI) coined by the Government of India to describe them, their problems and grievances have proliferated, sans any legislative remedies or administrative redress. It is in this milieu that the innovative writing of the authors throws light on their perspectives which concerns India and the NRIs. This pioneer work is a beacon in the dark firmament of the dilemma which ail the NRIs and all those who are connected with them.

The contents of the book are a focused study on every conceivable issue with which an NRI is confronted. Various aspects of these problems include subjects like marriage, divorce, spousal maintenance, child abduction, domestic and inter-country adoptions, succession, inheritance, probate and wills, nationality, immigration, citizenship as also the new questions on the issue of surrogate motherhood. The perceptions on immigration, managed migration, citizenship and nationality are grey areas which have been very well described in the book. Due to lack of authentic material and proper guidance on these new subjects, a large number of fellow citizens are sometimes misguided to utilize channels of illegal immigration which at times impacts severely on their lives.

In this backdrop, the book serves as a good eye opener in highlighting these problem areas with practical answers. Likewise, the quest of the NRI to become an Indian citizen is well handled. In the myriad predicament zone of Family Law relating to abandoned spouses, foreign divorce decrees, inter- parental child removal and inter-country adoptions, the book contains very good references which would provide realistic legal options. Surrogacy, an unchartered and adrift concept, is dealt with succinct clarity. The appraisal of Family Laws vis a vis Customs and Religion has been well evaluated from the NRI outlook or the foreign viewpoint which may be perplexed by components which compromise Law and Religion in the absence of a Uniform Civil Code in India. In a different breath, concerns of NRI property conflicts relating to tenancy, succession and inheritance find simplified responses arising from matters professionally looked at by the authors. Some original thoughts of the authors on reformatory ideas or examples for India to emulate, which have been gathered from their experience gained from foreign travels, are ingenious and thought provoking. Reports of some of the

A-28, Neeti Bagh, New Delhi-110049 Ph.: 26855323, 26528841 Fax: 91-11-28882957 E-mail: solisorabjee@gmail.com deliberations arising from participation in international conferences and seminars held in India on NRI legal issues and subject matters add a noteworthy dimension to the book.

The presentation of the book is admirably crafted in simple readable language. For those who need to delve into details, case law references lead them to wider horizons. The book is an invaluable source of ready and dependable information. The book has generous meaningful references to Strasbourg jurisprudence, especially in context of the right to family life of the NRI community vis a vis family migration.

I, have no doubt that the book will be extremely useful to academicians, Judges, policy makers, lawyers in India, overseas lawyers and also to foreign readers. The book will provide invaluable guidance to Foreign Offices, Consular Directorates besides Consular Sections of Embassies and High Commissions worldwide by providing answers to the unresolved problems in new emerging areas of the vast Indian Diaspora scattered around the world.

19 October 2011

**Soli J. Sorabjee**
Former Attorney-General for India

# PREFACE

The present book is culmination of further research attempting to assimilate as also to answer some of the dilemmas in the area of international family law, with special reference to "the legal baggage," of the non-resident Indian Community spread all over the globe. The phrase "legal baggage," was coined by the late The Right Hon'ble Lord Slynn of Hadley in his Foreword to our earlier book "Acting for Non-Resident Indian Clients," published by Jordan Publishing Limited, UK in December 2004.

To some extent, the book is an interface between academics and practitioners in the area of private international law, but at the same time, providing clear cut cogent solutions in the area of family law having a substantial cross border legal element of immense significance.

Principally, in this book we have attempted to identify the areas in the arena of International Family Law, which have attracted maximum attention professionally from the legal fraternity in major jurisdictions spread across the globe.

We have now been interacting with our dear colleagues and accomplished personalities from the legal fraternity specialising in international family law in different jurisdictions for more than last two decades in professional capacity as also at various international platforms, and conferences of key international global legal organisations, right from Vancouver in Canada to Perth in Australia. Certainly, we have benefited immensely from interaction with our distinguished fellow colleagues from different parts of the world, which in turn has motivated us to compile the present book.

We have noticed that a clear consistent theme and a pattern emerges from the nature, thinking and analysis of the key stand alone international family law conferences and major international annual conferences in the last couple of years i.e., the International Family Justice Judicial Conference for Common Law and Commonwealth Jurisdictions 2009 held in August, 2009 in The United Kingdom comprising of a gathering of 42 Hon'ble Judges from 22 jurisdictions, the European Chapter meeting of the International Academy of Matrimonial Lawyers held in Munich, Germany in May, 2010, the International Child Abduction, Relocation and Forced Marriages Conference organised by The London Metropolitan University in London in July, 2010, the International Law Association Conference held in the Hague, Netherlands in August, 2010, the International Bar Association Annual Conference held in Vancouver, Canada in October, 2010, the Commonwealth Law Conference held in February, 2011 at Hyderabad, India and the Annual Family Law Conference organised by Miller Du Toit Cloete Inc and the University of the Western Cape in March, 2011, at Cape Town, South Africa.

The hot topics identified are as follows: inter-parental child removal/ abduction, forced marriages in the Asian sub-continent, inter-country adoptions, surrogacy and the position of law with regard to pre-nuptial agreements followed by the much anxiously awaited judgment of the Supreme Court of England and Wales in the case of **Radmacher** in the latter part of 2010. Of course, mediation attracts a huge amount of interest as well, especially when divorce lawyers act on behalf of high net worth individuals having assets in multiple jurisdictions. We have attempted to cover the said topics as well in our present book. Obviously, there are other areas of family law which are of immense significance, but have not been covered within the scope of this book.

In the area of international child abduction, the Hague Conference on Private International Law, Permanent Bureau, has been making very vigorous laudable efforts to persuade more and more member States to join the Hague Convention on the Civil Aspects of Child Abduction. Notable are the efforts made by Mr. Hans Van Loon, Secretary General and Mr. William Duncan, Deputy Secretary General at the Hague.

The international family law fraternity would be failing in its duty if it does not acknowledge the renewed tireless tremendous global efforts made by the office of The Rt. Hon. Lord Justice Thorpe, Head of International Family Justice for England and Wales. He has spearheaded a unique pioneering movement to promote the cause and facilitation of cross border International Family Law Issues by constantly engaging into meaningful interaction and dialogue with his colleagues in different parts of the world.

The law stated is as of 12 October, 2011. Lastly, the responsibility for all the remaining errors in the present book is of course completely ours.

12th October 2011 ANIL AND RANJIT MALHOTRA

# CONTENTS

# PROFESSIONAL PROFILE OF ANIL MALHOTRA

*Anil Malhotra is a practising Advocate in India since September, 1983 at the Punjab and Haryana High Court at Chandigarh. He appears as Counsel in the Supreme Court of India at New Delhi and before other Courts, Commissions, Boards and Tribunals. He holds Bachelor of Science and Bachelor of Laws (Professional) degrees from the Punjab University, Chandigarh, India. He attained an LLM degree from SOAS, University of London, London in November, 1985. He studied comparative family law at the London School of Economics. He has taught civil procedural laws and matrimonial remedies for six years as a part-time lecturer at the Faculty of Laws, Panjab University, Chandigarh, India. For over 25 years he has had extensive exposure in handling civil, matrimonial, criminal and overseas litigation on behalf of non-resident Indians residing abroad. He represents a large number of overseas clients in Indian courts and regularly opines on matters of Indian law in cases arising in related matters in foreign jurisdictions. He has conducted a vast variety of matters in Indian Courts pertaining to interpretation and application of foreign Court Orders regarding divorce decrees, child abduction, custody, maintenance, adoption and property related issues of non-resident Indians. He interacts extensively with a worldwide Indian population settled overseas in advising them regularly on all issues of civil, matrimonial and criminal law. He is a member of Lawasia, International Law Association, International Bar Association, Commonwealth Lawyers Association and Indian Society of International Law besides being Country Representative (Family Law) Lawasia. His law firm, Malhotra & Malhotra Associates are empanelled Lawyers for several key embassies and High Commissions at New Delhi for advisory, opinion and other legal work.

Has contributed significantly to issues of Inter-Country Adoptions, Inter-Parental Child Removal and Surrogacy by convening seminars, discussions and debates at the India International Centre, New Delhi and other law faculties in association with Law Commission of India and Mr Soli Sorabjee, Senior Advocate. Has to his credit Amicus and Joint Expert appointments by Courts in India and abroad.

Has co-authored book titled "Acting for Non-resident Indian Clients" (London 2005) published by Jordan Publishing Limited, Bristol, UK. Have authored booklet on "An Overview of Legal Issues" for the Punjab Government (2008).

Has authored book titled "India, NRIs and the Law" published by Universal Law Publishing Company Private Limited, New Delhi in 2009.

Has written regular newspaper articles on family law and allied issues with about 100 articles to his credit.

On January 29, 2007 was elected as Fellow of The International Academy of Matrimonial Lawyers, London.

In May, 2010, the Executive Council of the International Law Association, London has nominated him as a Member of the International Family Law Committee of the International Law Association.

He is the Indian family law Correspondent for the International Family Law journal published by Jordan Publishing Limited, Bristol. As an author he has to his credit substantial published works in international legal journals. He is the Indian representative for Reunite Child Abduction Agency.

Was invited to speak at Wilton Park conference on "Migration: Towards a Comprehensive Approach" at San Lorenzo de El Escorial, Madrid, Spain in October, 2007.

He was invited by the International Law Association as a Speaker to the 73rd Biennial Conference to be held at Rio De Janerio, Brazil to speak in the session on Rights of Children on August 18, 2008, where he made a presentation titled "India, Inter Country Parental Child Removal and the Law."

From December 4 to 6, 2008, he was invited to speak at and attend Wilton Park Conference – "The Future of Migration" held at Wiston House, West Sussex, UK.

Was invited to speak on "Inter-Parental Child Removal Issues at the 11th Annual Family Law Conference at Cape Town, South Africa on March 12-13, 2009 and at the 16th Commonwealth Law Conference 2009 at Hong Kong on April 5-9, 2009.

Was also invited to speak on "Surrogacy Issues and Inter-Parental Child Abduction in India" at the Lawasia "Children and Law Conference" in Singapore on May 21-23, 2009. He was the only legal practitioner amongst Judges who had been invited to speak at the International Family Justice Judicial Conference for the Common Law & Commonwealth Jurisdictions held at Windsor, UK from August 4-7, 2009.

Was invited by the Government of India to make a special presentation on Property Problems of Non-Resident Indians at a special seminar held at New Delhi on January 7, 2010.

Was invited to speak on "Indian Civil Aspects of International Child Abduction Bill, 2007 and the Indian Perspective on International Child Abduction" at the Conference on International Child Abduction, Relocation and Forced Marriage held from June 30 to July 2 at the London Metropolitan University, London.

Was invited as a Panelist in the 74th Biennial Conference of the International Law Association to be held in the Hague, Netherlands from August 15 to 19, 2010 to speak in the session on "Out of Concern for the Child : Transnational Co-operation in Cases of Child Protection, Maintenance and Abduction."

Participated in the 17th Commonwealth Law Conference held from 5-9 February, 2011 at Hyderabad by making interventions in sessions on Honour Crimes, Forced Marriages and Inter-Country Parental Child Removal issues prevailing in India.

Invited to present a paper on Surrogacy Titled "All aboard for the fertility express" at the 14th Annual Family Law Conference 2011, Cape Town, South Africa, organised by Miller Du Toit Cloete Inc and the University of the Western Cape on 17 and 18 March, 2011.

(* anilmalhotra1960@gmail.com)

# PROFESSIONAL PROFILE OF RANJIT MALHOTRA

Ranjit Malhotra, qualified as a lawyer in India in the year 1990 and was the first Indian lawyer to be awarded the prestigious Felix Scholarship to read for the LLM degree at the School of Oriental and African Studies, University of London. He attained his Degree with merit in 1993, specialising in immigration laws and South Asian family laws. He is an India-based lawyer handling substantial international work. He is a member of the International Bar Association and has been until recently the Regional Representative for India of the Migration and Nationality Law Committee of the IBA. He is presently the Newsletter Editor of the Family Law Section of the IBA and the Co-Chair of the Family Law and Family Law Rights Section of Lawasia. He is also a nominated life member of the Indian Society of International Law, Immigration Law Practitioners Association, London, American Immigration Lawyers Association, Washington, Reunite Child Abduction Agency in London, Indian Council of Arbitration at New Delhi, the Inter Pacific Bar Association at Tokyo, Lawasia at Australia, Fellow of the International Academy of Matrimonial Lawyers, Commonwealth Lawyers Association at London and International Law Association at London. He is also enrolled with The International Association of Youth and Family Judges and Magistrates.

He frequently travels abroad to present papers at international legal conferences. Mr. Ranjit Malhotra has travelled extensively in the UK, USA, Canada, Europe, South Africa, Australia and the Far East in connection with professional assignments as also to attend conferences. He was the only Indian speaker at the first AILA Global Immigration Summit held in New York in September, 2002 and the second Summit in New York in October, 2004. He also presented papers at the Global Immigration Conferences jointly organised by AILA, IBA and ILPA held in London in November, 2007, November 2009 and September, 2011. Previously, he has made presentations at AILA Annual conferences held in New Orleans in 2003, Salt Lake City in 2005 and Vancouver in 2008. Recently he was awarded the AILA Berger memorial scholarship to make a presentation at the AILA Annual Conference held in San Diego, California in June, 2011.

In October, 2007, he was nominated by the British High Commission, New Delhi, India to attend the Wilton Park Conference titled "WP 890 Migration

Towards a Comprehensive Approach", held in Spain from 8-10 October, 2007. He had attended another Wilton Park conference as a special invitee on migration issues in the UK in December, 2008.

He has substantial published work in different major jurisdictions to his credit. He is one of the principal authors in the recently published book titled "Acting for Non-resident Indian Clients," by Jordan Publishing Limited at Bristol in U.K. The book carries a foreword by the late Lord Slynn of Hadley, Senior Judge of the erstwhile House of Lords in London, U.K.

Mr. Ranjit Malhotra, specialising in areas of private international law is a managing partner in his firm Malhotra & Malhotra Associates. The firm has a broad-based practice with a reputation for offering a full range of quality personalised legal services. The firm handles legal work for several Fortune 500 companies. He also extensively advises foreign lawyers in the area of private international law, while acting on behalf of the non-resident Indian community, besides rendering expert testimony in foreign litigation, involving Indian laws.

Mr. Ranjit Malhotra has also been extensively handling inbound and outbound corporate immigration work for software companies, banks, consulting companies, multinationals etc., including lodging business and settlement applications at Embassies and Consulates throughout India. He has rich experience of consular representation.

His firm, Malhotra & Malhotra Associates, is on the panel of lawyers for seven major Embassies in New Delhi, including the Australian High Commission, Canadian High Commission, British High Commission and New Zealand High Commission, German Embassy, Austrian Embassy, at New Delhi, and the office of the Canadian Consul General at Chandigarh.

Mr. Malhotra is also the Honorary Consular Correspondent for the Italian Embassy, New Delhi for the State of Punjab and Chandigarh, since December, 2007.

He can be contacted at malhotraranjitindia@rediffmail.com

# TABLE OF CASES

## A



## B

## R



## S

**T**



**U**



**V**



**W**



**Y**



**Z**

# A SALUTE TO A PATRIARCH

The doyen of the enlightened faculty of academics, politics, law, art, culture, agriculture, international relations, sports and above all a zealous social reformist is no more. At the ripe age of 86, respected late Ram Niwas Mirdha has left behind a rich legacy. He touched the hearts of all those who came in contact with him.

Starting his innings as a member of the Rajasthan Legislative Assembly in 1953, he held successive Cabinet Portfolios with the Central Government from 1970 to 1989. A member of the Tenth Lok Sabha from 1991 to 1996, his grand daughter Jyoti Mirdha now adorns the Lok Sabha. Even though he was a professional agriculturist, he studied law at Allahabad and international studies at Geneva. Leading Indian delegations to the United Nations and Commonwealth Conferences, he was an articulate speaker and an erudite scholar.

Even at his age he was yearning to learn and share knowledge in any and every subject. Having been in contact with him for the past about 10 years in his capacity as President of Indian Society of International Law (ISIL), he was always encouraging and prompting students, law teachers and legal practitioners to look into the deeper insights in the realm of different laws. He pioneered the first indigenous research project for the Ministry of External Affairs to make a blueprint for reform of law for Non-Resident Indians and Private International Law. His zest and zeal for the cause of law reform led him to regularly hold international law conferences, seminars and regular study programmes for law students in which he himself participated. His attendees were law pupils, their teachers and law scholars. No one else was invited as according to him the conference was not for them. He believed in promoting and sharing the cause of good education for pupils.

We have never known a person so composite in every faculty of life. He blended with art and culture so well in his assignment as Chairman of the Sangeet Natak Akademi that it was impossible to believe that he was the President of the Indian Society of International Law and head of a host of UN Associations in India. He headed the Indian Heritage Society and the Institute of Constitutional and Parliamentary Studies (ICPS). He had matured in politics and was a die-hard social reformist. It was unbelievable that his daily routine was full of activity. Moving from one office he headed to the other in Delhi, it was difficult to meet him at times. Regardless, he was a tireless bundle of energy and a source of immense inspiration.

He keenly followed-up every Pravasi Bharatiya Divas and stressed upon the need for his brain-child idea, a special seminar on problems of NRIs. His efforts saw light. On his asking, the recent special conference on property problems of

NRIs was held on 6 January before the 2010 Divas. It was a huge success. Braving the foggy ice winter cold, he arrived at Vigyan Bhawan to deliberate in its proceedings. Over lunch with a diplomat from Mauritius, an animated discussion ensued for over two hours after the seminar. His deep knowledge, instant wit and humour and rational analysis on whatever we discussed left everybody spellbound. That was the man.

An educationist to the core, he always lent unflinching support to those who wanted help. We can never forget that in 2004, he very gracefully took us informally to the residence of Sh. Bhairon Singh Shekhawat, then Vice-President, to release our book "Acting for Non-Resident Indian Clients." Later, in 2009, he lent his august presence to the release of "India, NRIs and the Law," and insisted on delivering an extempore speech standing upright without the need of a dais or a microphone to speak. His next mission was to organise a seminar in the Parliament Annexe under the banner of ICPS and ISIL to impress upon the Ministry of Overseas Indian Affairs to carry out substantial reforms in the realm of Private International Law.

Addressed by senior statesmen as "My esteemed Leader," he never let his private grief overcome his feelings. When he lost his elder son in 2009, he surprised visitors who went to pay condolences. He discussed with them issues of public concern and refused to be let into polite words of his personal loss. He lived alone in a small first floor accommodation in Delhi with an office and secretarial staff dominating and monitoring his academic time. An ardent and voracious reader, he would ask to be read if his eyesight failed him at times. He kept a big magnifying lens in his close proximity to read the fine print whenever he wanted to. Every conference programme in minutest detail was discussed, deliberated and explained before it touched finality. Merit, perfection, humility and thoughtfulness were the hallmarks of the man. He even went to the extent of personally checking the name tags of foreign delegates at international conferences organised by ISIL. Never failing to speak to students, he mingled with them to learn their views and share his thoughts. Such a teacher will now be rare to find.

Grief overwhelms us. A bout of pain and sorrow touches us and a tear wells up in the eye. The great man is no more. However, his great thoughts will be immemorial. In his memory and honour, the Government of India would do well in installing a Chair on studies in Private International Law to fulfil his dreams. The flame must burn. The baton must move in the relay. His message must be carried.

---

## MERCHANTS OF DEATH

Sad but true, human smuggling is a trade in which Indian youth have been bought and sold as literal slaves like any other commercial merchandise recently in Iraq. These horror stories emerged recently when about 60 Indian youth returned from Baghdad to recount these chilling and shocking stories. Baffling and mesmerizing, these are not movie stories but are real life accounts which hit you beyond oblivion.

Gullible, semi-literate, economically weak and under-privileged youth are tempted by human trafficking agents with promises of dollars and rich fortunes to go abroad. They sell ancestral lands, mortgage family property, pawn jewellery and force family members to incur loans for financing the foreign trip of their dreams. Destination nowhere is all set. The purpose is earning wealth. The means to secure foreign passage is immaterial. The trafficking agents extract and extort full advance payment in cash and sell them to death merchants while these gullible youth are still lost in their dreams of foreign pastures.

These innocent youth board flights to unknown destinations and land in the hands of human sharks who trade them for profit. In the recent case, innocent youth proceeded to Baghdad from Dubai and were re-sold to sub-agents. Their assignments were phenomenal. Under the watchful eyes of AK 47 toting guards, they were forced to clear explosives from agricultural fields in which remnants of the 2003 Gulf war i.e. bombs, rockets, shells, missiles, cartridges and other ammunition were scattered. With bare hands, these youth were to run after tractors which unearthed these deadly explosive materials and thereafter physically pick them up to clear the fields for agricultural plantation. Any resistance was severely dealt with. Passports were confiscated and locked.

The working conditions of the Indian youth were pathetic and bone chilling. No defined working hours, no wages, no protective equipment or gear and no contact with the outside world. 20 youths were cramped in a single room with inedible meagre food, limited water and no toilet facilities. Beatings, physical assault and painful cigarette stubs were inflicted as a routine. Any protest fetched further inhuman treatment and more torture.

The story in hell in Iraq continued for almost eight months till desperate youth made contact with the Indian media which publicized their plight. The Punjab and Haryana High Court intervened upon an application in a Public Interest Litigation and issued directions to the Government of India on 12 August to act promptly before there is any loss of life. Resultantly, some of the youth were abandoned on streets by panicky agents of death who feared retribution. These harassed and intimidated youth reached the Indian Embassy in Baghdad and ultimately managed to return back to India to narrate their woeful plight. Today, they are shattered but happy and lucky to be alive. They say that there are many more like them, trapped, helpless and disadvantaged with no help.

In a modern day scenario, the story is unbelievable but shockingly it is true. It seems baffling and revolting that it has happened. Exploitation, abuse, torture, material gain are elements which were mixed with it. Those who came back are happy to be alive. Those who will come back will be lucky to return. But, for how long and till when will this go on. Human smuggling, unfortunately is not defined as an offence or a wrong under any Indian law. The Government of Punjab took the initiative of enacting, "The Punjab Prevention of Human Smuggling Act, 2010" which was passed by the Punjab Vidhan Sabha on 1 October, 2010 and sent for Presidential assent in accordance with the provisions of article 254 (2) of the Constitution of India. Till date the status of the Bill is unknown. At the Central level, there is no statutory enactment of the Government of India which attempts to define or punish this menace of human smuggling. It is thus, a lawless proposition. Today, law does not consider it a specific offence and the business goes on.

Experience shows that all dubious travel agents booked under the offence of cheating defined in the Indian Penal Code find no conviction under criminal law. There is no documentary evidence of money changing hands and the loosely phrased offence escapes the noose of punishment. The trapped and defrauded youth, if alive, is happy if a portion of the illegal cash amount is refunded. The matter is compromised, the case is buried and the agent returns to catch more innocent youth for business trading. The merchants of death continue unabated without fear or favour. Law turns a blind eye.

In this milieu, what is to be done and what can stop this menace. The prognosis is two-fold. One is legal and the other is social. It is time that the Parliament seriously endeavoured to enact a Central law defining human smuggling and its dangerous parameters which engulf society and feast on innocent youth daily. The long arm of law must reach out with its tentacles to capture those who indulge in this business of human trafficking. Till a law is made, the trade flourishes with impunity.

At the same time, the social issue is paramount. Indoctrination to youth whether in Andhra Pradesh, Tamil Nadu, Punjab or Kerala is concerned, the message is common. Find meaningful resources of self-employment or vocational avenues at home. If you have to travel or migrate, use legal means. Beware of pitfalls and traps. Do not adopt unethical means. Undertake proper documentation and do valid paper work before you depart. Do not venture into dubious and unethical pastures of illegal immigration. Take a meaningful decision and do not be led by verbal promises or rosy pictures. Likewise, meaningful campaigns and publicity of migrating the right way would be advantageous.

It is also time, that the Government seriously remedied the situation. Official agencies particularly the Consular Sections of Indian Embassies abroad must be pro-active. They must reach out to Indian citizens in distress. The External Affairs and the Overseas Indian Affairs Ministries must not be silent spectators. They must rise to the occasion. Indian citizens abroad must be rescued and not be permitted to be traded like slaves. This is offensive against human dignity. It is time that the step forward must be taken to remedy the situation.

# TRIAL OF NRI MATRIMONIAL CRIMINAL OFFENCES

The vexed jurisdictional question for seeking relief in split NRI marriages for criminal wrongs has been set at rest by the Apex Court Judgment of 2 September, 2011 in *Thota Venkateswarlu* v. *State of Andhra Pradesh*, JT 2011 (10) SC 281 wherein it has been held that Indian Courts, with the prior consent of the Central Government, can try offences committed by an Indian citizen in a foreign country. The case related to a Hindu traditional marriage solemnized in Andhra Pradesh with allegations of torture meted out to the wife in Botswana. Accordingly, abandoned brides, jilted spouses, destitute children and offended families back home can now find solace with Indian Courts under criminal law.

Allegations of cruelty by the husband or his relatives, criminal breach of trust by misappropriation of a woman's personal property, dowry wrongs, criminal neglect to maintain spouse, children or parents, bigamous marriages and commission of adultery are commonly cited criminal offences in NRI marriages. Thirty million NRIs in 180 countries abroad makes their occurrence a high risk number. However, the process of criminal investigation and trial in India can be tardy and hedged with jurisdictional objections to thwart and delay award of punishment. In this bleak scenario, the Supreme Court judgment provides succour to unfortunate victims in dire straits on Indian soil. Interpreting these provisions, the Apex Court has culled out a clear mandate of law providing an authoritative import to be followed by all Indian Courts as the law of the land.

In terms of section 4 of the Indian Penal Code (IPC), Indian criminal Courts can try an accused Indian citizen even if the offence was committed outside India. Under section 188 of the Code of Criminal Procedure (CrPC), if a criminal offence is committed by an Indian citizen outside India, he may be dealt with in respect of such an offence as if it had been committed at any place within India at which the Indian citizen may be found. However, no such offence shall be inquired into or tried in India except with the previous sanction of the Central Government.

Considering a mixed bag of criminal wrongs of matrimonial cruelty, the Apex Court had crystallized the crux question whether in respect of a series of such offences, some of which were committed within India and some outside India, could such offences be tried together without the previous sanction of the Central Government as envisaged under section 188 Cr.P.C. Having done so, the salutary verdict of the Supreme Court, proceeds to conclusively decide the issue and an analysis of the settled law on the proposition can be interpreted to lay down the following conclusions:

- Stated offences under the Dowry Prohibition Act occurring within the territorial jurisdiction of the criminal Courts in India can be tried without having to obtain the previous sanction of the Central Government.

- Alleged offences of matrimonial cruelty and criminal breach of trust committed by an Indian spouse outside India, where the couple resided, may be dealt with as if they had been committed in India. Previous sanction of the Central Government would be necessary in such cases.
- In respect of offences alleged to be committed outside India, previous sanction is required to be taken by the prosecuting agency before the trial can commence. However, this fetter is imposed only when the stage of trial is reached and no sanction is required till commencement of trial. It is only after the decision to try the offender in India was felt necessary, sanction would be required for trial to commence. Upto the stage taking cognizance, no previous sanction is necessary.
- The Magistrate is free to proceed against the accused in respect of offences allegedly committed in India, complete their trial and pass judgment therein, without being inhibited by the other alleged offences for which sanction would be required.
- As the IPC extends to extra-territorial offences, Indian citizens would be amenable to Indian criminal law subject to limitations of sanction required under law.

The vivid, erudite and meaningful pronouncement will enable criminal Courts in India to proceed within clarity in the dispensation of justice to wronged NRI marriages. The jurisdiction of the Indian Courts in respect of NRI marital offences will no longer be lost by reason of the venue of the offence. Clearly, the object of prior sanction of the Central Government is only to prevent the accused from being tried over again in two different places for the same offence and not to escape the noose by jurisdictional immunity. Logically, the phrase "dealt with" for being proceeded within India under criminal law does not impede or infringe the process of investigation into marital wrongs committed abroad. Axiomatically, the bar of sanction operates before the Magistrate in India after the investigating authority presents the charge sheet for the alleged offences. However, it can also be stated that for all overt criminal acts committed in India, in furtherance of a conspiracy and confabulation with NRIs abroad, sanction of Central Government of prosecution in India may not be necessary.

In, a different breath, in another previous decision, the Supreme Court, in *Fatima Bibi* v. *State of Gujarat*, AIR 2008 SC 2392, had earlier come to the rescue of a mother-in-law, a Mauritius national, who was accused by her Indian daughter-in-law in Gujarat of torture, intimidation and instigation, as offences under the IPC in respect of physical and mental cruelty faced at the hands of her husband while residing with him in Kuwait. The Apex Court allowing her appeal had quashed the criminal proceedings holding that since the offences were said to have been committed in Kuwait, the IPC or CrPC would have no application. Further, as a citizen of Mauritius, the mother-in-law was not liable for prosecution under the IPC in India for offences committed outside India. Substantial justice resulted thereupon.

Thus, marriages in vain abroad cannot be remedied or dissolved in India if they are not within the ambit of Indian law. The Courts have drawn a well defined dividing line. But then, such fractured and fragmented human relationships need to be resolved. If Indian law is beyond the scope and purview of application, the solutions and answers may lie elsewhere. Seeing to the phenomenal number of increasing Indian diaspora abroad, principles of private international family law seriously need to be debated to assemble mechanisms within legal frameworks of the respective countries who face these global family law problems. This needs urgent and immediate deliberation at international platforms for common unified humane solutions. The Apex Court judgments point to this much needed path of resolution.

# FRESH DIRECTIONS IN CUSTODY BATTLES

A recent judgment of the Supreme Court provides some direction in the ever-increasing battles for custody of children. But a legislative framework is also urgently required so that decisions are not just left to judicial subjectivity

The world has shrunk. Inter-continental travel is easier, affordable, faster and comfortable. As a corollary, it has led to a surge in relationships between individuals of different nationalities and diverse backgrounds. International mobility has dismantled inter-cultural taboos. But when marriages break down, the children become the worst victims. Caught in the cross-fire of broken human relationships with ensuing disputes over custody and relocation, children are traumatised and torn between parents. Attempts are often made to remove the children and take them to other countries. The hazards of international child removal are accentuated by the chronic problems of maintaining access or contact internationally and have often defied legal solutions.

However, the Supreme Court of India on 13 May, 2011 in *Ruchi Majoo* v. *Sanjeev Majoo*, JT 2011 (6) SC 167, in a cross-border child custody battle, has laid down principles and created a precedent which is bound to have a wide-ranging impact. The matter arose in a US-based NRI couple's case. The wife left her husband in the US and returned to India with her son. She moved a Delhi Guardian Court and got custody rights. In a suit filed in the USA by her estranged husband, who claimed that his wife had abducted the child, a US Court issued a red corner notice against the wife and directed her to return to the USA.

**Courts differ**

While the wife, who had decided to settle down in India, took refuge in a Delhi District Court order allowing her custody of her son, the husband filed an appeal before the Delhi High Court, which set aside the lower court's order. It upheld the appeal and ruled that since a US Court had already issued an order in the custody case and since the parents and the child were all American citizens, Indian Courts had no jurisdiction in the matter and all issues needed to be agitated before Courts in the USA. The wife then preferred an appeal to the Supreme Court.

The Apex Court set aside the judgment of the Delhi High Court and directed that the proceedings shall go on before the Delhi Guardian Judge. It further directed that the proceedings be disposed off as expeditiously as possible, and till then, the interim custody will remain with the mother and the father will enjoy visitation rights only.

The Apex Court culled out three questions for determination. The first question related to the jurisdiction of the 'Guardian Judge' to entertain the petition for adjudicating custody issues. Interpreting the phrase "ordinarily resident", the

Court held that the intention of parties would also go to determine this important question. The fact that the child was studying and residing in Delhi for the past three years, the Court held, had clearly established that both the mother and the child were 'ordinarily residents of Delhi'. E-mails produced by the wife as evidence also established that the father of the child was a party to this arrangement. Hence, it concluded, that the Guardian Judge in Delhi had the jurisdiction and competence to decide the custody rights.

The Court also held that the jurisdiction of the Guardian Judge could not be declined on the principle of comity of Courts. Examining earlier precedents, the Court ruled that proceedings in *Habeas Corpus* matters are summary in nature which may lead to determination of custody issues when the child is within the jurisdiction of the High Court. Distinguishing and contrasting guardianship proceedings based on evidence, it has been held that if the removed child is not ordinarily resident within its jurisdiction, the Guardian Judge has no jurisdiction to entertain the proceedings even if it is an act of violation of a foreign Court custody order.

Disapproving of the application of the "Comity of Courts" principle in the matter, the Supreme Court held that no foreign Court order had been violated by the wife. There was no final decision by any US Court, the minor was voluntarily in India and there was no intention of the wife and the child to return to the USA. The Supreme Court held that the interest of the minor would be better served if the mother continued to have the custody of the child, which was also a more acceptable option.

**Balanced view**

With all fairness to the husband, the Supreme Court in the third question also modified the order of the Guardian Judge and granted visitation rights to him during the pendency of the petition before the Court in Delhi. Holding that the "father's care and guidance" is necessary at the "formative and impressionable stage" of the child's life, the Court viewed that for the "child's healthy growth and to stay in touch and share moments of joy, learning and happiness with each other", the father be granted visitation rights through telephonic contact, video conferencing and visits during vacations as determined by the Guardian Judge. This was indeed a humane and a benevolent view of the whole situation.

The well-settled and balanced verdict is a harmonious blend of legal principles, a positive interpretation of parental rights, a decisive pronouncement of jurisdictional issues and brings out a confluence of earlier precedents by distinguishing them on factual basis. It is a much needed decree of the Apex Court on legal battles over child removal and normally fought on uncertain grounds with no legislation on the subject. There is, therefore, a dire need to enact a statutory law on inter-parental child removal to be uniformly followed in all such matters. An appropriate legislative solution will be in the larger interests of children. The yeoman effort by the Courts to carve out solutions on a case-to-case basis can only be a time consuming exercise which cannot be stretched indefinitely.

With the increasing number of Indians migrating to other countries and the growing number of Overseas Citizens of India status, inter-parental child removal needs to be resolved on an international platform. It is no longer a local problem. The phenomenon is global. Parallel Court proceedings in two jurisdictions by warring parents reduce the child to be won over as a trophy at the end of a legal war. Steps have to be taken by joining hands globally to resolve these conflicts by interaction of Courts and countries.

Till India does not become a signatory to the Hague Convention on Civil Aspects of International Child Abduction, this cannot be achieved. It is equally important to create a domestic uniform law with clear, authentic and universal child custody principles before India accedes to the Convention. The machinery to implement the convention must first be devised. Divergent views only divide children. Removed children cannot be allowed to live on a no man's land. The temptation to wrongfully remove children must be deterred. The cruel abduction of children must find a legislative solution forthwith.

**Fresh guidelines laid down by the Supreme Court of India in *Ruchi Majoo* v. *Sanjeev Majoo*,** JT 2011 (6) SC 167

The Supreme Court laid down the following principles in its judgment on the case delivered on 13 May, 2011.

The expression "ordinarily resides" in Guardian & Wards Act is to be determined also by 'intention' of parties and not merely on residence abroad or overseas nationality.

Custody orders issued by foreign Courts are not to be taken as conclusive and binding but should be considered as just one of the factors or consideration that would go into the making of a final decision by an Indian Court. "Objectivity and not abject surrender is the mantra in such cases, " says the Apex Court's order.

*Habeas Corpus* petitions being summary in nature can determine custody issues of children present in its jurisdiction and also embark upon a detailed enquiry in cases where welfare of a minor is in question. In *Habeas Corpus* proceedings, the legality of the detention of the alleged detenue in the territorial jurisdiction of the Court will be gone into.

The principle of "Comity of Courts" in child custody cases has generally held that foreign judgments are unconditionally conclusive. However, welfare of the minor being paramount, the Supreme Court now says that, Indian Courts are duty bound to examine the matter "taking the foreign judgment only as an input for final consideration."

## NO QUICK FIX SOLUTION IN CUSTODIAL CONFLICTS

THE number of cases related to inter-parental child custody conflicts has gone up sharply. As more and more marriages fall apart, Non-Resident Indian parents often remove their children to India or to foreign jurisdictions either in violation of a foreign Court custody order or in infringement of the other spouse's parental rights.

• The Hague Convention, a multilateral treaty developed by the Hague Conference on Private International Law provides an expeditious method of returning a child taken from one-member nation to another.

• Though the Convention concluded on 25 October, 1980 and the treaty became effective from 1 December, 1983, India is still not a signatory despite the fact that it has been accepted by 80 nations so far.

• The Convention was drafted to "ensure the prompt return of children who have been abducted from their country of habitual residence or wrongfully retained in a contracting state not their country of habitual residence."

• The primary intention of the Convention is to preserve whatever *status quo* child custody arrangement existed immediately before an alleged wrongful removal or retention thereby deterring a parent from crossing international boundaries in search of a more sympathetic Court. The Convention applies only to children under the age of 16.

• The phrase "inter-parental child abduction" is neither defined nor is it an offence under any statutory law in India. Hence, it is extremely difficult to prove or establish child removal at the hands of a parent who is a natural guardian of the child.

• The most expeditious remedy is to file a Writ of *Habeas Corpus* in the High Court or the Supreme Court for return of custody by a parent on the strength of a foreign Court order or in violation of parental rights.

• The alternative remedy is to initiate guardianship proceedings under the Guardians and Wards Act, 1890 by leading evidence and placing all cogent material on the record before a Guardian Judge. The process is cumbersome, tedious and time consuming. It is also difficult and slow for a foreign parent.

• In 1984, in *Surinder Kaur* v. *Harbax Singh Sandhu* 1984 HLR 780 SC and in 1987, in *Elizabeth Dinshaw* v. *Arvind M. Dinshaw*, AIR 1987 SC 3, the Apex Court exercising its summary jurisdiction returned the removed minor children to the foreign country of their origin on the basis of foreign Court custody orders.

• In 1998, in *Dhanwanti Joshi* v. *Madhav Unde* 1998 (1) SCC 112 and in 2000, in *Sarita Sharma* v. *Sushil Sharma*, 2000 (3) SCC 14, the Courts favoured keeping the child's welfare and best interests in mind over all other aspects. Accordingly, foreign Court orders became only one consideration in child custody disputes which were to be decided on the merits of each case without any summary return.

• In 2010, in *V. Ravi Chandran* v. *UOI* 2010 (1) SCC 174, and again in 2010 in *Shilpa Aggarwal* v. *Aviral Mittal*, 2010 (1) SCC 591, the Apex Court, following *Habeas Corpus* petitions, directed the summary return of children to USA and UK respectively, leaving all aspects relating to child welfare to be investigated by Courts in the foreign jurisdiction.

• In May 2011, in *Ruchi Majoo* v. *Sanjeev Majoo*, JT 2011 (6) SC 167 in an appeal, in a Guardians and Wards petition, the Apex Court has directed that the proceedings for deciding custody rights shall go on before the Guardian Judge at Delhi and till then the interim custody shall be with the mother. The father has been given visitation rights.

**Why should India be interested in joining the 1980 convention?**

• India is no longer impervious to international inter-parental child removal.

• The present situation plays into the hands of the abducting parent.

• The offending parent at times usurps the role of the competent Court.

• India's non-signatory status has a negative influence on a foreign Judge who often declines a parent from taking the child to India fearing non-return.

• The Convention avoids the problems that may arise in Courts of different countries which are equally competent to decide such issues.

The best possible solution would be to become a signatory to the Hague Convention and enact a Indian International Child Abduction Law and create a Central Authority for liaison and for seeking adjudication before designated existing Indian Courts to resolve such disputes to decide summary return or to render decisions on merit. In the interest of children, the stalemate must end.

## CAN A BROKEN MARRIAGE BE STITCHED TOGETHER?

'Irretrievable breakdown of marriage' as a ground for divorce should be introduced cautiously along with safeguards to prevent misuse.

On 10 June, 2010 the Union Cabinet approved the introduction of a Bill, *i.e.*, the Marriage Laws (Amendment) Bill, 2010, to be tabled in the ongoing monsoon session of Parliament. It seeks to amend the Hindu Marriage Act, 1955 (HMA) and the Special Marriage Act, 1954 (SMA) to provide for irretrievable breakdown of marriage as a ground for divorce.

The long-awaited move comes more than a year after the Law Commission of India *suo motu* took up the study of the subject and in its 217th report in March 2009 strongly made the above recommendation.

The Commission examined the existing legislation as well as a number of judgments of the Supreme Court and the High Courts on the subject and was of the view that "irretrievable breakdown of marriage" should be incorporated as another ground for granting divorce under the provisions of the Hindu Marriage Act, 1955 and the Special Marriage Act, 1954. The Commission also recommended that before granting a decree for divorce on the ground that the marriage has irretrievably broken down, the Court should examine whether adequate financial arrangements had been made for the parties and their children.

Although such a ground for divorce is currently not mentioned in HMA, the Supreme Court has, in appropriate cases, granted a decree of divorce on grounds of "irretrievable breakdown of marriage" by virtue of the powers vested in it under article 142 of the Constitution of India. However, different Benches of the Supreme Court have taken separate stands over this issue.

In March, 2006, a three-Judge Bench of the Supreme Court granted divorce in *Naveen Kohli* v. *Neelu Kohli,* 2006 (4) SCC 558. But in February, 2009, a two-Judge Bench of the Court in *Vishnu Dutt Sharma* v. *Manju Dutt Sharma,* 2009 (6) SCC 379, refused to grant divorce on the ground of irretrievable breakdown of marriage. The Court observed that it could not add such a ground to section 13 of HMA as it would amount to amending the Act which is a function of the legislature.

In the most recent view in May, 2010, in *Neeti Malviya* v. *Rakesh Malviya,* 2010 (6) SCC 413, the Supreme Court, while examining the question of waiving the six-month waiting period for divorce by mutual consent by invoking its extraordinary powers under article 142 of the Constitution of India, has referred the question for consideration to a Bench of three Judges.

Clearly, the underlining note of invoking irretrievable breakdown of marriage as a ground for divorce did not find favour with the Bench. Thus, from the views in the judgment of the Supreme Court in *V. Bhagat* v. *D. Bhagat*, 1994 (1) SCC 337 allowing a divorce on the ground of irretrievable breakdown of marriage to the pronouncement of the Supreme Court in *Anil Kumar Jain* v. *Maya Jain*, 2009 (10) SCC 415, not allowing so, there has been a variant view on this controversial subject for 15 years. The Supreme Court, however, has been consistent in its view that neither the High Courts nor the subordinate Courts can exercise such power vested only in it.

Realistically speaking, a broken marriage limps to dissolution. Law cannot reunite parties if the matrimonial bond has severed. Consequently, a peaceful parting is necessary if the parties cannot reconcile despite best efforts. Thus, the adding of irretrievable breakdown of marriage as a ground for divorce by Parliament by amending the marriage laws may be the best possible solution for the future of limping marriages.

However, the power of the Court to grant divorce on the ground of irretrievable breakdown should be exercised with extreme caution only in circumstances warranting so and when it is in the interest of both the parties. Due regard for maintenance of the dependent spouse, besides welfare of children, must be safeguarded by enabling legislation. Hence, simultaneous amendments to other provisions of marriage laws in this regard must follow forthwith whenever such a law is made.

A balance needs to be maintained wherein the sanctity of the institution of marriage should be protected as well as the individual interests of aggrieved spouses addressed. Moral and cultural values are embedded in Indian ethos and emulation of western principles in matrimonial matters is not appreciable and should not be adopted with ease. Hence, the ground of irretrievable breakdown of marriage should be introduced cautiously and hedged with safeguards so that the provision is not misused.

Nevertheless, there is also an urgent need to set up a Family Court in every district of the country for adjudicating all kinds of matrimonial disputes. It is really unfortunate that even after more than 25 years of enactment of the Family Courts Act, 1984, only a miniscule number of such Courts have been set up only in metropolitan cities.

Also, there must be marriage and divorce laws not just for Hindus but also for Muslims, Christians, Parsis and other religious denominations in line with contemporary practices of young generations who receive higher education and have more cosmopolitan thinking of the brave new world. Times have changed and the people of India must move ahead without living in the past. Harmony at home and peace at work is the most important component and quality of successful Indians in the 21st century. A stable family is an epitome of Indian society.

# DISPUTE RESOLUTION IN THE FAMILY THE LAW FORGOT

Matters of the family which can be repaired must be mediated and settled by sewing and patchwork.

Today, the nuclear Indian family is plagued by new generation ills. Forced marriages, honour killings, live-in relationships, parental child removal, inter-country adoptions, and surrogacy defy solutions in codified laws. Conventional family law framers never visualised these societal complexities which have mushroomed recently. The statutory law has not caught up with the maze of intricacies which dog these family law issues.

Provisions for settlement of disputes outside the court find a prominent place in the Civil Procedure Code, the codified marriage laws and the Family Courts Act. However, settlement, reconciliation and mediation in family law matters are largely unutilised. Upholding the salutary provisions to endeavour reconciliation in the first instance, the Supreme Court in *Jagraj Singh* v. *Birpal Kaur* 2007 (2) SCC 564 clearly confirms that settlement efforts in matrimonial matters are not an empty, meaningless ritual. Matters of the family which can be repaired must be mediated and settled by sewing and patchwork. Human relationships must be bonded by settlement and, as far as possible, not litigated in Court.

Litigation — whether divorce, maintenance, alimony, child custody or any other matrimonial cause — should not be viewed in terms of failure or success of legal action. The amicable settlement of family conflicts is a social therapeutic problem. These disputes should be reconciled within the family fold so as not to disrupt the family structure. Adjudication is entirely different from conventional civil or criminal proceedings. Reverberations of a family dispute are felt in society. Their effective resolution by mediation or conciliation may provide lasting solutions for overall good.

The Supreme Court in *Gaurav Nagpal* v. *Sumedha Nagpal* 2008 (2) HLR 584 emphasised that efforts should be made to bring about conciliation to bridge communication gaps and to prevent people from rushing to Courts. The pressing need in the current social milieu is to create an infrastructure machinery for Alternative Disputes Resolution (ADR) mechanisms. Particularly, marriages solemnised in India and fractured abroad in the 30-million NRI community can be mended and settled. It is these limping unions which need reconciliatory formulas in India to prevent them from being split. Conflicts arising locally or overseas should not deteriorate into other ancillary issues multiplying the problem.

The mediation cell of the Punjab and Haryana High Court, which attempts to patch up matrimonial disputes, is an extremely positive development. The culture of settlement needs propagation. ADR cannot see the light of day unless citizens participate in the movement.

The conventional people's Courts can be a means to this end. Individual initiatives need awakening by self-consciousness, and not by the implementation of laws. Spouses, parents and families need to realise the advantages of ADR in the family structure. Matrimonial relief carved out of settlement will serve better than the results obtained by adversarial litigation involving time, effort, finances and, above all, breaking-up of a family.

Issues of marriage, divorce and children ought to be put before Family Courts. Trained counsellors, mediators and advisers should resolve them mutually. Superior Courts themselves must inject the spirit of mediation in appellate jurisdictions. A unanimous consensus saves a home, a family and a societal foundation. Mandatory reconciliation procedures should be affirmed with the seal of the court conclusively without any challenge.

Creating more Courts under the Family Courts Act will contribute to the resolution of family law disputes through ADR. The current handling of matrimonial litigation by conventional Courts is a poignant reminder of what prevails.

Trained counsellors, professional mediators and, above all, specialist family law judges could all form part of a well-organised adjudication team. This would give a new dimension to ADR in family law.

Laws to promote ADR exist but the infrastructure, professional assistance and the medium through which these beneficial reconciliatory mediation procedures are to be implemented are lacking. The package is wholesome. The numbers are huge. The need is dire. The solution is inbuilt. An effective implementation machinery is required. The lawmakers must aid, assist and implement ADR.

# NO BULL IN A CHINA SHOP OF NRI DIVORCES AND ANTI-SUIT INJUNCTIONS

Hindu marriages made in heaven and solemnised in India are now wantonly dissolved abroad. This is sad, but true. A prelude follows. Over 30 million overseas Indians are domiciled in 180 countries abroad. The parallel adjudication of their matrimonial disputes in the Courts simultaneously in India and abroad activates a new *inter se* marital discord.

This clash of jurisdictional battles also germinates a conflict amongst the authority of Courts. Foreign Courts often impose penal sanctions oblivious of prior directions of the existing Indian Courts of superior hierarchy. Rules of Private International Law offer little resolution. Spouses, children and extended families bear the brunt of multi-faceted parallel directives of Courts of different overseas territories.

The Supreme Court in *Neerja Saraph* v. *Jayant Saraph,* 1994 (6) SCC 641, proposed feasibility of enacting a legislation to ensure that no marriage between an NRI and an Indian which has taken place in India may be annulled by a foreign Court. Earlier in *Y. Narasimha Rao* v. *Y. Venkata Lakshmi,* 1991 (3) SCC 451, the Apex Court spelt out guidelines for recognition of foreign Court matrimonial judgments to decide when Hindu marriages solemnised in India were said to be dissolved by unenforceable foreign decrees.

The Bombay High Court in *Sondur Rajini* v. *Sondur Gopal,* 2006 (2) HLR 475, ruled that a foreign domicile of parties will not take away the jurisdiction of Indian Courts to decide the annulment of their ceremonial Hindu marriage solemnised when they were domiciled in India.

In *Naveen Chander Advani* v. *Leena Advani,* 2005 (2) HLR 582, the matrimonial dispute of a ceremonial marriage of Hindus celebrated in the US, was held by the Bombay High Court to be amenable for adjudication by the Family Court, Pune. The Delhi High Court in *Veena Kalia* v. *Jatinder Kalia,* AIR 1996 Del 54, ruled that an *ex-parte* decree of divorce of a foreign Court being a nullity, would not bar a subsequent petition for divorce in India even though maintenance had been accepted under the foreign judgment.

In *Harmeeta Singh* v. *Rajat Taneja,* 2003 (2) RCR (Civil) 97, the Delhi High Court temporarily restraining the foreign Court divorce proceedings held that even if the Hindu marriage is dissolved in the US, it would still have to be confirmed by an Indian Court. In *Moina* v. *Amardeep,* AIR 1986 Del 399, a foreign domicile was held by the Delhi High Court to be no deterrent to a divorce petition preferred in India to dissolve a Hindu marriage celebrated here. These authoritative and laudable verdicts clearly reflect that Indian Courts rightly have a prerogative to adjudicate matrimonial disputes falling in their domain.

In this backdrop, a new dimension of matrimonial litigation is coming in practice in the matrimonial arena in the shape of anti-injunction suits. A petition preferred in India for restraining an opposing spouse from pursuing or continuing with a complaint for matrimonial relief in a foreign court would be such an anti-injunction suit. Lack of jurisdiction, both regarding the corpus of the Hindu marriage and the physical presence of an Indian spouse in the territory abroad, are the grounds of such suits in India. However, even the reverse application now finds popular practice.

An extreme view finds enunciation in a judgment rendered on September 20, 2010, in an anti-injunction suit. The Federal Magistrates Court of Australia at Canberra restrained the wife from taking any action, as also for causing, allowing or assisting any other person, to pursue a complaint in India against the husband under the Dowry Prohibition Act, 1961. Both parties were Australian citizens married according to Sikh rites in India. By Australian consent orders, settlement of maintenance, property and child custody were resolved. The Canberra Court found that on evidence presented, Ms Singh had not established that a dowry was either requested or paid as alleged. Accordingly, the Court held "that the injunction acts only in relation to Ms Singh, and does not, either in terms or otherwise, purport to affect the administration of justice in India". The judgment was said to be based on considerations of equity and justice.

Consequently, the thought proposed for conscious deliberation which reverberates in the minds of those who live on home soil is the dire need for evolving an Indian jurisprudence in matrimonial litigation to deal with anti-injunction suits in India. If an American Court imposes a fine of US $ 1 lakh a day for not complying with a US Court child custody order contrary to an Indian Court order or a divorce petition on grounds of irretrievable breakdown of marriage is proceeded with the US despite a pending Indian divorce litigation, such oppressive litigation must be restrained by the dictates of equity, good conscience and comity of Courts. Such unconscionable acts are estoppel by conduct. If foreign Courts can evolve principles, similar thinking must develop at home too.

A foreign Court matrimonial order may at times invade the privacy of the home and leave the hapless Indian spouse to abject surrender without a remedy. Surely, law must come to the rescue of the victims. The yeoman verdicts of Indian Courts are a big crutch.

However, the need for a preventive remedy is stronger than a powerful cure at the end. What can be prevented must be stopped. What should not be suffered should not be endured. Anti-injunction suits in matrimonial matters in fit cases must deter oppressive foreign Court orders without technicalities. The majesty of Indian law must prevail.

## HINDU MARRIAGES : MADE IN HEAVEN, CELEBRATED IN INDIA AND DISSOLVED IN USA

A recent judgment of the Bombay High Court setting aside the parallel proceedings for divorce of the Family Court, Pune and upholding a divorce decree passed by the Court of Oakland, State of Michigan, USA, dissolving a Hindu marriage on the principle of breakdown, has evoked a new stream of thought with which the authors respectfully differ. The verdict, *Kashmira Kale* v. *Kishore Kumar Mohan Kale*, 2011 (1) HLR 333 lending sanctity to a US divorce decree in preference to proceedings under the Hindu Marriage Act. 1955 between the same parties upsets the settled law.

The parties married in Mumbai in 2005 according to Hindu rites, lived in USA and intermittently visited Mumbai and Pune. In September 2008, the wife filed divorce proceedings in the US whose jurisdiction was challenged by the husband in the US. Simultaneously, in October 2008, the husband filed a divorce petition in the Pune Family Court, claiming it to be the competent forum for adjudication of their dispute. The husband did not pursue the wife's divorce petition in the US any further and in January 2009, the US Court dissolved the marriage and divided the assets of the parties. However, the Family Court in Pune in September 2009 held that it still had the jurisdiction to try the husband's petition for divorce in India. In appeal, the Bombay High Court set aside the order of the Family Court, Pune, and upheld the US divorce decree dissolving the Hindu marriage.

The conclusions drawn by the Bombay High Court that the parties were domiciled in the US and hence the Hindu Marriage Act (HMA) cannot apply to them is *per se* erroneous. Furthermore, the non-application of the HMA to Hindus was misconstrued and the application of the breakdown principle without considering the written statement of the husband challenging the jurisdiction of the US Court were factors which did not lend a imprimatur to the foreign decree which did not take into consideration the provisions of the HMA under which the parties were married.

Noticing that section 1(2) of HMA applies only to Hindus in the territories to which the HMA applies but not considering that it also "applies to Hindus domiciled in the territories to which this Act extends who are outside the said territories" left the contention only half noticed. To add to it, section 2 of HMA prescribing application of the Act to Hindus, irrespective of domicile, nationality or citizenship, renders the decision of the Bombay High Court fallacious. Earlier precedents on the point enunciated by different High Courts stipulate that HMA applies to all Hindus irrespective of domicile or residence if they have married in India according to Hindu rites. Thus, it has been held that HMA has extra territorial application as a Hindu carries with him his personal law of marriage and Courts in India have jurisdiction to try their matrimonial disputes regardless of change of nationality or new domicile.

The Bombay High Court in *Sondur Rajini* v. *Sondur Gopal*, 2006 (2) HLR 475, had held that the provisions of the HMA do not cease to apply on change of domicile which is determined when the parties tie the nuptial knot under the HMA and not on the date when an application is made for matrimonial reliefs. In *Naveen Chander Advani* v. *Leena Advani*, 2005 (2) HLR 582, the Bombay High Court held that the Family Court in Pune wrongly declined to entertain a matrimonial petition relating to a marriage where parties, who last resided and married in USA according to Hindu rites and ceremonies, as the Family Court has jurisdiction to deal with matters under the HMA/SMA. The Delhi High Court had earlier echoed similar views in *Harmita Singh* v. *Rajat Taneja*, 2003 (2) RCR 197, holding that in consonance with principles of Private International Law, a US divorce decree would have to be confirmed by a Court in India. Even in *Moina* v. *Amardeep*, AIR 1986 Del 399, it had been held that under section 1(2) of HMA, the Canadian domicile of the husband could not be a ground to decline jurisdiction of Delhi Courts.

Equally flawed is the view of the Bombay High Court that since the parties last resided together in Michigan, USA, the U.S Court has territorial jurisdiction to decide their divorce dispute. This conclusion falls foul of the settled law laid down by the Supreme Court in *Jagir Kaur* v. *Jaswant Singh*, AIR 1963 SC 1521, that prescribing the limits of jurisdiction, speaking of last residence of a person with his wife, can only mean his last residence in the territories of India. It cannot obviously mean his residing with her in a foreign country for such an Act cannot confer jurisdiction on a foreign Court. The Bombay High Court in *Meera* v. *Anil Kumar*, 1992 (2) HLR 284, also held that "last resided" in section 19 of HMA means last residence in India and the High Court in India within whose jurisdiction the parties last resided together can take cognizance of the matter. Flowing from the same stream of thought, the Punjab and Haryana High Court has held that any temporary residence would confer jurisdiction to try the matrimonial dispute. This settled view militates against the erred conclusion of the Bombay High Court that temporary stay at Pune or Mumbai could not mean last residence in India as parties last resided together in USA.

Above all, the view of the Bombay High Court disagrees with the celebrated view of the Apex Court in *Y. Narasimha Rao* v. *Y. Venkata Lakshmi*, 1991 (3) SCC 451, clearly holding the rule that the jurisdiction assumed by the foreign Court as well as the grounds on which the relief is granted must be in accordance with the matrimonial law under which the parties are married. Three exceptions were culled out to this rule by the Supreme Court. Firstly, permanent foreign residence and invoking of relief on a ground available in matrimonial law under which parties were married. Secondly, voluntary submission to foreign jurisdiction coupled with contest on merits abroad on grounds available under matrimonial law under which parties were married. Thirdly, parties unconditionally consent to grant of relief although jurisdiction of foreign Court is not in accordance with provisions of matrimonial law of parties. The Apex Court in *Neerja Saraph* v. *Jayant*

*Saraph*, 1994 (6) SCC 641, thereafter had even suggested feasibility of a legislation to hold that "no marriage between a NRI and an Indian woman which has taken place in India may be annulled by a foreign court". Not noticing the above precedents of the Apex Court, the recent view of the Bombay High Court *per se* appears to be disagreeable if not *per incuriam*.

With due deference, the verdict of the Bombay High Court neither agrees with precedent on the point, does not adapt to Hindu law of marriage of the parties, nor is it conclusive. Parties may be treated as divorced in USA and still married in India. Confusion confounded. In this breath, the line of action adopted in a number of matrimonial disputes in the Punjab and Haryana High Court is most useful to quote. Limping marriages are taken before the mediation and conciliation centre at the High Court premises where the hatchet is peacefully buried and matters are amicably compromised to convert the matrimonial feuds to divorce petitions by mutual consent. Matters thereafter rest without contest on written settlements. Warring claims are put to sleep harmoniously. This is the better path than allowing foreign Courts to decide Hindu marriage disputes without conflict of laws. Indian Courts are better suited to decide them without foreign interference. Domestic law must prevail.

## INTER-COUNTRY ADOPTIONS: NEW GUIDELINES ATTRACTIVE, BUT ILLUSORY

The Guardian and Wards Act, 1890 (GWA), the 116-year-old Indian legislation plays spoilsport. A whopping 12 million orphan children in India need parents but the law does not allow Muslims, Christians, Jews and Parsis to become their adoptive parents. They can be appointed as guardians only.

The Hindu Adoption and Maintenance Act, 1956 (HAMA) does not allow non-Hindus to adopt a Hindu child. Consequently, non-Hindus and foreign nationals can at most become guardians under the GWA but cannot adopt children from India.

The Central Adoption Resource Authority (CARA) is the nodal Central body in New Delhi. To facilitate implementation of the norms, principles and procedures relating to adoption of children from India to foreign countries, the Supreme Court in three successive decisions in *Lakshmi Kant Pandey* v. *Union of India*, AIR 1984 SC 469, AIR 1986 SC 272 and 1988 (1) HLR 699 (SC) had directed the Government of India to issue guidelines for the above purposes. Accordingly, CARA from time-to-time has issued guidelines for adoption of children from India to foreign jurisdictions besides in-country adoptions.

The new guidelines by CARA for full and final "adoption" of children in India before they are sent abroad with prospective parents and that will mandate "final adoption of Indian children" under HAMA and the Juvenile Justice (Care and Protection of Children) Act, 2000 (JJ Act), seem attractive but illusory. This is because unless non-Hindu parents are statutorily permitted not to "adopt" and be merely guardians. Hence, any guidelines cannot overreach statutory law.

Till such time adoption is permitted only to Hindus, any foreigner who is a non-Hindu cannot adopt a child in India simply because no law permits so. In such event, the exercise of CARA to frame guidelines to allow foreign couples to adopt children in India may be flawed and defective. Any guidelines can supplement the law but not supplant it. Consequently, CARA cannot enact a law of its own.

HAMA permits adoption to a male or a female Hindu through a process of adoption enacted by Indian Parliament to codify the law relating to adoptions among Hindus. Even the JJ Act, permits adoption of orphaned, abandoned, neglected and abused children through institutional and non-institutional methods. But there is no statutory law which permits non-Hindus who are foreign nationals or professing other religions to adopt children in India.

For them, the limited recourse is under the GWA to become guardians which enables them to use the guardianship order obtained in India under the GWA to ultimately gain adoption in foreign jurisdictions. In this event, Indian statutory law does not permit adoption to foreign nationals and persons professing other religions to adopt in India.

HAMA gives a conclusive status to an adoption deed recording an adoption in compliance with its provisions. However, all foreign Embassies or the High Commissions in India still insist that the adoption deed is not enough. Rules of foreign jurisdictions stipulate that the adoptive parents have to thereafter obtain guardianship orders from a Guardian Judge under the Hindu Minority and Guardianship Act, 1956 (HMGA) for Hindus and a similar order under the GWA for non-Hindus.

Genuine transfer of parental responsibility by an irrevocable adoption deed is rendered redundant. This results in a paradox in law. A valid adoption deed under HAMA is not acceptable to foreign jurisdictions for immigration purposes unless it is supported by a guardianship order under the GWA or HMGA. Strange but true, that is how the law is read by foreign Embassies and High Commissions in India.

Against this backdrop, what should CARA do? It should resolve the conflicts and not compound them. CARA could well send a recommendation that before it enacts any guidelines, they should confirm to statutory law. Any guidelines which differ from the codified law will only add but not subtract to the current muddle of inter-country adoptions law.

The mechanics of inter-country adoptions, stringent adoption procedures, insurmountable technicalities, high refusal rates of visas for children in adoption matters and inordinate delay in Indian Court procedures have been a deterrent to adopt a child from India. What do we need? Where is the change desired?

A general law for adoption in India enabling any person, irrespective of his religion, race or caste to adopt a child from India will help. Further, keeping in view the Supreme Court's guidelines in adoption by foreign nationals to prevent trafficking of children and to protect their welfare, a uniform streamlined statutory procedure acceptable to foreign jurisdictions would also serve the purpose better to mitigate the plight of the adoptive child.

# PRE-NUPTIAL AGREEMENTS: UNSUITED IN THE INDIAN CONTEXT

Pre-nuptial agreements are not recognised in India under any existing matrimonial legislation, neither under the Indian Code of Civil Procedure, 1908, nor under any of the prevalent criminal laws in the Indian jurisdiction. The concept of pre-nuptial agreements is alien to the Indian legal system. Although, the concept of pre-nuptial agreements, is now a subject matter for discussion, especially in the metropolitan cities in India, but little guidance is available on the subject, in the Indian context. Clearly, this is on account of the fact that pre-nuptial agreements are not popular at all in the Indian jurisdiction, only to be found in minority and isolation in metropolitan and urban India only.

If at all any pre nuptial agreement is sought to be executed by the parties to the marriage, principally the contents of the same (a) should not be opposed to public policy, (b) should not violate the principles of natural justice (c) should not be fraudulent in letter and spirit and of course (d) recognise rights of both the parties, so that if the said pre-nuptial agreement is tested in a Court of law, it can stand judicial scrutiny. This is a highly debatable proposition given the Indian social milieu, the fabric of the Indian society, and of course the facts and circumstances of the case. This prerogative shall depend entirely on the discretion of the Court hearing the matter, depending on the cumulative facts and circumstances of the case before the Court.

In UK, its Law Commission has embarked on an examination of the status and enforceability of agreements between spouses and civil partners considering their property and finances. This was following the decision of the UK Supreme Court in October 2010 in the case of *Radmacher* v. *Granatino*, (2010) UKSC 42, which ruled that pre-nuptial agreements can be decisive in determining the financial decision on divorce. The process of consultation closed on 11 April, 2011. This report is anticipated in 2012. The key issues regarding the validity of the pre-nuptial agreements have been addressed in the above-mentioned judgment of the UK Supreme Court, which are also discussed in the latter part of the chapter.

It is pertinent to mention that article 142 of the Constitution of India vests the Supreme Court of India with vast inherent powers, and the same provides that the Supreme Court in the exercise of its jurisdiction may pass such decree or make such order as is necessary for doing complete justice in any cause or matter pending before it, and any decree so passed or orders so made shall be enforceable throughout the territory of India in such manner as may be prescribed by or under any law made by the Parliament of India.

By way of instance, it is pertinent to mention that the concept of irretrievable breakdown is not recognised as a ground for divorce under the existing matrimonial laws, but over the years the Apex Court has been recognising irretrievable breakdown as a ground for divorce, by using its above-mentioned inherent powers in its wisdom in appropriate cases only. This is only, when the matrimonial litigation reaches the last Court of Appeal.

The point to be conveyed is that if the Apex Court, can recognise irretrievable breakdown as a ground for divorce in India, although not existing in the statue book, it well may be the case that the Apex Court in the time to come can possibly adjudicate upon the validity/enforceability of pre-nuptial agreements or lay down suitable comprehensive guidelines on the subject in an suitable case. There is hardly any caselaw on the subject, in the Indian jurisprudence or in the Indian context.

That given the background of the concept of pre-nuptial agreements being alien to the Indian legal system, the validity of the marriage will not be affected in any manner, so long as a valid marriage has been performed between the parties to the marriage. It is very important that the marriage should be duly registered in terms of the relevant matrimonial legislation, as applicable to the parties. Of course, there are no consequences on the martial regime in India, in the absence of a pre-nuptial agreement. This aspect of the matter is of immense concern in international marriages, where parties have substantial assets in multiple jurisdictions.

In the cross-border perspective, queries are raised as to what would be the impact of child custody provisions in a pre-nuptial agreement in the Indian context. It is important to mention that India is not a party to the Hague Convention of the Child Abduction of 1980. The predominant consideration with regard to the relocation of the minor children will be the welfare and the best interest of the minor children. That under the provisions of the Hindu Minority and Guardianship Act, 1956, the mother is the natural guardian of a Hindu minor who is below the age of five years. The controlling consideration governing the custody of the children is the welfare of the children and not the right of the parents.

The Supreme Court of India in the matter of *Vikram Vir Vohra* v. *Shalini Bhalla* JT 2010 (3) SC 213, decided on 25 March, 2010, decided a case of relocation of a minor child. It was held by the Supreme Court of India that child custody orders are interlocutory in nature and can be altered for the welfare of the child. Consequently, the Supreme Court permitted the mother to take her minor son aged about ten years to Australia as per the wishes of the child to stay with the mother, upholding the welfare of the child as a paramount consideration.

It is important to mention that what is more prevalent in India, is the practice of post marriage settlement, in the event of divorce proceedings, allied matrimonial litigation especially when criminal proceedings have been initiated by either of the parties to the marriage. Generally, these criminal proceedings would be for cruelty/desertion and/or demand for dowry on part of the erring spouse, possibly arraying immediate family members as respondents in the said criminal litigation, which could well be from the family of either of the parties to the marriage. The Supreme Court of India in two recent meaningful decisions mentioned below has very aptly and tersely emphasised the need to encourage Court settlements in genuine matrimonial disputes.

The Apex Court in the matter of *B.S Joshi* v. *State of Haryana* 2003 (4) SCC 675, in para 13 (at page 682) of the judgment reiterated the law earlier laid down by the Apex Court itself in the matter of *G.V Rao* v. *L.H.V Prasad* 2000 (3) SCC 693. Para 12 (at page 698) of this judgment, has been reiterated as para 13 (at page 682) in the above mentioned matter of *B.S Joshi* (supra) and the same reads as follows:

> "13. The observations made by this Court, though in a slightly different context, in *G.V. Rao* v. *L.H.V. Prasad* are very apt for determining the approach required to be kept in view in a matrimonial dispute by the Courts. It was said that there has been an outburst of matrimonial disputes in recent times. Marriage is a sacred ceremony, the main purpose of which is to enable the young couple to settle down in life and live peacefully. But little matrimonial skirmishes suddenly erupt which often assume serious proportions resulting in commission of heinous crimes in which elders of the family are also involved with the result that those who could have counseled and brought about rapprochement are rendered helpless on their being arrayed as accused in the criminal case. There are many other reasons which need not be mentioned here for not encouraging matrimonial litigation so that the parties may ponder over their defaults and terminate their disputes amicably by mutual agreement instead of fighting it out in a court of law where it takes years and years to conclude and in that process the parties lose their "young" days in chasing their "cases" in different courts."

The point to be conveyed is that there is far greater emphasis in the Indian context to settle post marriage matrimonial disputes in the event of divorce related litigation, rather than focusing on pre-nuptial agreements. Traditionally, Indian society views marriage as a sacramental union and not as a contractual relationship. Although, media reports in the recent years indicate that a miniscule percentage of affluent urban couples have at times opted for executing pre-nuptial agreements. Typically in Indian society at first blush, even the thought of exercising a pre-nuptial agreement would seem abhorrent, rather face stiff resistance from family members. This is because when people marry in India, they do not readily anticipate divorce between the couple. Although, it is a matter of fact that divorce is on the rise in urban India, and even in smaller cities. It is common knowledge that, in some higher sections of Indian society, divorce is not considered to be stigmatic.

A quick survey of some of Mumbai's top divorce lawyers revealed that roughly 10 percent of marriages; mainly in the affluent socio-economic group are opting for pre-nuptial agreements. Hence, this concept has gained wide social acceptance. [For more details see article titled 'It's about my money, honey!' dated 15 March 2005, Times of India, Mumbai Edition.]

A matter agitating the validity of an elaborate memorandum of family settlement in ongoing divorce proceedings reached the portals of the Supreme Court of India. This is the reported case of *Ravi Singhal* v. *Manali Singhal*, 2001 (8) SCC 1. Here, it was argued by the appellant that an order for interim maintenance as part of the settlement made under special circumstances was void and is opposed to public policy. Attention had been drawn to Section 25 of the Hindu Marriage Act, 1955, where reference is made to agreements entered into by the parties regarding the amount of maintenance. Appellant further pleaded financial incapacity. The counsel for the respondents, on the other hand, contended that there could be a family settlement and was not against any public policy.

Hence, it becomes manifest from the above mentioned decision that the concerns as to the memorandum of settlement did find favour with the Hon'ble Apex Court, and the Judges without expressing any opinion on the merits of the matter, remanded back the matter to the single Judge as a Court of first instance for a detailed consideration of the matter.

Pre-nuptial agreements have generated immense debate internationally. One of the landmark judgment laid down by the Court of Appeal in Singapore is in the case of *Kwong Sin Hwa* v. *Lau Lee Yen*, 1993 (1) SLR 457. In this significant case, the parties were married on 1 April, 1991. They had agreed to cohabit, and to consummate the marriage after they had celebrated the traditional Chinese customary rites. Later on, the respondent refused to go through the Chinese ceremony. It was contended by the applicant that this refusal would amount to a willful refusal to consummate the marriage within the meaning of the S 100(b) of the Women's Charter and accordingly sought a decree of nullity.

It was held by the Court of Appeal in paras (E) and (F) (at page 469) of the judgment that:

> "It is clear to us that not every pre-nuptial agreement regulating or even restricting the marital relations of the husband and wife is void and against public policy. Much depends on the relevant circumstance and in particular, the nature of the agreement, the intention of the parties and the objective the agreement was designed to achieve. Consequently, where such a pre-nuptial agreement has been made and one of the parties after the marriage at the registry refuses to proceed with the religious or customary ceremony, it is not wrong for the court to give recognition to such agreement and to hold the party in default as having in effect willfully refused to consummate the marriage."

Lord Justice Thorpe of the British Court of Appeal, held in *Radmacher (formely Granatino)* v. *Granatino,* [2009] WLR (D) 227 observed at para 27 of the judgment as follows:

> ".....due respect for adult autonomy suggest that, subject of course to proper safeguards, a carefully fashioned contract should be available as an alternative to the stress, anxiety and expense of a submissions to the width of the judicial discretion....."

Although the judgment of the Court of Appeal was hailed as a victory for pre nuptial agreements in Britian, the Court of Appeal Judges had made it clear that it is for Parliament and not the Judges to change the law. But at the same time, the Court of Appeal had also articulated that Courts should continue to use their discretion to uphold pre nuptial agreements in certain circumstances. The Court of Appeal ruling had, however, emphasised the long overdue need for the Government to introduce new legislation to end the present uncertainty in the UK and make pre nuptial agreements binding.

This ruling was challenged before the Supreme Court of England and Wales. The much awaited judgment was handed down by the Supreme Court on 20 October 2010, and the same is briefly discussed hereunder:

DETAILS OF JUDGMENT OF THE SUPREME COURT OF ENGLAND AND WALES IN THE CASE OF RADMACHER (FORMERLY GRANATINO) V GRANATINO (APPELLANT) [2010] UKSC 42 ON APPEAL FROM: 2009 EWCA CIV 649: EMPHASISING ON THE PRINCIPLES TO BE APPLIED IN CONSIDERING THE IMPORTANCE OF PRE-NUPTIAL AGREEMENTS MADE BETWEEN THE HUSBAND AND WIFE BEFORE MARRIAGE, FOLLOWING THE BREAKDOWN OF MARRIAGE

The present appeal before the Supreme Court was mainly concerned with the question as to whether the Court of Appeal erred in finding that pre-nuptial contracts ought to be given decisive weight, where entered into freely by both parties, in an assessment under section 25 of the Matrimonial Causes Act, 1973.

The concept of nuptial agreements in the English jurisdiction has been summed-up in the introduction of the judgment of the UK Supreme Court.

The facts of the present case until the Supreme Court stage are as follows: Nicolas Granatino had married Katrin Radmacher in 1998. At the time of their wedding Mr Granatino had embarked on a lucrative career working for JP Morgan and Katrin. Radmacher was running a boutique in Central London. She already had some inherited wealth with the likelihood of more to come. Prior to the marriage they signed a German marriage contract at the instigation of Ms Radmacher and her family. Both the husband and wife came from countries (France and Germany) where prenuptial agreements are recognised in law, but were living in England where prenups are not legally binding. Mr Granatino did not take legal advice prior to signing the marriage contract and was not fluent in German. However, he understood what he was signing and that the nature and effect of the agreement was that he and his wife would keep their premarital assets separate and also keep separate any assets acquired during the marriage.

As a result of the contract Ms Radmacher's father advanced money and assets to her during the marriage and by the time the marriage broke down she was worth more than £100 million. When divorce proceedings had started not only had Ms Radmacher's wealth increased significantly, but Mr Granatino had given up his banking career and was studying for a doctorate at Oxford. They had two daughters.

In the High Court the trial Judge found that the agreement was manifestly unfair and awarded Mr Granatino a housing fund of £2.5 million, capitalised maintenance of £2,335,000 to provide him with an income for life as well as a sum to pay off his debts (which were mostly legal fees). Ms Radmacher appealed to the

Court of Appeal who attached far greater weight to the prenuptial agreement. The provision of a home was limited to the period of their children's education so that the house would revert to Ms Radmacher once their youngest daughter reached the age of 22 years. The capitalised maintenance was reduced to approximately £1 million to provide Mr Granatino with an income for 15 years, *i.e.* to cover the period to when his children were likely to finish their full-time education.

Mr Granatino appealed to the Hon'ble Supreme Court of England and Wales for further consideration. The Supreme Court (by a majority of 8 to 1) dismissed the appeal. The substantive judgment is given by Lord Phillips (President), with an additional judgment from Lord Mance. Lady Hale gave a dissenting judgment.

The conclusion of the judgment of the UK Supreme Court can be crystallised to be that the law in England and Wales is governed by the Matrimonial Causes Act 1973 which requires the Court "to have regard to all the circumstances of the case".

The up-shot of this very lengthy judgment can be summed-up as follows: the court should give effect to nuptial agreements that are freely entered into by each party with a full appreciation of its implications unless in the circumstances prevailing it would not be fair to hold the parties to their agreement.

## SUMMING UP THE INDIAN PERSPECTIVE

In sum, in the present day and age, the new India in the twenty first century is not ready to usher, leave alone to accept diluting the traditional sacramental notion of marriage into a somewhat commercially sounding agreement called pre-nuptial agreements. But, like the UK perspective it is believed that it is perhaps wiser to accept the concept of a prenuptial agreement in India that clearly states a fair division of property, personal possessions and financial assets than having the parties fighting over these small issues for years after filing of a divorce.

The larger issue that looms in the Indian set up is the fact that any pre-nuptial or post-nuptial agreements/settlements could well be struck down by the Courts on the ground of public policy, depending on the facts and circumstances on a case to case basis. However, the enforcement of pre-nuptial agreements may prove to be an effective check on some false or implicating prosecutions by some unscrupulous women who misuse section 498A IPC or the provisions of the Domestic Violence Act, 2005 to blackmail or to extort money.

# MORE QUESTIONS THAN ANSWERS OVER RENT-A-WOMB MARKET

Ethically, should women be paid for being surrogates? Can the rights of women and children be bartered away? If the arrangements fall foul, will it amount to adultery? Is the new law a compromise in surpassing complicated Indian adoption procedures?

**UNCERTAINTY: Emiko Yamada looked at her 11-day-old granddaughter Manji Yamada at a hospital in Jaipur on 5 August, 2008. The custody of the child, born to an Indian surrogate mother at Anand, Gujarat, and intended for a Japanese couple, Ikufumi Yamada, 45, and his then wife Yuki Yamada, 41, was in limbo after they divorced. Later, the Supreme Court intervened, and the baby left for Japan to unite with the father.**

The primordial urge to have a child of one's own flesh, blood and DNA — aided by technology, money and the Indian entrepreneurial spirit — has generated the "reproductive tourism industry," which in medical parlance is known as Assisted Reproductive Technology (ART).

In the U.K., no contract or surrogacy agreement is legally binding. In most States in the U.S., compensated surrogacy arrangements are either illegal or unenforceable. In some States in Australia, arranging commercial surrogacy is a criminal offence and any surrogacy agreement giving custody to others is void. In Canada and New Zealand, commercial surrogacy has been illegal since 2004, although altruistic surrogacy is allowed. In France, Germany and Italy, surrogacy, whether commercial or not, is unlawful. In Israel, the law only accepts the surrogate as the real mother and commercial surrogacy is illegal. What then prompts India to enact a law to make surrogacy agreements legally enforceable to protect the genetic parents, the surrogate mother and the child?

India's surrogacy boom began in January 2004 with a grandmother delivering her daughter's twins. The success flashed over the world literally spawned a virtual cottage industry in Gujarat. Would-be parents from the Indian diaspora in the U.S., the U.K. and Canada and foreigners from Malaysia, the UAE, Afghanistan, Indonesia, Uzbekistan and Pakistan, besides Nepal, are descending on sperm banks and In-Vitro Fertilization (IVF) centres in India looking for perfect sperm donors with South Asian genetic traits. Equally, renting wombs is another easy and cheap option in India. The relatively low cost of medical services, the easy availability of surrogate wombs, the abundant choices of donors with similar racial attributes and the lack of any law to regulate these practices are attracting both foreigners and Non-Resident Indians to sperm banks and surrogate mothers in India.

India has surreptitiously become a booming centre of a fertility market with its "reproductive tourism" industry reportedly estimated at Rs. 25,000 crore today. Clinically called ART, it has been in vogue in India since 1978 and today an estimated 200,000 clinics across the country offer artificial insemination, IVF and surrogacy.

So much so, the Supreme Court in 2008 in the *Baby Manji Yamada's* case, AIR 2009 SC 84 observed that "commercial surrogacy" reaching "industry proportions is sometimes referred to by the emotionally charged and potentially offensive terms wombs-for-rent, outsourced pregnancies or baby farms." It is presumably considered legitimate because no Indian law prohibits surrogacy. But then, as a retort, no law permits surrogacy either. However, the changing face of law is now going to usher in a new rent-a-womb law as India is set to be the only country to legalise commercial surrogacy.

In the absence of any law to govern surrogacy, the Indian Council of Medical Research (ICMR) issued guidelines in 2005 to check malpractices in ART. These national guidelines for accreditation, supervision and regulation of the ART clinics are, however, non-statutory, have no legal sanctity and are not binding.

Silent on major issues, they lack teeth and are often violated. Exploitation, extortion, and ethical abuses in surrogacy trafficking are rampant, go undeterred and surrogate mothers are often misused with impunity.

Surrogacy in the U.K., the U.S. and Australia costs more than $50,000, whereas advertisements on websites in India give varying costs in the range of $10,000 and offer egg donors and surrogate mothers. It is a free trading market, flourishing and thriving in the business of babies.

In a phenomenal repeat exercise to legalise commercial surrogacy, the ART (Regulation) Bill & Rules, 2010 — a draft Bill prepared by a 12-member committee including experts from the ICMR, medical specialists and other experts from the Ministry of Health and Family Welfare — was posted online recently for feedback.

Originally floated in 2008, this Bill is stated to be an Act to provide for a national framework or the regulation and supervision of Assisted Reproductive Technology and matter connected therewith or incidental thereto as a unique law proposed to be put before Parliament.

Abetting surrogacy, it legalises commercial surrogacy for single persons and married or unmarried couples, stating that the surrogate mother shall enter into a legally enforceable surrogacy agreement, she may receive monetary compensation and will relinquish all parental rights.

The 2010 draft Bill states that foreigners or NRIs coming to India to rent a womb will have to submit documentation confirming that their country of residence recognises surrogacy as legal and that it will give citizenship to the child born, through the surrogacy agreement, to an Indian mother. This, perhaps, is in view of the two-year legal battle over Nikolas and Leonard, surrogate sons of the German couple Jan Balaz and Susan Lohlad. Born to an Indian surrogate mother in January 2008, the children were rendered stateless with neither German nor Indian citizenship. The Supreme Court's intervention got them exit permits in May 2010. Likewise, after being stranded in Mumbai, a gay Israeli couple were granted

Israeli passports only after a DNA paternity test established in May 2010 that gay Dan Goldberg was the father of Itai and Liron born to a surrogate mother in Mumbai. This was after the matter was debated in the Knesset, the Israeli Parliament, and the Jerusalem District Court ruled on appeal that it was in the children's best interest to hold the DNA test to establish their paternity.

Before the law is put on the anvil, it needs a serious debate. Ethically, should women be paid for being surrogates? Can the rights of women and children be bartered away? If the arrangements fall foul, will it amount to adultery? Is the new law a compromise in surpassing complicated Indian adoption procedures? Is it compromising with reality in legitimising existing surrogacy rackets? Is India promoting "reproductive tourism?" Does the law protect the surrogate mother? Should India take the lead in adopting a new law not fostered in most countries? These are only some questions which need to be answered before we drape the new law. Let us pore into our hearts and with introspection decide carefully. Are we looking at a bane or boon? We should not wait for time to test it. We should decide now.

The surrogacy Bill needs to be discussed threadbare. Despite the legal, moral and social complexities that shroud surrogacy, there is no stopping people from exploring the possibility of becoming a parent. Women who rent their womb for surrogate pregnancy are slowly shaking off their inhibition and fear of social ostracism to bring joy to childless couples. However, the draft Bill has legal lacunae, lacks the creation of a specialist legal authority for adjudication and determination of legal rights of parties by a judicial verdict and falls foul of the existing laws. These pitfalls may be the graveyard of this proposed new law.

## ONE STOP SHOP FOR RESOLUTION OF NRI PROBLEMS

Our overseas Non-Resident Indians (NRIs) have been impressing upon the Union Government to resolve various problems confronting them. On its part, the Government holds the Pravasi Bharatiya Divas every year to take stock of their grievances. However, it is more a ritual to appease the NRI sentiment than to identify and tackle their problems on priority.

All that the NRIs want is a patient hearing by the Government and effective, expeditious and timely resolution of their problems in India. Of course, having been accustomed to practical dispute resolution systems abroad, they draw parallels and baffled Indian authorities, in turn, offer instant out-of-the-box remedies to save face. The result is an avoidable mess.

Consider some examples. A distraught husband from Patiala settled in Australia litigates for divorce while his Tamil wife settled in Hong Kong petitions Courts for maintenance and child custody. A separated US Green Card-holder husband relocated in Mumbai sues for divorce while the US-based wife from Varanasi seeks child support and benefits sitting in the US. A separated NRI couple in the UK seeks the British Court intervention to settle terms for children to visit India (with their mother) and ensure their return to the UK.

A divorced NRI husband in the US seeks child custody from mother resettelled in Hyderabad. A harried British Asian Muslim husband in the UK seeks to dissolve Nikahnama contracted in Lucknow. An embittered Swiss father of Punjabi origin seeks quick dissolution of a marriage solemnised in New Delhi. A traumatised Indian doctor in the UK seeks return of children removed to Gujarat by his wife who has launched proceedings under the Domestic Violence Act in Satara. These are real-life professional encounters which defy legislative solutions.

Today, the huge Indian diaspora nearing 30 million in 180 countries abroad pose and export from their foreign homes unique family law problems in the Indian domain which do not find ready answers in the existing Indian matrimonial legislations. Hence, judicial innovation to carve out individual relief in distinct NRI family disputes has become imperative on a case-to-case basis. But these are not consistent statutory remedies.

Recent media reports reflect a new pitch and euphoria to generate overnight answers to these NRI problems. They range from creating an NRI Commission, constituting NRI Cells, deputing designated authorities for NRI problems and forming special NRI Committees. However, such half-baked administrative measures soon fade away and resurface with the NRIs' participation in the Pravasi Bharatiya Divas in the following year. Unfortunately, the haunting ghosts return every year to resurrect with new dimensions.

The multifaceted problems of NRIs arise in the realm of validation and dissolution of marriages, enforcement of divorce decrees, maintenance obligations, matrimonial property regime, child custody/abduction, inter-country adoptions, testate/intestate succession, tenancy of property, land ownership, property investments and surrogacy issues. NRIs seek resolution of their problems from an Indian legal system not designed and created for resolving their new age issues.

Times have changed but statutory Indian laws have not kept pace. Most NRI problems do not even find definition or recognition in Indian laws. Our legislators have no time to amend them.

Against this background, measures such as NRI cells, commissions, committees or other bodies will not help. No such authority without statutory powers will have any credibility in the framework of the existing legal system. Parallel set-ups without statutory sanction are redundant. Such bodies will at best be recommendatory offices whose decisions will need judicial sanction. The aggrieved NRI or affected party will still need to invoke powers of a Court of competent jurisdiction for actual relief.

Accordingly, the Government needs to seriously enact new laws or amend existing laws to define the NRI problems and prescribe solutions. One such notable example is found under section 13 of the East Punjab Urban Rent Restriction Act, 1949. Its amendment in 2001 created a special class of NRI landlords who had a special right to recover immediate possession from tenants occupying their premises by a special summary procedure.

Likewise, in the family law arena, limping NRI marriages, abandoned spouses, abducted children, overseas adoption and surrogate relationships need statutory solutions. Family laws for NRIs need an exhaustive overhaul. Either all existing family law legislations should be amended or a single comprehensive Indian legislation should be enacted for all family-related legal problems of NRIs.

Similar is the situation in the field of property laws. Tenancy, succession, registration, investment and transfer of ownership of property form a bulk segment of NRI problems. But again, scattered, outdated legislations will serve no purpose.

Thus, there is a dire need for multiple amendments or for enacting a new NRI property law dealing with their problems comprehensively. Special legislative overhaul measures will fail if the legal system does not create or empower special Courts to deal with these legal NRI issues. There is a need to evolve a complete responsive machinery with proper rules under the newly enacted or amended NRI laws.

The time has come for a change. The answer lies in not creating cells or other toothless bodies but in enacting appropriate NRI laws, making corresponding procedural rules to implement them and vesting authority in competent Courts to adjudicate NRI disputes. This alone can provide an effective remedy. This must be done on an all-India basis. Piecemeal state legislations will not do. Above all, there is need for a sincere commitment and resolve on the part of the Government to enact or amend laws for NRIs.

## PUNJAB STATE COMMISSION FOR NRIs – AN ADVENTEROUS AGENDA

Come September and our migrated Indian brethren living overseas descend on Indian soil to reconnect with their roots. This year, there is a role reversal. With Punjab going to the hustings in 2012, Ministers in waiting and poll managers have flown in advance to UK, USA and Canada to lobby for support and seek green backs. Indigenous vote banks in rural belts in Punjab are immensely influenced by the provocative thinking of philanthropic cash rich prosperous NRIs in the matter of casting the ballot back home. This is regardless of the fact that only a 38 miniscule number of NRI voters have actually registered themselves for casting votes now allowed only by physical presence in Punjab. For wooing vote banks, the hard sell is who can devise the best mechanism for resolving the NRI problems in Punjab. This advertisement plank fuels innovative and ingenious ideas to strike emotional chords and open the threads of transatlantic NRI purse strings.

Estimated 30 million NRIs who have migrated from Indian shores reside in 180 countries abroad. About 5 million originate from Punjab and are bound with family, property and business interests back home. Their problems need solutions. Conventional laws and tardy procedures leaves them disenchanted. In this backdrop, NRIs seek alternative mediums for efficacious dispute resolution. The moot question is, can such mechanisms be created without conflict or collision with the prevalent Indian adjudication system.

Announcements in the media about the decision of the Government of Punjab for setting-up of a five-member State Commission for NRIs with a view to protect and safeguard the interest of NRIs in the State of Punjab and to recommend remedial measures to the State Government was the subject of a recent discussion aired by a news channel. Six participants representing different cross-sections debated the subject. Though the deliberations remained inconclusive but it was an introspection which established further delving. Hence, the need for a public thought is essential before a law is put on the anvil after being passed on 8 October 2011.

Who is an NRI? This is the first question to answer while seeing who is a PIO or an OCI.

A description of these terminologies answering frequently arising questions in this array of nomenclatures may be useful to summarise as follows:

- **NRI :** Section 2 of the Foreign Exchange Management Act, 1999 (FEMA) defines a person resident in India and a person resident outside India but does not define the term NRI. However, a notification defines NRI to mean a person resident outside India who is either a citizen of India or is a person of Indian origin. Under FEMA, a person "resident" in India is one who resides in India for more than 182 days in the preceding financial year and who comes or stays in India for any purpose and a "Non-Resident" is merely defined as a person who is not a resident in India. Therefore, an NRI can be summed up as an Indian citizen who is ordinarily residing outside India and holds an Indian passport.

- **PIO:** It means a foreign citizen who at any time held an Indian passport; or he/she *or* either of his/her parents or grand parents or great grand parents was born in and was permanently resident in India; or he/she is a spouse of a citizen of India or of a person of Indian origin. PIO Card holders can visit India without visa for 15 years and will be required to register with Foreigner's Registration Officer (FRO) in India when the stay exceeds 180 days continuously. PIOs enjoy parity with NRIs in respect of certain facilities but have no political rights and can apply for Indian citizenship after residing in India for a minimum of seven years.
- **OCI:** A foreign national who was eligible to become a citizen of India on 26 January, 1950, or was a citizen of India on or at any time after the said date or belonged to a territory that became part of India after 15 August, 1947 and, his/her children and grand children are eligible for registration as OCIs. They enjoy multiple entry, multipurpose lifelong visa for visiting India, are exempted registration with FRO/police authorities for any length of stay in India and are entitled to benefits notified under section 7B of the Citizenship Act. An OCI registered for 5 years and residing in India for one year can be granted Indian citizenship but have no political rights.

The enacted law labelled "the Punjab State Commission for NRIs Act, 2011" is stated to be "An Act to provide for the constitution of the Commission for NRIs in the State of Punjab with a view to protecting and safeguarding the interests of the NRIs in the State of Punjab, and to recommend remedial measures to State Government." It defines a "Complaint" by stating that it "means all petitions/communications received in State Commission for NRIs from an NRI or any other person on his behalf, in person, by post, by telegram, by fax or by any other means whatsoever, alleging, disputes or violations or abetment thereof or negligence in the prevention of such dispute or violation, by a public servant or a private person or the material on the basis of which the Punjab State Commission for NRIs takes *suo motu* cognizance." The law however, does not define what is an NRI dispute or a violation. Consequently, the authority, jurisdiction and powers of the Commission, are hazy, undefined and in a limbo. Though the proposed body has extensive investigative powers through the existing official machinery but its actual implementation for practical relief by passing effective orders will be questionable, doubtful and difficult. The uncertain jurisdiction treads on no foundation. Without defining the realm in which the powers will work, the exercise is in futility, as the NRI commission cannot usurp power of judicial courts.

A perusal of the enactment reveals that its focus is more on what concerns those who will be members of the proposed Commission and what they will get as benefits. The actual emphasis on what the body in making would actually do and how it would dispense justice in relation to a defined arena of NRI disputes or violations is blissfully missing. The contents of the proposed law seriously need a deliberated work up.

Whether it is a NRI, PIO or an OCI, their grouses revolve around family law related issues, property disputes, immigration related questions and trysts with criminal law. But then, a hierarchical system of civil and criminal Courts in accordance with existing jurisprudence mandates that all disputes shall be adjudicated by Courts of competent jurisdiction as per statutory laws made by Parliament and applicable throughout India. Consequently, identifying an "NRI dispute" for being heard and decided by a different realm will clearly fall foul of the system of prevalent adjudication by existing Courts. A civil, matrimonial or criminal dispute in India cannot carry separate tags and are bound to one system. Therefore, vesting an NRI Commission with such supposed powers may not be agreeable. Parallel hearings which cannot achieve finality will only compound problems. The aggrieved NRI will still need to invoke the powers of a competent Court for actual relief as an NRI Commission cannot enjoy parallel statutory adjudication powers.

In the alternative function of the NRI Commission of being a recommendatory body, the existing Law Commission of India and Punjab State Law Commission, are adequately saddled with this exclusive role of suggesting changes in laws on all fronts. In any case, no major exercise is needed to identify where amendments are required as both the problems and desired solutions are well known to all. Most of them relate to Central Laws within the ambit of Parliament. Hence, any State-level exercise to achieve independent changes will be an exercise in futility. Moreover, gullible NRIs would be more keen on a practical and empirical solution and not its process of change.

The solution lies in making exhaustive amendments in existing laws. In the family law arena, abandoned spouses, abducted children, limping marriages, inter country adoptions, surrogate relationships and marital property disputes need statutory resolution. Current family laws need exhaustive overhaul. Hence, either all existing family law legislations made by Parliament should be amended or a single comprehensive Indian law should be enacted for all family law related problems of NRIs.

Similarly, in the realm of property issues related to tenancy, succession, registration, investment of funds, transfer and ownership of assets, need a fresh look at a national level. Likewise, human smuggling and illegal trafficking not defined under Indian law require urgent legislation. Even problems in criminal laws need Central law changes.

The need is dire for enacting new laws to deal with the new generation NRI problems more comprehensively. But, at the same time, legislative changes will fail if they are not backed-up with specially created or empowered Courts to deal with these legal issues of NRIs. Therefore, enacting appropriate NRI laws, making corresponding procedural statutory rules and vesting authority in competent Courts to adjudicate NRI disputes is the wholesome answer on an all India basis. Piecemeal State endeavours by creating bodies in conflict will not be *in tandem*. The purpose though laudable will lead nowhere.

---

## VOTING RIGHTS FOR NRIs: AN OPTICAL ILLUSION

On the eve of the Pravasi Bharatiya Divas (PBD), 2011, announcements were made in Parliament with much fanfare by the Centre that a "Gazette Notification has been issued giving voting rights to Non-Resident Indians." In the debate on the Representation of People (Amendment) Bill, 2010, to allow NRIs to exercise their franchise in Indian elections, the Government stated that comprehensive electoral reforms are on the cards as the Union Cabinet has cleared amendments to the Bill. The Parliament has now passed the Bill and the law stands amended.

The Representation of Peoples Act, 1951, has undergone some changes. Previously, NRIs were barred under section 19 of the Act from voting if they remained outside India for six months for whatever reasons. The Government has inserted sub-section 1AA under section 20 of the Act to do away with this disability to give voting rights to NRIs.

The definition of NRI is elusive in the citizenship laws. However, section 2 of the Foreign Exchange Management Act, 1999 (FEMA) defines a person resident in India and a person resident outside India but does not define the term NRI. However, a notification defines NRI to mean a person "resident" outside India who is either a citizen of India or a person of Indian origin. Under FEMA, a person "resident" in India is one who resides in India for more than 182 days in the preceding financial year and who comes to stay in India for any purpose.

A "Non-Resident" is merely defined as a person who is not a resident of India. Therefore, an NRI can be summed up as an Indian citizen who is ordinarily residing outside India and holds an Indian passport. This is easier said than done.

For whom are these voting rights meant? It is stated that they are meant for three categories of 11 million NRIs who are not residents in India. **First**, they are Indian citizens who stay abroad for employment or business or vocation or any other purpose indicating an indefinite period of stay abroad. **Secondly**, they are Indian citizens working abroad on assignments with foreign Government agencies. And **thirdly**, they are Indian officials of Central or State Governments deputed abroad on temporary assignments or posted in Indian Missions abroad.

The voting rights for NRIs are otherwise an optical illusion. This is because the Government notification excludes Indian citizens who have become foreign nationals. And secondly, eligible voters can exercise their franchise only if they are present in the constituency on the polling day. There is no provision for postal ballots or provision for casting votes at Indian Embassies and Consulates abroad. Electronic voting is yet a far cry. Clearly, the announcement is illusory. The announcement is, therefore, a pre-PBD public relations exercise. Even NRIs gain little.

The principal issue remains. Both the Constitution of India and the Indian Citizenship Act, 1955, categorically prohibit dual citizenship and debar holding of two nationalities simultaneously of two different countries. To strike a compromise, the government amended the Citizenship Act, in 2005 to create a class of Overseas Citizens of India (OCI). This was primarily the only grant of a multiple-entry life-long visa for Indians-turned foreigners who could visit India anytime without a normal visa for any purpose whenever they like. However, the amended section 7B of the Citizenship Act specifically prohibits political, voting and other rights for OCIs. Thus, the bar of dual citizenship will never give way to any voting rights to Indians who are foreigners under the label of OCIs.

Consequently, only the 11 million NRIs with Indian passports qualify for voting rights if they are physically present in India on the polling day. The remaining 19 million NRIs do not even qualify to vote. The 11 million NRIs have to ensure their physical presence on the day of the polling to vote. Patriotism to vote is not so strong that the NRI will travel to India only for purposes of exercising his/her franchise. Clearly, the purpose of voting proves futile.

In the World Bank's recently released Migration and Remittances Fact Book, 2011, it is stated that India continued to be the largest recipient of remittances in 2010 with figures stated to be rising from $49.6 billion in 2009 to $55 billion in 2010. India is also stated to be the country with the second largest number of emigrants after Mexico. Over 30 million NRIs live in 180 countries abroad but we only want their euros, dollars and pounds. If we wish to have the best of both worlds, the serious option is not voting rights but dual nationality. The homing pigeons must be allowed the flight home with landing rights.

The time has now come for Indians to be recognised as citizens of India irrespective of their current nationality and place of residence abroad. Partial compromises will not do. The package and deal should be wholesome. Indians abroad should be given Indian citizenship irrespective of parallel identities of foreign citizenship.

Dual nationality should be a reality and not a dream. Our Indian brethren are not step-children. There is need for a relook at the issue which may warrant a constitutional amendment. This exercise must start in the new year. It may take a while but it would be worthwhile.

# CANCELLED INDIAN PASSPORTS

The question of nationality or citizenship of individuals, the conferment as well as its deprivation are complicated issues, which entail numerous legal implications. There is still another side to the coin, so far as Indian law is concerned. The Constitution of India provides for a single citizenship for the entire country in the territory of India. The provisions relating to citizenship in the Constitution of India are contained in articles 5 to 11 in Part II of the Constitution of India. Article 9 of the Constitution of India clearly mandates that no person shall be a citizen of India by virtue of article 5, or be deemed to be a citizen of India by virtue of article 6 or article 8, if he has voluntarily acquired the citizenship of any foreign State.

Thus, it becomes abundantly clear that an Indian citizen cannot have dual nationality. Therefore, if an Indian citizen voluntarily acquires citizenship of any foreign state, then, such Indian citizen has to give up or relinquish all rights as an Indian citizen as the Indian Constitution does not permit an Indian citizen to simultaneously have citizenship of any other country. Further, termination of Indian citizenship is covered in section 9 of the Citizenship Act, 1955. The provisions for termination are separate and distinct under section 9 apart from the provisions for making a declaration of renunciation which are dealt with separately under section 8.

Section 9(1) of the Act provides that any citizen of India who by naturalisation or registration acquires the citizenship of another country shall cease to be a citizen of India. It also provides that any citizen of India who voluntarily acquires the citizenship of another country shall cease to be a citizen of India. Section 9 is a complete code in itself as regards the termination of Indian citizenship on voluntary acquisition of the citizenship of a foreign country.

In exercise of powers under section 18 of the Citizenship Act, 1955, the Government of India has made the Citizenship Rules, 1956. The acquisition of another country's passport is also deemed to be voluntary acquisition of another country's nationality under the Citizenship Rules, 1956. Rule 30 of the Citizenship Rules 1956 in this regard authorizes the Central Government to determine the acquisition of citizenship of another country.

Further, para 3 of Schedule III of the Citizenship Rules, 1956 states that "the fact that a citizen of India has obtained on any date a passport from the Government of any other country shall be conclusive proof of his having voluntarily acquired the citizenship of that country before that date".

In view of the position stated above, it may be commented that persons who acquire citizenship of another country lose Indian citizenship from the date on which they acquire such citizenship of a foreign country or another country's passport as both the Constitution of India and the Indian Citizenship Act,1955 prohibit dual citizenship and holding of two nationalities simultaneously of two different countries.

The recent announcements by Indian Consulates abroad stating that Indian citizens acquiring foreign citizenships are required to renounce their Indian citizenship and surrender their Indian passports for cancellation and obtain surrender certificates from concerned Consulates has perturbed the NRI community. Renunciation of Indian citizenship under section 8 may be different from termination of citizenship under section 9 of the Citizenship Act. Obtaining a foreign passport from any other country is conclusive proof of voluntary acquisition of the citizenship of that country under the Passports Act. Both the Constitution of India and the Passports Act, prohibit dual nationality and hence an Indian Passport is deemed to be cancelled from the day nationality of a foreign citizenship is acquired. However, a declaration of renunciation of citizenship under section 8 of the Citizenship Act to be made by a former Indian citizen who is now a national of another country is mandatory under law and must be adhered to. Such declarations must be strictly enforced and implemented to prevent travel on Indian passports by former citizens who have relinquished Indian nationality. The majesty of law must prevail.

Under section 17 of the Passports Act, 1967, a passport or a travel document shall at all times remain the property of the Central Government. Moreover, possession of an Indian passport simultaneously with the nationality of a foreign country would be violative of the essence of Indian law which prohibits dual nationality. The steps taken by the Government of India to enforce the renunciation of Indian citizenship is a welcome move as those who chose to adorn a foreign nationality must rightfully give up their Indian passport to which they are not entitled under law. They may find respite in the acquisition of an Overseas Citizen of India status which is a compromise on their rights and entitles them to lifelong return to India without any visa requirement.

# DYNAMICS AND DIMENSIONS OF HUMAN SMUGGLING: THE DARK SIDE OF THE MOON

## A. BASIC FEATURES OF INDIAN IMMIGRATION SCENARIO

- WTO Study says that India is seventh largest country in the world with a population of over one billion people which accounts for 16.7% of the world population.
- About 30 million persons of Indian origin live in 180 countries abroad. 400,000 Indians immigrate every year.
- Interpol study "Marco Polo" reports that India is one of the countries accounting for the largest number of illegal immigrants coming to Western Europe and UNODC has commissioned a special study on this issue.
- The UNODC report on "Smuggling of migrants from India to Europe and in particular to UK: A study on Punjab and Haryana 2009" released in Chandigarh on 11 March, 2010 quotes that over one lac illegal immigrants from India are behind bars in foreign jurisdictions and over 20,000 youths from Punjab alone attempt irregular immigration every year.
- A multi-million dollar illegal immigration racket where 20,000 to 30,000 USD is charged by unscrupulous agents to send gullible Indians abroad flourishes in India, unabated and unchecked. Three examples are cited:
  (a) In 1996, 289 South Asians including 170 Indians from Punjab found a watery grave in the Ionian Sea in their voyage of illegal immigration to Europe.
  (b) UNODC quoted Indian - American Centre for political awareness in U.S.A. to inform that 73 men from Punjab duped by employment agents in Punjab landed in Tehran after a 1500-mile journey on foot. They were frost-bitten and their toes had to be amputated.
  (c) On June 24, 2007, Indian police apprehended an agent with 300 fake travel documents including 25 forged passports, 114 fake visas of Schengen countries and duplicate passports with fake identities.
- UNODC committed to combating global human trafficking estimates that about 2 million migrants cross international borders without authorization every year. The reasons for this in India are high population growth, increasing unemployment rate, quest for a better economic life and for improvement in status besides seeking professional growth in life.
- U.K. visas in India deals with over 500,000 applications every year and over 300,000 visas are issued every year. 80% illegal immigration from India

takes place from Punjab. Over 500,000 illegal immigrants from India live in U.K. alone & thousands from Punjab attempt to sneak into U.K. every year.

- The problem is not in Punjab alone. About 400,000 illegal workers from Andhra Pradesh without passports, travel documents or visas live in labour camps in UAE desperate to be jailed to enable their return to India.

## B. A LAW IN THE MAKING – THE PUNJAB PREVENTION OF HUMAN SMUGGLING ACT, 2010

It is an Act to provide for the regulation of the profession of travel agents with a view to check and curb their illegal and fraudulent activities, and malpractices of the persons involved in the organized human smuggling in the State of Punjab and for the matters connected therewith or incidental thereto. **This law has seven noteworthy features:**

- It defines human smuggling and travel agent.
- Provides for a licensing regime for agents and requires compulsory bank guarantees.
- Gives power of search, seizure and arrest.
- Creates special designated Courts for trials under the Act.
- Identifies defined variable punishment for offences under the Act.
- Provides for making of complaints by aggrieved persons to Judicial Magistrates for trial before special Courts.
- Authorises special Court to decide whether any illegally acquired property is liable to be confiscated.

Travel agent is defined as a person in a profession that involves arranging, managing or conducting affairs related to sending people abroad. It includes consultancy for permit emigration, obtaining education, work, travel for tourism, cultural entertainment or musical shows, medical treatment, spreading or preaching religion, participating in sport tournaments, issuing advertisements for travel, holding seminars and lectures to promote emigration, arranging matrimonial alliances for purposes of emigration, and arranging overseas travel for any purpose whatsoever. **Dishonest misrepresentation with intention to have wrongful gain for inducing, deception, cheating or allurement for above activities is punishable under the Act.** If any travel agent wants to advertise or hold seminars, he will have to notify the competent authority in writing giving complete details of advertisement of seminars.

## C. THEME FOR DISCUSSION AND ANALYSIS

- The urge for illegal migration cannot be curbed. The need for migration needs to be channelised and need for sustainable solutions needs to be explored. Legalized, managed, integrated and organised migration must be opted for. The only way of migration by legal means must be publicized
- The suggested solutions possible are a comprehensive approach on migration, setting out legal migration opportunities, selective migration, migration profiling, regularization of over stay (and not amnesty) short –

term visas and comprehensive policy determination by categorization of classes of visas

- A two-fold approach can be seen in the Indian context in the perspective of India where managed migration is currently in experimental stages. One set of ideology practices promotion whereas the other thinking is based on regulation of migration. Both follow an educative thought-oriented process. An active Government participation is a must for effective resolution of managed migration at operational levels in both these schools of thought.
- The first approach looking at promotion of migration sees channelised migration programmes. These visualize bi-lateral localized agreements for immigration between sending and receiving countries. A Government bureau in the States of Punjab and Haryana for assisting State residents to route immigration through Government channels with visas facilitation by VFS will eliminate traffickers with their illegal operations. This will have the following advantages with participation of the State machinery. These are:
  (a) Economic interests in promoting migration can be insured. The remittances for sending countries and special manpower needs for receiving countries can be identified in this process by channelised migration through local agreements.
  (b) Selective migration of special trades fulfills the need of receiving countries while simultaneously providing the need for employment and professional avenues of sending countries.
  (c) Localized agreements eliminate larger complicated issues of bigger arrangements on country basis, involving political and conflicting interests.
  (d) Such localised arrangements are more practical, more workable and easy to manage and administer by a bi–lateral participation between a State Government & a Foreign Embassy whose interests are limited to that State.
- The second approach looks at selective regulation of immigration by a system of checks and balances created and put in the system of migration. This process of regulation visualizes the following practices:
  (a) Tougher checks using biometrics, iris and other identity tests
  (b) Compulsory identity cards for foreign nationals.
  (c) Employee checking services and penalties for employers in employment of illegal workers from sending countries working in receiving countries
  (d) Imposition of nationality tests and English speaking tests
  (e) Enforcement networks by Government partnership to crack down on human trafficking.
- However, a tightening visa regime will deter clandestine illegal operators only if it is coupled with awareness, aids, publicity and education for enabling prospective migrants to take a conscious decision themselves to

migrate or not. In India today, with booming economic growth and increasing employments opportunities, it may be necessary to educate the youth whether they need to migrate. In this context, the role of the MOIA and State Governments supported by Foreign Missions to launch an outreach campaign into villages in Punjab where vans, banners, posters, newspapers and other publicity material in Hindi and Punjabi languages to carry the message of Migration–the right way would be extremely beneficial. This may be the second mode of helping all concerned to take a conscious decision for oneself for deciding to migrate or not and thus helping managed migration.

# HUMAN SMUGGLING: WHAT PUNJAB MUST DO

**Human smuggling, illegal trafficking and unethical immigration businesses are on the rise in India and other countries. The Punjab Prevention of Human Smuggling Act is a welcome move. Once it gets the President's assent, the State Government should draft comprehensive rules to enforce the legislation in letter and spirit**

The Punjab Prevention of Human Smuggling Act, 2010, is awaiting the President of India's assent. It is an important piece of legislation as it seeks to regulate the profession of travel agents to check their illegal and fraudulent activities and malpractices of those involved in the organised human smuggling in Punjab.

It has several noteworthy features. 'Human smuggling' and 'travel agent' are well defined. Travel agent is defined as a person in a profession that involves arranging, managing or conducting affairs related to sending people abroad. It includes consultancy for permanent emigration, obtaining education, work, travel for tourism, cultural entertainment or musical shows, medical treatment, spreading or preaching religion and so on.

The key focus of the legislation is on human smuggling as opposed to human trafficking. The distinction is crucial. Human smuggling facilitates illegal entry of people from one country to another. It has a cross-border element of voluntary cooperation without any coercion or undue influence. In contrast to human trafficking, there are no victims in human smuggling. Human trafficking entails slavery and possibly has no international element.

The Act provides for a much-needed licensing regime for agents and requires compulsory bank guarantees. Clearly, this will nail down middlemen of all sorts and fly-by-night street operators.

The legislation is not without teeth because it gives the power of search, seizure and arrest. Under the existing Central legislation, travel agents can be booked under section 420 of the Indian Penal Code, in terms of which it is very difficult to prove the offence of cheating as most transactions take place in cash. But the Punjab legislation gives more powers to the police in terms of offences being cognisable and non-bailable.

A separate mechanism has been carved out as the legislation seeks to create specially designated Courts for trials under the new Act. It identifies defined variable punishments for offences.

There is a provision for filing complaints by aggrieved persons to Judicial Magistrates for trial before the special Courts. The special Court is authorised to decide whether any illegally acquired property is liable to be confiscated.

Dishonest misrepresentation to have wrongful gain for inducing, deception, cheating or allurement for the activities carried out by the travel agents are punishable. There is also a caveat for legitimate business promotion. If any travel agent wants to advertise or hold seminars, he must notify the competent authority with details of advertisement of such seminars.

As the rules so framed by the Punjab Government after the Presidential assent should be comprehensive and free from ambiguity, the authorities concerned would do well to consider the following issues.

The *locus standi* of aggrieved persons should be given a broad sweep without hinging on technicalities. Quite often, the victims of human smuggling are stranded *en route* in hostile conditions in foreign countries. Their next of kin in such a situation should be empowered to file criminal complaints or claims for compensation against erring parties. Foreign Missions in the consular district of New Delhi should also be brought within the ambit of aggrieved persons so that they can lodge criminal complaints against habitual offenders who deal in bulk fraudulent applications.

In a world without borders, the 2010 Act like the provisions of the Hindu Marriage Act, 1955, should also have extra-territorial application. It is common knowledge that cross-border cartels operate from different jurisdictions right from the sending country to the receiving country. No complaint should fail on the ground that monetary consideration was paid outside India and that part of the cause of action took outside the territories of India.

There is need for a strict code for advertising by travel agents and immigration consultancies. There should be an express prohibition on all immigration-related advertisements in the media — print and electronic — for not advertising or canvassing the number of visas allegedly procured by their consultancies. Quite often, such figures of successful applicants are exaggerated and inflated and there is no way by which the innocent and gullible members of the public can check such projected figures.

As for offences, the rules should be applicable to any immigration consultancy, agent, franchisee operating even outside Punjab, if the principal office of the branch of such a concern is situated within Punjab. There should be a clear embargo on canvassing projected time schedules for permanent residency/ settlement in any foreign country.

The provision for a bank guarantee to be furnished by all such licensed immigration operators and travel agencies should be on *ad valorem* basis and the amount of the bank guarantee should be directly proportional to the number of applications handled by any such consultancy or agency.

In terms of compliance requirements, the rules under the said legislation should provide that any licensed immigration consultancy/travel agency or operator, should file a mandatory quarterly return on the number of applications handled by any such agency or operator with the steering committee constituted under the rules or with the Deputy Commissioner of the respective district, which shall be a pre-condition for the renewal of the annual licence.

To protect students, the rules should prohibit payment of the handsome commission paid to the local agents and franchisees in India by low level foreign universities from the tuition fees paid by the students in India. Over the years, this has promoted a different type of an industry giving fillip to lot of illegal activities on the side to exploit the student avenue.

Mass awareness is important. The rules should direct Regional Passport Offices (RPOs) in Punjab to adequately publicise this beneficial piece of legislation, in their respective offices. For the convenience of public, especially rural youth hailing from the far flung areas of Punjab who are victims of cheating by unscrupulous agents and dubious touts, copies of the legislation translated in Punjabi should be made available at the said RPOs.

One needs to look at the entire gamut of human smuggling. The NRI marriages in Punjab are a very serious problem, especially in terms of abandoned brides. Marriage is also used as a very convenient camouflage for human smuggling. Marriage palace operators provide complete packages to facilitate such commercial marriages. The rules under the legislation in question should bring within its ambit, abettors and perpetrators of such sham marriages, or victims of marriages of convenience.

As part of corporate social responsibility obligations, business houses in Punjab should be motivated to take suitable initiatives to publicise the evil effects of human trafficking and the dangers involved in patronising fly-by-night travel agents.

The Chief Secretary of Punjab, after constituting a Core Steering and Monitoring Committee, should regularly review the enforcement of the legislation and maintain comprehensive data of complaints and convictions under the said legislation. The Chief Secretary can include in the committee people from different walks of life. This could as well give an opportunity to review the working of the legislation. The core panel could have a dedicated a website and an email address to create a direct access for the public for their viewpoints.

The rules could well stipulate that the Punjab Government in close cooperation with the Ministry of External Affairs (MEA) and Ministry of Overseas Indians Affairs (MOIA) should also interact with all the Embassies and Foreign Missions in the consular district of New Delhi to share their international data of habitual immigration offenders, networks and cartels engaged in the business of human trafficking and human smuggling with the MEA and the MOIA so that they can further share and transmit the available data with the Punjab Government. This will prevent illegal migration and ensure greater cross-border cooperation with all member states.

The rules could provide for an immigration *Ombudsman* at the regional and district level. This soft option could be organised by complainants who do not have the resources to invoke the due process of law. A savings clause regarding the Consumer Courts' jurisdiction for deficiency in service and for refund/ compensation should also be there explicitly in the rules so that the offenders cannot possibly attempt to take refuge of the technicalities of law.

We have to wait and see which way the pendulum swings down the road. Hopefully, the letter and spirit of the rules will be at par with the Punjab Government's laudable effort in framing the 2010 legislation.

## MIGRATION GLOBAL PERSPECTIVES

- Over the years, Wilton Park, a leading UK-based think-tank for discussion of key international policy changes, has been debating key issues relating to migration policies, themes, perceptions, perspectives, trends and its future policy options. According to its 2007 report, legal migration is the most sensitive subject for discussion, particularly in terms of the public debate over numbers.

- The Interpol estimates that India contributes to the largest illegal population in Europe, and an estimated two million Indians cross international borders illegally every year.

- Human trafficking has now become a larger 'industry' worldwide than drug trafficking. In India alone, it is a multi-million dollar business.

- Globally, remittances are estimated to be equivalent to three times development aid.

- Members of the European Union already co-operate on shared mechanisms within borders such as Eurodac, a European Union-wide electronic system for the identification of asylum-seekers and illegal immigrants.

- FrontEx is an independent European agency funded by the EU and individual member states. With headquarters in Warsaw, it aims to coordinate the operational co-operation of their external borders.

### Patterns of immigration

- According to Wilton Park's 2008 findings, patterns of immigration and emigration are generally shaped by the long-term economic performance of a country.

- There is likely to be increased competition amongst the more developed countries for highly skilled migrants. On current demographic projections, China, for example, may change from being a source to a destination country.

- Political, religious and ethnic persecution are the key drivers of forced migration, but new displacement scenarios are evolving, including environmental degradation, declining resource, population growth and climate change.

- Factors vary regionally. In South Asia, migration is a well-established livelihood option. In the European Union, migration has been facilitated by the right to free movement of labour.

- Governments will continue to control illegal migration to facilitate the migration flows which they want.

- Public attitudes to migration are frequently negative.

- Policy responses from South Asian countries have been *ad hoc*; it is one of the few areas where no regional process is in place for strategic management of migration.

■ There are no real indications of the emergence of a leading international migration agency. The International Organisation for Migration could be a candidate.

**Areas of concern & reform**

■ Need to enact a Central legislation to check illegal trafficking, human smuggling and thriving unethical immigration businesses.

■ Imperative need for a consolidated work permit visa regime in India for inward foreign migration especially for highly skilled foreign workers which could also be a good source of revenue.

■ Spreading of awareness and education of the pitfalls of illegal immigration.

■ Need to establish managed migration channels.

# GOING ABROAD — IN JAIL

Upon petitioning the Punjab and Haryana High Court in Chandigarh, the London Borough of Ealing was recently successful in securing an emergency travel document for 12-year-old Gurinderjit Singh abandoned on the streets of Southall in the UK in 2008.

Sadly, he was a victim of illegal immigration as those who deserted him preferred to remain in hiding to stay in the UK to conceal their wrongful immigration status. Perhaps, they harboured a belief that deserting the boy would lead to the regularisation of his immigration status in the UK. This did not happen. The Borough through the British Courts became the boy's guardian and moved for his repatriation.

Fortunately, the boy was reunited with his extended family to celebrate his 12th birthday at home in his village in Punjab. Gurinderjit was happily back home on 29 March, 2010, after the Guardian Judge took a decision on his custody.

At a recent seminar in Chandigarh of the United Nations Office on Drugs and Organised Crime (UNODC), it was revealed in a report that 20,000 persons from Punjab try to migrate abroad illegally every year.

It was also reported that over one lakh persons who migrated illegally landed up behind bars. Many languish in jails abroad with no hope of return. Others, who stay on for economic and social reasons, are compelled to remain away from their homeland forever to keep their illegal status intact. Their return becomes a myth. No wonder, human trafficking agents thrive.

The Passports Act, 1967, and the Passports Rules, 1980, recognise the grant of emergency travel certificates authorising persons to enter India. Citizens of India abroad whose passports are lost, stolen or damaged and who cannot be issued a new passport without verification and persons who produce insufficient evidence to justify Indian citizenship, as also Indian citizens whose passports have been impounded, revoked or refused or have to be repatriated to India qualify for the grant of emergency travel certificates.

The Indian Missions abroad within whose jurisdiction such Indian citizens exist are competent to issue emergency travel certificates. However, neither the law nor any policy actually helps the illegal immigrants who attempt to return home in desperation abroad. The procedure for obtaining an emergency travel certificate is cumbersome and technical.

Proving Indian nationality for an Indian citizen in the absence of any documentation can be difficult. The verification of antecedents in India by the Indian Mission abroad as a precondition poses a major challenge.

The result: a large number of Indian nationals languish in jails abroad. Communication problems, lack of money and an inhospitable climate abroad can perpetuate their agony. Such hapless Indian citizens are a condemned lot.

Perhaps, the best possible solution to commence the return procedure is for every State Government to ask the Central Government to request all Foreign Embassies and High Commissions in New Delhi to give them a list of all Indian nationals detained in their respective countries on account of illegal immigration.

Thereafter, the Centre can pass on such lists to the States to which illegal immigrants belong. Once the antecedents of such Indian nationals are verified, emergency travel certificates can be issued to them through the Indian Missions abroad.

Leaving things in a flux and carrying on with the *status quo* will not help. As of now, the inclination, initiative and incentive to adopt a positive path seems to be lacking. States will have to prompt the Centre to start a fast-track process for the return of illegal immigrants. Once immigrants start returning home, their cases would deter others who wish to go abroad illegally. The enactment of a deterrent law may also help.

## LEGALISING SURROGACY — BOON OR BANE?

The Union Cabinet will examine the draft Assisted Reproductive Technology (Regulation) Bill, 2010, and then table it in Parliament.

Floated earlier in 2008, it envisages a national framework for the regulation and supervision of Assisted Reproductive Technology (ART). It legalises commercial surrogacy for single persons, married or unmarried couples. When it becomes law, the surrogate mother will have to enter into a legally enforceable surrogacy agreement.

It states that foreigners or NRIs coming to India to rent a womb will have to submit documentation confirming that their country of residence recognises surrogacy as legal and that it will give citizenship to the child born through the surrogacy agreement from an Indian mother. This, perhaps, is in view of the two-year legal battle of the surrogate sons, Nikolas and Leonard, born to the German couple Jan Balaz and Susan Lohlad. The two kids, born to an Indian surrogate mother in January 2008, were rendered stateless with neither German or Indian citizenship. Subsequently, the Supreme Court got them exit permits in May 2010.

Similarly, after being stranded in Mumbai, a gay Israeli couple was granted Israeli passports only after a DNA paternity test established in May 2010 that gay Dan Goldberg was the father of Itai and Liron born to a surrogate mother in Mumbai. This followed a debate in Knesset (Israeli Parliament) and the Jerusalem District Court ruled in appeal that it was in the children's best interest to hold the DNA test to establish their paternity.

Before Parliament passes the Bill, it must be debated thoroughly. Ethically, should women be paid for being surrogates? Can the rights of women and children be bartered? If the arrangements fall foul, will it amount to adultery? Is the Bill a compromise in surpassing complicated Indian adoption procedures?

Is the new law compromising with reality in legitimising existing surrogacy rackets? Is India promoting "reproductive tourism"? Does the law protect the surrogate mother? Should India take the lead in adapting a new law not fostered in most countries?

The draft Bill lacks the creation of a specialist legal authority for adjudication and determination of legal rights of parties by a judicial verdict and falls in conflict with the existing laws. These pitfalls need to be examined closely before enacting the legislation.

In the UK, no contract or surrogacy agreement is legally binding. In most states in the US, compensated surrogacy arrangements are either illegal or unenforceable. In some states in Australia, arranging commercial surrogacy is a criminal offence and any surrogacy agreement giving custody to others is void. In Canada and New Zealand, commercial surrogacy has been illegal since 2004, although altruistic surrogacy is allowed. In France, Germany and Italy, surrogacy, whether commercial or not, is unlawful.

What, then, prompts India to plan a legislation to protect the genetic parents, surrogate mother and the child? India's surrogacy boom began in January 2004 with a grandmother delivering her daughter's twins. The success spawned a virtual cottage industry in Gujarat. Today, India boasts of being the first to legalise commercial surrogacy soon to legitimise both intra-and inter-country surrogacy.

The would-be parents from the Indian diaspora in the US, the UK and Canada and foreigners from Malaysia, the UAE, Afghanistan, Indonesia, Uzbekistan, Pakistan besides Nepal are descending on sperm banks and In-vitro Fertilisation (IVF) centres in India looking for South Asian genetic traits of perfect sperm donors.

Moreover, renting wombs has become an easy and cheap option in India. Relatively low cost of medical services, easy availability of surrogate wombs, abundant choices of donors with similar racial attributes and the lack of any law to regulate these practices is attracting both foreigners and NRIs to sperm banks and surrogate mothers.

Surreptitiously, India has become a booming centre of a fertility market with its "reproductive tourism" industry reportedly estimated at Rs. 25,000 crore today. Clinically called ART, it has been in vogue in India since 1978 and today an estimated 200,000 clinics across the country offer artificial insemination, IVF and surrogacy.

In *Baby Manji Yamada's* case, AIR 2009 SC 84, the Apex Court observed that "commercial surrogacy reaching industry proportions is sometimes referred to by the emotionally charged and potentially offensive terms like wombs for rent, outsourced pregnancies or baby farms". It is presumably considered legitimate because no Indian law prohibits surrogacy. But then, as a retort, no law permits surrogacy either. Surely, the proposed law will usher in a new rent-a-womb law as India is set to be the only one to legalise commercial surrogacy.

In the absence of any law to govern surrogacy, the Indian Council of Medical Research Guidelines (2005) for accreditation, supervision and regulation of ART clinics in India are often violated. Exploitation, extortion and ethical abuses in surrogacy trafficking are rampant and surrogate mothers are misused with impunity.

Surrogacy in the UK, the US and Australia costs more than US $ 50,000 whereas advertisements on websites in India give varying costs in the range of US $ 10,000 and offer egg donors and surrogate mothers. It is a free trading market, flourishing and thriving in the business of babies.

# LAW FOR NON-RESIDENT INDIAN FAMILIES – A DILEMMA

## I. THE PROBLEMS IN BRIEF

Abandoned bride in distress due to runaway foreign country resident Indian spouse. Stressed Non-Resident Asian parent frantically searching spouse in India who has removed their child from a foreign jurisdiction in violation of a foreign Court order. Desperate spouse seeking child support and maintenance. Non-Resident spouse seeking enforcement of foreign divorce decree in India. Agitated children of deceased Non-Resident Indian turning turtle in trying to seek transfer of property in India and its repatriation to foreign shores. Anxious and excited foreign adoptive parents desperately trying to resolve Indian legal formalities for adopting a child in India. Bewildered officials of a foreign High Commission trying to understand the customary practices of marriage and divorce exclusively saved by Indian legislation. Foreign police officials trying to understand intricacies of Indian law in apprehending offenders of law on foreign soil. These are some instances of problems arising every day from cross-border migration.

There are a large number of legal issues that concern a sizable section of the Global Indian Community residing abroad. Though the Non-Resident Indians have increased multifold in foreign jurisdictions, but family law disputes and situations are handicapped for want of proper professional information and advice on Indian laws. The lure for settling in foreign jurisdictions attracts a sizable Indian population but the problems created by such migration largely remain unresolved.

## II. THE SEARCH FOR SOLUTION IN LAW

Solicitors and litigants overseas worldwide frantically look for professional opinions and advice when the problems come to the Indian resident abroad. Instances of conditions of validity of marriages solemnized in India, modes and means of divorce under Indian law, legal formalities to be complied with for adopting children from India, remedies available in Indian law for enforcing parental rights in child abduction and other family law issues are abound relating to Non-Resident Indians. Likewise, there are a plethora of problems in matters concerning succession and transfer of property, banking affairs, taxation issues, execution and implementation of wills and other commercial propositions for Non-Resident Indians. However, application of multiple laws, their judicial interpretation & other legalities often leaves the problems unresolved even though remedies partially exist in Indian law and partly need new urgent legislation.

The number of Non-Resident Indians has multiplied in every jurisdiction abroad. However, family, property, kith and kin or the love for the motherland keeps bringing the NRI back on Indian soil in body or in soul. With this return the NRI seeks a remedy for his legal problem connected with his temporary or permanent return to India. This invariably makes the NRI import the foreign law of the overseas jurisdiction from where he has migrated. Such a situation is created because either Indian law provides him no remedy or because he finds it easier and quicker to import a foreign Court judgment to India on the basis of alien law which has no parallel in the Indian jurisdiction. This clash of jurisdictional law is commonly called conflict of laws in the realm of private international laws which is not yet a developed jurisprudence in the Indian territory.

## III. DIFFICULTIES FACED UNDER INDIAN LAW

Areas of family law in which the problems of jurisdiction of law is seen occurring very frequently relate to dissolution of marriage, inter-parental child abduction, inter-country child adoption and succession of property of Non-Resident Indians. In matters of divorce, since irretrievable breakdown of marriage is not a ground for dissolving the marriage under Indian law, Indian Courts in principle do not recognise foreign matrimonial judgments dissolving marriage by such breakdown. Surprisingly, even very little help is available in areas of matrimonial offences and problems arising out of child abduction. Leaving a helpless deserted Indian spouse on Indian shores confronted with a matrimonial litigation of a foreign Court which he or she neither has the means or ability to invoke often results in despair, frustration and disgust. Likewise, enforcement of a foreign Court order in whose violation a child of the family has been removed and brought to Indian soil brings a parent to India desperately seeking a legal remedy. The list of problems is myriad but the solutions are few or non-existent.

Unfortunately, no special Indian legislation exists to combat such remedies. The number of Indians on foreign shores have increased multi-fold but the multiple problems which bring them back to India are still left to be resolved by the conventional Indian legislation. Times have changed but laws have not. However, the dynamic, progressive and open minded judicial system in the Indian jurisprudence often comes to the rescue of such problems by interpreting the existing laws with a practical application to the new generation problems of immigrant Indians. Fortunately, judicial legislation is the only crutch available.

## IV. INTERPARENTAL CHILD REMOVAL – A PECULIAR PROBLEM

A very interesting, human and engrossing area of cross-border litigation arises in cases of inter-parental child abduction from foreign shores when a spouse removes the child to India in violation of a foreign Court order. Unfortunately, India is not a party to the Hague Convention on the Civil Aspects of International Child Abduction, 1980. Neither was Pakistan. But the UK-Pakistan Judicial Protocol was signed on January 17, 2003 by the President of the Family Division of the High Court of England and Wales and by the Chief Justice of the Supreme Court of Pakistan. It incorporated the effective provisions of the Hague Convention for the return of the abducted children to the country of the habitual residence. Perhaps, the crying need of the day exists for one in India also. Even though the British and Indian Governments have recently signed a treaty to extradite offenders of criminal law but in respect of matrimonial problems there is no such agreement, treaty or protocol. Even Legislative changes are still a far cry.

## V. SUGGESTED SOLUTIONS AND REMEDIES

What then is the remedy as a panacea for all such ills and legal problems.

A reading in totality of the matters in the overseas family law jurisdiction gives an indication that in such affairs, it is the judicial precedents which provide the much available guidance and judicial legislation on the subject. With the large number of Non-Resident Indians now permanently living in overseas jurisdictions, it has now become important that some composite legislation is enacted to deal with the problems of Non-Resident Indians to avoid them from importing judgments from foreign Courts to India for implementation of their rights. The answer therefore lies in giving them law applicable to them as Indians rather than letting them invade the Indian system with judgments of foreign jurisdictions which do not find applicability in the Indian system. Hence, it is the Indian legislature which now seriously needs to review this issue and come out with a composite legislation for Non-Resident Indians in family law matters. Till this is done, foreign Court judgments in domestic matters will keep cropping up and Courts in India will continue with their salutary efforts in interpreting them in harmony with the Indian laws and doing substantial justice to parties in the most fair and equitable way. However, in this process, the Indian judiciary has made one thing very clear that is the Indian Courts would not simply mechanically enforce judgments and decrees of foreign Courts in family matters. The Indian Courts have now started looking into the merits of the matters and deciding them on the considerations of Indian law in the best interest of the parties rather than simply implementing the orders without examining them. Fortunately, we can hail the Indian judiciary for these laudable efforts and till such time when the Indian Legislature comes to rescue with appropriate legislation, we seek solace with our unimpeachable and unstinted faith in the Indian judiciary which is rendering a yeoman service.

In the context of the NRI, the following suggestions are mooted for improving the existing family law problems posed daily before NRIs and faced by effected people resident in India when they come in contact with NRIs. The solutions partly exist in proper implementation of existing laws, framing of proper regulations, creation of Family Courts and Fast Track Courts and by amendment of existing legislation. The six-point charter summary is set down as hereunder in the following sequence.

**1.** Registration of marriages must be made compulsory. This will in turn ensure compliance of conditions of a valid marriage, provide proof of marriage and act as a deterrent for bigamous practices. Section 8 of the Hindu Marriage Act, 1956 makes it optional for State Governments to provide for rules for providing for registration of marriages. It is opined that States with significant NRI migration must make marriage registration compulsory particularly when one of the spouses is an NRI. Simultaneously, it should be made obligatory that the NRI spouse must give intimation of his registration of marriage to the concerned Embassy/High Commission in India, in which country he is presently resident. The States in India with high migration incidence should make and notify rules under section 8 providing for compulsory registration of marriages and incidental matters related thereto.

**2.** Dissolution of marriage on the ground of breakdown of marriage as an additional ground for divorce should be introduced when at least one of the spouses is an NRI subject to safeguards provided by legislation. This would require amendment of the provisions of the Hindu Marriage Act, 1955 and Special Marriage Act, 1954. Such a ground would provide NRI spouses a judicial forum in India to seek a remedy on Indian soil rather than importing foreign judgments of alien Courts on breakdown grounds and give a chance to the Indian spouse to defend on convenient and equitable terms in Indian Courts. The need for this amendment must be strongly mooted by the States with high NRI population to the Government of India to enact appropriate legislation by suitable amendments in the existing Hindu Marriage Act, 1955 and Special Marriage Act, 1954 since inter-country migration from such States is significant and in large numbers.

**3.** Wherever one of the spouses is an NRI, parallel additions must be made in Hindu Marriage Act, 1955 and Special Marriage Act, 1954 to provide for provisions for maintenance and alimony of spouses, child custody and child support as also settlement of matrimonial property. This will ensure that the spouse/children on Indian soil are maintained and provided for in accordance with the income and standard of the NRI spouse in the foreign jurisdiction. It may also be worthwhile to suggest that under section 3 of the Family Courts Act, 1984, the respective State Governments where Family Courts have not been established should be directed to provide for Family Courts. The States with high NRI population which essentially needs Family Courts as a matter of dire urgency should immediately create such Courts to deal with family law problems and give priority to settlement of family law issues where parties are NRIs.

**4.** In the matters of succession, transfer of property, making/execution/ implementation of Wills, repatriation of NRI funds, the respective State Governments must simplify and streamline procedures. Ideally speaking, in matters having property problems, Fast Track Courts must be set up to deal with such cases expeditiously in accordance with a time bound schedule. The Punjab Government has made amendments in the East Punjab Rent Restrictions Act and the Punjab Security of Land Tenures Act for the summary trial of disputes regarding agricultural, commercial and residential property. However, no special Fast Track Courts exist in most States with high NRI population to settle these matters on priority. A fresh proposal should be mooted to set up such Courts as soon as possible.

**5.** In the area of inter-parental child abduction or removal of children to India from foreign jurisdictions against Court orders, India must become a signatory to the Hague Convention on Civil Aspects of International Child Abduction, 1980 to provide a treaty to be followed for observance and implementation of foreign Court orders. As of now, there is no international convention or treaty applicable in India since India is not a signatory to the said convention and other than conventional procedures, there are no remedies for enforcing such rights. Till such time there is no signing of such treaty, the State Governments with high NRI population should permit liaison with Foreign Missions/Embassies in New Delhi through whom Courts should be assisted to ensure return of children to the Country of their foreign residence if they are removed in violation of foreign Court Orders. The administrative and police authorities in Indian States with high NRI population should give some uniform guidelines to observe to assist such parents in distress and who often land in such States in India with no clue on whom to approach for assistance.

**6.** Inter-country child adoption procedures must be simplified and a single uniform legislation must be provided for in matter of adoption of Indian children by NRIs. This should be hedged with ample checks and safeguards but at the same time should provide a unified, straightforward and single agency procedure. The present system is lengthy, complicated, involves multiple agencies, is very time consuming and thus needs to be suitably amended. Further, again the States in India with high NRI population should lay down some uniform policy guidelines to be observed by State agencies, adoption homes and administrative authorities so that proper help and guidance is available in adoption matters.

In the view of the authors, the above changes can be made either by providing a new composite legislation for NRIs or suitable changes can be made in existing legislations for streamlining the laws and procedures. It is suggested that a core committee of specialists in the field of private international law should be constituted at the earliest to prepare a comprehensive draft to suggest the said changes in legislation in the best possible way. The Law Commission of India has already submitted reports to suggest reform and change in law on the above perspectives affecting the lives of NRIs in Indiaeveryday. It is the endeavour of the Law Commission to suggest to the Government of India to do whatever possible to improve the life of the NRIs in India. It is important to see what India can do for the NRI and not what the NRI can do for India.

## SIGN THE HAGUE CONVENTION FOR CHILDRENS' SAKE

The London Borough of Ealing seeks advice for the repatriation of an abandoned 10-year-old Indian boy in Southall after the Indian High Commission refused temporary travel documents unless the missing passport is cancelled and the Indian Court guardianship order is produced.

An agitated British father in the UK obtains the London High Court's order to seek the return of his minor daughter retained in India by her mother in Punjab contravening the British Court orders.

An Indian mother in the UK moves to Chennai with a 10-year-old son. His father seeks registration of the UK Court order in an Indian Court so that it is enforceable should the mother breach the UK Court order and violate his custody rights.

A distraught Australian mother desperately seeks child support from an Indian father who has abandoned his daughter and fled from Australia.

Of late, increasing cases of inter-parental child abduction have become a big problem. Unresolved conflicts have generated parallel legal proceedings with no resolution at either end. Sadly, India is not a signatory to the Hague Convention on Civil Aspects of International Child Abduction, 1980.

Consequently, Indian Courts decide these cases invariably on the principle of child welfare. The Writ of *Habeas Corpus* is invoked as an effective remedy. The foreign Court custody order forms the basis of invoking this.

The Supreme Court of India has held that a foreign Court's custody order shall be only one consideration while determining the matter on merits where the principle of child welfare will be the clinching factor.

Thus, whenever a *Habeas Corpus* petition seeks a child's summary return to a foreign country and the Court opines that it requires determination by requiring evidence to be led by warring spouses, parties are relegated to conventional Court custody proceedings.

Clearly, the issue being no longer a local problem needs to be resolved on an international platform. India should sign the Hague Convention because Indian Courts cannot stretch their limits to adapt to different foreign Court orders arising in different jurisdictions. India needs a uniform law on child custody by following the Hague Convention.

Earlier, cases of foreign children brought to India against parental consent were common citations. Now, the reverse is also true and child removal from India makes it a two-way street.

However, how would Indian Courts deal with situations when Indian children are removed to foreign jurisdictions in violation of local Court orders or parental wishes? Which law would apply and how would it extend to a foreign country?

The International Family Justice Judicial Conference for Common Law and Commonwealth Jurisdictions, 2009 held at Cumberland Lodge (UK) from 4 to 8 August 2009, which these authors attended, had resolved that a common law and Commonwealth judicial network be established for implementing international instruments involving international family and child protection.

It endorsed the need to encourage the States' right to ratify the Hague Convention and provide assistance to the left behind parents in non-convention countries.

It was agreed that mediation should be provided in cross-border child abduction disputes and common principles be applied in the judicial resolution of relocation disputes in the best interest of children.

The conference felt the imperative need for a Judge hearing a return application to consider the child's objection to return, grave risk of harm or intolerable situation and settlement of a child in a new environment.

The universal solution to both domestic and international problem of our global NRI community in the matter of inter-parental child conflicts cannot be resolved on a universal platform until India becomes a part of the global family of contracting countries who are signatories to the Hague Convention.

India did frame the Civil Aspects of International Child Abduction Bill, 2007. However, it is yet to be tabled in Parliament. We need a new synergy and commitment to the cause of the removed child. A law must be put in place expeditiously for the welfare of the child.

## SINGLE LAW NEEDED FOR NRIs

As many NRIs have settled abroad, there is need for composite legislation to deal with their legal problems. Parliament should enact a law for NRIs on family matters.

Till this is done, foreign Court rulings in domestic matters will crop up and Indian Courts will continue to interpret them in harmony with the Indian laws.

Solutions partly exist in the proper implementation of the existing laws, framing of regulations, the creation of Family Courts and Fast-Track Courts. The following suggestions are imperative for solving the NRIs' existing family law problems:

Registration of marriages must be made compulsory to provide proof of marriage and check bigamy. The NRI spouse must inform his registration of marriage to the Embassy/High Commission concerned.

Divorce due to an irretrievable breakdown of marriage should be introduced as an additional ground when at least one of the spouses is an NRI. This would require an amendment to the Hindu Marriage Act, 1955, and the Special Marriage Act, 1954.

This would give the NRI spouses a judicial forum in India to seek a remedy on Indian soil rather than depend on alien courts. States must impress upon the Centre the need for this amendment.

The Hindu Marriage Act, 1955 and the Special Marriage Act, 1954, must provide for maintenance and alimony, child custody and support as also settlement of matrimonial property. This will ensure maintenance of the spouse/children on Indian soil in accordance with the income of the NRI spouse abroad. Family Courts should be set up in all States.

In matters of succession, transfer of property, implementation of Wills and repatriation of NRI funds, the State Governments must simplify and streamline procedures. Ideally, Fast-Track Courts must be set up to deal with property cases.

The Punjab Government has made amendments to the East Punjab Rent Restrictions Act and the Punjab Security of Land Tenures Act for the summary trial of disputes regarding agricultural, commercial and residential property. However, no special Fast-Track Courts exist in most states with a high NRI population to settle these matters on priority. A fresh proposal should be mooted to set up such Courts soon.

India must become a signatory to the Hague Convention on Civil Aspects of International Child Abduction, 1980. Till such a treaty is signed, the States should permit liaison with Foreign Missions/Embassies in New Delhi through which Courts should be assisted to ensure children's return to the country of their foreign residence if they are removed in violation of foreign Court orders. The administrative and police authorities in India should give uniform guidelines to assist such parents in distress.

The inter-country child adoption procedures must be simplified and single uniform legislation introduced for the adoption of Indian children by NRIs. A unified and single agency procedure is the need of the hour. The present system is too complicated and time-consuming.

These changes can be made either by providing new composite legislation for NRIs or through suitable changes in the existing legislation. A core committee of specialists in Private International Law should be constituted for preparing a comprehensive draft to suggest the changes in legislation.

---

# INDIA'S DILEMMA ON INTER-PARENTAL CHILD REMOVAL

London Borough of Ealing seeks advice for repatriation of abandoned ten-year old Indian boy in Southall after Indian High Commission refuses temporary travel documents unless missing existing passport cancelled and Indian Court guardianship order is produced.

Agitated British father in U.K. obtains orders from High Court at London to seek return of minor daughter retained in India by mother in Punjab contravening British Court Orders.

Anxious Parents of Indian origin currently in Hong Kong litigating over minor son's custody rights seek prior enforcement measures of orders of Court of Hong Kong in High Court of Delhi in case of anticipated subsequent violation by either parent.

Indian mother in U.K. moving to Chennai with ten years old son. Father of child seeks registration of U.K. Court order in an Indian Court so that it is enforceable should the mother breach the U.K. Court order and violate his custody rights.

Distraught Australian mother desperately seeks child support from Indian father who has abandoned his daughter and fled from Australia.

Harried British Asian parents with two surrogate children from India with U.K. passports upon migrating to New Zealand seek advice whether according to Indian Law they can adopt their surrogate children.

Of over 1.1 Billion Indians, about 30 million Non-Resident Indians constituting the largest diaspora in the world live in 180 nations abroad. India itself is spread over 3.28 million square kilometres over 28 States and 7 Union Territories. These high number and volume statistics show immense potential for free cross border movement of Non-Resident Indians. This conversely has given rise to new dimensions of inter-country family oriented disputes. Inter-Parental Child Abduction is one such emerging problem which defies legislative solution in India. Unresolved inter-parental custody conflicts of children have recently generated parallel conflicting legal proceedings in different jurisdictions without any resolution at either end. A British police appeal in the international media for tracing a missing ten-year Indian girl and another recent Supreme Court order directing the CBI to trace a young boy shows the alarming nature of the problem which defies resolution in Indian law.

Inter-Parental Child removal is not defined in any Indian legislation and is not specified as an offence under any statutory law. The problem is compounded by the fact that India is not a signatory to the Hague Convention on Civil Aspects of International Child Abduction, 1980, which is signed by 80 countries worldwide. Hence, inter-parental child custody conflicts are invariably decided by Indian

Courts on the principle of the welfare of the child as the paramount consideration and the best interest of the child. The prerogative Writ of *Habeas Corpus* as a expedient remedy is thus invariably invoked being the most effective, emergent and efficacious remedy to a distressed parent whose child has been removed to India from foreign borders. The foreign Court custody order forms the basis of invoking this extra-ordinary constitutional remedy.

A case-law analysis reveals that till 1997, Indian Courts invariably exercised a power of summary return of a removed child to the country of habitual residence in compliance with a foreign Court order to restore parental rights of an aggrieved parent. However, from 1998 onwards, the Supreme Court has held that a custody order of a foreign Court shall be only one consideration while determining the matter on merits where the welfare of the child principle will be the clinching factor. Resultantly, whenever any *Habeas Corpus* petition seeks summary return of a child to a foreign country and the Court opines that it requires determination by requiring evidence to be led by warring spouses, parties are relegated to conventional Court custody proceedings. A protracted, time-consuming and tedious custody petition results and the unfortunate removed child is fought over as a trophy to be won in a battle of egos of litigating parents. Sometimes, the love and affection of an isolated child is monopolized by one parent to such an extent that the tender mind of a alienated child gets permeated with ill will towards the other parent who for no fault has even access to his loved one.

The world is a far smaller place now than it was a decade ago. Inter-country and inter-continental travel is easier and more affordable than it has ever been. The corollary to this is an increase in relationships between individuals of different nationalities and from different cultural backgrounds. Logically, the world in which we and our children live has grown immensely complex. It is filled with opportunities and risks. International mobility, opening up of borders, cross-border migration and dismantling of inter-cultural taboos have all the positive traits but are fraught with a new set of risks for children caught up in cross-border situations. Caught in cross-fire of broken relationships with ensuing disputes over custody and relocation, the hazards of international abduction loom large over the chronic problems of maintaining access or contact internationally with the uphill struggle of securing cross-frontier child support.

With the increasing number of Non-Resident Indians abroad and multiple problems arising leading to family conflicts, inter-parental child removal to India now needs to be resolved on an international platform. It is no longer a local problem. The phenomenon is global. Steps have to be taken by joining hands globally to resolve these conflicts through the medium of Courts interacting with each other. Till India does not become a signatory to the Hague Convention, this may not be possible. A time has now come where it is not possible for the Indian Courts to stretch their limits to adapt to different foreign Court orders arising in different jurisdictions. It is equally important that to create a uniform policy of law some clear, authentic and universal child custody law is enacted within India by adhering to the principles laid down in the Hague Convention. Divergent views emerging at different times may not be able to cope up to the rising number of such cases, which come up from time to time for interpretation. We in India are thus wanting for an expeditious acceptance and implementation of the International principles of inter-parental child removal which are couched in the Hague Convention.

Today, removal of children across borders has also acquired a dual carriageway dimension. Earlier, cases of foreign children brought to India against parental consent were common citations. Now, the reverse is also true and child removal from India makes it a two-way street. However, how would Indian Courts deal with situations when Indian children were removed to foreign jurisdictions in violation of local Court orders or parental wishes. Which law would apply and how would it extend to a foreign country. Clearly, there is no international law instrument that can be invoked and the only remedy with the aggrieved parent would be to invoke the national law of the foreign country where the child is wrongfully retained. Easier said than done. Visa formalities, traveling expenses, litigation costs and above all foreign Court procedures would be insurmountable deterrents. It seems the problem defies solutions and workable remedies.

At the International Family Justice Judicial Conference for Common Law and Commonwealth Jurisdictions, 2009 held at Cumberland Lodge, England from 4-8 August 2009, about 70 Judges and jurists from 22 jurisdictions seriously deliberated on the above issue and its related consequences in a global perspective. The authors, as the only lawyer participants presented the Indian perspective. In the conclusions and resolutions of this exclusive conference, it was unanimously resolved that a Common Law and Commonwealth Judicial Network be established forthwith to facilitate processes of implementing international instruments involving international family and child protection. The endeavour to encourage States to ratify the Hague Convention and provide assistance to left behind parents in non-convention countries was also endorsed. Providing mediation in cross-border child abduction disputes and the search for common principles to be applied in the judicial resolution of relocation disputes in the best interest of children internationally found acceptance to all. The need for a Judge hearing a return application to consider the child's objection to return, grave risk of harm or intolerable situation and settlement of a child in a new environment was viewed with favour. Lord Justice Matthew Thorpe, Head of the International Family Justice for England and Wales and Judge Court of Appeal concluded the meet by stating that the baton had to be passed on to a new jurisdiction, who would be the host after a gap of three years.

Be that as it may, the universal solution to both domestic and international problem of our global NRI community in the matter of inter-parental child conflicts cannot be resolved on a universal platform until India becomes a part of the global family of contracting countries who are signatories to the Hague Convention. There was an Indian endeavour to do so by framing of a Civil Aspects of International Child Abduction Bill, 2007. But, alas, it was never tabled before Parliament and it never saw the light of the day. India cannot be a beneficiary of an international conclave unless it joins the table with the convention countries by acceding to the Convention. We now need a new synergy, a motivated effort and a commitment to the cause of the removed child to shape a law to prevent the unfortunate removal of children. The child should not suffer. A law must be put in place forthwith for the cause of the child.

# NRIs PROPERTY RELATED PROBLEMS – THE PUNJAB MODEL

## INTRODUCTION – THE GIST OF THE IDENTIFIABLE PROBLEMS

➢ A foreign based second or third generation descendant of an NRI seeks transfer of title of family property willed to him in rural or urban India. An aging NRI battles in Court to recover possession of urban property in metropolitan India wrested away by unscrupulous elements. Enthusiastic NRI owner sitting abroad desperately seeks remedies to locate share in rural agricultural property to claim ownership on the basis of inheritance. NRI families battle over division of land and property in exclusive control with custodians in India. Horrified NRI shockingly discovers divested share of family property on arriving in India on the basis of fraudulent documentation. Frantic NRI family members try to implement family settlement thwarted by local relatives occupying property locally. These real life instances are now common to NRIs & PIOs.

➢ During the last over 50 years, large number of Indians have migrated and permanently settled in foreign countries leaving behind their homes, ancestors and landed properties. Now, when the NRIs wish to recover their properties, they find them in forceful or illegal occupation of their trusted childhood guardians or overstaying tenants who have designs to grab the property. Agreements are dishonoured, trust is violated and faith is destroyed. Commercial real estate property of NRIs is grabbed with impunity. The NRI has neither the patience nor the time to fight a protracted legal battle in an Indian law Court which may last a life time, if fought, waged and litigated till the Apex Court. Legal processes are cumbersome, tedious, technical and move at a snail's pace. The bottom line is that the NRIs are at a great disadvantage leaving them disillusioned and disappointed. No existing legislation comes to their rescue or aid.

➢ Gullible, excited and patriotic NRIs with a fervor happily invests huge sums of Pounds, Sterling, Dollars or Euros in real estate, flats, or immovable property in India. When it comes to taking actual physical possession of their prized immovable asset in their homeland, the vulnerable NRI discovers to his horror that either the land or the flat does not exist or that he has been cheated into buying property which does not exist. Unscrupulous, unethical and unprofessional brokers, builders or real estate agents who had made these deals with the NRIs and promised the moon have either disappeared, are untraceable or flatly deny having made any commitment. The dumbfounded NRI is to stunned to react. With little time at his hand on his Indian visit or sitting in a foreign land, he does not know what to do. Who will help him. Should he go to the police or the administrative authorities or to a Court of law for a judicial remedy. Where should he seek advice and how does he pursue the case. The questions are myriad but the solutions and answers lie submerged in a complicated web of long winded procedures which on initiation will proceed endlessly at a snail's pace. The frustrated, dejected and defeated NRI gives up not knowing what to do.

➢ The above summarization is in brief a nutshell of the NRIs ailing property problems for which he seeks a consolidated, composite, timely and effective remedy. The NRI wants to reconnect with his homeland but is disillusioned, disenchanted and disheartened. It is in this backdrop that this article looks at these peculiar problems with a focus on the State of Punjab which contributes highly to the migratory numbers.

➢ Broadly, property related problems can be divided under four heads as follows:

(A) Issues relating to landlord-tenant relationships in Punjab and Chandigarh.

(B) Issues relating to succession, Wills and inheritance - INDIA, NRIs and Wills.

(C) Problems arising out of revenue records and agricultural land disputes - the position prevailing in the State of Punjab.

(D) Propositions arising out of property investment related issues in India.

➢ It is in the above perspective, that this article looks at the above issues and how they are handled and attempted to be resolved in the framework of the existing laws which prevail in the State of Punjab and the Union Territory of Chandigarh in the matters of tenancy and agricultural property related issues which are governed by State legislations.

➢ In so far, problems related to succession, Wills and inheritance, as also propositions arising out of property investment related issues, the same are governed by Central legislations (except where there are separate State laws), the problems and solutions are by and large common throughout the territory of India. Hence, wherever there is a Central legislation enacted by Indian Parliament, the Indian law will have universal application throughout the Territory of India. To that extent, the issues and laws arising for succession and property investment related issues may be common for the entire Indian Jurisdiction and applicable in all States of India.

**(A) Issues relating to landlord-tenant relationships in Punjab and Chandigarh**

In 2001, the Government of Punjab upon receiving representations from various NRI individuals, and through their associations highlighting the plight of Indian residents returning to India after long years abroad decided to amend the existing East Punjab Urban Rent Restriction Act, 1949, to provide NRIs a right to recover immediate possession of their properties. It was represented that the NRIs having spent long years of their life abroad did not find conditions congenial in their own country on their return either to settle down or to take up any business. On account of rigid legal provisions of existing rent laws, the NRIs were unable to recover possession of their own residential/non-residential buildings from the tenants. Accordingly, the Government of Punjab having considered the situation had decided that the existing rent legislation viz. East Punjab Urban Rent

Restriction Act, 1949, should be amended to provide relief to NRIs to enable them to recover possession of a residential or scheduled building and/or one non residential building for their own use. By a notification dated 9 October, 2009, the Central Government has extended to the Union Territory of Chandigarh the benefit of the said amendment and hence as of now, NRI landlords are entitled to the benefit of immediate recovery of immediate possession of their properties in accordance with this Law as per details below.

**Summary eviction of tenants from properties of NRIs in Punjab and Chandigarh.**

➢ The East Punjab Urban Rent Restriction Act, 1949 (EPURRA), which extends to all urban areas in Punjab as also the Union Territory of Chandigarh, is an Act to restrict the increase of rents of certain premises and to provide for eviction of tenants therefrom. Other than prescribing a normal process for eviction of tenants, it also provides a summary procedure for recovering immediate possession of residential or scheduled buildings to certain specified landlords. By an amendment in 2001, the Act also created a special class of NRI landlords reposing in them a special right to recover immediate possession from tenants occupying their premises by a special summary procedure.

➢ Now under Section 13-B of the EPURRA, once in a lifetime, possession can be given to a NRI landlord to get one building vacated in a summary manner. A NRI landlord is accordingly required to prove that he is an NRI, he has returned to India permanently or temporarily, the requirement of the accommodation by him or his dependent is genuine and that he is the owner of the property for the last five years before the institution of the ejectment proceedings.

➢ By a 2005 landmark judgment titled *Baldev Singh Bajwa* v. *Monish Saini*, AIR 2006 SC 59, the Supreme Court has given far reaching positive dimensions both to the definition of an NRI landlord and to the concept of 'his return' to India in the context of the NRIs right to recover possession of his property under the summary procedure under section 13-B of the EPURRA. It does not distinguish between a Non-Resident Indian, Person of Indian Origin or an Overseas Citizen of India.

➢ To be an NRI, it is sufficient that a Person of Indian Origin establishes that he has permanently or temporarily settled outside India for his business or on account of his employment or for any other purpose which would indicate his intention to stay outside India for an uncertain period.

➢ A person to be an NRI should be of Indian origin. Since "Indian Origin" is not defined in the EPURRA, any person whose parents, grandparents or great grand parents were born in India and permanently resided in India would be an NRI. It is not necessary that the NRI should be a citizen of India. It is immaterial that the NRI holds a foreign passport or has shifted to a foreign country.

➢ Return to India cannot be read as return to India permanently with an intention to settle in India permanently. There is no requirement that the NRI has to permanently settle in India on his return or he has returned to India with an intention to permanently settle in India. Hence, "return to India" may not be of permanent nature as the premises may be required for the use of any dependent ordinarily living with the NRI. All that is required under section 13-B is that a NRI should return to India to claim the premises.

**(B) Issues relating to succession, Wills and inheritance - INDIA, NRIs and Wills**

As far as succession, inheritance and Wills is concerned, the Hindu Succession Act, 1956 and the Indian Succession Act, 1925 being Central legislations are applicable throughout the territory of India. Hence, in so far these issues are concerned, they apply uniformly throughout the territory of India to all States and Union Territories. The Indian Succession Act, 1925 is an Act to consolidate the law applicable to testamentary succession for Hindus and the Hindu Succession Act, 1956 is an Act to amend and codify the law relating to intestate succession among Hindus. Hence, in respect of the matter of Wills i.e. testamentary succession, all NRIs with movable and immovable property in India shall be governed by the Indian Succession Act, 1925.

• The global Indian diaspora has some problems on the home soil which needs intercontinental solutions. In this perspective, the disposition of property of an NRI living in a foreign domicile, when such property is located partly in India and partly situated abroad, often poses awkward questions. Must an NRI make a Will or leave his property to natural succession. Should the NRI make a joint, composite or common Will of his assets and properties in India and abroad. If so, should such a Will be registered and where. Need a person be appointed to execute the Will in different jurisdictions. Would it be better if there are different Wills for separate properties in India and abroad. Should such different Wills be registered individually in separate jurisdictions. How should inheritance rights of beneficiaries of NRIs be safeguarded in India and abroad. Which law Indian or foreign would apply to assets and properties of NRIs in different countries.

• Two distinct Indian legislations exist. The Hindu Succession Act, 1956 (HSA) contains the codified law relating to intestate succession among Hindus i.e. when there is no Will. The Indian Succession Act, 1925 (ISA) consolidates the law applicable to persons other than Hindus for intestate succession and testamentary succession for all persons in India including Hindus. Hence, all NRIs (whether Hindus or non-Hindus) can make Wills governed by the provisions of the Indian Succession Act, 1925. To begin with, for an NRI, it is advisable to execute a written Will, get it witnessed and registered to avoid any intricate problems of succession and inheritance. With the abundance of problems of NRI properties in India, natural succession in the absence of a Will may pose problems from third party claimants. An NRI ought to Will his property by choice to his natural heirs or others and thus eliminate speculation or bogus claims from claimants and pave a smooth succession. Thus, what ought to follow naturally must be better confirmed by a Will also.

• The HSA/ISA unlike the Hindu Marriage Act does not have extra territorial application. In the wisdom of the Legislature, there are well defined principles of international law, which regulate succession to the movable and immovable properties of a Hindu NRI domiciled outside the territory of India. Thus, on the basis of international comity, the following three principles can be deduced regarding the application of HSA/ISA:—

- **Firstly,** for a Hindu domiciled outside India, succession to his immovable property in India is governed by HSA/ISA whereas succession to his movable property shall be governed by the law of the country of his foreign domicile.

- **Secondly**, where a Hindu is domiciled in India, succession to his immovable property outside India shall be governed by the law of the country where the property is situated. Movables outside India will be governed by HSA/ISA or by the local law of the foreign country in which the movable property is situated.

- **Thirdly**, in respect of a Hindu domiciled outside India, succession to his movable and immovable property outside India shall not be governed by HSA/ISA but by the law of the foreign domicile of the Hindu.

- In the event of there being no Will, natural succession among the category of heirs as per the order of succession will flow as per the HSA. Then, speculation, outsider claims, disputes among heirs and third party rights are rife. Hence, it is in the best interest of an NRI to pen a Will and put down his wishes and leave nothing to doubt.

- In the light of non-application of HSA/ISA outside India, it is strongly recommended that NRIs of Hindu origin having immovable assets in different countries should execute a joint composite Will pertaining to all their immovable properties located in different jurisdictions. For NRIs, execution of separate Wills for separate immovable properties in different countries is not advisable. Establishing genuineness of a composite Will is easier than proving multiple Wills. It is also recommended that the NRI must register the Will separately in every jurisdiction even though it is optional in India to do so. It may be mentioned that the registration in a particular country may hold good in respect of properties of the NRIs in that jurisdiction. Accordingly, separate rules of registration of different countries ought to be complied with as per rules of the foreign domicile of the NRI.

- It is also advisable that the NRI should specifically appoint an executor to execute the Will in the particular jurisdiction where the property is situated. This assists the beneficiaries and simplifies the division of assets as per the Will. A written Will of an NRI duly witnessed and registered in respect of Indian properties identifies the claimants and legal heirs. Its multiple registration assures the seal of finality. The message for the NRI therefore is, to act well in advance and simplify the task of the beneficiaries who are to inherit their properties.

- Thereafter, the law of the jurisdiction, where the property is situate will govern the process of succession on the basis of rights established under the Will. The global Indian must take advantage of this well codified position of Indian succession law. This is to ensure that there is no uncertainty and ambiguity.

**(C) Problems arising out of revenue records and agricultural land disputes - the position prevailing in the State of Punjab**

The love of land and the need to reconnect with his homeland are an ingrained part and parcel of every NRI originating from Punjab. The landed agricultural properties left by forefathers, ancestors and well wishers always creates the innate desire in the Punjabi NRI to visit his homeland and stake his ownership claim to his land he loves. Sometimes, the landed property in the hands of relatives, tenants, family members or employees is difficult to recover, creating a plethora of unforeseen problems which can take a long time to resolve in the Revenue Courts. At times, title disputes are difficult to resolve and lack of documents to establish ownership can be difficult to obtain. This creates a very unpleasant and disturbing situation for the NRI. It is in this perspective that the State of Punjab has made some special endeavours to expedite the process of settling such disputes by simplified procedures and fast track resolution of such cases in this regard, the following summarized points are enumerated as under:

- Superseding its earlier orders under which existing Courts of Tehsildars and Naib-Tehsildars were designated as Fast-Track Courts for NRI's, the Department of Revenue and Rehabilitation in a directive issued on December 28, 2005 declared that four Fast-Track Courts would be set-up at Jalandhar, Hoshiarpur, Moga and Nawanshahr to which neighbouring districts would be attached.

- The District Revenue Officer heads a Fast-Track Court and has the powers to decide on the correction of "Khasra girdwari", partition, contested and un-contested mutations, registered and un-registered Wills, "lambardari", demarcation, rent suit, and ejection under the Punjab Land Revenue Act. They also hear "chowkidari" cases. The Additional Deputy Commissioner or the Divisional Commissioner decide appeals against the orders of the Fast-Track Courts.

- The Government of Punjab by Notification dated 16 November, 2006, has also appointed District Revenue Officers at four district headquarters to decide Suits under the Punjab Tenancy Act, 1887, for Non-Resident Indians by conferring powers of Assistant Collector Ist Grade upon them.

**(D) Propositions arising out of property investment related issues in India**

Investing in real estate, urban property, flats or apartments with builders, colonizers, estate agents and building companies can sometimes be a nightmare for NRIs. Colourful brochures, fancy promises, pictures of properties and attractive installment plans are used as inducement measures to extract huge sums of money from innocent NRIs who walk into such traps. At times, flats, houses, or apartments are not constructed as per the schedule and escalated costs are demanded failing which money already paid is forfeited. There are also times when the same property is sold to multiple owners and the unfortunate NRI has to face insurmountable problems. It is in this context that the following safeguards and remedies can be advocated which are applicable uniformly throughout the territory of India in all States & Union Territories.

• Before any investment in any property, flat or apartment is made in India, unless and until a physical verification is done through a reliable source or agency to conclusively establish the title or ownership of the builder, colonizer, company or estate agent, no money should be invested blindly without checking

• Every step should be taken by an NRI to ask, confirm and verify whether the person, builder, colonizer or company possesses a valid license, permission or sanction as per local laws to build a colony, set of apartments or the prescribed number of flats which are advertised or propagated at the time of sale.

• If possible, through the assistance of local agencies or contacts, the title of the owner who is selling the property should be verified from the local land records to establish the ownership of the vendor. This will rule out the issues relating to ownership being disputed at a later stage.

• It should be an absolute certainty that proper documents must be executed at the time of paying any initial deposit and no payment should be made unless and until proper contracts or agreements are executed and signed by the builder, estate agent, colonizer or company selling any property.

• It must be clarified in writing that in case the property is not handed over in the stipulated time, there shall be no escalation clause in terms of building costs. Similarly, adequate caution and care should be taken not to sign any agreement or document by which consent is given to agree to escalated building costs. Agreements or documents should be signed only after consultation with solicitors and no blank documents should be signed at all.

• In case there is any failure to hand over property in a stipulated period of time or there is any breach of promise, an NRI should not wait indefinitely. Every effort should be made to put the grievance or complaint in writing to the concerned colonizer, builder, estate agent or property developer which can serve as written proof and evidence for initiating any legal proceeding later.

• The Consumer Protection Act, 1986, an Act for better protection of the interests of consumers and for the purpose to make provisions for establishment of Consumer Courts for settlement of consumer disputes is a very effective remedy in India against errant builder, colonizers and property developers. Consumer Courts exist in every district in India and complaints can be made in simple language with a very small amount of fee payable as court-fee. The complaints can be followed up in person and the procedure of hearing is simple. Trial is expeditious and quick. It serves as a very effective remedy. Hence, it is strongly advised that in case of any deficiency in service or restrictive trade practice suffered by an NRI at the hands of any such errant builder, colonizer or estate agent, the provisions of the Consumer Protection Act, 1986 applicable throughout India should be invoked at the earliest possible. This is a easy, friendly and quick method for getting relief.

**CONCLUSION:**

As a common conclusion to all the above problems, some general suggestions can be mooted which can be a panacea to the NRI for the ills which ail him for his property problems. Though, no solution is universal but for the betterment of the properties of the NRI, these possible remedies can improve and make the situation better. These suggestions can be summarized in the following headings:

- At the outset it may be most useful for States and Union Territories all over India to constitute nodal cells for NRI affairs at State headquarters. These NRI cells with memberships of administration, police and legal authorities can be nodal bodies for entertaining NRI complaints online and in person from NRIs. They can forward these complaints to the respective departments to which they pertain to and advise NRIs what remedy to adopt for resolving the problem. If the issue can be resolved by seeking a response from the Government machinery internally, the matter can be concluded or the NRI can be guided to approach the appropriate Court for relief.
- The Constitution of the NRI nodal cell by the Chandigarh administration on August 12, 2009 which is headed by a retired High Court Judge and various officials including one of the authors as member is a role model for other States and Union Territories to adopt. This experiment is definitely worth emulating by other States in India.
- It is strongly advocated that in matters of landlord-tenant relationship, all States and Union Territories in India should enact local legislations on the lines of the special provisions for the Right to recover immediate possession of residential and non-residential buildings of NRIs. The Union Territory of Chandigarh by a notification dated 9 October, 2009 has made applicable the provisions of section 13(B) of the East Punjab Rent Restriction Act to the territory of Chandigarh whereby NRI landlords in Chandigarh can now recover immediate possession of their property. Wherever such a law does not exist in India, States and Union Territories should endeavour to make changes in local laws to incorporate such fast track changes in rent laws for NRIs.
- Further, it may be suggested that individual States and Union Territories should endeavour to create Fast Track NRI Courts in matters of agricultural properties, revenue affairs and land revenue disputes besides maintenance of revenue records. The changes in the State of Punjab in this regard are a helpful model to adapt.
- It may also be suggested that appropriate legislative changes may be brought about in matters of properties of NRIs involving cases where NRI properties have been retained, forcibly occupied or grabbed by unscrupulous or unethical persons. It may be in order if the Central Government seriously considers enacting a Central legislation applicable throughout the territory of India to take cognizance of such issues of NRI properties and bring them under them purview of such Legislation. Such an enactment can create special Courts for speedy trials of property disputes of NRIs.
- In so far issues concerning obtaining copies of land revenue records, title deeds, title documents, ownership records, transfer of ownership papers etc. are concerned, the Government of India should endeavour having a module

of public private partnership to whom the limited function of preparation and handing over copies can be out sourced. By commercial bidding, an agency can be identified either at Central or State level to handle this limited function of preparing copies of records on the basis of a regularly updated website to be prepared on the instructions of the respective State Governments and Union Territories within India. This out sourced agency can fix rates at which copies of all individual ownership records can be supplied on payment of requisite charges either online or in person to the concerned NRI on a written request supported by his identity and his connection with the property. The local administration in every State can monitor the function of such agency & restrict its function only to disseminate limited information to concerned NRI.

By no means, the above suggestions are exhaustive or conclusive. They are the beginning of a new thought process initiated by the Government of India in the very useful deliberation on property problems of NRIs/PIOs. However, to generate more thoughts, have more suggestions and consider other view points, these limited views have been put forth for a fruitful, interactive and participative consideration for the NRI brethren. It is a beginning without an end and a start of a new era for the NRI.

# NRI MARRIAGES – PROBLEMS AND POSSIBLE SOLUTIONS

## (I) INTRODUCTION

Of a population of over one billion Indians, nine million Punjabi NRIs constitute the biggest community from any Indian State to contribute to the total of thirty million NRIs living worldwide in 180 nations. Times have changed but family law legislations enacted by the Indian Parliament in 1955 and 1956 have left Indians where they were. The result, an influx of family law problems arising out of NRI marriages with no practical solutions in the legislative enactments as they exist today. To compound the problem, registration of marriages, which is optional under Hindu family laws, has not been made compulsory in most States including Punjab. The result: multiple marriages by the NRI often without a previous divorce, invariably by duping the previous spouse and providing no maintenance to the abandoned wife and the unfortunate child of such union if any. Legal recourse is difficult, time consuming, expensive and complicated. Despite a Family Courts Act, 1984, Punjab has none despite 27 years having elapsed since this law was made. The end result: about thirty thousand abandoned women in Punjab fending for themselves in an uphill legal system which provides no solutions or answers. These figures have been compiled by the National Commission for Women and the Ministry of Women and Child Development. [For more details see newsreport titled "Runaway NRI grooms now risk losing their passports," dated 5 February 2011, the Indian Express, Chandigarh Edition.]

## (II) COMMON ISSUES ARISING FROM NRI MARRIAGES

(A) Women go overseas after the wedding only to find themselves abandoned with no one to turn to, no money, no ability to speak the foreign language and no knowledge of the customs of the alien country and having no friends to turn to.

(B) Women who are battered or kept prisoner in the foreign home are often treated like domestic workers and sometimes not allowed to work outside the house.

(C) Innocent woman who later finds that her NRI husband is already married in the foreign country of his residence or has a live-in partner in close contact.

(D) Appalling but true there are also cases of "holiday brides" - women abandoned in India within days or weeks of marriage, with the husband promising to return once visa arrangements have been made, but never to be seen or heard again.

(E) Women who later realise that their NRI husband had furnished false information about his job, immigration status, earning, property, marital status and other material particulars about his personal life.

(F) Women whose husbands taking advantage of more lenient divorce grounds in other legal systems in foreign jurisdictions obtain ex-parte divorce by fraudulent representations and the helpless women remain oblivious of such a divorce. Recent cases have shown that women are duped, returned to India and abandoned without a passport in their parental home. They have thus no recourse to return to the foreign land.

(G) Women who are denied maintenance in India on the technical ground that her NRI husband had already procured a divorce abroad and she has no proof of his income, financial status and his assets abroad. Consular protection obligations in this regard need serious introspection and deliberation, at a policy level involving meaningful cross-border cooperation between member states.

(H) Women running from pillar to post fighting never ending legal battles but repeatedly encountering technical impediments relating to jurisdiction, service of notice, enforcement of orders etc. Often, on the passing of a three-year separation period, sometimes Courts decline to interfere, quoting a bar of limitation.

(I) Women who sought the legal recourse to bring the erring NRI spouse to task by initiating proceedings under the criminal law but failing because the NRI husband does not respond to the summons or even the warrant of arrest. Sometimes the women have no address or contact details to serve the summons overseas.

(J) Women have to fight legal battles for the custody of their children after their divorce abroad or after they are forced to leave the foreign home. Often such women also have to face charges of illegal abduction in addition to the emotional trauma of being duped. Such women are embroiled in time-consuming Court cases

## (III) LEGAL ISSUES INVOLVED IN NRI MARRIAGES

(1) **Conflict of laws**: On the issue of the validity of the marriage, the choice of law of marriage and divorce i.e. whether the Indian law would apply or the law of the husband's country of habitual residence would apply in dissolving the marriage.

(2) **Issue of jurisdiction:** Whether the Courts in India or the Courts of the country of the husband's residence have the jurisdiction to deal with the matrimonial dispute, issues relating to maintenance and other ancillary matters of child custody.

(3) **Maintenance and custody laws:** Whether the Indian law on these issues will apply or the law of the husband's country of habitual residence will apply to them.

(4) **Validity of foreign Court orders:** Situations are abound when a Non-Resident Indian invokes the jurisdiction of the foreign Court where he is resident and convinces the overseas Court to pass favourable Orders in such matters which are thereafter sought to be executed in the Indian jurisdiction through the Courts of law in India. Another very important question, which comes up at, the end

relates to enforcement and execution of foreign judgments when they are sought to be implemented in India. The Indian Courts do not accept foreign Court judgments, which violate sections 13 and 44 of the Indian Code of Civil Procedure, 1908.

(5) **Power of the Indian Courts:** Whether the Indian Courts have the power to restrain legal proceedings in the foreign Courts and/or pass contrary judgments/ orders. The foreign Courts mostly do not accept Indian Court orders.

(6) **Property rights and other ancillary issues:** Does the abandoned wife and her children out of the broken wedlock have property rights in the ancestral or the property of her in law's in India. Indian Courts mostly decline any such rights.

(7) **Other legal remedies available:** Whether the abandoned wife can avail other remedies like extradition, impounding of passport, cancellation of citizenship, attachment of property, look out orders, suit for damages, injunction, declaration or invoking the Writ of *Habeas Corpus*. Experience shows that foreign Missions and Embassies in India of the respective foreign countries offer little or no help. For the abandoned spouse to reach the foreign country is expensive, difficult and cumbersome, if in the first place the spouse manages to obtain a visa at all.

## (IV) RECOMMENDATIONS/PROPOSALS FOR REFORM AND CHANGE

(a) India should sign the Hague Conventions. In particular the following conventions which are directly related to the issue of NRI marriages: Till the decision for signing the Hague Conventions remains pending, India can contemplate signing bilateral or multilateral treaties especially with countries having considerable population of Indian origin. However, mechanical enforcement of foreign orders should not take place as provided under sections 13,44 and 44A of the CPC. Recent trends of the Indian Supreme Court show that in matters of marriage, divorce, child custody and maintenance, there is no mechanical application of a foreign Court order and the Courts go into the merits of the matter.

(b) To review the existing legal system and to formulate new laws which are in conformity with the Hague Conventions and help achieve the purpose of marriage related Hague conventions.

(c) **Specific amendments to:** (I) The Passport Act, 1967 providing for cancellation of the passport of the offending NRI spouse and including more details of the spouse in the passport; (II) The Extradition Act, 1962 to incorporate offences relating to NRI marriages like fraud, dowry , abandonment and cruelty; (III) The Indian Penal Code, 1860 in order to recognise specific offences relating to NRI marriages; IV) The Code of Criminal Procedure, 1973 and The Code of Civil Procedure, 1908 laying down clear and definite procedures where NRIs are concerned; (V) The Citizenship Act, 1955 for the cancellation of the citizenship of the offending spouse.

(d) Enact special Indian enactments to address the various issues that arise in NRI marriages and at the same time incorporating progressive principles being evolved in the field of private international law especially through the Hague Conventions. These enactments should specifically cover issues like validity of the marriages in the NRI context, choice of law of marriage and divorce, jurisdiction of Courts, enforceability of foreign Court orders, offences relating to marriages and the right of the abandoned spouse to property.

(e) Registration of marriages must be made compulsory. The marriage certificate of the NRI spouse must carry his social security number of his foreign home and the certificate must be lodged with the Embassy in India compulsorily. There should be specific columns in the marriage registration certificates for NRIs having complete substantive details about the foreign spouse.

(f) Adopt the convergence approach among official Indian agencies like the Ministries of Government of India: Women and Child Development, Overseas Indian Affairs and External Affairs. Also efforts should be made to coordinate the initiatives on the issue of NRI marriages and to jointly set up "special cells" for dealing with problems relating to NRI marriages. Ongoing efforts of the Ministry of Overseas Indian Affairs in this regard are indeed laudable.

(g) Involve the Indian Embassies to provide crisis assistance and support to abandoned brides through welfare officers. Make arrangements for providing extended residence permits or permanent residence status to abandoned spouses. Also to extend legal, monetary support and shelter to them.

(h) To provide free legal aid to distressed abandoned women in India and to try and explore joining hands with agencies in other countries to aid and advice women stranded in other countries.

(i) To set-up help lines to educate people about this growing menace and to provide counseling to women in need.

(j) To sensitise the police and the judiciary on the problem being faced by women in NRI marriages.

(k) Undertake specialised training of lawyers to deal with the problems relating to NRI issues. NRI related issues especially with regard to international family law should be part of the curriculum and continuing legal education programme for the legal fraternity.

(l) To develop cooperation between the non-Governmental organisations and the Government agencies to deal with this specific problem.

## (V) CONCRETE LEGAL PROPOSALS TO ACT AS IMMEDIATE DETERRENTS

In the context of the State of Punjab, the following suggestions are being put forward for improving the existing family law problems posed daily before NRIs and faced by effected people resident in the State of Punjab consequentially when they come in contact with NRIs. The solutions partly exist in proper implementation of existing laws, framing of proper regulations, creation of Family Courts and Fast Track Courts and by amendment of existing legislation. The seven point charter summary is set down as hereunder in the following sequence.

1. **REGISTRATION OF MARRIAGES MUST BE MADE COMPULSORY**. This will in turn ensure compliance of conditions of a valid marriage, provide proof of marriage and act as a deterrent for bigamous practices. Section 8 of the Hindu Marriage Act, 1955 makes it optional for State Governments to provide for

rules for providing for registration of marriages. It is opined that states with significant NRI migration must make marriage registration compulsory particularly when one of the spouses is an NRI. Simultaneously, it should be made obligatory that the NRI spouse must give intimation of his registration of marriage to the concerned Embassy/High Commission in India, in which country he is presently resident. The State of Punjab should make and notify rules under section 8 providing for compulsory registration of marriages and incidental matters related thereto.

2. **CREATION OF FAMILY COURTS:** It may also be worthwhile to suggest that under section 3 of the Family Courts Act, 1984, the respective State Governments where Family Courts have not been established should be directed to provide for Family Courts. The State of Punjab which essentially needs Family Courts as a matter of dire urgency should immediately create such Courts to deal with family law problems and give priority to settlement of family law issues where parties are NRIs. Wherever one of the spouses is an NRI, these Family Courts can better provide for provisions for maintenance and alimony of spouses, child custody and child support as also settlement of matrimonial property. This will ensure that the spouse/children on Indian soil are maintained and provided for in accordance with the income & standard of the NRI spouse in the foreign jurisdiction.

3. **CREATION OF FAST TRACK COURTS AND SIMPLIFICATION OF PROCEDURES:** In the matters of succession, transfer of property, making/ execution/implementation of Wills, repatriation of NRI funds, the respective State Governments must simplify and streamline procedures. Ideally speaking, in matters having property problems, Fast Track Courts must be set-up to deal with such cases expeditiously in accordance with a time-bound schedule. The Punjab Government has made amendments in the East Punjab Rent Restriction Act, 1949 and the Punjab Security of Land Tenures Act, 1953 for the summary trial of disputes regarding agricultural, commercial and residential property. However, no special Fast Track Courts exist in the State of Punjab to settle these matters on priority. A fresh proposal should be mooted to set-up such Courts as soon as possible.

4. **AMENDMENT OF FAMILY LAWS:** Dissolution of marriage on the ground of breakdown of marriage as an additional ground for divorce should be introduced when at least one of the spouses is an NRI subject to safeguards provided by legislation. This would require amendment of the provisions of the Hindu Marriage Act, 1955 and Special Marriage Act, 1954. Such a ground would provide NRI spouses a judicial forum in India to seek a remedy on Indian soil rather than importing foreign judgments of alien Courts on breakdown grounds and give a chance to the Indian spouse to defend on convenient and equitable terms in Indian Courts. The need for this amendment must be strongly mooted by the State of Punjab to the Government of India to enact appropriate legislation by suitable amendments in the existing Hindu Marriage Act, 1955 and Special Marriage Act, 1954 since inter-country migration from the State of Punjab is significant and in large numbers.

5. **DEDICATED CENTRAL/STATE GOVERNMENT REGULATED WEBSITE OF ERRING NRI SPOUSES.** The Ministry of Overseas Indian Affairs at a Central level, and in coordination with the respective State Governments should maintain a dedicated website of erring NRI husbands and habitual NRI offenders, who contract multiple marriages. This will to some extent act as a major deterrent, but more importantly it will be a source of information/caution to general members of the public so that they are not trapped into marrying a NRI groom, who is already guilty of contracting multiple marriages on the Indian soil and escaped the clutches of law. Such a website could also be translated into regional languages, for reasons of greater and easier accessibility.

6. **MEANINGFUL CONSULAR ASSITANCE AS PART OF CONSULAR PROTECTION OBLIGATIONS.** That as part of consular protection obligations, Foreign Embassies, Missions and Consulates in India should mandatorily furnish all the relevant data to aggrieved spouses of erring spouses of NRI marriages, who are habitually resident and domiciled in foreign countries. Some sort of practice directions by the Ministry of External Affairs in conjunction with the Ministry of Overseas Indian Affairs, Ministry of Women and Child Development can well be framed to direct Embassies and Foreign Missions to provide meaningful consular assistance to abandoned NRI brides. In fact all such Foreign Missions, should have dedicated desks or officers exclusively to provide proper assistance to such spouses in distress.

7. **Lastly**, the Punjab Government in the year 2010 enacted the Punjab Prevention of Human Smuggling Act, 2010 which is currently awaiting the assent of the President of India. Likewise, the Central Government as also the Punjab Government could well seriously consider enacting the NRI abandoned legislation, also having extra territorial application like the provisions of the Hindu Marriage Act, 1955.

In view of the authors, the above changes can be made either by providing a new composite legislation for NRIs or suitable changes can be made in existing legislations for streamlining the laws and procedures. It is suggested that a core committee of specialists in the field of private international law should be constituted at the earliest to prepare a comprehensive draft to suggest the said changes in legislation in the best possible way.

# MEDIATION, CONCILIATION AND THE ROLE OF COURTS

## (I) INTRODUCTION

Conciliation is the process of bringing together persons or organisations in dispute with each other in order to try to reach to a settlement. Mediation, on the other hand, is assisted negotiation of a dispute settlement. It is one of the most important techniques of resolving disputes and can be defined as non-binding negotiation process in which impartial third party assists the disputing parties in resolving the disputes.

The terms conciliation and mediation appear to be one and the same. But there is a fine distinction between the two. In conciliation process, the conciliator is called upon by the parties to make a non-binding recommendation or finding, concerning the factual and legal issues of a dispute as well as what the conciliator considers could be an appropriate resolution to the dispute. However, in the mediation process, the mediator is not duty bound by the parties either to make a finding or decision or to recommend jointly to the parties' any mode of resolution of the dispute involved. In mediation process, the role of mediator is only participatory in nature whereas the conciliator is guided by the principles of objectivity, fairness and justice. A significant difference between a mediator and a conciliator is that the mediator generally shares opinions in confidence and his function is to act as a mirror of reality for the parties whereas the conciliator acts as a fact finder or if required as a decision-maker through such decision is not binding.

In simple terms, mediation is known as private informal dispute resolution process in which a neutral third person, the mediator, helps disputing parties to reach an agreement. Mediation and conciliation processes are very similar to each other in that they interject a third party between the disputing parties either to mediate a specific dispute or to reconcile their relationship. Conciliation is formally recognized in India by the Arbitration & Conciliation Act, 1996 and the conciliated settlement agreement is given the same status as of a Court decree.

Abraham Lincoln advocated settlement through conciliation and mediation. Also a famous statement by John F. Kennedy, former US President – he said:

"Let us not negotiate with fear but let us not fear to negotiate."

None can deny that our cultural heritage is no different. Mahatma Gandhi advocated conciliation and mediation as a practicing lawyer in South Africa and said that it was the duty of lawyers to make efforts to settle disputes and that by doing so, lawyers would not be losers. He said that he, in fact, built up a reputation that he would always appear for the party whose case was invariably the just one. Therefore, the systems of conciliation and mediation are as much part of our cultural heritage as they are in any other country.

Parties are generally more satisfied with a mediated resolution, rather than one imposed upon them, as happens with a Court judgment, because the parties have created the solution themselves. In recent years, the use of binding mediation has developed as an alternative to arbitration and incorporates the negotiation aspects of mediation with the certainty of an outcome. Mediation is also much less costly than arbitration and protracted litigation.

## (II) REASONS FOR GROWTH OF MEDIATION AND CONCILLIATION

The litigant is today fairly sure that justice to his opponent, even if it cannot be denied ultimately, can be delayed as long as possible, may be for years. Unfortunately, successive Governments have not paid optimum attention to the judiciary. The numbers of Courts have not increased at least upto a basic minimum requirement and everybody finds it easy to blame the judiciary for the backlog. The judiciary is no doubt accountable, but there are other players who control the purse. It has been rightly said that the judiciary has neither the purse nor the sword.

Mounting arrears and delay in disposal of cases has put our Justice delivery system under severe strain and requires immediate attention. We need to take remedial measures to avoid total collapse of the system. The need of the hour today, therefore, is the speedy disposal of cases. How to curb the delays and clear the backlog? We have to find out - effective alternative methods of dispute resolution. We have to search for an alternative forum, which may be less formal, more effective and speedy. This is where conciliation and mediation come into picture. These two methods form part of ADR (Alternative Dispute Resolution) mechanism.

## (III) THE PROCESS OF MEDIATION

Unlike in regular Court litigation, in mediation proceedings, each party may, on his own initiative or at the invitation of the mediator, submit to the mediator suggestions for settlement of the dispute. When it appears to the mediator that there exist elements of a settlement, which may be acceptable to the parties, he shall formulate the terms of a possible settlement and submit them to the parties for their observations. After receiving the observations of the parties, the mediator may reformulate the terms of a possible settlement in the light of such observations. If the parties reach agreement on the settlement of the dispute, they may draw up and sign a written settlement agreement. If requested by the parties, the mediator and the institution may draw up, or assist the parties in drawing up, the settlement agreement. When the parties sign the settlement agreement, it shall be final and binding on the parties and persons claiming under them respectively and it shall have the same status of a decree of a Court of law.

The use of binding and non-binding mediation has increased greatly in both the private and public sectors, particularly for legal and business disputes. Many companies have chosen to insert mediation clauses into standard contracts as a preliminary dispute resolution step before arbitration or litigation.

Mediation can also be made of present or future disputes where the parties seek amicable settlement of such disputes by an agreement to mediate.

To provide finality to a dispute resolution clause, many parties include an arbitration provision that is, in the event their dispute is not settled during mediation. Essentially, an arbitration clause follows the mediation clause, and requires the parties to submit all disputes not settled in mediation to a final and binding arbitration. The mediator should never serve as an arbitrator in a subsequent arbitration, since he or she would have been exposed to confidential and privileged communications during the mediation process.

Mediation proceedings are settlement negotiations, and all offers, promises, conduct and statements, whether written or oral, made in the course of the proceedings, are inadmissible in any litigation or arbitration of their dispute. However, evidence that is otherwise admissible shall not be rendered inadmissible as a result of its use in the mediation session. Any information disclosed to the mediator in a private meeting shall remain confidential unless the party agrees that it may be disclosed.

## (IV) GROWTH OF MEDIATION AND CONCILLIATION IN INDIA

Today, all over the world and especially in the western countries, the corporate community is making use of mediation and conciliation to its fullest advantage for resolving the business disputes in a cost-effective and time-effective manner. However, the Indian business world is still content with adjudicative ways like litigation and arbitration. The business owners in India are yet to comprehend fully the importance of mediation as an effective tool to resolve the business disputes.

An attempt is made below to state the likely reasons explaining why the mediation is a less practiced process in India and to offer the possible suggestions to enhance the use of mediation in business dispute resolution

Mediation and conciliation are not new to us. The traditional method of resolution of disputes in India was by the Panchayat comprising of five members of village committees where the dispute originated. It has existed in our county in one form or the other. Mediation has been practiced in China and other countries for many centuries as the normal means of dispute resolution and now it has recently been adopted in western world as well.

As far as machinery for deciding the dispute under the Industrial Disputes Act is concerned, 'Conciliation' must precede the adjudication. Only when the conciliation proceedings fail that the matter can be referred to Labour Court or Industrial Tribunal or Arbitration (if the parties agree) by the Government for adjudication.

The Code of Civil Procedure, 1908, requires/enjoins the Court to make endeavour to assist the parties in arriving at the settlement in respect of subject matter of the suit or proceedings. Those disputes can be in relation to matrimonial life; for declaration of the legitimacy of any person in relation to guardianship of a person or the custody of the minor; for maintenance; validity of adoption; validity and legality of wills and succession etc. The Family Courts Act makes it compulsory for the Court to engineer a settlement. A duty is cast on the Family Court to make efforts for settlement in every proceeding or suit before it by persuading the parties to do so. In this regard, the Parliament has enacted the Civil Procedure Code (Amendment) Act, 1999 with a view to bring down the arrears in the various Courts especially in the Courts at the district level.

Section 89 of the amended Code of Civil Procedure, has made it obligatory for the Courts to refer the disputes, after issues are framed, for settlement either by way of (a) Arbitration; (b) Conciliation; (c) Judicial settlement; including settlement through Lok Adalats; or (d) Mediation. Further Proceedings in the Court are dependent upon the parties and the Court, to get the dispute settled through any of the Alternative Dispute Resolution Methods and it is only upon the failure of such alternative methods that the suit proceeds further.

Michel B. Shane, an authority in the field of 'Arbitration' has distinguished conciliation, arbitration and mediation. According to him, the conciliator is called upon to make a recommendation which is not binding in respect of factual or legal issues and suggest the appropriate resolution of such issues, the mediator is required to facilitate a consensus among the parties and not required to record a finding and convey his decision. Arbitration involves a binding resolution of a dispute by the third party. It would be thus clear that the process moves from a negotiation model (in mediation) to a litigation model (in arbitration) with conciliation falling somewhere in the middle.

### (V) BENEFITS/ ADVANTAGES OF MEDIATION AND CONCILIATION

Mediation has certain benefits like:

1. Parties get an opportunity to have their say and tell others how they see the problem in a friendly atmosphere without prejudice to any right.
2. Mediation helps the disputing parties understand how others see and feel about the problem.
3. Mediation is cheaper and quicker and can be arranged to suit the convenience of the parties.

Conciliation also has many advantages of resolution of dispute like:—

1. It offers a more flexible alternative, for a wide variety of disputes small as well as large.
2. It is committed to maintenance of confidentiality throughout the proceedings and thereafter of the dispute, the information exchanged, the offers and counter-offers of solutions made and the settlement arrived at.
3. It is cost-effective.

Keeping in view these advantages, it is high time that machinery of conciliation and mediation, as an effective ADR system, is exploited by us. Negotiations and settlement option must become part of the process of planning and development strategies adopted by advocates. Opportunities for negotiations and settlement must be pursued seriously when they arise. They exist almost in every civil case. Skill in negotiations, in due course of time will become much more important to the lawyers in time to come.

Conciliation and mediation are effective modes of resolution of disputes but these are required to be institutionalized.

Towards this end, mediation/conciliation, family and labour welfare centres have been set up by Delhi Legal Services Authority. Such centres are now functioning at Delhi High Court Complex, Patiala House Courts Complex and at 15 other places in different parts of Delhi. One centre at district Court complex at Tis Hazari is also functional.

## (VI) CONCLUSION

Mediation and conciliation can resolve the complex techno-commercial issues in a cost-effective and time-effective manner and help the disputing parties in protecting their long-term interests and preserving their ongoing business relationships.

In India, the increased level of awareness about mediation and conciliation, and the existence of a comprehensive code applicable uniformly to mediation and conciliation, besides the sufficient availability of the mediation services would certainly accelerate the use of mediation and conciliation in resolving the business disputes.

# ALTERNATIVE DISPUTE RESOLUTION AND THE ROLE OF INDIAN COURTS

*"My joy was boundless. I had learnt the true practice of law. I had learnt to find the better side of human nature and to enter men's hearts. I realized that the true function of a lawyer is to unite parties' driven asun'der. The lesson was so indelibly burnt into me that a large part of my time during the twenty years of my practice as a lawyer was occupied in bringing about private compromises of hundreds of cases. I lost nothing thereby – not even money, certainly not my soul."*

- Late Sh. Mohandas K. Gandhi

## (I) INTRODUCTION

There is an old Chinese curse, "may you live in interesting times". From a legal point of view, we cannot think of a time in the recent past that is more interesting than the present. Whatever our individual views may be on the merits or otherwise of the changes that are taking place, there is no doubt that we are experiencing a sea change in all aspects of the law – and this change is not merely one of practice and convenience, but of fundamental underlying theory as well.

Alternate Dispute Resolution or "ADR", as it is more commonly known, means the wide variety of methods by which conflicts and disputes are resolved other than through litigation and in a country like ours, where the backlog of cases is ever increasing and the common man is capable of losing his faith in the system of administration of justice, it is imperative that this faith be restored and a mechanism be adopted which does not have the complexities of long drawn litigation procedures but be as effective and binding on the parties adopting it.

ADR is a non-judicial means of settling disputes outside of the courtroom, avoiding costly and time-consuming litigation after a complaint or dispute arises. The use of ADR mechanisms is intended to supplement, not supplant, other enforcement mechanisms.

## (II) THE CONTENT OF ADR

**Alternative Dispute Resolution (ADR)** includes dispute resolution processes and techniques that fall outside of the Government judicial process. Despite historic resistance to ADR by both parties and sometimes their counsel, ADR has gained widespread acceptance among both the general public and the legal profession in recent years. In fact, some Courts now require some parties to resort to ADR of some type, usually mediation, before permitting the parties' cases to be tried. The rising popularity of ADR can be explained by the increasing caseload of traditional Courts, the perception that ADR imposes fewer costs than litigation, a preference for confidentiality, and the desire of some parties to have greater control over the selection of the individual or individuals who will decide their dispute.

"Alternative" Dispute Resolution is usually considered to be alternative to litigation. It also can be used as an expression for allowing a dispute to be resolved without Court intervention or as an alternative to other crude methods of concluding litigation. ADR includes mediation, arbitration and other ways of resolving conflicts with the help of a specially trained neutral third party and without the need for a formal trial or hearing. Sometimes a fifth type of ADR i.e, conciliation, is included as well, but for present purposes it can be regarded as a form of mediation.

Thus, the goals of ADR can be summarised for ready reference as hereunder:

(i) Early resolution of disputes;

(ii) More satisfying procedure for disputes resolution;

(iii) An outcome that reflects the parties' interests and values;

(iv) Litigant's satisfaction and result oriented compliance;

(v) Finality of resolution of disputes;

(vi) Win-win situation and preservation of relationship;

(vii) Reducing backlog and freeing judicial resources;

(viii) Cost savings for parties and Courts.

**(III) THE DOMESTIC PERSPECTIVE**

Alternative Dispute Resolution in India is not new and it was in existence even under the previous Arbitration Act, 1940. The Arbitration and Conciliation Act, 1996 has been enacted to accommodate the mandates of the UNCITRAL Model. To streamline the Indian legal system, the traditional civil law in the Code of Civil Procedure, (CPC), 1908 has also been amended and section 89 was introduced. Section 89 (1) of the CPC provides an option for the settlement of disputes outside the Court. It provides that where it appears to the Court that there exist terms, which may be acceptable to the parties, the Court may formulate the terms of a possible settlement and refer the same for arbitration, conciliation, mediation or judicial settlement.

ADR is by no means a recent phenomenon in India, though now it has been organised and systematised, expressed in clearer terms and employed more widely in dispute resolution in recent years than before. In earlier times, disputes were peacefully decided by intervention of kulas (family or clan assemblies), srenis (guilds of men following the same occupation), parishads (assemblies of learned men who knew law) before the king came to adjudicate on disputes. There were Nyaya panchayats at grassroots level before the advent of the British system of justice. Later on, Lok Adalats (people's Courts) have provided speedy and inexpensive justice in both rural and urban areas in India. The resolution of disputes forms a large part of the justice delivery system. India has a long tradition of resolving disputes through ADR methods viz Nyaya Panchayat System. At present there are about 30 million cases pending in the Indian Courts. A major step to expedite judicial process in this direction was initiated by the Central

Government by enactment of the Arbitration and Conciliation Act, 1996 which made significant changes in the law of arbitration. Institutions such as Lok Adalats have been given statutory recognition by the Legal Services Authorities Act, 1987. The Code of Civil Procedure, 1908 has been amended by incorporating section 89 and Order X, rules 1A, 1B and 1C, making it obligatory on the Courts to explore the settlement of disputes by ADR Methods in pending suits, which will create more demand for trained arbitrators, conciliators and mediators, to cater to the needs of more than 10,000 Courts spread all over the country. The need of the hour is to create an awareness of ADR methods among the people and to prepare a large pool of trained professionals in the field of ADR who will be able to practice these ADR Methods to resolve disputes.

The Constitution of India has defined and declared the common goal for all of us as — "to secure all the citizens of India justice social, economic and political; Liberty, Equality and Fraternity". ADR is a vehicle to achieve these principles and objectives.

## (IV) GROWTH OF ADR IN INDIA

Inspired by the United Nations Commission on International Trade Law's Conciliation Rules, which were adopted by the General Assembly of the United Nations in 1985, and the recommendation made by the General Assembly, the Parliament of India passed the Arbitration and Conciliation Act, 1996 which came into force on 25 January, 1996. The said Act intends to achieve consolidation and amendment of the law relating to domestic arbitration, international arbitration and enforcement of foreign arbitral awards as also to define the law relating to conciliation and the matters connected therewith or incidental thereto. Proceedings pending on arbitration commenced on or before 25 January, 1996 will continue to be governed by the Act of 1940.

For the promotion and development of arbitration and other Alternate Dispute Resolution techniques, Indian Society of Arbitrators (hereinafter referred to as ISA) was constituted. ISA has contributed substantially to the formulation and enactment of the Arbitration and Conciliation Act 1996, and is a leading arbitral institution in the country

## (V) ROLE OF COURTS

In India, laws relating to resolution of disputes have been amended from time-to-time to facilitate speedy dispute resolution. The judiciary has also encouraged out of Court settlements to alleviate the increasing backlog of cases pending in the Courts. To effectively implement the ADR mechanism, organizations like ICA, and ICADR were established, besides, Consumer Redressal Forums and Lok Adalats were revived. The Arbitration Act, 1940 was repealed and a new and effective arbitration system was introduced by the enactment of the Arbitration and Conciliation Act, 1996.This law is based on the United Nations Commission on International Trade Law (UNCITRAL) model law on international commercial arbitration.

The Legal Services Authorities Act, 1987 has also been amended from time to time to endorse use of ADR methods. Section 89 of the Code of Civil Procedure as amended in 2002 has introduced conciliation, mediation and pre-trial settlement methodologies for effective resolution of disputes. Mediation, Conciliation, Negotiation, Mini Trial, Consumer Forums, Lok Adalats and Banking Ombudsman have already been accepted and recognised as effective Alternative Dispute Resolution methodologies.

**(VI) ESTABLISHMENT OF ICADR**

At the initiative of some of the leading legal luminaries the International Centre for Alternative Dispute Resolution (ICADR) was established and registered as a society under the Societies Registration Act, 1860 for the promotion and development of ADR facilities and techniques to facilitate early resolution of disputes and to reduce the increasing burden of arrears in Courts. The ICADR is an autonomous organisation working under the aegis of the Ministry of Law and Justice, Government of India, with its Headquarters at New Delhi and Regional Centers at Hyderabad and Bangalore. It was inaugurated by the then Prime Minister of India at New Delhi on 6 October, 1995 and The Hon'ble Chief Justice of India is its Patron.

**(VII) ENACTMENT OF ARBITRATION & CONCILIATION ACT, 1996**

In the wake of globalisation of markets and liberalisation of our economy, it became necessary for the Government of India to enact a new legislation based on UNCITRAL, it also became essential to make Model Law Conciliation Rules to provide for an arbitral procedure which is fair, efficient, and capable of meeting the needs of the international business community. This is how the Arbitration and Conciliation Act, 1996, came into existence. The said Act makes significant changes in the entire process of arbitration, right from the time of the appointment of arbitrators till the completion of the process of arbitration. The supervisory role of the Court is reduced to a minimum and once the process of arbitration commences the intervention by the Court can be only after the arbitral award is made. The grounds for challenging an arbitral award are precise and specific. The arbitral award has been given the same status and force as that of a Court decree under the Code of Civil Procedure, 1908.

Several cases were filed in Courts with regard to the interpretation of some of the provisions of the Arbitration and Conciliation Act, 1996. The High Courts and the Supreme Court consistently upheld the provisions of the said Act. The Code of Civil Procedure, 1908 has been amended by inserting several new provisions and all of them aimed to reduce the delays in Court litigation. Section 89 has been inserted into CPC under which an obligation is placed upon the Courts to try ADR methods before the cases are taken up for trial. The constitutional validity of this amendment to CPC was challenged and the Supreme Court while upholding the constitutional validity of section 89 observed, inter alia, by its judgement dated 25 October, 2002 in *Salem Advocate Bar Association, Tamil Nadu* v. *Union of India,* AIR 2003 SC 189 that—

> "...keeping in mind the laws delays and limited number of Judges which are available it has now become imperative that resort should be had to Alternative Dispute Resolution mechanism with a view to bring to an end litigation between the parties at an early date".

A committee has been constituted by the Supreme Court to prepare the rules to be followed by all the Courts uniformly for implementation of the provisions of section 89 of CPC. The committee has prepared tentative rules to be followed by all the Courts in trying these ADR methods. Therefore, as a concluding note it can be stated that the success of ADR both now and in times to come will go a long way in reducing the mounting arrears and backlog of cases pending in Courts.

## ALTERNATE DISPUTE RESOLUTION

### *I. BACKGROUND OF ADR*

Alternate Dispute Resolution (ADR) is a very important and stimulating theme of contemporary relevance. The world is becoming increasingly small; and distances are being cut down with the increase in connectivity between nations. The world is evolving into a global village!

With the increase in the interaction between global citizens, their disputes have also increased. Courts are flooded with cases but neither the number of Courts nor the strength of Judges to resolve these disputes has increased. This has culminated in large number of unresolved disputes pending in the Courts as a natural consequence. Moreover, since adversary litigation is based on the win-loose theory, the animosity between the parties increases which is not congenial for a peaceful society.

Litigation involves a lot of delay and given the procedural formalities that are to be followed in appeals, revision and review, besides the constitutional remedies which can be invoked, the process of law can be unending. Once there is delay, obviously, the litigation process will become expensive. When we say expensive, it is not just the fee paid to the counsel and the Courts, it includes the other expenses of the litigants, besides the costs incurred by the infrastructure of the Courts, advocates office, loss of mandays and the psychological trauma one goes through in sustaining the litigation. Ultimately, when the Apex Court finally decides on the dispute, invariably one of the parties to the litigation will not be happy because of losing the case, despite the fact that the other party has incurred a very heavy expenditure and costs in the process of being victorious in the legal battle.

### *II. COMPONENTS OF ADR*

It is in this background, ADR methods gain importance. ADR is an alternative to litigation as a method of dispute resolution. The different modes of ADR are – Negotiation, Mediation, Conciliation, Mini Trial, Arbitration and the hybrid forms of these methods are Conciliation-cum-Arbitration, mediation settlements being converted to compromise decrees etc. The term ADR has been used to describe various systems that attempt to resolve dispute through methods other than litigation in Courts or tribunals. India has a very rich tradition of ADR methods, which were existent in the form of medieval Panchayats. In fact, the Panchayat's decisions were respected by the Judiciary also. In *Sitanna* v. *Viranna*, AIR 1934 SC 105, the Privy Council affirmed the decision of the Panchayat in a family dispute.

There is lot of flexibility in the use of ADR methods. The flexibility is available in the procedure as well as the way the solutions are found to the dispute. The solutions can be problem specific. Moreover, the rigidity of precedent as used in adversarial method of dispute resolution will not come in the way of finding solutions to the disputes in a creative way.

### *III. ADVANTAGES OF ADR*

**Firstly**, if the ADR method is successful, it brings about a satisfactory solution to the dispute and the parties will not only be satisfied, the ill-will that would have existed between them will also end. ADR methods especially mediation and conciliation not only address the dispute, they also address the emotions underlying the dispute. In fact, for ADR to be successful, first the emotions and ego existing between the parties will have to be addressed. Once the emotions and ego are effectively addressed, resolving the dispute becomes very easy. This requires wisdom and skill of counselling on the part of the mediator or the conciliator.

**Secondly**, the ADR method is participatory and there is scope for the parties to the dispute to participate in the solution finding process. As a result, they honour the solution with commitment. Above all this, the ADR methods work out to be cheaper and affordable by the poor people also. As of now, there are some variations when it comes to the expenses incurred in arbitration. In course of time when there are adequate number of quality arbitrators, the expenses of arbitration will also decrease. The promotion of institutional arbitration will go a long way in improving the quality of ADR services and making them cost-effective.

**Thirdly**, the development of ADR methods will provide access to many litigants. It helps in reducing the enormous work load that is imposed on the judiciary. Once the litigation that is pending before the judiciary becomes manageable, the Courts will be able to improve the quality of their decisions. All this will go a long way in improving not only the access to justice, but even the quality of justice.

### *IV. LAWS AIDING ADR*

The Indian scenario reveals that there are many legislations in India facilitating ADR and sometimes making it compulsory.

The Code of Civil Procedure contains the following provisions:

(i) Order 23, rule 3 provides for compromise of suit;

(ii) Order 32A, rule 3 requires the Courts to make efforts for settlement in case of family disputes;

(iii) Section 80 of the Code of Civil Procedure (CPC) requires giving of a 60 days mandatory notice in case of suits by or against the Government with a view to facilitate settlement of disputes amicably wherever possible;

(iv) Under Order XXXIIA CPC inserted by Amendment Act 104 of 1976, dealing with suits relating to matters concerning the family, an endeavour shall be made by the Court in the first instance, where it is possible to do so, consistent with nature and circumstances of the case, to assist the parties in arriving at a settlement in respect of the subject matter of the suit.

Even section 23 of the Hindu Marriage Act, 1955 (HMA) provides that before proceeding to grant any relief, the Court, at the first instance, should make an endeavour to bring about re-conciliation between the parties. Though such in-built mechanisms are there, in the CPC and the HMA for speedy disposal of cases by resorting to settlements, yet such provisions remain only on the statute book with no practical application and implementation by the Courts and the counsel. Such state of affairs should not be allowed to continue any longer. Every concerted effort is to be undertaken to make such salient provisions to be enforced and followed.

The above provisions of the CPC & the HMA and the duty cast upon the Court came for interpretation before the Supreme Court in *Jagraj Singh* v. *Bir Pal Kaur*, JT 2007 (3) SC 389 wherein upholding the order of the Hon'ble High Court summoning the Respondent-husband by non-bailable warrants, it was held as follows:

> "26 From the above case law in our judgment, it is clear that a court is expected, nay, bound, to make all attempts and section (2) of section 23 is a salutary provision exhibiting the intention of he parliament requiring the court 'in the first instance' to make every endeavor to bring about a reconciliation between the parties. If in the light of the above mentioned intention and paramount consideration of the legislature in enacting such provision, an order is passed by a Matrimonial Court asking a party to the proceeding (husband or wife) to remain personally present, it cannot successfully be contented that the court has no such power and in case a party to a proceeding does not remain present, at most, the court can proceed to decide the case *ex parte* against him/her. Upholding of such argument would virtually make the benevolent provision nugatory, ineffective and unworkable, defeating the laudable object of reconciliation in matrimonial disputes. The contention of the learned counsel for the appellant therefore cannot be upheld."

The above judgment of the Apex Court now make it mandatory for reconciliation to be attempted as provided by law. On another note, I may also point out that the Supreme Court has issued repeated directions that whenever there is any dispute between any two Government Departments or Public Sector Undertakings, they will first approach a dispute settlement committee setup on the directions of the Court by the Government of India to attempt to settle the matter by negotiation. Only upon the matter not being resolved by the committee, would the issue be taken up in Court. These directions have a very helpful role in facilitating the process of ADR by making it mandatory to resort to such procedures.

Section 9 of the Family Courts Act, 1984 provides for compulsory conciliation. The Industrial Disputes Act, 1947, provides for the process of conciliation and constitution of the Boards of Conciliation. In sections 4, 5, 12, 13 & 18. The Family Courts Act, 1984 (Central Act No. 66 of 1984) had been enacted to provide for the establishment of Family Courts with a view to promote conciliation in, and secure speedy settlement of disputes relating to marriage and family affairs and for matters connected therewith.

## *V. SOME VIEW POINTS ON ADR*

The Law Commission, in its 59th Report, 1974 had also stressed that in dealing with disputes, concerning the family, the Courts ought to adopt an approach radically different from that adopted in ordinary civil proceedings and that it should make reasonable efforts of settlement before the commencement of the trial.

In selecting persons for appointment as Judges, every endeavour shall be made to ensure that those given this responsibility are committed to the need to protect and preserve the institution of marriage and to promote the welfare of children and are qualified by reason of their experience and expertise to promote the settlement of disputes by conciliation and counselling.

The Arbitration and Conciliation Act, 1996 facilitates the parties to resolve disputes either through conciliation or arbitration. The settlement reached in conciliation or the award of the arbitrator is a deemed decree. It will be enforced by the Courts as if it were a decree. The Lok Adalats organized under the Legal Services Authorities Act, 1987, facilitates settlement between the parties. The settlement will have the status of a deemed decree. If pending disputes go before the Lok Adalat and are settled in the Lok Adalat, the court-fee paid to the Court will be returned to the person who has filed the suit.

## *VI. SIGNIFICANCE OF ADR*

From the above description the importance of ADR and how legislations are made to promote the same is very clear. The unfortunate thing is that we have not been able to develop a cadre of persons who will be able to use these ADR methods in dispensing justice. Lawyers by and large still believe that litigation is the way of resolving disputes. Litigants are also advised accordingly. The challenge that we are facing today is bringing about awareness among the people about the utility of ADR and simultaneously developing personnel who will be able to use ADR methods effectively with integrity.

The experiment of 'Lok Adalat' as an alternate mode of dispute settlement has come to be accepted in India, as a viable, economic, efficient and informal one.

Another right and welcome step taken was the enactment of the Consumer Protection Act, 1986 (Act No. 68 of 1986), for short "CP Act" for the settlement of consumer disputes and for matters connected therewith. The aim of CP Act is to provide for an effective, inexpensive, simple and speedy redressal to consumer grievances, which the civil Courts are not able to provide. This Act is nothing, but an alternate arrangement for the effective adjudication of consumer disputes. The protection as envisaged by the CP Act is for protection of consumers as a class.

In matters of arbitrations clauses in agreements between the parties, they have the option to go for *ad hoc* arbitration or institutional arbitration depending on their convenience. In *ad hoc* arbitration, the fees of the arbitrator will have to be agreed by the parties and the arbitrator. The present Indian experience is that the fee of the arbitrator is proving to be quite expensive in *ad hoc* arbitration.

## *VII. INSTITUTIONAL ARBITRATION*

Institutional Arbitration is an arbitration administered by an arbitral institution. The parties may stipulate in the arbitration agreement to refer an arbitral dispute between them for resolution to a particular institution. Some of the Indian institutions in this regard are Indian Council of Arbitration (ICA), Federation of Indian Chamber of Commerce and Industry (FICCI), International Centre for Alternate Dispute Resolution (ICADR), Hyderabad.

### Why Institutional Arbitration

The advantages of institutional arbitration are as follows:

(a) In *ad hoc* arbitration, the procedures will have to be agreed by the parties and the arbitrator. This needs cooperation between the parties. When a dispute is in existence, it is difficult to expect cooperation among the parties. In institutional arbitration, the rules are all ready there. There is no need to worry about formulating rules or spend time on making rules. Hence, institutional arbitration is beneficial.

(b) In institutional arbitration, the arbitral institution will have infrastructure facilities to conduct arbitration; they will have trained secretarial and administrative staff. There will also be library facilities. There will be professionalism in conducting arbitration. The costs of arbitration should work out to be cheaper in institutional arbitration.

(c) In institutional arbitration, the institution will maintain a panel of arbitrators along with their profiles. The parties can choose from the panel. It also provides for specialized arbitrators while in *ad hoc* arbitration, these advantages are not available.

(d) In institutional arbitration, the arbitrator's fee is fixed by the arbitral institution. The parties know before hand what will be the cost of arbitration. In ad hoc arbitration, the arbitrator's fee is negotiated and agreed. The Indian experience shows that it is quite expensive.

Accordingly, institutional arbitration is preferential and beneficial. We must encourage ICADR to empanel the Diploma & Certificate Holders as conciliators for Lok Adalats and also for the purpose of adoption of ADR methods for expeditious resolution of disputes in a peaceful and satisfactory manner. Unless these ADR methods are sincerely encouraged simultaneously by the judiciary, the executive and the advocate fraternity, the strife in the society will not end and the resort by the people out of frustration to other unsocial elements which disturbs the peace and harmony in the society will not be put an end to. It is therefore the duty of the judiciary and the executive to give maximum encouragement to ADR methods. We should endeavour to inspire the parties to settle disputes out of Court by utilizing provisions like section 89 of CPC and other legislations which provide out of Court settlement procedures. These are very important provisions to be implemented in letter and spirit both by litigants by Courts.

## *VIII. LOK ADALAT*

The experiment of 'Lok Adalat' (People's Court) as an alternate mode of dispute settlement has come to be accepted in India, as a viable, economic, efficient and an informal process.

Generally speaking, it is not a 'COURT', as understood by the common people, though they may find the attributes of a COURT in it and may be called by that name. A significant difference is that a law Court sits in its premises, where the litigants come with their lawyers and witnesses to seek justice, whereas in a LOK ADALAT, the informal 'Adalat' itself goes to the people to deliver justice at their doorsteps. Thus, it is a kind of forum provided by the people themselves or by interested parties, including social activists, legal-aid societies and public-spirited people belonging to every walk of life to bring inexpensive justice to the common man.

The procedural provisions in respect of disputes referred to Lok Adalat are contained in sections 19 to 22 of the Legal Services Authority Act, 1987. Under section 22 relating to powers of Lok Adalat, the Lok Adalat has been conferred with the powers of a civil Court under the CPC, 1908 in respect of the matters specified therein.

The present new section has been inserted by the CPC (Amendment) Act, 1999. It provides for the settlement of disputes outside the Court. The provisions of this section are based on the recommendations made by Law Commission of India and the Malimath Committee. It was suggested by the Law Commission of India that the Court might require attendance of any party to the suit or proceedings to appear in person with a view to arriving at an amicable settlement of disputes between the parties and make an attempt to settle the disputes between the parties peacefully, without any delay and with minimal expenditure.

Lastly, we wish to recall what Abraham Lincoln said more than a century ago:

> "Discourage litigation, persuade your neighbours to compromise, whenever you can. Point out to them the normal winner is often a real loser; in fees, expenses and waste of time. As a peace –maker, the lawyer has a superior opportunity of being a good person." (Notes for a Law Lecture – Home Book of American Quotations (by Dodd, Near) New York, 1967 p. 226).

# KEY ISSUES OF INTERNATIONAL COMMERCIAL ARBITRATION

## INTRODUCTION

In the recent decades, arbitration as a mechanism of dispute resolution has gained global acceptability. It is evolving as a principal method of settlement of commercial disputes. Technical advancement and world economic growths taken together has rendered arbitration an efficacious mechanism of dispute resolution. Fortunately, on account of the efforts made by the Untied Nations Commission on International Trade Law (UNCITRAL), some nationals have fallen in line with the model law made available by the UNCITRAL. This was pursuant to the recommendation of the General Assembly of the United Nations to the member nations to go in for legislation in conformity with the aforesaid model law. Arbitration, in a sense, is securing "private justice" through a chosen adjudicatory mechanism that has appropriate legislation sanction.

Since the past 50 odd years, there has been an upraise of this so-called international body which is a set up to settle disputes from contractual and other civil law relationships arising in the course of foreign trade and other forms of international economic relations, provided that the place of business of at least one of the parties is abroad, as well as dispute arising between enterprises with the foreign investments, international associations and organizations etc. It has now become a fancy more than a business to have a commercial arbitration committee of one's own state in this world community.

International commercial arbitration is one of the several forms of dispute resolution for international commercial agreements. The use of arbitration has increased alongwith the growth of international trade and commerce and the accompanying disputes springing from these pursuits. In a broader sense, arbitration is a vehicle of dispute resolution in which parties to a contract select a neutral arbitrator(s) to present their dispute for a legally binding ruling. Arbitration is often selected for the reasons of confidentiality, and to eliminate the uncertainties in the choice of arbitrator and forum. Parties from different national origins may also be reluctant to accept national Court litigation with the potential for national bias. Arbitration offers the parties more control over how proceedings will be conducted.

## COMMERCIAL ARBITRATION

In international commercial arbitration, it is important to characterize the nature of the underlying transaction and whether or not the relevant dispute is commercial; the involvement of commercial persons may be of relevance but should not be guiding principle. For instance, States, their ministries and agencies may be involved in a commercial activity although they do not qualify, strictly speaking, as a commercial person.

***Characteristics Defining Commercial Arbitration:***

Commercial Arbitration has several defining characteristics:

1. Arbitration is consensual, the parties must agree to arbitrate their differences.
2. Arbitrations are resolved by non-Governmental decision makers, arbitrators do not act as Government agents, but private persons selected by the parties.
3. Arbitration produces a definitive and binding award, which is capable of enforcement through national courts.

Another defining characteristic of arbitration is its flexibility, which generally permits to agree upon the procedures that will govern the resolution of their dispute. As a consequence, the procedural conduct of arbitrations varies dramatically across industrial sectors, arbitral institutions, and categories of disputes. In particular fields, or individual cases, parties often agree upon procedural rules that are tailor made for their individual needs. Apart from specialized fields, commercial arbitration often bears significant resemblances to commercial litigation: Arbitration will usually involve the submission of written pleadings and legal arguments, the presentation of written evidence and oral testimony, the application of law and the rendition of a binding award.

International commercial arbitration is similar, in important respects, to domestic arbitration. As in domestic matters, international arbitration is a consensual means of dispute resolution, by a non-Governmental decision maker that produces a legally binding and enforceable ruling. In addition, however, international arbitration has several features that distinguish it from domestic arbitration. Most importantly, international arbitration is often designed and accepted particularly to assure parties from different jurisdiction that their disputes will be resolved neutrally. Among other things, the parties seek a neutral decision maker. In addition, international arbitration is frequently regarded as a means of mitigating the peculiar uncertainties of transitional litigation, by designating a single, exclusive dispute resolution mechanism for the party's disagreements. Moreover, international arbitration is often seen as a means of obtaining an award that is enforceable in diverse jurisdiction.

## INTERNATIONAL COMMERCIAL ARBITRATION EXPOUNDED

Section 2(1)(f) of the Arbitration and Conciliation Act, 1996, defines international commercial arbitration as:

> "International Commercial Arbitration: means an arbitration relating to disputes arising out of legal relationships, whether contractual or not, considered as commercial under the law in force in India and where at least one of the parties is—
>
> (i) an individual who is a national of, or habitually resident in, any country other than India; or
>
> (ii) a body corporate which is incorporated in any country other than India; or

(iii) a company or an association or a body of individuals whose central management and control is exercised in any country other than India; or

(iv) the Government of a foreign country;

The expression "international commercial arbitration" has been defined to mean, in short, an arbitration relating to a commercial dispute which has at least one of the parties belonging to a foreign country. Such party may be an individual, firm or a company. It has been noticed that Public Sector Undertakings (PSUs) i.e. State-owned corporations in India and other business entities normally do not object to the arbitration in an international contract to take place outside India. corporations such as Oil and Natural Gas Commission (ONGC), the National Hydro Power Corporation (NHPC), Steel Authority of India Ltd. (SAIL), Food Corporation of India (FCI) in their international contracts agree to arbitration being held outside India as Government of India and/or State-owned corporations are amenable to subscribing to an arbitration clause making arbitration subject to the rules of an internationally recognized arbitral organization.

## THE KEY ISSUES

The international or domestic character of commercial arbitration may result in the application of a different set of rules. Several legal systems have special rules for domestic and international arbitration while other systems opt for a unified regulation. There are three ways of establishing the international character of arbitration. Arbitration may be international because:

(a) its subject-matter or its procedure or its organization is international; or

(b) the parties involved are connected with different jurisdictions; or

(c) there is a combination of both.

The objective criterion focuses on the subject-matter of the dispute and the international or national character of the underlying transaction. Hence, the international commercial interest, or the cross-border element of the underlying contract, or the fact the dispute is referred to a genuinely international arbitral institution, such as the ICC, the ICLA or ICSID, would be sufficient for the arbitration to qualify as international. To the subjective criterion, the focus is on the different nationality or domicile or place of business of the parties to the arbitration agreement. It follows that parties, individuals or companies, should come from different jurisdiction. The modern combined criterion, a third approach combines both the subjective and objective criteria.

## EFFECTS AND CHANGES

The rapid development of international commercial arbitration has forced national legal systems not only to tolerate international commercial arbitration, but also to provide for favourable, legal regimes within which it can flourish. It has been rightly suggested that in the 1980s and the 1990s we have experienced a period of competition amongst legislature and judiciary, they all tried to attract more international arbitration. The two main effects of this competition were the modernization and liberalization of arbitration regimes and the transfer of the favourable treatment of international arbitration onto the domestic level. This was also reflected in the new trend for unified regulation of international and domestic arbitrations. The principle that what is good for international arbitration is also good for domestic arbitration was adopted by Sweden, Germany and other countries. In England, although different systems were anticipated in the Arbitration Act, the domestic rules were not put into effect. The modern unified arbitration system minimizes the importance of the distinction of the national and international arbitration.

An undisputed significant role towards unification and internationalization of international commercial arbitration is ascribed to the success of the model law.

It appears that unified regulatory model, which is often referred to as monism, is the emerging trend. The internationalization of arbitration appears to be a welcome move globally. There is a gradual convergence of national arbitration systems, greatly enhanced by modern arbitration laws, the revised international and institutional arbitration rules and the increased acceptance of party autonomy, which can be found in the vast majority of international commercial contracts.

## MEASURES TO MAKE INTERNATIONAL COMMERCIAL ARBITRATION MORE EFFECTIVE IN INDIA

**In order to make India the Global Hub for Arbitration, certain obstacles have to be overcome by taking proper remedial measures.**

1. **A separate law for domestic and international matters**
   - An intrinsic mistake in the 1996 law is that there is a common law for both domestic and international matters. There should be different laws for both as done in Singapore. **There is a need for separation of law for domestic and international matters.**
   - Bills which encourage domestic and international arbitration should be brought up so that India would become the arbitration hub of the world.
2. **Parties to arbitration should ensure that there is no delay in the process of arbitration.**
   - While preparing the contract, parties need to be very clear what all they want regarding arbitration like venue of arbitration, composition of arbitral tribunal etc.
   - Delay by parties on various accounts like scope of jurisdiction should be avoided.
   - Language in the contract should not be erred. It should be very clear what kinds of matters are open for arbitration, whether any dispute or a particular dispute. Generally, the arbitration agreement/clause says, "matters arising out of the contract". Sometimes, there is a dispute whether there is something arising from the contract.
   - Appointment of arbitrators is really important and so the parties should be very careful while appointing the arbitrator and both parties should be satisfied as to the impartiality of the arbitrator.
3. **A separate tribunal for monitoring the arbitration process**
   - There is a need of a tribunal whose main function would be monitoring the process which ensures quality arbitration.

- Both parties should be allowed to plead. If a party fails to plead, the arbitral tribunal should go on with the arbitration process. For this, the arbitral tribunal has to be given more authority and power.

4. **Efforts should be made to reduce costs**

- Cost of arbitration is very high and so first of all efforts should be made to bring the costs down. 82% of the cost is constituted by the fees of the arbitrators and counsels of both the parties. The arbitrators should discuss with the counsel what steps should be taken to resolve the dispute so that both the parties are satisfied with the procedure.
- The time for resolving the dispute should be reduced, which will further help in reducing the cost of arbitration. This can be done by fixing the time for arbitration in the arbitration agreement itself for by agreement between the parties in the preliminary hearing the arbitral tribunal.
- Reduction in costs will allow matters of small claims to come for arbitration which will enlarge the scope of international commercial arbitration and even parties who are not financially capable of going for arbitration in case of disputes (at the present costs), will be able to get the benefit of the arbitration process.

## CONCLUSION

International commercial arbitration has proved to be a very effective mechanism for resolving disputes but it faces certain obstacles which can be overcome by adopting certain measures such as reducing costs, avoiding delay, setting up a separate monitoring institution and making separate laws for domestic and international matters. By adopting the aforesaid measures, international commercial arbitration will not only enlarge its scope but also promote arbitration for small claims. Especially, in developing countries like India, where the economy is developing at a very high rate and also with the advent of globalisation, the economy has expanded a few notches. A dispute resolving mechanism such as international commercial arbitration can help in fostering the growth of the economy.

## SOME SUGGESTIONS

On the other hand, most of the time countries, such as Singapore have opted for arbitration as they have separate laws for domestic and international matters and the Courts interference is minimal. India can also become the arbitration hub of the world, if proper arbitration mechanisms are developed international commercial arbitration in India should be made much easier and accessible or else the main purpose of its existence will be deprived. It should also be less technical and more responsive to the canons of justice and fair play and make the arbitrator adhere to such process and norms which will create confidence not only by doing justice between the parties, but by creating the sense that justice appears to have been done, and this being emphatically done. So are we ready for the next global arbitration hub Incredible India!

# INTERFERENCE IN ARBITRAL AWARDS ON GROUNDS OF PUBLIC POLICY – A KEY ISSUE IN INTERNATIONAL ARBITRATION

## INTRODUCTION: ARBITRATION LAW IN INDIA

Prior to 1996, arbitration in India was governed substantially by three enactments:

(1) The Arbitration Act, 1940;

(2) The Arbitration (Protocol and Convention) Act, 1937; and

(3) The Foreign Awards (Recognition and Enforcement) Act, 1961.

Thereafter, with the advent of the United Nations Commission on International Trade Law ('UNCITRAL') Model Law on Arbitration in 1985 and with a view to further the process of reforms undertaken, the Indian Parliament passed the Arbitration & Conciliation Act, 1996 ('the Act of 1996'). The said Act encompasses the principles laid down under the UNCITRAL Model Law.

## COMMERCIAL CONSIDERATION

The principal need for this enactment was the consensus that the earlier laws governing arbitration in India were outdated and not aiding the process any longer. The commercial realities had changed a lot and dispute resolution processes needed a change as well. An arbitral procedure which was in line with internationally prevalent arbitral procedure for arbitration in India, including international commercial arbitration, would enable India to implement her economic liberalisation programme with more confidence.

## MINIMAL COURT INTERVENTION

One of the most attractive features of arbitration is the minimal supervisory role and interference of Courts in the arbitral process. In line with this objective, the Arbitration and Conciliation Act, 1996 (Act of 1996) sets out the reliefs for which parties to arbitral proceedings can approach a Court when arbitration proceedings are pending. Wide powers are given to the arbitral tribunal under the Act of 1996, whereas under the old enactments, the parties would be entitled to and would often approach the Courts, rendering the theoretically efficient process of arbitration nugatory.

## PUBLIC POLICY CHALLENGE TO ARBITRAL AWARDS

Challenges to arbitral awards are governed under the provisions of section 34 of the Act of 1996. Section 34(2)(b)(ii) deals with a situation where the arbitral award is sought to be set aside on the ground that it (the arbitral award) is in conflict with the public policy of India. Section 34(2)(b)(ii) of the Act of 1996 states:

> "34. Application for setting aside arbitral award—(1) Recourse to a Court against an arbitral award may be made only by an application for setting aside such award in accordance with sub-section (2) and sub-section (3).
>
> (2) (b) the Court finds that—
>
> (ii) the arbitral award is in conflict with the public policy of India.
>
> *Explanation*—Without prejudice to the generality of sub-clause (ii), it is hereby declared, for the avoidance of any doubt, that the award is in conflict with the public policy of India if the making of the award was induced or affected by fraud or corruption or was in violation of section 75 or section 81."

Sub-section (ii) provides an explanation with respect to public policy and states that it includes an award which was induced or affected by fraud or corruption or which violated the provisions of section 75 or 81 of the Act of 1996. Whilst the explanation demystifies the said sub-section (2)(b)(ii) up to a certain extent, the generality of the concept of public policy clearly remains inherent in the said provision and therefore is left to the Courts to expound.

## EXPOUNDING OF PUBLIC POLICY GROUND

Public Policy is not defined under the Act of 1996 or any other enactment in India. Public policy can be referred to as a branch of common law, concerning public good or public interest, which is governed by precedents. It does not pertain to Government policy. In a world where change is said to be the only constant, the concept of public policy is in flux and therefore the onus of maintaining certainty in the concept of public policy must fall on the use of precedents by the Courts.

## INDIAN COURT DECISIONS

The Honourable Supreme Court of India has expounded the term 'Public Policy' in *Delhi Transport Corporation v. DTC Mazdoor Congress* , 1991 Supp (1) SCC 600: 'The phrases "public policy," "opposed to public policy" or "contrary to public policy" are incapable of precise definition. It is valued to meet the public good or the public interest. What is public good or in the public interest or what would be injurious or harmful to the public good or the public interest vary from time to time with the change of circumstances. New concepts take the place of old ones. The transactions which were considered at one time as against public policy were later held by the Courts to be in public interest and were found to be enforceable. Therefore, this Court held in *Central Inland Water Transport Corpn. Ltd.* v. *Brojo Nath Ganguly,* 1986 (3) SCC 156 that "there has been no well recognized head of public policy, the Courts have not shirked from extending it to new transactions and changed circumstances and have at times not even flinched from inventing a new head of public policy."

It can be seen that the power of the Court to expound the theory of public policy is thus far-reaching and judicious use of such power is required. To date, section 34 has been subject to various interpretations, varying as per the facts and circumstances of each matter.

Deciding whether an award is opposed to public policy is therefore not a simple task. The Courts have always looked at that question keeping public interest and good in mind. They are no doubt guided by the principles laid down in various precedents. In situations where there exist no precedents, the Courts always can be guided by the principles underlying the fundamental rights and the directive principles as set out in the Constitution of India.

## A COMPARATIVE PERSPECTIVE

An apparent distinction between the Act of 1996 and the English Arbitration Act, 1996, is the absence of a provision empowering the Court to correct an error of law in the award. Needless to say, any error of law would leave the aggrieved party at the receiving end of substantial injustice and that would be a scenario that no Court would like to see. This absence is clearly a weakness of the Act of 1996 which it appears only can be filled by giving the doctrine of public policy the widest possible amplitude.

There is a school of thought that does not agree with this proposition. This school is of the view that the legislature in his own wisdom, and possibly to ensure finality and a speedier disposal of a dispute, has chosen not to include such a provision in the Act of 1996. That again has been held to be incorrect by the Honourable Supreme Court which states that for achieving the object of the speedier disposal of dispute, justice in accordance with law cannot be sacrificed.

## ENLARGED INTERPRETATION BY THE INDIAN SUPREME COURT

The Hon'ble Supreme Court has therefore, in *ONGC* v. *Saw Pipes*, 2003 (5) SCC 705, held that section 34(2)(b)(ii) of the Act of 1996 is required to be given a wider interpretation. Thus, quoting from the judgment:

'The result would be – award could be set aside if it is contrary to:

(a) Fundamental policy of Indian law; or
(b) the interest of India; or
(c) justice or morality; or
(d) in addition, if it is patently illegal.'

These heads under which the doctrine of public policy is applied to arbitral awards are by no means comprehensive. Rather, they are indicative of the development of the said doctrine. Whilst the first three heads above were laid down first in the *Renusagar* case, 1994 Supp (1) SCC 644, the fourth one was added in the Oil and Natural Gas Commission case (supra) (whilst re-affirming the first three as laid down in Renusagar). Nothing prevents the Courts from expounding the doctrine of public policy to fill a void left by the legislature by addition to or deleting from the indicative list of heads.

## BENEFICIAL INTERPRETATIONS BY COURTS

The Courts have never refrained from interfering with an arbitral award which has caused substantial injustice to any of the parties. Whilst the hesitancy in applying the said doctrine due to the ever-changing nature of the concept of public policy is understandable, its judicious use is integral to fill the 'void' left by legislature, albeit in its own eternal wisdom.

**CONCLUSION**

Needless to say, a situation where, due to a void in the Act of 1996, the Courts are required to give the widest possible amplitude to the term 'public policy', can given rise to situations where a party will challenge any arbitral award on this ground. This will of course negate the basic feature of the Act of 1996 and the concept of arbitration which envisages the quickest possible resolution of disputes in a timely and efficient manner. Thus, due care must be taken by the Courts to harmonise unwarranted interference in arbitral awards using the said section 34(2)(b)(ii) of the Act of 1996.

# TRANSPARENCY AND ACCOUNTABILITY IN DELAY IN CRIMINAL JUSTICE

## (I) INTRODUCTION: THE BACKGROUND

The jurisprudence of Ancient India, which was essentially Hindu-ruled, was shaped by the concept of 'Dharma', or rules of right conduct, as outlined in the various manuals explaining the Vedic scriptures such as 'Puranas' and 'Smritis'. The King had no independent authority but derived his powers from 'Dharma', which he was expected to uphold. The distinction between a civil wrong and a criminal offence was clear. While civil wrongs related mainly to disputes arising over wealth, the concept of pataka or sin was the standard against which crime was to be defined.

India was subjected to a series of invasions by the Muslims beginning in the 8th Century A.D. and ending in the 15th century when a mixed race of Persians, Turks and Mongols set up the Moghul Empire. They occupied most of the Northern region and enforced a Mohammedan criminal law that classified all offences on the basis of the penalty which each offence merited. These included retaliation (blood for blood), specific penalties (as for theft and robbery) and discretionary penalties.

India became a nation under the British who arrived in the early 17th Century as traders of the East India Company. The Company slowly acquired territory across the sub-continent, strictly for commercial operations in the beginning, but gradually assumed considerable powers of governance. Considering the Muslim criminal law to be irrational and draconian, the Company brought about several reforms through a series of regulations which modified or expanded the definitions of some offences, introduced new offences and altered penalties to make them more logical and reasonable. The Indian Penal Code (IPC) defining crime and prescribing appropriate punishments was adopted in 1860, following the painstaking work of the First Law Commission, particularly its Chairman Lord Macaulay. The IPC has stood the test of time. As a sequel to the IPC, a Code of Criminal Procedure was enacted in 1861 and established the rules to be followed in all stages of investigation, trial and sentencing. This Code was repealed and a new Code came into effect in 1974. These two Codes, along with parts of the Indian Evidence Act 1872, forms the essence of India's criminal law. A large number of special and local laws such as the Arms Act, Prohibition Act, Immoral Traffic (Prevention) Act, etc., take care of various other anti-social activities.

## (II) THE PURPOSE OF CRIMINAL JUSTICE: AN ASSESSMENT

The purpose of the criminal justice system is to deliver justice for all, by convicting and punishing the guilty and helping them to stop offending, while protecting the innocent. It is responsible for detecting crime and bringing it to justice; and carrying out the orders of Court, such as collecting fines, and supervising community and custodial punishment. The key goals for criminal justice are to help reduce crime by bringing more offences to justice, and to raise public confidence that the system is fair and will deliver justice to the law-abiding citizen. The victim and the witnesses also expect from the criminal justice system a satisfaction level that justice has been done and not only appears to have been done. These are some elementary perceptions of justice of a common man.

## (III) CRIMINAL LAW ADMINISTRATION IN INDIA: SOME PERCEPTIONS

Rules of evidence coupled with otherwise cumbersome procedures have burdened the system in favour of the accused besides turning it against the investigation and the victim. Appearing acquittal decisions leave little doubt that crime is today a high-profit, low-risk business. Our criminal law jurisprudence is based on distrust towards the police and the investigation. Procedural fairness has been the most relevant consideration in the matter of deprivation of liberty. There appears to be a presumption of innocence even when the accused appears to be *prima facie* guilty. The investigation has to discharge the onerous burden of proving the guilt of the accused beyond reasonable doubt. The accused invariably attempts to delay the trial. A delayed trial ensures dissipation of evidence. With its seemingly inadequate evidence, the prosecution stands handicapped. The accused then attacks the prosecution's case and seeks acquittal with benefit of doubt. The criminal Court has little choice except to let the criminal go free. This is normally the sad story of criminal law justice administration.

Efforts in the past to reform the rules of evidence and simplify procedure have met with opposition. Opponents of change always caution you that tightened provisions would lead to a higher conviction rate and strengthen enforcement in the hands of the police. In a nutshell, the criminal law justice system now depends on two rules of practice. The police arrests and chargesheets a person on suspicion. The Court acquits the accused on the basis of benefit of doubt. Success in a criminal law trial is very scarcely achieved through the process of cross-examination. Winning over of witnesses in the absence of any witness protection programme has become the most misused avenue available to the accused. Convictions or acquittals are decided on whether witnesses depose or turn hostile. The hostility of witnesses added with the unwillingness of eye witnesses to depose, displays public apathy. Courts under such a situation do not know the truth; as they are expected to know only the available evidence. The gap between truth and evidence is the pitfall of the legal system. How does one fill this void. The Law Commission of India in its 178th Report analysed the problem of the hostile witnesses. The Report stated: "To protect public interest and to safeguard the interests of society, measures need to be devised to eliminate, as far as possible, scope for such happenings." The Justice Malimath Committee also suggested changes in criminal law administration. The committee also made some meaningful recommendations. Both the above reports concluded that perjury in judicial proceedings and hostile witnesses, coupled with the backlog of the criminal cases, was a major problem which affected our criminal justice system.

## (IV) DELAY IN CRIMINAL JUSTICE: SOME DIFFERENT VIEWS

Often it happens that after spending years in prison, a person is acquitted not because there was not enough evidence on record or because material witnesses turned hostile but because he was actually innocent. Can the State compensate him for the lost years, for the time spent away from children; for the loss of livelihood; and for the loss of reputation and dignity or for loss of life and liberty.

More than two-thirds of the stated over 3,20,000 prisoners languishing in jails across the country are said to be undertrials. Perpetual delays in criminal trials must be looked into. The Supreme Court has consistently maintained that the right to a speedy trial is part of the guarantee of the fundamental right to life and personal liberty under article 21 of the Constitution of India. The Law Commission of India, in its report on Delays and Arrears in Trial Courts (1978), recommended that a criminal case should be endeavoured to be disposed off within six months.

In 1987, the Law Commission stressed the need to raise the ratio of Judges to the population from 10.5 per one million people to 50 Judges per one million. However, even after almost two decades, there has been little progress on this score. Today, we have reportedly over 56 lakh pending criminal cases in the Courts. The National Crime Records Bureau reports that only 31 per cent criminal trials are completed in less than a year. Some are said to take even more than 10 years.

The lack of Judges is not the sole reason for the delays. It is the long procedures, cumbersome processes and, most significantly, the indifference besides the lack of accountability of the criminal justice system. In *Hussainara Khatoon & others v. Home Secretary, State of Bihar*, AIR 1979 SC 1369, the Supreme Court lamented that it is a travesty of justice that certain people end up spending time in custody not because they are guilty but because the Courts are too busy to try them, and they, as the accused, are too poor to afford bail. An elaborate set of guidelines to enable the release of poor and indigent prisoners, without having to arrange for someone to stand as surety for them, was laid down.

In *Common Cause v. Union of India & others*, 1996 (4) SCC 33, the Supreme Court issued another set of guidelines to enable the release on bail of persons in custody whose trials had dragged on for inordinately long periods. Unfortunately, lack of accountability in the system of criminal administration of justice has led to the problem being perpetuate and the jails continue to be filled up by undertrials whose cases have dragged on much beyond the permissible limits of a just and fair system.

## (V) WHAT SHOULD BE DONE: SOME PRACTICAL THOUGHTS AND SUGGESTIONS

(A) The pursuit of life, liberty and peace includes freedom from crime. The State's foremost duty is to provide these basic rights to each citizen. The success of a criminal justice system can only be measured by how successful it is in ensuring these rights in word and spirit. The extent, to which these are successfully guaranteed, will be reflected in the confidence of the public in the system.

(B) On the one hand particularly with improving information technologies, the availability of information on the incidence of crime is increasing; as is the rise in the expectations of the people from the State.

(C) Some of the laws, rules and procedures which were good for the bygone era do not serve the purpose today. The people who run the system also need to be trained, motivated and finally made accountable. This is essential in a democracy, which requires both transparency and accountability. It is difficult to expect the laws and procedures to make up for the deficiencies of the people who administer it and *vice-versa*. Perceptions of justice have undergone a change and levels of accountability are required to achieve transparency. Society changes, and so do its values. A system as vital and critical to the society as the criminal justice system cannot be static. Reforms ought to be a continuous process, keeping pace with the emerging challenges. No worthwhile reform is possible without deep study and intensive research

(D) The Constitution, the Indian Penal Code and the Code of Criminal Procedure prescribe the rights and duties of the people to ensure their life, liberty and dignity. Generally, people hesitate to come forward to assist the criminal justice authorities unless compelled by circumstances or personal interests. With a view to securing justice to the people and punishing the offenders, the functionaries of the criminal justice system should motivate the people to discharge their duties under various laws. Orientation programmes should be evolved and implemented to educate and awaken the people about their responsibilities. There is a necessity for a meaningful and healthy dialogue between the people and criminal justice functionaries, especially the police. Formation of voluntary schemes can help bring the people closer to the police.

(E) It appears that crime trends disclose significant increase in the crime rate, especially violent crime. The pendency of cases in Courts has increased and the seemingly declining rate of conviction of criminal cases reflects the difficulties of the machinery to deliver speedy justice. Law Commissions and eminent persons have pointed out flaws in the working of different agencies and indicate that the system of criminal justice administration is found wanting in its efficacy in keeping crime under control.

(F) The Law Commission has pointed out that quite often, the police sometimes refrain from producing all material witnesses on the same day, with the object of clearing lacunae in the prosecution evidence once the defence's case is revealed through cross-examination. Many times, the reason for the absence of the accused from Court proceedings, resulting in adjournment of the case is improper planning. In this regard video conferencing of accused directly from the jail without actually transporting them to the Courts has proved to be a boon.

(G) Sometimes a single unplanned absence or leave by a Magistrate or Judge, whether on account of personal reasons or official duties sets the trial back by a couple of months, causing undue delay and suffering to the person facing trial. Sometimes the accused and their representatives also contribute to the delay, to buy time to turn the case in their favour. Structural and procedural deficiencies apart, non-enforcement of existing legal provisions by criminal justice enforcement agencies to ensure attendance of witnesses, prosecutors, defence counsel and support staff leads to inexcusable delays in the completion of criminal trials. This can be curtailed by preventing unnecessary adjournments or postponements.

(H) Lasting solutions to procedural delays may lie in the adoption of new methods like the recent introduction of plea-bargaining for certain categories of offences. Amendments in the Code of Criminal Procedure now allow the accused to negotiate lenient punishment on an admission of guilt. This will avoid protracted trials involving lengthy and cumbersome procedures if the matter can be resolved by newer methods legally permissible in the system of criminal justice.

## (VI) CONCLUSION : SOME THOUGHTS

The famous adage justice delayed is justice denied is an eye opener to begin reform. Changes and evolution are a continuing process. Neither criminal law nor administration of justice can be static. Criminal law jurisprudence demands that perceptions of law and justice must keep pace with changing times. Holistic reform entails that the police, the prosecution, the prisons department and the Courts, introspect and review their own processes before seeking changes from outside to rectify problems in the system. Besides, those responsible for nourishing the system that is the executive and the legislature need to fulfil their part of the obligation. Not only justice delayed is justice denied but justice delayed is truly injustice. Transparency and accountability to citizens of this proud country demands that justice should not believe to be done but must appear to be done.

# HUMAN RIGHTS: LIMITATIONS AND JUDICIAL REVIEW – THE INDIAN PERSPECTIVE

## (I) INTRODUCTION: THE INDIAN BACKGROUND

The Constitution of India enacted on the 26 November, 1949 resolved to constitute India as a Union of States and a Sovereign, Socialist, Secular, Democratic Republic. Today, a population of over one billion Indians live in twenty-eight States and seven Union Territories within India besides about twenty five million Indians who reside in foreign jurisdictions and are called Non-Resident Indians. Within the territory of India spread over an area of 3.28 million Sq. Kms, the large Indian population comprised of multicultural societies professing and practicing different religions and speaking different local languages coexist in harmony in one of the largest democracies in the world.

The Indian Parliament at the helm of affairs legislates on central subjects in the Union and Concurrent lists and State legislatures enact laws pertaining to State subjects as per the State and Concurrent lists with regard to the subjects enumerated in the Constitution of India. Likewise, pertaining to the judiciary, under article 214 of the Indian Constitution there shall be a High Court for each State and under article 124 there shall be a Supreme Court of India. Under article 141 of the Constitution, the law declared by the Supreme Court shall be binding on all Courts within the territory of India. However, the Supreme Court may not be bound by its own earlier views and can render new decisions.

Part III of the Constitution of India secures to its citizens "Fundamental Rights" which can be enforced directly in the respective High Courts of the States or directly in the Supreme Court of India by issue of prerogative Writs under articles 226 and 32 respectively of the Constitution of India. Under the Constitutional scheme, the fundamental rights guaranteed under part III of the Constitution are sacrosanct, inviolable and are enforceable through Writ petitions mentioned above. Such rights invariably take shape and find expression as 'Human Rights' since The Protection of Human Rights Act, 1993 defines "Human Rights" as the rights relating to life, liberty, equality and dignity of the individual guaranteed by the Constitution or embodied in the international covenants and enforceable by Courts in India. Their justiciability is manifested through the process of judicial review under articles 32 and 226 of the Constitution directly to the Supreme Court and the High Courts respectively.

Simultaneously Part IV of the Indian Constitution lays down "Directive Principles of State Policy" which are not enforceable by any Court but are nevertheless fundamental in the governance of the country and it shall be the duty of the State to apply these principles while making laws. Under article 44 of the

Constitution in this Part, the State shall endeavour to secure for the citizens a Uniform Civil Code throughout the territory of India. However, realistically speaking, till date a Uniform Civil Code remains an aspiration which India has yet to achieve and enact.

## (II) NEED FOR LIMITATIONS OF HUMAN RIGHTS

Juristically, no individual right can be absolute since no such rights can be protected unless there is a social order in which the rights of one person shall be respected by others and, in case of interference, would be enforced by the State. Conversely, if an individual in the exercise of his individual rights affects the interest of other individuals or of the society, the State must intervene to curb such violations as human rights are both enforced and checked by the State. Hence, the guarantee of human rights must contain the necessary limitations so that the collective interest of society may not be jeopardised. The justification for these limitations is the common good, the collective welfare of all and the establishment of justice and peace in a larger world perspective for orderly society. The Indian Constitution acknowledges that there cannot be absolute liberty and the rule of law enjoins that law must protect the rights of others.

## (III) RIGHTS AND THEIR LIMITATIONS

Article 19 of the Constitution (hereinafter called article 19) guarantees the principal Right of Freedom in the following forms to all its citizens:

(a) freedom of speech and expression;

(b) freedom to assemble peacefully and without arms;

(c) freedom to form associations or unions;

(d) freedom to move free throughout the territory of India;

(e) freedom to reside and settle in any part of the territory of India;

(f) freedom to practice any profession, or to carry on any occupation trade or business;

These salient fundamental freedoms find manifestation as human rights due to their exalted status in the Indian Constitution which in article 14 guarantees to all persons equality before law and equal protection of laws in addition to the guarantee provided by article 21 that no person shall be deprived of his life or personal liberty except according to procedures established by law. However, etched in article 19 are also inbuilt the limitation clauses found in articles 19(2) to (6) which can be invoked as a shield provided the conditions of reasonableness of the restrictions imposed and the grounds specified in the relevant limitation clause are satisfied. The grounds of limitation to Freedom of Speech as stated in article 19(2) are summed up as follows:

(i) Sovereignty and integrity of India;

(ii) Security of the State;

(iii) Friendly relations with foreign States;

(iv) Public order;

(v) Decency or morality;

(vi) Contempt of Court;

(vii) Defamation;

(viii) Incitement to an offence.

With respect to freedom of assembly, the grounds of limitation under article 19(3) are as hereunder:

(i) Sovereignty and integrity of India;

(ii) Public Order;

For the freedom of association, morality constitutes an additional ground besides sovereignty and integrity of India and public order as limitations under article 19(4). 'Interests of General Public' is mentioned as a composite ground of limitation for the freedom of movement [article 19(5)], residence [article 19(5)] as well as freedom of profession or business [article 19(6)]. However, in the case of freedom of profession or business, there are two additional grounds of limitation namely:

(a) imposing technical or professional qualifications; and

(b) State Trading.

Perhaps, at the time of the enactment of the Indian Constitution, the object of specifying the restrictions in article 19(2) to (6) was to define with certainty the limitations that might be imposed upon the freedoms instead of leaving that to the disposal of the Courts of law. In this perspective support can be drawn from what Dr Ambedkar explained in the Constituent Assembly Debates, Vol VII at page 41:

> "...what the Draft Constitution had done is that instead of formulating fundamental rights in absolute terms and depending upon our Supreme Court to the rescue of Parliament by inventing the doctrine of police power, it permits the state directly to impose limitations upon fundamental rights."

However, the passage of time has shown that it is the intervention in judicial review which is the harbinger of human rights as the restrictions upon fundamental freedoms cannot be left to the exclusive discretion of the Parliamentary machinery. A brilliant 9-Judge Constitution Bench Supreme Court judgment in *I.R. Coelho* v. *State of Tamil Nadu,* 2007 (2) SCC 1, while examining the permissibility for Parliament under article 31B to immunize legislations from fundamental rights by inserting them into the ninth schedule, was pleased to lay down the following law as enumerated in para 151 (at page 111) as hereunder:

> "(i) A law that abrogates or abridges rights guaranteed by Part III of the Constitution may violate the basic structure adopted or it may not. If former is the consequence of the law, whether by amendment of any article of Part III or by an insertion in the Ninth Schedule, such law will have to be invalidated in exercise of judicial review power of the court. The validity or invalidity would be tested on the principles laid down in this judgment."

Thus, in expounding the scope of judicial review, the Supreme Court has clearly held that even though Parliament has power to amend provisions of Part III of the Constitution relating to fundamental rights, but as held above, that power "shall have to be tested on the touch stone of the basic or essential features of the Constitution as reflected in article 21 read with article 14 and article 19: article 15 and article 14 read with articles 16(4), (4A) & (4B):, articles 20 and 32 etc., and the principles underlying them or if the law(s) concerned infringe the essence of fundamental rights". Hence, the guarantee of fundamental freedoms and human rights are now the beneficial interpretations of the Supreme Court in judicial review where both the freedom and its limitation is tested on the touch stone of the basic structure doctrine.

## IV. INTERPRETATION OF HUMAN RIGHTS IN JUDICIAL REVIEW

Indian Courts have been evolving the concept of social justice in some recent pronouncements in which fundamental freedoms and their limitations have been questioned. The following decisions are cited in support of these interpretations:

(i) Rickshaw Pullers – A policy decision taken by the State Government not to renew licences of rickshaw pullers to abolish slow moving vehicles was illegal and violative of article 19 (1) (g) of the Constitution as held in *All Bengal Rickshaw Union* v. *State of West Bengal*, AIR 2000 Cal 186.

(ii) Street Hawkers – The right of street hawkers to transact business while going from place-to-place is subject to proper regulation in the interest of general convenience of the public including health and security considerations, as held in *South Calcutta Hawkers Association* v. *Government of West Bengal*, AIR 1997 Cal 234.

(iii) Policy decision on water - The State authorities having taken a policy decision on the question of the best utilisation of available water and pragmatic assessment of the situation in public interest, does not infringe fundamental rights guaranteed under article 21 of the Constitution, was held in *Pennar Delta Auyacutders Association* v. *Government of Andhra Pradesh*, AIR 2000 AP 317.

(iv) Begging – Eunuchs are indeed entitle to their fundamental rights guaranteed to citizens and persons under Part III of the Constitution, but they cannot claim a fundamental right to beg in the face of Bombay Prevention of Begging Act, 1959, was held in *Sushila Kanwar* v. *State of Gujarat*, AIR 2000 Guj 194.

(v) Stray Dogs – After insertion of article 51-A in the Constitution, it has become the duty of every citizen to have compassion for living creatures. Section 112 of Hyderabad Municipal Corporation Act casts a mandatory duty on the Corporation to made adequate provision for prevention of infectious diseases, but does not include the duty to destroy unlicensed and unclaimed stray dogs, was held in *J. Gopalan* v. *Municipal Corporation of Hyderabad*, AIR 1996 AP 371.

(vi) Expulsion of a Foreigner – The Foreigners Act 1946, vests the Central Government with absolute discretion to expel a foreigner. Where the application of a foreigner seeking extension of his stay in India is rejected, he has no right to claim to stay in the country. Thus, the order of expulsion of a foreigner does not amount to deprivation of life of personal liberty under article 21 of the Constitution, was held in *Gilles Pfeiffer* v. *Union of India*, AIR 1996 Mad 322.

(vii) Providing Security – The Court is not powerless to issue directions to concerned authorities to make arrangements for security of the lives of citizens and provide security guards in appropriate cases of imminent danger to life and liberty, was held in *Ramveer Upadhaya* v. *State of Uttar Pradesh*, AIR 1996 All 131.

(viii) Environment Protection – Any person in a locality has a right to complain to authorities who are obliged to monitor environmental degradation and ecological imbalance that a tyre retreading plant set up in a residential area emitting obnoxious gases was causing harm to the environment and was directed to be wound up, was held in *Sitaram Chhaparia* v. *State of Bihar*, AIR 2002 Pat 134.

(ix) Speedy disposal of waste – Without awaiting directions of the High Court, it was entirely for the Pollution Control Board and its officers to take speedy and determined action against culprits, who were dumping hazardous waste so as to ensure public health, was held in *Suo Moto* v. *Vatva Industries Association*, AIR 2000 Guj 33.

(x) Noise Pollution – Noise Pollution being wrongful contamination of the environment can be well regarded as a pollutant if it exceeds a reasonable limit because it contaminates environment and affects the health of persons and therefore offends article 21 of the Constitution, which was held in *Free Legal Aid Cell* v. *Government of NCT of Delhi*, AIR 2001 Del 455.

A reading of the above clearly demonstrates that Indian Courts are alive to the human rights of people and where the executive or the administrative machinery fails to provide necessary redressal, the power of judicial review has been exercised to give immediate relief by issue of a mandate to uphold basic human dignities.

## V. HUMAN RIGHTS AND NATURAL JUSTICE

Articles 14 and 21 of the Constitution guarantees to all "persons" equality before law and ensures that no "person" shall be deprived of his life of personal liberty except in accordance with law. However, the fundamental freedom under article 19 are guaranteed only to all "citizens" of India. Irrespective of this dividing line, in a landmark decision by the erudite Bench of the Madras High Court in *S.Nalini Srikaran* v. *Union of India*, AIR 2007 Mad 187, the Court did substantial justice by holding that a person found to be a citizen of India cannot be treated as a foreigner as long as the Central Government does not record a decision to that effect and the termination of Indian citizenship does not merely depend upon the action of a foreign country in issuing a passport to the Indian citizen.

The backdrop of the case was unique. The appellant and her husband were arrested, tried and convicted in connection with the murder of former Prime Minister Late Rajiv Gandhi. While in prison, the appellant gave birth to a female child in 1992. Till 1998, the child lived with her mother in prison. In 1998, on the appellant being awarded the death penalty by the special Court, the appellant's mother-in-law, a Sri Lankan citizen took the minor child to Sri Lanka on an emergency passport given by the Sri Lanka Government to the minor. Later, in appeal, the appellant's death penalty was converted into life imprisonment and she was confined in a special prison for women at Vellore.

In 2004, the Appellant's minor daughter applied for permission to travel to India and since the Indian High Commission in Sri Lanka took no decision, the Madras High Court directed the Union of India to take a decision whereupon the appellant's daughter was permitted to meet her mother and whereafter the minor returned to Sri Lanka. Subsequently, the appellant again moved the Madras High

Court stating that due to escalated ethnic conflict in Sri Lanka and fast deteriorating conditions, schools and colleges in Tamil areas have been closed and a large number of displaced families are coming to India as refugees to be rehabilitated on humanitarian considerations. The appellant concerned with her daughter's education contended that as the minor was an Indian citizen, her daughter should be permitted to return to India permanently. The Indian Government rejected the request stating that since the minor had voluntarily acquired a Sri Lankan passport, she ceased to be a citizen of India.

The Madras High Court in determining the question whether the minor has ceased to be a citizen of India on acquisition of a Sri Lankan passport held that as long as the Central Government does not determine the question of cessation of Indian citizenship as also go into the issue as to whether the foreign citizenship was voluntarily acquired by conducting a quasi-judicial enquiry and affording reasonable opportunity, a citizen of India cannot be treated as a foreigner till a decision is recorded in the above terms. Further, the Court held that the termination of Indian citizenship does not merely depend upon the action of foreign country in issuing a passport.

The above decision given by the Court interpreting the provisions of the Citizenship Act 1956 and the Citizenship Rules, 1956 is a salutary pronouncement. Rendering the verdict in exercising its powers of judicial review, the Court did substantial justice to a minor child who was forced to go to Sri Lanka at a tender age of six years which was by no means a voluntary exercise. Regardless, the mandate of the Court that cession of Indian citizenship requires a conscious determination by the Central Government by passing an order under section 9(2) of the Citizenship Act having due regard to rules of evidence, clearly demonstrates the true import of the principles of natural justice. In expounding this principle, the Court has indeed reiterated a new perspective of human rights by weaving colours in the fabric of a thought process to rectify arbitrariness and discrimination in an administrative decision.

## VI. HUMAN RIGHTS AND BOUNDARIES OF TERROR

Laws of Terror are tough and defy all boundaries. The most living recent example is the 27 year old Indian doctor Mohammad Haneef from Bangalore who was a "terror prisoner" in a solitary cell in the Wolston prison in Queensland, Australia. He was arrested at Brisbane airport on 2 July, 2007 and without any charges spent 12 days in custody before being questioned. On being granted bail pending trial in the Brisbane Magistrate's Court after being charged with "recklessly" providing support to a terrorist organization, within one hour his multi-year work visa was cancelled on "character grounds" under the Australian Migration Act because he failed the character test. The Australian authorities invoked immigration laws to keep him in detention.

But on home turf, a recent decision of the Bombay High Court in Writ Petition No. 450 of 2007, *Satish Nambiar* v. *Union of India*, 2007 (5) Bom CR 247 pronounced on 21 June, 2007, did not generate much media attention despite pronouncing that a foreigner who had been registered as an Overseas Citizen of India (OCI) cannot claim the same rights as an Indian citizen upon cancellation of his OCI status and revocation of his permanent Indian visa in public interest without any hearing.

The above decision related to a 1950 Mumbai-born American citizen of Indian origin employed with the American Consulate from 1973 to 1999 at Mumbai. On being granted a special immigrant visa to USA in 1999, he resigned from his position as a security investigator at the US Consulate and left for America with his wife, where he lived till 2005. His wife returned to India to look after her ailing mother and did not go back. For himself, he applied and was granted an OCI Card and permanent Indian visa on May 18, 2006. He also took up an appointment at the American Consulate in Mumbai.

On 14 February, 2007, the Central Government cancelled in public interest his OCI card by invoking section 7D(e) of the Citizenship Act 1955 wherein if "it is necessary so to do in the interest of the sovereignty and integrity of India, the security of India, friendly relations of India with any foreign country, or in the interest of the general public", registration of an OCI can be cancelled. Since no opportunity of pre-decisional hearing was granted, the petitioner challenged it in the Bombay High Court on the ground that it was not preceded by any enquiry, it suffers from arbitrariness, it violates the constitutional mandate of equality before law and withdraws without hearing benefits granted to him in accordance with law. The petitioner claimed that he had no criminal record, he had not violated any law, he was a law abiding citizen and no case had ever been registered against him.

The Court held that the Indian Government could not be faulted in its decision considering the adverse reports by the security agencies on post-verification of his antecedents which have been placed before the Court in sealed cover. The Court held that it was not mandatory for the Government to give any hearing to the petitioner keeping in view the fact that it was likely to affect the security of the country and the relationship with a foreign state. The Court held that this decision could hardly be examined by it so as to measure the extent of threat or degree of adverse effect to the interest and sovereignty of the country. The Court further held that the action was not vitiated for want of compliance with principles of natural justice nor on any other grounds.

With due deference, the authors differ. The proposition held by the Court that an OCI cannot be equated to an Indian citizen for purposes of enjoying fundamental rights guaranteed under article 14 (Equality before Law and Equal Protection of Laws) and article 21 (Protection of Life and Personal Liberty) of the Indian Constitution guaranteed to Indian citizens is thought provoking. Section 7B(2) of the Citizenship Act enumerates the rights to which an OCI is not entitled. Under it, neither the protection of article 14 nor the mandate of article 19 (Fundamental Rights) or article 21 (Personal liberty) is excluded from application to OCIs. In any case, articles 14 and 21 extend to any "person" and are not limited to Indian citizens alone unlike article 19 which is confined to "citizens" alone. However, the Court has held that their protection is guaranteed only to Indian citizens under the Indian Constitution and not to OCIs defined under the Citizenship Act. Hence, the Court concluded that an OCI is capable of being deprived of his legal status as an OCI without any pre-decisional hearing, enquiry or compliance with rules of natural justice.

Striking a balance between individual human rights, civil liberties and national security with the responsibility of the Government to protect its citizens from terrorism is indeed the need of the hour. However, in generalizing this proposition, the denial of principles of natural justice cannot be said to be inbuilt in the Citizenship Act to revoke the registration of an OCI without an opportunity of hearing in accordance with law. Articles 14 and 21 do not differentiate or discriminate between "persons" or "citizens". Equality is the hallmark of Indian law. Rights conferred by the Constitution on human beings must be given to them. In this regard there cannot be any difference between a citizen of India, an NRI or an OCI. Human rights are equal for all as they do not discriminate between "persons" or "citizens" in the territory of India.

**VII. SUPREMACY OF HUMAN RIGHTS**

The decision of the Supreme Court in *I.R. Coelho* v. *State of Tamil Nadu*, 2007 (2) SCC 1, is a landmark and historic pronouncement and a watershed in the annals of judicial history. The wisdom elucidated by the Apex Court in upholding fundamental freedoms can be best described in the views of the Court as follows in paras 109, 140, 141, 146 and 149 (extracted at page 17):

> "The golden triangle of articles 14, 19 and 21 as it stands for equality and rule of law clearly forms part of the basic structure of the Constitution and cannot be abrogated. These articles stand on altogether different footing. Article 21 is the heart of the Constitution. It confers right to life as well as right to choose. Article 15, article 21 read with articles 14 and 19 which constitute the core values which if allowed to be abrogated would change completely the nature of the Constitution. The fact that some articles in Part III stand alone has been recognised even by Parliament, for example, articles 20 and 21. Article 359 provides for suspension of the enforcement of the rights conferred by Part III during Emergencies. However, by the Constitution (Forty-fourth Amendment) Act, 1978, it has been provided that even during Emergencies, the enforcement of the rights under articles 20 and 21 cannot be suspended. This is the recognition given by Parliament to the protections granted under articles 20 and 21. No discussion or argument is needed for the conclusion that these rights are part of the basic structure or framework of the Constitution. Same would be the position in respect of the rights under article 32, again, a part of the basic structure of the Constitution. Exclusion of fundamental rights would result in nullification of the basic structure doctrine, the object of which is to protect basic features of the Constitution as indicated by the synoptic view of the rights in Part III."

The authoritative pronouncement of the Supreme Court is unequivocal. Without equality, the rule of law would fail. Fundamental freedoms and human rights have been placed at a very high pedestal and they cannot be subjugated except as per law which must stand the test of judicial scrutiny.

Another very illustrative decision of the Calcutta High Court in *Association for Protection of Democratic Rights* v. *State of West Bengal*, 2008 (1) ICC 153 Cal, is a illuminating verdict upholding the supremacy of human rights in what is popularly known as the Nandigram case. It would be most appropriate to quote from the judgment itself in this regard. In para 110 (at page 497), the view of the Court is very well described in the following words:

> "In this country, all citizens enjoy certain fundamental rights even a prisoner is entitled to certain basic rights. The State cannot therefore have unbridled power to take away those fundamental rights of the citizens which include their lives, except in accordance with procedure prescribed by law. In various affidavits and petitions, the State has been accused of State indulging in sponsored terrorism. In this case, the villagers had gathered to prevent the State from taking forcibly acquisition of their lands. This gathering cannot be termed as an unlawful assembly. The allegations are that brute force has been used to crush the agitation against the acquisition of villagers land. The atrocities had been committed by the police in collaboration with known and unknown persons. In such circumstances it would be wholly erroneous to permit the local police to investigate. The petitioners are not asking for an investigation to be conducted under Delhi Special Establishment Act, 1946. They are asking that the CBI should investigate the case on orders of the Court which have been made to secure the ends of justice. There are numerous examples where investigation by the CBI has been directed, when direct allegations have been made against the police. In this case, the allegations are so serious there is no scope for doubt that the only course open for this Court is to direct the CBI enquiry to continue"

Furthermore, in para 148 (at page 513), the Calcutta High Court has further elucidated the significance of the platter on which it places human rights and fundamental dignities, which are quoted as follows:

> "It is too late in the day to accept the submission that the orders issued, by the executive, which lead to the death of 14 innocent persons, cannot be the subject-matter of judicial review. The allegation made is that police firing that erupted on 14th March, 2007 was a State sponsored terrorism. These allegations cannot simply be ignored by the High Court. In public proceedings the Court passes orders for the benefit of the general public for passing effective orders. The Court can examine the decision making process, which leads to a particular action of the State. Fundamental rights are guaranteed under article 21 of the Constitution of India. These rights have been given a unique place in the scheme of the Indian Constitution. The fundamental rights have also been described as negative obligation of the State which does not permit encroachment on individual liberties except within the well defined limits of law. The object of fundamental rights is to foster an atmosphere which would be conducive to the fulfillment of the aims and objectives enacted in the Preamble of the Constitution of India. Indeed fundamental rights are so important that they occupy a unique place in all civilized societies. Part-IV of the Constitution contains the directive principles which are to be followed by the State to enable this country to fulfill the dream projected in the Preamble of the Constitution of India. Therefore any abrogation of the fundamental rights must be strictly in

conformity with law validly enacted by a competent legislature. Therefore, the action of the State authorities in directing the police to open fire on the crowd that had gathered at Nandigram cannot be said to be beyond the pale of judicial review."

Undoubtedly, it is sacrosanct that human rights can be regulated to achieve a greater public purpose and that fundamental freedoms are hedged with limitations and safeguards. However, in the brilliance of the innovative judicial system in India, the Courts strike a balance between human rights and public good in adjudicating upon the action of State authorities. No doubt, the scales are tilted in favour of public good. Regardless, this cannot curtail personal liberties to negate human rights and render fundamental freedoms illusory. Free expression, human rights and personal liberty cannot be compromised except when they endanger similar rights of others.

Another dimension of fundament freedoms had erupted in public life. A Court intervention on 4 March, 2008 saw the Apex Court lifting till further hearing on 14 March, 2008, the ban on screening of the film "Jodha Akbar" upon the film producer challenging the ban imposed by certain State Governments on the screening of the film. Quoting from the earlier Supreme Court judgment in *S. Rangarajan* v. *P. Jagjivan Ram*, 1989 (2) SCC 574, it was agitated that "freedom of expression cannot be suppressed on account of threats of demonstration and violence. That would tantamount to negation of the rule of law and surrender to blackmail and intimidation". It was urged that the screening of a film is a fundamental right covered under free speech and can be restricted only if it threatens public order. But then who is to decide this. The Apex Court has already ruled earlier in this regard by holding in 1989 (2) SCC 574 (at pages 598-599) that "it is the duty of the State to protect the freedom of expression since it is a liberty guaranteed against the State. The State cannot plead its inability to handle the hostile audience problem. It is its obligatory duty to prevent it and to protect the freedom of expression." However, the fact remains that there is nothing higher than the fundamental freedoms which are guaranteed under the Constitution of India. Fundamental human rights and freedoms are the essence of the rule of law which must be upheld and protected.

## VIII. CONCLUSION

Human rights universally are based on principles of equality, dignity and respect. They require a balance to be struck between the rights of an individual and the rights of others and the community at large. The Human Rights Act, 1998 of United Kingdom which came into force in Britain on 2 October, 2000, as an Act to give further effect to sixteen key rights and freedoms guaranteed under the European Convention on Human Rights (ECHR) derive strength from the aspirational terms of the Universal Declaration of Human Rights issued by the United Nations in 1948. We, in India, derive our human rights from the fundamental freedoms enshrined in Part III of the Constitution as the Protection of Human Rights Act, 1993 defines "Human Rights" as the rights relating to life, liberty, equality and dignity of the individual guaranteed by the Constitution or embodied in the international covenants and enforceable by Courts in India. The Protection of Human Rights Act, 1993, in India, is itself an Act to provide for the constitution of a National Human Rights Commission, State Human Rights Commission in States and Human Rights Courts for better protection of human rights and for matters connected therewith or incidental thereto. Thus, our bedrock of human rights is embedded in the fundamental rights guaranteed by the Indian Constitution. The saviour for fiercely guarding these rights and protecting them lie in the judicial arms which exercise prerogative Writs to enforce them. Illustrations, precedents and quotes from cited cases above clearly prove the point. Our inbuilt system of checks and balances provides an excellent functioning system for interpretation of fundamental freedoms guaranteed to Indian citizens under the Constitution. Recent interpretations of Courts have clearly shown that there is no compromise on fundamental freedoms so long as they do not infringe or impinge upon similar rights of others. The dynamic jurisprudential system under which we co-exist ensures that a balance is struck in equalizing the fundamental rights of all citizens in our democratic horizon. The balancing strength is thus maintained under our vibrant constitutional scheme which ensures the equality of law and equal protection of laws.

# THE DOCTRINE OF JUDICIAL PRECEDENT: STARE DECISIS & PER INCURIAM

## (I) INTRODUCTION:

Borrowed largely from usage and practice in English Law, the phrases *stare decisis* and *per incuriam* are primarily common law concepts. In general, Court decisions in common law jurisdictions are lengthy and go into great detail as to how the decision was reached. They can briefly be explained as follows:

### *(1a) EXPOUNDING STARE DECISIS:*

The doctrine of judicial precedent is concerned with the importance of case law in our system. The American Judge, Oliver Wendell Holmes JNR once said that "The life of the law has not been logic; it has been experience." But then, if judicial precedent is simply experience in legal jargon, why does it deserve our attention. An important and distinctive element of both Indian and English law is that the reasoning and decisions founded in preceding cases are not simply considered with respect or as a good guide but are binding on inferior Courts. This is known as the principle of *'stare rationibus decidendis'*; usually referred to as *'stare decisis'* which is a Latin legal term. It translates simply as "Let the decision stand". The phrase 'Rationibus '(reasoning) is the vital binding element in judicial precedents. Thus, what *stare decisis* means in practice is that when a Court makes a decision in a case then any Courts which are of equal or lower status to that Court *must* follow that previous decision. More fully, the legal term is *"stare decisis et non quieta movere"* meaning "stand by decisions and do not move that which is quiet." The phrase *"quite non movere"* is itself a famous maxim akin to "let sleeping dogs lie".

### *(1b) EXPLAINING PER INCURIAM:*

Literally translated as "through want of care", *per incuriam* refers to a judgment of a Court which has been decided without reference to a statutory provision or an earlier judgment which would have been relevant. The significance of a judgment having been decided per incuriam is that it does not have to be followed as a precedent. Ordinarily the rationale of a judgment must be followed thereafter by lower Courts hearing similar cases. But, a lower Court is free to depart from an earlier judgment of a superior Court where that earlier judgment was decided *per incuriam*. Thus, *per incuriam* can be said to be an exception to the doctrine of judicial precedent.

## (II) THE ENGLISH BACKGROUND:

### *(IIa) THE COURT HIERARCHY AND STARE DECISIS*

• *THE EUROPEAN COURT OF JUSTICE (ECJ)*

Under Section 3(1) of the European Communities Act 1972, decisions of the ECJ are binding, in matters of community law, on all Courts up to and including the House of Lords.

• *THE HOUSE OF LORDS*

This is the highest British Court unless a matter of European Community law is involved. For some hundred years the Law Lords considered themselves bound. The House of Lords was bound by its own previous decisions until 1966 when Lord Gardiner LC announced a change of practice. The Practice Statement (Judicial Precedent) 1966 (1) WLR 1234 stated that although the House of Lords would treat its decisions as normally binding it would depart from these when it appeared right to do so by holding " too rigid adherence to precedent may lead to injustice in a particular case and also unduly restrict the proper development of the law." This power has been used sparingly. A decision of the House of Lords binds all lower Courts. Its pronouncements only about 100 a year are seen as creating an air of certainty in the realm of law.

• *COURT OF APPEAL (CIVIL DIVISION)*

The Court of Appeal is bound by decisions of the House of Lords even if it considers them to be wrong. In *Young* v. *Bristol Aeroplane Co Ltd.* [1944] KB 718, the Court of Appeal held that it was bound by its own previous decisions subject to the following three exceptions:

* Where its own previous decisions conflict, the Court of Appeal must decide which to follow and which to reject.

* The Court of Appeal must refuse to follow a decision of its own which cannot stand with a decision of the House of Lords even though its decision has not been expressly overruled by the House of Lords.

* The Court of Appeal need not follow a decision of its own if satisfied that it was given *per incuriam* (literally, by carelessness or mistake).

Decisions of the Court of Appeal itself are binding on the High Court and the County Courts.

• *COURT OF APPEAL (CRIMINAL DIVISION)*

In principle there is no difference in the application of stare decisis in the civil and criminal divisions of the Court of Appeal. In practice, however, in addition to the *Young case* (supra) exceptions, because a person's liberty may be at stake, precedent is not followed as rigidly in the criminal division.

In *R* v. *Taylor,* 1950 (2) KB 368 the Court of Appeal held that in 'questions involving the liberty of the subject' if a full Court considered that 'the law has either been misapplied or misunderstood' then it must reconsider the earlier decision. This rule was followed in *R* v *Gould* 1968 (1) All ER 849 and *R* v. *Newsome,* 1970 (2) QB 711.

• *THE HIGH COURT*

The High Court is bound by the Court of Appeal and the House of Lords but is not bound by other High Court decisions. However, they are of strong persuasive authority in the High Court and are usually followed. Decisions of individual High Court Judges are binding on the County Courts.

A Divisional Court is bound by the House of Lords and the Court of Appeal and normally follows a previous decision of another Divisional Court but may depart from it if it believes that the previous decision was wrong: *R* v *Greater Manchester Coroner*, ex parte Tal [1985] QB 67.

• *CROWN COURTS*

Decisions made on points of law by Judges sitting at the Crown Court are not binding, though they are of persuasive authority. Therefore, there is no obligation on other Crown Court Judges to follow them.

• *COUNTY COURTS AND MAGISTRATES' COURTS*

The decisions of these Courts are not binding. They are rarely important in law and are not usually reported in the law reports.

***(IIb) PER INCURIAM DECISIONS AND BRITISH LAW:***

A decision which is reached *per incuriam* is one reached by carelessness or mistake, and can be avoided. In *Morelle* v. *Wakeling,* 1955 (2) QB 379, Lord Evershed MR stated that "the only case in which decisions should be held to have been given per incuriam are those of decisions given in ignorance or forgetfulness of some inconsistent statutory provision or of some authority binding on the court concerned".

In *Secretary of State for Trade and Industry* v. *Desai,* (1991), The London Times 5 December 1991, Scott LJ said that to come within the category of *per incuriam* it must be shown not only that the decision involved some manifest slip or error but also that to leave the decision standing would be likely, inter alia, to produce serious inconvenience in the administration of justice or significant injustice to citizens.

However, this rule does not permit the Court of Appeal to ignore decisions of the House of Lords. In *Cassell* v. *Broome,* [1972] AC 1027 Lord Denning MR held the House of Lords' decision in *Rookes* v. *Barnard,* [1964] AC 1129 to be per incuriam on the basis that it ignored previous House of Lords' decisions. He was rebuked sternly by the House of Lords when *Broome* v. *Cassell* went the House of Lords who considered that the Court of Appeal 'really only meant' that it 'did not agree' with the earlier decision as put in the words of Lord Halisham, the then Lord Chancellor:

> "Even if this is not so, it is not open to the Court of Appeal to give gratuitous advice to judges of first instance to ignore decisions of the House of Lords."
>
> "I am driven to the conclusion that when the Court of Appeal described the decision in Rookes v Barnard as decided 'per incuriam' or 'unworkable' they really only meant that they did not agree with it . . . [I]n the hierarchical system of courts which exists in this country, it is necessary for each lower tier, including the Court of Appeal, to accept loyally the decisions of the higher tiers". [1972] AC 1027, 1054.

Lord Denning's decision was thus reversed by the House of Lords. With the retirement of Lord Denning as the principal crusader, the conflict came to a halt. Thus it can be commented that 'per incuriam 'does not simply mean that the earlier Court got things wrong.

**(III) THE INDIAN POSITION:**

The Supreme Court of India was created on 28 January, 1950 after the adoption of a new Constitution. The doctrine of *stare decisis* is embodied in article 141 of the Constitution of India. This article mandates that the law declared by the Supreme Court shall be binding on "all Courts" in the territory. The expression "law declared" is wider than the "law found or made" and implies the law creating role of the Court.

However, the decision or judgment of a Judge may fall into two parts: the *ratio decidendi* (reason for the decision) and obiter dictum (something said by the way).

RATIO DECIDENDI - The *ratio decidendi* of a case is the principle of law on which a decision is based. When a Judge delivers a judgment in a case he outlines the facts which he finds have been proved on the evidence. Then he applies the law to those facts and arrives at a decision, for which he gives the reason *(ratio decidendi).*

OBITER DICTUM - The judge may go on to speculate about what his decision would or might have been if the facts of the case had been different. This is an *obiter dictum.*

The binding part of a judicial decision is the *ratio decidendi.* An *obiter dictum* is not binding in later cases because it was not strictly relevant to the matter in issue in the original case. However, an *obiter dictum* may be of persuasive (as opposed to binding) authority in later cases.

A difficulty arises in that, although the Judge will give reasons for his decision, he will not always say what the *ratio decidendi* is, and it is then up to a later Judge to "elicit" the ratio of the case. There may, however, be disagreement over what the ratio is and there may be more than one ratio.

Thus the doctrine of judicial precedent is not simply a mechanical process of matching similarities and differences. It is not merely a science of comparisons for it embodies the art of interpretation; the art of propounding the principle to be derived from each case.

However, it seems the doctrine of precedent appears to have been overplayed. The principle of *Stare decisis* and precedents has to be viewed in a rational and selective way. Apart from law reporting, a duty is cast on the Courts to be meticulously selective in the application of the principle of *stare decisis.* No doubt, the doctrine of precedent has been established in Indian Jurisprudence (M.C. Setalvad "The Common law of India" – Hamlyn Lectures, pages 47-50, and Law Commission's 14 Report Page 628) conferring certain advantages like uniformity, certainty and avoidance of delays, but too much reliance on precedents obstructs the free development of legal jurisprudence. Precedents while they may be good as general doctrine, if abused, will render law too technical, restricted and narrow in its outlook. Even in England, the trend appears to be in the words of Lord Gardiner, L.C., who made a general statement in a decision of the House of Lords (*London Street Tramways* v. *London County Council*, 1966 (1) WLR 124:1966 AER 77) "Their Lordships nevertheless recognise that too rigid adherence to precedent may lead to injustice and also unduly restrict the proper development of the law. They propose, therefore, to modify their present practice and while treating former decisions of this House as normally binding to depart from a previous decision when it appears necessary."

In India too, Judges of late are prone to discourage technical adherence to the practice of following precedents for all conceivable situations. The trend is to recognise the fundamental and basic concepts in law as laid down in the recognised leading decisions of the highest Courts of the land. Where the law is so settled, there is no need of getting into the intricacies of case-law around such a decision. Where, however, it is not so settled, then there is a need to evolve the law with certainty and authority with or without the aid of past precedent. If the decided cases are canalised into a few selective cases, the problem of evolution of law becomes easier.

However, there is also the emerging trend in India to develop its own jurisprudence even in well settled matters as observed in *Commissioner of Police* v. *Syed Hussain,* 2006 (3) SCC 173, the Apex Court observed that the time has come where this Court can develop " administrative law" by following the recent decisions of the House of Lords where the doctrine of proportionality should be invoked. The Wednesbury doctrine laid down in *Associated Provincial Picture Houses Limited* v. *Wednesbury Corporation,* 1947 (2) All ER 680 was itself under consideration in *Huang* v. *Secretary of State,* 2005 (3) All ER 435 and in *R* v. *Secretary of State,* 2001 (3) All ER 433(HL). In the light of these decisions , this Court in *Syed Hussain's* Case (supra) examining the exercise of powers of judicial review on grounds available under general administrative law held that the doctrine of proportionality did not warrant interference in the penalty of removal from service of a constable who had betrayed public trust by aiding criminals to jump bail.

**(IV) CONCLUSIONS:**

**(A)** There is much discussion about the virtue and irrationality of using case law under the system. The supporters of the system argue that following precedent makes decisions "predictable". But in answer it can be stated that by distinguishing a precedent, the conclusion can be different in a given case. Both the common law and the civil law traditions utilise the concept of precedent. No case has a meaning by itself; each case stands in a relationship to other cases. Like tracing one's ancestors, therefore, it is at least theoretically possible to go backwards in time, step by step, to see how a complicated principle emerged from perhaps a single case. It is not uncommon to find gross inconsistencies or jumps in logic, but for the most part the changes will be evolutionary rather than revolutionary. Inevitably one will face the same problem as with the 'Big Bang' theory of how the Universe began: what came before the original case?

**(B)** The great value of the doctrine of stare decisis is that it provides certainty. On the other hand, there are dangers: first, that in order to avoid the conclusions of stare decisis Courts are sometimes forced to find hair-splitting distinctions between cases; secondly, the doctrine limits flexibility and can make unassailable some principles which should have been abandoned long ago. To sum up, the advantages and disadvantages of precedent can be highlighted as hereunder:

• ***ADVANTAGES***

* There is certainty in the law. By looking at existing precedents it is possible to forecast what a decision will be and plan accordingly.

* There is uniformity in the law. Similar cases will be treated in the same way. This is important to give the system a sense of justice and to make the system acceptable to the public.

* Judicial precedent is flexible. There are a number of ways to avoid precedents and this enables the system to change and to adapt to new situations.

* Judicial precedent is practical in nature. It is based on real facts, unlike legislation.

* Judicial precedent is detailed. There is a wealth of cases to which to refer.

• ***DISADVANTAGES***

* Difficulties can arise in deciding what the ratio decidendi is, particularly if there are a number of reasons.

* There may be a considerable wait for a case to come to Court for a point to be decided.

* Cases can easily be distinguished on their facts to avoid following an inconvenient precedent.

* There is far too much case law and it is too complex.

**(C)** The Constitution of India in its wisdom laid down the binding jurisdiction of the Supreme Court in article 141. In turn this Court has categorized instances where its decisions have no binding force. Thus, where a decision is *obiter dicta*, is *per incuriam*, is *sub silentio* (without any argument or debate on the relevant question) and where an order is made with the consent of parties on the reservation that it is not to be treated as a precedent, this Court does not pronounce *stare decisis*. Thus the beauty of the Constitutional scheme with self limiting powers of this Court creates the barriers but gives it the liberty to cross them within judicial parameters. Article 137 further reserves the power of this Court to review its own judgments and orders subject to well defined limitations. In such a backdrop, the entire system is well defined and permits ample scope for growth and development of law. The dynamic power to develop the jurisprudence is well defined where precedents are not stare decisis. To grow law must evolve new interpretations. Law cannot be limited to precedent. Development cannot be stunted by barriers of precedent. Time, technology, social changes and research necessitate new interpretations of law. Even though judicial interpretation cannot be a substitute for legislation, the concept of justice requires that the Constitutional mandate of law must be met. Matters purely *per incuriam* being a class apart are free from shackles of precedent. Self imposed limits however, must limit this exercise wherever necessary.

# GLOBALISATION OF LAW AND THE COMMON MAN

**(I) Introduction**

Immanuel Kant wrote over two hundred years ago that we as people are 'unavoidably side-by-side'. A violent challenge to law and justice in one place has consequences for many other places and can be experienced everywhere. While he dwelt on these matters at length, he could not have known how profound his concerns would become.

Since Kant, our mutual inter-connectedness and vulnerability have grown rapidly. We no longer live, if we ever did, in a world of discrete national communities. Instead, we live in a world of what would be called 'overlapping communities of fate' where the trajectories of countries are deeply enmeshed with each other. In our world, it is not only the violent exception that links people together across borders; the very nature of everyday problems and processes joins people in multiple ways.

The story of our increasingly global order - 'globalisation ' - is not a singular one. Globalisation is not just economic; for it also involves growing aspirations for international law and justice. From the United Nations to the European Union, from changes to the laws of war to the entrenchment of human rights, from the emergence of international environmental regimes to the foundation of the International Criminal Court, there is also another narrative being told – a narrative which seeks to reframe human activity and entrenches it in law, rights and responsibilities.

**(II) What is Globalisation**

The technological development that characterizes the past two decades has triggered a communicational enhancement around the globe. Inter-connectedness between people is greater everyday. Jet airplanes, cheap telephone service, email, computers, huge oceangoing vessels, instant capital flows, all these have made the world more interdependent than ever. Along with products and finances, ideas and cultures circulate more freely. As a result, laws, economies, and social movements are forming at the international level. Many politicians, academics, and journalists treat these trends as both inevitable and (on the whole) welcome. International travel and communication now represent ordinary aspects of life. This phenomenon is commonly described as globalisation. The global social justice movement, itself a product of globalisation, proposes an alternative path, more responsive to public needs.

**(III) Globalisation of law**

The term *'globalisation of law'* refers to the degree to which the whole world lives under a single set of legal rules. Such a single set of rules might be imposed by an international body, adopted by global consensus, or arrived at by parallel development in all parts of the globe. In today's world of increasing international trade and inter-dependence, the need for transnational law has increased many folds. Since more and more countries open their economy, either partially or completely, there is a growing need to recognize and work towards a uniform system of law. This process of globalisation is evident in all facets of law.

The common man on the streets of India hardly ever understands World Trade Organisation (WTO) and trade talks. Instead, he feels the impact of globalisation in several direct ways in today's world: increased fuel prices at the petrol pump, global brand names in shopping malls, mobile phone connectivity, broadband-induced knowledge of what is going on around the world, besides secondary demand created on high-quality farm produce and fruits seen at super markets all around in cosmopolitan cities, et al. The most common man does not even view all these as threats: the farmer in the hinterlands of India welcomes the advantages and benefits of the internet and the knowledge it disseminates.

### (IV) Categories of Globalisation

We can identify two distinct inter-related aspects of globalisation and the law. **Firstly**, the adoption and implementation across large segments of the globe of what are now widely accepted as significant legal norms and approaches, for example, the basic principles of trial by jury and the discovery of evidence. **Secondly**, is the increasing number of areas of the law which are now subject to international agreements more or less binding on the States party to them. Most obviously, we perhaps think of trade law and the international sale of goods, which between them cover a vast variety of issues ranging from agricultural tariffs to contract enforcement and intellectual property rights. From a different perspective, one could of course add the UN convention on Human Rights too, like the roots of a great tree these are slow, sometimes faltering, often unpredictable growths.

### (V) Merits and Demerits of Globalisation

Globalisation is helping to reduce world poverty. According to the World Bank, income inequality has narrowed since its peak in 1970, and the number of people in extreme poverty (defined as those living on less than a dollar a day) has declined by 200 million since 1980. The figure is still far too high, but it does represent a fall from 31% of the world's population to 20%.

Globalisation has helped to spread improvements in basic hygiene, vaccinations against many communicable diseases, and lower rates of infant mortality. In 1950, life expectancy in developing countries was only 44 years and infant mortality was 179 per thousand infants. Today, the equivalent figures are 64 years and 59 per thousand. Undoubtedly, death control has gone hand-in-hand with birth control.

But there are *problems* too. As the foundations are shaken, the world becomes an unstable place to live in. Customs, traditions and values that have sustained communities for innumerable years are undermined. The values that we in the richer, developed and developing countries cherish, protect and promote are not always and everywhere seen as unalloyed goods. Globalisation has led to the disintegration of these values, traditions and cultural systems. Individual freedom can seem like extravagance, which is a liberty at times uncalled for. Even universal human rights may challenge particular customary social relations. For those who are alienated, the temptation to ancestral revolt, spurred on by religious fundamentalism, can be strong. These are the other extremes of globalisation

**(VI). Globalisation of Commercial and Contract Law**

In today's world of inter-dependence and international commerce, there is an increasing importance of growth of harmonization of international commercial law. Most of the countries have now recognized the need for a uniform, predictable and transparent system of law for encouraging foreign investment and international trade with other countries. As a result of this, the Courts and law of most of the countries recognize and enforce the judgments of other nations. Hence, there is a tentative movement towards the formulation of transnational commercial law through contracts. In the global context, because of the economic position of the United States and some of the countries of Europe, these countries substantially influence the process of globalisation of law. The obvious reason being that they contribute substantially to foreign investments in other parts of the world and have a strong role to play in international trade.

**(VII) Globalisation of Public Law**

Certain global commonalities in law develop from a universal, and apparently growing, popular distrust of Governments. Sometimes a Government has undertaken many welfare activities and also expanded its role to the commercial front. The need to put appropriate checks on Governments has also increased. This has paved the way for administrative law and now many nations have accepted the Rule of Law and used it to check the Government. The world has unanimously recognized that appropriate checks are needed on the Government and that there now exist certain fundamental principles that have been recognized as basic to all populations for checking the Government from abuse of power.

It is also clear that across that world, attention is being paid to the use of law to achieve these goals. This concept has rapidly spread all over the globe and is now increasingly recognized in U.K. and India too. In India, we have land mark decisions where administrative discretions and quasi-judicial functions have been checked and rectified by the Courts in accordance with the Rule of Law. The principles of natural justice are now acknowledged the world over and Courts around the globe are now giving effect to the two famous maxims of natural justice namely, *Audi Alterem Partem* (no one should be condemned without a hearing) *and Nemo Debit Juris in Propria Causa* (No man shall be a judge in his own cause). The countries around the world now openly acknowledge these two principles as *pillars of public law*. The import of these two maxims implies that no person shall be the judge in his own cause and that every person shall have a right to be heard before an order is passed against him. Globalisation has firmly entrenched these symbols of law in different societies, systems, political setups and administrative establishments. Those who do not accept them have been isolated.

**(VIII) Globalisation of Protective Law**

The constitutional rights momentum is one aspect of a global movement that is based on the distrust of concentrations of power. The individual is seen as needing protection from all the larger forces that threaten to crush him, and not simply from the Government alone. Law is seen as one instrument for such protection. Thus, in speaking of globalisation, we move from the realm of constitutional law to the realm of torts, product standards, consumer protection, and occupational health and safety.

Global patterns are, however, far from uniform here. India has experienced a tort explosion in the form of landmark cases concerning CNG buses for environmental protection, relocation of industrial and commercial activity in housing areas as well as preservation of monuments of national heritage. Many other nations too have now under the wake of environmental consciousness have started considering active legislations or laws in this regard.

It can be said without exaggeration that the face of our planet in the coming decades will depend on what path of ensuring its security the world community will choose in the conditions of globalization. It is hoped that the imperative of joint actions in the face of common dangers will prevail over the reflex of "every man for himself" and that humanity will opt for a democratic multi-polar world order that guarantees progressive development and equal security for all the states. At the same time the fallout of globalisation to protect our natural resources from being frittered away is an appreciable factor.

**(IX) Globalisation and International Law-Conclusion**

Law has traditionally been the province of the nation state, where Courts and police enforce legal rules. By contrast, international law has been comparatively weak, with little effective enforcement powers. But, globalisation is changing the contours of law and creating new global legal institutions and norms. On one hand, the International Criminal Court promises to bring to justice odious public offenders based on a worldwide criminal code, whereas on the other hand inter-governmental cooperation increasingly brings to trial some of the most notorious international criminals. Business law is globalizing fastest of all, as nations agree to standard regulations, rules and legal practices. Diplomats and jurists are creating international rules for bankruptcy, intellectual property, banking procedures, commercial interests and many other areas of corporate law. In response to this internationalization, and in order to serve giant, transnational companies, even law firms are globalizing their practice. The biggest firms are merging across borders, creating mega practices with several thousand professionals in dozens of countries, Business process outsourcing is now spreading to knowledge process outsourcing and legal process outsourcing.

In several Indian cities, one comes across stores sporting the names 'China Bazaar', and the like, which essentially sell made-in-China goods for the price-conscious Indian consumer. This is globalisation for the common man, opening up of the economy for the ordinary citizen and bringing India-China co-operation to the street corner socialist. Neither the Indian shopkeepers nor the consumers are concerned about China adhering to World Trade Organisation rules or workers' rights. All that matters is the full freedom to enjoy cheap goods from even the not-so-free nations. This is perhaps the best manifestation of 'enlightened self-interest'.

---

# THE SUPREME COURT OF UNITED KINGDOM

"Judges ought to be more Learned than Witty, more Reverent than Plausible and more Advised than Confident". So reads an inscription in the majestic library of the new Supreme Court of United Kingdom.

Great Britain sees a new transformation in its high judiciary. The Supreme Court of England functional from 1 October, 2009 has 11 Judges who hold Court in the former Middlesex Guildhall in Parliament Square, fully renovated and refurbished recently. Most of the Courts first Justices were professional Law Lords who were earlier able to vote on legislation. Now, they only decide points of law of the greatest public importance. The symbolic location of the new Court building is chosen to represent the United Kingdom's separation of powers with judiciary and legislature balanced on opposite sides of Parliament Square. The other two sides are formed by the executive, that is the treasury and the established church, that is the Westminster Abbey. The Court now undertakes the work previously carried out by the Appellate Committee of the House of Lords which earlier presided in the Parliament building.

Created in 2009, the Supreme Court is the Highest Court of Appeal in United Kingdom and was created to achieve complete transparency and separation between the judiciary and the upper house of British Parliament. The Supreme Court was established by the Constitutional Reform Act, 2005 and sat for the first time in October 2009 with 11 Judges most of whom were members of the House of Lords.

The most appealing feature of the Highest Court is its simplicity. Shorn of the splendour and regalia of robes, wigs and formal Court attire, the Judges dressed in formal suits and neck ties sit at the same floor level as advocates, assistants and clients in simple chairs to hear civil and criminal cases from England, Wales, Northern Ireland and Scotland. Right to appeal to Supreme Court is not automatic. Cases must be generally referred from a lower Court on the basis of public importance. Proceedings are routinely filmed and televised. Each case is heard by a panel of five Justices sitting in a semi-circle and selected by the President of the Supreme Court according to expertise, availability and other factors. Simplicity of form, procedure, attire and address are the hallmark of this new monumental justice system. Since points of law are the subject of adjudication rather than the rights and wrongs of a particular case, the court-rooms are specially designed to encourage the atmosphere of a learned participative debate. Members of public are welcome to observe proceedings from the public seating area with 28 seats available for them in each court room. The justices always sit in odd numbers to make sure of a majority decision. In most difficult or important constitutional cases, seven or even nine Justices may sit to decide issues of significance.

Most of the current eleven justices used to be Lords of Appeal or members of the House of Lords. For new justices, a new selection process has been created based on merit. The justices appointed with a fixed remuneration have no added facilities of housing, transport, security or other perquisites. Proceedings at the Supreme Court are routinely filmed for archiving purposes and footages made available to broadcasters. The five senior Judges of the Supreme Court also sit as the Judicial Committee of the Privy Council which originated as the Highest Court of civil and criminal appeal of the erstwhile British Empire. It has still been asked for final rulings in appeals from different kinds of law from many countries which are amenable to the judicial committee of the Privy Council.

Recently, visiting the Court at London and interacting with Lord Phillips, President of the Supreme Court and Lord Kerr, Judge of the Supreme Court left a very impressionable impact. It certainly has broken from tradition, heritage, a conventional decorum of dress and has parted from a strict procedural style. Emphasis is more on simplicity of form and substance with attention towards expeditious decision making. The focus on regalia, pomp and style is non-existent. Administration of justice and adjudication of law on matters of public importance are the restricted portfolios of the new British Supreme Court as the Highest Court of civil and criminal appeal in UK. It appears to be a well designed, smoothly working justice system proposed to be free of the burden of conventional appeals which may add monumental numbers to pending arrears. Liberated from formality, it is a simple justice system of the highest Court. It is definitely a new experiment to emulate for creating a new sense of Justice for the Apex Court of a jurisdiction from which many countries have inherited their legal systems. As a logical corollary, the need for change likewise is also desirable.

## CORBETT'S LEGACY

Reading "Man Eaters of Kumaon" by Jim Corbett before visiting Corbett National Park in Uttarakhand was highly recommended. It proved true to the hilt. Jim Corbett (1875-1955) India's most famous hunter of man-eater tigers was a conservationist committed to the cause of environment. He helped establish India's first national park whose expansive virgin forest with its unique wildlife offers the most exquisite, enthralling, enriching and enchanting fairly tale experience. But more than that it carries a message for your progeny. Keep your ecology and environment intact.

A visit to Corbett's home, now a museum, proved to be a touching experience for the family children. Corbett had bought 40 acres of land in 1917 and had let it out to 15 families. He called his model village "Chotti Haldwani" and took initiative for the welfare of its residents. Corbett was a visionary. He built houses for tenants, arranged irrigation canals and had a wall raised around the village to protect crops and villagers from wild animals. "Chotti Haldwani" is a integral part of Corbett's folklore in his famous treasured books called the Corbett Corpse. Corbett did not charge any fee from his tenants for using his land not did he accept any agricultural produce in kind. In turn, they paid him back with their love, sincerity and devotion to him and his ideology.

Today, the entire tourism in Corbett dwells around the vision of a man who developed it. But for him the huge Corbett National Park may have been another jungle ravished and plundered by mankind for natural wealth, resources and wild life. A reading of his short stories further depicts his focus on the life revolving around the common man whom he called "the poor of India". He lived with them, loved them and dedicated his life to them. This is the best message the children learnt from him.

In modern times, Corbett still lives. His famous books, Man Eaters of Kumaon (1944), The Man Eating Leopard of Rudraprayag (1947), My India (1952), Jungle Lore (1953), The Temple Tiger and more Man Eaters of Kumaon (1954), and Tree Tops (1955) are veritable classics. Written in simple language, they narrate sheer excitement of the jungle. The advice given was correct. Read the books before you go. For the children it was reliving the Corbett experience in the jungle as it was narrated in the book. Corbett's legacy is thus still preserved in his books.

Driving through the enchanting forest in specially available jeeps upon permits being issued by the forest department, the family children live an experience which today's urban towns with computers, laptops, i-pods and note books cannot offer. The movement of a bush showing the magnificence of the majestic tiger was a memorable experience. The guide warned us not to step of the open jeep. The view of the tigress with her two cubs in tow by the flowing water viewed by us from a distance gave a magnificent spectacle which probably will live with the children for the rest of their lives. Blending with nature has a unique flavour in itself.

Most importantly what has the treasured legacy passed on to today's generation. Probably, the values imbibed by the simple life of Jim Corbett who lived like a common man. Today, he is revered and remembered for his commonness and his unique qualities. If there were more Jim Corbetts today, we would leave a better future for our forthcoming generations. Humility, simplicity and generosity were Corbett's biggest qualities. To carry the legacy, we brought two volumes of Corbett's short stories which make excellent reading at the end of the day. Reading aloud and sharing them with children is the best way to disseminate Corbett's message of love, bonding, sharing, affection and generating feelings of humanity. May Corbett live long in our minds, in our thoughts and in our deeds. He is immortal.

# CUSTOM AS AN IMPORTANT SOURCE OF HINDU LAW: ITS USAGE IN INTERNATIONAL FAMILY MIGRATION

## INTRODUCTION

As practitioners in the area of private international law, when dealing with major Embassies and High Commissions in New Delhi on behalf of intending settlement applicants in the context of family migration, it is essential for foreign immigration and family law lawyers to understand the legal position in India as to family law issues such as the statutory recognition of customary marriages and divorces as also registration of marriages under the provisions of the Hindu Marriage Act, 1955, (hereafter, HMA, 1955) as also applicable to the Non-Resident Indians staying abroad. This is the main thrust of this article. Due to local variations and the recognition of customs under Indian law, immigration law at the Indian end has a very different complexion. These differences are critical to the foreign immigration lawyers preparing immigration applications, at the initial stages at the time of lodging the family re-union applications and of course in the event of any litigation before immigration adjudicators and tribunals.

That apart from statutory recognition by the Hindu Marriage Act, 1955 this article also traces the case-law analysis on the subject of customary marriages and divorces. The case-law analysis in the present article is in chronological order from the year 1969 even with reference to some very old decisions of the Privy Council to the year 2010 taking into account the important relevant judgments. The Judgments quoted are of the Supreme Court of India and various High Courts in the country, especially the Punjab and Haryana High Court, within whose jurisdiction bulk of the population of Punjabi origin resides, apart from the neighbouring states as well. Customary Karewa marriages are popular among certain agricultural sects in rural parts of Punjab. Also, it is manifest from the case-law analysis that customary marriages including the custom of Karewa marriages which are defined below have not been overruled; modified or diluted in any form at all, whatsoever.

It is pertinent to mention over here that Karewa marriage is just one of the many forms of customary marriages, but as a matter of fact customary marriages, in India vary within different communities and regionally as well.

Karewa marriage was way back defined by Sir W.H. Rattigan, before the partition of India took place. Para 75 of Chapter 5 of Rattigan's celebrated treatise relating to customary marriage, divorce and dower defines Karewa marriage as follows:

> "A "Karewa" marriage with the brother or some other male relative of the deceased husband requires no religious ceremonies, and confers all the rights of a valid marriage."

## CODIFICATION OF CUSTOM AS FIRST RULE OF DECISION: PRIOR TO PARTITION OF INDIA AND BEFORE SUBSEQUENT ENACTMENT OF COMPREHENSIVE FAMILY LAW LEGISLATION IN THE REALM OF HINDU LAW

For further details see pages 525 to 555 of "A Digest of Customary Law," by Sir W.H Rattigan as at present ascertained in the Fifteenth reprinted edition of 1989, revised by Om Prakash Aggarwal, with a foreword by Dr. Bakshi Tek Chand and published by the University Book Agency, Allahabad. The first edition of this book was published in the year 1880, and further six editions of this book were brought out by the celebrated author himself and the last of his original work having been published in 1901. This of course has been followed by revised editions subsequently by eminent authors. The introduction at page 1 of this book reads as follows:

> "A Digest of Civil Law for The Punjab Chiefly Based On The Customary Law. Preliminary: Custom in this Province is the first rule of decision in all questions regarding succession, special property of females, betrothal, marriage, divorce, dower, adoption, guardianship, minority, bastardy, family relations, wills, legacies, gifts, partitions, any religious usage or institution, alluvion and diluvion."

The relevant case-law analysis on customary marriages and customary divorces in the present article is to drive home the point, that custom traditionally is an important source of Hindu law, and that continues to be the position even to-date.

## FAMILY IMMIGRATION ISSUES

### *Indian Marriages: Registration of Marriages Law and Custom*

Both formally registered and customary marriages are recognised under the laws of India. Visa officers have full information about the state of origin of the applicants. They are quite up-to-date on issues like land value, monies earned from cultivation per acre, Indian customs, etc. In Hindu marriage cases they view the Saptapadi photographs with a jeweller's focus. Saptapadi is the taking of seven steps by the bridegroom and the bride jointly before the sacred fire. The marriage becomes complete and binding when the seventh step is taken.

At the major Embassies and High Commissions in New Delhi including the office of the Canadian consulate at Chandigarh, the capital of the State of Punjab, most visa officers will be aware that in certain areas in the State of Punjab especially in Jalandhar and Hoshiarpur districts which are famous for outbound family migration, fake marriages are performed with all pomp and show without the religious ceremonies actually taking place at all. This is to facilitate migration through the family route.

A typical case is where the British Asian boy or girl is from the Midlands in the U.K. or a spouse from Maryland in the USA or from areas having dense Indian population in Canada, who is being married to a spouse from the State of Punjab. And the parents, being wary of the outcome of the spouse application, insist on such a contingent arrangement. In such a situation, a fake marriage certificate is submitted to the immigration authorities. To attempt to safeguard the interests of their children, the parents fall prey to bad advice. It is sad to mention that dubious travel agents and unqualified local consultants thrive on this Non-Resident clientele.

Under section 8 of the Hindu Marriage Act, 1955 (HMA 1955), the principal law governing Hindu marriages, registration of marriages is not compulsory. This is primarily because Hindu marriages and most marriages in India have been always performed in public with wide publicity. Section 8(2) provides that any State Government may make rules for the compulsory registration of Hindu marriages. Furthermore, section 8(5) specifically expresses that failure to register a Hindu marriage does not affect its validity. Even where compulsory registration of marriage is laid down under the rules, non-registration does not affect the validity of the marriage, but merely entails a nominal fine. Moreover, mere registration of a marriage under section 8 will not ipso facto make the marriage valid.

In light of the prevailing law in India, registration of marriages in this region by Non-Resident Indians is only undertaken to satisfy the immigration authorities. It is not very difficult to obtain fake marriage certificates in the above-mentioned areas of Punjab. Such false practices have a direct bearing on genuine applicants. Even their documentation and circumstances leading to the marriage are viewed cautiously.

Customary marriages are also performed in limited situations where one of the spouses, is resident abroad. Generally, it is the husband who is resident abroad.

## CUSTOM AS AN IMPORTANT SOURCE OF HINDU LAW

The HMA, 1955, is an Act of the Parliament of India to amend and codify the law relating to marriage among Hindus.

At the outset, it is important to mention that section 5 of the Hindu Marriage Act, 1955, which deals with the conditions for a valid Hindu marriage, also by virtue of section 5(iv) of the HMA, 1955 allows marriage within the prohibited relationship degree as and when permitted by the custom or usage governing the parties to the marriage, as is generally the situation in customary marriages.

It is also important to mention that section 29 of the HMA, 1955 recognises customary marriages before the enactment of the HMA, 1955 while also simultaneously recognising customary divorces even after the enactment of the HMA, 1955 and of course as of-date. To make matters explicitly clear customary divorces, subject to conditions of compliance are clearly recognised under the provisions of section 29 of the HMA, 1955.

Customary marriages within the prohibited degrees of relationship are specifically recognised by virtue of section 5(iv) of the HMA, 1955 after the said legislation came into force, that is on 18 May 1955, and this continues to be the position even to-date.

It is important to advert to the relevant provisions of the Hindu Marriage Act, 1955. The relevant sections relating to the territorial jurisdiction as also the extra territorial application are defined in section 1 of the HMA, 1955. The application of the said Central legislation is defined in section 2 of the HMA, 1955, while the definition clause is contained in section 3 of the HMA, 1955. The conditions for a valid marriage are stipulated in section 5 and registration of marriages under the said legislation is provided in section 8 of the HMA, 1955. The savings clause has explicit recognition in section 29 of the HMA, 1955.

The relevant clauses of the HMA, 1955 with regard to the scope of the present article are reproduced below.

**"1. Short title and extent.**—(1) This Act may be called the Hindu Marriage Act, 1955.

(2) It extends to the whole of India except the State of Jammu and Kashmir, and applies also to Hindus domiciled in the territories to which this Act extends who are outside the said territories.

**2. Application of Act.**—(1) This Act applies – (a) to any person who is a Hindu by religion in any of its forms or developments, including a Virashaiva, a Lingayat or a follower of the Brahmo, Prarthana or Arya Samaj, (b) to any person who is a Buddhist, Jaina or Sikh by religion, and (c) to any other person domiciled in the territories to which this Act extends who is not a Muslim, Christian, Parsi or Jew by religion, unless it is proved that any such person would not have been governed by the Hindu law or by any custom or usage as part of that law in respect of any of the matters dealt with herein if this Act had not been passed.

Explanation.-The following persons are Hindus, Buddhists, Jainas or Sikhs by religion, as the case may be:—

(a) any child, legitimate or illegitimate, both of whose parents are Hindus, Buddhists, Jainas or Sikhs by religion;

(b) any child, legitimate or illegitimate, one of whose parents is a Hindu, Buddhist, Jaina or Sikh by religion and who is brought up as a member of the tribe, community, group or family to which such parent belongs or belonged; and

(c) any person who is a convert or re-convert to the Hindu, Buddhist, Jaina or Sikh religion.

(2) Notwithstanding anything contained in sub-section (1), nothing contained in this Act shall apply to the members of any Scheduled Tribe within the meaning of clause (25) of article 366 of the Constitution unless the Central Government, by notification in the Official Gazette, otherwise directs.

(3) The expression "Hindu" in any portion of this Act shall be construed as if it included a person who, though not a Hindu by religion, is, nevertheless, a person to whom this Act applies by virtue of the provisions contained in this section.

**3. Definitions.**—In this Act, unless the context otherwise requires.—

(a) the expressions "custom" and "usage" signify any rule which, having been continuously and uniformly observed for a long time, has obtained the force of law among Hindus in any local area, tribe, community, group or family:

Provided that the rule is certain and not unreasonable or opposed to public policy; and Provided further that in the case of a rule applicable only to a family it has not been discontinued by the family;

(b) "district court" means, in any area for which there is a city civil court, that court, and in any other area the principal civil court of original jurisdiction, and includes any other civil court which may be specified by the State Government, by notification in the Official Gazette, as having jurisdiction in respect of the matters dealt with in this Act;

(c) "full blood" and "half blood"-two persons are said to be related to each other by full blood when they are descended from a common ancestor by the same wife and by half blood when they are descended from a common ancestor but by different wives;

(d) "uterine blood"- two persons are said to be related to each other by uterine blood when they are descended from a common ancestress but by different husbands;

Explanation.-In clauses (c) and (d), "ancestor" includes the father and "ancestress" the mother;

(e) "prescribed" means prescribed by rules made under this Act;

(f) (i) "sapinda relationship" with reference to any person extends as far as the third generation (inclusive) in the line of ascent through the mother, and the fifth (inclusive) in the line of ascent through the father, the line being traced upwards in each case from the person concerned, who is to be counted as the first generation;

(ii) two persons are said to be "sapindas" of each other if one is a lineal ascendant of the other within the limits of sapinda relationship, or if they have a common lineal ascendant who is within the limits of sapinda relationship with reference to each of them;

(g) "degrees of prohibited relationship"-two persons are said to be within the "degrees of prohibited relationship"—

(i) if one is a lineal ascendant of the other; or

(ii) if one was the wife or husband of a lineal ascendant or descendant of the other; or

(iii) if one was the wife of the brother or of the father's or mother's brother or of the grandfather's or grandmother's brother of the other; or

(iv) if the two are brother and sister, uncle and niece, aunt and nephew, or children of brother and sister or of two brothers or of two sisters;

*Explanation.*—For the purposes of clauses (f) and (g), relationship includes—

(i) relationship by half or uterine blood as well as by full blood;

(ii) illegitimate blood relationship as well as legitimate;

(iii) relationship by adoption as well as by blood;

and all terms of relationship in those clauses shall be construed accordingly."

It is important to mention that similar definition of the above mentioned section 3(a) of the HMA, 1955 also finds mention as section 3(a) the Hindu Adoptions and Maintenance Act, 1956 (hereafter HAMA,1956).

Section 5 of the HMA, 1955 prescribes the valid conditions for a Hindu marriage, which are stated below. It will be noticed that section 5(iv) of the HMA, 1955 explicitly recognises customary marriages.

**"5. Conditions for a Hindu marriage.**—A marriage may be solmenised between any two Hindus, if the following conditions are fulfilled, namely:—

(i) neither party has a spouse living at the time of the marriage;

(ii) at the time of the marriage, neither party—

(a) is incapable of giving a valid consent to it in consequence of unsoundness of mind; or

(b) though capable of giving a valid consent, has been suffering from mental disorder of such a kind or to such an extent as to be unfit for marriage and the procreation of children; or

(c) has been subject to recurrent attacks of insanity;

(iii) the bridegroom has completed the age of twenty one years and the bride the age of eighteen years at the time of the marriage;

(iv) the parties are not within the degrees of prohibited relationship unless the custom or usage governing each of them permits of a marriage between the two;

(v) the parties are not sapindas of each other, unless the custom or usage governing each of them permits of a marriage between the two".

Clearly, it will be noticed from the above mentioned provision that section 5(iv) statutorily permits marriage between the degrees of prohibited relationship on the basis of custom or usage.

Section 8 of the HMA, 1955 provides for registration of marriages, and even validly performed customary marriages can be very much registered under section 8 of the HMA, 1955 which reads as under:

**"8. Registration of Hindu marriages.**—(1) For the purpose of facilitating the proof of Hindu marriages, the State Government may make rules providing that the parties to any such marriage may have the particulars relating to their marriage entered in such manner and subject to such conditions as may be prescribed in a Hindu Marriage Register kept for the purpose.

(2) Notwithstanding anything contained in sub-section (1), the State Government may, if it is of opinion that it is necessary or expedient so to do, provide that the entering of the particulars referred to in sub-section (1) shall be compulsory in the State or in any part thereof, whether in all cases or in such cases as may be specified, and where any such direction has been issued, any person contravening any rule made in this behalf shall be punishable with fine which may extend to twenty-five rupees.

(3) All rules made under this section shall be laid before the State Legislature, as soon as may be, after they are made.

(4) The Hindu Marriage Register shall at all reasonable times be open for inspection, and shall be admissible as evidence of the statements therein contained and certified extracts therefrom shall, on application, be given by the Registrar on payment to him of the prescribed fee.

(5) Notwithstanding anything contained in this section, the validity of any Hindu marriage shall in no way be affected by the omission to make the entry."

Section 29 of the HMA, 1955 gives statutory recognition to customary divorce and the same is stated below for ease of reference.

**"29. Savings.**—(1) A marriage solemnised between Hindus before the commencement of this Act, which is otherwise valid, shall not be deemed to be invalid or ever to have been invalid by reason only of the fact that the parties thereto belonged to the same gotra or pravara or belonged to different religions, castes or sub-divisions of the same caste.

(2) Nothing contained in this Act shall be deemed to affect any right recognised by custom or conferred by any special enactment to obtain the dissolution of a Hindu marriage, whether solmenised before or after the commencement of this Act.

(3) Nothing contained in this Act shall affect any proceeding under any law for the time being in force for declaring any marriage to be null and void or for annulling or dissolving any marriage or for judicial separation pending at the commencement of this Act, and any such proceeding may be continued and determined as if this Act had not been passed.

(4) Nothing contained in this Act shall be deemed to affect the provisions contained in the Special Marriage Act, 1954 (43 of 1954) with respect to marriages between Hindus solmenised under that Act, whether before or after the commencement of this Act."

## ESSENTIALS OF A VALID CUSTOM

It is important to refer to the essential ingredients of a valid custom, which essentially require that the custom should be ancient, certain, reasonable and not opposed to public policy. That way back in 1969, in the reported case of *Rabindra Nath Dutta* v. *The State,* AIR 1969 Cal 55, the Calcutta High Court laid down that the provisions of the HMA, 1955 do not provide for any particular kind or form of ceremonies to be observed in a Hindu marriage. Para 20 (at page 58) of the said judgment reads as follows:

> "20. The Hindu Marriage Act does not lay down any special or particular kind or form of ceremonies to be compulsorily observed in all Hindu marriages. In fact, the form of marriage, prescribed by the Sastras, is subject to modifications by custom or usage. But the expression `Customary Ceremonies' cannot be taken to mean that `Sastric Ceremonies' have been totally ignored. The expression `Customary Rites and Ceremonies' naturally means such sastric ceremonies, which the caste or community to which the party belong is customarily following. Customary rites and ceremonies to be accepted must be shown that such custom as an essence of marriage ceremony had been followed definitely from ancient times and that the members of the Caste, Community or Sub-Caste had recognised such ceremonies as obligatory. Once it is proved by evidence what ceremonies had been followed as customary rites, it is no longer left to the will of the Caste, Community or Sub-Caste to alter them as the essence of custom is that

on account of its definiteness it had been recognised and adopted by the caste or community with certainty and without any variation."

The Supreme Court of India in the case of *Harihar Prasad Singh* v. *Balmiki Prasad Singh*, AIR 1975 SC 733, held that the specific family custom pleaded in a particular case should be proved. The initial onus lies on the plaintiffs to prove the special custom. It must be proved that the custom has been acted upon in practice for such a long period and with such invariability as to show that it has by common consent been submitted to as the established governing rule of the particular family.

## TRADITIONAL REASONS AND OBJECTIVES BEHIND CUSTOMARY MARRIAGES

The Chadar ceremony, that is the second marriage which is one of the forms of Karewa marriage, is a brief marriage ceremony which is basically handing over the bride to the bridegroom. This custom of low key marriages is uniformly followed within the Jatts and certain sections of the Sikh community which is an established ongoing practice of Karewa marriages within the Sikh community. There is no dispute as to the validity of such a custom.

The said customary wedding ceremony is generally a small low-key ceremony. That given the circumstances of the said wedding, no celebrations are held at all. No guests are invited and neither are any pictures taken at all. That all such Karewa marriages, generally as per custom, are usually performed in such a low-key manner. That, as per the tenets of the Sikh religion, no actual wedding ceremony is also performed in a Sikh temple, like a wedding ceremony in normal circumstances. The main reason for following such a practice is that it is a remarriage of a widow, quite often within the immediate family itself.

Traditionally, one of the prime objectives of such a customary marriage is the rehabilitation of the widow within the family-fold, and to retain the land holding within the family fold itself. Since, Karewa marriages emanate from the State of Punjab, which is known for its flourishing agriculture, hence, the size of the land holdings have added significance for the family name. Land holdings in the State of Punjab are considered to be the pride of the family and of course more valuable than the family silver.

## ADDITIONAL MODES OF PROVING VALID CUSTOMARY MARRIAGES : CREDIBLE EVIDENCE BY WAY OF AFFIDAVITS AND EXPERT LEGAL REPORTS

Evidence as to the usage and continuance of such customary marriages and practices can be put forward in the shape of affidavits, to demonstrate the genuineness of the same to the satisfaction of the immigration authorities, where they doubt the existence and usage of such customary practices and additionally supported by expert reports from lawyers of repute, in the event of any post-refusal appeal proceedings or in any litigation in any foreign Court or tribunal.

That such affidavits should be tendered by the aggrieved beneficiary applicant wife, to the Sarpanch, that is the elected village headman including several respectable elderly people from the village from different walks of life. There should be atleast 8-10 such affidavits couched in very specific terms as to the applicability, specific practice, usage and continuity of the custom within the community.

The Supreme Court in para 6 (at page 737) of the above judgment of *Harihar Prasad* (supra) has traced the history of the usage of the family customs, also placing reliance on some of the very early decisions of the Privy Council.

Para 6 of the above-mentioned judgment of *Harihar Prasad* (supra) (at page 737) reads as follows:

> "6. Now on whom does the burden rest and what is the scope of the evidence that is admissible? The earliest decision on the question regarding proof of custom in variance of the general law is found in *Ramalakshmi Ammal* v. *Shivanatha Perumal*, (1872) 14 Moo. Ind. App. 570 at p 585 (PC) to the effect;
>
> "It is of the essence of special usages modifying the ordinary law of succession that they should be ancient and invariable; and it is further essential that they should be established to be so by clear and unambiguous evidence. It is only by means of such evidence that the Courts can be assured of their existence, and that they possess the conditions of antiquity and certainty on which alone their legal title to recognition depends."

This passage was quoted by this Court with the approval in its decision in *Pushpavathi Vijayaram* v. *P. Visweswar*, AIR 1964 SC 118, and this Court went on further to observe:

> "In dealing with the family custom, the same principle will have to be applied, though, of course, in the case of a family custom, instances in support of the custom may not be as many or as frequent as in the case of customs pertaining to a territory or to the community or to the character of any estate. In dealing with family customs, the consensus of opinion amongst the members of the family, the traditional belief entertained by them and acted upon by them, their statements, and their conduct would all be relevant and it is only where the relevant evidence of such a character appears to the Court to be sufficient that a specific family custom pleaded in a particular case would be held to be proved, *Abdul Hussein Khan* v. *Bibi Sona*, 45 Ind. App. 10: AIR 1917 PC 181".

That the above-mentioned observations of the Supreme Court of India way back in the year 1964 in the case of *Pushpavathi Vijayaram* v. *P. Visweswar*, (supra) subsequently reiterated in the above mentioned case of *Harihar Prasad* (supra) in the year *1975*. Obviously, affidavits of local village people should state that the customary marriage of the applicant was on the basis of family custom, consensus of the applicant wife and also the family and the community and they acted accordingly upon the traditional belief entertained by them.

It should not be the case at all that the usage of the custom of Karewa marriage, other forms of customary marriages or divorces by the either of the spouses with his/her consent and the support of the family has sprung up overnight, possibly to circumvent immigration rules. The pleaded custom should be supported by affidavits of respectable community members and there should exist no such infirmity in the pleadings made by them.

## CUSTOMARY DISSOLUTION OF MARRIAGES, UNDER SECTION 29(2) OF HMA, 1955

Customary dissolution of marriages is permitted under section 29 (2) of the HMA, 1955. There is a direct judgment of the Jammu and Kashmir High Court in the case of *Rano Devi* v. *Rishi Kumar,* AIR 1981 J&K 2. The interpretation of section 29(2) of the HMA, 1955 in crystal clear terms in para 6 (at page 4) of the said judgment reads as follows:

> "It clearly states that marriage may be dissolved in accordance with a custom governing the parties, or under any other law providing for the same. This sub section is couched in a stronger language and says that notwithstanding anything contained in the Act, including sections 4 and 13, a Hindu marriage may be dissolved even under the customary law of the parties, by adopting a mode different from the one provided under the Act. This is what has happened here also. Instead of approaching the District Court in a petition under section 13, the parties, by mutual agreement, dissolved their marriage by executing a deed of divorce, a mode permissible under the customs followed by them. The trial Court was, therefore, right in dismissing the appellant's petition on the ground that since the marriage between the parties already stood dissolved through a customary divorce, no decree for the restitution of conjugal rights could be passed in her favour."

There is a custom among the Sikh Jats of Amritsar, by which a husband can dissolve a marriage out of Court, preferably by written instrument, which of course is saved by section 29(2) of the HMA, 1955. Thus, a second marriage after such customary divorce was held not to be void. This was held in the case of *Balwinder Singh* v. *Gurpal Kaur,* AIR 1985 Del 14. Para 20 of this judgment has elucidated the position of customary divorces in very eloquent terms as follows:

> "20. The upshot of the whole discussion, therefore is that there is ample oral as well as other evidence on record to warrant the conclusion that there does exist a custom amongst Sikh Jats of District Amritsar under which a marriage can be dissolved out of court preferably through a written instrument. The very fact that dissolution of marriage amongst Sikh Jats of that district has been taking place even after the enactment of the Act is in itself a strong proof of its recognition by the community concerned. It would show that despite the relief of dissolution of marriage by divorce being available under the Act people still prefer to resort to customary law rather than seek redress in a court of law under the Act. So, the mere fact that the appellant has not furnished any old instance would not undermine the evidentiary value of the instances cited by various witnesses in Court; rather they tend to establish beyond doubt that such a custom is firmly rooted and is still prevalent despite the remedy of divorce being available under statutory law. Hence, I hold accordingly. "

Quite often, there are refusal letters by the Embassy authorities in instances of Karewa marriages or other forms of valid customary marriages. That such an assertion in the case of a valid customary marriage that the beneficiary has married her former brother-in-law, which of course is not legally sustainable also in light of the law laid down in *Parkash Chander* v. *Parmeshwari,* AIR 1987 P&H 37.

Para 12 (at page 42) of the said judgment is most relevant in so far relating to interpretation of Karewa marriages and reads as follows:

> "12. The next question of definite importance which arises in this case is whether during the lifetime of Ishwar Singh who was very much present in the village, any Karewa marriage could be legally entered into between the respondent and the appellant, or had it in fact so taken place. There is no doubt whatsoever in my mind that in the presence of Ishwar Singh, who was very much alive in the village, no valid marriage could take place between the parties. Such a marriage would be void in the face of the provisions of section 5(1) of the Act wherein it is laid down that a marriage may be solemnised between any two Hindus if neither party has a spouse living at the time of the marriage. It has been held by the Supreme Court in *Mohd. Ikram Hussain* v. *State of Uttar Pradesh,* AIR 1964 SC 1625, that in view of provisions of sections 5 and 11 of the Act, such a marriage would be null and void. In para 74 of the Digest of Customary Law by Sir W.H. Rattigan (13th edition), it has been laid down that until the former marriage is validly set aside, a woman cannot marry a second husband in the lifetime of her first husband."

**WIFE SHOULD NOT HAVE A LIVING SPOUSE FOR A VALID KAREWA MARRIAGE**

It is very important that for a Karewa marriage to be valid the wife, should have no living spouse at the time she solemnised her subsequent Karewa marriage.

In the above-mentioned case of *Parkash Chander* (supra), the Karewa marriage was held to be invalid because the original husband of the wife was subsequently found not to be dead. He was found to be alive after a certain period of time. Meanwhile, the wife had entered into a Karewa marriage with her brother-in-law. In this particular case, the wife pleaded the custom raising the presumption that since her first husband had not been heard for 2-3 years, he was presumed to be dead. This contention was outrightly rejected on the ground that the alleged custom was contrary to section 108 of the Indian Evidence Act, 1872.

The Punjab and Haryana High Court tersely held in para 20 (at page 46) of the said judgment as follows:

> "20. ...In the instant case what the respondent had pleaded was that since Ishwar Singh, her husband, had not been heard of and his whereabouts were not known for a period of 7-8 years, she entered into a Karewa marriage with the appellant. Therefore, it is not necessary to probe into the facets of the issue whether there is a custom prevalent in the community of the parties which permits dissolution of marriage on the ground that either party had been mentally insane, had become impotent or was incapable of performing the duties of husband/wife. The only aspect that needs examination and determination is whether a divorce is permissible in the community of the parties under custom where one of the spouses is unheard of or his whereabouts are not known. Before examination of this

aspect of the issue, it has to be kept in mind that a custom to be valid must not contravene any express provision of the law. It should not be against public policy nor it should be contrary to justice, equity and good conscience and it should be ancient, certain and invariable. These ingredients of a valid custom are laid down in para 1 of Rattigan's digest of Customary Law ibid..."

In the event of refusal of a settlement visa for a wife to join her husband overseas in the case of a valid customary marriage, support can very much be drawn by the beneficiary wife from the above-mentioned observations of the Punjab and Haryana High Court judgment. This is to the effect that the custom of Karewa marriage pleaded by the beneficiary wife is very much valid, does not contravene any express provision of law and neither is it against public policy.

That under the provisions of the HMA, 1955 both parties to the marriage are at full liberty otherwise to solemnise their marriage by way of customary rites and ceremonies generally prevalent in their community. But, such ceremonies and rites should essentially qualify the requisites of essential ingredients of a custom, as already stated above. But, if Saptapadi (taking of seven steps around the holy fire) and invocation before the sacred fire are made, the marriage is validly solemnised under the Shastric law.

## CUSTOMARY MARRIAGES WILL NOT BE RECOGNISED IN ABSENCE OF COGENT RELIABLE PROOF

That in a particular customary marriage case, where there is no proof of custom, and neither is a customary marriage pleaded, such a customary marriage will not be recognised. In this particular regard, it is important to advert to the observations of the Kerala High Court in the case of *Chakki* v. *Ayyappan,* AIR 1989 Ker 89.

The Kerala High Court held at para 10 (at page 92) of the said judgment as follows:

> "10. The appellant cannot succeed only by a showing that in other marriages of the community there were exchange of rings and pooja and thali etc. Those can be accepted as requirements of customary marriage only if they are proved to be sufficiently ancient and definite and that members of the community recognise them as obligatory. It should also be shown that those formalities were unalterable. As we indicated earlier, there are no pleadings, much less any proof of an ancient, definite and unalterable custom in this regard."

By way of clarification, in the above-mentioned Kerala High Court judgment, the marriage was held to be valid on the basis of the performance of the statutory essential requirement of a Hindu marriage that is invocation before the sacred fire, and Saptapadi, that is taking seven steps by the groom and bride jointly before the sacred fire.

## KAREWA MARRIAGES GENERALLY PREDOMINANT IN AGRICULTURAL TRIBES OF PUNJABI ORIGIN.

That in the case of *Garja Singh* v. *Surjit Kaur,* AIR 1991 P&H 177, it was held that a marriage will be valid only if the ceremony through which it is solemnised is sanctioned by the religion of either party as a customary ceremony. Therefore, merely going through some ceremonies like distribution of Gur and Shakkar (Sugar) with the intention that the parties be taken to have been married will not make them the customary ceremonies prescribed by law or sanctioned by custom. Even in the general customary law in Punjab as applicable to the predominantly agricultural tribes, the 'Karewa' marriage with the brother or some male relative of the deceased husband requires no religious ceremonies and confers all the rights of a valid marriage. However, the bride in the instant case had no connection whatsoever with the deceased alleged to be her husband prior to the execution of the 'Karewa Nama'. The marriage with a stranger has to be performed in accordance with the customary rights or ceremonies as prescribed by law. There is no allegation much less proof, as to what were the customary ceremonies performed for solemnising the marriage between the deceased and the defendant claiming share in the estate of the deceased, as his widow.

This is also one of the judgments which categorically notices that such Karewa marriages are generally predominant in agricultural tribes of Punjabi origin.

**CUSTOM SHOULD BE PROVED IN THE FOLLOWING TERMS:**

Furthermore, the Punjab and Haryana High Court in the case of *Asha Rani* v. *Gulshan Kumar,* AIR 1995 P&H 287, has elaborated in para 10 (at page 289), the way in which custom should be proved in the following terms:

> "10. A custom must be proved to be ancient, certain and reasonable if it is to be recognised and acted upon by Courts of Law. The specific family custom pleaded in a particular case should be proved by the party pleading it. It must be proved that the custom has been acted upon in practice for such a long period and with such invariability, as to show that it has, by common consent, been submitted to as the established governing rule of the particular family. Custom no doubt can be proved by oral evidence of witnesses acquainted with custom, instances and general pronouncements. Section 29(2) of the Act does not disturb the position which a customary divorce occupied before the enactment of the Act."

Clearly, it is manifest, that as stated above customary marriage and divorce, *qua* the aggrieved beneficiary applicant can additionally be proved by key credible witnesses from the community and possibly community leaders as well, in the shape of affidavits.

**NOT NECESSARY FOR PARTIES TO OBTAIN DIVORCE FROM COURT, ON GROUND ALREADY REGOGNISED BY CUSTOM**

In the case of *Rita Rani* v. *Ramesh Kumar,* 1995 (2) HLR 338 (P&H), it was held that if there is a local custom by which marriage can be dissolved either by brotherhood or by executing an agreement, such a customary dissolution of marriage is saved by section 29(2) of the HMA, 1955. And more importantly the parties are not required to obtain a decree of divorce through Court, after such a customary divorce has been effected.

The Punjab and Haryana High Court held in para 7 (at page 339) as follows:

> "7. Relying on *Balwinder Singh* v. *Smt. Gurpal Kaur,* AIR 1985 Del 14: [1985(1) AIHLR 442 (Del)]; *Smt. Sudarshan Kaur* v. *Major Manmohan Singh*

> *Bhatt*, AIR 1978 P&H 115; A Digest of Customary Law by Sir W.H. Rattigan (Fourteenth Edition) page 470; and Hindu Law by Mula 16th edition page 745, he contended that from the pleadings and sole testimony of Ramesh Kumar, it is evident that in the cast of the parties, there is customary mode of marriage and customary mode of dissolution of marriage also. Therefore, Ramesh Kumar himself dissolved his earlier marriage with Rita Rani under this customary mode i.e. dissolution of marriage by 'biradari'. He stressed that under section 29(2) of the Act, it is not necessary for parties in any such case to go to Court to obtain divorce on ground recognised by custom. It is not the case of Ramesh Kumar that this customary mode of dissolution of marriage is either against the public policy or is not upheld by Courts."

The ruling in the above-mentioned case is of immense significance. It has been categorically held by the Punjab and Haryana High Court at Chandigarh in the above-mentioned decided case that it is not necessary for the parties to go to Court on the ground that such a divorce is recognised by custom. Likewise, it is argued by analogy that it is not mandatory for the parties to the marriage as in the present case to go to Court for validation of their customary marriage. Generally, there is an assertion in the refusal letters in settlement cases by the Embassy authorities to the effect "also please provide a Court order stating that this relationship is allowed." Clearly, in light of the above settled position of law as stated above, the assertion of a Court declaration by the Embassy authorities to the effect that the relationship is permitted by law is not a sustainable action.

**COURTS CAN TAKE JUDICIAL NOTICE OF GENERAL CUSTOMS:**

The Punjab and Haryana High Court in *Ranbir Kaur* alias *Harjit Kaur* v. *Gurnam Singh,* 1996 (2) HLR 71, held that the Courts can take judicial notice of general customs. The Court elaborated that the term general custom is used in the sense that it has, by repeated recognition by Courts over a period of time, become entitled to judicial notice. Paragraph 8 (at page 74) of this judgment crystallises the law on judicial notice of general customs by consolidating the earlier case-law as follows:

> "8. Whoever sets up a custom must prove the same. Sometimes the custom is recognised by Courts and it passes into the law of land. This question was considered by the Supreme Court in the case of *Ujagar Singh* v. *Mst. Jeo,* AIR 1959 SC 1041. In paragraph 14 it was held:
>
> 14. It therefore appears to us that the ordinary rule is that all customs, general or otherwise, have to be proved. Under S.57 of the Evidence Act however nothing need to be proved of which courts can take judicial notice. Therefore, it is said that if there is a custom of which the courts can take judicial notice, it need not be proved. How the circumstances in which the courts can take judicial notice, it need not be proved. How the circumstances in which the courts can take judicial notice of a custom were stated by Lord Dunedin in *Raja Ram Rao* v. *Raja of Pittapur*, 45 Ind App 148 (154, 155): AIR 1918 PC 81 (83), in the following words, " When a custom or usage, whether in regard to a tenure or a contract or a family right, is repeatedly brought to the notice of the Courts of a country, the Courts may

> hold that custom or usage to be introduced into the law without necessity of proof in each individual case." When a custom has been so recognised by the courts, it passes into the law of the land and the proof of it then becomes unnecessary under section 57(1) of the Evidence Act. It appears to us that in the courts in the Punjab the expression "general custom" has really been used in this sense, namely, that a custom has by repeated recognition by courts, become entitled to judicial notice as was said in *Bawa Singh* v. *Mt. Taro*, AIR 1951 Punj 239; *Sukhwant Kaur* v. *Balwant Singh*, AIR 1951 Punj 242."

The judgment above, specifically highlights the importance of general custom. This term is used in the sense that the same by repeated recognition by the Courts has become entitled to judicial notice.

Thus, it can be stated that the onus of proving and establishing a custom would lie on the party who claims its benefit. As already stated before, that from the catalogue of evidence in the shape of affidavits furnished by the beneficiary applicant, other members of the family, as also by respectable people from the community, the practice of customary marriages and divorces can be proved successfully. Whether the same is acceptable for judicial notice or it is to be proven separately, would depend on the facts and circumstances of each case.

It is clear that in northern Indian State of Punjab, customary divorce and customary widow re-marriage is an acceptable customary practice in some local communities. [For further details see: A Digest of Customary Law (in Punjab), authored by Sir W.H. Rattigan in 1880, and re-printed subsequently by other authors, discusses in great detail customary law practices prevalent in Punjab in all walks of life.] In the most recent edition (1995), Chapter V specifically reports and discusses known prevalent customary practices of Marriage and Divorce in different classes and communities in Punjab.

The scheme and object of the HMA, 1955 is not to override any such custom which recognises divorce and explicit recognition is given to the same by the saving clause contained in section 29(2) of the HMA, 1955. It is not necessary for parties in any such case to go to Court to obtain divorce on the grounds recognised by custom. The custom, as already elaborated above in sufficient detail must of course, be a valid custom.

Section 29(2) of the Act saves customary divorce but the party relying on a custom needs to prove the existence of such custom and also that it is ancient, certain, reasonable and not opposed to public policy. In *Mariammal* v. *Padmanabhan* AIR 2001 Mad 350, the Madras High Court overruled the finding of the trial Court that there cannot be customary divorce after the coming into force of the Hindu Marriage Act, 1955. It held that divorce was recognised by custom even before the Act, and after the Act also Courts uphold such custom if not opposed to public policy. Such custom being saved under section 29(2), it is not necessary for the parties in such cases to go to the Court to obtain divorce on grounds recognised by custom.

That from the discussion and also case-law analysis on section 29 of the HMA, 1955 it is manifest that the said section specifically saves customs regarding marriage and divorce from the operation of the provisions of the HMA, 1955 and they are legally recognised. In *Jasbir Singh* v. *Inderjit Kaur,* AIR 2003 P&H 317, the husband sought annulment of his marriage on the ground that at the time of marriage, his wife was already married. The wife's contention was that she had obtained a customary divorce from her previous husband and the petitioner was aware of this as he had seen the written deed of customary divorce; he was, therefore, estopped from taking the plea that the wife was already married and not divorced. The wife was a Jat Sikh from district Sangrur in Punjab. After going through the evidence, the Court held that it was established that there is a custom among the Jat Sikhs of district Sangrur which permits divorce and the wife had obtained the divorce according to that custom. The validity of the custom being saved, it is not necessary for the parties to go to Court to obtain divorce on grounds recognised by custom; it is open for the parties to dissolve the marriage out of Court, in accordance with the custom. The Court relied on, inter alia, *Gurdit Singh* v. *Mst. Angrez Kaur,* AIR 1968 SC 142 where the Apex Court held that there can be valid divorce where custom allows dissolution and on dissolution of a marriage by custom, the party can enter into second marriage in the lifetime of the first divorced spouse. The husband's petition for annulment was consequently dismissed in *Jasbir Kaur* (supra) as, the wife having obtained customary divorce from her previous husband, the marriage with the petitioner was legal and valid.

The Punjab and Haryana High Court held in para 9 (at page 319) of the judgment as follows:

> "9. In AIR 1978 P&H 98 (supra) relied upon by the learned counsel for the appellant-husband, it has been held that a party relying upon a particular custom is called upon to allege and to prove that custom. It was further held that entries in a Riwaj-e-am, which pertain to a special custom applicable to a locality or a class of persons, should also be presumed to be correct unless rebutted. ..."

The Punjab and Haryana High Court further held in paras 20 and 21 (at pages 323 and 324), as follows:

> "20. ...In *Gurdit Singh* v. *Mst. Angrez Kaur,* AIR 1968 SC 142, it was held by the Hon'ble Supreme Court that a custom exists among the Hindu Jats of the Jalandhar District which permits a valid divorce by a husband of his wife which dissolves the marriage. It was further held that on the dissolution of such a marriage the divorced wife can enter into a valid marriage with a second husband in the lifetime of the first husband. The law laid down by this Court in (1962) Punj LR 1179, was affirmed by the Hon'ble Supreme Court, in the said authority. In *Balwinder Singh* v. *Smt. Gurpal Kaur,* 1985 MLJ 414: AIR 1985 Del 14 it was held by the Delhi High Court that on a plain reading of section 29(2) of the Hindu Marriage Act, it is manifest that a marriage may still be dissolved in accordance with a custom governing the parties or under any other law providing for the same. It was further held that the validity of any custom recognising the right to dissolve a marriage is expressly saved by this sub-section. It was further held that as a necessary corollary, it follows that it would not be necessary for the parties in any such case to go to Court to obtain divorce

on grounds recognised by custom and it would be open to dissolve the marriage out of Court in accordance with such custom. It was further held that the net result will be that a Hindu marriage may now be dissolved under section 13 of the Hindu Marriage Act or under any other special enactment or in accordance with any custom applicable to the parties. Reliance was also placed on the law laid down by Hon'ble Court, in Gurdit Singh's case (supra), in respect of the existence of such a custom in District Jalandhar. It was also held that the existence of such a custom permitting dissolution of marriage by divorce amongst Hindu Jats was also prevalent in District surrounding Jalandhar District, including Amritsar, Hoshiarpur and Ludhiana.

21. In view of the above, in my opinion, it can safely be held that there is a custom among Jat Sikhs of District Sangrur, permitting dissolution of marriage by divorce through writing executed by the parties in this regard and such a divorce would be recognised, in view of section 29(2) of the Hindu Marriage Act and the law laid down by the Hon'ble Supreme Court and Delhi High Court, in the cases referred to above. I am further of the opinion, that the learned Additional District Judge had rightly found that the marriage between the petitioner and respondent could not be annulled under section 11 of the Hindu Marriage Act, inasmuch as respondent had validly obtained a divorce from her previous husband Lachhman Singh, at the time when her marriage had taken place with the petitioner. Accordingly, I affirm the findings of the learned Additional District Judge in this regard."

The above-mentioned ruling in the case of *Jasbir Singh* (supra) laying down similar tenor of law as in the above-mentioned case of *Rita Rani* (supra) is again of immense significance. This is because it has been yet again categorically reiterated by the Punjab and Haryana High Court at Chandigarh in the above mentioned decided case of *Jasbir Singh* (supra): that it is not necessary for the parties to go to Court on the ground that such a divorce is recognised by custom. Hence, if the denial letter by the Embassy authorities in the case of a valid Karewa marriage states to the effect "also please provide a Court order stating that this relationship is allowed," clearly the same would not be legally sustainable as per the settled position of law, as elaborated above.

## CUSTOMARY DISSOLUTION OF MARRIAGE DOES NOT REQUIRE VALIDATION FROM COURT- RECENT SUPREME COURT OF INDIA JUDGMENT

Much more recently, the Supreme Court of India in *Mahendra Nath Yadav* v. *Sheela Devi*, 2010 (9) SCC 484, upheld the judgment of the Allahabad High Court stating that the High Court rightly held that dissolution of marriage through the panchayat (local elected village council at the grassroot level) as per custom cannot be a ground for granting divorce under section 13 of the HMA, 1955.

The facts of this case as recorded paras 4 and 5 (at pages 485-486) of the judgment are as follows:

"4. According to appellant, it was customary in the locality and in the community to which both parties belong to have a divorce through the Panchayat. Thus, the Panchayat was convened on 7-6-1997. The said Panchayat decided that the appellant should pay a sum of Rs. 30,000 to the respondent's family. It was paid and a document was prepared which was duly signed by the parties. Thus, the marriage came to an end. In order to give legal effect to the said customary divorce, the appellant tried to persuade the respondent to get divorce from the Family Court under section 13B of the 1955 Act, by consent. However, she did not agree. Thus the appellant approached the Family Court by filing Petition No. 370 of 1998 under section 13 of the 1955 Act, seeking divorce on the ground of desertion and cruelty.

5. The respondent filed the counter-case i.e. Petition No. 57 of 1999 under section 9 of the 1955 Act, for restitution of conjugal rights. The Family Court decreed the suit mainly on the ground that the marriage stood dissolved through Panchayat and dismissed the petition filed by the wife for restitution of conjugal rights vide order dated 15-09-2000. Being aggrieved, the respondent preferred appeals against both the orders before the High Court and the High Court has reversed the said order in both the cases. Hence this appeal."

The reasoning clearly elucidated by the Apex Court in not interfering with the judgment of the High Court advanced in para 7 (at page 486) of the judgment is as follows:

"7. The High Court has rightly held that dissolution of marriage through Panchayat as per custom prevailing in that area and in that community permitted cannot be a ground for granting divorce under section 13 of the 1955 Act. We fully agree with the said decision for the reason that in case the appellant wanted a decree on the basis of customary dissolution of marriage through Panchayat held on 7-6-1997, he would not have filed a petition under section 13 of the 1955 Act. Filing this petition itself means that none of the parties was of the view that the divorce granted by the Panchayat was legal. In view of the above, we do not see any reason to interfere with the well-reasons judgment of the High Court."

## DIFFERENT TYPES OF CUSTOMS

The Supreme Court of India in an elaborate judgment handed down in the year 2007 has very clearly elucidated the three types of different customs in the case of *Ass Kaur (Deceased) by L.Rs.* v. *Kartar Singh (Dead) by L.Rs.*, JT 2007 (9) SC 118. One of the key issues in this case was succession rights on the basis of Karewa marriage.

Paras 10 to 12 (at pages 121 and 122) of the said judgment of the Apex Court are most relevant and read as follows:

"10. Hindu law recognises three types of customs : local custom, class custom and family custom. The courts below have held that the parties were governed by Zimindara custom. Whether the said custom is a general custom, or a special custom or for that matter a family custom has not been stated. The customary law prevailing in the State of Punjab has received a statutory sanction by reason of the Punjab Laws Act, 1872, sections 5 and 7 whereof read as under:

> 5. Decisions in certain cases to be according to Native law.- In questions regarding succession, special property of females, betrothal, marriage divorce, dower, adoption, guardianship, minority, bastardy, family relations, wills, legacies, gifts, partitions, or any religious usage or institution the rule of decision shall be—
>
> (a) any custom applicable to the parties concerned, which is not contrary to justice, equity or good conscience, and has not been by this or any other enactment altered or abolished, and has not been declared to be void by any competent authority.
>
> (b) the Muhammadan law, in cases where the parties are Muhammadans and the Hindu law, in cases where the parties are Hindus, except in so far as such law has been altered or abolished by legislative enactment, or is opposed to the provisions of this Act, or has been modified by any such customs as is above referred to.
>
> 7. Local customs and mercantile usages when valid.-All local customs and mercantile usages shall be regarded as valid, unless they are contrary to justice, equity or good conscience, or have, before the passing of this Act, been declared to be void by any competent authority.

11. Amongst the Sikh Jats of Punjab province, there exists a custom, where the widow marries her first husband's brother in the Karewa form, remarriage would not cause forfeiture of her own share. [See *Chunnilal* v. *Mst. Attar Kaur,* AIR 1933 Lah 69].

12. In respect of Jats belonging to Ferozepur district, it has been held that a widow who remarried her first husband's brother succeeds to a co-widow in preference to collaterals. But the widow's right only accrues on husband's death, and if it does not accrue then, it cannot accrue later by the death of subsequent heir. The fact, if the widow is a Karewa widow it would not affect her right in a suit the parties to which were the two widows of a Manhas Rajput resident in the Shakargarh Tehsil of Gurudaspur District, had that the plaintiff (upon whom under the circumstances the onus lay) had failed to prove a custom in her favour, excluding the defendant, who was a co-widow by a Karewa marriage, from succeeding to a share in the deceased husband's estate [*Mst. Dakho* v. *Mst. Gano,* 22 PR 889]. Even a woman who had contracted such marriage may not forfeit her life estate, if any, in her deceased husband's property despite the provisions of the Hindu widows Remarriage Act, 1856. However, the said principle would not apply where a remarriage is not with the brother of her deceased but with some other relative. "

Furthermore, the Apex Court in paras 17 to 19 of the said judgment has reiterated the settled position of law that Courts can take judicial notice of custom and as and when the custom has been recognised by the Courts, the same need not be proved. Paras 17 to 19 (at pages 123 and 124) read as follows:—

> "17. We may, however, notice that customary law has been recorded in Rattigan's Digest of Customary Laws. The courts below have categorically held the law to be applicable in the instant case is the customary law having regard to the fact that the parties belonged to the community of Sidhu Jats.
>
> 18. In *R.B.S.S. Munnalal* v. *S.S. Rajkumar*, AIR 1962 SC 1493, this Court was considering the question as to whether a Jain widow could adopt a son to her husband without his express authority, being governed by the custom which had by long acceptance become part of the law applicable to them. Therein, it was observed:
>
> ...It is well-settled that where a custom is repeatedly brought to the notice of the Courts of a country, the courts may hold that custom introduced into the law without the necessity of proof in each individual case....
>
> 19. The court can also take judicial notice of such customs in terms of Section 57 of the Evidence Act, 1872. As and when custom has repeatedly been recognised by the courts, the same need not be proved. Reference in regard to the Punjab 'general custom' may be made to *Ujagar Singh (supra),* and *Bawa* v. *Taro,* AIR 1951 Punj 239."

That certainly the law reiterated and the law laid down by the Supreme Court of India in the above mentioned case of *Ass Kaur (Deceased)* (supra), would clearly support the case of a beneficiary wife, who is affected by the refusal of her settlement visa application. The Apex Court has yet again given clear cut recognition to Karewa marriages, even in rights of succession.

Furthermore, the observations in para 25 (at pages 124 and 125) of the above judgment are also very important in a situation where a wife has performed a valid customary marriage.

Para 25 of *Ass Kaur (deceased)* (supra) reads as follows:

> "25. As statutory law did not exclude the applicability of the customary law, the principle that customary law would prevail over the statutory law would apply. It was so found by the courts below."

The point to be conveyed is that in the case of a valid customary marriage, the customary law would prevail over statutory law.

Lastly, in so far relating to the present judgment, support is drawn from the observations in para 29 (at page 125) of the *Smt. Ass Kaur (deceased)* (supra) judgment which reads as follows:—

> "29. In *Daya Singh (dead) through L.Rs.* (supra), paragraph 23 of Rattigan's Digest of Customary Law of Punjab has been noticed. It was held:
>
> > It is on the basis of this Customary Law that the reversioners succeeded in the suit filed by them questioning the gift made by the respondents mother to her. There is no doubt that Rattigan's work is an authoritative one on the subject of Customary Law in Punjab. This Court in *Mahant Salig Ram* v. *Musammat Maya Devi* said:

The customary rights of succession of daughters as against the collaterals of the father with reference to ancestral and non-ancestral lands are stated in para 23 of Rattigan's Digest of Customary Law. It is categorically stated in sub-para (2) of that paragraph that the daughter succeeds to the self-acquired property of the father in preference to the collaterals even though they are within the fourth degree. Rattigan's work has been accepted by the Privy Council as a book of unquestioned authority in the Punjab. Indeed, the correctness of this para was not disputed before this Court in *Gopal Singh* v. *Ujagar Singh*."

The Andhra Pradesh High Court in the year 2008 has in relation to the constant usage of customary law has reiterated the relevant operative parts of earlier judgments of the Supreme Court of India and the Privy Council. This is in the case of *Atluri Brahmanandam* v. *Anne Sai Bapuji*, AIR 2008 AP 235. Paras 16 to 19 (at page 239) of the said judgement read as follows:

"16. In *Gokal Chand* v. *Parvin Kumari*, AIR 1952 SC 231, Supreme Court laid down general principles, to be kept in view, in dealing with the question of customary law. Inter alia it is laid down that, "a custom in order to be binding must derive its force from the fact that by long usage it has obtained a force of law, but English rule that, 'a custom in order that it may be legal and binding, must have been used so long that the memory of man runneth not to the contrary' should not be strictly applied to Indian conditions. All that is necessary to prove is that the usage has been acted upon in practice for such a long period and with such invariability as to show that it has, by common consent, been submitted to as the established governing rule of a particular locality".

17. In *Raja Ram Rao* v. *Raja of Pittapur*, AIR 1918 PC 81, the Privy Council held as under:

This proposition, it must be noted, does not negative the doctrine that there are members of the family entitled to maintenance in the case of an impartible zamindari. Just as the impartibility is the creature of custom, so custom may and does affirm a right to maintenance in certain members of the family. No attempt has been, as already stated, made by the plaintiff to prove any special custom in this zamindari. That by itself in the case of some claims would not be fatal. When a custom or usage, whether in regard to a tenure or a contract or a family right, is repeatedly brought to the notice of the Courts of a country, the Courts may hold that custom or usage to be introduced into the law without the necessity of proof in each individual case. It becomes in the end truly a matter of process and pleading. (Emphasis supplied)

18. In *Bai Sakar*, AIR 1937 Bom 65, Supreme Court laid down as under:

The fact that a particular custom has been judicially recognized establishes that the custom is reasonable and not opposed to public policy so that it will be upheld whenever it is proved. This is the legal aspect of custom: *Moult* v. *Halliday*, (1898) 1 QB 125. But, subject to what I shall presently state, judicial recognition of a custom in another suit leaves untouched the proof of the fact that the custom is applicable to the particular parties who are before the court. (Emphasis supplied)

> 19. In *Ujagar Singh,* AIR 1959 SC 1041, while observing that every general custom relied on a person must be clearly proved to exist, the Supreme Court ruled that if the Court takes judicial notice of such custom under section 57 of Indian Evidence Act, 1872, no further proof is required. Keeping this in mind, the submission of learned Counsel for the appellant that the plaintiff did not plead and prove the existence of such custom is without any merit...."

Much more recently, the Punjab and Haryana High Court in *Rajinder Kaur* v. *Kuldeep Singh,* 2011 (1) HRLR 205 (Haryana Law Reporter), refused to recognise a customary divorce in the absence of any evidence on record to prove that divorce through a Panchyatnama that is the written agreement executed before the local elected village council at the grassroots level, was actually permissible under any custom or usage prevalent in the society. In this particular case, the second marriage of the wife, without legally nullifying the earlier marriage, was held to be a nullity. The decree earlier passed by the trial Court declaring the second marriage null and void on the petition of the husband was upheld by the High Court in no uncertain categorical terms.

Para 11 (at pages 207 and 208) of the said judgment in this regard is most relevant and is reproduced hereunder:

> "11. As already observed above learned matrimonial court also found as a fact, that no evidence was led to establish that there was any custom or usage prevalent in the community of the appellant under which divorce through writing of panchayatnama was permissible. Hon'ble Supreme Court in the case of *M.M. Malhotra* v. *Union of India,* AIR 2006 SC 80, has laid down as under:—
>
>> "11. For appreciating the status of a Hindu woman marrying a Hindu male with a living spouse some of the provisions of the Hindu Marriage Act, 1955 (herein referred to as the "Marriage Act") have to be examined. Section 11 of the Marriage Act declares such a marriage as null and void in the following terms:
>>
>>> 11. "Void marriage—Any marriage solemnised after the commencement of this Act shall be null and void and may, on a petition presented by either party thereto against the other party, be so declared by a decree of nullity if it contravenes any one of the conditions specified in clauses (i), (iv) and (v) of section 5."
>>
>> Clause (i) of section 5 lays down, for a lawful marriage, the necessary condition that neither party should have a spouse living at the time of the marriage. A marriage in contravention of this condition, therefore, is null and void. By reason of the overriding effect of the Marriage Act as mentioned in section 4, no aid can be taken of the earlier Hindu law or any custom or usage as a part of that law inconsistent with any provision of the Act. So far as section 12 is concerned, it is confined to other categories of marriages and is not applicable to one solemnised in violation of sections (i) of the

Act. Sub-section (2) of section 12 puts further restrictions on such a right. The cases covered by this section are not void abinitio, and unless all the conditions mentioned therein are fulfilled and the aggrieved party exercises the right to avoid it, the same continues to be effective The marriages covered by section 11 are void ipso jure, that is, void from the very inception, and have to be ignored as not existing in law at all if and when such a question arises. Although the section permits a formal declaration to be made on the presentation of a petition, it is not essential to obtain in advance such a formal declaration from a court in a proceeding specifically commenced for the purpose. The provisions of section 16, which is quoted below, also throw light on this aspect."

> **16. Legitimacy of children of void and voidable marriages:**—(1) Notwithstanding that a marriage is null and void under section 11, any child of such marriage who would have been legitimate if the marriage had been valid, shall be legitimate, whether such child is born before or after the commencement of Marriage Laws (Amendment) Act, 1976 (68 of 1976), and whether or not a decree of nullity is granted in respect of that marriage under this Act and whether or not the marriage is held to be void otherwise than on a petition under this Act.
>
> (2) Where a decree of nullity is granted in respect of a voidable marriage under section 12, any child begotten or conceived before the decree is made, who would have been the legitimate child of the parties to the marriage if at the date of the decree it had been dissolved instead of being annulled, shall be deemed to be their legitimate child notwithstanding the decree of nullity.
>
> (3) Nothing contained in sub-section (1) or sub-section (2) shall be construed as conferring upon any child of a marriage which is null and void or which is annulled by a decree of nullity under section 12, any rights in or to the property of any person, other than the parents, in any case where, but for the passing of this Act, such child would have been incapable of possessing or acquiring any such rights by reason of his not being the legitimate child of his parents.

Sub-section (1), by using the words underlined above clearly implies that a: void marriage can be held to be so without a prior formal declaration by a court in a proceeding. While dealing with cases covered by section 12, sub-section (2) refers to a decree of nullity as an essential condition and sub-section (3) prominently brings out the basic difference in the character of void and voidable marriages as covered respectively by sections 11 and 12. It is also to be seen that while the legislature has considered it advisable to uphold the legitimacy of the paternity of a child born out of a void marriage, it has not extended a similar protection in respect of the mother of the child. The marriage of the appellant must, therefore, be treated as null and void from its very inception."

In view of the authoritative pronouncement of Hon'ble Supreme Court marriage between the parties was nullity, therefore, learned matrimonial court rightly allowed the petition and dissolved the marriage by way of a decree of nullity."

The judgment above is significant for two reasons. **Firstly**, the Court tersely refused to recognise an invalid customary marriage. **Secondly**, the judgment explicitly lays down that no formal declaration from the Court of competent jurisdiction is necessary in case of void ipso jure marriages.

## CONCLUSION

Clearly, it emerges that custom is an important source of Hindu law, having due statutory recognition by virtue of the saving clauses under the provisions of the Hindu Marriage Act, 1955. Huge case-law is available on the subject.

There is a clear consistency of approach by the Supreme Court of India and various High Courts in different parts of the country in reiterating the earlier settled position of customary law with regard to marriage and divorce. The underlying aim of this chapter is to attempt to ensure that the principled approach in customary marriages and divorces, as applicable under the relevant provisions of the Hindu Marriage Act, 1955 is duly availed of by the parties to such genuine customary marriages and divorces in limited situations, especially in the area of international family migration.

Sometimes, from practical experience it is noticed that parties who genuinely perform customary marriages and enter into customary divorces depending on the facts and circumstances of each case, intending to join their spouses resident abroad on the basis of family re-union, in the context of the present article, are not properly and professionally guided. This of course results in outright refusals, at the hands of the Embassy authorities. The problem is compounded by the fact of lack of specialist knowledge on part of visa and consular officers, obviously for which they cannot be blamed. Clearly, this is an avoidable situation. The fact of the matter is that such a gap needs to be plugged appropriately by proper paper work substantially highlighting the statutory provisions and the settled position of law.

Lastly, as it will be noticed that knowledge of Indian family law also becomes essential for foreign immigration lawyers acting on the behalf of sponsors in appeal proceedings in the event of unsuccessful applications. Specialist domestic family law expertise is pivotal in customary marriages and divorces. The relevant provisions of Indian law in this regard, will hopefully prevent foreign practitioners from unwarily walking into traps created by conflicts between local Indian laws and laws of their own jurisdiction.

# SOCIO-LEGAL PERSPECTIVE OF FORCED MARRIAGES IN THE INDIAN CONTEXT: PERCEPTIONS AND POSSIBLE SOLUTIONS

## I. Introduction and background

*Content of this paper*

This chapter deals with the problem of forced marriages, specifically in the Indian context, and the socio-legal problems associated with this practice. Connected with this topic is the problem of honour killings, which takes place in rural parts of India and even outside the territories of India. This chapter also looks at the types of forced marriages, the motives of forced marriages, causes and factors of forced marriages, effects of a forced marriage and the consequences of forced marriages.

To give an insight into the problem, decided cases by the various High Courts in the country and the Supreme Court of India have also been discussed in the main body of the chapter.

This chapter also looks at the various remedies provided in different legislations in the Indian jurisdiction, both civil and criminal to combat the menace of forced marriages. It is pertinent to mention at the outset that in India, we do not have any exclusive consolidated legislation on the issue of forced marriages, barring forced marriages and providing consequential relieves to aggrieved parties.

Further, the chapter touches some of the European legislative approaches to the problem. Europe, among other parts of the Western world, is a major hub of international immigration, also of Indian nationals. The Non-Resident Indian (NRI) community carries their cultural values into their countries of immigration. It is such a serious issue in the UK, for instance, that the British Government had to enact the Forced Marriages legislation in the year 2007. Other countries do not have a comprehensive legislation on the topic, but have made changes in their private international law so as to fight the problem of forced marriages.

Finally, this chapter attempts to advance suggestions to prevent the solemnisation of forced marriages.

*Marriages and Forced Marriages*

Although "marriage" and the whole gamut concerning it have been dealt with differently in different cultures, it finally all boils down to marriage being a social union or legal contract between individuals that creates kinship. Various religions and cultures over the time had and have their own connotations of marriage. It is an institution in which interpersonal relationships, usually intimate and sexual, are acknowledged in a variety of ways, depending on the culture or sub-culture in which it is found, [see, http://en.wikipedia.org/wiki/Marriage#cite_note-81]. In some cultures marriage is viewed as a sacrament and in some others it is viewed as a contract. According to traditional Hindu beliefs in ancient India, marriage was considered to be a pure sacrament: A permanent (indissoluble) and eternal union (connecting husband and wife for several lives) of holy (not contractual) character. In modern times, Hindu law has come to regard the institution of marriage as a blend between sacrament and contract, having semblance of both. Consent to marriage is, according to modern Hindu law, only necessary to a certain extent, which will be discussed later in this chapter, [for more details see: Paras Diwan, Law of Marriage and Divorce, 5th Edition, 2008, p. 14, 21, 22.]

In certain societies or sections of societies, marriage can be subject to imperative of a higher order than the spouses' individual wishes, for example the wishes of the spouses' families or prohibitions on marriage that are imposed for social reasons. In India, caste and "gotra" (a term denoting all persons who trace descent in an unbroken male line from a common male ancestor) can be the reason for forcing (or violently prohibiting) marriages. More to this problem which is specific to India will be covered in this chapter.

**Forced marriage** is a term used to describe a marriage in which one or both of the parties are married without consent or against his or her will. It is important to distinguish between a forced and an arranged marriage: in an arranged marriage, both parties consent to the assistance of their parents or a third party (such as a matchmaker) in choosing the spouse. Forced marriages are generally made because of family pride, the wishes of the parents, or social obligation. The practice of forced marriage was common amongst the upper classes in Europe until the 1900s, and is still practiced in parts of South Asia, East Asia, the Middle East, and Africa. In Western Europe and North America, forced marriages now are generally committed within the migrant communities from the above-mentioned areas of the world. In forced marriages, it is generally perceived that it is more often the female (rather than the male) who is the involuntary, not consenting spouse, [see, http://en.wikipedia.org/wiki/Forced_marriage].

## II. Definition of "forced marriages"

### *1. Definition*

A forced marriage is a marriage that is performed under duress and without the full and informed consent or free will of both parties. Being under duress includes feeling both physical and emotional pressure. Some victims of forced marriage are tricked by their families into travelling to another country where the marriage takes place. Victims fall prey to forced marriage through deception, abduction, coercion, fear, and inducements. A forced marriage may be between children, a child and an adult, or between adults. Forced marriages are not limited to women and girls, as boys and men are also forced to marry against their will. A forced marriage is considered to be domestic violence. Victims of forced marriages often experience physical violence, rape, abduction, torture, false imprisonment and enslavement, sexual abuse, mental and emotional abuse even murder, [For more details see the website of the organization Child Rights Information Network (CRIN), http://www.crin.org/email/criminal_detail.asp?crinmailID=2280].

***2. The problem in defining the term "forced marriage"***

The term "forced marriage" can be used to cover various different concepts, like arranged marriage, marriage for reasons of customs, child marriage, early marriage, marriage of convenience, marriage to acquire nationality, bogus or sham marriage, undesirable marriage. In all of those marriages the consent to marriage is the crucial issue. The marriages listed above have their own particular characteristics and a certain overlapping of those characteristics takes place as long as the marriage has not been solemnised. Due to this a certain difficulty arises in defining precisely what constitutes a "forced marriage".

The term "forced marriage" is defined differently in different countries. Not all nations, cultures or individuals share a common conception of marriage or regard it as the same institution in terms of its content or form. In some cultures, consent to marriage is not regarded to be essential. "Consent" is both a mental process, a psychological or internal commitment to going ahead with the marriage, and the external expression of that, in a form required by law. So to constitute consent, both internal and external element have to be there. In cases other than those where there is actual physical proof that a person's freedom of consent has been denied by physical force or violence, it is not always easy to determine the relationship between the individual's inner intent and the psychological phenomena associated with the explicit content of the marriage contract. The intent expressed when a marriage is concluded depends on all the circumstances in which it is expressed. Feelings of fear and subordination can rule out all thoughts of resistance – under such circumstances there cannot be any genuine consent to a marriage. However, it is very difficult to prove emotional threats that may have prevented individuals from opposing a marriage which is against their will, [see, Edwige Rude-Antoine, Forced marriages in Council of Europe member states, A comparative study of legislation and political initiatives, Strasbourg 2005, p. 7, retrieved from http://www.coe.int/t/dghl/standardsetting/equality/03themes/violence-against-women/CDEG(2005)1_en.pdf]

**III. International Prevalence of Forced Marriages**

Forced and early marriages mainly affect young women and girls, although there are cases of young men and boys being forced to marry. Reliable statistics on forced marriages are difficult to compile due to the unofficial and, therefore, undocumented nature of most forced marriages. According to the 2007 report by Sigma Huda, victims' resistance to speaking out against their typically "closed" families or communities poses another obstacle to collecting reliable data. The lack of a birth certificate leads to an impossibility for the concerned to prove that they are a victim of early marriage, [see, Sigma Huda, Report of the Special Rapporteur on the Human Rights Aspects of the Victims of Trafficking in Persons, Especially Women and Children, http://daccess-dds-ny.un.org/doc/UNDOC/GEN/G07/104/10/PDF/G0710410.pdf?OpenElement]

While forced and early marriages as well as early motherhood are becoming increasingly less common among the wealthiest sectors of society in all regions of the world, they persist in Africa and South Asia, as well as certain areas of the Former Soviet Union. In 2003, the International Centre for Research on Women estimated that more than 51 million girls under 18 years were married and they expected the figure to rise to over 100 million within the next ten years. Similarly, in 2006, experts estimated that thirty-eight percent of young women aged 20 to 24 in the fifty least developed countries were married before the age of 18.

In its 2005 publication "Early Marriage: A Harmful Traditional Practice," UNICEF estimates that among women aged 15 to 24, 48% were married before the age of 18 in South Asia. In Bangladesh, 27.3% of women aged 15 to 19 years old were married by the age of 15, and 65.3% of women aged 20 to 24 were married before the age of 18. UNICEF estimates that in Africa 42% of women aged 15 to 24 were married before the age of 18. In Niger, 27.3% of women aged 15 to19 were married before the age of 15, and 76.6% of women aged 20 to 24 were married before the age of 18. According to surveys conducted by the National Committee on Traditional Practices of Ethiopia (NCTPE), the prevalence of marriage by abduction is as high as 92 per cent in Southern Nations Nationalities and Peoples Region (SNNPR), with a national average of 69%, [UNICEF Annual Report 2005, Early Marriage – A Harmful Traditional Practice, retrieved from http://www.unicef.org/publications/files/Early_Marriage_12.lo.pdf].

In the region of Kyrgyzstan, Kazakhstan, Turkmenistan, Uzbekistan, Azerbaijan, Georgia, Tajikistan, and Albania, the practice of bride kidnapping or bride abduction is the most common form of forced marriage. In the 18th and 19th centuries, bride abduction was used by consenting couples who could not otherwise marry due to financial difficulties or social constraints. Today, most bride abductions occur in spite of a girl or young woman's protestations and often involve men's families, who sometimes instigate and conspire in the abduction. In Kyrgyzstan, "bride-kidnapping" is on the rise: The organisation Human Rights Watch found that approximately 40% of women in cities had been victims of bride kidnapping while 60 to 80% of village women had been victims, [see, http://www.stopvaw.org/Forced_and_Early_Marriage.html].

Also in countries such as Afghanistan, Pakistan and India, various kinds of forced marriages are prevailing in society, sidelining the basic principles of humanity and one's freedom to choose a partner and a life of dignity.

## IV. Types of Forced Marriages

### *1. Shotgun Marriage*

A shotgun marriage is a marriage that is forced upon the participants usually because the bride is pregnant. Such a wedding has the aim to protect the family of the bride from embarrassment due to her pregnancy, [see, http://marriage.about.com/od/arrangedmarriages/g/shotgun.htm]. The pregnant woman's father, almost by accepted custom, resorts to coercion (such as threatening the would-be-groom with a shotgun) to ensure that the man who had sexual intercourse with his daughter marries her also.

The purposes of shotgun weddings are: to ensure that the woman has enough material means of support and that the child is raised by both parents as well as to make the male responsible for his act of impregnation of the female. A major objective is the restoring of social honour to the mother and her family. The practice of shotgun marriages also prevents the birth of illegitimate children and conceals the fact that the conception took place before marriage, [see, http://en.wikipedia.org/wiki/Shotgun_wedding#Shotgun_wedding].

Shotgun weddings have become uncommon in Western countries as out-of-wedlock births have become socially acceptable and the number of such births has increased, mainly in the context of stable live-in relationships. Moreover, the modern methods of birth control and abortion as well as the availability of material support to unmarried mothers such as State welfare schemes has also reduced the perceived need for such measures, [see, http://en.wikipedia.org/wiki/Forced_marriage]. Yet in developing countries and traditional societies which do not accept illegitimate children, such kind of forced marriages still exist.

In India, a special kind of shotgun weddings occurs with a high frequency in the poor State of Bihar. The practice of men abducted by prospective in-laws for purpose of marriage has grown to be an established custom in parts of the State. As per a comprehensive report in the magazine India Today, edition of 5 April 2010, Bihar's shotgun weddings consist of the forcible abduction of young boys by the families of young girls for the purpose of a forced child marriage. It is thus boys and young men who are abducted by the prospective in-laws for marriage to their daughters. This is an established custom in some regions of Bihar known as "Pakaraua Vivah" ("capture and marry off"), [see, Amitabh Srivastava, Bihar's Shotgun Weddings, India Today, 5th April 2010, page 68].

The reason for the Bihari type of shotgun weddings is the difficulty which daughter's parents face when trying to marry off their daughter. In India, the still very much prevailing social evil of dowry (high sums of money or properties, asked for by the boy's family from the girl's family in order to marry off their son to that girl) plays a major role in the development of this practice. It is the bride's family who has to carry the financial burden of arranging the marriage and paying the dowry. For parents of boys, marriages have become a money-minting enterprise; girl's parents are being ruined by the marriages. No wonder many families have adopted such desperate measures as abducting a possible bridegroom at an early age and forcing him into marriage, knowing well that they cannot arrange the necessary dowry for their daughter's marriage. Snatching a young boy is the easiest method to marry off one's daughter to a valuable bridegroom without having to afford the dowry, [see, Amitabh Srivastava, Bihar's Shotgun Weddings, India Today, 5th April 2010, page 69].

After capturing the bridegroom, a traditional Hindu marriage ceremony in the temple is performed. The ceremony is videotaped and the priest, fully cooperating with the girl's family, issues a marriage certificate. The marriage is widely accepted and supported among the other villagers. Interestingly enough, the Bihar practice of shotgun marriages often does not lead to annulments of marriage due to lack of consent or the like. As soon as the sacred marriage ceremony has been solemnised, the boy's parents eventually agree to the marriage, accepting a much lower dowry as they would have without the marriage yet being performed. This must be seen in the context of marriage being regarded as a sacrament in Hindu religion and culture, and not a contract. Therefore, the marriage ceremony is to be respected. There seems to be a high degree of reconciliation between the two involved families which is being reached at by the assistance of the village elders, [see, Amitabh Srivastava, Bihar's Shotgun Weddings, India Today, 5th April 2010, page 69].

In certain Bihari villages, up to 90% of marriages have been solemnised by kidnapping a bridegroom. In spite of the social acceptance of this custom, the number of First Information Reports (FIRs) launched due to kidnapping for marriage in the state of Bihar shows that people have started to fight against this kind of forced marriage, [see, Amitabh Srivastava, Bihar's Shotgun Weddings, India Today, 5th April 2010, page 70].

**2. *Compensation Marriage***

This ancient custom, prevalent in Pakistan's Northwest Frontier Province, Afghanistan, and parts of the Middle East, refers to the practice of forcing girl children into arranged marriages as compensation for a murder perpetrated by her family, to offset debts, or to settle other inter-clan or family disputes.

In Pakistan this practice is called *Swara,* in other regions it is known as *Vanni.* Whatever it is called, compensation marriages are widely accepted as a way of keeping the peace between tribes and families. However, under-aged girls torn from their homes in this manner often end up systematically abused and forced into a life of virtual slavery in the homes of their "enemies". The real victim of this ancient custom is the girl who is forced to pay for the "sins" of her family. Such girl is being denied her basic human rights and even a proper marriage. Moreover, she bears the stigma of shame for the rest of her life, [see, http://www.unfpa.org/gender/docs/fact_sheets/marriage.doc].

**3. *Arranged marriages and marriages for reason of custom***

An arranged marriage is a marriage arranged by someone other than the couple getting married. Such marriages were earlier very common in royal and aristocratic families around the world. In some cultures, arranged marriage is a tradition handed down through many generations. Parents, who take their son or daughter's marriage into their own hands, have themselves been married by the same process.

An arranged marriage does not necessarily mean "forced marriage". An arranged marriage depends on an "arrangement", *i.e.* negotiation and conciliation between families and in-laws and between parents and children. All parties concerned need to reach a common understanding and an agreement. In this type of marriage the "fiancés" are involved in the procedure and prepared over a long period for the idea of the wedding. In some cases they are also entitled to a say in the discussions. An arranged marriage is not, by definition, negative as the couple is given the chance to make up their own mind. However, a forced marriage is one in which the young people involved have nothing to say. All decisions are taken by the parents and the family and the young people are forced to enter the matrimonial bond. These two forms of marriage can overlap and boundaries between the two forms may blur, [see, Edwige Rude-Antoine, op. cit., page 18].

In India, the tradition of arranged marriages is still prevailing in most layers of society, whether educated or not. Since this is Indian tradition, the spouse to be married agrees to the intervention of the family members in making the match as well as to the match itself. Studies in India show that culture, tradition, caste and community are still the crucial factors in the institution of marriage and in families. Love and other emotions have very little to do with marriage. A study conducted in India, involving 3850 literate young people aged between 15 and 29 years, revealed that 51% of them would prefer to have their marriage arranged. Clearly attitudes are changing, however, 41.8% said they would prefer to marry for love, [see, Sex Education, Counselling, Research, Training and Therapy Department of the Family Planning Association of India (SECRT), "Attitudes and Perceptions of Educated, Urban Youth to Marriage and Sex", report of a survey conducted by the Family Planning Association of India (FPAI), 1990, page 33.; as quoted by Edwige op. cit., page 18].

***4. Bogus Marriage, Sham Marriage, Marriage of Convenience, Putative Marriage, Marriage to acquire Nationality and Undesirable Marriage: absence of marital intent***

The terms "bogus marriage", "sham marriage" and "marriage of convenience" describe forced marriages in specific legal contexts. Object and purpose of such marriages is primarily to circumvent the immigration rules that various countries apply to foreign nationals. The primary intention involved is not to find a family but rather, in most cases, to use the marriage as a means of obtaining a residence permit or nationality.

In the Resolution of the Council of the European Union of December 1997, however, they are defined as marriages of convenience, i.e. "marriage concluded between a national of a Member State or a third-country national legally resident in a member state or a third-country national, with the sole aim of circumventing the rules on entry and residence of third-country nationals and obtaining for the third-country national a residence permit or authority to reside in a Member State". This complex formulation constitutes a realistic response to the types of union described, in which there is no intent to create a lasting relationship, [see, Edwige Rude-Antoine, op. cit., page 19 f].

***5. Marriage under Constraint: violation of the will and restriction of freedom***

Forced marriage and marriage under constraint are similar concepts: "A marriage is forced where at least one of the parties does not consent to it and constraint is used." This is similar to the position taken in the 1956 United Nations Supplementary Convention on the Abolition of Slavery, which lists under practices similar to slavery "any institution or practice whereby […] a woman, without the right to refuse, is promised or given in marriage on payment of a consideration in money or in kind to her parents, guardian, family or any other person or group".

### *6. Child Marriage and Early Marriage: where lack of maturity makes consent impossible*

Under article 1 of the United Nations Convention on the Rights of the Child, which was concluded in 1989, "a child means every human being below the age of eighteen years unless, under the law applicable to the child, majority is attained earlier". Marriages of parties below the age of majority thus constitute child marriages. Although many countries have laws that prevent "child marriages" – also known as "early marriages" – by laying down rules about minimal age for marriage and marital capacity which have regard both to puberty and the procreative function of marriage and to the need for a certain degree of maturity in order to marry, in some cases there is explicit provision for minors to marry subject to parental authorization or official dispensation.

In situations where marriage can take place between partners aged under 18 years, indeed much doubt arises as to whether such young people are capable of taking an informed decision about a marriage partner and indeed about the implications of marriage. It thus matters little whether we refer to "child marriage" or "early marriage". In all such situations the marriage involves at least one partner who has not attained physical, intellectual and emotional maturity, and has therefore been unable to express full consent to marriage.

In many parts of the world, traditional, custom-based and/or religious rules and practices may also play a significant role. Marriages continue to be solemnised according to established rituals and are not necessarily registered. For example in India although a law of 1978 raised the minimum age for marriage from 18 to 21 for men and from 15 to 18 for women, [E.g. Section 4 of the Special Marriage Act, 1954] , the impact of the reform has been limited because people in rural areas have remained attached to their own traditions.

## V. Motives, causes & factors of Forced Marriages

### *1. Motives of parents*

Parents, who force their children to marry, often justify their behaviour as protecting their children, building stronger families and preserving cultural or religious traditions. Some parents come under significant pressure from their extended families to get their children married. In some instances, agreements have been made about marriage while the children were very young. Some of the key motives that have been identified are:

- family honour;
- peer group or family pressure;
- maintaining and strengthening family links;
- ensuring that the land, property and wealth of the family remains within the family;
- protecting perceived cultural ideas (which can be misguided or out of date);
- protecting religious ideals that are misguided;
- preventing "unsuitable" relationships, *e.g.* outside the ethnic, cultural, religious or caste group;

- long standing family commitments;
- controlling unwanted behaviour and sexuality (including perceived promiscuity or being gay, lesbian, bisexual or transgender);
- in case of international migrants: to form and maintain cultural identity and to strengthen their own culture in the foreign country;
- in case of international migrants: for the purpose of claims for residence and citizenship.[see,http://www.accmuk.com/?target= forced_marriage & menuitem =Campaigns & submenuitem=Forced%20Marriage].

**2. *Motives for Shotgun Weddings***

The reason for the already discussed Bihar type of shotgun weddings is the financial difficulty which in India parents face when trying to marry off their daughter. The still very much prevailing social evil of dowry (high sums of money or properties, asked for by the boy's family from the girl's family in order to marry off their son) plays a major role in the development of this practice in India. It is the bride's family who has to carry the financial burden of arranging the marriage and paying the dowry. For the boys' families, marriages bring them money whereas girls' families can hardly afford a regular marriage including a regular dowry. No wonder many families have adopted such desperate measures as abducting a possible bridegroom at an early age and forcing him into marriage, as they might not be able to arrange the necessary dowry for their daughter's marriage.

**3. *Further causes and factors for Forced Marriages***

In The United Kingdom, the working group on forced marriage found that most cases were a result of loving manipulation, whereas parents genuinely felt that they were acting in their children and family's best interests. To families living in poverty or economic instability, a daughter may be seen as an economic burden who must be married as soon as possible to take financial strain off of the family. Marriage can also be used to settle a debt, or to strengthen the family or caste status through social alliances. Fears about sexual activity before marriage, or fear of rumours about such activity ruining a daughter's opportunity to marry well, may also be a reason for an early and a forced marriage. A girl will sometimes be married off soon after her first menstruation so as to "protect" her virginity, as in many cultures the honour of a whole family depends on a girl's virginity.

It has grown more and more common to send a victim back to an immigrant family's country of origin to marry or to force the victim to sponsor a spouse from the country of origin (usually to enable the sponsored spouse to migrate to a Western country).

In some cases, forced marriages also take place for the purpose of trafficking. In societies with highly disproportionate ratio of men to women, women are trafficked for the purpose of marriage. In China, for example, where the one-child policy and a cultural preference for male children has led to a "shortage" of women (due to a widespread female foeticide) a large number of North Korean women are being trafficked into the country. In situations of armed conflict, such as in Sierra Leone, women are sometimes trafficked for the purpose of marrying soldiers, [see, http://www.stopvaw.org/Forced_and_Early_Marriage.html].

## VI. Effects & Consequences of Forced Marriages

### *1. Psychological and emotional problems*

Forced marriage is closely connected with risks of psychological, sexual and/ or domestic violence. Victims tend to be isolated from their peers and friends which places the girls or boys concerned in a vulnerable position: problems of loss of self-confidence can occur when minors are being forcibly married and sexual violence may be involved. The concerned girls (and boys) fear that their younger brothers or sisters may be made to pay if they refuse a forced marriage. Opposing the forced marriage means often deciding to break with one's own family. This is an extremely hard choice to make, [see, Edwige Rude-Antoine, op. cit., page 31].

"Those who flee from the family sometimes do so at great cost. A girl who runs away exposes herself to reproach from all her relatives because, through her desire for independence, she has diminished the family's standing in the eyes of friends and neighbours. Young girls who flee refuse to explain why they have done so and they are then accused of being selfish and immoral. If they have to stay away from their families for long periods they often lose contact with other members of their entourage, to whom they are close. Very few girls have a circle of friends outside the family. When they leave the family their school friends reject them, accusing them of lacking respect for their parents. The notion of freedom, which is often idealised, can prove illusory. The emphasis that is placed in Germany and other western societies on autonomy and individuality masks a reality of isolation and fear of weakness or failure. Independence can come at the same heavy price even for young German girls. They often find themselves in one-to-one relationships in which family patterns are recreated, and they end up making a precipitate return to the family." [for more details see, Bikim Bayam Tekeli, L'association Papatya et l'accueil des jeunes filles à Berlin, in Hommes et Migrations - Femmes contre la violence, p. 110; as quoted by Edwige Rude-Antoine, op. cit. page 31].

### *2. Health damage*

Rape and sexual or domestic violence, self-hurt or suicide often occur in the context of forced marriages. [see, http://www.accmuk.com/?target= forced_ marriage & menuitem = Campaigns & submenuitem = Forced% 20 Marriage]. Husbands in forced and early marriages are more likely than normal marriages to become violent because the relationship between the spouses is based on the power of one spouse over the other. Rape occurs frequently in forced and early marriages and has severe consequences, especially for young brides. Young women are more susceptible to sexually transmitted diseases. In general, younger women enter into marriages with partners who are significantly older and more sexually experienced. A lack of education concerning sexual transmitted diseases and social norms preventing young girls from asking questions about their partners sexual history, and a limited amount of power in their marriage make these young women more susceptible to getting infected. Sexually transmitted diseases such as HIV, Hepatitis B and others are known to be contracted more easily in defloration, [see, http://www.stopvaw.org/Forced_and_ Early_ Marriage.html].

The girls or young men involved in forced marriages often suffer psychological troubles such as insomnia, nightmares, eating disorders (typically anorexia and bulimia), behavioural difficulties (including irritability, loss of interest in school, running away and even drug addiction), and various somatic disorders (notably abdominal pain). Some get caught into severe depressions. Other health consequences that occur frequently are early pregnancy, [see, Edwige Rude-Antoine, op. cit., page 31]. Complications during childbirth are much more common among child mothers. They can result in severe disabilities, such as obstetric fistula (a tearing of the vagina) which can leave women incontinent. Maternal mortality rates are much higher among such young women.

The loss of the victim's lives by honour killings can be the ultimate consequence in those cases where a forced marriage is refused (mainly by the girl) and/or where an own boyfriend or spouse is chosen. Some families resort to "honour based violence" as the girl is considered to have dishonoured the family, and (in migrant communities) they often employ people or send male relatives to find her, bring her back to the family, sent her back to the country of origin or even kill her in the name of "honour". Ten years ago, the UNFPA estimated the annual world–wide number of honour killing victims at 5,000, [For details see article titled "The casteaways", dated 13 June 2010, published in the Chandigarh edition of The Pioneer newspaper].

### 3. *Financial and legal difficulties*

A girl or boy resisting a forced marriage is often compelled to leave the family home. If the victim wants to escape the forced marriage and the clutches of the family, an alternative accommodation and financial support is needed. In case the person married wants to resolve the matrimonial bond he or she was forced to enter into, he or she will require legal assistance and support. In many cases, identity documents such as passports have been taken away from the victims by their families. Under such circumstances, it is most difficult for the victims to defend their human rights and basic freedoms, [see, Edwige Rude-Antoine, op. cit., page 32].

The unofficial nature of many of these marriages means that they often go unregistered, leaving a woman with no legal protections in cases of separation.

### 4. *Further consequences*

Forced and early marriages have other consequences also: Victims rarely have access to social services that could assist them. Early marriages often interrupt a victim's education. This deprives them of their right to education and limits any future possibility of economic independence from their spouse, making it more difficult to escape from an unwanted marriage.

## VII. Another Dimension of the Problem: Honour Killings

### 1. *Forced Marriages and Honour Killings*

Forced marriages and honour killings are often intertwined. Marriage can be forced to save honour, and women can be murdered for rejecting a forced marriage and marrying a partner of their own choice who is (due to family status, economical status, caste etc.) not acceptable for the family of the girl. In traditional societies, honour killings are basically "justified" as a sanction for "dishonourable" behaviour.

### 2. *Origin and background of Honour Killings*

In Muslim communities, honour killings date back to the pre-Islamic era. In those times men killed their baby daughters to avoid the possibility that they might dishonour their family. The Prophet Mohammed called for this to end. However, the practice spread throughout Arab-dominated countries such as Pakistan, Afghanistan, Iran, India and Bangladesh, the West Bank of Israel and Jordan. Members of Muslim communities implement this practice also in their western immigration countries. *e.g.* members of the Turkish community in Germany or Pakistani immigrants in the UK, [see, http://en. wikipedia. org/ wiki/ Honor_ killing]. However, honour killing is not at all confined to Muslim communities: in India, where the ancient Hindu caste system – although officially abolished – still holds its strong grip on society, honour killings occur with a ghastly frequency.

Recently, award-winning Jordanian journalist Rana Husseini has drawn international attention to the struggle against honour killings in her country, Jordan, by publishing a book about her investigations about the widespread occurrence of the crime, [see, Rana Husseini, Murder in the Name of Honour, Oneworld Publications, Oxford, 2009].

### 3. *Perpetrators of Honour Killings*

Honour killings are mainly committed by fathers and brothers, whereas females in the family (mothers, mothers-in-law, sisters, and cousins) frequently support the attacks against teenage daughters and daughters in their early twenties. Wives and older-age daughters may also be victims. Death threats are often used as a means of control. The planning and execution involve multiple family members and can include mothers, sisters, brothers, male cousins, uncles, grandfathers, etc. If the girl escapes, the extended family will continue to search for her to kill her. The reason given for the honour killing is that the girl or young woman has "dishonoured" the family. At least half the time, the killings are carried out with barbaric ferocity. The female victim is often raped, burned alive, stoned or beaten to death, cut at the throat, decapitated, stabbed numerous times, suffocated slowly, etc. The murderers do not show any remorse, but instead experience themselves as "victims" who had to defend themselves from the girl's actions and to restore their lost family honour.

### 4. *Prevalence of Honour Killings in India*

In India, honour killings happen regularly in the northern States of Punjab, Haryana and western Uttar Pradesh. But, it is not just a north Indian phenomenon. Honour killings have also been reported from other parts of the country like the far flung States of Chhatisgarh, Tamil Nadu, Jharkhand and Andhra Pradesh, [see, Himanshi Dhawan, "Honour Killing not just a North Indian phenomenon", dated 6 July, 2010, The Times of India]. This happens not only within the Muslim community, but within all the major religious groups: Muslims, Sikhs and Hindus regard honour and morality as a collective family matter, [see, http://ibnlive.in.com/cfs/blog/53796/1541]. Rights are collective, not individual. Family, clan and tribal rights supplant individual human rights. Women who are killed in honour killings are targets if they refuse an arranged marriage or a forced marriage, or seek to obtain an advanced education, or seek a divorce from a violent husband or seek to marry against their parents wishes. When young people wish to get married to a person of another caste or community, their families might not only disapprove and prohibit this alliance, but in extreme cases also commit an honour killing of that person. Although this does not only concern women but men also, the problem of honour killing affects the physically weaker sex more. It is a serious violation of the right to life of those women, [see, Narender Kumar, Constitutional Law of India, 7th Edition 2008, Allahabad Law Agency, page 311].

There is no nationwide data on the prevalence of honour killings in India as the National Crime Records Bureau does not collect separate data on the crime due to it not yet being separately classified under Indian law. Indian journalist Ammu Joseph takes the figures of the India Democratic Women's Association (AIDWA) of 2007 and estimates that the annual toll in the North Indian State of Haryana (where honour killings occur most frequently) must be around 300. The total figure across the three States of Punjab, Haryana and Uttar Pradesh would be then at least 900 per year. She estimates that if another 100-300 were added for the rest of the country, the total figure for India would be about the same as estimated for Pakistan (which researchers suggest has the highest per capita incidence of honour killings in the world), [see, Ammu Joseph, No Honour in Murder, The Hindu Magazine, 23rd May 2010, page 1].

***5. Role of caste Panchayats in Honour Killings in North Indian society***

Especially in the State of Haryana, honour killings are ordered and socially sanctioned by so-called "Khap Panchayats". Regular Panchayats are democratically elected Indian village councils with certain judicial competencies. Khap Panchayats, however, are extra-constitutional bodies without legal sanction.

A "Khap" is a cluster of villages united by caste and geography. It is as old as 14th century when upper castes consolidated their power and position. A Khap Panchayat governs the "Khap" formed by same + (clan) families from several neighbouring villages. Khap Panchayats are prevalent in Haryana, western Uttar Pradesh and parts of Rajasthan, [see,http://www.azadindia.org/social-issues/khap-panchayat-in-india.html].

The word "*gotra*" means "lineage" in the Sanskrit language. A *gotra* is the lineage or clan assigned to a Hindu at birth. In most cases, the system is patrilineal and the *gotra* assigned is that of the person's father, however in some communities such as the Nairs of Kerala, the *gotra* is passed through the mother. The *gotra* system is part of a system of classification or identification of various Brahmin families in ancient times. Like caste does not change, *gotras* also do not change. In The Concise Oxford Dictionary of World Religions, it has been defined in the Indian context as the exogamous group of all persons (especially brahmans) related by descent through the male line from a common male ancestor. Exogamous is defined as a section of society within which marriages are prohibited.

The main rule is that all boys and girls within a Khap are considered siblings. Those living in a Khap are not allowed to marry in the same *gotra* or even in any *gotra* from the same village. Most victims of honour killings which are reported are young people who choose to love and marry outside their caste, sub-caste or religion or within the same *gotra*. The socially and economically dominant castes, represented by the Khap Panchayats, are responsible for those acts of reprisal, [see, Ammu Joseph, op. cit., page 5], Khap Panchayats pass orders annulling marriages, telling married couples to live like brothers and sisters and socially obstructing them (by ordering social boycott in the village against the couple and its families) in case they disobey their dictate. In some cases, they order to kill the persons disobeying them, [see, The Tribune, Chandigarh, 12 March 2010]. Their orders – which constitute social sanctions for disapproved behaviour – are mainly based on ancient Hindu customs. The Khaps mainly prohibit and sanction so-called "sagotra marriages", *i.e.* marriages within the same *gotra* (a term denoting all persons who trace descent in an unbroken male line from a common male ancestor). According to ancient Hindu law, sagotra marriage was within the ambit of prohibited relationship. Yet the Hindu Marriage Disabilities Removal Act, 1946, introduced that a marriage between Hindus which is otherwise valid shall not be invalid by reason of the fact that the parties belong to the same *gotra*. The same rule is contained in the Hindu Marriages Act, 1955. Khap Panchayats, however, do not recognise and accept the reformative direction which the State has taken over half a century back, [see, Virendra Kumar, Vicissitudes of gotra row, dated 14 March 2010, The Sunday Tribune, Chandigarh, page 13].

### 6. *The killings and problems in investigation*

Honour killings are ordered by caste Panchayats and carried out by mobs with the connivance of family members or by family members themselves. Not only women are targets and victims of honour killings, but more often except in inter-caste or inter-community love marriages, the male involved will also be killed. According to a study commissioned by the National Commission for Women, reveals that 72% of the 326 cases surveyed were in fact inter-caste marriages while same *gotra* marriages were only 3%. Marriages within the caste were 15% while only 1% were inter-religious marriages, [see, "Honour Killings not just a north Indian phenomenon," dated 6 July, 2010, The Times of India, New Delhi].

The usual remedy to such murders is to suggest that society must be prevailed upon to be more gender-sensitive and shed prejudices of caste and class. Efforts should be made to sensitise people on the need to do away with social biases. But equally, it should be made clear that there is no escape for those who take justice into their own hands. So far, there is no specific law to deal with honour killings. The murders come under the general categories of homicide, murder or manslaughter. When a mob has carried out such attacks, it becomes difficult to pinpoint a culprit. The collection of evidence becomes tricky and eyewitnesses are never forthcoming.

It is no secret that the caste-based, extra-legal bodies that are Khap Panchayats enjoy at least tacit support from a number of political leaders, civil servants, police officers, lawyers and even Judges, [see, Ammu Joseph, op. cit., page 5]. This makes the punishments of the abettors difficult and nearly impossible.

### *7. Recent developments in North India*

In March 2010, a landmark judgment was passed by the District and Sessions Judge at Karnal, Haryana, regarding the honour killing of a young couple, Manoj and Babli Banwala, a young couple belonging to the same caste and *gotra* who had eloped with each other to marry against the will of the girl's family. The heinous murder had taken place after the local Khap Panchayat had ruled against the couple's marriage. The Judge awarded death sentence to five out of six persons involved in the brutal murder of the couple. All five were close relatives of the girl (one brother, two cousins and two uncles). The judgment is considered to be a landmark one not only due to the capital punishment awarded to five of the culprits but also due to the leader of the Khap Panchayat being sentenced to life imprisonment for abetting the murder.

Recently, the Chief Justice of the Punjab & Haryana High Court issued directions to the Deputy Commissioners and the Superintendents of Police for them to monitor the working and conduct of Khap Panchayats, [see, Indian Express, 4 April, 2010].

The Ministries of Home Affairs and Law and Justice are preparing to amend the Indian Penal Code (IPC) to define the act of "honour killing". The demand for such a law was made repeatedly with the objective of stamping out this social evil. The aim is to provide for deterrent punishment for caste and community panchayats which should be booked for aiding and abetting such killings and as accomplices to the murder, [see, Nitin Mahajan, IPC will define honour killing, Asian Age, 14 January 2010].

The Central Government has indicated that it would bring in a new law that will make the punishment for honour killings, extremely stringent. The new law is likely to target Khap Panchayats, irrespective of whether they have actually approved of the killing. Further, the Government has suggested that unlike ordinary criminal law, which requires the prosecution to establish guilt, the new law will reverse the onus of proof, leaving those accused to prove their innocence, [see, Editorial titled, "Of marriage and murder", dated 26 June 2010, The Hindu].

### *8. Recent Landmark Judgment by the Hon'ble Supreme Court of India Condemning the Barbaric and Feudal Practice of Honour Killings Directing the Subordinate Courts Countrywide to Award Death Sentence to the Accused Perpetrating Such Offences*

In a recent judgment by the Hon'ble Supreme Court of India in the case of *Bhagwan Dass* v. *State (NCT) of Delhi,* JT 2011 (6) SC 345, the question of punishment for "honour killings" was the key issue in the case before the Hon'ble Apex Court. This was yet another case of gruesome honour killing, this time by the accused-appellant of his daughter.

In the present case, the appellant was very annoyed with his daughter, who had left her husband Raju and was living in an incestuous relationship with her uncle, Sriniwas. This infuriated the appellant as he thought this conduct of his daughter Seema, had dishonoured his family, and hence he strangulated her with an electric wire. The trial Court convicted the appellant and this judgment of the trial Court was upheld by the High Court. Ultimately, both these judgments were also upheld by the Supreme Court of India.

The facts and circumstances of the case are best described in paras 5 and 6 (at pages 346 and 347) of the judgment, as also reproduced hereunder:

> "5. This is a case of circumstantial evidence, but it is settled law that a person can be convicted on circumstantial evidence provided the links in the chain of circumstances connects the accused with the crime beyond reasonable doubt vide *Vijay Kumar Arora* v. *State (NCT of Delhi)*, (2010) 2 SCC 353 (para 16.5), *Aftab Ahmad Ansari* v. *State of Uttaranchal*, (2010) 2 SCC 583 (vide paragraphs 13 and 14), etc. In this case, we are satisfied that the prosecution has been able to prove its case beyond reasonable doubt by establishing all the links in the chain of circumstances.
>
> 6. In cases of circumstantial evidence motive is very important, unlike cases of direct evidence where it is not so important vide *Wakkar* v. *State of Uttar Pradesh*, (2011) 3 SCC 306 (para 14). In the present case, the prosecution case was that the motive of the appellant in murdering his daughter was that she was living in adultery with one Sriniwas, who was the son of the maternal aunt of the appellant. The appellant felt humiliated by this, and to avenge the family honour he murdered his own daughter."

Hence, it is manifest as also categorically noticed by the Hon'ble Apex Court that it was a clear cut case of a honour killing.

Para 8(i) (at page 347) of the said judgment while also taking into account the recent judgments of the Supreme Court of India itself, strongly deprecates the practice of honour killings in the following categoric terms:

> "8. The circumstances which connect the accused to the crime are:
>
> (i) The motive of the crime which has already been mentioned above. In our country unfortunately 'honour killing' has become common place, as has been referred to in our judgment in *Arumugam Servai* v. *State of Tamil Nadu* Criminal Appeal No.958 of 2011 (@SLP(Crl) No.8084 of 2009) pronounced on 19-4-2011.
>
> Many people feel that they are dishonoured by the behaviour of the young man/woman, who is related to them or belonging to their caste because he/she is marrying against their wish or having an affair with someone, and hence they take the law into their own hands and kill or physically assault such person or commit some other atrocities on them. We have held in *Lata Singh* v. *State of U.P.*, (2006) 5 SCC 475, that this is wholly illegal. If someone is not happy with the behaviour of his daughter or other person, who is his relation or of his caste, the maximum he can do is to cut off social relations with her/him, but he cannot take the law into his own hands by committing violence or giving threats of violence."

Further, the complete factual circumstances of this horrendous crime have been set out in detail in the remaining sub-paragraphs of para 8 (at pages 347 and 348) of the said judgment, which ultimately led to sustaining of the conviction of the accused-appellant father who was unfortunately guilty of killing his own daughter.

That (at pages 350 and 351) of the said judgment, the Hon'ble Apex Court has highlighted the fact that independent witnesses in such situations are not forthcoming by noticing and reiterating earlier judgments of the Supreme Court of India as follows:

> "It has been contended by the learned counsel for the appellant that there was no independent witness in the case. However, as held by this Court in *State of Rajasthan* v. *Teja Ram,* AIR 1999 SC 1776:
>
> > "The over-insistence on witnesses having no relation with the victims often results in criminal justice going awry. When any incident happens in a dwelling house, the most natural witnesses would be the inmates of that house. It is unpragmatic to ignore such natural witnesses and insist on outsiders who would not have even seen anything. If the court has discerned from the evidence or even from the investigation records that some other independent person has witnessed any event connecting the incident in question, then there is a justification for making adverse comments against non-examination of such a person as a prosecution witness. Otherwise, merely on surmises the court should not castigate the prosecution for not examining other persons of the locality as prosecution witnesses. The prosecution can be expected to examine only those who have witnessed the events and not those who have not seen it though the neighbourhood may be replete with other residents also."

Similarly, in *Trimukh Maroti Kirkan* v. *State of Maharashtra,* 2006 (1) SCC 681 this Court observed:

> "These crimes are generally committed in complete secrecy inside the house and it becomes very difficult for the prosecution to lead evidence. No member of the family, even if he is a witness of the crime, would come forward to depose against another family member. The neighbours, whose evidence may be of some assistance, are generally reluctant to depose in court as they want to keep aloof and do not want to antagonize a neighbourhood family. The parents or other family members of the bride being away from the scene of commission of crime are not in a position to give direct evidence which may inculpate the real accused except regarding the demand of money or dowry and harassment caused to the bride. But, it does not mean that a crime committed in secrecy or inside the house should go unpunished." (emphasis supplied)"

The Apex Court in the penultimate part of the judgment strongly and very critically, rightly so deprecated the merciless practice of barbaric honour killings, (at page 351) of the said judgment in the following stern directions:

> "In our opinion both the trial court and High Court have given very cogent reasons for convicting the appellant, and we see no reason to disagree with their verdicts. There is overwhelming circumstantial evidence to show that the accused committed the crime as he felt that he was dishonoured by his daughter.
>
> For the reason given above we find no force in this appeal and it is dismissed.
>
> Before parting with this case we would like to state that 'honour' killings have become commonplace in many parts of the country, particularly in

Haryana, western U.P., and Rajasthan. Often young couples who fall in love have to seek shelter in the police lines or protection homes, to avoid the wrath of kangaroo courts. We have held in *Lata Singh's* case (supra) that there is nothing 'honourable' in 'honour' killings, and they are nothing but barbaric and brutal murders by bigoted, persons with feudal minds.

In our opinion honour killings, for whatever reason, come within the category of rarest of rare cases deserving death punishment. It is time to stamp out these barbaric, feudal practices which are a slur on our nation. This is necessary as a deterrent for such outrageous, uncivilized behaviour. All persons who are planning to perpetrate 'honour' killings should know that the gallows await them.

Let a copy of this judgment be sent to the Registrar Generals/Registrars of all the High Courts who shall circulate the same to all Judges of the Courts. The Registrar General/Registrars of the High Courts will also circulate copies of the same to all the Sessions Judges/Additional Sessions Judges in the State/Union Territories. Copies of the judgment shall also be sent to all the Chief Secretaries/Home Secretaries/Director Generals of Police of all States/Union Territories in the country. The Home Secretaries and Director Generals of Police will circulate the same to all S.S.Ps/S.Ps in the States/Union Territories for information."

Clearly, the judgment aims to send out a clear stern message to the society at large, and of course in no uncertain terms. This now leads us to the next question, as to why there is a need for a separate exclusive legislation within the Indian criminal legal system to combat the menace of honour killings, which are increasing in number day by day. This question was put forward to us at the forced marriages session by Justice Peter Singer of the Family Law Division of the Royal Courts of Justice, High Court of London, as then he was at the London Metropolitan University Conference on" International Child Abduction, Relocation and Forced Marriages," held from 30 June, 2010 – 2 July, 2010. The answer to this question is precisely summed-up by Mr. Soli Sorabjee, our distinguished former Attorney General of India, in his fortnightly column "'Honour' killing?" dated, 12 September, 2010, in The Sunday Indian Express, where he advances the following precise reasoning:

"The fact that 'honour killing' is a crime punishable under one or more provisions of the IPC is not a valid argument against the enactment of a special law to extirpate this practice as in the case of sati. We need a specific law criminalising this evil practice, providing stiff penalties and also making the offence non-bailable. States must act firmly and promptly ignoring electoral and political considerations."

## VIII. Case Law on Forced Marriages and Honour Killings

### 1. *Moniram Hzarika v. State of Assam,* 2004 Cri LJ 2553

*Facts of the case*

Paresh Sailkia lodged a complaint in Bebrapara police out-post alleging that his younger sister Bibi Saikia had been kidnapped by the appellant herein who was also a resident of the same village. His sister was a student of 8th standard and a minor. He had been informed that she had been seen in the company of the appellant after the kidnapping. Paresh had gone to the house of the appellant where he was not allowed to enter the house by the appellant and his brother. However, he had noticed there that arrangements were made for performing the marriage ceremony between the appellant and Bibi Saikia.

*Judgment*

The appellant was held guilty of kidnapping a minor from legal guardianship, section 361 of Indian Penal Code, IPC, 1860. It was held that unlawfully taking away or taking away by incitement a minor from the lawful custody of his or her parent or guardian without parent's or guardian consent; amounts to kidnapping within the meaning of this section as and when read with section 366 of IPC.

**2. *Madho Singh* v. *State of Rajasthan,* 1997 Cri LJ 2641**

Sections 5, 6 and 8 of Child Marriage Restraint Act, 1929 and section 29(1) of Criminal Procedure Code, 1898 – Order of committal passed by Judicial Magistrate challenged – jurisdiction of Court of Sessions to try offences under consideration – in view of sections 8 and 29(1), the Court of Session had no jurisdiction to try offences under sections 5 and 6 of Act – power to take cognizance of and jurisdiction to try such offences by any other Court being excluded by clear prohibition in provisions of section 8 – Judicial Magistrate has jurisdiction to try offences under section 5 and 6.

*Facts of the Case:*

Kumari Nain Kanwar, daughter of Loon Singh was living with her maternal grandmother. She was kidnapped at night from her residence. The girl was aged about 16 years. Thanks to a rigorous search it was found that the girl was kidnapped by the neighbour Madho Singh with the intent to get married with her.

**3. *The State of Gujarat* v. *Fulsinh Bimsinh,* AIR 1971 Guj 1**

***Facts of the Case***

In this case 8 people were involved in the kidnapping of a minor girl below 16 years. Two of them kidnapped a girl Bai Vada, daughter of Bhikhsingh Kalusingh with the intent to compel her to marry against her will or to force or seduce her to illicit intercourse. The other accused abetted the commission of the said offence. One of the accused married Bai Vada.

*Judgment*

The boy marrying the girl below 16 years committed an offence punishable under section 5 of the Child Marriage Restraint Act, 1929. The other accused failed to prevent the said marriage being performed and thereby committed an offence punishable under section 6 of the Child Marriage Restraint Act, 1929 (abetment). All the offenders involved in the kidnapping were held guilty under section 366 read with section 34 of the IPC (joint liability).

**4. *Sujit Kumar* v. *State of Uttar Pradesh,* AIR 2002 NOC 265**

In this case, the Allahabad High Court took serious note of honour killing, harassment and ill-treatment in the context of socially not approved marriages and directed the police to take strong measures against those who committed such offences.

**5. *Dilip Remnarayan Tiwari* v. *State of Maharashtra*, 2010 (1) SCC 796**

*Facts of the Case*

College girl Sushma fell in love with Prabhu who lived in her neighbourhood. For about 5-6 years, a secret love affair went on between the two. Sushma's family disapproved of the relationship from the start as Prabhu was a Keralite belonging to the Ezhava caste whereas Sushma was a Brahmin hailing from Uttar Pradesh. Sushma's elder brother Dilip as well as her mother threatened the girl during the love affair various times. At some point Dilip even assaulted his sister with kicks and fist-blows on account of her love affair with Prabhu and threatened that if she married this man, both would be eliminated. Ultimately, on 29 October, 2003 Sushma got married to Prabhu and moved to his family. Her brother Dilip or other family members many times tried to convince her to come back, which the young woman refused. Seven months after the marriage she was pregnant and it was obvious that she would not join her parental home anymore. In the night of 16 May, 2004 to 17 May, 2004, Dilip along with his three friends knocked on the back side of Prabhu's home at 1.15 am and upon Prabhu's father opening the door, they entered with knifes in their hands, assaulted him and stabbed him to death. Upon intervention of them they also stabbed Prabhu's cousin, his neighbour and Prabhu himself to death.

*Judgment*

The matter before the Supreme Court mostly turned around the question whether the capital punishment could be awarded to the three accused for the honour killing. The Supreme Court while considering the mitigating circumstances of the accused number 1, Dilip, went into the background of the honour killing and the mindset of the accused. The Court considered that the accused must have been prey of the so-called insult on the family honour which his younger sister had imposed on his family. It is a common experience that when the younger sister commits something not approved by her family (in this case an inter-caste and inter-community marriage), then in society it is the elder brother justifiably and morally held responsible for not having stopped such an affair. The issue becomes a family defeat (page 795, para 62). Family members such as Dilip, are subject to constant spite of the society. In inter-caste marriage cases, the fact of the so-called higher status of a Brahmin family over the non-Brahmin status of the rejected groom aggravates the situation. The Supreme Court held that the killer had become victim of his wrong but genuine caste considerations which did – in this case – not justify the award of the death sentence for his participation in murder. "The murders were the outcome of social issue, *i.e.* a marriage of a high caste girl with a person hailing from a lower caste. ... Caste is a concept which grips a person before his birth and does not leave him even after his death. The vicious grip of the caste, community, religion, though totally unjustified, is a stark reality. The psyche of the offender in the background of a social issue like an inter-caste/ community marriage, though wholly unjustified, would have to be considered in the peculiar circumstances of this case." (page 796, para 64).

**IX. Media Reports on Forced Marriages/Honour Killings**

The importance of the subject in the present day and age is reflected from the large number of press reports all over India. Some of the prominent instances published in the print and electronic media, find discussions hereunder.

**1.** ***Child marriage rampant in Bengal*** **(Indianexpress.com, Kolkata, Tuesday, 10 March 2009)**

Mariam, a resident of Deganga in North 24 Parganas, was married by her parents at the age of 13 years. Her husband later brought her to Kolkata and she was forced into prostitution. Mariam's case does not stand alone. The State of Bengal witnesses many instances of child marriages.

**2.** ***Fight against child marriages in India,*** **[http://www.merinews.com/article/fight-against-child-marriages-in-india/154850.shtml]**

A widow and mother of six children married her 12-year-old daughter to a 35-year-old man in Channa Bakhar village of Jodhpur. The marriage took place clandestinely in the village last weekend in the presence of a few relatives and was kept hidden from other villagers. But when the news leaked, the village Panchayat and Sen Samaj declared the marriage illegal. The villagers worked together to save the girl. Balika Vadhu has purportedly gone into hiding even as her husband Gajendra Sen and his parents were running away.

**3.** ***Wife pays the price for forced marriage*** **(The Hindu Online edition of India's National Newspaper, Saturday, 15 November 2008, ePaper)**

In Bangalore: Software engineer S. Manoj Kumar was forced by his family into an arranged marriage although he was involved with someone else. Three months into the marriage, his bride, Lakshmi, also a software engineer, had to pay the ultimate price. She was beaten to death. And the suspected murderer: her husband. The two were working in the same company.

*Facts of the case*

On Thursday, the HAL Airport police took Manoj Kumar into custody as they found inconsistencies in his version of events. The police said he broke down during interrogation and confessed to the murder. On November 7, Kumar, a resident of Vinayak Nagar near HAL Airport, lodged a complaint with the police that when he came home from work he found his wife Lakshmi murdered and that jewellery estimated at Rs. 30,000 was missing. The police initially suspected murder for gain. During routine questioning of Kumar's colleagues, the police came upon leading facts. Kumar had apparently reached office at 9 a.m. that morning, gone home in the afternoon and not returned to work. "We found this suspicious," city Police Commissioner Shankar M. Bidari told presspersons here.

**4.** ***Forced child marriage in Bihar*** **(AndhraNews.net, Gaya, Bihar, 5 May 2009)**

Personnel of Bihar Police arrested a few persons involved in the kidnapping of a young boy and conducting his marriage with a girl child by force in Gaya district.

*Facts of the case*

A 15-year-old boy named Lal Babu was kidnapped on Sunday for the wedding, which was solemnised under compulsion and at gunpoint. A student of 10th standard, Lal Babu was rounded-up when he came out of his coaching centre and soon a crowd gathered at the spot. Reportedly, the kidnappers opened fire to scare away the crowd. Although the police nabbed Babu, they could not foil the child marriage that was conducted earlier. However, after instant investigations, the child bride was also arrested. It was also confirmed by the police officials that both girl and boy were below the legal age of marriage, 18 and 21 years respectively. Police arrested the girl child's mother along with a few others, who according to primary investigations were involved in the kidnapping.

**5. *Another child marriage solemnized in Bihar* (Samay, Bihar, 6 June, 2009)**

A 13-year-old boy was kidnapped for wedding, which was solemnized under compulsion. The boy was thrashed badly by the people of bride's side for opposing to marry, said sources. He was allegedly abducted and was forced to marry an 8 year old girl.

**6. *Woman files case against parents, husband for forced marriage* (Sulekha.com Newshopper, Patna, Bihar, 5 October, 2009)**

Shabnam Kumari, in her 20s, filed the case early this week in the Court of Chief Judicial Magistrate in Begusarai district, about 125 km from here. Shabnam, a resident of Bashi village in Begusarai, said in her complaint that she was married to Sagar Ram of Suro village this July against her wish. She alleged that her parents married her off after taking money from her husband. After marriage, her husband pressured her to have sex with another man, Shabnam alleged, adding that she was assaulted and humiliated by Sagar Ram when she refused. She informed her parents but they did not help. She then left her husband's house and shifted to the house of a relative, who is also a friend. After she fled from her husband's house, her parents lodged a case of kidnapping against two men - Gagan Kumar and Santosh Ram. Both surrendered in Court and were sent to jail last month. Shabnam said in Court that she was not kidnapped by the two. She also refused to live with her husband or parents and requested the Court to allow her to live with her relative.

**7. *Landmark case on forced marriage: mother jailed* (The Centre for Social Cohesion, May 2009)**

A mother has been sentenced, in what has been called a 'landmark case' in the UK, for three years for forcing her two teenage daughters to marry their first cousins in Pakistan in July 2007. The mother duped the children, aged 14 and 15, into thinking they were visiting Pakistan on a holiday. However, when they arrived they discovered that their marriage preparations were underway for a joint ceremony. Returning to the UK in September 2007, the girls confided in their teachers in February 2008 who immediately informed the police. The 39 year old mother was arrested. The mother was charged and convicted for inciting or causing a child to engage in sexual activity, arranging or facilitating the commission of a child sex offence, and intending to pervert the course of justice. She pleaded not guilty.

**8. *A Judgment by the Calcutta High Court* (21 December 2009)**

Shubhendu Ray, a resident of Bakultala in West Bengal is a businessman and a local leader of a political party. His daughter Anita is a 15-year-old girl. Shahidul, a local Muslim boy seduced Anita and forcefully abducted her on 14 October, 2009. Later on, she was forcefully converted to Islam and on the next day Shahidul married her. On 20 October, 2009 Shubhendu Ray, with the help of the police, went to Shahidul's house and recovered his daughter Anita. A case was moved against Shahidul and then onwards he was absconding.

Meanwhile, Shahidul filed an anticipatory bail petition to the Court at Barhamour but the petition was rejected. Then Shahidul moved his petition to the Calcutta High Court and a Division Bench, comprising of Justice Pinaki Ghosh and Justice Shailendra Prasad Talukdar (both of them are Hindus), granted the anticipatory bail to Shahidul, on 16 December. While delivering their verdict, the Judges said that, though marriage of a girl below 18 is unlawful according to Hindu Marriage Act, it is not applicable in the present case. Since Anita was converted to Islam prior to her marriage, the case falls under the purview of the Muslim Marriage Act and as the Muslim Marriage Act permits one to marry a 15 year-old girl, hence Shahidul has done no offence.

The question therefore arises – Is conversion of a minor girl of 15 valid in law? If not, then the conversion of minor girl Anita stands null and void in the Court of law. So treating her marriage according to Muslim Marriage Act does not arise. Furthermore, eloping with a minor girl of 15 without the consent of her parents is a clear case of kidnapping, which is a highly criminal offence and how the honourable Judges have overlooked this crime on the part of Shahidul before granting him the said anticipatory bail. Such carelessness and callousness of the honourable Judges of a High Court is unpardonable.

***9. UK official rescues Punjabi girl from forced marriage* (Indianexpress.com 6 January 2005, Nawanshahr)**

A UK-based Punjabi couple's attempt to marry off their daughter, a British national, against her wishes in Nawanshahr, Punjab, has been thwarted by the British High Commission in India.

Lesley Beaton, director, Consular Services was in town today to assist the 21-year-old woman from Northern England, whose parents had taken away her passport, ticket and money to force her to marry a man of their choice in India.

The victim, working in North England, came to Nawanshahr four months ago, where her parents introduced her to a few Punjabi men for matrimonial purpose. The woman, who was raised in the UK, wanted to go back and continue studies. She felt she was too young to marry.

***10. High Court orders security for couple* (The Tribune, 20 February, 2010)**

Reena, a resident of Narwana, seeks the Court's intervention for killing herself "honourably" rather than face her relatives, angry that she had tied the knot against their wishes. In her petition, seven months' pregnant Reena has sought directions for protection. In an apparent attempt to build up the argument in favour of direction for protection, Reena said she cannot imagine the kind of death her relatives will give after catching up with her. So to save her from the "brutality", she should be allowed to take the extreme step. Coming to her rescue, Chief Justice Mukul Mudgal and Justice Jasbir Singh directed instantaneous police protection for Reena and her husband after according the matter utmost priority.

***11. HC slams cops after girl killed for "honour"* (The Times of India, 10 March 2010)**

Despite the orders of the Delhi High Court the Delhi Police failed to prevent the death of a woman allegedly at the hands of her parents for marrying outside their caste. The Delhi High Court now made the Police Commissioner of Delhi Police personally responsible for ensuring the safety of the husband.

***12. Reining in Khaps*** **(The Tribune, Chandigarh, 12 March 2010)**

A Division Bench of the Punjab and Haryana High Court observed that the State Government cannot absolve itself of blame for the continued menace of the extra-constitutional bodies that are Khap Panchayats in the State. The State Government so far failed to rein in these bodies. Chief Justice Mukul Mudgal directed the State Government to initiate exemplary action against one or two Khap Panchayats. He mentioned that unfortunately, these bodies represent the region's dominant caste which is why the political leadership is reluctant to lay its hands on them for fear of losing vital vote banks. However, Khap Panchayats and their members form 27 per cent of the votebank in northern State of Haryana.

***13. Forced Marriage runaways' bounty hunters*** **(The Hindu, Chandigarh, 31 August, 2010)**

Desperate families who want to find and bring back their runaway teenage daughters employ bounty hunters in the community in Bradford, Northern England. For around GBP 5'000, taxi-driver Zakir tracks down women and girls who had run away to escape a forced marriage. He does not harm them but returns them to their parents to face their "destiny," of being made to marry somebody their parents had chosen. Zakir uses his knowledge acquired in the taxi business and his contacts with fellow drivers, shopkeepers etc. to hunt the runaways down. Zakir proclaims that he does not do this work for the money, but as a favour to the families in order to save their honour as he shares their values.

South-Asian families are under huge pressure to conform to the traditional values of their community. They are fearful of a negative and an embarrassing reputation spread about them and see their daughters as the embodiment of their family honour which is why their sexual and moral behaviour needs to be controlled. Those families will do anything in the name of honour, as taxi-driver Zakir summarises it.

Campaigners now demand a "witness protection scheme," for forced marriages runaways which would help them in not being traced anymore.

## X. Legal Framework to combat Forced Marriages

### *1. International Legal Framework*

Numerous international legal instruments prohibit forced and early marriage, including the Universal Declaration of Human Rights, the United Nations Convention on Consent to Marriage, Minimum Age for Marriage and Registration of Marriages, the Convention on the Elimination of All Forms of Discrimination against Women. The Universal Declaration of Human Rights states in article 16 clause 2 that any marriage may only be solemnized with the free and full consent of the future spouses. Although most countries have signed onto these documents, many countries have not taken sufficient steps to implement these treaties. For example, many signatory countries still lack domestic laws specifying 18 as the minimum age to marry. In the United States, some states have no minimum age to marry (although they typically require court and parental approval), and others make exception to their minimum age if there is a pregnancy involved, which can conflict with States statutory rape laws.

In 2005, the Council of Europe adopted Resolution 1468 on forced marriages and child marriages. The resolution defines forced marriage as the "union of two persons at least one of whom has not given their full and free consent to the marriage" (Para. 4), and child marriage as the "union of two persons at least one of whom is under 18 years of age" (Para. 7). It urges states, *inter alia,* to ratify relevant international treaties, comply with the Council of Europe Committee of Ministers' Recommendation (2002) on the protection of women against violence, set the minimum age for marriage at eighteen years, and consider criminalizing acts of forced marriage.

In 2008, the United Nations Division for the Advancement of Women released a legislative model framework in an expert group report entitled "Good practices in legislation on violence against women." This model code includes provisions outlawing forced and early marriage.

For the first time in history, the act of forced marriage was prosecuted as a crime against humanity under international law. According to the 2007 report by Sigma Huda, in May 2004, the Special Court for Sierra Leone charged six individuals with the act of forced marriage. Forced marriage during the war in Sierra Leone involved not only the acts of rape and sexual slavery, but forcing a woman to do other tasks, such as cook or clean. These "marriages" lasted for years. Many of these bush wives have been unable to return home due to the associated stigma of their marriage, a "Stockholm Syndrome" attachment to their commanders, threatened separation from their children, or a lack of resettlement support, [see, http://www.stopvaw.org/Forced_and_Early_Marriage.html].

### 2. *National legal framework*

Some European countries have adopted measures to combat the phenomenon of forced marriages. There are several ways to tackle this problem: it can be approached by introducing new provisions into civil law relating to marriage, into private international law (*e.g.* under which circumstances should marriages solemnised abroad be recognised in a European country? Should there be any provisions allowing exceptions from the usual age for marriage of 18 years for foreign nationals?), into criminal law (by creating offences or more severe punishment) and even into migration law (by not allowing a spouse under 18 to join her spouse in the European country etc.).

#### *2.1 Switzerland*

(a) Existing legal provisions

(aa) Civil (Matrimonial) Law

In Switzerland, marriage is considered to be a legal contract of its own kind. Any sacramental ceremony such as a church wedding can only be performed after the legal wedding and does by itself have no effect. Swiss substantial law requires bride and groom to be 18 years or above and of sound mind, both not having any living spouse and not being within the prohibited degree of relationship (articles 94-96 Swiss Civil Code). The procedure of preparation of the marriage is initiated with an application of bride and groom. The marriage officer at the civil status authority checks whether the requirements for a valid marriage are fulfilled. The couple has to appear personally in the offices of the civil status authority which will check on their identity and will determine whether the requirements for entering into a valid marriage are fulfilled (article 96 Swiss Civil Code). If they are, bride and groom, they can marry within the next 3 months after brief respite of 10 days (article 100 Swiss Civil Code). Out of the prescribed procedure of the legal marriage it becomes evident that the contract of marriage is based on consent of both parties: bride and groom have to answer each the question whether they want to enter into marriage (article 102 Swiss Civil Code).

The marriage is voidable under certain circumstances. One of the reasons, according to article 107 of the Swiss Civil Code is that if one spouse is forced into marriage by being threatened with a near and substantial danger for life and limb or of the honour of himself or herself or of another closely connected person. If the spouse had not entered the marriage, had he or she been free to decide, his or her will to marry is considered to be formed under the influence of a threat. Only the spouse so threatened can file the suit for declaring the marriage invalid and only within 6 months from the moment of lapse of the threat and in any case only within 5 years after marriage (article 108 Swiss Civil Code).

In severe cases, the Swiss authorities can deprive parents, who are known or must be assumed to have made arrangements for marrying their child abroad, of their right to determine the place of residence of that child. The guardianship authorities can further withdraw the parent's right to live with the child or even the parent's custody over the minor (article 311 Swiss Civil Code).

So to protect young women from violence, threats and stalking of family members the Courts can pass protection orders so to prohibit her relatives to enter into contact, to approach her or to enter her home (article 28b Swiss Civil Code). Such protection measures would be necessary if a concerned woman or girl has run away so to oppose to the forced marriage or tries to escape from an already solemnised arranged marriage, [see, Andrea Buechler, Zwangsehen in zivilrechtlicher und internationalprivat-rechtlicher Sicht, FamPra.ch, 2007 pages 725, 732, 743].

(b) Private international law

One important aspect with regard to the existing legal framework to deal with forced marriages is the recognition of marriages solemnised abroad (outside of Switzerland). Switzerland's Act on Private International Law (LDIP) provides that any marriage solemnised in a foreign country will be recognised in Switzerland if it is valid according to the law of the *loci celebrationis* or the law applicable at the foreign domicile of one of the parties' or applicable in the foreign State of which one of the parties' is citizen. In case bride and groom have solemnised their marriage outside Switzerland in order to circumvent Swiss impediments to marry, the authorities will not recognise their marriage if one of the two spouses is Swiss citizen or both are residents of Switzerland, [see, Article 45(1) and (2) of Switzerland's Act on Private International Law (LDIP); see Kurt Siehr, Das Internationale Privatrecht der Schweiz, Zurich 2002, 22 ff]. A forced marriage is violative of the public policy (the so-called order public) and cannot be recognised in Switzerland. This stands in contradiction to the substantial Swiss matrimonial law which provides that a marriage is validly solemnised once both parties have stated their "yes" in front of the marriage officer. This contradiction can, as Swiss law Professor and renowned international family law expert Prof. Andrea Buechler suggests, only be dissolved by reforming the substantial law and by permitting the parties whose forced marriage was solemnised in Switzerland to file a law suit so to declare the marriage voidable without any time limitation. With respect to child marriages solemnised abroad involving a minor spouse it is the practice of the Swiss authorities to deny recognition of such marriage, if the spouse was below 16 years, [see, Andrea Buechler, op. cit., page 747].

(b) Present reform of Swiss law with relation to forced marriages

In 2004, a discussion on forced marriages was launched in Switzerland which had led to legislative activity. Several members of Parliament and parliamentary commissions raised the issue of whether the above-mentioned provisions of Swiss law would suffice to deal with the emerging problem of forced marriages. The Swiss Government published on 14 November 2007 a report on forced marriages in Switzerland. It came to the conclusion that mainly the existing statutory provisions in the Civil Code and the Act on International Private Law should be amended, [see, http://www.bsv.admin.ch/themen/gesellschaft/01643/01927/01938/index.html?lang=de]. In November 2008, the Swiss Government suggested the following concrete measures, [see, http://www.ejpd.admin.ch/ejpd/de/home/dokumentation/mi/2008/2008-11-05.html]:

- duty of marriage officers performing the legal marriage to examine whether or not there is any sign that there is force, coercion or threatening of a partner involved in the marriage; if there is any doubt, the officers have to hear each of the spouses separately;
- law suits for rendering a marriage which was solemnised under force voidable should not be time-barred anymore;
- law suits for rendering a marriage voidable can also be filed by the competent State authority if the marriage was not entered out of free will or if one of the spouses was not 18 at the time of marriage;
- Article 44 clause 2 of the LDIP, which so far allowed foreign nationals in Switzerland to get married under the substantial law of their foreign country, even if one of the partners was below 18 years old, is to be deleted;
- marriages solemnised abroad which involve persons below 18 years should not be recognised anymore in Switzerland;
- however, no amendments or changes in the criminal law were considered to be necessary, as the existing provisions regarding the offences of duress and coercion were considered to be sufficient to cover the offence of forced marriages.

In October 2009, a report considering the legislative inputs of the different committees was published. Many inputs had been made as to the introduction of a new offence of forcing a person into marriage. This offence would make any person taking part by exercising force with regard to a marriage or abetting or instigating of a forced marriage punishable. This and other suggestions as mentioned above had mainly been approved and the Swiss government will until the end of the year 2010 provide a draft Bill for the necessary changes in existing law, [see, http://www.news.admin.ch/message/?lang=de&msg-id=29604].

**2.2 *United Kingdom***

In response to the problem of forced marriages in the UK, the Forced Marriage (Civil Protection) Act 2007 was passed, which enables the victims of forced marriage to apply for Court orders for their protection, [see, http://www.accmuk.com/?target=forced_marriage &menuitem= Campaigns & submenuitem =Forced%20Marriage]

*(a) Short synopsis of the Forced marriage (Civil Protection) Act, 2007*

The Forced Marriage (Civil Protection) Act, 2007 came into force in late 2008. The aim of the Act is to provide protection to those at risk of forced marriage and to provide recourse for those who have already been forced into marriage. The Act also sends out a strong signal that forced marriage is unacceptable and will not be tolerated. The object of the Forced Marriage Act is to allow Family Courts to prevent the occurrence of a forced marriage and to protect victims of a forced marriage by removing them from the marriage through a Forced Marriage Protection Order. The legislator's policy was not to criminalize forced marriage, but to provide civil remedies in the Act. The Act acknowledges that forced marriage is an abuse of human rights and is a manifestation of violence against women and children. The Act speaks of a forced marriage when at least one spouse does not or cannot consent to the marriage, [see, http://www.stopvaw.org/uk_examines_forced_marriage_law.html].

The Act itself provides the legal base for the Courts to make a Forced Marriage Protection Order. The Courts enjoy wide discretion to deal flexibly and sensitively with the circumstances of each individual case, employing civil remedies that will offer protection to victims without criminalising members of their family.

If the victim of a forced marriage due to permanent control and surveillance is not able to ask for help himself or herself, an application for a Protection Order can be filed by a third person (section 63C of the Act). In certain cases the Court can pass orders ex officio (section 63C(1)(b) read along with (6) of the Act), [see, http://www.justice.gov.uk/docs/cp0208.pdf].

*(b) Implementation of the Forced Marriage (Civil Protection) Act 2007.*

In November 2009, the government of the United Kingdom published a report examining the effects and implementation of the Forced Marriage (Civil Protection) Act within the first year of its being in operation, [see, Report of Ministry of Justice of the UK, One year On: the initial impact of the Forced Marriage (Civil Protection) Act 2007 in its first year of operation, November 2009]. In the course of the study, Judges and court staff, law enforcement, forced marriage voluntary support groups, and members of the Forced Marriage Unit were interviewed by researchers. The study concluded that the Act is being made use of throughout the nation, however not uniformly. A certain under use has been noticed and attributed to a fear of the parties and victims to approach the Courts or agencies.

Within the first year of the Act's implementation, Judges and Courts have become familiar with the process and have developed standard templates. The processes which have been established within the Act have been rated as direct and straightforward. The success of the working of this innovative legislation, can be substantiated by the data obtained from the Foreign and Commonwealth Office, London.

**Recent data provided by the Foreign and Commonwealth Office, London with regard to Forced Marriages.**

**Statistics for 2009:**

The Forced Marriage Unit (hereafter, FMU) of the Consular Assistance Group of Foreign and Commonwealth Office London, received 1682 reports relating to possible forced marriage and dealt with 377 assistance (overseas and UK) and immigration cases, wherein 8% of the cases where the FMU gave advice or support relating to possible forced marriage were associated with India. That out of the 152 overseas assistance cases where the FMU provided direct support, 6 cases involved British nationals in India. That out of the 137 immigration cases dealt with by the FMU, 14 cases involved spouses from India.

**Statistics for 2008:**

The FMU received 1618 reports relating to possible forced marriage and dealt with 430 assistance cases (both overseas and within the UK) and immigration cases. That in 7% of the cases where the FMU gave advice or support relating to possible forced marriage were associated with India. That out of the 178 overseas assistance cases, where the FMU gave direct support, 3 cases involved British nationals in India. That out of the 208 immigration cases dealt with by the FMU, 15 cases involved spouses from India

The report also contains recommendations. **First,** there is a call for a stronger focus on co-operation between the different agencies to make the process as beneficial as possible for the victim. **Second**, the research indicates that more publicity and training is necessary to increase awareness within specific, "closed" communities. **Third,** more research and resources should be directed towards long-term protection and support of the victims. Finally, the report warns of the danger of regarding forced marriage as a problem that is easily solved. "There is a need for action, but also a need for caution and understanding of the impact of an application on a young person who then loses family and community, and will need long term protection and support."

**UK COURT OF APPEAL JUDGMENT IN THE CASE OF DIEGO ANDRES AGUILAR QUILA AND AMBER AGUILAR, SHAKIRA BIBI AND SUHYAL MOHAMMED v. SECRETARY OF STATE FOR THE HOME DEPARTMENT: REPORTED AS [2010] EWCA Civ 1482 ON THE ISSUE OF AGE BAR IMPOSED BY THE CURRENT UK IMMIGRATION RULES.**

The above-mentioned case is being cited with a view to highlight the interpretation of the ban contained in the amended para 277 of the current UK immigration rules HC 395, on the entry of foreign spouses between the ages of 18 and 21. The major upshot of this ruling is that the age bar imposed in the amended immigration rules is one of the lawful ways of dealing with the problem of forced marriages.

Basically, this judgment upheld age bar imposed in the amended marriage immigration rules *qua* para 277 of HC 395, which expressly prohibits marriages between the ages of 18 and 21 in the UK, as also extended to the settlement applications outside the UK on the basis of marriage lodged and processed at other British Consular Posts and Missions situated overseas. This of course is with the principal logic and rational of the vulnerability of forced marriages with regard to certain ethnic communities in the UK, even in cross-border marriages.

Lord Justice Sedley, as then he was has summarised in paras 1 to 3 of the said judgment, the social and cultural reasons in so far relating to the amendment of para 277 of HC 395 in the following words:

"1. These two appeals raise the question whether the ban contained in paragraph 277 of the immigration rules on the entry for settlement of foreign spouses between the ages of 18 and 21 is a lawful way of dealing with the problem of forced marriages.

2. Forced marriage is not merely a cultural or social problem. A woman forced into marriage is in the law of this country a victim of false imprisonment and rape, and those arranging and procuring it are likely to be guilty of kidnapping and conspiracy. In these circumstances, the Home Office is justified in doing everything it properly can to prevent or inhibit it. But the question is whether the immigration control is an appropriate means of doing so, and if it is, is the method adopted in the rules lawful?

3. It might seem at first sight that a rule restricting the age at which spouses can be united here has no appreciable bearing on the problem. But research and other data have satisfied the Home Secretary, first, that the targeted age-group is particularly vulnerable to this form of abuse, and secondly that there is no practical way of differentiating within it between forced and voluntary marriages. The Home Secretary has concluded that the unavoidable cost in terms of innocent casualties is justified by the expectation that the rule will frustrate a significant number of forced marriages."

Both the appeals in the case of *Diego Andres Aguilar Quila and Amber Aguilar, Shakira Bibi and Suhyal Mohammed* v. *Secretary of State for the home department*, reported as [2010] EWCA Civ 1482 had been clubbed together as both the appeals raised a common question relating to the age bar as contained in the amended para 277 of the UK immigration rules. The facts of the case have been summarised in paras 14 to 17 of the judgment as follows:

> "14. Diego Andres Aguilar Quila is a Chilean national, born on 12 July, 1990 and therefore still under 21. He entered the United Kingdom on a student visa which expired on 3 August, 2009. By then – in fact in 2006 when he first came here with his parents – he had met and fallen in love with Amber Jeffery, a British citizen. On 22 November, 2008, when she was 17, they married.

15. Amber Aguilars date of birth is 25 April, 1991. At the time of marriage Diego Aguilar would have been eligible for a visa as a spouse when his wife reached 18, but before that date arrived the new rule was introduced. Mr Aguilar therefore applied before the announced rule-change took effect, but the application was refused on the ground that his wife was still only 17. By the time she turned 18 the amended rule was in force and the Home Office refused to waive it. A notice of refusal to vary Mr Aguilars leave to enter was simultaneously issued.

16. The effect has been severe. Since he still had an unexpired period of leave to remain, Mr Aguilar had no right of appeal. Had he done what many entrants do and overstayed, he would have acquired rights of appeal to which we will come later in this judgment. Instead he behaved responsibly and on 31 July, 2009 left the United Kingdom. His wife, as was to be expected, left with him. To do so she had to give up a place which she had been offered, on the basis of A-level results which included distinctions in French and Spanish, on the joint honours degree course in modern languages beginning that autumn at Royal Holloway College of London University. There was no equivalent course available in Chile, and her plans to become a modern language teacher here have had to be put on hold. The couple went to live in cramped conditions with the Aguilar family in a suburb of Santiago. They have since moved to the Republic of Ireland; but they are still forbidden to live together here.

17. Shakira Bibi is a Pakistani national, born on 7 July, 1990. She was married on 30 October, 2008 in Pakistan, of which she is a national, to Suhayl Mohammed, a United Kingdom citizen and resident, born on 8 April, 1990. Their marriage was a traditional arranged marriage, but there is no suggestion that it was forced. On 1 December 2008 Ms Bibi applied for entry clearance to join her husband here. It was refused by the entry clearance officer in Islamabad on the ground that both parties were under 21. The couple is still apart."

Both the appellants claimed that since their respective cases did not fall in the category of forced marriages, hence, the ban effecting them in terms of the amended rule 277 of the UK immigration rules would not be applicable to either of them.

It is important to advert to the relevant UK immigration rules in this regard. That in terms of the rule 277 of the immigration rules a ban is imposed on the entry for settlement of foreign spouses between the ages of 18 and 21. The chronology of amendments with regard to different prescribed age limits has been elaborated by the Court in paras 5 to 8 of the said judgment. Paras 5 to 8 read as follows:

"5. Subject to a variety of conditions which are not presently material, a foreign national may in principle be granted entry clearance or leave to enter or remain as the spouse or civil partner of a person lawfully present or settled in the United Kingdom. For procedural purposes the UK-based spouse is known as the sponsor. Among sponsors are United Kingdom citizens with an indefeasible right of abode and a constitutional right to marry; but a sponsor may also be present in the United Kingdom only by virtue of leave to enter or remain. The material rule does not differentiate between these classes.

6. Until November 2008, rule 277 of the Immigration Rules (HC 1113) required the sponsor and the incoming spouse both to be aged over 18. (Until 2003 the sponsor could be as young as 16; in 2003 this was raised to 18, as was the age of the incoming spouse in 2004.) While this too is capable of having had an impact on bona fide marriages, no point is taken or arises on it in the present appeals, and I treat it as a lawful restriction, whatever its purpose.

7. With effect from 27 November 2008, however, rule 277 was amended to read:

Nothing in these Rules shall be construed as permitting a person to be granted entry clearance, leave to enter, leave to remain or variation of leave as a spouse or civil partner of another if either the applicant or the sponsor will be aged under 21 on the date of arrival in the United Kingdom or (as the case may be) on the date on which the leave to remain or variation of leave would be granted.

8. With effect from 6 April 2010 the rule was amended by interposing after the words "aged under 21":

(or aged under 18 if either party is a serving member of HM Forces)"

By virtue of the present above-mentioned immigration rules, it can be well argued that at the time of grant of entry clearance, leave to enter, leave to remain or variation of leave, it is mandatory that the sponsor spouse resident in the UK should be 21 years of age before such permission is granted. The entry clearance officers have to take into account the import of rule 277 of the immigration rules, before granting the entry clearance.

Basically, the Court of Appeal was of the opinion that the question in law in the present case was the impact of article 8 of the ECHR qua the amended rule 277, as summed up in para 33 of the judgment in the following terms:

"33. The first question of law is whether the court is required to consider the proportionality of the rule at all. Mr McCullough submits that all that counts is its legality and its rationality. There are two parallel reasons why the appellants contend that the rule, even if not unlawful in itself, cannot lawfully be applied to them if its operation is disproportionate. One is that, because it interferes with a fundamental right, it is required at common law either to be proportionate in principle or to operate proportionately. The other is that, because it engages article 8(1) of the Convention by denying respect to the appellants family life, it requires justification under article 8(2). I will consider these in turn."

In the present judgment, the question as to whether the spouse of a United Kingdom national who exercises the right to marry is entitled prima facie to the benefit of the other spouse's right of abode without interference under the immigration rules has been answered in paras 48 and 49 of the judgment in the following terms:

"48. In my judgment rule 277 represents a direct interference with what the common law and Convention both value as a fundamental right. In the eyes of the common law it is not simply the right to marry and not simply the right to respect for family life but their combined effect which constitutes the material right: that is to say a right not merely to go through a ceremony of marriage but to make a reality of it by living together. For the state to make exile for one of the spouses the price of exercising the right to marry and embark on family life requires powerful justification considerably more powerful, in my judgment. In Convention terms the two rights are discrete, but their practical relation to each other is in my view very much the same.

49. It is not disputed, even so, that there will be measures which a state is entitled to take which impede the right, for instance by excluding spouses with serious criminal records or – materially – parties to forced marriages. In deciding whether to apply such measures it is established by *Abdulaziz* that the state may place weight on the fact (if it is a fact) that neither spouse has a citizens right of abode here. But I accept the appellants case that the starting point is not, as the Home Secretary suggests, a thin entitlement which, so long as it can be exercised somewhere in the world, can legitimately be stultified here. It is a fundamental right which, whether at common law or by virtue of article 8 read with article 12 of the Convention, the state is ordinarily required to respect."

Further, the Court of Appeal in paras 58 to 60 has answered the question as to whether the rule exceeds as to what is necessary and proportionate in terms of family life to accomplish the objective of the age bar introduced in the amended para 277 of the UK immigration rules.

Para 58 gives a detailed account of the view-point from the other side of the fence i.e the reasoning advanced on behalf of the UKBA. Paras 58 to 60 read as follows:

"58. This is not the end of the proportionality exercise. It is also appropriate to consider the strength of the case that rule 277 will have the intended effect. A proven case that an important social objective will be achieved by limiting certain individual rights may suffice to justify an invasive measure. By parity of reasoning, a speculative or conjectural case will carry far less weight as justification for such restrictions. The Home Offices reasoning on proportionality – not ex post facto but at the time when the rule was formulated – is set out in the witness statements of Nicola Smith, a deputy director of immigration policy and the head of the permanent migration team in the Home Offices Borders Agency. It confirms that the scale of forced marriage in the UK is "very difficult to estimate". I have mentioned above that such estimates as there are indicate that only a small fraction of the many marriages caught by rule 277 are likely to be forced marriages. As to these, Ms Smith gives the following reasons for introducing the rule:

i. To help tackle the problem of forced marriage by allowing young people extra time to develop maturity and life skills which would help them to resist inappropriate family pressure to marry.

ii. To provide an opportunity to complete education and training

iii. To delay sponsorship and therefore time spent with a (sometimes abusive) spouse if the sponsor returns to the UK.

iv. To allow a victim of forced marriage an opportunity to seek help and advice during the period when they cannot sponsor their spouse and extra time to make a decision about whether to sponsor.

59. It has to be observed that the first of these reasons assumes that no marriage has taken place. If so, the rule has no bearing on it. The second and third purposes may be palliative but are in no way preventative. The fourth does seek to address the situation of a victim of forced marriage. The last part of it, however, assumes the very free will which forced marriage overbears. It is only the first part of it which has a concrete bearing on the problem, but it bears only on cases where the sponsor is the victim – that is, where a female UK Citizen has been forced to marry a foreign national. There may well be good reason to suspect that this class of case – where entry to the UK can be sold to a foreign national by forcing a woman with British nationality to marry him – is the major and most pernicious sub-group. This, in fact, was the primary group identified as in need of protection in the 2008 consultation paper *Marriage Visas: the Way Forward* (see §1.3). But it is only on this sub-group that the first part of reason iv can have a bearing.

60. While therefore we must be careful to refrain from substituting our judgment for that of the Home Secretary on policy issues, we are not entitled to refrain from evaluating the strength of the policy imperative and its rationale in deciding whether its impact on innocent persons is proportionate. In my judgment the policy imperative is only obliquely, partially and in large part speculatively related to the measure under scrutiny."

Lord Sedley while allowing the two appeals in question on the ground that the application of rule 277 to the two appellants and their sponsors is unlawful. He also in the concluding portion of his judgment explicitly made it clear that he would not strike down the rule 277 of the UK immigration rules. His conclusion in paras 66 and 67 is summed up as follows:

"66. I would limit the courts judgment, for the reasons we have respectively given, to allowing these two appeals on the ground that the application of rule 277 to the two appellants and their sponsors is unlawful. I would not strike down the rule, since we have not been dealing with its impact on couples where neither spouse is a United Kingdom national. Whether to keep it in limited form or to drop it altogether is a matter for the Home Secretary, not for the court.

67. What is a matter for us is what is now to happen to Ms Bibi and Mr Aguilar. In my view each is entitled, in the absence of any other valid objection to their admission, to enter this country forthwith as the spouse of a British citizen. We will welcome counsels submissions, in the first instance in writing and if possible by agreement, as to the form of order which is appropriate."

Further, Lord Justice Pitchford in the concurring portion of his judgment agreed with the principle judgment handed down by Lord Justice Sedley. He has concluded that the amended rule 277 of the UK immigration rules is not applicable in the facts and circumstances of the present two cases. This is elaborated in para 68 of the judgment in the following terms:

> "68. I am grateful to Sedley LJ for his compelling analysis. For the reasons he has given I agree that the court should confine itself to a consideration of the impact of rule 277 upon these particular appellants. I understand it to be common ground that the sole basis for declining leave to enter was the age restriction imposed by rule 277. I agree, with the reasons given by Sedley LJ, that refusal of leave on the ground of age alone represents such a disproportionate interference with a fundamental right that the decisions cannot stand. I propose to make only a small contribution of my own on the subject of interference by the state with a fundamental right under Art 8. I accept that Art 12 has in the present appeal no life of its own."

Finally, Lord Justice Gross in the penultimate part of the judgment has yet again highlighted in eloquent terms the non applicability of rule 277 of the immigration rules in the facts and circumstances of the present two cases in paras 73, 80 and 81 of the said judgment as follows:

> "73. I have read with great respect the judgments of Sedley LJ and Pitchford LJ in draft. I agree entirely with the outcome they propose, namely, that although we do not strike down the rule itself, rule 277 of the Immigration Rules (HC 1113) ("rule 277") cannot lawfully be applied to the present appellants. However, I find myself in the invidious position of reaching the same conclusion....
>
> 80. Although much less is known on the facts about Ms. Bibi and Mr. Mohammed than is apparent as to Mr. and Mrs. Aguilar, no grounds have been presented for distinguishing them, in the event that the *Aguilar* appeal succeeds.
>
> 81. Accordingly and for the very simple common law reason/s outlined above, I would allow these appeals, though joining with Sedley LJ and Pitchford LJ in their tribute to the judgment of Burnett J, from which the *Aguilar* appeal has been brought."

Clearly, the judgment is notable of the impact of the omnipotent right to family life contained in article 8 of the ECHR on the amended para 277, of the current UK immigration rules. But, the fact of the matter is that this judgment is only case specific.

However, it is important to add that an appeal has been filed by the Secretary of State to the Supreme Court of UK against the judgment of the UK Court of Appeal (UKSC 2011/0022). Permission has been granted to the Secretary of State to appeal to the Supreme Court against the judgment of the Court of Appeal in the case of *Quila* v. *Secretary of State for the Home Department,* [2010] EWCA Civ 1482. This is concerning the increase in the sponsor spouse visa age from 18 to 21. The appeal has been expedited and the matter was listed for 8 and 9 June, 2011. The Hon'ble Supreme Court has heard the arguments raised by the respective parties and the judgment of the Hon'ble Supreme Court of the UK is awaited, at the time the present book has gone to the press.

### *2.3 Further strategies adopted by various countries*

Various European countries have started to introduce provisions into their legal systems according to which marriages solemnised outside their territory will be denied recognition in case that the marriage solemnised abroad does not fulfil all the requirements of the domestic law (*e.g.* age of one of the spouses below 18 years).

However, there are various international agreements on the issue of marriages which set a minimum age for marriage of 15 years, *e.g.* article 16 of the Declaration of Human Rights of 10 December, 1948, article 16 clause 2 of the Convention on the Elimination of all Forms of Discrimination Against Women (CEDAW) of 18 December, 1979, article 11 clause 1 no. 3 and 4 of the Convention of 14 March, 1978 on Celebration and Recognition of the Validity of Marriages and article 1 and 2 of the Convention on Consent to Marriage, Minimum Age for Marriage and Registration of Marriages of 7 November, 1962. With regard to the latter convention a recommendation of the Office of the United Nations High Commissioner for Human Rights exists. It holds that a minimum age of 15 years is mandatory; however it also acknowledges the autonomy in legislative matters of all UN member states (Principle II Recommendation on Consent to Marriage, Minimum Age for Marriage and Registration of Marriages from 1 November, 1965). Considering this international framework it does not seem to be justified to deny marriages solemnised outside the territory recognition in domestic law, only based on the fact that the requirement of a minimum age of 18 years of any domestic law is not met.

Moreover, any country trying to combat the problem of forced marriages by the above-mentioned restriction has keep in mind the respect of other countries' legal systems; the parties' freedom to marry (some marriages below 18 might be genuine) and the target to avoid voidable marriages, [see, Andrea Buechler, op. cit., page 747 f].

## *3. Indian legal framework*

### *3.1 Indian Penal Code, 1860 (IPC)*

"Section 361 IPC:

Kidnapping from lawful guardianship.—

Whoever takes or entices any minor under sixteen years of age if a male, or under eighteen years of age if a female, or any person of unsound mind, out of the keeping of the lawful guardian of such minor or person of unsound mind, without the consent of such guardian, is said to kidnap such minor or person from lawful guardianship.

*Explanation.*—The words "lawful guardian" in this section include any person lawfully entrusted with the care or custody of such minor or other person

Section 362 IPC:

Abduction.—

Whoever by force compels, or by any deceitful means induces any person to go from any place, is said to abduct that person.

Section 366 IPC:

Kidnapping, abducting or inducing woman to compel her marriage, etc.—

Whosoever kidnaps or abducts any woman with the intent that she may be compelled or knowing it to be likely that she will be compelled to marry any person against her will, or in order that she may be likely forced or seduced to illicit intercourse, or knowing it to be likely that she will be forced or seduced to illicit intercourse, shall be punished with imprisonment of either description for a term which may either be extended upto 10 years, and shall also be liable to fine; and whoever; by means of criminal intimidation as defined in this Code or of abuse of authority or any other method of compulsion, induces any woman to go from any place with intent that she may be, or knowing that it is likely that she will be, forced or seduced to illicit intercourse with another person shall also be punishable as aforesaid."

**COMMENT**

**Ingredients** - This section consist of the following:

1. Kidnapping or abducting any woman.
2. Such kidnapping or abducting must be:
   (i) With intent that she may be compelled or knowing it to be likely that she will be compelled to marry any person against her will;
   or
   (ii) in order that she may be forced or seduced to illicit intercourse or knowing it to be likely that she will forced or seduced to illicit intercourse; or
   (iii) by means of criminal intimidation or otherwise by inducing any woman to go from any place with intent that she may be, or knowing that she will be, forced or seduced to illicit intercourse.
3. It is immaterial whether the woman kidnapped is married or not. [see, S.N. Mishra, Indian Penal Code, 16th Edition 2008, page 601].

The provision of section 361 IPC punishes the kidnapping or abduction of a minor male under 16 years or a minor female under 18 years from lawful guardianship and without the guardian's consent, e.g. for a forced marriage (such as the discussed "shotgun marriage" in Bihar). It further makes punishable the kidnapping or abduction of a female of any age for purpose of marriage. However, it does not contain any provisions regarding criminal liability of persons forcing somebody into marriage.

The following two enactments, the Child Marriage Restraint Act, 1929, and the Prohibition of Child Marriage Act, 2006, declare certain actions in relation to child marriages punishable.

### *3.2 Child Marriage Restrain Act, 1929 and 1978*

The object of the 1929 Act was to eliminate the evil of early marriage of a female child. The Act fixed the age of marriage for girls at 14 years. A contravention of the provisions of the 1929 Act did not render the marriage invalid as the validity of the marriage was a subject beyond the scope of the Act. It was considered that a marriage under the Hindu Law by a minor male was valid even though the marriage was not brought about on his behalf by the natural or lawful guardian as well as that the minority of an individual could operate as a bar to his or her incurring contractual obligations, but it could not be an impediment in the matter of performing the necessary sacrament for marriage. A minor's marriage without the consent of the guardian could thus be held to be valid on the application of the doctrine of *factum valet*, [see, http://wcd.nic.in/cmr1929.htm].

Section 5 of the 1929 Act provided punishment for anybody who performs, conducts or directs any child marriage, unless he proves that he had reasons to believe that the marriage was not a child marriage. Section 6 provided that any person having charge of the minor, whether as parent or guardian or in any other capacity, lawful or unlawful, who does any act to promote the marriage or permits it to be solemnised, or negligently fails to prevent it from being solemnised, shall be punished with simple imprisonment which may extend to three months and shall also be liable to fine.

The Act was amended in 1949 and newly adopted in 1978 in the Child Marriage Restraint Act, 1978, setting 18 as the minimum age for women to get married and 21 for men.

### 3.3 The Prohibition of Child Marriage Act, 2006

The Prohibition of Child Marriage Act, 2006, superseded the Child Marriage Restrain Act, 1929. It contains both civil and criminal provisions.

The Prohibition of Child Marriage Act, 2006, provides for the prohibition of the solemnisation of child marriages and for matters connected with child marriages. It prohibits marriage below 18 for girls and 21 for boys. Section 15 of the Act makes any offence under the Act cognizable and non-bailable. The Act also enhanced the penalty for violation of the provisions as compared to the previous Child Marriage Restraint Act of 1929.

Sections 9 and 11 provide respectively for punishment for a male adult above 18 years of age marrying a child as well as for any person having charge of the child promoting or permitting the solemnisation of a child marriage.

The 2006 Act declares in its section 3 child marriages to be voidable at the option of that party to the marriage which is a child. The marriage can thus be annulled by the Court upon a petition for annulment. If a girl below the age of 18 has thus been married off without her consent, she has now the choice to annul her marriage, [see, Himanshi Dhavan, Child brides may declare marriage void, The Times of India, 15the September 2006, retrieved from http://timesofindia.indiatimes.com/articleshow/1992687.cms].

The Act further declares the marriage of a minor child to be null and void when the minor child

(a) is taken or enticed out of the keeping of the lawful guardian; or

(b) by force compelled, or by any deceitful means induced to go from any place; or

(c) is sold for the purpose of marriage and made to go through a form of marriage or is married and afterwards sold or trafficked or used for immoral purposes, [see, Section 12 of the Prohibition of Child Marriage Act, 2006].

The 2006 Act not only provides for punishment for solemnizing marriages in contravention to the Act (as already the 1929 Act did), but also declares child marriages void or voidable in certain situations: If a child below the prescribed age of 18 or 21, as the case may be, is forced to marry against her or his will, the child can file a petition for annulment of the marriage. If a child is being abducted for the purpose of a forced marriage, such marriage is null and void. The Act does thus have some potential to fight against forced marriages of young men below 21 years or young women below 18 years, whether the coercion comes from the own parents or from outsiders. However, it is pertinent to mention that some 70-80% of the Indian population lives in villages where family, caste and community pressures are much more effectual than any remote legislature. Implementation and enforcement of this legislation in those sections of society is therefore a difficult task. For example, as the reality in Bihar shows, parents of kidnapped child bridegrooms tend to respect the sacrament of marriage, although it was entered without their consent and forcibly, and do not know nor care about the legal situation, [see, Amitabh Srivastava, op. cit., page 68 ff].

### *3.4 Hindu marriages - The Hindu Marriage Act, 1955*

Section 1(2) of the Hindu Marriage Act, 1955, provides that the Act only applies to parties which are Hindus and either are living in India or domiciled in India with a residence abroad. It is not necessary that they should be Indian nationals (Section 2 of HMA). This means that the provisions of the HMA, 1955, are having extra-territorial effect outside of India for people residing abroad, but being domiciled in India.

With regard to the domicile of a person, the Indian law follows the Common Law doctrine of domicile. A domicile of origin is attributed by law to all persons at birth, whereas it is usually the domicile of the father. It adheres to a person until a domicile of choice is acquired. A domicile of choice is acquired by an individual residing in a country other than the country of his/her origin, with the intention of remaining there permanently.

Section 5 sets the conditions for a marriage between two Hindus, out of which one refers to consent to the marriage:

A marriage can be solemnised if "(ii) at the time of marriage, neither party is incapable of giving a valid consent to it in consequence of unsoundness of mind". Further requirements as per clause (iii) of this section is the minimum age of the couple, *i.e.* the bridegroom must have completed the age of 21 years and the bride, the age of 18 years at the time of the marriage. (Section 5 of the Hindu Marriage Act, 1955). The latter requirement is concurring with the Prohibition of Child Marriages Act, 2006.

Section 12 of the HMA provides that any marriage solemnized after the commencement of this Act shall be voidable and may be annulled by a decree of nullity if the marriage was in contravention of the condition specified in clause (ii) of section 5 (no valid consent given due to unsoundness of mind) or if the consent of the petitioner (or where the consent of the guardian in marriage to the petitioner the consent of such a guardian) was obtained by force or by fraud as to the nature of the ceremony or as to any material fact or circumstances concerning the respondent.

In clause (2) of section 12 bars the filing of a petition for the annulling a marriage based on the ground of consent obtained by force or by fraud if

(i) the petition has been presented more than one year after the force had ceased to operate or, as the case may be, the fraud had been discovered; or

(ii) the petitioner has, with his or her full consent, lived with the other party to the marriage as husband or wife after the force has ceased to operate or, as the case may be, the fraud has been discovered. (section 12 of the Hindu Marriage Act, 1955)

The Hindu Marriages Act, 1955, thus enables a party to get a marriage annulled if his/her consent to the marriage was obtained by coercion (or fraud). Due to the extra-territorial application of the Act it applies also to people domiciled in India with a residence abroad, *e.g.* Non-Resident Indians living in the UK.

### *3.5 Comment to the existing legal framework in India*

Marriage in India is not regarded as a pure contract, but has still remained mainly a sacrament. This spirit reflects in the lesser importance which the consensual element in marriage enjoys in Indian legal framework (which is of utmost importance in any law which regards marriage as a special kind of civil contract) and maintains the tradition of the ancient Hindu law in which marriages without consent were valid. With respect to the minimum age for marriage, the Prohibition of Child Marriage Act, 2006, adopts a policy of overlooking (since it declares a marriage of people below the prescribed age only as voidable and not as void): a marriage without consent is perfectly valid; only if one is able to prove that consent was obtained by fraud or force, the marriage is voidable. Marriages without consent are thus valid under the Hindu Marriage Act, 1955, since a consenting mind is not condition precedent to a marriage, [see, Paras Diwan, op. cit, page 21 f].

## XI. Suggestive Measures to prevent Forced Marriages

Although legislation for honour killings is on the anvil, there is an equally crying need for separate consolidated forced marriages legislation in India as done in the UK, considering that India is a society in which forced marriages occur with a high frequency. It is suggested that this legislation should have extra-territorial application as well, just as the provisions of the Hindu Marriage Act, 1955: Section 1(2) of this Act provides that the Act only applies to parties which are Hindus and either are living in India or domiciled in India with a residence abroad. It is not necessary that they should be Indian nationals (section 2 of HMA). This means that the provisions of the HMA, 1955, are having extra-territorial effect outside of India for people residing abroad but domiciled in India.

An example will make the extra-territorial effect of Indian law more clear: A third generation Punjabi girl, having the UK citizenship, is supposed to be married off forcibly to a Punjabi boy, living in Punjab. The girl, although having grown up in the UK and although having the UK citizenship, has kept her domicile of origin in Punjab, India, so does the boy. The Indian legislation would be applicable to them.

Although forced and early marriages are widespread, many efforts to prevent such marriages have proven successful. "Stop Violence Against Women" (STOPVAW) is a forum for information, advocacy and change in the promotion of women's human rights in countries of Central and Eastern Europe and the former Soviet Union. It has compiled the following measures taken up in different parts of the world which have proved effective in postponing marriages for girls and helping to stop forced marriages:[1]

With respect to India, an example is quoted out of the Maharashtra region, where the Institute for Health Management runs a Life Skills Program which teaches young women and girls in a one year life skills course. The course focuses on self-sufficiency and encourages parents to actively participate. Since the introduction of the course, the median age of marriage for the region has risen from 14.5 years to 17 years. Also in the regions of Rajasthan, Karnataka and Haryana, India, a small sum is deposited in a savings account at the birth of a daughter into a low-income family. If the girl reaches 18 and is unmarried, she may then collect the sum.

With regard to India's neighbouring country Bangladesh, the example of a secondary school scholarship program for girls, introduced in the early 1990s, is cited. To participate, parents had to sign a contract promising their daughters would not marry before the age of 18. Schools waived fees for books and school fees, and parents received some compensation for the diminished agricultural production resulting from the loss of the daughter's labour. This program has seen great success in postponing marriages.

Such programmes have emboldened girls to take action on their own behalf. There have been reports of cases where a victim's classmates, hearing of a forced or early marriage of a peer, have lobbied against it and even sent petitions to local law enforcement, [see, http://www.stopvaw.org/Forced_and_ Early_ Marriage.html].

**XII. Conclusion**

Forced and early marriages entrap women and young girls in relationships that deprive them of their basic human rights. Forced marriage constitutes a human rights violation in itself: article 1 of the Convention on Consent to Marriage, Minimum Age for Marriage and Registration of Marriages states that "No marriage shall be legally entered into without the full and free consent of both parties, such consent to be expressed by them in person after due publicity and in the presence of the authority competent to solemnize the marriage and of witnesses, as prescribed by law." The negative effects and consequences of forced marriages are various.

In India, the whole range of the kinds of marriages which fall in the ambit of the wide term "forced marriages" can be found. Several reasons lead to the high frequency of forced marriages: Traditions prescribe that it is the parents that are responsible for the marriage of their children. Accepting the free choice of young men and women of their life partner is still the exception and not the rule. Parents feel and are generally believed to have a better knowledge of what is good for their children which is the reason why the practice of arranged marriages is still prevalent throughout the country, whether in educated or non-educated layers of society. Marriage is not considered to be an individual affair, but a family affair: a union of families rather than of individuals. However, the step from an arranged marriage to a forced marriage is only a small one; the borders between the two forms are overlapping. Consent to a marriage was in older times not regarded necessary and is still not a condition precedent to a valid marriage.

Moreover, although there is a change in attitude occurring these days, children's rights are still not valued high in India, which is manifest in the widespread child prostitution, child labour and the lack of children's education (although hopes are high that the latter is now about to change with the recent entering into force of the Right to Free and Compulsory Education Act, 2009, which is, if fully implemented, going to provide free and mandatory primary school education to each Indian child).

An additional problem in India is the still prevailing division of society by caste and the power which certain non-legal institutions such as the mentioned Khap Panchayats have. In the same way as parents have the actual power to force their children in an unwanted marriage, those bodies have the power to prohibit an unapproved marriage and order for social sanctions in case their judgment is not being followed. Brutal honour killings, committed by the own family on innocent young people, is the consequence.

Comparing the legal framework adopted by various countries shows that a co-ordinated approach is necessary to effectively combat the problem of forced marriages. Measures on different levels and in different areas are required. Some jurisdictions have opted for preventive measures, others put the main weight on providing possibilities to dissolve a forced marriage (by means of declaration as null and void or divorce). The principle, valid for many European countries, that the applicable law to marriages of migrant spouses shall be the substantial law of the country of origin of the spouses is more and more restricted by the order public or by setting their own minimal requirements for a valid marriage. Since in forced marriages the age of the spouse is often very low and below 18 years, one of the preventive plans of action taken on in the context of migration laws is the setting of a minimal age of the migrating spouse. The reason behind this solution is simple: if there is no possibility for the spouses to live together (by way of migration of one spouse to the other) then there is no sense in a forced marriage solemnized only for the purpose of claims for residence and citizenship. However, this measure violates the right to family life of those people who have entered into marriage out of their own free will.

India has adopted the concept of offering the possibility to dissolve a Hindu marriage which was solemnized due to force and without the free and full consent of a spouse. Also, Indian legislation provides with section 366 IPC and the Prohibition of Child Marriage Act, 2006, the necessary criminal law to punish abduction of a female for purpose of marriage as well as child marriages and to declare child marriages as void if solemnised after an abduction. However, the existing legal framework in India is in desperate need of a coherent legislation on the topic of forced marriages. Moreover, Courts and the Government have to take stringent action against the rule of the extra legal Khap Panchayats, which have so far been shielded from any State intrusion due to political reasons.

It is the State's and the society's responsibility to protect the human rights of its young citizens, to avoid forced marriages, to create possibilities and opportunities for the people concerned to break free and to find protection, support and aid. Education of the young women and men as well as their parents is just as much necessary as a broad concept to empower the young people concerned with the problem.

**Postscript :Decision of the Supreme Court of England and Wales pronounced on 12 October 2011 to the effect that Rule 277 of the British Immigration Rules infringes Article 8 of the ECHR**

However, the Supreme Court, by a 4-1 majority, dismissed the appeal of the Secretary of State on the ground that the refusal to grant marriage visas to the Respondents was an infringement of their rights under Article 8 of the ECHR. According to the judgment of the Supreme Court of the UK pronounced on 12 October, 2011, the Secretary of State had failed to establish that the interference with the Respondents' rights to a family life was justified under Article 8(2) ECHR. The Supreme Court further stated, that para 277 of the immigration rules has a legitimate aim, namely the protection of the rights and freedoms of those who might be forced into marriage and is rationally connected to that objective, but its efficacy is highly debatable. The Supreme Court further held that the restriction under para 277 was automatic and indiscriminate as it failed to detect forced marriages and imposed a delay on cohabitation in the country of choice, which was a deterrent that could impair the essence of the right to marry under Article 12 ECHR. The Supreme Court was of the further opinion that it is hard to conceive that the Secretary of State could avoid infringement of Article 8 ECHR when applying Paragraph 277 to an unforced marriage. Hence, the Supreme Court of the UK, upheld the earlier judgment of the British Court of Appeal.

# ALL ABOARD FOR THE FERTILITY EXPRESS

## I. INTRODUCTION

Mythological surrogate mothers are well known in India. Yashoda played mother to Krishna though Devki and Vasudeva were the biological parents. Likewise, in Indian mythology Gandhari made Dhritarashtra the proud father of 100 children though he had no biological relation with them.

(A) The primordial urge to have a biological child of one's own flesh, blood and DNA aided with technology and the purchasing power of money coupled with the Indian entrepreneurial spirit has generated the "reproductive tourism industry" estimated at Indian Rupees 25,000 crores (US dollars 5,000 million) today. This comes as a boon to childless couples all round the world. At the same time it raises serious ethical and legal concerns and mirrors the plight of the poor of an underdeveloped country who are willing to sell something as sacrosanct as their women's motherhood.

(B) In a developed country like UK no contract or surrogacy agreement is legally binding. In most States in the US, compensated surrogacy arrangements are either illegal or unenforceable. In some states in Australia arranging commercial surrogacy is a criminal offence and any surrogacy agreement giving custody to others is void. In Canada and New Zealand, commercial surrogacy has been illegal since 2004, although altruistic surrogacy is allowed. In France, Germany and Italy, surrogacy, commercial or not is unlawful. In Israel, law only accepts the surrogate mother as the real mother and commercial surrogacy is illegal. What then prompts India to enact a proposed law to make surrogacy agreements legally enforceable is to protect the genetic parents, surrogate mother and the child.

(C) India's surrogacy boom began in January 2004 with a grandmother delivering her daughter's twins. The success flashed over the world literally spawned a virtual industry in the State of Gujarat in India. Today, while Iceland has the first openly gay lady politician as its Prime Minister, India boasts of being the first country intending to legalise commercial surrogacy to legitimize both intra and inter-country surrogacy which is rampantly abound.

(D) Would-be parents from the Indian Diaspora in the US, UK and Canada and foreigners from Malaysia, UAE, Afghanistan, Indonesia, Uzbekistan, Pakistan besides Nepal are descending on sperm banks and In-Vitro Fertilisation (IVF) centres in India looking for South Asian genetic traits of perfect sperm donors. Equally, renting wombs is another easy and cheap option in India. Relatively low cost of medical services, easy availability of surrogate wombs, abundant choices of donors with similar racial attributes and lack of any law to regulate these practices is attracting both foreigners and Non-Resident Indians (NRIs) to sperm banks and surrogate mothers in India.

(E) India, surreptitiously, has become a booming centre of a fertility market with its "reproductive tourism" industry reportedly estimated at Indian Rupees 25,000 crores (US dollars 5,000 million) today. Clinically called "Assisted Reproductive Technology" (ART), it has been in vogue in India since 1978 and today an estimated 200, 000 clinics across the country offer artificial insemination, IVF and surrogacy.

(F) So much so, in the recent decision of the Supreme Court on 29 September 2008 in *Baby Manji Yamada v. Union of India*, AIR 2009 SC 84, it was observed that "commercial surrogacy" reaching "industry proportions is sometimes referred to by the emotionally charged and potentially offensive terms: wombs for rent, outsourced pregnancies or baby farms". It is presumably considered legitimate because no Indian law prohibits surrogacy. But then, as a retort, no law permits surrogacy either. However, the changing face of law is now going to usher in a new rent-a-womb law as India is set to be the only country in the world to legalise commercial surrogacy.

## II. SOME RECENT HAPPENINGS

(G) The complicated case of Japanese baby Manji born on 25 July 2008 to an Indian surrogate mother with IVF technology upon fertilization of her Japanese parents eggs and sperms in Tokyo and the embryo being implanted in Ahmedabad, triggered off complex, knotty issues. The Japanese biological parents got divorced and the mother disowned the infant upon its birth in India. The grandmother of the infant petitioned the Supreme Court challenging the directions given by the Rajasthan High Court relating to production and custody of baby Manji Yamada. Her request to the Apex Court for permission for the infant to travel with her and for issuance of a passport under consideration with the Central Government was directed to be disposed off expeditiously. Following the directions of the Supreme Court dated 29 September 2008, the Regional Passport Office in Jaipur issued an "Identity Certificate" to the baby on 1 November 2008. Thereupon, the grandmother Emiko Yamada flew out to Japan with the baby. A pandora's box has opened with a floodgate of questions and issues related to ethics and legality surrounding surrogacy with Japanese *baby Manji's* case (supra). However, her citizenship status remained unclear.

(H) In another separate case, Israeli gay couple Yonatan and Omer Gher became parents in India on 12 October 2008, when their child was conceived with the help of a Mumbai based surrogate mother in a fertility clinic in Bandra. It is reported that a 3.8 kilo baby boy was born to them at Hiranandani Hospital in Powai (Mumbai) on 12 October 2008.

Reportedly, Yonatan and Omer had been together for the past seven years and had decided to start a family. But since Israel reportedly does not allow same sex couples to adopt or have a surrogate child, India became their choice to find a surrogate mother. Yonatan and Omer reportedly first came to Mumbai in January 2008 for an IVF cycle when Yonatan is stated to have donated his sperm. Thereafter, they selected an anonymous "mother". Accordingly, the child was conceived with the help of a Mumbai based surrogate mother in a fertility clinic in Bandra. After the child was born, the gay couple left for Israel with the child on 17 November 2008.

(I) Subsequently, in the year 2010, another gay couple, Dan Goldberg and Arnon Angel from Israel to whom twin baby boys were born in Mumbai from an Indian surrogate mother, were stranded in India after the refusal of the Jerusalem Family Court to allow a paternity test to initiate the process for Israeli citizenship for the twins. The issue was debated in the Knesset (Israeli Parliament) where Prime Minister Benjamin Netanyahu had to intervene so that the infants could be brought to Israel following legal procedures. Ultimately, in appeal, the Jerusalem District Court, accepted the claim that it was in the best interest to hold a DNA paternity test to establish that Dan Goldberg was the father of the twin baby boys Itai and Liron. The DNA samples of Goldberg and the twins were brought to the Sheeba Medical Centre in Israel which established Goldberg as the father of the infants. After being stranded in Mumbai for over 3 months, Goldberg and his twin baby boys returned to Israel in May 2010 after being granted Israeli passports.

(J) After a frustrating two-year legal battle in India on behalf of their surrogate sons – Nikolas and Leonard – German couple Jan Balaz and Susan Anna Lohald got to go to Germany after the Supreme Court of India intervened and in a Court hearing on 26 May 2010, the Indian Government agreed to provide them exit permits. The twin babies were born in the State of Gujarat in January, 2008, and registered as children born of a foreign couple through an Indian surrogate mother. Upon being declined birth certificates, Jan Balaz moved the Gujarat High Court which ruled that since the surrogate mother is an Indian national, therefore, the children will also be treated as Indian nationals and will be entitled to Indian passports. However, the Government of India challenged this decision stating that the toddlers being surrogate children, they could not be granted Indian citizenship, which rendered the twins stateless as they got neither German nor Indian citizenship. The German authorities had also refused visas to the twins on the ground that German law did not recognize surrogacy as a means to parenthood. Ultimately, Jan Balaz and Susan Lohald went through an inter-country adoption process in India, upon which the Indian Government granted exit permits to the German surrogate twins to enable their journey back home to Germany.

(K) As of now, homosexuality is no longer an "Unnatural Offence" in India. Previously, section 377 of the Indian Penal Code, which criminalizes homosexuality, was struck down as unconstitutional by the High Court of Delhi on 2 July 2009 to decriminalize homosexuality [For more details see: *Naz foundation v. Government of NCT of Delhi*, 160(2009) DLT 277]. However, there is no bar to gay couples hiring a surrogate mother to deliver children for gay couples in India. Thus, there are reports in the media that there are numerous gay couples coming to India to look for surrogate mothers, as India does not disallow such surrogacy arrangements.

## III. THE POSITION OF INDIAN LAW ON THE SUBJECT OF SURROGACY: PRINCIPALLY UNDER THE 2005 GUIDELINES

(L) In the absence of any law to govern surrogacy, the Indian Council of Medical Research (ICMR) issued Guidelines in 2005 to check the malpractices of Assisted Reproductive Technology (ART). These national guidelines for accreditation, supervision and regulation of ART Clinics in India, 2005 are non statutory, have no legal sanctity and are not binding. Silent on major issues, they lack teeth and are often violated. Exploitation, extortion, and ethical abuses in surrogacy trafficking are rampant, go undeterred and surrogate mothers are often misused with impunity. Surrogacy in UK, USA and Australia costs more than US Dollars 50,000 whereas advertisements on websites in India give varying costs of about US Dollars 10,000 besides offering the services of egg donors and surrogate mothers. It is a free trading market, flourishing and thriving in the business of babies.

(M) At a time when the world's first test-tube baby Louise Brown born in 1978 in UK has now herself become a mother and high profile international adoptions by celebrities like Madonna and Angelina Jolie are glorifying international adoption, India does not lag behind. Noted Indian film actress Sushmita Sen inspires single women both in India and abroad to adopt children breaking conventional taboos and age-old practices. Resultantly, orphan girls are finding mothers in India and abroad.

(N) Genuine adoptive foreign and NRI would be parents too are pitted against an insurmountable wall. Child adoption in India is a complicated issue. It is over burdened with knotty legal processes and complicated lengthy procedures for those who want to give a new home and a new life to reported 12 million Indian orphans. Even though the Indian Constitution ordains it to be a sovereign, socialist, secular, democratic republic, 64 years of Independence have not given a comprehensive adoption law applicable to all its citizens, irrespective of the religion they profess or the country they live in as Non-Resident Indians (NRIs), Persons of Indian Origin (PIOs) or Overseas Citizens of India (OCIs). Resultantly, those who cannot by law adopt and can be appointed only as guardians under personal Indian laws, turn to options of IVF clinics or rent surrogate wombs. It is in this perspective that India now needs to adopt another law to turn to actual reality, the dreams of those who live abroad rather than turning to unhappy and sometimes unethical practices.

(O) A silent revolutionary change is fast heralding a new dawn in matter of inter-country adoptions. However, the plethora of Indian laws, does not improve the plight of 12 million orphaned children in India who need adoptive parents. The Guardian and Wards Act (GWA), 1890 permits guardianship and not adoption. The Hindu Adoption and Maintenance Act (HAMA), 1956 does not permit non-Hindus to adopt a Hindu child. Requirements of immigration have further hurdles even after adoption. Should law not change because these children need adoptive parents? May be the urge to be a parent has now taken over in the form of "embryo adoption" wherein fertilized sperms and eggs developed into an embryo are successfully implanted in Indian clinics and nurtured by foreign mothers in their homeland ensuring hassle free adoption of Indian embryos without complicated procedures. Technology has overtaken law. Time is now ripe for Indian laws also to legitimize adoptions. It must be pointed out here that the laws would only be successful in achieving their ends if and only if an international viewpoint is visibly reflected. Society has engineered changes. Indians whether NRIs, OCIs or PIOs are all Indians and must get the first benefit of adopting Indian children.

## IV. THE NEW LAW IN THE MAKING: THE ASSISTED REPRODUCTIVE TECHNOLOGY (REGULATION) BILL & RULES, 2010

(P) In a phenomenal exercise to legalise commercial surrogacy, The Assisted Reproductive Technology (Regulation) Bill & Rules, 2010, a draft bill prepared by a 12 members committee including experts from ICMR, medical specialists and other experts from the Ministry of Health and Family Welfare, Government of India has been posted online recently for feedback. This Bill, earlier also floated in 2008 for comment, is stated to be an Act to provide for a national framework or the regulation and supervision of Assisted Reproductive Technology and matter connected therewith or incidental thereto as a unique proposed law to be put before the Indian Parliament. Abetting surrogacy, it legalizes commercial surrogacy stating that the surrogate mother may receive monetary compensation and will relinquish all parental rights. Single parents can also have children using a surrogate mother. Foreigners, upon registration with their Embassy can seek surrogate arrangements. It also legalizes commercial surrogacy for single persons, married or unmarried couples stating that the surrogate mother shall enter into a legally enforceable surrogacy agreement. The 2010 draft bill states that foreigners or NRIs coming to India to rent a womb shall have to submit documentation confirming that their country of residence recognizes surrogacy as legal and that it will give citizenship to the child born through the surrogacy agreement from an Indian mother.

(Q) Before the law is put on the anvil, it needs a serious debate. Ethically, should women be paid for being surrogates? Can the rights of women and children be bartered? If the arrangements fall foul, will it amount to adultery? Is the new law a compromise in surpassing complicated Indian adoption procedures? Is the new law compromising with reality in legitimising existing surrogacy rackets? Is India promoting "reproductive tourism"? Does the law protect the surrogate mother? Should India take the lead in adapting a new law not fostered in most countries? These are only some questions which need to be answered before we drape the new law. Let us delve into our hearts and with introspection decide carefully. Are we looking at a bane or a boon? We should not wait for time to test it. We should decide now. The surrogacy bill needs to be discussed threadbare.

Despite the legal, moral and social complexities that shroud surrogacy, there is no stopping people from exploring the possibility of becoming a parent. Women who rent their womb for surrogate pregnancy are slowly shaking off their inhibition and fear of social ostracism to bring joy to childless couples.

(R) The proposed Bill which is called an Act "to provide for a national framework for the regulation and supervision of Assisted Reproductive Technology and matters connected therewith or incidental thereto" provides the constitution of a National Advisory Board for Assisted Reproductive Technology, comprising of members not exceeding 21, whose functions are confined to promoting the cause of reproductive technology. The salient details are:

- The new Assisted Reproductive Technology (Regulation) Bill & Rules, 2010, legalises commercial surrogacy, stating that the surrogate mother may receive monetary compensation for carrying the child in addition to health-care and treatment expenses during pregnancy.

- Both the couple or individual seeking surrogacy through the use of Assisted Reproductive Technology, and the surrogate mother shall enter into a surrogacy agreement which shall be legally enforceable.
- The surrogate mother will relinquish all parental rights over the child once the amount is transferred and birth certificates will be in the name of commissioning parent/s.
- The prescribed age-limit for a surrogate mother is between 21 and 35 years. The proposed Bill also states that no women shall act as a surrogate mother for more than five children including her own.
- Single persons, men or women or single parents, unmarried couples can also have children using a surrogate mother. In case of a single man or a woman, the baby will be his/her legitimate child. A child born to an unmarried couple using a surrogate mother and with the consent of both the parties shall be their legitimate child.
- All foreigners seeking infertility treatment in India will first have to register with their embassy. Their notarised statement will then have to be handed over to the treating doctor. The foreign couple will also state whom the child should be entrusted to in case of an eventuality such as a genetic parent's death.
- A foreigner or foreign couple not resident in India or an NRI individual or couple seeking surrogacy in India shall appoint the local guardian legally responsible for taking care of the surrogate child during and after pregnancy.
- The party seeking surrogacy must ensure and establish to the ART clinic that the party would be able to take the child born through surrogacy outside India to the country of the party's origin or residence as the case may be.
- A child born out of surrogacy shall be the legitimate child of both the parties or of the single man or woman as the case may be. The birth certificate will contain the name or names of the genetic parent or parents (as the case may be) who sought such use. If parties get divorced or separated, the child shall be the legitimate child of the couple. The birth certificate of a child born through the use of Assisted Reproductive Technology shall contain the name or names of the parent or parents, as the case may be, who sought such use.
- If a foreigner or a foreign couple seeks sperm or egg donation, or surrogacy, in India, and a child is born as a consequence, the child, even though born in India, shall not be an Indian citizen.
- Foreigners or NRIs coming to India seeking surrogacy in India shall appoint a local guardian who will be legally responsible for taking care of the surrogate during and after pregnancy till the child is delivered to the foreigner or foreign couple or the local guardian. Further, the party seeking surrogacy must ensure and establish through proper documentation that the country of their origin permits surrogacy and that the child born

through surrogacy in India will be permitted entry in the country of their origin as a biological child of the commissioning couple/individual. If the foreign party seeking surrogacy fails to take delivery of the child born to the surrogate mother, the local guardian will be legally obliged to take the child and be free to hand over the child to an adoption agency. In case of adoption or the legal guardian having to bring up the child in India, the child will be given Indian citizenship.

- Surrogacy be recommended for patients for whom it is medically impossible/undesirable to carry a baby to term.
- ART clinic must not advertise surrogacy arrangements. The responsibility should rest with the couple or a semen bank.
- ART clinic must ensure that the surrogate woman satisfies all the testable criteria (sexually transmitted or communicable disease that may endanger the pregnancy).
- A prospective surrogate mother must be tested for HIV and shown to be a seronegative for this virus just before embryo transfer.

## V. LEGAL ISSUES CURRENTLY PLAGUING THE FIELD AND THEIR POSSIBLE SOLUTIONS

(S) Position of Indian law today *viz-a-viz* surrogacy arrangements:

➢ The questions now often posed professionally are (i) as to what would be the remedy available to biological parent/s to obtain exclusive legal custody of surrogate children; (ii) how can the rights of the surrogate mother be waived off completely; (iii) how can the rights of the ovum or sperm donor be restricted; and (iv) how can the genetic constitution of the surrogate baby be established and recorded with authenticity.

➢ As of now, in the case of foreigners or non-Hindu couples, single parents or gay parents, they can only claim guardianship of a child under the GWA in respect of children born out of surrogacy arrangements. The adoption process can take place only in the foreign parent's country of nationality or permanent residence as the case may be. This is because the HMGA and HAMA do not allow any adoption proceedings to non-Hindus and thus any foreign non-Hindu parent cannot invoke HAMA/HMGA for adoption proceedings in India. Unless, these Indian enactments are amended or a new provision is enacted, adoption may be difficult for non-Hindu couples or foreigners.

➢ Surrogacy in India is legitimate because no Indian law prohibits surrogacy. To determine the legality of surrogacy agreements, the Indian Contract Act would apply and thereafter the enforceability of any such agreement would be within the domain of section 9 of the Indian Code of Civil Procedure (CPC). Alternatively, the biological parent/s can also move an application under the Guardian and Wards Act for seeking an order of appointment to be declared as the guardian of the surrogate children.

➢ In the absence of any law to govern surrogacy, the 2005 ICMR Guidelines apply. But, being non-statutory, they are not enforceable or justiciable in a Court of Law. Under para 3.10.1 a child born through surrogacy must be adopted by the genetic (biological parents). However, this may not be possible in case of non-Hindu foreign parents who cannot adopt in India.

➢ Under Section 10 of the Indian Contract Act, 1872 all agreements are contracts, if they are made by free consent of parties competent to contract, are for a lawful consideration, are with a lawful object, and are not expressly declared to be void. Therefore, if any surrogacy agreement satisfies these conditions, it is an enforceable contract. Thereafter, under Section 9 CPC, it can be the subject of a civil suit before a civil Court to establish all/any issues relating to the surrogacy agreement and for a declaration/injunction for the reliefs prayed for.

➢ Other issues, which have now cropped up for opinion are as to whether a single or a gay parent can be considered to be the custodial parent of a surrogate child. As of today, it may be stated that a single or a gay parent can be considered to be the custodial parent by virtue of being the genetic or biological father of the surrogate child born out of a surrogacy arrangement. Japanese *baby Manji Yamada's* case (supra), and the Israel gay couple case who fathered the child in India are clear examples to establish that this is possible. Under para 3.16.1 of the 2005 ICMR Guidelines dealing with legitimacy of children born through ART (which were the basis of the claim in the Japanese baby's case in the Supreme Court), this claim can be made. However, only in a petition for guardianship under GWA and/or in a suit for declaration in a civil Court, the exclusive custodial rights can be adjudicated by a Court of competent jurisdiction upon appreciation of evidence and considering all claims made in this regard.

➢ What would be the status of divorced biological parents in respect of the custody of a surrogate child. Essentially, this is a question which will require determination in accordance with the surrogacy agreement between the parties. There would be apparently no bar to either of the divorced parents claiming custody of a surrogate child if the other parent does not claim the same. However, if the custody is contested, it may require adjudication by a Court of competent jurisdiction.

➢ Would biological parent/s be considered the legal parent of the children. In answer to this question it can be stated that the biological parents would be considered to be the legal parents of the children by virtue of the surrogacy agreement executed between the parties and the surrogate mother. Under para 3.16.1 of the 2005 ICMR Guidelines dealing with legitimacy of the child born through ART, it is stated that "a child born through ART shall be presumed to be the legitimate child of the couple, born within wedlock, with consent of both the spouses, and with all the attendant rights of parentage, support and inheritance. Even in the 2010 Draft Bill and Rules, a child born to a married couple, an unmarried couple, a single parent or a single man or woman shall be the legitimate child of the couple man or woman as the case may be.

➢ How the domain of international law can provide an amiable solution to the rising complexities arising out of inter-country surrogacy settlements.

However, the moot question which may arise for determination whether a judicial verdict for determination of rights of parties in a surrogacy arrangement is essential in respect of a foreign biological parent who wishes to take the surrogate child to his/her country of origin or permanent residence, it can be said that either a declaration from a civil Court and/or a guardianship order ought to be a must to conclusively establish the rights of all parties and to prevent any future discrepancies arising in respect of any claims thereto.

## VI. POSITION OF LAW UNDER THE 2010 BILL

- Under the ART Regulation Bill 2010, Assisted Reproductive Technology, Surrogacy, "gamete", and Surrogacy agreement have been defined as follows:

  "Assisted Reproductive Technology", with its grammatical variations and cognate expressions, means all techniques that attempt to obtain a pregnancy by handling or manipulating the sperm or the oocyte outside the human body, and transferring the gamete or the embryo into the reproductive tract;

  "Surrogacy", means an arrangement in which a woman agrees to a pregnancy, achieved through Assisted Reproductive Technology, in which neither of the gametes belong to her or her husband, with the intention to carry it and hand over the child to the person or persons for whom she is acting as a surrogate;

  "Gamete", means sperm and oocyte (that is egg);

  "Surrogacy Agreement", means a contract between the person(s) availing of Assisted Reproductive Technology and the surrogate mother;

- Chapter 2 of the Bill describes the constitution of authorities to regulate Assisted Reproductive Technology. A 21-member National Advisory Board comprising of various experts is sought to be created with functions to promote Assisted Reproductive Technology related issues. State boards are recommended in States and State registration authorities are sought to be created for procedural purposes. Proceedings before the National and State Boards are deemed to be civil Court proceedings for limited purposes & are sought to be treated as judicial proceedings even though the constitution of the National or State Advisory Board have no judicial officers, Judges or designated Courts as constituents.

- Chapter 3 of the Bill talks for procedures for registration and complaints in respect of Assisted Reproductive Technology clinics. Chapter 4 talks of the duties of such clinics. Chapter 5 talks of sourcing, storage, handling and record keeping for gametes, embryos and surrogates. Chapter 6 relates to regulation on research on embryos.

- Chapter 7 discusses rights and duties of patients, donors, surrogates and children in extensor. The rights and duties are well defined and determination of the status of the child is laid out in detail irrespective of the status of parties as a couple, as an unmarried couple, as single parents, gay parents or otherwise. The duty to take children born through surrogacy from India to the country of origin or residence of the biological parents or residence is spelt out.

- Chapter 8 talks of offences and penalties for contravening the provisions of the Act and chapter 9 in the miscellaneous section talks of maintenance of records, power to search and seize, power to make regulation and rules. The Act is stated to be in addition to and not in derogation with any other law for the time being in force.

## VII. ANOMALIES IN THE ART REGULATION BILL, 2010

- The Bill has neither designated, nor authorised nor created any Court or judicial forum to resolve issues which will require adjudication in problems arising out of surrogacy, ART and surrogacy agreements. This is a very big lacunae in the Bill. There has to be a designated or a defined Court as in the Hindu Marriage Act or the Guardian and Wards Act which has to be vested with the authority in law to decide disputes arising under the proposed law.
- The National and State Advisory Boards are only authorities who will promote ART, surrogacy arrangements and related procedures. The proceedings of these boards have been deemed to be "judicial proceedings" before civil Courts for limited purposes. There is no designated Court, judicial officer or Judge appointed, created or nominated for this purpose. Therefore, how far these advisory boards will be able to perform the "judicial proceedings" "deemed to be a civil Court" remains to be seen.
- Chapter 3 talks of complaints, chapter 4 talks of duties, chapters 5 and 6 talks of more ART related issues. Chapter 7 talks of duties. Chapter 8 talks of offences and penalties which carry serious consequences. But the question is who will adjudicate these and decide them to impose penalties. Who will determine these "offences." Unless and until a Court is designated, created or nominated, all this will remain inconclusive, indecisive and incomplete.
- There are already serious issues of determining parentage, nationality, issuance of passport, grant of visas and problems of disputed parentage. There is no forum defined, designated or created which will look into these problems or determine how they have to decided or dealt with.
- *Baby Manji Yamada's* case (supra), is an eye opener. Thereafter, the Israeli gay couple's case and the German couple's case, are a follower in the sequel of problem areas. Embassies, Foreign Missions and High Commissions of different countries in India are looking at a resolution on these issues by means of a law in the making. But, parentage, nationality, passport, visa and related issues remained undetermined in the law in making. There is already a conflict on adoption and guardianship as non-Hindus cannot adopt in India. Therefore, would it not be better to make it mandatory to create a Court for adoption/guardianship purposes by proper statutory enactments before a child is removed from India to a foreign country. This will not only provide a system for uniform application to check malpractices but will also conclusively ascertain rights of parties in case of a dispute. Moreover, all Embassies, Foreign Missions and High Commissions will be guided by a proper procedure. Thus, the Indian law cannot afford to remain a *kupa manduka* or the frog in a well approach and must embrace the concept of *vasudevayakatumbakam*, ie the whole world is my family.

- In the light of the above thoughts, it may be necessary to create a procedure for adoption, guardianship, determination of rights etc. to be mandatory through a nominated Court, designated Court or specified authority to be compulsorily followed in case of any inter-country surrogacy arrangement. Likewise, this forum, Court, authority can also be the adjudicating authority to determine disputes decide offences and determine penalties under the Bill. Without this, the proposed Act is not meaningful, is inconclusive and will only create more uncertainty leading to more disputes and inconsistent views. Day in and day out, problems arise but there is no solution in the existing legal system. Hence, it is extremely necessary to enact a suitable legislation forthwith.

## VIII. ABSENCE OF CODIFIED LAW ON SURROGACY IN INDIA

In the absence of any codified law as the situation exists today, in respect of surrogacy arrangements, the ordinary civil law of the land would be applicable in respect of surrogacy also since there is no specific law on the subject to govern such arrangements. The Code of Civil Procedure, 1908, is an Act made by the Indian Parliament for the entire territorial jurisdiction of India as a federal/central law to consolidate and amend the laws relating to the procedure of the Courts of civil judicature. Section 9 of this Code permits Courts to try all civil suits unless they are expressly or impliedly barred.

Section 9 of the Civil Procedure Code, 1908 provides as follows:

> "9. *Courts to try all civil suits unless barred*—The Courts shall subject to the provisions herein contained have jurisdiction to try all suits of a civil nature excepting suits of which their cognizance is either expressly or impliedly barred."

Resultantly, in the law as it exists in India today, both the validity and enforceability of any surrogacy arrangement or agreement can be achieved in a civil Court by preferring a civil suit under section 9 of the Code above by seeking appropriate relief as is admissible to parties under Indian law. This option can be exercised to enforce a surrogacy agreement if it is valid in law. However, the touchstone of the validity of such a civil suit would have to be tested under the provisions of the Indian Contract law to see if such agreement can be a contract.

In the above backdrop, it may thus be necessary to also see the position of surrogacy arrangements or agreements under the Indian law of contract. It may thus first be pertinent to quote section 10 of the Indian Contract Act 1872, which specifies as to what agreements are contracts. In this regard, section 10 may be quoted in its own words for the present context:

> "10. *What agreements are contracts* – All agreements are contracts if they are made by the free consent of parties competent to contract, for a lawful consideration and with a lawful object, and are not hereby expressly declared to be void."

For the present context, any surrogacy arrangement or agreement, which is arrived at by the free consent of the parties who are competent to contract and who have entered into the arrangement or agreement for a lawful consideration as also with a lawful object which is not expressly declared to be void, would be a contract. It may be added here that since as per the prevalent law in India commercial surrogacy procedures are legal in India, subject to the fulfillment of other conditions of section 10 of the Contract Act quoted above, a surrogacy arrangement or agreement would be a contract. In the face of this conclusion, a surrogacy agreement or arrangement would be an enforceable contract by preferring a civil suit under section 9 of the Code of Civil Procedure. This possible option can be exercised at the option of parties whenever necessary and to adjudicate any determination of disputed rights.

For the present purposes, it may be helpful to note certain observations of the Supreme Court of India interpreting section 9 of the Code of Civil Procedure. The Supreme Court of India in the case of *E. Achuthan Nair* v. *P. Narayanan Nair,* AIR 1987 SC 2137, has held in this regard as hereunder:

> "In India, the question whether a suit is cognizable by a civil court is to be decided with reference to Section 9 of the Civil Procedure Code. If the suit is of a civil nature, the court will have jurisdiction to try the suit unless it is either expressly or impliedly barred."

Further, the Supreme Court of India in another case, *Srikant Kashinath Jituri* v. *Corporation of the City of Belgaum,* AIR 1995 SC 288, has held as hereunder:

> "The expansive nature of the Section 9 is demonstrated by use of phraseology with positive and negative. The earlier part opens the door widely and later debars entry to only those, which are expressly or impliedly barred. The two explanations, one existing from inception and latter added in 1976 bring out clearly the legislative intention of extending operation of the section to such religious matters where right to property or office is involved irrespective of whether any fee is attached to the office or not. The language used is simple but explicit and clear. It is structured on the basic principle of a civilized jurisprudence that absence of machinery for enforcement of right renders it nugatory. The heading which is normally key to the civil suits are cognizable unless barred. What is meant by it is explained further by widening the ambit of the section by use of the word 'shall' and the expression, 'all suits of a civil nature' unless 'expressly or impliedly barred'. Each word and expression casts in obligation on the Court to exercise jurisdiction for enforcement or right. The word 'shall' makes it mandatory. No Court can refuse to entertain a suit if it is of description mentioned in the section. That is amplified by use of expression, 'all suits of civil nature'. The word 'civil nature' is wider than the word 'civil proceeding'. The section would, therefore, be available in every case where the dispute has the characteristic of affecting one's right which are not only civil but of civil nature."

The above decisions of the Supreme Court of India can be relied upon to state that any enforceable surrogacy agreement which is a valid contract under Indian law can be the subject of adjudication in a civil suit by a Court of competent civil jurisdiction in India and there would be no bar to maintainability of such a civil suit.

In the face of the above interpretations of section 9 of the Code of Civil Procedure by the Supreme Court of India, it can be safe to conclude that only such surrogacy agreements or arrangements which satisfy the ingredients of section 10 of the Indian Contract Act would be contracts which are enforceable in a civil Court since the cognizance of such a civil suit would neither be expressly or impliedly barred. Hence, every surrogacy agreement will have to be tested on the touch stone of the above ingredients to confirm whether such agreement is a valid contract under Indian Law which can be enforced in a Indian Court of law.

It may also be necessary to point out that there also exists in India another federal/Central legislation applicable throughout the territory of India called 'The Guardian and Wards Act, 1890 (GWA,1890) which is an Act to consolidate and amend the law relating to guardians and wards prevalent in India. Section 4 of the Act specifies the persons entitled to apply for a guardianship order and section 9 prescribes the Court having jurisdiction to entertain the guardianship application. Section 10 lays down the form of the application and section 11 prescribes the procedure on admission of the application. Section 13 lays down the requirement of hearing of evidence before making of an order under the Act and section 26 permits the removal of a ward from the jurisdiction of the Court. This is the second possible option which can be availed of by the biological parent at the option of parties, if desired for enforcement of the rights of parties arising from the surrogacy arrangements or agreements. Any surrogate parent can in terms of the valid surrogacy agreement executed between the parties seek to take out guardianship proceedings in India under the GWA to enforce biological parentage rights for establishing exclusive custody of the surrogate children on the basis of genetic (DNA) evidence and other rights spelt out in the surrogacy agreement. This optional legal proceeding can be availed of in India by a biological parent optionally, if required at all in the event of any eventuality or dispute between the parties to the agreement and considered necessary in such a situation.

## IX. COMMERCIALISED PACKAGE COSTS OF SURROGACY ARRANGEMENTS FROM INDIA

A very recent detailed article titled "Moms on the Market," published on 13 March 2011 in a renowned Indian national newspaper The Hindustan Times, which is published simultaneously from a large number of major cities in India. We are referring to the Chandigarh edition of the Hindustan Times.

The relevant rates and figures with regard to surrogacy arrangements as highlighted in box format within the said one complete page article are tabulated hereunder:

**"THE SURROGACY SUPERMART**

From being a centre of cheap reproductive labour, India is now virtually a surrogacy supermarket where deals are available off the shelf and bonuses are thrown in for good measure. Here's what it takes to go baby shopping:

**Surrogate charges: INR 1,00,000-3,50,000**

This fee varies across various cities, IVF clinics and the third party (recruitment agents) involved. To claim this, surrogates need to be "healthy", married, have at least one child and be "mature enough" to understand/handle the surrogacy. Specific demands can be made by parents. For instance, Israeli couples don't want Muslim women. Some couples want to ensure that the women don't smoke, drink and are "religious-minded." Clinics can also be choosy: not all will agree to do surrogacy for gay couples.

**IVF procedure costs: INR66,000**

Some IVF packages include upto 4 embryo transfer attempts. So, a surrogate could be implanted with about 3-4 embryos to ensure pregnancy.

**Egg donor (Indian): INR1,80,000 extra**

Highly qualified, post graduate, fertile, fair complexioned egg donors can demand uptoR 50,000.

**Egg donor (Blonde, blue-eyed):**

Add another **INR**1,80,000 for donors flown in from the US, UK, Russia

**Twins:** R 1,35,000 extra for handling complications, C-section etc

**Hiring a second surrogate:**

Add another **INR**4 lakh to the package. There will be an extra cost if both surrogates get pregnant and foetal reductions need to be done.

**Surrogate compensation:**

**INR** 2,000-3,000 for food.

This varies across cities. Some surrogates say they get even lesser than **INR** 2,000. Some parents send across gifts, for the surrogate, clothes for her children, religious texts and songs and also end up offering any other monetary help.

**Other add-ons:** Spa packages, Agra tours, airport pick-up, drop."

Also, the source to the said article states that fertility clinic costs, and other costs are approximate figures. The said article also gives figures of complete packages offered by some of the fertility clinics and medical tourism agencies.

Queries are often put forward by instructing solicitors and attorneys in so far relating to the issue of costs, which have been very pin-pointedly answered on the basis of the above-mentioned comprehensive article appearing in one of the India's leading national newspapers.

## X. ARRANGEMENTS RELATING TO THE REGISTRATION OF BIRTHS REGARDING CHILDREN BORN OUT OF SURROGACY ARRANGEMENTS IN INDIA

In India at the moment, we do not have any legislation on legal parentage as a result of surrogacy arrangements. At the moment, in India we have the Registration of the Births and Deaths Act, 1969 which does not contain any provision regarding parentage as a result of a surrogacy arrangement. The said enactment laid down by the Parliament of India came into force on 31 May 1969. Surrogacy parentage was not an issue at the time the said legislation came into being. Neither, have there been any amendments or additions with regard to any surrogacy issues in the said enactment pertaining to the registration of births and deaths in the Indian jurisdiction.

That in so far relating to arrangements for registration of births of child born out of surrogacy arrangement is concerned, in India reference is drawn to the relevant provisions of the 2005 ICMR Guidelines and the 2010 Bill.

Para 3.5.4 (at page 63) of the 2005 ICMR Guidelines clearly provides that the birth certificate of children born out of a surrogacy arrangement, shall be in the name of the genetic parents.

Para 3.5.4 of the 2005 ICMR Guidelines provides as follows;

> "A surrogate mother carrying a child biologically unrelated to her must register as a patient in her own name. While registering she must mention that she is a surrogate mother and provide all the necessary information about the genetic parents such as names, addresses, etc. She must not use/ register in the name of the person for whom she is carrying the child, as this would post legal issues, particularly in the untoward event of maternal death (in whose names will the hospital certify this death?). The birth certificate shall be in the name of the genetic parents. The clinic, however, must also provide a certificate to the genetic parents giving the name and address of the surrogate mother. All the expenses of the surrogate mother during the period of pregnancy and post-natal care relating to pregnancy should be done by the couple seeking surrogacy. The surrogate mother would also be entitled to a monetary compensation from the couple for agreeing to act as surrogate; the exact value of this compensation should be decided by discussion between the couple and the proposed surrogate mother. An oocyte donor can not act as a surrogate mother for the couple to whom the ooctye is being donated."

Likewise, attention is drawn to chapter VII of the 2010 Bill, which deals with rights and duties of patients, donors, surrogates and children. In this regard attention is invited to para 34 (10) of chapter VII which provides as follows:

> "The birth certificate issued in respect of a baby born through surrogacy shall bear the name(s) of individual/individuals who commissioned the surrogacy, as parents."

Hence, from a combined reading of the relevant provisions in the 2005 ICMR Guidelines and the 2010 Bill, it can be safely asserted that the birth certificates of children born out of surrogacy arrangements should be in the name of the commissioning parents.

The said certificates are issued under sections 12 and 17 of Births and Deaths Act, 1969. For ease of reference, section 12 of the 1969 act reads as under:

> "**12. Extracts of registration entries to be given to informant.**—The Registrar shall, as soon as the registration of a birth or death has been completed give, free of charge, to the person who gives information under section 8 or section 9 an extract of the prescribed particulars under his hand from the register relating to such birth or death."

It is important to mention, normally the practice followed by Government hospitals and nursing homes in India, is that they forward particulars of all births with the relevant details to the designated authorities under the provisions of the registration of Births and Deaths Act, 1969. This is a mandatory and a statutory duty of the medical officer of such an institution, prescribed under section 8 of the Registration of Births and Deaths Act, 1969. Furthermore, the certified copy of the birth certificate is a public document in terms of section 76 of the Indian Evidence Act, 1872.

It is equally important to refer to section 17 of the 1969 Act. The same reads as under:

> "**17. Search of births and deaths register** – (1) Subject to any rules made in this behalf by the State Government, including rules relating to the payment of fees and postal charges, any person may—
>
> (a) cause a search to be made by the Registrar for any entry in a register of births and deaths;
>
> (b) obtain an extract from such register relating to any birth or death:
>
> Provided that no extract relating to any death, issued to any person, shall disclose the particulars regarding the cause of death as entered in the register.
>
> (2) All extracts given under this section shall be certified by the Registrar or any other officer authorised by the State government to give such extracts as provided in section 76 of the Indian Evidence Act, 1872 (1 of 1872), and shall be admissible in evidence for the purpose of proving the birth or death to which the entry relates."

Here it is submitted that in terms of clause 2 of section 17 of the 1969 Act, a birth certificate is admissible in evidence as far as the factum of birth is concerned. So, it can be argued that this is the legal position as to parentage of children born as a result of surrogacy arrangements in the Indian jurisdiction.

## XI. POSITION IN TERMS OF THE NATIONALITY OF CHILDREN BORN OUT OF SURROGACY ARRANGEMENTS IN INDIA

The legislation which deals with the acquisition and determination of Indian citizenship is the Citizenship Act, 1955. This enactment provides four modes of acquisition of citizenship which are contained in Sections 3, 4, 5 and 6 and the same are reproduced hereunder:

> "**3. Citizenship by birth**—
>
> (1) Except as provided in sub-section (2), every person born in India,—
>
> (a) on or after the 26th day of January, 1950, but before the 1st day of July 1987;
>
> (b) on or after the 1st day of July,1987,but before the commencement of the Citizenship (Amendment) Act, 2003 and either of whose parents is a citizen of India at the time of his birth;
>
> (c) on or after the commencement of the Citizenship (Amendment) Act, 2003, where—
>
> (i) both of his parents are citizens of India ; or
>
> (ii) one of whose parents is a citizen of India and the other is not an illegal migrant at the time of his birth,

shall be a citizen of India by birth.

(2) A person shall not be a citizen of India by virtue of this section if at the time of his birth—

(a) either his father or mother possesses such immunity from suits and legal process as is accorded to an envoy of a foreign sovereign power accredited to the President of India and he or she, as the case may be, is not a citizen of India; or

(b) his father or mother is an enemy alien and the birth occurs in a place then under occupation by the enemy.

**4. Citizenship by descent—**

(1) A person born outside India shall be a citizen of India by descent,—

(a) on or after the 26th day of January, 1950, but before 10th day of December, 1992, if his father is a citizen of India at the time of his birth ; or

(b) on or after the 10th day of December, 1992, if either of his parents is a citizen of India at the time of his birth:

Provided that if the father of such a person referred to in clause (a) was a citizen of India by descent only, that person shall not be a citizen of India by virtue of this section unless—

(a) his birth is registered at an Indian consulate within one year of its occurrence or the commencement of this Act, whichever is later, or, with the permission of the Central Government, after the expiry of the said period; or

(b) his father is, at the time of his birth, in service under a Government in India:

Provided further that if either of the parents of a person referred to in clause (b) was a citizen of India by descent only, that person shall not be a citizen of India by virtue of this section, unless—

(a) his birth is registered at an Indian consulate within one year of its occurrence or on or after the 10th day of December, 1992, whichever is later, or with the permission of the Central Government, after the expiry of the said period; or

(b) either of his parents is, at the time of his birth, in service under a Government in India:

Provided also that on or after the commencement of the Citizenship (Amendment) Act, 2003, a person shall not be a citizen of India by virtue of this section, unless his birth is registered at an Indian consulate in such form and in such manner as may be prescribed,—

(i) within one year of its occurrence or the commencement of the Citizenship (Amendment) Act, 2003, whichever is later ; or

(ii) with the permission of the Central Government, after the expiry of the said period:

Provided also that no such birth shall be registered unless the parents of such person declare, in suchform and in such manner as may be prescribed, that the minor does not hold the passport of another country.

(1A) A minor who is a citizen of India by virtue of this section and is also a citizen of any other country shall cease to be a citizen of India if he does not renounce the citizenship or nationality of another country within six months of attaining full age.

(2) If the Central Government so directs, a birth shall be deemed for the purposes of this section to have been registered with its permission, notwithstanding that its permission was not obtained before the registration.

(3) For the purposes of the proviso to sub-section (1),[any person] born outside undivided India who was, or was deemed to be, a citizen of India at the commencement of the Constitution shall be deemed to be a citizen of India by descent only.

**5. Citizenship by registration—**

(1) Subject to the provisions of this section and such conditions and restrictions as may be prescribed, the Central Government may, on an application made in this behalf, register as a citizen of India any person not being an illegal migrant who is not already such citizen by virtue of the Constitution or of any other provisions of this Act and belongs to any of the following categories, namely:—

(a) a person of Indian origin who is ordinarily resident in India for seven years before making an application for registration;

(b) a person of Indian origin who is ordinarily resident in any country or place outside undivided India;

(c) a person who is married to a citizen of India and is ordinarily resident in India for seven years before making an application for registration;

(d) minor children of persons who are citizens of India;

(e) a person of full age and capacity whose parents are registered as citizens of India under clause (a) of this sub-section or sub-section (1) of Section 6;

(f) a person of full age and capacity who, or either of his parents, was earlier citizen of independent India, and has been residing in India for one year immediately before making an application for registration;

(g) a person of full age and capacity who has been registered as an overseas citizen of India for five years, and who has been residing in India for [one year] before making an application for registration.

*Explanation 1.*—For the purpose of clauses (a) and (c), an applicant shall be deemed to be ordinarily resident in India if—

(i) he has resided in India throughout the period of twelve months immediately before making an application for registration ; and

(ii) he has resided in India during the eight years immediately preceding the said period of twelve months for a period of not less than six years.

*Explanation 2.*—For the purposes of this sub-section, a person shall be deemed to be of Indian origin if he, or either of his parents, was born in undivided India or in such other territory which became part of India after the 15th day of August, 1947.

(2) No person being of full age shall be registered as a citizen of India under sub-section (1) until he has taken the oath of allegiance in the form specified in the Second Schedule.

(3) No person who has renounced, or has been deprived of, his Indian citizenship or whose Indian citizenship has terminated, under this Act shall be registered as a citizen of India under sub-section (1) except by order of the Central Government.

(4) The Central Government may, if satisfied that there are special circumstances justifying such registration, cause any minor to be registered as a citizen of India.

(5) A person registered under this section shall be a citizen of India by registration as from the date on which he is so registered; and a person registered under the provisions of clause (b)(ii) of article 6 or article 8 of the Constitution shall be deemed to be a citizen of India by registration as from the commencement of the Constitution or the date on which he was so registered, whichever may be later.

(6) If the Central Government is satisfied that circumstances exist which render it necessary to grant exemption from the residential requirement under clause (c) of sub-section (1) to any person or a class of persons, it may, for reasons to be recorded in writing, grant such exemption.

***6. Citizenship by naturalisation***

(1) Where an application is made in the prescribed manner by any person of full age and capacity [not being an illegal migrant] for the grant of a certificate of naturalisation to him, the Central Government may, if satisfied that the applicant is qualified for naturalisation under the provisions of Third Schedule, grant to him a certificate of naturalisation:

Provided that, if in the opinion of the Central Government, the applicant is a person who has rendered distinguished service to the cause of science, philosophy, art, literature, world peace or human progress generally, it may waive all or any of the conditions specified in Third Schedule.

(2) The person to whom a certificate of naturalisation is granted under sub-section (1) shall, on taking the oath of allegiance in the form specified in

Second Schedule, be a citizen of India by naturalisation as from the date on which that certificate is granted."

Since there is no exclusive and separate legislation governing nationality and citizenship issues of children born out of surrogacy arrangements in India, hence, in such a situation all nationality and citizenship issues will be governed by the above-mentioned provisions of the Indian Citizenship Act, 1955.

## XII. PRESENT POSITION OF THE PETITION INSTITUTED IN THE SUPREME COURT OF INDIA FOR SPECIAL LEAVE TO APPEAL (CIVIL) NUMBER(S)31639/2009 (FROM THE JUDGMENT AND ORDER DATED 11/11/2009 IN LPA NO. 2151/2009 OF THE HIGH COURT OF GUJARAT AT AHMEDABAD) UNION OF INDIA & ANR. PETITIONER(S) v. JAN BALAZ & ORS. RESPONDENT(S). THIS CASE IS STILL PENDING FOR CONSIDERATION OF IMPORTANT PUBLIC ISSUES AT LARGE, WHILE THE NECESSARY RELIEF TO FACILITATE THE ONWARD MOVEMENT OF TWO MINOR SURRGOATE CHILDREN TO GERMANY STOOD GRANTED.

The above-mentioned case is an important case of a German couple, who had entered into a surrogacy arrangement in India. They encountered serious problems and had to invoke the jurisdiction of the Gujarat High Court. They had a High Court verdict in their favour, which was ultimately challenged by the Government of India before the Hon'ble Supreme Court of India. The operation of the Gujarat High Court judgment was stayed by the Hon'ble Supreme Court of India. The appeal in this particular case is still pending in the Hon'ble Supreme Court of India.

Nonetheless, the Hon'ble Supreme Court of India devised a unique way to facilitate the onward movement of the surrogate children to Germany. The visa problems were compounded by the fact that surrogacy is illegal in Germany and surrogacy does not have any sort of legal recognition at all in Germany.

The Hon'ble Supreme Court of India made the Central Adoption Resource Agency (hereafter CARA) which is an autonomous body under the aegis of the Women and Child Development, Government of India, a party to the said case. CARA principally deals with inter-country adoptions only. That when CARA was impleaded as a party before the Supreme Court of India, they contended that a surrogate child is not subject to the process of inter-country adoption, but on the intervention of the Supreme Court of India, the learned Solicitor General of India made a suggestion for issue of directions to CARA to take up the issue of adoption of the said children as a special case. And, these directions were successfully implemented. The German commissioning parents were successfully granted the relevant relief, while the case remains pending before the Hon'ble Supreme Court of India.

The entire factual background to this case, including reference judgments of Gujarat High Court, followed by the relevant orders past by the Hon'ble Supreme Court of India find mentioned below:

The citation of this case before the Gujarat High Court was as follows: *Jan Balaz v. Anand Municipality,* AIR 2010 Guj 21. Although, the operation of the said judgment was stayed by the Hon'ble Supreme Court of India on 25 November, 2009 but it is important to refer to the said Gujarat High Court judgment, because it gives important perspective related to surrogacy issues in India as also the legal dimensions at this moment in time.

The facts of this case in so far relating to the issuance of the birth certificates and the passports of the minor children have been elaborated in para 17 of the said judgment. In this particular case, birth certificates had been issued to the two minor children born out of a surrogacy arrangement. The said birth certificates issued by the Registrar of Births and Deaths of the competent jurisdiction showed the name of the mother as the gestational surrogate, and an Indian national. The German father's name also stood recorded in the said birth certificates. The Gujarat High Court noticed that the egg donor was also reported to be an Indian woman, of course her identity was not disclosed.

The Gujarat High Court held in the penultimate part of para 17 (at page 26) of said judgment as follows:

> "...Either way the mother of the babies is an Indian national. Petitioner, it is true, has not married Khristi Marthaben Immanuel, surrogate mother of the children or the egg donor. Children are born not out of a subsisting marriage. Even if the children are described as illegitimate children, even then they are born in this country to an Indian national and hence, they are entitled to get Citizenship by birth as per Section 3(1)(c)(ii) of the Citizenship Act, 1955, since of the their parent is an Indian citizen..."

Accordingly, the Gujarat High Court directed the local regional passport authorities to release the passports of the two minor children which were earlier issued to them, but they were subsequently withdrawn by the passport authorities.

Finally, the Gujarat High Court held that the two minor babies born out of a surrogacy arrangement in the facts and circumstances of the said case were Indian citizens by birth. Hence, they could not be denied passports to travel abroad, which would be otherwise violative of article 21 of the constitute of India.

Para 9 (at page 23) of the said judgment highlights the legal, moral and ethical issues in the area of surrogacy in the Indian jurisdiction and the same reads as follows:

> "9. We may at the outset point out that lot of legal, moral and ethical issues that arise for our consideration in this case, which have no precedents in this country. We are primarily concerned with the rights of two new born innocent babies, much more than the rights of the biological parents, surrogate mother, or the donor of the ova. Emotional and legal relationship of the babies with the surrogate mother and the donor of the ova is also of vital importance. Surrogate mother is not the genetic mother or biologically related to the baby, but, is she merely a host of an embryo or a gestational carrier? What is the status of the ova (egg) donor, which in this case is an Indian national but anonymous. Is the ova donor, the real mother or the gestational surrogate? Are the babies motherless, can be brand them as legal orphans or Stateless babies? So many ethical and legal questions have come up for consideration in this case for which there are no clear answers, so

far, at least, in this country. True, babies conceived through surrogacy, encounter a lot of legal complications on parentage issues, this case reveals. Legitimacy of the babies is, therefore, a live issue. Can we brand them as illegitimate babies disowned by the world. Further, a host of scientific materials are made available to us to explain what is traditional surrogacy, gestational surrogacy, altruistise surrogacy, commercial surrogacy etc. and also the response of various countries with regard to the surrogacy, especially commercial surrogacy."

Para 10 (at pages 23 and 24) of the said judgment adverts to the 220th report on need for legislation to regulate Assisted Reproductive Technology. This particular paragraph has summed up the recommendations of the Law Commission of India report on the subject of surrogacy in the following words:

> "10. Commercial surrogacy is never considered to be illegal in India and few of the countries like Ukraine, California in the United States. Law Commission of India in its 220th Report on need for legislation to regulate Assisted Reproductive Technology Clinics as well as rights and obligations of parents to a surrogacy has opined that surrogacy agreement will continue to be governed by contract among parties, which will contain all terms requiring consent of surrogate mother to bear the child, agreement of a husband and other family members for the same, medical procedures of artificial insemination, reimbursement of all reasonable expenses for carrying the child to full term, willingness to hand over a child to a commissioning parents etc. Law Commission has also recommended that legislation itself should recognize a surrogate child to be the legitimate child of the commissioning parents without there being any need for adoption or even declaration of guardian. Further, it was also suggested that birth certificate of surrogate child should contain names of the commissioning parents only and that the right to privacy of the donor as well as surrogate mother should be protected. Exploitation of women through surrogacy was also a worrying factor, which is to be taken care through legislation. Law Commission has expressed its desire that Assisted Reproductive Technology Bill with all safeguards would be passed in the near future."

Para 14 (on pages 24 and 25) of the above-mentioned Gujarat High Court judgment succinctly reiterates the fact that there is no law in India prohibiting surrogacy and the crying need for a comprehensive legislation on the subject in the following words:

> "14. We have indicated, in India there is no law prohibiting artificial insemination, egg donation, lending a womb or surrogacy agreements. No civil or criminal penalties are also imposed. Public pressure, for a comprehensive legislation defining the rights of a child born out of surrogacy agreement, rights and responsibilities of a surrogate mother, egg donor, commissioning parties, legal validity of the surrogacy agreement, the parent child relationship, responsibilities of Infertility Clinic etc. are gaining momentum. Legislature will have to address a lot of emotional, legal and ethical issues. Question as to whether surrogacy can be seen as a ray of

hope to otherwise a childless couple, so as to build up a family of their own, necessary for human happiness and social stability also calls for attention. Few are the case laws and precedents defining the rights of those who have a vital role to play in this reproductive technology. One case worth mentioning in India is **Baby Manji's case decided by the apex court of India (2008) 13 SCC 518: (AIR 2009 SC 84)**. Various issues which we have highlighted in this case were not discussed or answered in that case. That was a case where the Japanese Embassy in India refused to grant the child, born to surrogate Indian mother, VISA or Passport on the ground that the Japanese Civil Code recognizes a mother only to be a woman who gives birth to a baby. Attempts made to adopt Manji also did not fructify since Guardians and Wards Act, 1890 did not allow single man to adopt those babies. Efforts were made to obtain Indian Passport, which also required a birth certificate. Question arose as to who was the real mother whether it was anonymous egg donor or the surrogate mother. Birth certificate was then issued by the local Municipality, by showing the father's name. Later the Regional Passport Office, Rajasthan issued a certificate of identity as part of a transit document and not the Passport. Certificate did not contain nationality, mother's name or religion of the baby."

Lastly, para 20 (at page 26) of the Gujarat High Court judgment has highlighted further remaining gray areas in so far relating to children born out of cross border surrogacy arrangements by observing as follows:

"20. Further, under the Indian Evidence Act, no presumption can be drawn that child born out of a surrogate mother, is the legitimate child of commissioning parents, so as to have a legal right to parental support, inheritance and other privileges of a child born to a couple through their sexual intercourse. The only remedy is a proper legislation drawing such a presumption including adoption. Further the question as to whether the babies born out of a surrogate mother have any right of residence in or citizenship by birth or mere State orphanage and whether they acquire only the nationality or the biological father has to be addressed by the legislature."

That the above-mentioned Gujarat High Court judgment has been challenged in the Supreme Court of India primarily on the following grounds among other legal issues.

### XIII. Grounds of Appeal Advanced by the Government of India in the Supreme Court of India Against the Above Mentioned Gujarat High Court Judgment *Jan Balaz* v. *Anand Municipality*, AIR 2010 Guj 21

(1) The present petition raises following substantial question of law of general importance as to:—

(i) Whether a surrogate mother could be treated as one of the parents by excluding commissioning parents, for the purpose of section 3(1)(c)(ii) of the Indian Citizenship Act, 1955, which provides that every person born in India, one of whose parents is a citizen of India, shall be a citizen of India by birth.

(ii) Whether the gestational carrier/surrogate mother will have any parental right to a child so born, even if there is a valid and legally enforceable agreement of surrogacy, having contrary stipulations.

(iii) Whether, an agreement of surrogacy between the parties (i.e. surrogate mother and the commissioning parents, executed in India) will not hold field in absence of any valid legislation passed by the Parliament.

(iv) Whether, a foreign national would have any enforceable right to seek *mandamus* against the petitioner/Union of India to suit his convenience and to suit the domestic laws of another country (Germany) where the surrogacy is not recognised.

(v) Whether, the interpretation to section 3(1)(c)(ii) of the Indian Citizenship Act, 1955 as given by the Hon'ble High Court is justified, thereby a conclusion has been drawn that the surrogate children in question are Indian nationals by birth, without having any legal foundation and by ignoring the terms of agreement of surrogacy between the surrogate mother and commissioning parents and also by ignoring the recommendations of Law Commission of India on the subject in report number 220.

(2) It is submitted that the Law Commission of India vide report number 220 recommended that India requires legislation which recognises the surrogate child to be the legitimate child of commissioning parent without there being any need for adoption or even declaration of guardian. The Law Commission of India in the said report further recommends that birth certificate of the surrogate child should contain; names of the commissioning parents only. Though, these facts have been noticed by the Hon'ble Gujarat High Court, however, by ignoring the agreement of surrogacy validly executed between the parties and by ignoring the admission of the respondent number 1 in its Writ petition itself, erroneously held that section 3(1)(c)(ii) of the Indian Citizenship Act, 1955, provides for citizenship by birth where one of the parents is a citizen of India and in the present case the surrogate mother satisfies, the ingredients of section 3(1)(c)(ii) of the Indian Citizenship Act, 1955. It was further submitted in the grounds of appeal that the Hon'ble Gujarat High Court erroneously came to conclusion that under the present legal frame work in India, the two babies born in India to the gestational surrogate mother are citizens of India and are therefore entitled to Indian passports. It was also submitted, that the Hon'ble High Court has ignored the above-mentioned recommendations of the Law Commission of India, which in absence of any valid legislation, will have persuasive effect and the Courts generally follow such recommendations except in cases where the Court after having discussed its pros and cons, differ with recommendations by assigning reasons.

(3) Further, the agreement of surrogacy is a valid contract in India which has to be honoured and given effect to as well. The *mandamus* issued by the Hon'ble Gujarat High Court in exercise of its power under article 226 has virtually superseded a valid agreement of surrogacy, which is totally unwarranted. It was also averred that though, there is no legislation on the subject but there are sufficient materials including the binding agreement of surrogacy between the

parties and the above-mentioned recommendations of the Law Commission of India on the subject. The issues raised in the initial Writ petition under article 226 of the Constitution of India (which is equivalent of judicial review proceedings in the UK) could have been adjudicated within such frame work. However, without any legal foundation the Hon'ble Gujarat High Court came to the conclusion that since the surrogate mother is Indian national therefore, the surrogate children would also be treated as Indian nationals and accordingly entitled to the Indian passports.

That the orders passed by the Hon'ble Supreme Court of India in the Special Leave Petition instituted against the above-mentioned Gujarat High Court judgment from 25 November 2009 i.e. the first time when the Special Leave Petition first came up for hearing in the Supreme Court until as of this book going to the press for publication are by and large short orders passed during the course of the hearing including interim directions as well on certain crucial hearings.

The Hon'ble Apex Court after taking a very sympathetic and a compassionate approach awarded the necessary relief to facilitate the onward movement of the two minor surrogate children to Germany.

The case has now being carrying on for adjudication of larger issues in public interest and given the lack of specific direct legislation on the subject of surrogacy in India.

Certainly, it is important to cite some of the interim orders, so as to demonstrate the workable solution devised by the Hon'ble Supreme Court of India so as to facilitate the onward movement of the surrogate children to Germany.

CARA was added as a party in the said case on 25 February, 2010, and on this date the Hon'ble Apex Court was apprised of the fact that CARA was sympathetically considering the issue of adoption in the peculiar facts of the case, although surrogate children are outside the scope of CARA Guidelines.

The said order dated 25 February, 2010 is reproduced hereunder:

"Petition(s) for Special Leave to Appeal (Civil) No(s).31639/2009

(From the judgement and order dated 11/11/2009 in LPA No.2151/2009 of The HIGH COURT OF GUJARAT AT AHMEDABAD)

*UNION OF INDIA & ANR.* Petitioner(s)

v.

*JAN BALAZ & ORS.* Respondent(s)

(With prayer for interim relief)

**Date: 25/02/2010**

This Petition was called on for hearing today.

**CORAM:**

HON'BLE MR. JUSTICE ASOK KUMAR GANGULY

HON'BLE MR. JUSTICE R.M. LODHA

Upon hearing counsel the Court made the following

**ORDER**

Heard learned counsel for the parties.

Today, when the matter was taken up, the learned counsel representing Union of India submitted that procedure for temporary adoption is under process and Central Adoption Resource Authority (hereinafter referred to as 'CARA') which is an autonomous agency under the Ministry of Women and Child Development, Government of India is processing the adoption procedure. It has been represented to us that normally a surrogate child is not subjected to adoption but keeping in view the facts of the case, CARA may consider the case of adoption in the instant case sympathetically.

CARA be added as party respondent in the present case. Ordered accordingly. Issue notice to the newly impleaded respondent.

On the joint prayer of learned counsel for the parties and having regard to the urgency of the matter, list the matter on 16.03.2010.

In the meantime, CARA, if so advised, may file an affidavit."

The Hon'ble Apex Court further issued directions to CARA on 17 March 2010 to consider and process the case of adoption of the children as also to initiate appropriate steps in this regard. The said order passed by the Hon'ble Apex Court on 17 March 2010 is reproduced hereunder:

"Petition(s) for Special Leave to Appeal (Civil) No(s).31639/2009

(From the judgement and order dated 11/11/2009 in LPA No. 2151/2009 of The HIGH COURT OF GUJARAT AT AHMEDABAD)

*UNION OF INDIA & ANR.* Petitioner(s)

VERSUS

*JAN BALAZ & ORS.* Respondent(s)

(With prayer for interim relief)

**Date: 17/03/2010**

This Petition was called on for hearing today.

CORAM : HON'BLE MR. JUSTICE G.S.SINGHVI

HON'BLE MR. JUSTICE ASOK KUMAR GANGULY

UPON hearing counsel the Court made the following

**ORDER**

Yesterday, the case was adjourned for today with an understanding that arguments will be heard on the merits of the main case because Ms.Kamini Jaiswal, learned counsel appearing for the respondents gave out that the suggestion made by the learned Solicitor General for issue of directions to CARA to take up issue of adoption of children as a special case is not acceptable to her client Today, Ms. Jaiswal submitted that on a second thought she and her client felt that the offer made by the learned Solicitor General is reasonable and deserves consideration because the same may finally resolve the controversy at least in part.

In view of above, the case is adjourned to 3rd of May, 2010 with the direction to the concerned authorities of CARA to consider and process the case of adoption of the children and take appropriate action including consultation with the authorities of the Government of Germany within a maximum period of four weeks from today. This direction is being given by the Court keeping in view the peculiar facts of the case."

The earlier directions passed by the Hon'ble Apex Court on 25 February 2010 and 17 March 2010, certainly yielded positive results, as is evident from the orders passed by the Hon'ble Court on 5 May 2010. The same is reproduced hereunder:

"Petition(s) for Special Leave to Appeal (Civil) No(s).31639/2009

(From the judgement and order dated 11/11/2009 in LPA No.2151/2009 of The HIGH COURT OF GUJARAT AT AHMEDABAD)

*UNION OF INDIA & ANR.* Petitioner(s)

VERSUS

*JAN BALAZ & ORS.* Respondent(s)

(With prayer for interim relief)

**Date: 05/05/2010**

This Petition was called on for hearing today.

**CORAM:**

HON'BLE MR. JUSTICE G.S. SINGHVI

HON'BLE MR. JUSTICE ASOK KUMAR GANGULY

Upon hearing counsel the Court made the following

**ORDER**

Learned Solicitor General says that all the steps which could facilitate inter-country adoption have been taken by CARA and No Objection Certificate can be issued as soon as the willingness of the concerned agency of Germany is received.

Learned Solicitor General and Ms.Kamini Jaiswal request that having regard to the peculiar facts of the case, the Court may hear the same during the summer vacation. The request of the learned counsel is accepted. List the case on 26.05.2010."

It will be noticed that the directions passed by the Hon'ble Supreme Court of India in the above-mentioned case of Jan Balaz are case specific only and not meant to be used as a routine precedent for children born out of surrogacy arrangements. Perhaps, the time has now come for the Supreme Court of India to lay down guidelines with regard to children born out of surrogacy arrangements, especially when the commissioning parents are permanently domiciled and habitually resident overseas. These guidelines could well be akin to guidelines laid down by the Supreme Court of India in the case of *D K Basu v. State of West Bengal,*

AIR 1997 SC 610, where the Court laid down clear cut guidelines relating to the law of arrest and *Vishaka and others v. State of Rajasthan*, AIR 1997 SC 3011 providing guidelines for sexual harassment protection at work places.

## XIV. UK DOMESTIC LAW ON SURROGACY AND NO INTERNATIONAL AGREEMENTS OR CONVENTIONS REGULATING OR GOVERNING SURROGACY

That as per the information available on the UK Border Agency website on Inter-country surrogacy and the immigration rules, the department of health holds the lead responsibility for making law and policy on surrogacy in The United Kingdom. The Human Fertilisation and Embryology Act, 1990 (hereafter HFE Act, 1990) applies to all of The United Kingdom and it is this legislation which regulates parental orders. Other aspects of surrogacy are regulated by the Surrogacy Arrangements Act, 1985. There are no international agreements or conventions which regulate how surrogacy should be managed between countries. Hence, anyone considering entering into an inter-country surrogacy arrangement must remember that if they permanently reside in The United Kingdom, they are subject to United Kingdom law and the definitions which underlie surrogacy. This is of vital importance as the definition of who constitutes "a parent," for the purpose of United Kingdom law affects whether a child born abroad as the result of a surrogacy arrangement, may be brought into The United Kingdom under the immigration rules.

## XV. CONCLUSION AND RECOMMENDATIONS

(1) Surrogacy involves conflict of various interests and has inscrutable impact on the primary unit of society viz. family. Non-intervention of law in this knotty issue will not be proper at a time when law is to act as ardent defender of human liberty and an instrument of distribution of positive entitlements. At the same time, prohibition on vague moral grounds without a proper assessment of social ends and purposes which surrogacy can serve would be irrational. Active legislative intervention is required to facilitate correct uses of the new technology i.e. ART and relinquish the cocooned approach to legalisation of surrogacy adopted hitherto. The need of the hour is to adopt a pragmatic approach by legalizing altruistic surrogacy arrangements and prohibit commercial ones.

(2) The draft Bill prepared by the ICMR is full of lacunae, nay, it is incomplete. However, it is a beacon to move forward in the direction of preparing legislation to regulate not only ART clinics but rights and obligations of all the parties to a surrogacy including rights of the surrogate child. Most important points in regard to the rights and obligations of the parties to a surrogacy and rights of the surrogate child the proposed legislation should include may be stated as under:

(a) Surrogacy arrangement will continue to be governed by contract amongst parties, which will contain all the terms requiring consent of surrogate mother to bear child, agreement of her husband other family members for the same, medical procedures of artificial insemination, reimbursement of all reasonable expenses for carrying child to full term, willingness to hand over the child born to the commissioning parent(s), etc. But such an arrangement should not be for commercial purposes.

(b) A surrogacy arrangement should provide for financial support for surrogate child in the event of death of the commissioning couple or individual before delivery of the child, or divorce between the intended parents and subsequent willingness of none to take delivery of the child.

(c) A surrogacy contract should necessarily take care of life insurance cover for surrogate mother.

(d) One of the intended parents should be a donor as well, because the bond of love and affection with a child primarily emanates from biological relationship. Also, the chances of various kinds of child-abuse, which have been noticed in cases of adoptions, will be reduced. In case the intended parent is single, he or she should be a donor to be able to have a surrogate child. Otherwise, adoption is the way to have a child which is resorted to if biological (natural) parents and adoptive parents are different.

(e) Legislation itself should recognise a surrogate child to be the legitimate child of the commissioning parent(s) without there being any need for adoption or even declaration of guardian.

(f) The birth certificate of the surrogate child should contain the name(s) of the commissioning parent(s) only.

(g) Right to privacy of donor as well as surrogate mother should be protected.

(h) Sex-selective surrogacy should be prohibited.

(i) Cases of abortions should be governed by the Medical Termination of Pregnancy Act, 1971 only.

---

# CONFLICT OF LAW IN INTER-COUNTRY ADOPTIONS: THE INDIAN PERSPECTIVE WITH SPECIAL REFERENCE TO THE POSITION AFTER INDIA RATIFYING THE HAGUE CONVENTION ON ADOPTIONS

## I. INTRODUCTION

This article analyses the conflict of law position relating to inter-country adoption law and procedure, in the Indian jurisdiction. The paper in hand also looks at the relevant legislation to be complied with by foreigners and Persons of Indian Origin resident abroad permanently, seeking to adopt children from India. At the outset, it is important to emphasise that at present there exists no exclusive general law on adoption of children governing non-Hindus and foreigners. Adoption is permitted by statute among Hindus, and by custom among some other communities. In India, in the last few years a new dimension has also taken place on account of tedious and complicated inter-country adoption laws and procedures. This is giving rise to surrogacy arrangements, preferred especially by the Non-Resident Indian community overseas. This new emerging issue is also discussed in this article.

At present, non-Hindus and foreigners can only be guardians of children under the Guardian and Wards Act, 1890. In actual practice, foreign nationals and Persons of Indian Origin domiciled overseas wishing to adopt children from India first obtain guardianship orders from the District Court or the High Court, as the case may be, within whose territorial jurisdiction the child is residing. This is with a view to adopt formally under the legal system of the country of their habitual residence. A brief reference is also made to the enactment of the Juvenile Justice (Care and Protection of Children) Act, 2000 subsequently amended by Act 33 of 2006. This legislation introduces the concept of secular adoptions. This concept is discussed in the main body of the report.

The Indian Ministry of Welfare, pursuant to certain guidelines issued by the Supreme Court of India in a Public Interest Litigation petition, *Laxmi Kant Pandey* v. *Union of India,* AIR 1984 SC 469, framed guidelines governing inter-country adoptions. This case was monitored by the Supreme Court from time-to-time until 1991, when the Court scrupulously reviewed the existing procedure and practices followed in inter-country adoptions. The main objective was to prevent trafficking of children and to protect the welfare of adopted children.

In the further supplemental judgment of *Laxmi Kant Pandey* v. *Union of India,* AIR 1986 SC 272, the Apex Court pointed out that ordinarily the Court, entertaining an application on behalf of a foreigner seeking to be appointed guardian of a child with a view to eventual adoption, should not insist on the foreigner making a deposit by way of security for due performance of the obligations undertaken by him. However, in appropriate cases, the Court may exceptionally pass an order requiring him or her to make such deposit. The Court has also observed that it is at that point of time that the execution of a bond would ordinarily be sufficient.

The Apex Court in the second supplemental judgment of *Laxmi Kant Pandey* v. *Union of India,* AIR 1987 SC 232, once again, among other issues, clarified this aspect of the matter. The Apex Court held that the Guardian Judge need not insist on security or a cash deposit or bank guarantee, and it should be enough if a bond is taken from the recognised Indian placement agency which is processing the application. This agency may in turn take a corresponding bond from the sponsoring social or child welfare agency in the foreign country. Some directions issued in AIR 1984 SC 469 and AIR 1986 SC 272 were also modified.

More importantly, Justice Bhagwati in AIR 1987 SC 232, para 12 (at page 240) incorporated a vital note of clarification, as follows:

> '... We would, therefore, direct that in case of a foreigner who has been living in India for one year or more, the home-study report and other connected documents may be allowed to be prepared by the recognised placement agency which is processing the application of such foreigner for guardianship of a child with a view to its eventual adoption and that in such a case the Court should not insist on sponsoring of such foreigner by a social or child welfare agency based in the country to which such foreigner belongs nor should a home-study report in respect of such foreigner be required to be obtained from any such foreign social or child welfare agency, the home study report and other connected documents prepared by the recognized placement agency should be regarded as sufficient.'

After the implementation of the initial guidelines in 1989, it was felt necessary to revise them. Accordingly, a taskforce comprising a cross-section of representatives of adoption agencies under the chairmanship of former Chief Justice of India, Mr. Justice P.N. Bhagwati, was constituted on 12 August 1992. The taskforce submitted its report on 28 August, 1993, and the Indian Government accepted its recommendations. Accordingly, the Government of India circulated revised guidelines in 1994 (hereinafter 'the Guidelines') to regulate matters relating to the adoption of Indian children. These guidelines were published by the Government in the Gazette of India on 20 June, 1995. Subsequently, new further revised guidelines have come into place from 14 February, 2006. CARA has now submitted a draft of amended comprehensive guidelines to the newly created Ministry for Women and Child Development. These are called the Draft Guidelines on Adoption of Indian Children without Parental Care. These 2007 Guidelines have not been approved by the concerned Ministry as yet.

It may however be pertinent to point out that the Apex Court in *Anokha* v. *State of Rajasthan,* 2004 (1) HLR 351 has held that the above guidelines would not be applicable where the child is living with his or her biological parent(s) who have agreed that he or she is to be given in adoption to a known couple who may be of foreign origin. The Court in such cases has to deal with the application under section 7 of the Guardian and Wards Act, 1890 and dispose of the same after being satisfied that the child is being given in adoption voluntarily with the parents being aware of the implications of adoption, that is the child would legally belong to the adoptive parents' family; that the adoption is not induced by any extraneous reasons such as the receipt of money etc; that the adoptive parents have produced evidence in support of their suitability; and finally that the arrangement would be in the best interest of the child.

Much more recently the Supreme Court of India has again reiterated the guidelines in case of adoption of children by foreign parents, as originally laid down in the case of *Laxmi Kant Pandey* v. *Union of India*, (supra, 1984). While emphatically following these guidelines in *St. Theresa's Tender Loving Care Home* v. *State of Andhra Pradesh*, 2006 (1) HLR 122, the Apex Court pointed in para 10 (at page 128) of the judgment: "While making the requisite and prescribed exercise it has to be kept in mind that the child is a precious gift and merely because he or she for various reasons is abandoned by the parents that cannot be a reason for further neglect by the society...."

## II. BRIEF OVERVIEW OF PROCEDURE TO BE FOLLOWED IN INTER-COUNTRY ADOPTIONS UNDER REVISED CARA GUIDELINES OF 2006

CARA guidelines stipulates that every application from a foreigner wishing to adopt a child must be sponsored by a social or child welfare agency recognised or licensed by the Government of the country in which the foreigner is resident. Furthermore, the agency should be recognised by the Central Adoption Resource Agency (hereafter 'CARA') set up under the aegis of the Indian Ministry of Welfare. CARA is the principal monitoring agency of the Indian Government handling all affairs connected with national and inter-country adoptions.

No application by a foreigner to adopt a child should be entertained directly by any social or child welfare agency in India working in the areas of inter-country adoption or by any institution or centre to which the children are committed by the Juvenile Court. The reasons behind this directive have been summed up by M.N. Das in his book Guardians and Wards Act (Eastern Law House, 14th Edn, 1995) at pages 80–81:

> 'Firstly, it will help to reduce, if not eliminate altogether, the possibility of profiteering and trafficking in children, because if a foreigner were allowed to contact directly agencies or individuals in India for the purpose of obtaining a child in adoption, he might, in his anxiety to secure a child for adoption, be induced or persuaded to pay any unconscionable or unreasonable amount which might be demanded by the agency or individual procuring the child. Secondly, it would be almost impossible for the court to satisfy itself that the foreigner who wishes to take the child in adoption would be suitable as a parent for the child and whether he would be able to provide a stable and secured family life to the child and would be able to handle trans-racial, trans-cultural and trans-national problems likely to arise from such adoption, because, where the application for adopting a child has not been sponsored by a social or child welfare agency in the country of the foreigner, there would be no proper and satisfactory home study report on which the court can rely. Thirdly, in such a case,

where the application of a foreigner for taking a child in adoption is made directly without the intervention of social or child welfare agency, there would be no authority or agency in the country of the foreigner who could be made responsible for supervising the progress of the child and ensuring that the child is adopted at the earliest in accordance with law and grows up in an atmosphere of warmth and affection with moral and material security assured to it.'

## III. THE ROLE OF CENTRAL ADOPTION RESOURCE AUTHORITY

The Central Adoption Resource Authority (hereafter, CARA) is an autonomous body under the Ministry of Women and Child Development, Government of India. Its mandate is to find a loving and caring family for every orphan/destitute/ surrendered child in the country. The Central Adoption Resource Authority (CARA) was initially set up in 1990 under the aegis of the Ministry of Welfare in pursuance of Cabinet decision dated 9 May, 1990. Pursuant to a decision of the Union Cabinet dated 2 July, 1998, the then Ministry of Social Justice and Empowerment conferred the autonomous status on CARA with effect from 18 March, 1999 by registering it as a society under the Societies Registration Act, 1860. It was designated as Central authority by the Ministry of Social Justice and Empowerment on 17 July, 2003 for the implementation of the Hague Convention on Protection of Children & Cooperation in respect of inter-country adoption (1993). The Ministry of Women & Child Development has of late been mandated to look after the subject-matters 'Adoption' and 'Juvenile Justice (Care & Protection of Children) Act, 2000' pursuant to 16 February, 2006 notification of Government of India regarding reallocation of the business.

In-country adoption of Indian children is governed by in-country guidelines-2004 while inter-country adoption procedure is governed by a set of guidelines last issued on 14 February, 2006. These guidelines are a follow-up of various directions given by the Supreme Court of India in *L.K. Pandey* v. *Union of India,* (supra). These guidelines have been amended and updated from time-to-time keeping in mind the welfare of such child. While CARA is engaged in clearing inter-country adoption of Indian children, its principal aim is to promote in-country adoption. In fact, CARA ensures that no Indian child is given for inter-country adoption without him/her having been considered by Indian families residing in India. CARA also provides financial assistance to various NGOs and Government-run homes to promote quality child care to such children and place them in domestic adoption.

## IV. DETAILS OF PRESENT PROCEDURE TO BE FOLLOWED IN INTER-COUNTRY ADOPTIONS FROM INDIA UNDER REVISED CARA GUIDELINES OF 2006

**Step I) Enlisted Foreign Adoption Agency (EFAA)**

- The applicants will have to contact or register with an Enlisted Foreign Adoption Agency (EFAA)/Central authority/Government department in their country, in which they are resident, which will prepare the Home Study Report (HSR) etc. The validity of "Home Study Report" will be for a period of two years. HSR report prepared before two years will be updated at referral.

- The applicants should obtain the permission of the competent authority for adopting a child from India. Where such Central authorities or Government departments are not available, then the applications may be sent by the enlisted agency with requisite documents including documentary proof that the applicant is permitted to adopt from India
- The adoption application dossier should contain all documents prescribed in Annexure-2. All documents are to be notarised. The signature of the notary is either to be attested by the Indian Embassy/ High Commission or the appropriate Government department of the receiving country. If the documents are in any language other than English, then the originals must be accompanied by attested translations. A copy of the application of the prospective adoptive parents along with the copies of the HSR and other documents will have to be forwarded to RIPA by the Enlisted Foreign Adoption Agency (EFAA) or Central authority of that country.

**Step II) Role of Recognised Indian Placement Agency (RIPA)**

- On receipt of the documents, the Indian agency will make efforts to match a child who is legally free for inter-country adoption with the applicant.
- In case no suitable match is possible within 3 months, the RIPA will inform the EFAA and CARA with the reasons therefore.

**Step III) Child being declared free for inter-country adoption - Clearance by ACA**

- Before a RIPA proposes to place a child in the inter-country adoption, it must apply to the ACA for assistance for Indian placement.
- The child should be legally free for adoption. ACA will find a suitable Indian prospective adoptive parent within 30 days, failing which it will issue clearance certificate for inter-country adoption.
- ACA will issue clearance for inter-country adoption within 10 days in case of older children above 6 years, siblings or twins and special needs children as per the additional guidelines issued in this regard.
- In case the ACA cannot find suitable Indian parent/parents within 30 days, it will be incumbent upon the ACA to issue a clearance certificate on the 31st day.
- If ACA clearance is not given on 31st day, the clearance of ACA will be assumed unless ACA has sought clarification within the stipulation period of 30 days.
- NRI parent(s) (at least one parent) HOLDING Indian Passport will be exempted from ACA clearance, but they have to follow all other procedures as per the guidelines.

**Step IV) Matching of the Child Study Report with Home Study Report of FPAP by RIPA**

- After a successful matching, the RIPA will forward the complete dossier as per Annexure 3 to CARA for issuance of "No-Objection Certificate".

**Step V) Issue of No-Objection Certificate (NOC) by CARA**

- RIPA shall make application for CARA NOC in case of foreign/PIO parents only after ACA Clearance Certificate is obtained.
- CARA will issue the 'NOC' within 15 days from the date of receipt of the adoption dossier if complete in all respects.
- If any query or clarification is sought by CARA, it will be replied to by the RIPA within 10 days.
- No Indian Placement Agency can file an application in the competent Court for inter-country adoption without a "No-Objection Certificate" from CARA.

**Step VI) Filing of Petition in the Court**

- On receipt of the NOC from CARA, the RIPA shall file a petition for adoption/guardianship in the competent Court within 15 days.
- The competent Court may issue an appropriate order for the placement of the child with FPAP.
- As per the Hon'ble Supreme Court directions, the concerned Court may dispose the case within two months.

**Step VII) Passport and Visa**

- RIPA has to apply in the Regional Passport Office for obtaining an Indian Passport in favour of the child.
- The concerned Regional Passport Officer may issue the passport within 10 days.
- Thereafter the VISA entry permit may be issued by the Consulate/ Embassy/High Commission of the concerned country for the child.

**Step VIII) Child travels to adoptive country**

- The adoptive parent/parents will have to come to India and accompany the child back to their country.

As of now, all inter-country adoptions are governed by the 2006 guidelines. The authors have learnt from official sources, that the draft 2007 guidelines are likely to be finalised very soon. Nonetheless, the importance of the basic documentation cannot be undermined in inter-country adoptions. The starting point of course is the Home Study Report.

The importance of the Home Study Report is of paramount importance. In fact, it is like a clear cut balance sheet of the prospective adoptive parents. It is a very handy document, at the entire stage of the adoption process, especially when the guardianship proceedings are instituted in the Court of the Guardian Judge, within whose jurisdiction the minor child is residing. And, secondly at the time of the visa interview at the concerned Embassy or Consulate to impress upon the visa /consular officer as to the positive aspects of the application, with a view to enhancing the chances of the success of the application.

## HOME STUDY REPORT

Paragraph 2.14 of the earlier 1995 guidelines categorically and emphatically enumerates the required contents of the Home Study Report, which should include the following information tabulated below. Although, this is the list of documentation stipulated in the earlier guidelines of 1995, but from the experience of the authors in handling family migration issues, we would still recommend compliance of the exhaustive documentation mentioned below for two clear-cut reasons mentioned in the preceding paragraph.

(1) social status and family background;

(2) description of the home;

(3) standard of living as it appears in the home;

(4) current relationship between the husband and wife;

(5) current relationship between the parents and children (if there are any children);

(6) development of any already adopted children;

(7) current relationship between the couple and the members of each other's family;

(8) employment status of the couple;

(9) health details, such as clinical tests, hearing condition, past illness, etc, (medical certificate etc);

(10) economic status of the couple;

(11) accommodation for the child;

(12) schooling facilities;

(13) amenities in the home;

(14) reasons for wanting to adopt an Indian child;

(15) attitude of grandparents and relatives towards the adoption;

(16) anticipated plans for the adoptive child;

(17) legal status of the prospective adoptive parents.

CARA permissions not necessary in inter-country adoptions where both families are known to each other but not without the absence of the guardianship order from the Court of competent jurisdiction.

In the case of, *Zaveed Pharukhi* v. *Unknown*, 2005 (4) Bom CR 244, an appeal against the order of the learned single Judge dismissing the appellants petition had been filed in the Bombay High Court. The appellants had filed a petition for an order seeking a declaration to be appointed as guardians of a newly born baby boy. The appellants were husband and wife from Canada and had no children of their own and they used to visit India frequently. They were willing to adopt a child. The biological parents of the child were also co-appellants and they pleaded that they had four children and they were unable to maintain them. They were informed that the principal appellants were desirous of adopting a child. Since the natural parents/co-appellants were genuinely finding it difficult to provide for the fourth child, they agreed to give their newly born child in adoption to the principal appellants from Canada.

The two main issues of the case which came up for consideration before the Court can be summed up as follows: Whether mere consent of the biological parents to give the child in adoption per-se enough by itself? Only because the biological parents are financially underprivileged, can a petition to appoint affluent people as the child's guardian be maintainable?

The Bombay High Court in appeal against the decision of the single Judge of the Bombay High Court itself has dealt with the above-mentioned two issues keeping in mind the reasons and justifications given by the learned single Judge while dismissing the petition. According to the Bombay High Court on the appellate side, the petition was dismissed by the learned single Judge of the Bombay High Court on the ground that only because the biological parents of the child have agreed to give their child in adoption the same cannot be allowed to be so.

The Hon'ble High Court in appeal proceedings reiterated the position of law in cases where children are given in adoption by the biological parents as held by the Supreme Court of India in the case of *Smt. Anokha* v. *State of Rajastha,* (supra). Para 14 of *Zaveed Pharukhi* (supra) as follows:

> "14. The law regarding cases of adoption of children living with their biological parents who are sought to be given in adoption to a known couple willingly by the biological parents themselves is governed by the judgment of the Supreme Court in *Anokha's* case. In paragraph 15, the Supreme Court held as under:—
>
> > "15. None of these provisions in the several decisions of this Court impinge upon the rights and choice of an individual to give his or her child in adoption to named persons, who may be of foreign origin. The Court in such cases has to deal with the application under section 7 of the Guardians and Wards Act, 1890 and dispose of the same after being satisfied that the child is being given in adoption voluntarily after being aware of the implication of adoption viz. that the child would legally belong to the adoptive parents' family, uninduced by any extraneous reasons such as the receipt of money etc. ; that the adoptive parents have produced evidence in support of their suitability and finally that the arrangement would be in the best interest of the child.""

The Bombay High Court on the appellate side in the present case arrived at a conclusion on the issue at hand in terms of the law laid down in *Anokha* (supra). The appellate court in *Zaveed Pharukhi* (supra) in para 15 as stated below:

> "15. In Anokha's case the Supreme Court has also provided the guidelines for the nature of evidence necessary to satisfy the Court regarding the desirability of permitting such applications and the undertakings to be given by the parties and safeguards to be provided by the Court. However, it is clear that the Supreme Court has categorically stated that in cases such as the one before us, the Court has to deal with the application under section 7 of the Guardianship and Wards Act. It is necessary for the Court to be satisfied that the child is being given in adoption voluntarily; that the biological parents are aware of the nature and consequences of their act namely that the child would legally belong to their adoptive parents and that the act of the parties is not induced by any undesirable extraneous reasons such as the receipt of money."

Section 7 of the Guardianship and Wards Act, 1890 (hereinafter referred to as GWA,1890) deals with the powers of the Court to make an order as to guardianship. The Court rightly so had a caveat and a word of caution that there should not be mechanical application of mind in guardianship matters. Similar concerns are voiced in para 16 of the said judgment as hereunder:

> "16. We believe that an order allowing the adoption or permitting the persons other than the biological parents to be appointed as the guardians of a child ought not to be passed mechanically. Matters such as these cannot be treated like applications for consent decrees. Nor can they be permitted except for valid and desirable reasons. Indeed such orders ought not to permit a sale of children. Nor should parents be permitted to abdicate their duties of providing for their children not merely financially but emotionally as well. It is necessary to realize that orders such as these do not merely affect the parties to the application but primarily affect the child. The object ought not to be merely monetary. Socially and psychology to remove the child from the custody of the biological parents is a matter of utmost importance. The Court necessarily has to weigh cases such as these very carefully in the balance."

Clearly, the Court pointed out at the grave implications of the decision of biological parents to give their children in adoption. The Court is of the view that such adoptions should be carefully granted keeping in mind the best interests of the child.

Since in the present case the appellate Court was satisfied that the intention of the parties was bona fide and genuine, the application ought to be granted for justifiable valid reasons.

Further, in the present case of *Zaveed Pharuki* (supra) itself there is a balanced and a logical discussion after considering the facts and circumstances of case in hand, in allowing the petition on the sole ground that the petitioners were affluent people and the biological parents were financially not well off. And as to whether in light of section 19(b) of GWA, 1890 it is improper to allow any person as a guardian of the minor child in question unless parents were unfit to be guardians of the child.

The Bombay High Court on the appellate side in *Zaveed Pharukhi* (supra) has summed up the issue of a child being given in adoption because the biological parents were poor in para 22 of the judgment in the following terms:

> "22. Nor is it difficult to understand in the facts and circumstances of the case, why appellant No. 3 and 4 have consented to appellant Nos. 1 and 2 being the guardians and adoptive parents of the child. Appellant No. 3 is a domestic worker with a very meagre income. They have four children including the said child. The first three children are 13, 11 and 6 years old respectively. They will be dependent on appellant No. 3 and 4 for many years to come. The youngest of them will be dependent on appellant Nos. 3 and 4 for at least another 12 to 15 years. Appellant No. 3 and 4 have stated that they are not in a position to maintain their children. We see no reason to disbelieve them. Appellant No. 3 and 4 have by no means abdicated or

neglected to discharge their duties as biological parents by consenting to this petition. Indeed they have made an enormous sacrifice the nature of which requires no elaboration. It would be unkind to equate such a sacrifice to an abdication of parental duties. At the cost of repetition we must recall the words of the Supreme Court in *Laxmi Kant Pandey's* and *Anokha's* cases:—

"We may make it clear at the outset that we are not concerned here with cases of adoption of children living with their biological parents, for in such class of cases, the biological parents would be the best persons to decide whether to give their child in adoption to foreign parents""

In the present case, the Court categorically stated that they were unable to find any fault in the decision of the parents to give their child in adoption to the Canadian appellants.

Clearly, and rightly so the appellate Court in para 23 of the said judgment ruled that superior financial capacity of the prospective adoptive parents cannot let the pendulum swing entirely in their favour, simply on the strength of the sole factor of the affluence of the prospective adoptive parents. Para 23 of the said judgment has advanced balanced reasoning in the following terms:

"23. We are entirely in agreement with the learned Judge that merely because appellant No. 1 and 2 are financially well off, the Court ought not to appoint them as the guardians of the minor child. The fact that a party is financially well off can never be the sole consideration for an order appointing them as guardians. It is but a factor to be taken into consideration while deciding whether or not they would be able to provide for the child. Parents cannot be permitted to give their children in adoption without good cause. The importance of the role of the biological parents in every respect cannot be overstated. The importance of this aspect requires no elaboration for it is too obvious. If parents are allowed to give their children in adoption freely and without just cause, it would undoubtedly adversely affect the children emotionally and psychologically. In the ultimate analysis, the welfare of the child is of paramount important. This principle underlines the entire Act of 1890."

Eventually, the appellate Court reiterated the law earlier laid down by the Hon'ble Supreme Court of India in the principal judgment of *Lakshmi Kant Pandey* (supra) and *Anokha* (supra) by stating that the biological parents are the best Judge to decide the issue of adoption. Certainly, this is coupled with the safeguard/ caveat of guardianship order by the Court of competent jurisdiction.

The learned single Judge of the Bombay High Court did not consider himself to be bound by the judgment of the Hon'ble Supreme Court of India in the case of *Anokha* (supra) on the ground that in the case of *Anokha* (supra) the father of the child had expired and therefore, the provisions of section 19(b) of the GWA, 1890 were not applicable to the case. Section 19(b) of the GWA, 1890 provides for the appointment of guardian of the minor child.

To meet the above-mentioned negative interpretation of the learned single Judge, the appellate Court sought recourse with ingenuity to the law laid down in the case of *Gita Hariharan* v. *Reserve Bank of India,* AIR 1999 SC 228. That with regard to the section 19(b) of the GWA, 1890, High Court has dealt with the question by giving a detailed analysis of the celebrated judgment in the case of *Gita Hariharan* (supra). In the case the Constitutional validity of the section 6(a) of the Hindu Minority and Guardianship Act, 1956 and section 19(b) of GWA, 1890 was challenged on the ground that the mother of the minor was relegated to an inferior position since her right as a natural guardian was only made cognizable 'after' the father. But the Supreme Court held in the case that the term 'after' would mean 'in the absence of' and not 'after the life-time' of the father. Hence, in light of the law laid down in the case of *Gita Hariharan* (supra) it is implicit that even during the lifetime of the father, the mother could be considered to be natural guardian in certain circumstances.

Eventually, the Bombay High Court on the appeal side held with justifiable reasoning that the earlier judgment of Hon'ble Supreme Court of India in the case of *Anokha* (supra) was applicable in the present case and consequently the appeal was allowed.

**V. CARA PERMISSIONS NOT NECESSARY IN INTER-COUNTRY ADOPTIONS, WHERE FAMILIES ARE KNOWN TO EACH OTHER: REGIONAL PASSPORT OFFICER HAS NO AUTHORITY TO DIRECT ADOPTIVE PARENTS/GUARDIANS TO OBTAIN CARA PERMISSION**

In the case of, *Frank M. Costanzo* v. *The Regional Passport Officer*: Writ Petition Number 14880 of 2011, decided on 17 September, 2010, the petitioners were permitted to take their adopted son to USA by an order of the Family Court at Puducherry. This was by virtue of a guardianship order from the Court of competent jurisdiction. And thereafter, they submitted an application to the Regional Passport Officer for the issue of a passport to their minor son. But the petitioners received a reply from the Regional Passport Officer stating that, the adoption of Master Praveen Kumar is not in accordance with the extensive procedures laid down by the Government of India, meaning to refer to the CARA guidelines. Accordingly, they were directed to furnish a no objection certificate from Central Adoption Resources Agency (CARA).

The key issue which arose in this particular case was as follows: Whether the condition of CARA clearance imposed by the Regional Passport Officer for the issuance of the passport of the minor child was legally justifiable, where such a child has been taken in guardianship dually supported by a guardianship order granted by the Family Court, in a situation where both the families are known to each other?

The Madras High Court in the present case reiterated the law laid down by the Supreme Court of India in the principal judgment of *Lakshmi Kant Pandey* v. *Union of India,* (supra, 1984) and *Smt. Anokha* v. *State of Rajasthan,* (supra), as applicable to the facts and circumstances of the present case.

The Madras High Court in para 10 of the said judgment positively noted the law laid down in the case of *Anokha* (supra), and also noticing the fact that in the case of *Anokha* (supra), the prospective adoptive parents as then they were, had a judicially directed scrutiny of their Home Study Report which culminated into a judgment passed by the Court at Venice. The Supreme Court in effect applied section 13 of the Indian Code of Civil Procedure, 1908. All this has been eloquently reiterated in para 10 of the Madras High Court judgment as hereunder:

> "10. The Guidelines issued by the Government consequent to the direction of the apex Court would not apply to the voluntary adoption from the biological parents. This view was reiterated by the Apex Court in *Anokha (Smt)* v. *State of Rajasthan* reported in (2004) 1 SCC 382, wherein it has been clearly held that in the case of adoption from biological parents, the Guidelines do not apply. In paragraph 16, it has been held as follows:
>
> "In the case before us although the Guidelines do not apply, respondents 2 and 3 had produced evidence which fulfilled all the particulars required of a Home Study Report. The appellant has repeatedly affirmed her closeness to respondents 2 and 3 and her conviction that they would nourish and care for baby Alka as if she was their own. Respondents 2 and 3 have produced sufficient evidence to justify their suitability to be adoptive parents. There was a judicially directed scrutiny by a local government agency in Venice. The enquiry report has resulted in a judgment passed by the Court at Venice, Italy. That judgment can be accepted by this Court under section 13 of the Code of Civil Procedure, particularly, when the respondents have filed the investigation report and other material on the basis of which the judgment was delivered.""

Furthermore, the Madras High Court categorically turned down the contentions of the Regional Passport Officer, Government of India, Ministry of External Affairs at para 13 of the said judgment in the following terms:

> "13. (i) When the Central Adoption Resource Agency (CARA) does not impose such condition in respect of adoption from biological parents, the passport authority cannot the same. It has no legal basis;
>
> (ii) The guidelines issued by the passport authorities has no binding force in sofar as the petitioners are concerned. It is without authority of law and there is no legal basis for imposing such condition.
>
> (iii) In any event, insisting no-objection from Central Adoption Resource Agency (CARA) for issue of passport will run counter to the decisions of the Apex Court cited above."

Finally, the Writ petition of the adoptive parents was allowed by the Madras High Court and the respondents were directed "to issue the passport without any further delay."

In the case of, *Tim Cecil* v. *Unknown*; 13 June 2011; OP No. 247 of 2011; the Madras High Court had the occasion to elaborate at length the safeguards in the event of inter-country adoptions made by biological parents directly to foreign nationals. In this particular case, the petitioners were German nationals who did not have any biological child of their own. After coming to India they got acquainted with biological parents of child in question who were willing to give their fourth child to petitioners for being fostered and brought up by them as they already had three daughters.

The two key issues which arose in this case can be summed up as follows: Whether a blanket exemption of biological parents from the safeguards prescribed in inter-country adoptions in the interest of children? Whether the right of biological parents to give their child in adoption absolute and unfettered? The Court before answering these two questions of vital importance first dealt with the operative part of the judgment in such situations in the landmark case of *Lakshmi Kant Pandey* v. *Union of India,* (supra, 1984), also reiterating the law laid down by the Supreme Court of India in *Anokha* (supra) and finally made substantive references to most of the international instruments and conventions relating to child law. Certainly, the Court with its ingenuity carved out the necessary relief, but not without adequate monitored safeguards.

The Court first reiterated the position of law in cases of direct adoptions by biological parents as held by the Supreme Court of India in the primary case of *Lakshmi Kant Pandey* (supra, 1984). Para 11 of the order dated 13 June, 2011 in the case of Cecil stated as follows:

> "The Rules relating to Inter-Country Adoptions came to be framed in pursuance of the judgment of the Supreme Court in *Lakshmi Kant Pandey* v. *Union of India,* AIR 1984 SC 469. In paragraph 11 of the said decision, the Supreme Court made it clear that they were not concerned in that case with cases of adoption of children living with their biological parents, since in those cases, the biological parents would be the best persons to decide whether to give their child in adoption to foreign parents or not. It was also clarified in paragraph 11 of the said decision that it is only in cases where the children sought to be adopted are destitute or abandoned and are living in Social or Child Welfare Centres that it was necessary to consider what normative and procedural safeguards should be forged for protecting their interest and promoting their welfare. Therefore, drawing my attention to the observations of the Supreme Court, contained in paragraphs 11, 12 and 13 of the said decision, the learned counsel for the petitioners contended that there is no requirement of sponsorship by an Agency or the production of a Home Study Report."

The law laid down by the Hon'ble Supreme Court of India in *Lakshmi Kant Pandey* (supra, 1984) was reiterated by the Supreme Court in the case of *Smt. Anokha* v. *State of Rajasthan,* (supra). It was held by the Court in this judgment that the guidelines do not relate to regulation of adoption procedure in respect of children with biological parents. It is only where there is impersonalized attention of a placement authority that there is a need to closely monitor the process as per the guidelines.

In cases where children are given in adoption by the biological parents, the Court only has to deal with an application under section 7 of the Guardianship and Wards Act, 1890. And the application is to be adjudicated upon after being satisfied that the child is being given in adoption voluntarily by the natural parents after being aware of the implications of their decision to give their child in adoption.

The Madras High Court in the present case of *Cecil* (supra) in para 14 of the order dated 13 June, 2011 distinguished the facts of the case in-hand with the facts of the case of *Anokha* (supra) in the following terms:

> "14. But the said decision arose out of a case where the adoptive parents at least produced a Home Study Report, though not sponsored by an Agency. In the case on hand, there is neither a sponsorship by an Agency nor a Home Study Report. In such circumstances, the question that poses a challenge to me is as to whether the right of the biological parents to offer their children in adoption or foster care to foreigners can be said to be unfettered and uncontrolled by any guidelines, as appears to have been suggested in *Smt. Anokha*."

Clearly, the sensitivity of the Court was pointing out the absence of a Home Study Report in the case in-hand. Furthermore, the Court in para 15 of the said order dated 13 June 2011 noticed the published dissent of CARA in the following terms:

> "15. In a book titled "Every Child Deserves a Loving Family" published by the Central Adoption Resource Authority of the Ministry of Women and Child Development, Government of India, the following observations have been made with regard to the decision of the Apex Court in *Smt.Anokha*:-
>
> "Under a special situation, one direct case of inter-country adoption was allowed by Honourable Supreme Court of India which was not compatible with Hague Convention on Inter-country Adoption ratified by Government of India. This cannot be used as a precedent since Hague Convention on Inter-country Adoption-1999, ratified by Government of India does not recognise any case of direct adoption and the receiving country will not issue permission under article 5/17 to agree to such kind of adoption without involvement of recognised agencies and authorities.""

The Madras High Court order in *Cecil* (supra) in para 16 of the judgment itself furnishes shocking statistics with regard to the miserable plight of the underprivileged children in India.

> "16. The above observations have to be seen in the context of the statistics about the status of children in India. A recent report contained the following statistics:
>
> (i) There are 18 million street children;
>
> (ii) There are 100 million child labourers;
>
> (iii) Over 59 million children have no access to school;
>
> (iv) One out of two children between the ages of 6 and 14 has no access to primary education;
>
> (v) Out of 27 million children born every year, 2 million do not survive to celebrate their first birthday;
>
> (vi) Every year 27,06,000 children under 5 years die;
>
> (vii) Millions of children are denied even the most basic rights of survival and protection;

(viii) About 60 million children under the age of 6 live below the poverty line;

(ix) Children from 100 million families live without water at home;

(x) 500,000 children are forced into this commercial sex trade every year;

(xi) 1 out of every 3 girls does not live to see her 15th birthday;

(xii) Every sixth girl child's death is due to gender discrimination, 3 lakh more girls than boys die every year;

(xiii) Female mortality exceeds male mortality in 224 out of 402 districts in India;

(xiv) 53% of girls in the age group of 5 to 9 years are illiterate;

(xv) Unrecorded numbers of girl children are killed within hours of being born;

(xvi) While in 1960 there were 976 girls born for every 1000 boys, in 2001, there are only 927 girls for every 1000 boys.

Even if one does not give undue weightage to these statistics, the social picture presented by it, cannot be ignored in toto."

The Court further expressed serious concern for the view that in cases where children are given in adoption by the biological parents themselves, satisfaction per-se of the natural parents that the children are voluntarily given for adoption by the parents is simply not enough. The apprehensions of the Court are rightly so very strongly voiced in the following terms in para 17 of the judgment as follows:

> "17. In a newspaper report published on 14.6.2010 from Karnataka, it was stated that impoverished parents put up their children to sale for a few thousands of rupees. It was reported therein that in a week immediately preceding the date of the report, six families in Tiptur Taluk of Tumkur District of Karnataka sold their children to prosperous families and that adoption procedures were not followed in those cases. Therefore, I think that a blanket exemption of biological parents from the safeguards prescribed in other inter-country adoptions may not be in the interest of the children, to whom the Court owes an obligation as a Court of Wards. Children are not properties of their parents so as to entitle them to have absolute dominance over them. In a country where abject poverty drives a few families to sell their children for beggary, forced labour or prostitution, it is not safe to rely entirely upon the wisdom of the biological parents, to give their children in adoption or for foster care, to foreigners."

Going by the above mentioned newspaper report cited in the Madras High Court judgment, it is common knowledge that human trafficking of children as also abuse of children is rampant in our country in alarming proportions. But, it is most respectfully submitted that the view of CARA as stated in the above mentioned publication titled "Every Child Deserves a Loving Family," as also noticed in the Madras High Court order of *Cecil* (supra) as a sequel to the judgment handed down by the Supreme Court of India in *Anokha* (supra) is not correct. The same is not legally sustainable.

**Firstly,** CARA directives on the administrative side cannot possibly overwrite the law laid down by the Hon'ble Supreme Court of India in the case of *Anokha* in the year 2004.

**Secondly,** if CARA was aggrieved by the judgment in the case of *Anokha* (supra) they should have as a nodal institution or the Ministry of Welfare under the aegis of which CARA was set up filed an intervener application or a review application before the Supreme Court of India itself, at the time the judgment was handed down in the case of *Anokha* (supra). The law laid down in the case of *Anokha* (supra) is perfectly correct as it looks directly at genuine bona fide adoptions as also advocating the added safeguard of Court scrutiny and possibly intervention on guardianship applications, where the parties are known to each other.

**Thirdly,** CARA has taken shelter of India ratifying the Hague Convention on adoptions on 6 June 2003 in challenging in isolation the correctness of the law laid down by the Hon'ble Supreme Court of India in the case of *Anokha* (supra). As a matter of fact, CARA is yet to come out on any published opinion or material suitably highlighting the advantages of India signing the Hague convention on adoptions. This of course is much to the disadvantage of the NRI community, who are left in the lurch on account of an unnecessary deep void in this area of law despite India signing the Hague convention on adoptions. CARA or the Ministry of Welfare or the Ministry of Women and Child Development possibly in conjunction with the Law Ministry of India, should have taken timely and concrete steps in drafting as also implementing and enabling legislation specifically looking at the positive steps of India signing the Hague convention on adoptions, thereby, giving meaningful interpretation to India signing the Hague Convention on adoptions.

Further there is a discussion in the present order dated 13 June, 2011 itself, on the rights of the biological parents over their children. The Court in detail has referred to various international conventions and even reports of the Law Commission of India in order to arrive at a conclusion that the rights of the biological parents to give their children in adoption are not absolute and unfettered. This is by providing a home study report and a guardianship order from a Court of competent jurisdiction. The important international conventions dealing with inter-country adoptions which have been ratified by India include the Convention on the Rights of the Child, 20 November, 1989 and the Hague Convention on protection of children and cooperation in respect of inter country adoptions concluded on 29 May, 1993. And the 153rd report of Law Commission of India, dated 26 August, 1994 and the Juvenile Justice Act, 2000 are other important national documents discussed in the case on the point of rights of biological parents. The Court has summed up its concern in para 28 of the order dated 13 June, 2011 in the following categorical terms:

> "28. In the light of the mandate contained in the Convention on the Rights of the Child and the Hague Convention, both of which have been ratified by India and also in the light of the provisions of the Juvenile Justice (Care and Protection of Children) Act, 2000 as amended by Act 33 of 2006, the

> primary responsibility of providing care and protection to children is that of his birth family. Since the child has a fundamental right to be protected against any kind of exploitation, the biological parents cannot be held to have an absolute and unfettered right to give their children in adoption or for foster care to foreign nationals. It is true that the Personal Law of Hindus have always recognized the right of the biological parents to give their child in adoption. But this recognition under the Hindu Law, as pointed out by Sir Henry Maine and other Scholars, was a contrivance to prevent the interruption of succession. The origin of this institution amongst the Hindus was attributed to the religious belief of spiritual efficacy of the possession of a son and a belief that by leaving a male issue in this world, they would save themselves from the torments of the next. Consequently, there was to some extent an element of protection in the form of succession to property. Therefore, the same cannot, as on date, enable the biological parents to contend that their rights to give their children in adoption to foreign nationals is absolute and unfettered. In such circumstances, despite the fact that the parties involved in this case appear to be genuine, I am unable to order the original petition as prayed for unconditionally without even a Home Study Report."

Hence, it is manifest that the Court logically carved out the necessary relief, as already stated above. According to the Madras High Court the decision of the biological parents, however bona fide, need not always be an informed decision. And in view of the detailed reasoning in the order dated 13 June, 2011 the Court issued directions to the Central Adoption Resource Authority, Ministry of Women and Child Development, Government of India, to engage the services of a recognised and approved agency in Germany and have a home study conducted in respect of the petitioners and submit the same to the Court within a period of three months to enable the Court to allow the above original petition as prayed for, so as to allow the process of adoption without CARA intervention.

## VI. PREFERENCE TO PARENTS OF INDIAN ORIGIN

Another significant issue in inter-country adoptions, is locating prospective adoptive parents, preferably of Indian origin. The Supreme Court of India, in *Karnataka State Council for Child Welfare* v. *Society of Sisters of Charity St Gerosa Convent*, AIR 1994 SC 658, held that the rationale behind finding Indian parents or parents of Indian origin is to ensure that the children should grow up in Indian surroundings so that they retain their culture and heritage. This is definitely an issue, which has a bearing on the question of the welfare of the children. The best interest of the children is the main and prime consideration.

The Gujarat High Court in a progressive judgment in *Jayantilal* v. *Asha*, AIR 1989 Guj 152 upheld the validity of guardianship orders in favour of two Norwegian couples who were appointed as guardians of Hindu children. The Court held in para 12 (at page 156):

> '... if the biological parents have died rendering the child an orphan then the society owes a duty to the child that at least a semblance of comfort and care which the biological parents could have provided will be provided to

the child, if some people from howsoever distant a corner of this planet, come forth to do so. In such a case a petty contention like the change of religion or culture of the child can hardly stand in the way of the court in sanctioning inter-country adoption. Unfounded and imaginary apprehensions also are of little consequence and once the court is assured that there is no possibility of the child being abused which assurance can flow from the independent agencies which are ordained for the purpose then nothing can and need prevent the court from sanctioning an inter-country adoption.'

Thus, the procedure described above and the supervisory role of the Court serves as a double check on inter-country adoptions. Not only does this dual process ensures a check against suspected child abuse, but at the same time it also removes hyper-technical objections to facilitate the conclusion of the adoption process and to enable the adopted child to leave the country with his or her adoptive parents without further bureaucratic delays.

The Allahabad High Court in *Jagdish Chander Gupta* v. *Dr Ku Vimla Gupta*, 2004 (1) HLR 282 held that, under section 9 of the Guardian and Wards Act 1890, the application for guardianship of a minor shall be made to the District Court having jurisdiction in the place where the minor ordinarily resides. The supervisory role of the Court in placing the welfare of the minor as the primary consideration is best reflected in the following words of the Court in para 16 (at page 285):

'It should not be lost sight of and must be emphasised that in custody cases, a child has not to be treated as a chattel in which its parents have a proprietary interest. It is a human being to whom the parents owe serious obligations. One's own self-interest sometimes clouds his perception of what is the best for those for whom he or she is responsible. It takes a very high degree of selflessness and maturity – which is for most of the people probably unattainable degree for a parent/proposed guardian to acknowledge that it might be better for the child to be brought up by someone else.'

## VII. RATIFICATION OF THE HAGUE CONVENTION ON INTER-COUNTRY ADOPTION BY THE GOVERNMENT OF INDIA ON 6 JUNE, 2003

The Government of India has also ratified the Hague convention on Inter-Country Adoption on 6 June, 2003. Although, the Government of India has ratified the Hague Convention in this regard, but in actual practice the same has not been publicised. And, from the practical point of view not much tangible benefits are forthcoming at all to people residing abroad seeking to adopt children from India. In fact, one of the authors of this article at the Annual National Meet on Adoption organised in New Delhi on 3-4 May, 2007, by the CARA, now falling under the new created Ministry of Women and Child Development, strongly advocated the emergent need for setting up a committee or a task force to commission a comprehensive report to look at the potential benefits on India signing the Hague Convention on adoptions. If such a report is prepared, it can well be officially circulated to the Foreign Embassies and Missions in India. This is of course, with a view to creating awareness and publicising the advantages of India signing the

Hague Convention on adoptions, to prospective adoptive parents of foreign origin and Persons of Indian Origin domiciled overseas.

### VIII. DOCUMENTS REQUIRED FROM FOREIGN ADOPTIVE PARENTS AND OVERSEAS SOCIAL OR CHILD WELFARE AGENCY FOR INTER-COUNTRY ADOPTION APPLICATION

Experience of dealing with CARA and/or the concerned Ministry suggests that the documentation should be compiled meticulously in order to avoid bureaucratic delays. The following documents must be submitted by the foreign adoptive parents. It will be noted that the Indian requirements are quite similar to those prescribed in various appendices of RON 117 issued by the British Home Office:

(1) home study report;

(2) recent photographs of the adoptive family;

(3) marriage certificate of the foreign adoptive parents;

(4) declaration concerning the health of the foreign adoptive parents;

(5) certificate of medical fitness of the foreign adoptive parents duly certified by a medical doctor;

(6) declaration regarding financial status, together with supporting documents including employer's certificate, wherever applicable;

(7) employment certificate of the foreign adoptive parents, if applicable;

(8) income-tax assessment order(s) of the foreign adoptive parents;

(9) bank references for the foreign adoptive parents;

(10) particulars of properties owned by the prospective adoptive parents;

(11) joint declaration tendered by the foreign adoptive parents stating willingness to be appointed guardians of the child;

(12) undertaking from the social or child welfare enlisted agency sponsoring the foreigner to the effect that the child would be legally adopted by the foreign adoptive parents according to the law of the country within a period not exceeding two years from the time of arrival of the child;

(13) undertaking from the foreign adoptive parents to the effect that the child would be provided with the necessary education and upbringing according to status of the adoptive parents;

(14) undertaking from the recognised foreign social or child welfare agency that the report relating to the progress of the child along with his/her recent photograph would be sent quarterly during first two years and half-yearly for the next three years in the prescribed proforma through the relevant Indian diplomatic post;

(15) power-of-attorney conferred by the intending parents in favour of the social or the child welfare agency in India which will be required to process the case. Such power-of-attorney should also authorise the lawyer in India to handle the case on behalf of the foreign adoptee parents, if they are not in a position to come to India;

(16) certificate from the recognised foreign social or child welfare agency sponsoring the application to the effect that the adoptive parents are permitted to adopt a child according to the laws of their country;

(17) undertaking from the recognised foreign social or child welfare agency to the effect that, in case of disruption of the adoptive family before the legal adoption has been effected, it will take care of child and find a suitable alternative placement for the child with prior approval of CARA;

(18) undertaking from the recognised foreign social or child welfare agency that it will reimburse all expenses to the concerned Indian social or child welfare agency as fixed by the competent Court towards maintenance of the child and the processing charge fees.

It is important to reiterate that all the above certificates, declarations and documents in support of the application should be duly notarised by a notary public whose signature should be duly attested either by an officer of the Ministry of External Affairs, the Ministry of Justice or the Ministry of Social Welfare of the country of the foreign adoptive parents or by an officer of the Indian Embassy or the High Commission or Consulate in that country.

## IX. DOMESTIC LAW OF ADOPTION IN INDIA UNDER THE PROVISIONS OF THE HINDU ADOPTIONS AND MAINTENANCE ACT, 1956

Having elaborated the law and procedure relating to inter-country adoptions, brief reference is now made to the domestic law governing adoptions by Hindus.

The principal law relating to adoption in India by Hindus only is contained in the Hindu Adoptions and Maintenance Act, 1956 (HAMA 1956).

### (A) SECTION 6 OF THE HAMA, 1956 MANDATES REQUISITES OF A VALID ADOPTION

Section 6 stipulates four conditions for a valid adoption, namely:

(1) the person adopting has the capacity, and also the right, to take in adoption;

(2) the person giving the child in adoption has the capacity to do so;

(3) the person adopted is capable of being taken in adoption; and

(4) the adoption is made in compliance with the other conditions mentioned in chapter 2 of the HAMA 1956.

Section 6(iv) requires that the adoption should be made in compliance with other conditions mentioned in chapter 2 of the HAMA 1956. In other words, in order that the adoption should be valid, the provisions of sections 7–11 must be satisfied. Section 7 deals with the capacity of a male Hindu to take in adoption; and section 8 with the capacity of a female Hindu to take in adoption. Section 9 qualifies persons capable of giving children in adoption; section 10 categorises those persons who may be adopted; and section 11 enumerates other conditions for a valid adoption. Thereafter, section 12 elaborates the effects of a valid adoption.

**(B) SECTION 11 OF THE HAMA, 1956 STIPULATES OTHER ESSENTIAL CONDITIONS FOR A VALID ADOPTION**

Section 11 of the HAMA, 1956 stipulates other vital conditions for a valid adoption, and is reproduced below.

> '11. *Other conditions for a valid adoption.*—In every adoption, the following conditions must be complied with:—
>
> (i) if the adoption is of a son, the adoptive father or mother by whom the adoption is made must not have a Hindu son, son's son or son's son's son (whether by legitimate blood relationship or by adoption) living at the time of adoption;
>
> (ii) if the adoption is of a daughter, the adoptive father or mother by whom the adoption is made must not have a Hindu daughter or son's daughter (whether by legitimate blood relationship or by adoption) living at the time of adoption;
>
> (iii) if the adoption is by a male and the person to be adopted is a female, the adoptive father is at least twenty-one years older than the person to be adopted;
>
> (iv) if the adoption is by a female and the person to be adopted is a male, the adoptive mother is at least twenty-one years older than the person to be adopted;
>
> (v) the same child may not be adopted simultaneously by two or more persons;
>
> (vi) the child to be adopted must be actually given and taken in adoption by the parents or guardian concerned or under their authority with intent to transfer the child from the family of its birth [or in the case of an abandoned child or child whose parentage is not known, from the place or family where it has been brought up] to the family of its adoption:
>
> Provided that the performance of *datta homam* shall not be essential to the validity of adoption.'

**(C) SECTION 12 OF THE HAMA, 1956 SPECIFICALLY DEALS WITH THE EFFECTS OF A VALID ADOPTION**

Section 12 specifically deals with the legal effects of an adoption made in accordance with the provisions of the HAMA, 1956. It can be pointed out that section 12 of the HAMA, 1956 satisfies the requirements of clause (ix) of para 310 of HC 395 of the current British Immigration Rules governing adoption. This clause in very harsh terms states that the adopted child 'has lost or broken his ties with his family of origin'.

As to the legal effects of a valid adoption, it is important to cite certain decisions of the Supreme Court of India. It was held by the Supreme Court of India in *Sitabai* v. *Ramchandra,* AIR 1970 SC 343, in para 6 (at page 348):

> '... The true effect and interpretation of sections 11 and 12 of Act No 78 of 1956 therefore is that when either of the spouses adopts a child, all the ties of the child in the family of his or her birth become completely severed

and these are all replaced by those created by the adoption in the adoptive family ...'

Similarly, it was held by the Supreme Court in *Kartar Singh* v. *Surjan Singh,* AIR 1974 SC 2161, in para 7 (at page 2163):

> '... The words in section 11(vi) "with intent to transfer the child from the family of its birth to the family of its adoption" are merely indicative of the result of the actual giving and taking by the parents or guardians concerned referred to in the earlier part of the clause. Where an adoption ceremony is gone through and the giving and taking takes place, there cannot be any other intention ... .'

And, the Supreme Court of India in *Chandan Bilasini* v. *Aftabuddin Khan,* 1996 (1) HLR 79 SC, held in para 6 (at page 81):

> '... Section 12 of the Hindu Adoptions and Maintenance Act clearly provides that an adopted child shall be deemed to be the child of his adoptive father or mother for all purposes with effect from the date of the adoption and from such date all ties of the child in the family of his or her birth shall be deemed to be severed and replaced by those created by the adoption in the adoptive family ...'

## (D) SECTION 15 OF THE HAMA, 1956 PROVIDES THAT A VALID ADOPTION NOT TO BE CANCELLED

Finally, section 15 of the HAMA, 1956 underlines the irrevocability of the validly performed adoption by stating that it cannot be cancelled or renounced. Therefore, under Indian law, once a legitimate adoption is obtained, in accordance with the procedure established by law, the margin for interference is minimal, except in certain exceptional circumstances.

The adoption process once validly effected in terms of HAMA, 1956 is an irrevocable act and the biological parents cannot seek the custody of the child at a later point of time. The same principle applies in the interest of the children when children are given in foster care by their parents first voluntarily and later when they seek its return at their whims and pleasure.

The Bombay High Court in a decided case, reported as *Maroti Vithal Bhatwalkar* v. *Mahila Vikas Mandal, Chandrapur,* AIR 2007 (NOC) 965 Bom, has handed down a significant ruling in this regard. In this particular case, the biological parents gave their child to a childless couple, as they stayed away from each other and were not sure whether they would be able to or even wanted to take care of the child properly or not. The foster parents took good care of the child but six and a half years later, the biological parents filed an application with the scrutiny officer, that they wanted the child back with them. They were still living separately and were not sure as to who would keep the child. The matter went to the Court and dismissing their claim, the Court held that merely because of the report of the scrutiny officer the child cannot be handed over back to the biological parents. Biological parents cannot wait to receive back the child indefinitely and leave the fate of the child in suspended animation leaving to them the choice of exercising option of claiming child at a later point of time. In the interest of the child, its care and continuity should not be disturbed.

**(E) REGISTERED ADOPTION CAN BE CHALLENGED UNDER SECTION 16 OF THE HAMA, 1956**

Section 16 of the HAMA, 1956 reads as follows:

> '16. *Presumption as to registered documents relating to adoption.*—Whenever any document registered under any law for the time being in force is produced before any court purporting to record an adoption made and is signed by the person giving and the person taking the child in adoption, the court shall presume that the adoption has been made in compliance with the provisions of this Act unless and until it is disproved.'

In an important ruling concerning adoption by Hindus, *Jai Singh* v. *Shakuntala*, 2002 (3) SCC 634, the Supreme Court of India has recently held that, though a document registering an adoption should be treated as final proof of adoption, it could still be challenged in a Court of law if evidence to the contrary was put forward.

The Apex Court, in interpreting the statutory intent of section 16 of the HAMA 1956, said that the presumption about the registered document relating to adoption 'cannot be an irrebuttable presumption'. Justices Umesh C Banerjee and Brijesh Kumar held in para 2 (at pages 636 and 637):

> '2. The section thus envisages a statutory presumption that in the event of there being a registered document pertaining to adoption there would be a presumption that adoption has been made in accordance with law. Mandate of the statute is rather definite since the legislature has used "shall" instead of any other word of lesser significance. Incidentally, however, the inclusion of the words "unless and until it is disproved" appearing at the end of the statutory provision has made the situation not that rigid but flexible enough to depend upon the evidence available on record in support of adoption. It is a matter of grave significance by reason of the factum of adoption and displacement of the person adopted from the natural succession — thus onus of proof is rather heavy. Statute has allowed some amount of flexibility, lest it turns out to be solely dependent on a registered adoption deed. The reason for inclusion of the words "unless and until it is disproved" shall have to be ascertained in its proper perspective and as such the presumption cannot but be said to be a rebuttable presumption. Statutory intent thus stands out to be rather expressive depicting therein that the presumption cannot be an irrebuttable presumption by reason of the inclusion of the words just noticed above....'

In the above-mentioned ruling, the Supreme Court also concurred with the similar tenor of law laid down by the Punjab and Haryana High Court in *Modan Singh* v. *Sham Kaur*, AIR 1973 P&H 122.

Clearly, the ruling in *Jai Singh* (supra) will be of immense help to immigration officers of Foreign Missions/Consulates/Embassies in India in weeding out suspect adoption immigration applications lodged from within the applicant's own family designed to circumvent immigration controls.

## (F) CASE-LAW ANALYSIS OF ADOPTIONS: NOT TO BE DISTURBED AFTER A LAPSE OF LONG PERIOD OF TIME

From the ratio of the case-law handed down by the Supreme Court of India and other High Courts in the country, it emanates that when an adoption ceremony has been performed and the giving and taking of the child takes place, there cannot be any other intention other than effecting the adoption.

The catena of case law also holds that the process of adoption cannot be challenged after a significant lapse of time.

One of the early decisions handed down by the Hon'ble Supreme Court of India in the case of *L. Debi Prasad (dead) by L.Rs* v. *Tribeni Devi*, AIR 1970 SC 1286 (V 57 C 270), is a significant judgment on adoptions that cannot be challenged after a significant lapse of time.

Paragraphs 8 and 9 of the said judgment (at pages 1289 and 1290) state as under:

> "8. That is also the view expressed in Mayne's Hindu Law wherein it is observed that the giving and receiving are absolutely necessary to the validity of an adoption; they are the operative part of the ceremony, being that part of it which transfers the boy from one family to another; but the Hindu Law does not require that there shall be any particular form so far as giving and acceptance are concerned; for a valid adoption all that the law requires is that the natural father shall be asked by the adoptive parent to give his son in adoption, and that the boy shall be handed over and taken for this purpose.
>
> 9. There is no doubt that the burden of proving satisfactorily that he was given by his natural father and received by Gopal Das as his adoptive son is on Shyam Behari Lal. But as observed by the Judicial Committee of the Privy Council in *Rajendro Nath Holdar* v. *Jogendro Nath Banerjee*, (1870-72) 14 Moo Ind App 67 (PC) that although the person who pleads that he had been adopted is bound to prove his title as adopted son, as a fact yet from the long period during which he had been received as an adopted son, every allowance for the absence of evidence to prove such fact was to be favourably entertained, and that the case was analogous to that in which the legitimacy of a person in possession had been acquiesced in for a considerable time, and afterwards impeached by a party, who had a right to question the legitimacy, where the Defendant, in order to defend his status, is allowed to invoke against the claimant every presumption which arises from long recognition of his legitimacy by members of his family; that in the case of a Hindus, long recognition as an adopted son, raised even a stronger presumption in favour of the validity of his adoption, arising from the possibility of the loss of his rights in his own family by being adopted in another family. In *Rup Narain* v. *Gopal Devi*, (1909) 36 Ind App 103 (PC), the Judicial Committee observed that in the absence of direct evidence much value has to be attached to the fact that the alleged adopted son had without controversy succeeded to his adoptive father's estate and enjoyed till his death and that documents during his life and after his death were framed upon the basis of the adoption. A Division Bench of the Orissa

High Court in *Balinki Padhano* v. *Gopalkrishna Padhano,* AIR 1964 Ori 117; held that in the case of an ancient adoption evidence showing that the boy was treated for a long time as the adopted son at a time when there was no controversy is sufficient to prove the adoption although evidence of actual giving and taking is not forthcoming. We are in agreement with the views expressed in the decisions referred to above."

Another High Court ruling in the reported case of *Sauney Majhi* v. *Duli Dei,* AIR 1985 Ori 22, demonstrates the validity of the adoption process in absence of evidence where a significant amount of time has lapsed.

Paragraph 6 (at pages 24 and 25) of the said judgment above reads as under:

> "6. The law is fairly settled that the evidence in support of an adoption is sufficient to satisfy the very grave and serious onus that rests upon any person who seeks to displace the natural line of succession by alleging an adoption. The fact of adoption must be proved in the same way as any other fact, but where there is a lapse of long period between the date of adoption and the time when it is being questioned, every allowance for the absence of evidence to prove such fact must be favourably entertained, as after the lapse of a long period, direct evidence to prove adoption may not be available.

The Supreme Court in the case of *L. Debi Prasad* v. *Tribeni Devi,* (supra), observed:—

> "In the case of all ancient transaction, it is but natural that positive oral evidence will be lacking. Passage of time gradually wipes out such evidence. Human affairs often have to be judged on the basis of probabilities. Rendering of justice will become impossible if a particular mode of proof is insisted upon under all circumstances. In judging whether an adoption pleaded has been satisfactorily proved or not, we have to bear in mind the lapse of time between the date of the alleged adoption and the date on which the concerned party is required to adduce proof. In the case of an adoption said to have taken place years before the same is questioned, the most important evidence is likely to be that the alleged adoptive father held out the person claiming to have been adopted as his son; the latter treated the former as his father and their relations and friends treated them as father and son. There is no predetermined way of proving any fact. A fact is said to have been proved where after considering the matters before it, the Court either believes it to exist or considers its existence so probable that a prudent man ought, under the circumstances of the particular case, to act upon the supposition that it exists. Hence if after taking an overall view of the evidence adduced in the case, we are satisfied that the adoption pleaded is true, we must necessarily proceed on the basis, in the absence of any evidence to the contrary, that it is a valid adoption as well."

The aforesaid view of the Supreme Court has been followed in a number of cases of this Court and of other High Courts. The aforesaid principle only regulates the mode of proof of the factum of adoption. In the decision in the case of *Sri Kanchumarthi Venkata Seetharama Chandra Row* v. *Kanchumarthi Raju,* AIR 1925 PC

201, which has been approved by the Supreme Court in the case of *Voleti Venkata Ramarao* v. *Kesaparagada Bhasararao,* AIR 1969 SC 1359, it has been authoritatively said that in the case of an ancient adoption, it stands to reason that after a very long-term of years and a variety of transactions of open life and conduct upon the footing that the adoption was a valid act, the burden must rest heavily upon him who challenges its validity. The appellants in this case rely upon the aforesaid principles and have contended that the date of adoption as available from the evidence on record was 1909 and it is not possible to prove the factum of adoption by direct evidence. Thus, according to them the overall view of the evidence on record should lead to the conclusion that there was a valid adoption as alleged by them."

It will be noticed that the aforesaid view of the Supreme Court of India in the matter of *Debi Prasad* v. *Tribeni Devi,* (supra), has been followed in the above mentioned-case of *Sauney Majhi* v. *Duli Dei,* (supra). The aforesaid principle only regulates the mode of proof of the factum of adoption.

The third ruling in line to support the above-mentioned argument in favour of the validity of the adoption in absence of evidence is the reported case of *Sitaram Nai* v. *Puranmal Sonar,* AIR 1985 Ori 171.

Paragraphs 8 and 9 of the said judgment which are relevant are cited hereunder:

> "8. Before examining the correctness of rival contentions and examining the evidence adduced in this case to find out whether the adoption of defendant No. 2 by late Baluram has been proved in this case or not, it would be profitable to note the law on the point. Under the Hindu law, as it existed prior to the commencement of the Hindu Adoptions and Maintenance Act, the physical act of giving and receiving is absolutely necessary to the validity of an adoption. There is no particular form prescribed for giving and taking but what the law requires is that there should be some overt act to signify the delivery of the boy from one family to another. The natural parents should hand over the adoptive boy and the adoptive parents should receive him. In case of an old adoption, however, strict proof of the performance of the ceremonies may not be available. An adoption acquiesced in and recognized for a number of years by the person making the adoption and a long course of recognition on the part of the persons who would be expected to know of the fact and who were best acquainted with the circumstances, can give rise to the inference that the conditions relating to the adoption" were fulfilled. (See, Mulla's Hindu Law, section 489). There is no specific rule as to number of years necessary for the purpose to dub the adoption as an 'old adoption'. By judicial pronouncements, however, the Courts in India have more or less considered adoption, of 25 years and more to be an ancient adoption. In our opinion, no definite formula can be applied as to the number of years to find out whether the adoption is an old adoption or not. But according to us, where on account of lapse of time, it is not possible to give evidence of persons proving the ceremony of giving and taking, then a party can take recourse to the theory of ancient adoption, provided of course there has been a

sufficient lapse of time between the date of alleged adoption and the date on which the same is challenged. But if the evidence discloses that the persons who attended the adoption ceremony are available to give evidence, then in such a case one cannot discharge his burden of proving the factum of giving and taking merely by taking recourse to the fact that the adoption had taken place 25 or 30 years before the same is challenged. In our opinion, it depends upon the facts and circumstances of each case.

9. ....In this case of *Gouranga Sahu* v. *Bhaga Sahu,* AIR 1976 Ori 43, S.K. Ray, J (as he then was) considering the case of an old adoption and also the burden of proof and the mode of appreciation of evidence thereto. In that case, the adoption was 36 years old. In paragraph 6 of the judgment, his Lordship held:—

"…. So even though the normal rule is that one who seeks to deflect the natural line of succession to property by alleging adoption must discharge that heavy burden, in cases of ancient adoption every allowance for the absence of evidence to prove such fact must be favourably entertained. Where there is a long lapse of years between the adoption and the time when it is being questioned and during the period of interregnum a variety of transactions of open life and conduct upon the footing that the adoption was a valid act have taken place, the initial burden necessarily shifts to the person who challenges its validity…."

After applying the law to the facts of that case his Lordship held:—

"…. Considering the entire evidence on record, both documentary and oral, and the variety of transactions of open life and conduct upon the footing of adoption coupled with the weakness of the defence evidence, and absence of any casteman or relative coming forward in support of the defence case/it is impossible to say that the plaintiff is the adopted son of Mohana is erroneous......"

From the said judgment, it is not quite, clear as to what was the evidence which, his Lordship has considered in coming to the aforesaid conclusion.

A conspectus of the aforesaid authorities unequivocally lays down the rule that a person who claims title on the basis of adoption must prove the adoption and it has to be established that the essential ceremony of giving and taking did take place. That burden, however, shifts to the person who challenges the adoption to disprove the adoption when on account of long lapse of years, direct evidence of giving and taking has disappeared. But if direct evidence is available, then the burden would not shift and the person who claims title on the basis of adoption must discharge that burden."

Another recent example in support of the validity of adoptions where a significant amount of time has lapsed is the case of *Munivenkatappa* v. *Dodamuniyappa*, 2008 (2) HLR 308.

Para 13 (at page 311) of the judgment read as under:

"13. …… It is also to be noticed that under the Hindu Law giving and receiving of a boy are absolutely necessary to the validity of adoption. They are the operative part of the ceremony, which converts the boy of one family to another family. But, however, it is to be noticed that the Hindu Law does not require giving and receiving of a boy, so far as the acceptance is concerned. For a valid adoption all that the law requires is that the parent in adoption and that the boy shall be handed over and taken over by the parties. It is to be noticed that in the case of a long recognition of an adoption it raises a strong presumption in favour of the validity of the adoption arising from the loss of his rights from his own family and adopt the right of another family. In ancient adoptions, where the evidence by lapse of time is not available and there are documents evidencing the adoption, then in such circumstances, it is for them who challenge the adoption to prove that the said adoption has not taken place, as there is no circumstance sufficient to prove adoption is forthcoming."

In light of the above-mentioned rulings, it is noticed that even though grave and serious onus lies on the person who seeks to deflect from the natural line of succession, as it will be noticed that a clear exception has been made by the Hon'ble Supreme Court of India and various High Courts in the country in a number of cases dealing with the issue of ancient adoptions. A strong presumption is raised in favour of the validity of adoption in such cases. Meaning thereby, that where due to long lapse of years, it is not possible to get the evidence to prove the adoption, it is to be presumed that the adoption is valid and the burden to prove that the adoption did not take place actually and consequently shifts on the person challenging the said adoption in question. However, if direct evidence is available in such cases, the burden to prove the adoption does not shift in such a situation and the person claiming the title on the basis of the adoption has to prove the adoption satisfactorily.

## (G) POSITION OF CUSTOMARY ADOPTIONS BEFORE AND AFTER THE COMMENCEMENT OF THE HINDU ADOPTIONS AND MAINTENANCE ACT, 1956

### BRIEF CASE-LAW ANALYSIS ON POSTION OF RECOGNITION OF CUSTOMARY ADOPTIONS BEFORE AND AFTER THE COMMENCEMENT OF THE HINDU ADOPTIONS AND MAINTENANCE ACT, 1956

In the case of *Mohinder Singh* v. *Gurbax Singh*, 2004 (138) PLR 154, the Punjab and Haryana High Court has analysed the position of law relating to customary adoptions specifically before and after the commencement of the Hindu Adoptions and Maintenance Act, 1956 (hereinafter referred to as the HAMA, 1956).

The key issue in the present case was as to what was the effect of the provisions of the HAMA, 1956, after the commencement of the HAMA, 1956 on 21 December 1956 on customary adoptions made before the enactment of the said legislation.

Both the trial Court as well as the first appellate Court held that the adoption in the present case was valid under the customary rules and the same cannot be cancelled or set aside. Therefore, the Hon'ble High Court upheld in appeal the customary adoption made on 3 February 1946.

The issue in hand was discussed at length before the Hon'ble High Court by both the parties in the present case. The legal point of the difference in the position of customary adoptions before and after the enactment of the HAMA, 1956 was noticed and analysed by the Hon'ble High Court in para 14 (at pages 158 and 159) in the following terms:

> "14. While referring to section 30 of the Adoptions and Maintenance Act, learned counsel for the defendant further submitted that in this case, the alleged adoption was made in the year 1946 i.e. much prior to the commencement of the Adoptions and Maintenance Act, therefore, the validity and the effect of such an adoption has to be determined in accordance with the position existing prior to the Adoptions and Maintenance Act. He submitted that the adoption in question was customary, which was nothing but appointment of a legal heir. Though, such adoption has been abolished now under section 4 of the Adoptions and Maintenance Act, but the nature of the adoption in the instant case would not change, in view of section 30 of the Adoptions and Maintenance Act as the provisions of sections 4 and 12 of the said Act will not be applicable in the instant case. Section 12 of the Adoptions and Maintenance Act provides that an adopted child shall be deemed to be the child of his adoptive father or mother for all purposes with effect from the date of the adoption and from such date all the ties of the child in the family of his or her birth shall be deemed to be severed and replaced by those created by the adoption in the adoptive family. In view of this Section, now there is no scope for customary adoption i.e. appointment of legal heirs. But sections 4 and 12 of the Adoptions and Maintenance Act will not be applicable on an adoption, which was made prior to coming into force of this Act. The validity and effect of such adoption will be determined on the basis of law or custom prevailed at that time. In the instant case, the adoption was made in the year 1946 under the custom. The said adoption was nothing but the appointment of a legal heir. Thus, the status of the plaintiff will not change after coming into force of the Adoptions and Maintenance Act and the validity and effect of the adoption of the plaintiff by Dasondha Singh has to be analysed according to the position existing prior to the Adoptions and Maintenance Act. In nutshell, the contention of learned counsel for the defendant is that under the customary law of Punjab, the adoption of the plaintiff was nothing but an appointment of a legal heir and by such appointment, he was not transplanted to the family of the appointor or conversely he did not become grandson of Rur Singh, father of Dasondha Singh. Therefore, he could not form a coparcenary with Dasondha Singh, and without being a coparcener, he did not have any right to challenge any alienation made by his appointor i.e. Dasondha Singh. In support of his contention, learned counsel for the defendant relied upon a decision of the Hon'ble Apex Court in *Daniraiji Vrajlalji, Junagadh* v. *Maharaj Shri Chandraprabha*, AIR 1975 SC 784, wherein it was held that an adoption in 'Goda Datta' form made before the passing of the Adoptions and Maintenance Act can be cancelled or revoked even after coming into force of that Act. Neither section 4 nor section 15 of the Adoptions and Maintenance Act is retrospective in its operation. Any custom or usage as

part of the Hindu Law in force prior to the commencement of the Act has ceased to have effect in regard to any matter for which provision has been made in Chapter-II, except what has been expressly provided in the Adoptions and Maintenance Act, which prohibits cancellation of adoption, applies to an adoption which has been validly made in accordance with the provisions contained in Chapter II of the Adoptions and Maintenance Act and after its commencement. It does not do away with the incident and characterstic of revocability of the custom of Goda Datta. Validity of an adoption made before the commencement of the Adoptions and Maintenance Act and also its effect has to be examined and determined with reference to the law or the custom as it stood prior to the coming into force of the Adoptions and Maintenance Act and not in accordance with it. Thus, on the basis of the aforesaid, learned counsel for the defendant submitted that the plaintiff being only an appointed heir under the customary law was having no locus standi to contest the alienation made by Dasondha Singh. By such an adoption, he did not become the member of the family of his adoptive father and thus, he did not acquire the status of a coparcener. Therefore, neither he has any right in the coparcenary property being a coparcener nor he has right to challenge the alienation of the ancestral coparcenary property made by Dasondha Singh during his life time."

The Hon'ble High Court has given a detailed analysis of adoptions under the customary law of Punjab in paras 20 and 21 (at pages 162 and 163) of the said judgment in the following terms:

"20. Under the customary law of Punjab, there was distinction between customary formal adoption and adoption by way of customary appointment of heirs. Under the Hindu law or in case of customary formal adoption, the adoption is primarily a religious act intended to confer spiritual benefit on the adopter, and under the Customary Law in Punjab, adoption was a secular act the object of which was to appoint a legal heir. The formal adoption by customary method confers on the adopted son the status of a son in the adoptive family with a right of collateral succession in the family of the adoptive father. The formal adoption may be made in accordance with custom and by observing the customary forms. It is not necessary to comply with the rules of Hindu law in the matter of ritual or otherwise. In case of customary adoption the adoption was no more than a mere appointment of a legal heir creating a personal relationship between the adoptive father and the appointed heir only. There is no tic of kinship between the appointed heir and the collaterals of the adoptive father. The appointed heir does not acquire the right to succeed collaterally in the adoptive father's family. He acquires the right to succeed the property which his adoptive father leaves for him at the time of his death. He has no right to challenge any alienation made by the adoptive father during his life time. The status of the appointed heir is, thus, materially different from that of a son adopted under the Hindu taw or formal adoption under custom.

21. The adoption is formal if the parties manifest a clear intention that there should be a complete change of the family of the adopted son, so that he ceases to be a member of his natural family and loses his right of collateral succession in that family and at the same time becomes a member of the adoptive father's family and acquires a right of collateral succession in the family. This distinction has been clearly recognised by the Hon'ble Supreme Court in *Kehar Singh* v. *Dewan Singh*, AIR 1966 SC 1555 wherein it was held as under:—

"A customary adoption -in the Punjab is ordinarily no more than a mere appointment of an heir creating a personal relationship between the adoptive father and the appointed heir only, see *Mela Singh* v. *Gurdas*, ILR 3 Lah 362; AIR 1922 Lah 433 (FB). There is no lie of kinship between the appointed heir and the collaterals of the adoptive father. The appointed heir does not acquire the right to succeed collaterally in the adoptive father's family. The status of the appointed heir is thus materially different from that of a son adopted under the Hindu law.

The general custom negativing the right of the appointed heir to succeed collaterally in the family of his adoptive father is stated in article 49 of Rattigan's Digest of Customary Law, 13th Edn. D.572 thus:—

"49. Nor, on the other hand, does the heir acquire a right to succeed to the collateral relatives of the person who appoints him, where no forma! adoption has taken place, inasmuch as the relationship established between him and the appointer is a purely personal one."

The rule in article 49 does not apply to a formal adoption by the customary method. The customary formal adoption completely severs the connection of the adopted son with his natural family and transplants him from his natural family to the adoptive family. Such an adoption confers on the adopted son the right of collateral succession in the adoptive father's family and takes away the right of collateral succession in the natural family. The formal adoption may be made in accordance with custom and by observing the customary forms, and it is not necessary to comply with the rules of Hindu law in the matter of ritual or otherwise. See *Abdur Rehman* v. *Raghubir Singh*, (1949) 51 PLR 119; *Waryaman* v. *Kanshi Ram*, ILR 3 Lah I7: AIR 1922 Lah 105."

Further it was also held in *Mukand Singh* v. *Wazir Singh*, (1972) 4 SCC 178 that a Hindu governed by customary law in Punjab was not disentitled to make a formal adoption according to customary adoption or according to Hindu rites and ceremonies."

In effect in this particular judgment, the Hon'ble High Court has categorically held that customary adoption in the state of Punjab before the commencement of the HAMA, 1956 was no more than a mere appointment of a legal heir creating a personal relationship between the adoptive father and the appointed heir only. But in para 24 (at page 164) of the said judgment it has been upheld that the customary adoption in the present case was not a mere appointment of a legal heir but it was a formal adoption as well having the effect of the adopted child becoming a member of the family of the adoptive father.

In the case of *S T Krishanappa* v. *Shivkumar*, JT 2007 (6) SC 641, the Apex Court has dealt with the application of the "Dvyamushayana" form of adoption, which was the main question in the appeal proceedings before the Supreme Court of India. The said deed of adoption admittedly did not contain any form of evidence at all as to whether the adoption was in "dvyamushyayana" form or in any other form. The Hon'ble Supreme Court rejected the said appeal purely on the ground that there was no evidence on record to sustain the fact that the said adoption was in "dvyamushyayana" form.

The Apex Court cited with approval, some of its earlier decisions directly on the subject in para 11 of the judgment in the following terms:

> "11. What are the requisite ingredients of adoption in the said form came up for consideration in *Rajgopal (Dead) by LRs.* v. *Kishan Gopal,* (2003) 10 SCC 653, wherein a Division Bench of this Court upon taking into consideration a large number of decisions stated the law thus;
>
> "18. In every case of absolute dvyamushyayana form of adoption, there must be an agreement to the effect that the person given in adoption shall be the son of both i.e. the natural father as well as the adoptive father and such an agreement must be proved like any other fact by the party alleging the same. See *Laxmipatirao Shrinivas Deshpande* v. *Venkatesh Tirmal Deshpande* and *Mohna Mal* v. *Mula Mal.*""

The adoption deed in question in the above-mentioned case was executed on 15 February 1945 prior to the commencement of the HAMA, 1956 on 21 December 1956. This judgment in the year 2007 also reiterates the earlier law laid down by the Hon'ble Supreme Court in *Kartar Singh (Minor) through Guardian Bachan Singh* v. *Surjan Singh (Dead),* AIR 1974 SC 2161, wherein it was categorically held that adoptions according to custom stood abolished upon the commencement of the HAMA, 1956.

## (H) CUSTOMARY ADOPTIONS AND SUPPORTING PROOF THEREOF

In the case of *Salekh Chand* v. *Satya Gupta,* 2008 (13) SCC 119, the Hon'ble Supreme Court of India elaborated in an analytical and chronological manner the catalogue of evidence required for proving and establishing custom followed by customary adoptions in India, as applicable to various communities, more so before the commencement of the HAMA, 1956. The said judgment also elaborates in detail the Hindu mythological belief and age old tradition in effectuating adoptions.

The analysis of the Apex Court is contained in para 20 at sub-paras 13 to 20 (at pages 128 to 130) of the judgment in the following terms:

> "13. Custom must be ancient, certain and reasonable as is generally said. It will be noticed that in the definition in clause (a) of section 3 of the Act, the expression 'ancient' is not used, but what is intended is observance of custom or usage for a long time. The English rule that ' a custom, in order that it may be legal and binding, must have been used so long that the memory of man runneth not to the contrary' has not been strictly applied to Indian conditions. All that is necessary to prove is that the custom or

usage has been acted upon in practice for such a long period and with such invariability and continuity as to show that it has by common consent been submitted to as the established governing rule in any local area, tribe, community, group or family. Certainty and reasonableness are indispensable elements of the rule. For determination of the question whether there is a valid custom or not, it has been emphasized that it must not be opposed to public policy. I shall deal with the question of public policy later on.

14. The origin of custom of adoption assumes great importance. The origin of custom of adoption is lost in antiquity. The ancient Hindu Law recognized twelve kinds of sons of whom five were adopted. The five kinds of adopted sons in early times must have been of very secondary importance, for, on the whole, they were, relegated to an inferior rank in the order of sons. Out of the five kinds of adopted sons, only two survive today; namely, the Dattaka form prevalent throughout India and the Kritrima form confined to Mithila and adjoining districts. The primary object of adoption was to gratify the means of the ancestors' by annual offerings and therefore it was considered necessary that the offerer should be as much as possible a reflection of a real descendant and had to look as much like a real son as possible and certainly not be one who would never have been a son. Therefore, the body of rules was evolved out of a phrase of Saunaka that he must be 'the reflection of a son'. The restrictions flowing from this maxim had the effect of eliminating most of the forms of adoption. (See Hindu Law by S.V. Gupte, Third Edition at pages 899-906).

15. The whole law of Dattaka adoption is evolved from two important texts and a metaphor. The texts are of Manu and Vasistha, and the metaphor that of Saunaka. Manu provided for the identity of an adopted son with the family into which he was adopted. (See. Manu. Chapter IX, pages 141-142, as translated by Sir W. Jones). The object of an adoption is mixed, being religious and secular. According to Mayne, the recognition of the institution of adoption in early times had been more due to secular reasons than to any religious necessity, and the religious motive was only secondary; but although the secular motive was dominant, the religious motive was deniable. The religious motive for adoption never altogether excluded the secular motive. (See Mayne's Hindu Law and Usage, Twelfth Edition, page 329).

16. As held by this Court in *V.T.S. Chandrashekhara Mudalie* v. *Kulandeivelu Mudalier,* AIR 1963 SC 185, substitution of a son for spiritual reasons is the essence of adoption; and consequent devolution of property is mere accessory to it; the validity of an adoption has to be judged by spiritual rather than temporal considerations; and, devolution of property is only of secondary importance.

17. In *Hem Singh* v. *Harnam Singh,* AIR 1954 SC 581, it was observed by this Court that under the Hindu Law adoption is primarily a religious act intended to confer spiritual benefit on the adopter and some of the rules have therefore been held to be mandatory, and compliance with them

regarded as a condition of the validity of the adoption. The first important case on the question of adoption was decided by the Privy Council in the case of *Amarendra Mansingh* v. *Sanatan Singh*, AIR 1933 PC 155. The Privy Council said "Among the Hindus, a peculiar religious significance has attached to the son, through Brahminical influence, although in its origin the custom of adoption was perhaps purely secular. The texts of the Hindus are themselves instinct with this doctrine of religious significance. The foundation of the Brahminical doctrine of adoption is the duty which every Hindu owes to his ancestors to provide for the continuance of the line and the solemnization of the necessary rites."

18. With these observations it decided the question before it, viz.,that of setting the limits to the exercise of the power of a widow to adopt, having regard to the well established doctrine as to the religious efficacy of sonship. In fact the Privy Council in that case regarded the religious motive as dominant and the secular motive as only secondary.

19. This object is further amplified by certain observations of this Court. It has been held that an adoption results in changing the course of succession, depriving wife and daughters of their rights, and transferring the properties to comparative strangers or more remote relations. See *Kishori Lal* v. *Chaltibai*, AIR 1959 SC 504. Though undeniably in most of the cases motive is religious, the secular motive is also dominantly present. We are not concerned much with this controversy, and as observed by Mayne it is unsafe to embark upon an enquiry in each case as to whether the motives for a particular adoption were religious or secular and an intermediate view is possible that while an adoption may be a proper act, inspired in many cases by religious motives, courts are concerned with an adoption, only as the exercise of a legal right by certain persons.

20. The Privy Council's decision in Amarendra Mansingh's case (supra), has reiterated the well established doctrine as to the religious efficacy of sonship, as the foundation of adoption. The emphasis has been on the absence of a male issue. An adoption may either be made by a man himself or by his widow on his behalf. The adoption is to the male and it is obvious that an unmarried woman cannot adopt. For the purpose of adoption is to ensure spiritual benefit for a man after his death by offering of oblations and rice and libations of water to the manes periodically. Woman having no spiritual needs to be satisfied, was not allowed to adopt for herself. But in either it is a condition precedent for a valid adoption that he should be without any male issue living at the time of adoption.""

Clearly, the Hon'ble Supreme Court of India has outlined the origin of customary law of adoptions and the law on the subject as it existed before the enactment of the HAMA, 1956.

Further, the Court has emphasised on the proof of existence of customs in cases of adoptions. The Hon'ble Supreme Court has reiterated the earlier existing case-law in so far as relating to proving the validity of the customs so advanced, in paras 21 to 23 and 25 to 29 (at pages 130 to 132) of the judgment in the following terms:

"21. In *Mookka Kone* v. *Ammakutti Ammal,* AIR 1928 Mad 299 (FB), it was held that where custom is set up to prove that it is at variance with the ordinary law, it has to be proved that it is not opposed to public policy and that it is ancient, invariable, continuous, notorious, not expressly forbidden by the legislature and not opposed to morality or public policy. It is not disputed that even under the old Hindu law, adoption during the lifetime of a male issue was specifically prohibited. In addition, I have observed that such an adoption even if made would be contrary to the concept of adoption and the purpose thereof, and unreasonable. Without entering into the arena of controversy whether there was such a custom, it can be said that even if there was such a custom, the same was not a valid custom."

22. It is incumbent on party setting up a custom to allege and prove the custom on which he relies. Custom cannot be extended by analogy. It must be established inductively and not by a priori methods. Custom cannot be a matter of theory but must always be a matter of fact and one custom cannot be deduced from another. It is a well established law that custom cannot be enlarged by parity of reasoning.

23. Where the proof of a custom rests upon a limited number of instances of a comparatively recent date, the court may hold the custom proved so as to bind the parties to the suit and those claiming through and under them; but the decision would not in that case be a satisfactory precedent if in any future suit between other parties fuller evidence with regard to the alleged custom should be forthcoming. A judgment relating to the existence of a custom is admissible to corroborate the evidence adduced to prove such custom in another case. Where, however a custom is repeatedly brought to the notice of the courts, the courts, may hold that the custom was introduced into law without the necessity of proof in each individual case.

25. ...... All that is necessary to prove is that usage has been acted upon in practice for such a long period with such invariability as to show that it has, by consent, been submitted so as to establish governing rules of a particular locality or community.

26. A custom, in order to be binding must derive its force from the fact that by long usage it has obtained the force of law, but the English rule that "a custom in order that it may be legal and binding, must have been used long that the memory of man runneth not to the contrary" should not be strictly applied to Indian conditions. All that is necessary to prove is that the usage has been acted upon in practice for such a long period and with such invariability as to show that it has, by common consent, been submitted to as the established governing rule of a particular locality.

27. A custom may be proved by general evidence as to its existence by members of the tribe or family who would naturally be cognizant of its existence, and its exercise without controversy, and such evidence may be safely acted on when it is supported by a public record of custom such as the Riwaj-i-am or Manual of Customary Law.

28. In yet another decision reported in *Hem Singh* v. *Harnam Singh,* AIR 1954 SC 581, this Court observed that the custom recorded in the 'Riwaj-i-am' is in derogation of the general custom and those who set up such a custom must prove it by clear and unequivocal language. Similarly, when a custom is against the written texts of the Hindu Law then, one who sets up such a custom must prove it by a clear and unequivocal language. It may also be pointed out that the settled law is that for a valid adoption, not only the person adopting should be capable of lawfully taking in adoption; but the person giving must be capable of lawfully giving in adoption and the person adopted must be capable of being lawfully taken in adoption. It is necessary that all these three conditions should be satisfied and that it is not sufficient that one of them be satisfied.

29. In the case of Hem Singh (supra) this court quoted with approval of some of the observations in Mulla's Principles of Hindu Law at Page 541 of XI Edition with such observations in paragraph 434 to the following effect:

> "It has similarly been held that the texts which prohibit the adoption of an only son, and those which prohibit the adoption of an only son, those which enjoin the adoption of a relation in preference to a stranger, are only directory; therefore, the adoption of an only son, or a stranger in preference to a relation, if completed, is not invalid; that in cases such as the above, where the texts are merely directory, the principle of factum valet applies, and the act done is valid and binding."
>
> But just thereafter the following observations occurred in the same paragraph:
>
> "But the texts relating to the capacity to give, the capacity to take, and the capacity to be the subject of adoption are mandatory. Hence the principle of factum valet is ineffectual in the case of an adoption in contravention of the provisions of those texts.""

Therefore, the Court has given a detailed analysis of the ways in which the person alleging the existence of the custom may prove it.

Hence, in the present case the Hon'ble Supreme Court has laid down the guidelines on which it can be decided whether a particular act is a custom or not and has further, mentioned the ways in which a customary adoptions may be proved by the persons alleging its existence.

In the case of *Atluri Brahmanandam* v. *Anne Sai Bapuji*, JT 2010 (12) SC 441 the issue for consideration before the Hon'ble Supreme Court of India was whether the plaintiff was the adopted son of the auction-purchaser under the customary law, as he was adopted when he was more than 15 years of age and whether the said adoption was prohibited under section 10(iv) of the HAMA, 1956. The Supreme Court upheld the adoption to be valid in terms of the saving clause contained in section 10(iv) of the HAMA, 1956. The reasoning of the Apex Court supported by the statute law as also, earlier precedent of the Andhra Pradesh High Court judicially recognising the prevalence of the said "Kamma" custom in the community of Andhra Pradesh has been summed up in paras 12 to 16 of the judgment in the following terms:

> "12. We are concerned for the purpose of this case with clause (iv) of section 10 which provides that a person to be adopted should not have completed the age of 15 years. But there is also an exception provided therein to the aforesaid required qualification which provides that if there is a custom or usage applicable to the parties permitting persons who have completed the age of 15 years being taken in adoption, such a person could also be validly adopted. On the other hand, the effect and the implication of section 16 of the Act is that if there is any document purporting to record an adoption made and is signed by the person giving as well the person taking the child in adoption is registered under any law for the time being in force and if it is produced in any Court, the Court would presume that the adoption has been made in compliance of the provisions of the Act unless and until it is disproved.
>
> 13. There is no denial of the fact in the present case that the respondent was more than 15 years of age at the time of his adoption. But the respondent has relied upon the exception provided in section 10(iv) and has proved by leading cogent and reliable evidence like Ex. A-8 that there is a custom in the "Kamma" community of Andhra Pradesh for adoption of a boy even above the age of 15 years. Therefore, the aforesaid exception which is engrafted in the same part of the provision of section 10 of the Act was satisfied. Since the aforesaid custom and aforesaid adoption was also recorded in a registered deed of adoption, the Court has to presume that the adoption has been made in compliance with the provisions of the Act, since the respondent has utterly failed to challenge the said evidence and also to disprove the aforesaid adoption.
>
> 14. Reference has also been made to a Division Bench decision of the Andhra Pradesh High Court reported in 1964 Andhra Weekly Reporter p. 156. In the said decision, the Division Bench has recognized that there is a custom among the members of the "Kamma" caste to adopt a boy of more than 15 years old and that such custom is valid. The said decision rendered by a Division Bench in 1964 has stood the test of time and has remained binding till date.
>
> 15. In the case of *Ujagar Singh* v. *Mst. Jeo* reported in AIR 1959 SC 1041, this Court has held that the ordinary rule is that all customs general or otherwise have to be proved, but under section 57 of the Evidence Act, 1872 nothing need to be proved of which the Court can take judicial notice. It was also held that when a custom has been repeatedly recognized by Courts, it is blended into the law of land and proof of the same would become unnecessary under section 57 of Evidence Act, 1872.
>
> 16. The aforesaid decision is squarely applicable to the facts and circumstances of the present case. The Andhra Pradesh High Court has recognized such a custom among the "Kamma" community of Andhra

Pradesh of taking in adoption of a person even above the age of 15 years of age and has held the same to be legal and valid."

Hence, in light of the legal position as enunciated above, the said over aged customary adoption was held to be valid.

Summing-up the position of law in so far as relating to customary adoptions under the provisions of the HAMA, 1956, section 4 of the HAMA, 1956, expressly prohibits customary adoptions after the commencement of the HAMA, 1956 on 21 December 1956. Whilst, section 5 of the HAMA, 1956 categorically states that all the adoptions made after the enactment of the HAMA, 1956 have to be made in accordance with compliance of the provisions of the HAMA, 1956. Furthermore, under section 10(iv) of the HAMA, 1956 a limited relaxation has been made allowing customary adoptions in cases of persons who are over the age of fifteen years, provided there is existing ongoing established custom in support thereof. The above mentioned Supreme Court judgment in the case of *Atluri Brahmanandam* (supra) is a recent example of an adoption upheld under section 10 (iv) of the HAMA, 1956

## X. PROBLEMS FACED IN INTER-COUNTRY ADOPTION

This is an issue of immense significance. At present non-Hindus and foreign nationals can only be guardians of children under the Guardian and Wards Act, 1890. They cannot adopt children. The child loses out by being deprived of the benefits of a valid adoption. There have been disturbing press reports about 'greedy social activists'. Sharma Vinod, in his article titled 'Indian child losing out in adoption mart, dated 9 September 1997, The Hindustan Times, pointed out that at the root of the problem is certain placement agencies' desire for financial gain and their propensity to extort money from childless foreigners. In the same report, it was pointed out that in practice the paperwork is complex. The system is not working because of long delays at the different levels of scrutiny.

Additionally, according to in-vitro fertilisation experts in New Delhi, the number of infertile couples from foreign countries opting for in-vitro fertilisation is increasing. Low-cost and hi-tech treatment in India is helping Non-Resident Indian couples to realise their dreams of natural parenthood. Non-Resident Indian couples are reluctant to opt for adoption for two major reasons. First, religious and social factors are a major issue. Secondly, it has been highlighted that cumbersome adoption and immigration laws make it very difficult to take the child to the United Kingdom or the United States, after the adoptive child is chosen from the homeland. [For details see Sharma Jyoti, newspaper article titled 'How egg-citing! NRIs eye desi donors,' dated 29 August, 2003, The Times of India]

In a hard hitting editorial opinion, titled "Maternity for Hire," dated 24 February, 2006 published in The Times of India, New Delhi/Chandigarh Edition, it has been noticed that a new trend is emanating. India after becoming a hub for medical tourism, is entering another new platform. India is emerging as a sought after destination for surrogate mothers. Desperate childless NRI couples are rushing to India to rent a womb. Anand, in Gujarat, has seen as many as 14 commercial in-vitro fertilization surrogacy cases in the last two years. It is a disturbing trend. A woman's womb is not a piece of real estate to be rented out.

Going through such a commercial pregnancy, a woman undergoes considerable physical and psychological trauma.

This article sadly and rightly so laments: ".....It is particularly sad because there are over 12 million orphaned children in India who need parents. And another 44 million destitute children who are denied the warmth of a family. If only people could transcend the desire to have a baby that is genetically theirs, India would be the logical place where childless couples could seek parental happiness through adoption. Research shows that parental love has less to do with biological ties and more with shared experiences, and that adoptive parents love their children as much as biological parents. But our adoption figures don't go beyond a few thousand per year. Playing spoilsport is a 115-year-old Act – the Guardians and Wards Act – which does not allow Muslims, Christians, Jews and Parsis to become a child's adoptive parents. They can only be a "guardian." Even the more liberal Hindu Adoption and Maintenance Act, 1956, does not allow non-Hindus to adopt a Hindu child. The adoption process is tedious and hemmed in by all sorts of unnecessary restrictions. It is ironical that in a country with so many children without a home, there's a long waiting list of couples wanting to adopt. We urgently need to change the laws, make the process less cumbersome and allow India to become a popular adoption destination."

## XI. DIRECTIONS BY SUPREME COURT OF INDIA TO CARA TO CONSTITUTE EXPERT COMMITTEE INCLUDING MEDICAL EXPERT/S IN CASES OF ADOPTION OF CHILDREN WITH SPECIAL NEEDS

In a recent case of, *Craig Allen Coates* v. *State*, 2010 (8) SCC 794, the Hon'ble Supreme Court of India, adopted a very humane approach with a view to evaluate and facilitate the adoption of a mentally challenged child.

In this particular case, Ms Coates from USA having an extended experience in home based nursing, filed a petition for adopting minor child Anil who had developmental delays and difficulties with respect to learning and expressing and required special care for learning needs. But, both the District Court as well as the High Court rejected the petition. An appeal was then filed in Supreme Court of India to get permission and clearance for the adoption process.

The main issues that arose in the case can be summed up as follows: Whether the adoption of a child with special needs is in the best interest of the child? What procedure should be adopted in such cases?

Keeping in mind the circumstances of the case, the Supreme Court of India requested the learned Solicitor-General to get the matter examined by an expert committee as to whether the adoption of child by Ms Coates would be in the best interest of the child. According to the expert report of the board such a child with special needs will benefit from family-based care and nurturance rather than institutional care. From the records made available to the board it was of the view that Ms. Coates had adequate financial and emotional resources to provide for the adopted child. Thus, the board was of the clear opinion that the petitioner should be allowed to adopt the minor child.

After considering the report of the expert committee the Supreme Court of India allowed the appeal with some directions for future cases of adoption of children with special needs. The positive and meaningful directions are laid down in Para 5 (at page 796) of the judgment which states as follows:

> "We further direct that for inter-country adoptions the procedure followed heretofore could include a reference to an expert committee on the lines constituted in the present case to ensure that inter-country adoptions are allowed only after full and proper satisfaction is recorded by all agencies including a committee of experts wherever reference to such a committee is considered necessary. We are told that Central Adoption Resources Agency (CARA) has the power to make references but no expert committee as such has been constituted or identified for that purpose. In our opinion, it would be appropriate if CARA requests the director, All India Institute of Medical Sciences to constitute a committee of experts to be headed by professor and Head of the Department of Psychiatry, AIIMS. CARA may have similar expert committees constituted in other states also to facilitate references to them in regard to children who may be living at distant places from Delhi."

Certainly, the above-mentioned judgment is a good precedent for the future as well, where genuine and bona fide prospective foreign applicants who have the willpower, resources and determination to look after handicapped children are outrightly not denied an opportunity of a prospective inter-country adoption from India

## XII. NEW DIMENSIONS FOR THE BETTER: THE JUVENILE JUSTICE (CARE AND PROTECTION OF CHILDREN) AMENDMENT ACT, 2006

The Ministry of Women and Child Development has of late been mandated to look after the subject-matters 'Adoption' & 'Juvenile Justice (Care & Protection of Children) Act, 2000' pursuant to 16 February 2006 notification of Government of India regarding reallocation of the Business.

Also, the Government enacted the Juvenile Justice (Care & Protection of Children) Act, 2000 and further amended it in the year 2006 to ensure adequate protection and rehabilitation measures for children in need of care and protection.

It is important to advert to the historical perspective leading to the enactment of the above-mentioned legislation and the need to fill in the void on account of secular perspectives from the point of view of potential adoptive parents which are not just confined to Hindus. This has been very eloquently elaborated in para 3 of the judgment handed down the High Court of Kerala in the matter of *Andrew Mendez* v. *State of Kerala,* 2008(1) KLT 1000. Para 3 of the said judgment reads as under:

> "Then came the enactment of The Juvenile Justice (Care and Protection of Children) Act, 2000. It contained provisions relating to adoption. Adoptions a legal concept was available only among the members of the Hindu community except where custom permits such adoption for any sections of the polity. But in Chapter 6 of the Act dealing with rehabilitation and social re-integration of children, we find the legislature accepting the concept of secular adoption whereby without any reference to the community or the religious persuasions of the parents or the child concerned, a right appears to have been granted to all citizens to adopt and all children to be adopted.

The history of the attempt to bring in the concept of secular adoption into Indian system of laws narrates a sad tale of inaction and action without conviction on the part of the legislature. It is perhaps unfortunate that even now the republic of India does not have a codified law of adoption applicable to all Indians. The attempts of the Indian Parliament in this direction did not bear fruit. The history of the Adoption of Children's Bill 1972 and Adoption of Children's Bill 1980 do not, of courts, bring credit to the secular credentials of the Indian polity. Let us accept the reality. Awareness and acceptance of failure can be stepping stones to eventual success. We have not been able to bring in a secular law of adoption applicable to all Indians so far. It is in this context that a laudable attempt is undertaken by the legislature by the stipulations which have been made in Chapter IV of the Juvenile Justice (Care and Protection of Children) Act, 2000. There was still confusion as the concept of adoption was not defined in the Act. The provisions were criticized to be inadequate as the legal status of the adopted child has not by law been declared to be equal to that of a biological legitimate child. It is in this context that Act 33 of 2006 was introduced under which the concept of adoption was defined by enacting section 2(aa) of the Act which reads as follows:

> "Adoption" means the process through which the adopted child is permanently separated from his biological parents and become the legitimate child of his adoptive parents with all the rights, privileges and responsibilities that are attached to the relationship....

5. After the amendment by Act 33 of 2006, section 41 reads as follows:

"41. *Adoption.*—(1) The primary responsibility for providing care and protection to children shall be of his family.

(2) Adoption shall be resorted to for the rehabilitation of the children who are orphan, abandoned or surrendered through such mechanism as may be prescribed.

(3) In keeping with the provisions of the various guidelines for adoption issues from time-to-time, by the State Government, children may be given in adoption by a court after satisfying itself regarding the investigations having been carried out as are required for giving such children in adoption.

(4) The State Government shall recognize one or more of its institutions or voluntary organisations in each district as specialized adoption agencies in such manner as may be prescribed for the placement of orphan, abandoned or surrendered children for adoption in accordance with the guidelines notified under sub-section (3):

> Provided that the children's homes and the institutions run by the State Government or a voluntary organisation for children in need of care and protection, who are orphan, abandoned or surrendered, shall ensure that these children are declared free for adoption by the Committee and all such cases shall be referred to the adoption agency in that district for placement of such children in adoption in accordance with the guidelines notifies under sub-section (3).

(5) No child shall be offered for adoption:

(a) until two members of the Committee declare the child legally free for placement in the case of abandoned children;

(b) till the two months period for reconsideration by the parent is over in the case of surrendered children; and

(c) without his consent in the case of a child who can understand and express his consent.

(6) The Court may allow a child to be given in adoption—

(a) to a person irrespective of Marital status or;

(b) to parents to adopt a child of same sex irrespective of the number of living biological sons or daughters; or

(c) to childless couples."

The Juvenile Justice (Care and Protection of Children) Amendment Act, 2006 applies to all children as well as parents irrespective of their religion and gender. All adoptable children under category of children in need of care and protection (as defined under JJ Act), shall be processed under this specific legislation by district Courts, city civil Courts, Family Court and other appropriate Courts as may be defined under State JJ Rules to be framed based on the above Act. The legislation being child focused legislation, guarantees all rights to an adopted child and it is also recognized under international obligations by all Hague member countries.

On implementation of JJ Amendment Act, 2006 and its State rules, all cases of orphan, abandoned and surrendered children have to be processed under the Act so that unrelated children have adequate safeguards in their placement.

In an editorial article titled "Adopting New Guidelines," dated 19 November 2007, published in The Hindustan Times of India, it has been analysed "*...In a bid to put adoptive parents of all faiths on the same platform, amendments to the Juvenile Justice (Care and Protection of Children) Act (JJ Act) have now been notified and guidelines framed. One of the most important amendments to the Act made clear that adoption under this legislation would allow an adopted child to become the "legitimate child of his adoptive parents, with the rights, privileges and responsibilities attached to the relationship." This is a significant move considering till now, adoption by non-Hindus has been guided by the Guardian and Wards Act (GAWA), 1890, which gives them the status of 'guardians', a relationship that becomes void when the child entered adulthood. Conversely, it doesn't give the 'ward' legal rights due to a biological child.*"

In effect, non-Hindu parents can now claim full parenthood instead of just the interim "guardian" status that they were allowed until recently. That prior to the enactment of the JJ Act, 2006, only Hindu couples who adopted children could claim to be parents. Non-Hindus were just guardians to their adopted children. This of course, also led to children being denied rights to inherited property and besides also creating day to day problems for parents at the time of school admissions and such like matters.

Another major upshot of the JJ Act, 2006 is that inter-country adoptions are permissible under the same. The point to be noted is as to how would the

Embassies and Foreign Missions in India view adoption orders granted to Hindus and non-Hindus as well as foreigners. This is the moot point.

All opinions are not positive. The JJ Act had intitially drawn some amount of criticism as well. In an article titled "Time to Unscramble the Adoption Tangle," dated 20 November 2007, published in the Times of India, Swati Deshpande came out with some very valid criticisms as follows.

> "....Activists emphasise that there is no clarity on the provisions for adoption in the Juvenile Justice (Care and Protection) Act. "There is a lot of confusion on the issue of adoption under the Juvenile Justice (JJ) Act," said child-rights activist Sangeeta Punalekar. She noted that adoption was provided for under the JJ Act in 2000 itself to aid the rehabilitation and social integration of orphaned, abandoned or neglected children. "But even then it met with hardly any response," Punalekar said. To date, there are no known cases of adoption under the JJ Act in Maharashtra, though there have been a few cases in Delhi. Punalekar said the law stipulates that instead of getting the approval of higher courts—like district courts and high courts (in the case of inter-country adoption)—adoption should be done locally by child welfare committees and Juvenile Justice Boards. However, she and other activists said there seem to be no rules or infrastructure in place nor is there clarity on related issues, like if the law will apply to Muslims. As it stands, the amendment to the JJ Act defines adoption as the "process through which the adopted child is permanently separated from his biological parents and becomes the legitimate child of his adoptive parents with all the rights, privileges and responsibilities attached to the relationship" In other words, the Act would apply to all Indians. ....It is not clear how this law would override the provisions of other personal laws. The Muslim personal law, for instance, does not permit adoption, he noted. The government can't try and plug loopholes in one Act by amending another...."

In the above-mentioned judgment of Kerala High Court in *Andrew Mendez* v. *State of Kerala,* (supra) it was tersely held that only the District Court can have jurisdiction to entertain an application under section 41(6) of the Juvenile Justice Act read with rule 33(5) of the Central Rules. Initially, it was stipulated that the Juvenile Justice Board may allow the child to be adopted. It was also explicitly held in this judgment that the 'Court' and not the Board has powers under section 46 of the Act to allow adoptions. Also, this judgment is laudable for the fact, that it reiterates the provisions with regard to the time scales for adjudicating upon such applications, as laid down initially by the Supreme Court of India in the case of *Lakshmi Kant Pandey* in the year 1984. The concluding portion of para 27 of this judgment held:

> "...that such applications must be disposed of within a period of two months from the date of presentation. The courts have to sympathetically consider the plight of the guardians yearning for an order for adoption and the need of children being given in adoption with expedition."

## XIII. PROVISIONS OF THE JUVENILE JUSTICE ACT, 2000 TO PREVAIL OVER THE PROVISIONS OF THE HINDU ADOPTION AND MAINTENANCE ACT, 1956

In the case of, *In Re: Adoption of Payal @·Sharinee Vinay Pathak and his wife Sonika Sahay @ Pathak*: Petition no. 31 of 2009, the Bombay High Court gave a very lucid and meaningful interpretation to the provisions of the Juvenile Justice Act, 2000 (hereinafter referred to as JJ Act, 2000) especially with regard to the conflict of law position in so far relating to same sex adoptions as envisaged under the provisions of the Hindu Adoption and Maintenance Act, 1956 (hereinafter referred to as HAMA,1956).

The main issue in the petition revolved around the interpretation of HAMA, 1956 and the JJ Act, 2000 on the point as to whether a Hindu couple governed by the provisions of the HAMA, 1956 with a natural biological child of their own could possibly adopt a child of the same gender under provisions of JJ Act, 2000? And in case of conflict between the provisions of the HAMA, 1956 and the JJ Act, 2000, which act would prevail?

In the above-mentioned case, both the petitioners were Hindus and married on 29 June 2001. They were blessed with a daughter on 4 February 2003. In the present petition, the petitioners sought an order appointing them as the guardians of a female child subsequently born on 12 November 2004. The biological parents of the child executed a declaration on 16 November 2004, four days after the child was born, recording the circumstances in which they had decided to surrender the child at the nursing home where the said child was born. The declaration explicitly stated that the mother and the spouse had been counselled by a placement agency duly recognised by the Government of India and that they had voluntarily agreed to surrender their newly born child in adoption. The child was not claimed by the parents within the stipulated two months period of reconsideration. By an order of Justice A.M. Khanwilkar dated 8 June 2005 of the Bombay High Court itself, the petitioners were appointed the guardians of the minor child and the child has since then lived with them for over four years. In the present case, a petition was filed seeking a declaration that the petitioners were the adoptive parents of the child with all the consequential rights.

Justice D. Y. Chandrachud while dealing with the issue of the declaration in the said appeal petition, first dealt with the key issue of the interpretation of the relevant legislations enacted by the Parliament of India, comparing the contradicting provisions of the two enactments in question. The provisions of the said two relevant enactments are summed-up as follows:

> The HAMA, 1956 amends and codifies the law relating to adoptions and maintenance among Hindus and specifies conditions for valid adoption. One of them is that if the adoption is of a daughter, the father or mother who wish to adopt the child must not have a Hindu daughter (or a son's daughter) living at the time of adoption.

The Hon'ble Court stated whilst, the JJ Act, 2000, enacted to provide for the rehabilitation and social integration of orphaned, abandoned or surrendered children. Adoption is one of the techniques recognised by Parliament to facilitate the object of rehabilitation. The JJ Act, 2000 does not incorporate a restrictive condition foreclosing the right of parents who have a child to adopt another child of the same gender. The JJ Act, 2000 specifically recognizes the right of parents to adopt children irrespective of the number of living biological sons or daughters.

In the light of the provisions of the above-mentioned enactments, the key point of consideration was as to whether a Hindu couple with a child of their own, adopt another child of the same gender. The Hon'ble High Court has dealt with the relevant provisions of both the said enactments in a remarkable manner with crystal clear clarity, leaving no room for ambiguity at all before arriving at a perfectly workable solution.

Section 11 of the HAMA, 1956 provides certain conditions that must be complied with in every case of adoption. Since, section 11 of the HAMA, 1956 has already been reproduced in the earlier portion of this article the same is not being repeated again. Basically, section 11 of the HAMA, 1956 prohibits same sex adoptions by the same couple.

The High Court on the appellate side in the present case proceedings gave a logical interpretation of section 11 of the HAMA, 1956 in para 7 of the judgment as follows:

> "7. What these clauses stipulate is a prohibition on the adoption of a child of the same gender where the adoptive father or mother already have a child living at the time of the adoption. If the adoption is of a daughter, the adoptive father or mother must not have a Hindu daughter or a son's daughter living at the time of adoption. Where the adoption is of a son, the condition is more stringent because the adoptive father or mother should not have a Hindu son, son's son or son's son's son living."

The Court in the above-mentioned paragraph highlighted the restrictions and prohibitions on the adoption of a minor child by Hindus.

Further, in para 8 of the judgment the Court has reminded us of the Constitutional obligations warranted by the Constitution of India in so far as relating to the safety of health, welfare and education of the minor children. The Constitutional provisions in this regard as summed-up in paras 8 and 9 of the judgment are as follows:

> "8. Article 15 of the Constitution empowers the State, in clause (3), to make special provisions for women and children. Article 39 is part of the Directive Principles of State policy. Clause (e) of article 39 directs the State in framing its policies to secure that the tender age of children is not abused. In clause (f) the State has to ensure that children are given opportunities and facilities to develop in a healthy manner and in conditions of freedom and dignity so as to ensure that childhood and youth are protected against exploitation and against moral and material abandonment. By article 45 the State has to endeavour to provide early childhood care and education for all children until they complete the age of six. Article 47 requires the State to raise levels of nutrition. Under article 51-A it is the fundamental duty of every citizen who is a parent or guardian to provide opportunities for education to his or her child or, as the case may be, ward between the age of six and fourteen.

> 9. Fundamental as they are in the governance of the country, these provisions are part of a sensitive vision of the founding fathers. The human tragedy of the exploitation of children, of child abuse and of malnutrition among children was in contemplation as these provisions were drafted. Those provisions are a composite part of our constitutional ethos which places freedom and dignity as one of the foremost values of governance in civil society. Freedom and dignity of the young must count above all. The young are amongst the most vulnerable to disease and deprivation which follow upon abandonment and isolation. Poverty has no religion."

Furthermore, the Court has also emphasised on the Convention on the Rights of the Child, ratified by India on 11 December, 1992. Some of the provisions of the Convention mentioned in para 10 of the judgment are as follows:

> "10. India ratified the Convention on the Rights of the Child on 11th December, 1992. Article 3 of the Convention provides that in all actions concerning children, whether undertaken by public or private social welfare institutions, Courts of law, administrative authorities or legislative bodies, the best interests of the child shall be a primary consideration. All States have undertaken to ensure to children such protection and care as is necessary for their well being and to take all appropriate legislative and administrative measures. Article 20 of the Convention provides that a child temporarily or permanently deprived of his or her family environment shall be entitled to special protection and assistance provided by the State. Such care could include foster placement and adoption amongst other alternatives. Under article 21 States who are parties to the Convention recognized that the system of adoption shall ensure that the best interests of the child shall be the paramount consideration."

Certainly, the Court has laid emphasis on the safeguards and the measures for the protection of children that need to be kept in mind by the State while dealing with matters relating to delicate and sensitive subject of adoptions, which is all the more important in a country like India, where there is large scale abuse of under privileged children.

The Court has further discussed the provisions and the object of the JJ Act, 2000. The Court in paras 11 and 12 of the said judgment has elaborated the object with which the Parliament of India had enacted the JJ Act, 2000 in the following terms:

> "11. The Juvenile Justice (Care and Protection of Children) Act was enacted in 2000, "to consolidate and amend the law relating to juveniles in conflict with law and children in need of care and protection". The object of the Act is to provide for "care, protection and treatment by catering to their development needs and by adopting a child-friendly approach in the adjudication and disposition of matters in the best interest of children and for their ultimate rehabilitation". The Preamble to the Act makes reference to several constitutional provisions which have a bearing on the welfare of children and to the obligation assumed by India as a responsible member of the international community.

12. Parliament enacted the Juvenile Justice (Care and Protection of Children) Act, 2000 to effectuate constitutional provisions and fulfill India's international obligations. The Act is intended to provide effective provisions and various alternatives for rehabilitation and social reintegration such as adoption, foster care, sponsorship and aftercare of abandoned, destitute, neglected and delinquent juveniles and children. The Act was amended in 2006 in order to effectuate the beneficial objects of the legislation and in order to remove the anomalies which had arisen in the implementation of the Act."

The Hon'ble Court has further examined the provisions of the JJ Act, 2000 which are contradictory and in contrast to the provisions of HAMA, 1956. Few important provisions of the JJ Act, 2000 in this regard elaborated by the Hon'ble Court are as follows:

"13. Chapter IV of the Juvenile Justice Act is entitled "Rehabilitation and Social Reintegration". Section 40 of the Act provides that rehabilitation and social reintegration of a child shall be carried out alternatively by (i) adoption, (ii) foster care, (iii) sponsorship and (iv) sending the child to an after care organisation. Sub section (1) of section 41 provides that the primary responsibility for providing care and protection to a child is to be that of his or her family. By sub section (2) adoption is to be resorted "for the rehabilitation of children who are orphaned, abandoned or surrendered" through such mechanism as may be prescribed. Sub section (3) of section 41 empowers the Court to give children in adoption subject to satisfaction of investigations having been carried out, as are required for giving children in adoption. Sub section (4) empowers the State Government to recognize one or more of its institutions or voluntary organizations in each district as specialised adoption agencies for the placement of orphaned, abandoned or surrendered children for adoption. Sub section (5) of section 41 contains the following stipulations for offering children in adoption: "(5) No child shall be offered for adoption—

(a) until two members of the Committee declare the child legally free for placement in the case of abandoned children, (b) till the two months period for reconsideration by the parent is over in the case of surrendered children, and (c) without his consent in the case of a child who can understand and express his consent."

14. Sub section (6) emphasizes that the Court may allow a child to be given in adoption (a) to a person irrespective of marital status; or (b) to parents to adopt a child of the same sex irrespective of the number of living biological sons or daughters; or (c) to childless couples. These provisions of the Juvenile Justice Act must be read in the context of some of the definitions. The expression "adoption" is defined by clause (aa) of section 2 as follows:

"(aa) 'adoption' means the process through which the adopted child is permanently separated from his biological parents and becomes the legitimate child of his adoptive parents with all the rights, privileges and responsibilities that are attached to the relationship."

15. Section 2(d) defines the expression "child in need of care and protection". Clause (v) includes within this category a child who does not have a parent and whom no one is willing to take care of or whose parents have abandoned or surrendered the child.

16. Rules have been framed under the Act and rule 33 provides for rules for implementing Chapter IV which deals with rehabilitation and social integration."

In para 17 of the said judgment, the Court has drawn-up a crisp comparison as to the ethos and objective behind the above-mentioned two respective child-related Central legislations, the subject-matter of discussion in the present case i.e the provisions of the HAMA, 1956 and the JJ Act, 2000. The said analysis reads as follows:

"17. The Hindu Adoptions and Maintenance Act, 1956 regulates adoptions by or to a Hindu. The Act spells out requisites of valid adoptions, defines capacities for men and women professing the Hindu religion to take in adoption and to give in adoption, for persons who may be adopted and the conditions for adoption. The Act enunciates consequences or effects of a valid adoption in law. The Act establishes rules of general applicability to Hindus in specific areas of family law - adoption and maintenance. The Juvenile Justice (Care and Protection of Children) Act, 2000 is beneficent secular legislation. The Act makes special provisions for a limited sub class of children - those juveniles in conflict with law and children in need of care and protection. Adoption under the Act of 2000 is an instrument of legislative policy to rehabilitate and provide social integration to children who are in need of care and protection. The Preamble to the Act emphasizes that the legislation was enacted to consolidate and amend the law relating to juveniles in conflict with law and children in need of care and protection. Rehabilitation and social integration of orphaned, abandoned and surrendered children is a matter of legislative regulation by the Juvenile Justice Act. Adoption is a technique contemplated by the law in order to facilitate rehabilitation and reintegration of children of a particular class governed by Chapter IV. The mission of the law is to provide special rules to govern the adoption of a narrow sub class of children namely, those who are orphaned, surrendered or abandoned. In construing the provisions of the Juvenile Justice Act the effort of the Court must be to ensure that the beneficent object with which the legislation was enacted must be facilitated and furthered. Beneficial legislation, it is a trite principle of interpretation, must be construed liberally."

The Hon'ble Court in para 18 of the said judgment has touched upon the constitutionality of the JJ Act, 2000 being approved by the Supreme Court of India, in the following terms:

"18. The provisions of the Juvenile Justice Act came up for consideration before a Constitution bench of the Supreme Court in *Pratap Singh* v. *State of Jharkhand*. The Supreme Court held that the Act was not only beneficial legislation but that it was also remedial in character. The Constitution bench held that the statute must be construed in a manner that would make it effective and operative on the principle of ut res magis valet quam pereat. A similar approach had been adopted by a Bench of three Learned Judges of the Supreme Court in *Umesh Chandra* v. *State of Rajasthan,* (1982) 2 SCC 202. The Rajasthan Children Act, 1970 was regarded as a piece of social legislation which the Court held, would have to be "liberally and meaningfully construed"."

It is ought to mention that the Hon'ble Court has observed in para 19 of the said judgment that adoption is a facet of the right to life under article 21 of the Constitution of India.

Further, para 20 of the judgment demonstrates the creativity of the Court in finding an alternative solution, where a same sex adoption of a child, does not fit within the traditionally acceptable mould within the provisions of the HAMA, 1956 and emphasises that in practice the Courts will have to go to great lengths to protect the welfare of the abandoned, orphaned or surrendered children as envisaged within the provisions of the JJ Act, 2000. Para 20 of the said judgment reads as under:

"20. The Hindu Adoptions and Maintenance Act, 1956 and the Juvenile Justice Act, 2000 must be harmoniously construed. The Hindu Adoptions and Maintenance Act, 1956 deals with conditions requisite for adoption by Hindus. The Juvenile Justice Act of 2000 is a special enactment dealing with children in conflict with law and children in need of care and protection. While enacting the Juvenile Justice Act 2000 the legislature has taken care to ensure that its provisions are secular in character and that the benefit of adoption is not restricted to any religious or social group. The focus of the legislation is on the condition of the child taken in adoption. If the child is orphaned, abandoned or surrendered, that condition is what triggers the beneficial provisions for adoption. The legislation seeks to ensure social integration of such children and adoption is one method to achieve that object. The religious identity of the child or of the parents who adopt is not a precondition to the applicability of the law. The law is secular and deals with conditions of social destitution which cut across religious identities. The legislature in its wisdom clarified in sub section (6) of section 41 that the Court may allow a child to be given in adoption to parents to adopt a child of the same sex irrespective of the number of living biological sons or daughters. This provision is intended to facilitate the rehabilitation of orphaned, abandoned or surrendered children. The condition must apply to all persons irrespective of religious affiliation who seek to adopt children of that description. The object of rehabilitation and providing for social reintegration to orphaned, abandoned or surrendered children is a matter of high legislative policy. It is in effectuation of that policy that the legislature has stipulated that adoption of such a child must proceed irrespective of the marital status of a person taking in adoption and irrespective of the number of living biological children of the parents seeking adoption. Consequently, where the child which is sought to be adopted falls within the description of an orphaned, abandoned or surrendered child within the meaning of sub section (2) of section 41 or a child in need of care and protection under clause (d) of section 2, the provisions of the Juvenile Justice (Care and Protection of Children) Act, 2000 must prevail. In such a case the embargo that is imposed on adopting a child of the same sex by a Hindu under clauses (i) and (ii) of section 11 of the Hindu Adoptions and Maintenance Act, 1956 must give way to the salutary provisions made by the Juvenile Justice Act. Where, however, the child is not of a description falling under the purview of Chapter IV of the Juvenile Justice Act, 2000, a Hindu desirous of adopting a child continues to be under the embargo imposed by clauses (i) and (ii) of section 11 of the Act of 1956. If the two pieces of legislation, both of which are enacted by Parliament are harmoniously construed, there is no conflict of interpretation."

By analogy and judicial reasoning, the Court has skilfully navigated a conclusion that both the above pieces of central legislation enacted by the Parliament of India upon harmonious construction, have no conflict of interpretation at all.

However, in an alternative argument the Court has also dealt with a situation where both the enactments are in conflict with each other. The Hon'ble Court in such a situation has also provided a solution in para 21 of the said judgment as follows:

> "21. Alternatively, even if there were to be a conflict between the provisions of the Hindu Adoptions and Maintenance Act, 1956 and the Juvenile Justice Act of 2000, it is the latter Act which would prevail. This is on the well settled principle that when there are two special Acts dealing with the same subject matter, the legislation which has been enacted subsequently should prevail. The Supreme Court applied this principle in the context of a conflict between the Companies Act, 1956 and the Recovery of Debts Due to Banks and Financial Institutions Act, 1993 in its decision in *Allahabad Bank* v. *Canara Bank,* (2000) 4 SCC 406. Where a later enactment does not expressly amend (whether textually or indirectly) an earlier enactment which it has power to override, but the provisions of the later enactment are inconsistent with those of the earlier, the later by implication amends the earlier so far as is necessary to remove the inconsistency between them."

Hence, in terms of the law laid down by the Hon'ble Court, it is manifest that the provisions of the JJ Act, 2000 would prevail in the event of any conflict with the provisions of the HAMA, 1956.

The petition was, therefore, disposed of in terms of the reliefs sought by the appellants. The petitioners were declared to be the adoptive parents of the minor child in question with all the rights, privileges, responsibilities and consequences under the law.

There is no shadow of doubt that this beautifully carved out judgment has harmoniously blended the supremacy of the provisions of the JJ Act, 2000 over the provisions of the HAMA, 1956 with a view to a positive meaningful interpretation in the given circumstances of the case, as also taking into account article 21 of the Constitution of India and the Convention on the Rights of the Child with the ultimate relief standing out like a pyramid.

But, it is a matter of deep regret that the above-mentioned judgment has not been taken due note of by the CARA authorities. One would have expected that the CARA authorities would have issued some sort of clarification stating that provisions of the JJ Act, 2000 coupled with the added safeguard of guardianship orders from the Court of competent jurisdiction, would be applicable to the large Non-resident Indians fraternity, Overseas Citizens of India and Persons of Indian Origin. Also, any such addition in the existing guidelines should adequately clarify that foreign Missions and Embassies in India should recognise same sex adoptions within the ambit, scope and provisions of the JJ Act, 2000.

After a detailed analysis of the judgment in appeal proceedings relating to *In Re: Adoption of Payal* (supra), it is strongly felt that we need an immediate review of our existing adoption legislation and the creation of new adoption law, which acknowledges in reality the problems of our NRI community, who are sadly childless. Also, the new legislation also needs to be realistic with a pragmatic international perspective and of course to provide support as also succour to that section of the childless NRI community, in an increasingly globalised world without borders.

Having elaborated on the wide sweep of the enlarged ambit of the provisions of the Juvenile Justice (Care and Protection of Children) Act, 2000 as amended by Act no. 23 of 2006, it is now equally important to advert to the position of law relating to surrogacy, which is a new order of the day.

Surrogacy has indeed arrived in India. In our day-to-day practice; we are confronted with queries from foreign lawyers as to the legal position relating to surrogacy arrangements. Here, it would be pertinent to briefly elaborate as to the legal position in this regard.

### XIV. THE LAW AS APPLICABLE IN INDIA AS TO THE LEGAL PARENTAGE OF CHILDREN BORN IN THAT JURISDICTION AS A RESULT OF A SURROGACY ARRANGEMENT

In India at the moment, we do not have any legislation on legal parentage as a result of surrogacy arrangements. At the moment, in India we have the Registration of the Births and Deaths Act, 1969 which does not contain any provision regarding parentage as a result of a surrogacy arrangement. The said enactment laid down by the Parliament of India came into force on 31 May 1969. Surrogacy parentage was not an issue at the time the said legislation came into being. Neither, have there been any amendments or additions with regard to any surrogacy issues in the said enactment pertaining to the registration of births and deaths in the Indian jurisdiction.

As far as legislation on surrogacy is concerned draft surrogacy proposals were going through the Parliament at some stage. The current position in this regard is not very clear. Guidelines dealing with Artificial Reproductive Technologies (ART) have been prepared by an expert committee of the Indian Council of Medical Research in association with the National Academy of Medical Sciences (India), which could in the future become a part of the final draft of a proposed legislation. The preface to the guidelines as circulated in March 2004 specifically points out that ".....There are no guidelines for the practice of ART, accreditation of infertility clinics and supervision of their performance in India. This document aims to fill this lacuna and also provide a means of maintaining a national registry of ART clinics in India....."

For this purpose the National Guidelines for accreditation, supervision and regulation of ART Clinics in India have been framed. These guidelines provide a foundation for the proposed legislation relating to this field of law. These guidelines state that the surrogate mother is under no circumstances considered to be the legal mother.

Para 3.5.4 of the said guidelines provides that in cases where the surrogate mother is biologically unrelated to the child, the birth certificate shall have the name of the genetic parents. Therefore, if the genetic parents are the commissioning parents, who have contributed their genetic material for the unborn child, they shall be automatically recorded as the legal parents, if DNA tests prove the same. No adoption procedure needs to be followed by the genetic parents under such circumstances. Para 3.5.4 of the said guidelines reads as under:

> "3.5.4. – *A surrogate mother carrying a child biologically unrelated to her must register as a patient in her own name.*—While registering she must mention that she is a surrogate mother and provide all the necessary information about the genetic parents such as names, addresses, etc. She must not use/register in the name of the person for whom she is carrying the child, as this would pose legal issues, particularly in the untoward event of maternal death (in whose names will the hospital certify this death?). *The birth certificate shall be in the name of the genetic parents.* The clinic, however, must also provide a certificate to the genetic parents giving the name and address of the surrogate mother. All the expenses of the surrogate mother during the period of pregnancy and post-natal care relating to pregnancy should be borne by the couple seeking surrogacy. The surrogate mother would also be entitled to a monetary compensation from the couple for agreeing to act as a surrogate; the exact value of this compensation should be decided by discussion between the couple and the proposed surrogate mother. An oocyte donor can act as a surrogate mother."

However, in terms of the above-mentioned guidelines, in cases where the surrogate mother also donates her egg, the commissioning parents/infertile couple will have to legally adopt the child, and it is only after this legal procedure has been complied with, then the infertile couple become the legal parents of the child born through such an arrangement. This fact will also have to be recorded in the birth certificate issued to such a child.

Furthermore, where the genetic material is supplied by third party donors, in such cases the birth certificate issued to the child will initially have the names of the genetic parents. Here, it would become mandatory for the infertile couple to legally adopt the child so born, before they can be referred to as the legal parents of such a child.

In order to avoid conflicts at a later stage, the said guidelines categorically state that once the child has been legally adopted by the infertile couple, then the third party donor and the surrogate mother shall relinquish all parental rights connected with the child. Para 3.5.5. of the said guidelines mandates as under:

> "*3.5.5* - A third-party donor and a surrogate mother must relinquish in writing all parental rights concerning the offspring and vice versa."

However, it is submitted that the law relating to surrogacy in India is in its prenatal stage and unfortunately at the moment there is no legislation in existence prescribing a code of practice governing the moral, ethical and legal aspects of such surrogate arrangements. Hence, the said guidelines only have persuasive value at this moment in time.

## XV. CONFLICT OF LAWS IN INTER-COUNTRY ADOPTIONS

During our time as counsel dealing with adoption applications at the British High Commission and other major Embassies at New Delhi, we have quite frequently encountered a conflict of laws situation where Non-Resident Indians, who have been residing abroad for several decades, adopt children from within their own family. The preference for adoption by immediate blood relatives is a common South Asian phenomenon.

The unsuspecting adoptive parents duly comply with the requirements of the HAMA, 1956 for taking the child in adoption. The adoption deed is proudly presented to the immigration authorities; and this is where the trouble begins. The UK immigration authorities completely disregard the Indian adoption deed, and they are legally justified in doing so under the Adoption (Designation of Overseas Adoptions) Order 1973, SI 1973/19.

Under the 1973 Order, if a child has been legally adopted from a country whose adoption orders are recognised as valid under UK law, i.e. from a 'designated' country, then the parents may apply for the child to join them in the United Kingdom as their adopted child.

If the child has not been legally adopted from a 'designated' country or the adoption is from a country whose adoption orders are not recognised as valid in UK law, that is the child is from a 'non-designated' country, entry clearance will have to be obtained for the child to travel to the United Kingdom for adoption through the English Courts. India is specified as a 'non-designated' country under the 1973 Order.

The adoptive parents, then, are confronted with a refusal by the immigration authorities on the ground that the adoption deed is not valid under the 1973 Order, although there has been due compliance with the provisions of the HAMA, 1956. The only avenues available to the parents are to challenge the refusal by way of appeal or to lodge a fresh application.

The real dilemma in such a situation is to set back the clock to satisfy the requirements of British immigration law. How can a Non-Resident Indian adoptive couple obtain a guardianship order from a local Court once a formal irrevocable adoption process has taken place? Certainly, a guardianship order is on no better footing than a valid adoption under the HAMA 1956. This is a proposition, which, sooner or later, will have to be tested by the British Courts.

Rather, it has been done so by the Court of Appeal in a judgment, upholding a judgment under the provisions of the HAMA, 1956. But, the central plank to uphold the validity of such an adoption is on the basis of right to family life. This judgment of immense significance has been analysed by our co-author Rambert De Mello in our book titled "Acting for Non-resident Indian Clients," (Jordan Publishing Limited, First Edition, 2004) (at pages 221-222). His analysis is as follows:

> "Recently, the Court held that the bias against Indian adoption custom was wrong and that it was a breach of the right to family life and discriminatory to refuse an adopted child entry clearance to the United Kingdom by giving less weight to an adoption effected by customary law in India and which was recognised as valid there, on the ground that it was not a recognised practice in English law: *Singh* v. *ECO Delhi,* [2004] EWCA Civ 1075.

(1) The main principle arising for consideration in Singh was whether an adoption which does not meet the requirements of relevant international instruments should invariably be a reason for according little weight to it in determining whether family life exists or not. The adoption of the boy in the case of Singh was valid in India but not recognised in the United Kingdom.

(2) The Court concluded that such a rigid and formulaic approach is not justified and that the failure to satisfy the requirement of relevant international instruments will vary from case to case, and that of considerable importance will be the nature of the departure from the provisions of a relevant instrument. If the departure is one of substance rather than procedure and goes to the heart of the safeguards that the instrument is intended to promote, then it may well be appropriate to give the adoption order little weight ([2004] EWCA Civ 1075 at [33]).

(3) In this case much might be said of the fact that the children had not been adopted and that their biological link with their natural parents was fluid, continuing and developing.

(4) The principles enunciated in Singh which are relevant in determining whether family life exists between an adopted child and adoptive parents are equally applicable in a situation which needs to resolve whether there is family life existing between a child and his natural parents who are separated from each other.

(5) The best interests of the child will be relevant and may well be determinative at the stage at which the court has to decide the extent to which respect should be given to family life or whether interference with family life is justified under article 8.2 [2004] EWCA Civ 1075 at [34] per Dyson LJ, at [68] per Munby J.

(6) The potential for development of family life is relevant in determining whether family life already exists and this is not confined to cases involving children and their natural parents; unless some degree of family life is already established, the claim to family life will fail and will not be saved by the fact that at some time in the future it could flower into a full-blown family life or that the applicants have a genuine wish to bring this about [2004] EWCA Civ 1075 at [38].

(7) The fact is that many adults and children, whether through choice or circumstance, live in families more or less removed from what until comparatively recently would have been recognised as the typical nuclear family – the Convention is a living instrument [2004] EWCA Civ 1075 at [63]–[64] per Munby J). The law must adapt itself to these realities (at [65]. There is no bright line test that the law can set. The infinite variety of the human condition precludes arbitrary defining.

(8) The existence or non-existence of family life is a question of fact depending upon the real existence in practice of close personal ties – a close personal relationship which has sufficient constancy and substance to create de facto family ties – the parents' cohabitation with the child will often be highly significant but this is not decisive [2004] EWCA Civ 1075 at [79].

(9) The fact that the parents do not see their children frequently is not fatal to establishing family life; one must be cautious before setting too high a benchmark for the existence of family life certainly where there is the constancy and commitment which a parent has shown towards his child [2004] EWCA Civ 1075 at [90]."

It is strange, that this judgment has not got due recognition in the academic and the professional arena. This judgment should be publicised vigorously, so that prospective adoptive parents residing overseas can take due benefit of this path breaking judgment. No doubt, this ruling is indeed laudable for building the edifice of the right to family life to recognise, an adoption made in India under the provisions of the HAMA, 1956, which is otherwise in direct conflict with the provisions of British immigration law as contained in HC 395.

Likewise, the American Embassy and numerous European Embassies at New Delhi also outright refuse to accept the above-mentioned adoption deeds under the provisions of HAMA 1956. Hence, only guardianship orders are acceptable. These can be obtained only by lodging guardianship petitions under the provisions of the Hindu Minority and Guardianship Act, 1956 in the Court of the Guardian Judge, in whose jurisdiction the minor child is residing. It is like a full blown trial. It is very difficult to obtain guardianship orders. These petitions have to be supported by exhaustive documentation as to the background and standing of the proposed overseas adoptive parents. Sometimes, it can be a time consuming exercise, and it is very difficult in such a situation for the foreign couple to spend long periods of time in India awaiting custody orders. With these custody orders, the adoption ultimately takes place in the foreign country of habitual residence of the adoptive parents. In India, we have no exclusive law of adoption for foreigners or Non-Resident Indians.

Furthermore, adoptions within the family fold are not encouraged, while adoption applications by foreigners seeking to adopt children from orphanages and welfare homes are likely to receive positive treatment.

The noose of British immigration law has been further tightened by changes to HC 395, which were given effect by HC 538, and came into force on 1 April 2003. Reference in this regard is drawn to the observations of Richard McKee, a prominent Immigration Appeals Adjudicator:

'Now HC 538 has not only lifted the restriction on third party support, but it has introduced a provision for de facto adoption. For all adopted children coming from countries whose adoption orders (if they have such things) are not recognised in the UK, the adoptive parents must have been living abroad, having assumed the role of the child's parents, for at least 18 months, of which the last 12 must have been spent living together with the child. This is to show a genuine transfer of parental responsibility. The expectation that the adoptive parents be married has now been dropped.' [For details see *Richard McKee 'New Immigration Rules'* [2003] 17.2 IA & NL 127–129].

The most worrying issue about these changes is that it is next to impossible for Non-Resident Indian couples to come and spend one complete calendar year with the adoptive child in India. Certainly, no UK employer or any other overseas employer would grant such long leave to any employee. However, more positively, senior level expatriates posted in India could possibly comply with the time requirement stipulated by the newly introduced provisions of HC 538.

Furthermore, there has been an European Court of Human Rights decision on the basis of a friendly settlement having very wide ramifications, which could change the entire gamut of inter-country adoptions from India. This case was the fallout of the immigration officer's denial to permit an Indian couple to bring their adopted child to UK, which resulted in the Government of United Kingdom paying costs and damages totalling to more than £ 42,000 before the European Court of Human Rights. This was a friendly settlement in the case of Singh and Others Vs The United Kingdom, application number 60148/00 which was disposed off on 8.6.2006.The said application was lodged before the ECHR on 24 May 2000 and admitted for hearing thereafter, upon preliminary submissions and arguments.

Earlier on 11 March 1997 the immigration authorities had refused permission to the adoptive parents to bring the child into the UK. This was because adoptions from India are not recognised for the purposes of entry clearance. Thus, the child fell out of the rules for entry clearance as he was not adopted because of any inability on the part of his parents to care for him. But, there was a genuine transfer of parental responsibility. Incidentally, this adoption application was lodged by us at the British High Commission, New Delhi. This judgment has not received much publicity and academic analysis at this moment in time. This case was reported in the London Times on 21 June 2006. As a matter of fact, six years have elapsed ever since the settlement took place in the above-mentioned case, but the same has not been followed as a precedent at all and neither did it result in any changes in law or policy in this area of law by the British Government.

Recent relevant case-law on the ever expanding ambit of article 8 of the ECHR as possibly applicable to inter-country adoptions handed down by the House of Lords as then it was, the Supreme Court of England and Wales and the European Court of Human Rights is analysed hereunder.

## XVI. HOUSE OF LORDS JUDGMENT IN THE CASE OF HUANG (FC) (RESPONDENT) V. SECRETARY OF STATE FOR THE HOME DEPARTMENT (APPELLANT) AND KASHMIRI (FC) (APPELLANT) V. SECRETARY OF

**STATE FOR THE HOME DEPARTMENT (RESPONDENT) (CONJOINED APPEALS) SESSION 2006-07, 19TH REPORT, ([2007] UKHL 11), ON APPEAL FROM: [2005] EWCA CIV 105, ON APPLICATION OF ARTICLE 8 OF THE ECHR.**

The above-mentioned case is being cited with a view to draw support on the interpretation of article 8 of the ECHR in inter-country adoption cases, especially from India. It is common knowledge that it is a South Asian phenomena to adopt within the family fold, rather than going in for adoptions from orphanages and social organisations in the voluntary sector. The point to be conveyed is that there is potentially a genuine semblance of some form of established family life from the time the formal adoption process or the guardianship applications are lodged in the Court of competent jurisdiction, as the case may be until the time the adoptive parents or the prospective adoptive parents are entangled in the immigration hoops.

In the event of any appeal proceedings initiated post refusal, the issue of family life also assumes added significance, among other crucial factors. In these circumstances, law on the right to family life has to be canvassed vigorously as well to demonstrate established family life, which in turn is likely considerably to enhance the chances of the success of the appeal proceedings. Hence, there is brief analysis below of the above-mentioned judgment by the erstwhile House of Lords in the case of *Huang* (supra).

In *Huang (FC) (Respondent)* v. *Secretary of State for the Home Department (Appellant)* and *Kashmiri (FC) (Appellant)* v. *Secretary of State for the Home Department (Respondent) (Conjoined Appeals): House of Lords: Session* 2006-07, 19th Report, ([2007] UKHL 11), an appeal from: [2005] EWCA Civ 105, two appeals had been heard together as they raised a common question on the decision-making role or function of appellate immigration authorities (adjudicators, the Immigration Appeal Tribunal, immigration judges) when deciding appeals, on Convention grounds, against refusal of leave to enter or remain, under section 65 of the Immigration and Asylum Act 1999 and Part III of Schedule 4 to the said legislation. First, the facts are being set out, before adverting to the relevant legislation that is the Human Rights Act, 1998 and the case-law analysis in particular reference to article 8 of the ECHR.

Mrs Huang was a Chinese citizen born on 29 March 1942. Her husband (from whom she was separated), daughter, son-in-law and two grandsons were British citizens living in the UK. Mr Kashmiri was an Iranian citizen born on 4 July 1981. His parents and two siblings came to the UK in 2000 and were in due course granted indefinite leave to remain as refugees, but Mr Kashmiri's claim to asylum has been refused. As stated in the judgment, neither of the applicants qualified for the grant of leave to remain in the UK under the immigration rules and administrative directions promulgated at that time. Both of them claimed that their refusal of leave to remain was unlawful because it was incompatible by their Convention rights to respect for their family guaranteed by sections 2, 3 and 6 of and article 8 in Schedule 1 to the Human Rights Act, 1998.

It is important to advert to the relevant UK legislation in this regard. That in terms of the UK Human Rights Act, 1998 the public authorities as also the British

Courts are duty bound to follow the provisions of the ECHR as set out in schedule 1 of the Human Rights Act, 1998, as also held by the Court in para 8 of the said judgment of *Huang* (supra). Para 8 of the said judgment reads as follows:

> "8. In the Human Rights Act 1998 Parliament not only enabled but required the Convention rights set out in Schedule 1 to the Act (including article 8) to be given effect as a matter of domestic law in this country. It did so (section 2) by requiring courts or tribunals determining a question which had arisen in connection with a Convention right to take into account any relevant Strasbourg jurisprudence, by requiring legislation, where possible, to be read compatibly with Convention rights (section 3) and, most importantly, by declaring it unlawful (section 6) for a public authority to act in a way incompatible with a Convention right. Thus immigration officers, the appellate immigration authority and the courts, as public authorities (section 6(3)), act unlawfully if they do not (save in specified circumstances) act compatibly with a person's Convention right under article 8. The object is to ensure that public authorities should act to avert or rectify any violation of a Convention right, with the result that such rights would be effectively protected at home, thus (it was hoped) obviating or reducing the need for recourse to Strasbourg."

Para 9 of the said judgment talks of provisions relating to compliance of convention rights in terms of the above-mentioned domestic legislation in the UK in the following terms:

> "9. Two important steps were taken to ensure compliance with this new domestic legal obligation. The first was to amend (Cm 4851, September 2000) the then current Immigration rules so as to require immigration officers, entry clearance officers and all staff of the Home Office Immigration and Nationality Directorate to carry out their duties in compliance with the provisions of the Human Rights Act 1998. It is these officers who ordinarily decide, in the first instance, whether leave to enter or remain in the country should be granted."

By virtue of the above-mentioned domestic legislation in the UK, as also incorporated in the British immigration rules, it can be well possibly be argued even at the time of lodging the adoptions entry clearance applications at any of the British posts in India, the entry clearance officers to take into account article 8 of the ECHR, as also incorporated in the Human Rights Act, 1998. This argument of course, will depend on the facts and circumstances of each individual case.

Further, para 18 of the said judgment gives a brief overview of the convention jurisprudence i.e. the ECHR and more than that emphatically dwells on the sensitivity factor, while dealing and adjudicating upon family reunion issues in the following terms:

> "18. The authority must of course take account, as enjoined by section 2 of the 1998 Act, of Strasbourg jurisprudence on the meaning and effect of article 8. While the case law of the Strasbourg court is not strictly binding, it has been held that domestic courts and tribunals should, in the absence of special circumstances, follow the clear and constant jurisprudence of that

court: *R(Alconbury Developments Ltd)* v. *Secretary of State for the Environment, Transport and the Regions,* [2001] UKHL 23; [2003] 2 AC 295, para 26; *R(Ullah)* v. *Special Adjudicator,* [2004] UKHL 26: [2004] 2 AC 323, para 20. It is unnecessary for present purposes to attempt to summarise the Convention jurisprudence on article 8, save to record that the article imposes on member states not only a negative duty to refrain from unjustified interference with a person's right to respect for his or her family but also a positive duty to show respect for it. The reported cases are of value in showing where, in many different factual situations, the Strasbourg court, as the ultimate guardian of Convention rights, has drawn the line, thus guiding national authorities in making their own decisions. But the main importance of the case law is in illuminating the core value which article 8 exists to protect. This is not, perhaps, hard to recognise. Human beings are social animals. They depend on others. Their family, or extended family, is the group on which many people most heavily depend, socially, emotionally and often financially. There comes a point at which, for some, prolonged and unavoidable separation from this group seriously inhibits their ability to live full and fulfilling lives. Matters such as the age, health and vulnerability of the applicant, the closeness and previous history of the family, the applicant's dependence on the financial and emotional support of the family, the prevailing cultural tradition and conditions in the country of origin and many other factors may all be relevant. The Strasbourg court has repeatedly recognised the general right of states to control the entry and residence of non-nationals, and repeatedly acknowledged that the Convention confers no right on individuals or families to choose where they prefer to live. In most cases where the applicants complain of a violation of their article 8 rights, in a case where the impugned decision is authorised by law for a legitimate object and the interference (or lack of respect) is of sufficient seriousness to engage the operation of article 8, the crucial question is likely to be whether the interference (or lack of respect) complained of is proportionate to the legitimate end sought to be achieved. Proportionality is a subject of such importance as to require separate treatment."

Para 19 of the said judgment reminds adjudicators, now designated as immigration Judges to take into account the issue of proportionality, while adjudicating upon convention questions by referring to its earlier judgment, as follows:

"19. ....The House is recognised as much in *R (Razgar)* v. *Secretary of State for the Home Department* [2004] UKHL 27: [2004] 2 AC 368, paras 17-20, 26, 27, 60, 77, when, having suggested a series of questions which an adjudicator would have to ask and answer in deciding a Convention question, it said that the judgment on proportionality

"must always involve the striking of a fair balance between the rights of the individual and the interests of the community which is inherent in the whole of the Convention. The severity and consequences of the interference will call for careful assessment at this stage".

If, as counsel suggest, insufficient attention has been paid to this requirement, the failure should be made good."

Para 20, the penultimate part of the judgment is of utmost significance in international family migration matters. Para 20 in categorical terms provides as follows:

"20. In an article 8 case where this question is reached, the ultimate question for the appellate immigration authority is whether the refusal of leave to enter or remain, in circumstances where the life of the family cannot reasonably be expected to be enjoyed elsewhere, taking full account of all considerations weighing in favour of the refusal, prejudices the family life of the applicant in a manner sufficiently serious to amount to a breach of the fundamental right protected by article 8. If the answer to this question is affirmative, the refusal is unlawful and the authority must so decide. It is not necessary that the appellate immigration authority, directing itself along the lines indicated in this opinion, need ask in addition whether the case meets a test of exceptionality. The suggestion that it should is based on an observation of Lord Bingham in *Razgar* above, para 20. He was there expressing an expectation, shared with the Immigration Appeal Tribunal, that the number of claimants not covered by the Rules and supplementary directions but entitled to succeed under article 8 would be a very small minority. That is still his expectation. But he was not purporting to lay down a legal test."

Two recent developments in the UK are of relevance in the context of inter-country adoptions. First, section 55 of the Borders, Citizenship and Immigration Act, 2009 imposes a duty on all public authorities to safeguard and promote the welfare of children. The term public authorities of course includes, entry clearance officers at the British Posts/Missions dealing with settlement applications including adoption applications. Secondly, the Supreme Court of England and Wales in ZH (Tanzania) [2011] UKSC 4 has held that in article 8 cases where children are involved, the best interests of the child must be "a primary consideration," which can only be outweighed by very serious countervailing factors. This emphasis on the welfare and best interests of children will strengthen the argument of couples who have adopted children in countries whose adoption orders are not recognised in the UK. Hence, if genuine 'family life' has been established between the children and their adoptive parents, which of course is well documented by credible evidence on record, it will generally be a breach of article 8 if the children are not granted entry clearance.

Section 55 of the Borders, Citizenship and Immigration Act 2009 mandates as follows:

'*55 Duty regarding the welfare of children.*—(1) The Secretary of State must make arrangements for ensuring that—

(a) the functions mentioned in sub-section (2) are discharged having regard to the need to safeguard and promote the welfare of children who are in the United Kingdom, and

(b) any services provided by another person pursuant to arrangements which are made by the Secretary of State and relate to the discharge of a function mentioned in sub-section (2) are provided having regard to that need.

(2) The functions referred to in sub-section (1) are—

(a) any function of the Secretary of State in relation to immigration, asylum or nationality;

(b) any function conferred by or by virtue of the Immigration Acts on an immigration officer;

(c) any general customs function of the Secretary of State;

(d) any customs function conferred on a designated customs official.

(3) A person exercising any of those functions must, in exercising the function, have regard to any guidance given to the person by the Secretary of State for the purpose of sub-section (1).

(4) The Director of Border Revenue must make arrangements for ensuring that—

(a) the Director's functions are discharged having regard to the need to safeguard and promote the welfare of children who are in the United Kingdom, and

(b) any services provided by another person pursuant to arrangements made by the Director in the discharge of such a function are provided having regard to that need.

(5) A person exercising a function of the Director of Border Revenue must, in exercising the function, have regard to any guidance given to the person by the Secretary of State for the purpose of sub-section (4).

(6) In this section—

"children" means persons who are under the age of 18;

"customs function", "designated customs official" and "general customs function" have the meanings given by Part 1.

(7) A reference in an enactment (other than this Act) to the Immigration Acts includes a reference to this section.

(8) Section 21 of the UK Borders Act, 2007 (c. 30) (children) ceases to have effect."

**XVII. RECENT JUDGMENT OF THE SUPREME COURT OF ENGLAND AND WALES IN THE CASE OF ZH (TANZANIA) (FC) (APPELLANT) V. SECRETARY OF STATE FOR THE HOME DEPARTMENT (RESPONDENT) REPORTED AS [2011] UKSC 4 ON APPEAL FROM: [2009] EWCA CIV 691 AMPLIFYING THE SCOPE OF ARTICLE OF THE ECHR.**

The judgment of the Supreme Court of England and Wales in the case of *ZH (Tanzania) (FC) (Appellant)* v. *Secretary of State for the Home Department (Respondent) reported as* [2011] UKSC 4 on appeal from: [2009] EWCA Civ 691 has amplified the scope of article 8 of the ECHR, especially with regard to the best interests of the children. The same is discussed hereunder:

Basically, the crucial issue involved in the case has been summed-up in para 1 of the judgment in the following terms:

> "1. The over-arching issue in this case is the weight to be given to the best interests of children who are affected by the decision to remove or deport one or both of their parents from this country. Within this, however, is a much more specific question: in what circumstances is it permissible to remove or deport a non-citizen parent where the effect will be that a child who is a citizen of the United Kingdom will also have to leave? There is, of course, no power to remove or deport a person who is a United Kingdom citizen: see Immigration Act, 1971, section 3(5) and (6). They have a right of abode in this country, which means that they are free to live in, and to come and go into and from the United Kingdom without let or hindrance: see 1971 Act, sections 1 and 2. The consistent stance of the Secretary of State is that UK citizens are not compulsorily removed from this country (eg Phil Woolas, Hansard, Written Answers, 15 June 2009). However if a non-citizen parent is compulsorily removed and agrees to take her children with her, the effect is that the children have little or no choice in the matter. There is no machinery for consulting them or giving independent consideration to their views."

But, the present ruling takes into account the Strasbourg jurisprudence, as also the May 2008 UNHCR guidelines in determining the best interests of the child which also includes within its wide sweep adoption cases. The purpose of citing this judgment is to demonstrate as to how right to family life under article 8 of the ECHR, helps in supporting the case of genuine inter-country adoption cases from India, where there is strong and compelling established family life.

Basically, this case is central to the fact of the mother's deportation and the fate of her UK-born children if they were to be left behind in the UK or alternatively to accompany the mother to her country of origin, as stated in start of para 14 (at page 5) of the judgment as follows:

> "14. This is the mother's appeal on the ground that her removal will constitute a disproportionate interference with her right to respect for her private and family life, guaranteed by article 8 of the European Convention on Human Rights..."

The ruling in the present case also reiterates the right to respect family life in para 14 (at page 6) of the judgment as follows:

> "14. .... However, in *Beoku-Betts* v. *Secretary of State for the Home Department* [2008] UKHL 39, [2009] AC 115, the House of Lords held that both the Secretary of State and the immigration appellate authorities had to consider the rights to respect for their family life of all the family members who might be affected by the decision and not just those of the claimant or appellant in question. Lord Brown of Eaton-under-Heywood summarised the argument which the House accepted thus, at para 20:
>
> "Together these members enjoy a single family life and whether or not the removal would interfere disproportionately with it has to be looked at by reference to the family unit as a whole and the impact of removal upon each

member. If overall the removal would be disproportionate, all affected family members are to be regarded as victims...""

Quite often in adoption and marriage refusal cases, the arguments raised by Entry Clearance Officers in refusal cases is that article 8 of the ECHR does not recognise the choice of the country with regard to the right to family reunion. The present judgment at para 19, (page 9) has reiterated the law in this regard as follows:

"19. It was long ago established that mixed nationality couples have no right to set up home in whichever country they choose: see *Abdulaziz* v. *United Kingdom,* (1985) 7 EHRR 471. Once they have done so, however, the factors relevant to judging the proportionality of any interference with their right to respect for their family lives have quite recently been rehearsed in the case of *Rodrigues da Silva, Hoogkamer* v. *Netherlands,* (2007) 44 EHRR 729, at para 39:

". . . Article 8 does not entail a general obligation for a state to respect immigrants' choice of the country of their residence and to authorise family reunion in its territory. Nevertheless, in a case which concerns family life as well as immigration, the extent of a state's obligations to admit to its territory relatives of persons residing there will vary according to the particular circumstances of the person involved and the general interest [the reference is to *Gûl* v. *Switzerland,* (1996) 22 EHRR 93, at [38]]. Factors to be taken into account in this context are the extent to which family life is effectively ruptured, the extent of the ties in the contracting state, whether there are insurmountable obstacles in the way of the family living in the country of origin of one or more of them, whether there are factors of immigration control (e.g. a history of breaches of immigration law) or considerations of public order weighing in favour of exclusion [the reference is to *Solomon* v. *The Netherlands,* App No 44328/98, 5 September 2000]. Another important consideration will also be whether family life was created at a time when the persons involved were aware that the immigration status of one of them was such that the persistence of that family life within the host state would from the outset be precarious. The Court has previously held that where this is the case it is likely only to be in the most exceptional circumstances that the removal of the non-national family member will constitute a violation of article 8 [the reference is to *Mitchell* v. *United Kingdom,* App No 40447/98, 24 November 1998; *Ajayi* v. *United Kingdom,* App No 27663/95, 22 June 1999].""

The judgment above in the case of *ZH (Tanzania)* (supra) sufficiently takes into account the UNCRC and the best interests of the child. Paras 21 to 23 (at pages 11 and 12) are a terse reminder as follows:

"21. It is not difficult to understand why the Strasbourg Court has become more sensitive to the welfare of the children who are innocent victims of their parents choices. For example, in *Neulinger* v. *Switzerland,* (2010) 28 BHRC 706, para 131, the Court observed that "the Convention cannot be interpreted in a vacuum but must be interpreted in harmony with the general principles of international law. Account should be taken . . . of 'any relevant rules of international law applicable in the relations between the parties' and in particular the rules concerning the international protection of human rights". The Court went on to note, at para 135, that "there is currently a broad consensus – including in international law – in support of the idea that in all decisions concerning children, their best interests must be paramount".

22. The Court had earlier, in paras 49 to 56, collected references in support of this proposition from several international human rights instruments: from the second principle of the United Nations Declaration on the Rights of the Child 1959; from article 3(1) of the Convention on the Rights of the Child 1989 (UNCRC); from articles 5(b) and 16(d) of the Convention on the Elimination of All Forms of Discrimination against Women 1979; from General Comments 17 and 19 of the Human Rights Committee in relation to the International Covenant on Civil and Political Rights 1966; and from article 24 of the European Union's Charter of Fundamental Rights. All of these refer to the best interests of the child, variously describing these as "paramount", or "primordial", or "a primary consideration". To a United Kingdom lawyer, however, these do not mean the same thing.

23. For our purposes the most relevant national and international obligation of the United Kingdom is contained in article 3(1) of the UNCRC:

> "In all actions concerning children, whether undertaken by public or private social welfare institutions, courts of law, administrative authorities or legislative bodies, the best interests of the child shall be a primary consideration.""

Furthermore, para 23 of the said judgment also takes into account the import of section 55 of the Borders, Citizenship and Immigration Act, 2009, as follows:

> "23. .... This is a binding obligation in international law, and the spirit, if not the precise language, has also been translated into our national law. Section 11 of the Children Act, 2004 places a duty upon a wide range of public bodies to carry out their functions having regard to the need to safeguard and promote the welfare of children. The immigration authorities were at first excused from this duty, because the United Kingdom had entered a general reservation to the UNCRC concerning immigration matters. But that reservation was lifted in 2008 and, as a result, section 55 of the Borders, Citizenship and Immigration Act, 2009 now provides that, in relation among other things to immigration, asylum or nationality, the Secretary of State must make arrangements for ensuring that those functions "are discharged having regard to the need to safeguard and promote the welfare of children who are in the United Kingdom""

Para 25 of the said judgment dwells upon the legitimate expectation of the Supreme Court emanating from the recent Strasbourg Court jurisprudence for the national authorities to apply the relevant provisions of UNCRC in the following terms:

> "25. Further, it is clear from the recent jurisprudence that the Strasbourg Court will expect national authorities to apply article 3(1) of UNCRC and

> treat the best interests of a child as "a primary consideration". Of course, despite the looseness with which these terms are sometimes used, "a primary consideration" is not the same as "the primary consideration", still less as "the paramount consideration". Miss Joanna Dodson QC, to whom we are grateful for representing the separate interests of the children in this case, boldly argued that immigration and removal decisions might be covered by section 1(1) of the Children Act, 1989:
>
> "When a court determines any question with respect to—(a) the upbringing of a child; or
>
> (b) the administration of a child's property or the application of any income arising from it,

the child's welfare shall be the court's paramount consideration."

However, questions with respect to the upbringing of a child must be distinguished from other decisions which may affect them. The UNHCR, in its Guidelines on Determining the Best Interests of the Child (May 2008), explains the matter neatly, at para 1.1:

> "The term 'best interests' broadly describes the well-being of a child. . . . The CRC neither offers a precise definition, nor explicitly outlines common factors of the best interests of the child, but stipulates that:
>
> the best interests must be *the determining factor for specific actions,* notably adoption (Article 21) and separation of a child from parents against their will (Article 9);
>
> the best interests must be *a primary* (but not the sole) *consideration for all other actions* affecting children, whether undertaken by public or private social welfare institutions, courts of law, administrative authorities or legislative bodies (Article 3)."
>
> This seems to me accurately to distinguish between decisions which directly affect the child's upbringing, such as the parent or other person with whom she is to live, and decisions which may affect her more indirectly, such as decisions about where one or both of her parents are to live. Article 9 of UNCRC, for example, draws a distinction between the compulsory separation of a child from her parents, which must be necessary in her best interests, and the separation of a parent from his child, for example, by detention, imprisonment, exile, deportation or even death."

But, from the context of the present article, it is immensely significant to note that adoptions are covered in the ambit of article 21 UNCRC which of course can also be pleaded as part of consular representation at the time of lodging of the entry clearance applications at the British High Commission at New Delhi or the concerned British Deputy High Commissions in other parts of the country or in the appeal grounds in the event of refusal.

Further, Lord Hope in the concurring portion of his judgment while agreeing with the principle judgment handed down by Lady Hale has concluded that the precarious immigration status of the mother cannot be held against the children. This is in para 44 (at page 20) of the judgment in the following terms:

> "44. There is an obvious tension between the need to maintain a proper and efficient system of immigration control and the principle that, where children are involved, the best interests of the children must be a primary consideration. The proper approach, as was explained in *Wan* v. *Minister for Immigration and Multicultural Affairs*, [2001] FCA 568, para 32, is, having taken this as the starting point, to assess whether their best interests are outweighed by the strength of any other considerations. The fact that the mother's immigration status was precarious when they were conceived may lead to a suspicion that the parents saw this as a way of strengthening her case for being allowed to remain here. But considerations of that kind cannot be held against the children in this assessment. It would be wrong in principle to devalue what was in their best interests by something for which they could in no way be held to be responsible."

Finally, Lord Kerr in the penultimate part of the judgment has yet again highlighted in eloquent terms the primacy of the best interest of the child in para 46 (at page 20) of the judgment as follows:

> "46. It is a universal theme of the various international and domestic instruments to which Lady Hale has referred that, in reaching decisions that will affect a child, a primacy of importance must be accorded to his or her best interests. This is not, it is agreed, a factor of limitless importance in the sense that it will prevail over all other considerations. It is a factor, however, that must rank higher than any other. It is not merely one consideration that weighs in the balance alongside other competing factors. Where the best interests of the child clearly favour a certain course, that course should be followed unless countervailing reasons of considerable force displace them. It is not necessary to express this in terms of a presumption but the primacy of this consideration needs to be made clear in emphatic terms. What is determined to be in a child's best interests should customarily dictate the outcome of cases such as the present, therefore, and it will require considerations of substantial moment to permit a different result."

Clearly, in light of the analysis on the case-law relating to article 8 of the ECHR, the importance of the same cannot be overstated, in cases of family migration. But, the stumbling block even in genuine and bona fide cases, especially in marriage cases is the argument put forward by the entry clearance officers is that the family life can exist even in the habitual country of residence and domicile, of the applicant wanting to join his/her spouse or adoptive parents in the UK, as the case may be. Further, the stumbling block encountered is that such an intending immigrant, cannot choose the country of his/her choice where family life is further sought to be pursued in the future. This of course creates further serious problems. Either the existing relationship is put to serious disrepair forcing split family life in different countries, or if it is a marriage case, the spouse settled in the UK is left with no choice but to relocate to India more out of compulsion than choice.

## XVIII. CONCLUSION

There has been a growing demand for a general law of adoption enabling any person, irrespective of his religion, race or caste, to adopt a child. There is now a clear case for overhauling the existing adoption law in India.

As far as the mechanics of inter-country adoption are concerned, all the major Embassies in India are more than stringent in dealing with adoption applications. The refusal rates are very high. There is no room at all for compassion. The hurdles are almost insurmountable, causing lot of hardship to childless Non-Resident Indian couples.

The question that now remains to be answered is as to how successful the revised 2006 Guidelines discussed in this article have been. Sadly, the answer can be found in a very recent Andhra Pradesh High Court judgment, *John Clements* v. *All Concerned (AP)* 2003 (2) HLR 331. The Court lamented in paras 59-61 (at page 331):

> '59. Para 2.14 of the guidelines envisages that no application by foreigner for taking a child in adoption should be entertained directly by any social child welfare agency in India working in the areas of inter-country adoption or by any institution or centre or Home to which children are committed by the Juvenile Court. The very next paragraph says "the original application along with original documents as prescribed by the Supreme Court of India would be forwarded by the foreign enlisted agency to a recognised placement agency in India".
>
> 60. Taking advantage of the inconsistency in the guidelines and ignoring the judgment of the Supreme Court the foreign enlisted agencies started directly approaching the placement agencies in India and are trying to take the Indian children in adoption with their connivance and active support of VCA an CARA officials, who are simply putting their seal of approval on these adoptions without bothering whether the procedure prescribed for intercountry adoption of a child is followed or not. With the result, trafficking in female children is going on unabated in violation of the guidelines given by the Supreme Court.
>
> 61. After the present scam came to light, the Government of Andhra Pradesh issued the Andhra Pradesh Orphanages and other Charitable Homes (Supervision and Control) Rules in GO Ms No 16, dated 18.04.2001. In para 11 (VII) of the said GO it is stated that "relinquishment" of child by "biological parents" on family grounds of poverty, number of children, unwanted girl child will not be permitted. Such children should not be admitted in Homes or "Orphanages" and, it admitted, the license and recognition of Home or Orphanage shall be cancelled or withdrawn.'

Therefore, it can be concluded that, although there is no doubt that CARA is doing good work in its policing role, the negative media feedback has definitely not escaped judicial notice.

The finalisation of the 2007 Guidelines are eagerly awaited. Hopefully, the consolidated comprehensive guidelines shall carve out clear cut and precise uniformity in areas and legal issues addressed in this article and not provide piecemeal reforms and solutions. The same have not been finalised at the time of the preparation of the manuscript of this book.

While the Government has been grappling on an *adhoc* basis with lacunas arising out of the guidelines which have been revised from time to time, in the interim, new issues have cropped-up.

**Firstly,** there are legal issues connected with surrogacy. There is no legislation in India pertaining to surrogacy as yet.

**Secondly,** no practical tangible useful benefits are forthcoming at all to prospective NRI adoptive parents and persons of foreign origin arising out of India signing the Hague Convention Adoptions.

India has ratified the Hague Convention on Protection of Children and Cooperation in respect of inter-country adoptions on 6 June 2003. Sadly enough, this significant development in the area of child law has gone completely unnoticed. However, the CARA authorities in their existing guidelines are yet to recognise in any form the ratification of Hague Convention on adoptions by India. It is suggested that the CARA authorities working in tandem conjointly with the Law Ministry of India, the Ministry of Women and Child Development, the Ministry of External Affairs, the Ministry of Overseas Indians Affairs as also the Legal and Treaties Division should take concrete steps in drafting as also implementing enabling legislation specifically looking at the positive steps of India signing the Hague convention on adoptions. In actual practice and interface with the above-mentioned Government agencies during seminars and conferences of national importance, it appears that there is little co-ordination and interaction inter se within these important Government departments and ministries. Alternatively, if it is too late in the day to enact new enabling legislation with a view to seeking implementation of the Hague Convention on adoptions in the Indian jurisdiction, then in such a situation either of the ministries as mentioned above could well come out with a notification on the lines mentioned above. But, more importantly any such notification or directive should carry a specific direction to all the Embassies and Foreign Missions in India, to the effect that all Hague Convention adoptions made by the NRI community, subject to compliance of the due provisions of law, should be given due recognition. Also, any such notification or directive should clearly aim to define the concept of the "sending country," and the "receiving country," leaving little room for ambiguity.

**Thirdly**, the proposed revision of the guidelines of 2007 should also categorically attempt to provide a clear cut direction in no uncertain terms to all major Embassies, High Commissions and Consulates in India, that all adoptions under the provision of the Juvenile Justice (Care and Protection of Children) Amendment Act, 2006 by Non-Resident Indians, Persons of Indian Origin and foreigners as well, should be duly acknowledged and their validity accepted as well to facilitate movement of the adopted children in the country of the habitual residence of the adopting parents. This of course has to be hedged with safeguards and compliance of due process of law, both in India and abroad. But, the core issue is the recognition of adoption orders handed down by the designated Courts in

India under the provisions of the above mentioned amended provisions of the JJ Act of 2006. It is very important that these three new major issues also receive the due attention they warrant in the present day and age.

It is suggested that the concept of gender free adoptions as provided under the provisions of the JJ Act, 2006 should well be taken into account in the CARA guidelines which are presently under revision. And also the CARA authorities should take into account the provisions of the JJ Act, 2006 as also to specifically support the concept of gender free inter-country adoptions bearing in mind the plight of that particular section of NRI community, who are actually childless or even those who are willing to adopt children from India even though they have a child from an existing matrimonial relationship.

Lastly, the authors experience reveals that Guardian Judges, especially in small towns and cities in India, who deal with such cases are not particularly conversant with the interpretation of the inter-country adoption guidelines discussed in this article. Therefore, in sum and substance it can be stated that a uniform but strict procedure must be evolved which can be easily followed and adhered to both in letter and spirit. No doubt procedural hurdles and legal formalities are necessary to prevent abuse of the process but separate and intricate adoption and immigration procedures often leave foreign adopting parents in confusion over differing interpretations. Therefore, if the adoption process and procedures are overhauled so that they conform to a uniform pattern, it may make the process more convenient, less cumbersome and easier to follow. All of this would be in the best interests of the child, which is undoubtedly the paramount consideration, and at the same time would allow both the letter and spirit of law to be adhered to. Considered changes are thus urgently required in the field of inter-country adoption from India. Time has also come to enact legislation dealing with legal parentage issues of children born out of surrogacy arrangements.

# ALTERNATIVE DISPUTE RESOLUTION IN INDIAN FAMILY LAW – REALITIES, PRACTICALITIES AND NECESSITIES

## (I) INTRODUCTION: THE INDIAN BACKGROUND

The Constitution of India enacted on the 26 November 1949 resolved to constitute India as a Union of States and a Sovereign, Socialist, Secular, Democratic Republic. Today, a population of about 1.1 billion Indians live in twenty-eight States and seven Union Territories within India besides about twenty five million Indians who reside in foreign jurisdictions and are called Non-Resident Indians. Within the territory of India spread over an area of 3.28 million sq. kms, the large Indian population comprises of multicultural societies professing and practicing different religions and speaking different local languages co-existing in harmony in one of the largest democracies in the world.

The Indian Parliament at the helm of affairs legislates on Central subjects in the Union and Concurrent Lists and State legislatures enacts laws pertaining to State subjects as per the State and Concurrent Lists with regard to the subjects enumerated in the Constitution of India. Likewise, pertaining to the judiciary, under article 214 of the Indian Constitution there shall be a High Court for each State and under article 124 there shall be a Supreme Court of India. Under article 141 of the Constitution, the law declared by the Supreme Court shall be binding on all Courts within the territory of India. However, the Supreme Court may not be bound by its own earlier views and can render new decisions.

Part III of the Constitution of India secures to its citizens "Fundamental Rights" which can be enforced directly in the respective High Courts of the States or directly in the Supreme Court of India by issue of prerogative Writs under articles 226 and 32 respectively of the Constitution of India. Under the Constitutional scheme, amongst others, freedom of religion and the right to freely profess, practice and propagate it is sacrosanct and is thus enforceable by a prerogative Writ issued by the superior Courts.

Simultaneously Part IV of the Indian Constitution lays down "Directive Principles of State Policy" which are not enforceable by any Court but are nevertheless fundamental in the governance of the country and it shall be the duty of the State to apply these principles while making laws. Under article 44 of the Constitution in this Part, the State shall endeavour to secure for the citizens a Uniform Civil Code throughout the territory of India. However, realistically speaking, till date a Uniform Civil Code remains an aspiration which India has yet to achieve and enact.

It is seen that the Indian legal system has grown and evolved with the lives and aspirations of its people and its varied cultures, religious practices and personal laws. The Indian legal system is founded and fortified by age-old concepts and precepts of justice, equity and good conscience, which are, indeed, the hallmarks of common law.

The Constitution of India is the fundamental authority of law in India. The Constitution gives due recognition to statutes, case-law and customary law consistent with its dispensations. A single unified judicial system is the unique feature of the Indian judiciary system. The Supreme Court at the apex of the entire judicial system is followed by High Courts in each State or group of States. Under the High Courts exists a hierarchy of civil and criminal subordinate Courts. Panchayat Courts also function in some States under various names like Nyaya Panchayat, Panchayat Adalat, Gram Kachheri, etc. to decide civil and criminal disputes of petty and local nature. These are grassroots level petty Courts meant to decide small disputes at the lowest levels.

## (II) EXISTING FAMILY LAW LEGISLATIONS PREVALENT IN INDIA

India is a land of diversities with several religions. The oldest part of Indian legal system is the personal laws governing the Hindus and the Muslims. The Hindu personal law has undergone changes by a continuous process of codification. The process of change in society has brought changes in law reflecting the changed social conditions and attempts the solution of social problems by new methods in the light of experience of legislations in other countries of the world. The Muslim personal law has been comparatively left untouched by legislations.

The Indian legal system is basically a Common law system. The Indian Parliament has enacted the following family laws which are applicable to the religious communities defined in the respective enactments themselves. A brief description of each of these separate enactments is given as hereunder.

**(A)** The main marriage law legislation in India applicable to the majority population constituted of Hindus is known as The Hindu Marriage Act, 1955, which is an Act to amend and codify the law relating to marriage among Hindus. Ceremonial marriage is essential under this Act and registration is optional. It applies to any person who is a Hindu, Buddhist, Jaina or Sikh by religion and to any other person who is not a Muslim, Christian, Parsi or Jew by religion. The Act also applies to Hindus resident outside the territory of India. Nothing contained in this Act shall be deemed to affect any right recognized by custom or conferred by any special enactment. Likewise, in other personal law matters, Hindus are governed by the Hindu Succession Act, 1956, which is an Act to amend and codify the law relating to intestate succession among Hindus. The Hindu Minority and Guardianship Act, 1956 is an Act to amend and codify certain parts of the law relating to Minority and Guardianship among Hindus and the Hindu Adoptions and Maintenance Act, 1956 is an Act to amend and codify the law relating to adoptions and maintenance among Hindus.

It may be pertinent to point out that the Indian Succession Act, 1925, is an Act to consolidate the law applicable to intestate and testamentary succession in India unless parties opt and choose to be governed by their respective codified law otherwise applicable to them. In respect of issues relating to guardianship, the

Guardian and Wards Act, 1890 would apply to non-Hindus. Interestingly, section 125 of the Code of Criminal Procedure, 1973, provides that irrespective of religion, any person belonging to any religion can approach a Magistrate for being provided maintenance. Therefore, apart from personal family law legislations, both Hindus and non-Hindus have an independent right of maintenance under the general law of the land, if he or she is otherwise entitled to maintenance under this Code.

**(B)** The Indian Parliament also enacted the Special Marriage Act, 1954, as an Act to provide a special form of marriage in certain cases, for the registration of such and certain other marriages and for divorces under this Act. This enactment of solemnizing marriage by registration is resorted to by Hindus, non-Hindus and foreigners marrying in India who opt out of the ceremonial marriage under their respective personal laws. Registration is compulsory under this enactment. Divorce can also be obtained by non-Hindus under this Act. This legislation governs people of all religions and communities in India, irrespective of their personal faith. Likewise, under the Foreign Marriage Act, 1969, a person has only to be a citizen of India to have a marriage solemnized under this Act outside the territorial limits of India.

**(C)** The Parsi Marriage and Divorce Act, 1936 as amended in 1988, is an Act to amend the law relating to marriage and divorce among the Parsis in India.

**(D)** The Indian Christian Marriage Act, 1872, was enacted as an Act to consolidate and amend the law relating to the solemnization of the marriages of Christians in India and the Divorce Act, 1869 as amended in 2001, is an Act to amend the law relating to divorce and matrimonial causes relating to Christians in India.

**(E)** The Muslim Personal Law (Shariat) Application Act,1937, the Dissolution of Muslim Marriages Act,1939, the Muslim Women (Protection of Rights on Divorce) Act, 1986 and the Muslim Women (Protection of Rights on Divorce) Rules, 1986, applies to Muslims living in India.

For enforcement and adjudication of all matrimonial and other related disputes of any person in any of the different religious or non-religious communities under the respective legislations mentioned above, the designated judicial forum or Court where such petition is to be lodged is prescribed in the respective enactments themselves. There is an organized system of designated civil and criminal judicial Courts within every State in India which works under the overall jurisdiction of the respective High Court in the State. It is in the hierarchy of these Courts that all family and matrimonial causes are lodged and decided by the aggrieved party. In addition, the Indian Parliament has enacted the Family Courts Act, 1984 to provide for the establishment of Family Courts with a view to promote conciliation in and to secure speedy settlement of disputes relating to marriage and family affairs. Despite the existence of an organized, well regulated and established hierarchy of judicial Courts in India, there are still unrecognized parallel community and religious Courts in existence whose interference has been deprecated by the judicial Courts since such unauthorized and unwarranted bodies work without the authority of law and are not parts of the judicial system.

## (III) BACKGROUND NOTE TO ALTERNATIVE DISPUTE RESOLUTION IN INDIA

It is believed that the development of the country can be also understood from the capability of its legal system in rendering effective justice. The practice of amicable resolution of disputes can be traced back to historic times, when the villages' disputes were resolved between members of a particular relations or occupations or between members of a particular locality. In rural India, the 'Panchayats' (assembly of elders and respected inhabitants of the village) decided aproximately all the disputes between the residents of the village, while disputes between the members of a clan continued to be decided by the elders of the clan. These methods of amicable dispute resolution were recognized methods of administration of justice and not just an "alternative" to the formal justice system formed by the sovereigns, feudal lords or the adalat systems initiated by the British and the formal Court system. The two systems continued to function analogous to each other. The process followed by the traditional institutions was that of arbitration and conciliation, depending on the character of dispute.

In India we have a massive legal system comprising nearly 15000 Courts across the country. It is the constitutional obligation of the judiciary to exercise its jurisdiction to reaffirm the faith of the people in the judicial set up. Therefore, evolution of new juristic principles for dispute resolution is not only important but imperative. In India the need to evolve alternative mechanisms simultaneous with the revival and strengthening of traditional systems of dispute resolution have been reiterated in reports of expert bodies [For more details see: Report of the Committee on Legal Aid (1971), *Report of the Expert Committee on Legal Aid: Processual Justice to the People*, Government of India, Ministry of Law, Justice and Company Affairs (1973), *Report on National Juridicare Equal Justice – Social Justice*, Ministry of Law, Justice and Company Affairs (1977)]. Each of these reports saw the process of improving access to justice through legal aid mechanisms and Alternative Dispute Resolution (ADR) as a part of the systemic reform of the institution of the judiciary coupled with substantive reforms of laws and processes.

## (IV) EXISTING STATUTORY PROVISIONS FOR ADR IN LAW IN INDIA

The sensitivity of the legislature towards providing a speedy and efficacious justice in India is mainly reflected in a couple of enactments which are enumerated as hereunder:

- Arbitration under the Arbitration and Conciliation Act, 1996;
- Settlement under Order XXXIIA of the Indian Code of Civil Procedure, 1908;
- The incorporation of section 89 in the traditional Civil Procedure Code (CPC) read with Order X, rules IA, IB, and IC for settlement of disputes outside Court.
- The Establishment of Lok Adalat under the Legal Services Authority Act, 1987; looks to mediation, conciliation and informal settlement of disputes in litigation.

- ➢ Reconciliation under sections 23(2) and 23(3) of the Hindu Marriage Act, 1955 as also under section 34(3) of the Special Marriage Act, 1954;
- ➢ Duty of Family Court to make efforts for settlement under Family Courts Act, 1984;

**The Constitutional Mandate**

➢ **Article 21 of the Constitution of India** declares in a mandatory tone that no person shall be deprived of his life or his personal liberty except according to procedure established by law. The words "life and liberty" are not to be read narrowly in the sense monotonously dictated by dictionaries; they are organic terms which are to be construed meaningfully.

The right to speedy trial has been rightly held to be a part of right to life or personal liberty by the Supreme Court of India [for more details see: *Hussainara Khatoon (1)* v. *Home Secretary, State of Bihar,* 1980 (1) SCC 81. The Supreme Court has allowed article 21 to stretch its arms as wide as it legitimately can. The reason is very simple. This liberal interpretation of article 21 is to redress that mental agony, expense and strain which a person proceeded against in litigation has to undergo and which, coupled with delay, may result in impairing the capability or ability of the accused to defend himself effectively. Thus, the Supreme Court has held the right to speedy trial a manifestation of fair, just and reasonable procedure enshrined in article 21. A speedy trial encompasses within its sweep all its stages including investigation, inquiry, trial, appeal, revision and re-trial. In other words, everything commencing with an accusation and expiring with the final verdict falls within its ambit. The same has got recognition from the "legislature" as well in the form of introduction of "Alternative Dispute Resolution" (ADR) mechanism (ADRM) through various statutes [for more details see: See –"The Culture of ADR in India-by Praveen Dalal" [http://www.odr.info/THE% 20CULTURE%20OF%20 ADR%20IN%20INDIA.doc]

➢ **The Indian Arbitration and Conciliation Act, 1996**

The above is a generalized list of statutory enactments which govern the arena of Indian dispute resolution by finding expression in different words under separate laws. Arbitration generally is now a prevalent practice in the Indian civil jurisdiction. Due to pendency of mounting arrears of cases in Courts in India, there was a dire need for effective means of Alternative Dispute Resolution. India's first enactment on arbitration was the Arbitration Act, 1940. Other supporting legislations in existence were the Arbitration [Protocol and Convention] Act of 1937 and the Foreign Awards Act of 1961. Arbitration under these laws was never effective and led to further litigation as a result of rampant challenge of the awards rendered under these laws. The Indian legislature thus enacted the existing current Arbitration & Conciliation Act, 1996 to make arbitration, domestic and international both, more effective in India. The Act is based on the UNCITRAL Model Law (as recommended by the U.N. General Assembly) and facilitates international commercial arbitration as well as domestic arbitration and conciliation. Under the above 1996 Act, an arbitral award can be challenged only in the manner prescribed and on limited grounds. The 1996 Act also restricts Court intervention in arbitration proceedings to minimal interference. India is party to the New York Convention of 1958 on the Recognition and Enforcement of Foreign Arbitral Awards. As the name of the Act suggests, it also covers conciliation, which is a form of mediation. Accordingly, arbitration is a popular mode of dispute resolution in civil disputes and commercial agreements invariably contain an arbitration clause.

➢ **Provisions for ADR under the Code of Civil Procedure, 1908**

The Code of Civil Procedure, 1908 (CPC for short), as amended from time-to-time is an Act to consolidate and amend the laws relating to the procedure of the Courts of civil judicature in India. All litigation of a civil nature in India is essentially governed by the substantive provisions of law, contained in the various sections of the CPC and the corresponding implementing provisions are contained in various orders and rules of the CPC. There are three substantive and procedural provisions contained in the CPC which provide for settlement of disputes outside the Court. These can be identified briefly as the following before quoting the details of the respective provisions:

❖ ***Section 89 of the Code of Civil Procedure: Settlement of disputes outside the Court***

❖ ***ORDER X of the Code of Civil Procedure, 1908: Examination of Parties by the Court.***

❖ ***ORDER XXXIIA of the Code of Civil Procedure, 1908: Suits Relating to Matters Concerning the Family***

It may now be useful to quote the details of all the three provisions of the CPC mentioned above. They are extracted hereunder in the order given above:

❖ ***Section 89 of the Code of Civil Procedure: Settlement of disputes outside the Court***

With a view to implement the 129th report of the Law Commission of India, it was made obligatory for Courts to refer disputes after the issues were framed for settlement either by way of Arbitration, Conciliation, Mediation, Judicial Settlement or through Lok Adalat (a settlement Court). It was felt that only after the parties failed to get their disputes settled through anyone of the Alternate Dispute Resolution methods, should the litigation proceed further in the Court in which it was filed. Accordingly, section 89 CPC reads in the following terms:

> "*89. Settlement of disputes outside the Court.*—(1) Where it appears to the court that there exist elements of a settlement which may be acceptable to the parties, the court shall formulate the terms of settlement and give them to the parties for their observations and after receiving the observation of the parties, the court may reformulate the terms of a possible settlement and refer the same for—
>
> (a) Arbitration;
>
> (b) Conciliation;
>
> (c) Judicial settlement including settlement through Lok Adalat; or
>
> (d) Mediation.
>
> (2) Where a dispute had been referred—

(a) For arbitration or conciliation, the provisions of the Arbitration and Conciliation Act, 1996 (26 of 1996) shall apply as if the proceedings for arbitration or conciliation were referred for settlement under the provisions of that Act;

(b) to Lok Adalat, the court shall refer the same to the Lok Adalat in accordance with the provisions of sub-section (1) of section 20 of the Legal Services Authority Act, 1987 (39 of 1987) and all other provisions of that Act shall apply in respect of the dispute so referred to the Lok Adalat;

(c) for judicial settlement, the court shall refer the same to a suitable institution or person and such institution or person shall be deemed to be a Lok Adalat and all the provisions of the Legal Services Authority Act, 1987 (39 of 1987) shall apply as if the disputes were referred to a Lok Adalat under the provisions of that Act;

(d) For mediation, the court shall effect a compromise between the parties and shall follow such procedure as may be prescribed."

A perusal of section 89 CPC quoted above clearly spells out the statutory modes, mechanisms, machinery and procedure provided and stipulated for alternative modes of dispute redressal in all matters of civil litigation in India. These substantive provisions are procedurally supported by Order X, rules 1A, 1B and 1C as below:

❖ ***ORDER X of the Code of Civil Procedure, 1908: Examination of Parties by the Court.***

Rules 1A, 1B and 1C were inserted in Order X by the CPC (Amendment) Act, 1999. This was consequential to the insertion of section 89(1) CPC, making it obligatory upon the Courts to refer the dispute for settlement by way of Arbitration, Conciliation, Judicial Settlement including settlement through Lok Adalat or Mediation. A settlement can thus be made by adopting any of the said modes specified in the amended section 89. Order X of the CPC along with rules 1, 1A, 1B and 1C read in the following terms:

*"Order X: Examination of Parties by the Court:*

1. *Ascertainment whether allegations in pleadings are admitted or denied.* – At the first hearing of the suit of the Court shall ascertain from each party or his pleader whether he admits or denies such allegations of fact as are made in the plaint or written statement (if any) of the opposite party, and as are not expressly or by the necessary implication admitted or denied by the party against whom they are made. The Court shall record such admissions and denials.

*1A. Direction of the Court to opt for any one mode of alternative dispute resolution.* – After recording the admissions and denials, the Court shall direct the parties to the suit to opt either mode of the settlement outside the Court as specified in sub-section (1) of section 89. On the option of the parties, the Court shall fix the date of appearance before such forum or authority as may be opted by the parties.

*1B. Appearance before the conciliatory forum or authority.* – Where a suit is referred under rule 1A, the parties shall appear before such forum or authority for conciliation of the suit.

*1C. Appearance before the court consequent to the failure of efforts of conciliation.* – Where a suit is referred under rule 1A and the presiding officer of conciliation forum or authority is satisfied that it would not be proper in the interest of justice to proceed with the matter further, then, it shall refer the matter again to the Court and direct the parties to appear before the court on the date fixed by it."

As per the rule 1A above, the parties to the suit are given an option for settlement of the dispute outside Court. When the parties have exercised their option, it shall fix the date of appearance before such forum or authority as may be opted by the parties for settlement. As per the rule 1B, the parties are required to appear before such forum or authority opted by them. Rule 1C provides for the presiding officer of the forum or authority to refer the matter again to the Court in case it feels that in the interest of justice, the forum or authority should not proceed with the matter.

❖ ***ORDER XXXIIA of the Code of Civil Procedure, 1908:***

It may be pertinent to point out, that all proceedings under the Hindu Marriage Act and the Special Marriage Act in India are regulated by the provisions contained in the CPC. Accordingly, in so far as suits relating to matters concerning the family are concerned, by an amendment made in 1976, the Indian Parliament in its wisdom added Order XXXIIA to the Code of Civil Procedure to provide for mandatory settlement procedures in all matrimonial proceedings specifically. Order XXXIIA CPC which is relevant to the present context is quoted hereunder for purposes of ready reference:

*"Order XXXIIA: Suits Relating to Matters Concerning the Family:*

**1.** Application of the Order

(1) The provisions of this Order shall apply to suits or proceedings relating to matters concerning the family.

(2) In particular, and without prejudice to the generality of the provisions of sub-rule (1), the provisions of this Order shall apply to the following suits or proceedings concerning the family, namely:—

- (a) a suit or proceeding for matrimonial relief, including a suit or proceeding for declaration as to the validity of a marriage or as to the matrimonial status of any person;
- (b) a suit or proceeding for a declaration as to legitimacy of any person;
- (c) a suit or proceeding in relation to the guardianship of the person or the custody of any minor or other member of the family, under a disability;
- (d) a suit or proceeding for maintenance;
- (e) a suit or proceeding as to the validity or effect of an adoption;
- (f) a suit or proceeding, instituted by a member of the family relating to wills, intestacy and succession;
- (g) a suit or proceeding relating to any other matter concerning the family in respect of which the parties are subject to their personal law.

(3) So much of this Order as relates to a matter provided for by a special law in respect of any suit or proceeding shall not apply to that suit or proceeding.

**2.** Proceedings to be held *in camera*

In every suit or proceeding to which this Order applies, the proceeding may be held *in camera* if the Court so desires and shall be so held if either party so desires.

**3.** Duty of Court to make efforts for settlement

(1) In every suit or proceeding to which this Order applies, an endeavour shall be made by the Court in the first instance, where it is possible to do so consistent with the nature and circumstances of the case, to assist the parties in arriving at a settlement in respect of the subject-matter of the suit.

(2) If, in any such suit or proceeding, at any stage it appears to the Court that there is a reasonable possibility of a settlement between the parties, the Court may adjourn the proceeding for such period as it thinks fit to enable attempts to be made to effect such a settlement.

(3) The power conferred by sub-rule (2) shall be in addition to, and not in derogation of, any other power of the Court to adjourn the proceedings.

**4.** Assistance of welfare expert

In every suit or proceeding to which this Order applies, it shall be open to the Court to secure the services of such person (preferably a woman where available), whether related to the parties or not, including a person professionally engaged in promoting the welfare of the family as the Court may think fit, for the purpose of assisting the Court in discharging the functions imposed by rule 3 or this Order.

**5.** Duty to inquire into facts

In every suit or proceeding to which this Order applies, it shall be the duty of the Court to inquire, so far is reasonably can, into the facts alleged by the plaintiff and into any facts alleged by the defendant.

**6.** "Family"-meaning of

For the purposes of this Order, each of the following shall be treated as constituting a family, namely:—

(a) (i) a man and his wife living together;

(ii) any child or children being issue or theirs; or of such man or such wife;

(iii) any child or children being maintained by such man and wife;

(b) a man not having a wife or not living together with his wife, any child or children, being issue of his, and any child or children being maintained by him;

(c) a woman not having a husband or not living together with her husband any child or children being issue of hers, and any child or children being maintained by her;

(d) a man or woman and his or her brother, sister, ancestor or lineal descendant living with him or her; and

(e) any combination of one or more of the groups specified in clause (a), clause (b), clause (c) or clause (d) of this rule.

Explanation-For the avoidance of doubts, it is hereby declared that the provisions of rule 6 shall be without any prejudice to the concept of "family" in any personal law or in any other law for the time being in force."

A reading of the above clearly establishes the statutory mandate laid down by the Civil Procedure Code to make an endeavour in the first instance to assist the parties in arriving at a settlement in a matrimonial cause in any matrimonial proceeding before a Court of competent jurisdiction. Hence, in any suit or proceeding for matrimonial, ancillary or other relief in matters concerning the family, there is a separate and independent statutory provision providing for mandatory settlement proceedings. This is over and above the other statutory provisions applicable.

### ✣ *Lok Adalat system under the Legal Services Authority Act, 1987*

• The Legal Services Authorities Act, 1987, as per its preamble, was enacted as "An Act to constitute legal services authorities to provide free and competent legal services to the weaker sections of the society to ensure that opportunities for securing justice are not denied to any citzen by reason of economic or other disabilities, and to organise Lok Adalats to secure that the operation of the legal system promotes justice on a basis of equal opportunity." Under chapter VI of the Act, authorities may organise Lok Adalats (settlement Courts) at such intervals and places and for exercising such jurisdiction and for such areas as it thinks fit. Generally, the Lok Adalat consists of serving or retired judicial officers and other persons of eminence, specified by the respective Government in consultation with the judiciary. Over the passage of time, such Lok Adalats have become a popular mode for informal settlement of civil disputes of all nature. Written compromises, settlements and negotiated conclusions drawn up in Lok Adalats are returned to the Court of competent jurisdiction for passing an appropriate judicial award, decision, decree or compromise as the case may be. Even matrimonial matters are settled in Lok Adalats and thereafter such negotiated settlements are affirmed by the respective matrimonial Courts by appropriate orders or consent decrees/ judgments so drawn up.

• Lok Adalat generally means "People's Court". India has had a long history of resolving disputes through the mediation of village elders. The system of Lok Adalats is an improvement on that and is based on Gandhian principles. This is a non-adversarial system, where through mock Courts (called Lok Adalats) are held by the State Authority, District Authority, Supreme Court Legal Services Committee, High Court Legal Services Committee, or Taluk Legal Services Committee, periodically for exercising such jurisdiction as they think fit. These are usually presided by retired Judge, social activists, or members of the legal profession. Lok Adalats do not have jurisdiction on matters pertaining to non-compoundable offences.

• There is no court-fee and no rigid procedural requirement (that is no need to follow mandatory process laid down by the Civil Procedure Code or Evidence Act), which makes the process very fast. Parties can directly interact with the Lok Adalat Judges in vernacular language, which feature is not possible in regular Courts.

• Cases that are pending in regular Courts can be transferred to a Lok Adalat if both the parties agree and consent to it. A case can also be transferred to a Lok Adalat if one party applies to the Court in writing where matter is pending. If the Court sees some chances of settlement after giving an opportunity of being heard to the other party, the matter can be transferred to the Lok Adalat for settlement.

• The focus in Lok Adalats is on compromise and settlement. When no compromise is reached, the matter goes back to the regular Court. However, if a compromise is reached, an award is made by consent and is binding on the parties. It is enforced as a decree of a civil Court after it is affirmed as such by the regular Court. An important aspect is that the award is final and cannot be appealed, not even under article 226 because it is a judgement by consent and consent orders are not appealable.

• All proceedings of a Lok Adalat are deemed to be a judicial proceedings and every Lok Adalat is deemed to be a civil Court under the Legal Services Authorites Act, 1987.

• The Law Commission of India in its 129th Report recommended for the alternate modes of dispute redressal to be obligatory on the Courts after framing of issues. It is only after the parties fail to get their disputes settled through any one of the Alternate Dispute Resolution methods that the suit shall proceed further in the Court where it was filed and where the matter was pending before settlement was attempted.

### ❖ *Settlement under Indian Family Law Statutes*

Reconciliation is mandatory under the Hindu Marriage Act, 1955 (HMA) and the Special Marriage Act, 1954 (SMA). However, other Indian matrimonial statutes do not provide for it and there is therefore no statutory mandate to attempt settlement in other cases.

• *Reconciliation under section 23(2) & section 23(3) of the Hindu Marriage Act*

Section 23(2) HMA states that before proceeding to grant any relief under it, there shall be a duty of the Court in the first instance, in every case to make every endeavour to bring about reconciliation between parties where relief is sought on most of the faulty grounds for divorce specified in section 13 HMA. Section 23(3) HMA makes a provision empowering the Court on the request of parties or if the Court thinks it just and proper to adjourn the proceedings for a reasonable period not exceeding 15 days to bring about reconciliation. It must be borne in mind that a Hindu marriage is a sacrament and not a contract. Even if divorce is sought by mutual consent, it is the duty of the Court to attempt reconciliation in the first instance. Accordingly, Hindu law advocates rapprochement and reconciliation before dissolving a Hindu marriage. Sections 23(2) and 23(3) of the HMA, relevant for the present context are reproduced hereunder:

*Section 23 of the Hindu Marriage Act, 1955:*

"23. *Decree in Proceedings—*

(1) xx xx xx xx

(2) Before proceeding to grant any relief under this Act, it shall be the duty of the court in the first instance, in every case where it is possible so to do

consistently with the nature and circumstances of the case, to make every endeavour to bring about a reconciliation between the parties:

[Provided that nothing contained in this sub-section shall apply to any proceeding wherein relief is sought on any of the grounds specified in clause (ii), clause (iii), clause (iv), clause (v), clause (vi) or clause (vii) of sub-section (1) of section 13.

(3) For the purpose of aiding the court in bringing about such reconciliation, the court may, if the parties so desire or if the court thinks it just and proper so to do, adjourn the proceedings for a reasonable period not exceeding fifteen days and refer the matter to any person named by the parties in this behalf or to any person nominated by the court if the parties fail to name any person, with directions to report to the court as to whether reconciliation can be and has been, effected and the court shall in disposing of the proceeding have due regard to report."

- *Section 34 of the Special Marriage Act, 1954.—*

The provisions of sections 34(2) and 34(3) of the SMA are pari materia to the provisions contained in sections 23(2) and 23(3) of the HMA. Even though the marriage contracted under the SMA does not have the same sacramental sanctity as marriage is solemnized under the HMA, the Indian Parliament in its wisdom has retained the provisions for reconciliation of marriages in the same terms in the SMA as they exist in the HMA. The mandatory duty on the Court is thus in similar terms. For purposes of ready reference, sections 34(2) and 34(3) SMA are quoted hereunder:

*"34. Duty of Court in passing decrees—*

(1) xx xx xx xx

(2) Before proceeding to grant any relief under this Act it shall be the duty of the court in the first instance, in every case where it is possible so to do consistently with the nature and circumstances of the case, to make every endeavour to bring about a reconciliation between the parties:

[Provided that nothing contained in this sub-section shall apply to any proceeding wherein relief is sought on any of the grounds specified in clause (c), clause (e), clause (f), clause (g) or clause (h) of sub-section (1) of section 27 of the Special Marriage Act, 1954.

(3) For the purpose of aiding the court in bringing about such reconciliation, the court may, if the parties so desire or if the court thinks it just and proper so to do, adjourn the proceedings for a reasonable period not exceeding fifteen days and refer the matter to any person named by the parties in this behalf or to any person nominated by the court if the parties fail to name any person, with directions to report to the court as to whether reconciliation can be and has been, effected and the court shall in disposing of the proceeding have due regard to the report."

It may be noticed that the provisions under both the statutes is almost identical and accordingly every endeavour to bring about reconciliation is mandatory.

■ *Other Pre-emptive Measures under the Hindu Marriage Act, 1955*

*Section 14 of the Hindu Marriage Act, 1955* is another pre-emptive measure provided by the said Act, which was presumably designed with the object of preventing hasty recourse to legal proceedings by the spouses without making a real effort to reconcile and save their marriage from being dissolved. In this context, it may be useful to quote section 14(1) HMA which states that "Notwithstanding anything contained in this Act, it shall not be competent for any Court to entertain any petition for dissolution of marriage by a decree of divorce, [unless at the date of presentation of the petition one year has elapsed] since the date of marriage." Thus, section 14 HMA provides a deterrent from initiating divorce proceedings in the first year of marriage. The logic again being to advocate settlement and reconciliation between parties and avoid hasty divorces.

However, under the proviso to section 14 HMA, the Court is conferred a discretionary power to entertain a petition before the expiry of one year, if it finds on the allegation in the affidavit filed in the support of the petition that *prima facie* there is exceptional hardship to the petitioner or depravity on the part of the respondent [for more details see: *Gulzar Singh* v. *State of Punjab,* 1998 (2) HLR 204 (P&H)]. It presupposes an application for leave of Court to present a petition for divorce before the expiry of one year from the date of marriage. Hence, the statute provides discretion to the Court in entertaining a petition or divorce in the first year of marriage on the ground of exceptional hardship or exceptional depravity.

Section 14(2) *HMA* further states that "In disposing of any application under this section for leave to present a petition for divorce before the expiration of one yearfrom the date of marriage, the court shall have regard to the interests of any children of the marriage and to the question whether there is a reasonable probability of a reconciliation between the parties before the expiration of the said one year"

- Section 29 of the SMA contains similar provisions with similar bars.

■ *Petition for Divorce by Mutual Consent.* – Under section 13 B HMA and section 28 SMA, divorce by mutual consent is available. However, it is not granted instantly and a joint motion made by both parties in the first instance has to wait for 6 months but not longer than 18 months to be confirmed for granting a divorce by mutual consent in the second motion. It is evident that reconciliation may be out of question in a petition for divorce by mutual consent. But there is an inbuilt opportunity for reconciliation if parties wish to avail of it. When a joint petition is presented, it is adjourned for a minimum period of six months. This period is to enable them to think over the matter of divorce and if the parties want to prolong their consideration of reconciliation, they can do so for another year (total period is eighteen months, within which they can move the motion of a decree of divorce). Section 28 SMA contains similar provisions with similar bars. The logic in these enactments is again to provide for reconciliation in a thinking period between the first and the second motion.

Some precedents settled by Indian Courts may be cited in support. In *Hitesh Narendra Doshi* v. *Jesal Hitesh Doshi,* 2000 (2) HLR 45, the minimum six month waiting period from the date of the presentation of the petition for snapping the marital ties between the parties by mutual consent under section 13B(2) of the Hindu Marriage Act was held to be mandatory and it was held that the Court has no power to relax the said compulsory time wait of six months and cannot pass a decree of divorce forthwith.

However, in *Mohinder Pal Kaur* v. *Gurmeet Singh*, 2002 (1) HLR 537, it was held that the six months waiting period can be brought down in cases where an existing divorce petition is already pending for more than six months and efforts for reconciliation have been made earlier but without any success. Thus, the waiting period cannot be curtailed in a freshly instituted petition for divorce by mutual consent if in an earlier petition on fault or other grounds, the parties have already been litigating for more than six months and reconciliation between them has been of no avail.

■ *Matters to which reconciliation does not apply: Petition on certain faulty grounds.*— When a petition for divorce under the Hindu Marriage Act, 1955 is presented on the ground of change of religion [clause (ii) of section 13(1)], unsoundness of mind [clause (iii) of section 13(1)], leprosy [clause (iv) of section 13(1)], venereal disease [clause (v) of section 13(1)], renunciation of world [clause (vi) of section 13(1)], or presumption of death [clause (vii) of section 13(1)] reconciliation efforts need not be made, that is to say, the provisions of section 23(2) do not apply. The proviso to section 23(2) HMA exempts the mandatory requirement of attempting reconciliation between the parties when divorce is sought on any of the grounds in HMA above.

Similarly, when a petition for divorce is made under Special Marriage Act, 1954 on the ground of seven years sentence of imprisonment [clause (c) of section 27(1)], unsoundness of mind [clause (e) of section 27(1)], venereal disease [clause (f) of section 27(1)], leprosy [clause (g) of section 27(1)], or presumption of death [clause (h) of section 27(1)], no efforts at reconciliation need be made. The proviso to section 34(2) SMA exempts the mandatory requirement of attempting reconciliation between the parties when divorce is sought on any of the grounds in SMA stipulated above.

However, it may be added out of abundant clarification that on all other grounds of divorce, both under HMA and SMA, the Court has an obligation to make efforts at reconciliation [for more details see: *Pramila* v. *Ajit*, AIR 1989 Pat 163]. This mandatory and statutory duty of the Court cannot be waived.

*Reconciliation by the Court.* – Sub-section (2) of section 23 of the Hindu Marriage Act, 1955 and sub-section (2) of section 34 of the Special Marriage Act, 1954 lay down that at first instance it is the duty of the Court to make every effort to bring about reconciliation between the parties where it is possible to do so consistently with the nature and circumstances of the case. The words are "before proceeding to grant relief". At one time a view was propounded that the reconciliation endeavour should be made towards the end of the proceedings when the Court comes to a conclusion that it is going to grant "relief". But then the provision has also the words "at the first instance" and these have been interpreted to mean that before the Court takes up the case for hearing, it should make an effort at reconciliation. Presently, the latter is the prevalent view and hence reconciliation is to be attempted in the first instance.

### ➢ *Family Courts Act, 1984*

The Preamble to the Family Courts Act, 1984 enacted by the Indian Parliament states that it is "An Act to provide for the establishment of Family Courts with a view to promote conciliation in, and secure speedy settlement of disputes relating to marriage and family affairs and for matters connected therewith." In the statement of objects and reasons of the Family Courts Act, five essential requirements were pin-pointed in the context of providing reconciliatory efforts to litigating parties and these can be summarized in the following words stated in the statement of objects and reasons:

(a) make it obligatory on the part of the Family Court to endeavour, in the first instance to effect a reconciliation or a settlement between the parties to a family dispute. During this stage, the proceedings will be informal and rigid rules of procedure shall not apply;

(b) provide for the association of social welfare agencies, counsellors, etc., during conciliation stage and also to secure the service of medical and welfare experts;

(c) provide that the parties to a dispute before a Family Court shall not be entitled, as of right, to be represented by legal practitioners. However, the Court may, in the interest of justice, seek assistance of a legal experts as *amicus curiae* in the case;

(d) simplify the rules of evidence and procedure so as to enable a Family Court to deal effectively with a dispute, and

(e) provide for only one right of appeal which shall lie to the High Court.

In seeking to achieve the above objects, the endeavour of the Family Courts Act was to adopt a friendly, conciliatory and informal dispute resolution atmosphere which would enable parties to amicably settle their differences without the shackles of the technical rules of the law of procedure and evidence. These objects find expression in the Constitution of the Family Courts Act, its jurisdiction and procedure. The necessary provisions for reconciliations in the Family Courts Act, 1984 are dealt with under section 9 of the Act which reads as hereunder:

*Section 9 of the Family Courts Act, 1984:*

"9. *Duty of Family Court to make efforts for settlement*:—(1) In every suit or proceeding, endeavour shall be made by the Family Court in the first instance, where it is possible to do so consistent with the nature and circumstances of the case, to assist and persuade the parties in arriving at a settlement in respect of the subject-matter of the suit or proceeding and for this purpose a Family Court may, subject to any rules made by the High Court, follow such procedure as it may deem fit.

(2) If, in any suit or proceeding, at any stage, it appears to the Family Court that there is a reasonable possibility of a settlement between the parties, the Family Court may adjourn the proceedings for such period as it think fit to enable attempts to be made to effect such a settlement.

(3) The power conferred by sub-section (2) shall be in addition to, and not in derogation of any other power of the Family Court to adjourn the proceedings."

The Act also makes it open to the Family Courts under *section 12* "to secure the services of a medical expert or such person (preferably a woman where available), whether related to the parties or not, including a person professionally engaged in promoting the welfare of the family as the Court may think fit, for the purposes of assisting the Family Court in discharging the functions imposed by this Act." Clearly, the thought, logic and motive in the Act in making available services of professional experts is to provide counselling, expert help and assistance of trained mediators. Therefore, this enactment is a wholesome legislation on reconciliatory modes in family law disputes in the Indian matrimonial jurisdiction.

**(V) ANALYSIS OF THE STATUS OF ADR IN FAMILY LAW IN INDIA**

The duty of making or amending laws is on the legislature but to develop it and to interpret it to suit the needs, circumstances of the society is the call of the judiciary. Hence, unless and until the beneficial provisions of the matrimonial legislation promoting and advocating reconciliation in matrimonial disputes in India is favourably interpreted and strictly implemented by the Courts, the letter of law may be an illusory mirage which remains on the statute book only. It is therefore the solemn duty of the matrimonial Courts in India to ensure that the mandatory settlement efforts are actually put into practice and parties are encouraged to actually utilize them for out of Court settlements. Thus, there is a heavy burden on the Courts to discharge this solemn duty failing which it will neither be possible nor useful to enforce reconciliatory measure in matrimonial disputes in the Indian jurisdiction. Accordingly, it would be most useful to cite and quote some recent prominent verdicts of superior Indian Courts which have stressed and highlighted the dire necessity of the beneficial provisions of Indian legislation which provide mandatory reconciliation procedures.

Section 23 of the Hindu Marriage Act, 1955 and Order XXXIIA of the Code of Civil Procedure, 1908 and the duty enjoined upon the Court came up for interpretation before the Supreme Court recently in the case of *Jagraj Singh* v. *Bir Pal Kaur*, JT 2007 (3) SC 389. When the above provisions of the CPC and the HMA and the duty cast upon the Court came for interpretation before the Supreme Court in *Jagraj Singh* v. *Bir Pal Kaur* (supra), wherein upholding the order of the Hon'ble High Court summoning the Respondent husband by non-bailable warrants, the Indian Apex Court in its landmark judgment laid down and held as follows:

> "26 From the above case law in our judgment, it is clear hat that a court is expected, nay, bound, to make all attempts and section (2) of section 23 is a salutary provision exhibiting the intention of he parliament requiring the court 'in the first instance' to make every endeavor to bring about a reconciliation between the parties. If in the light of the above mentioned intention and paramount consideration of the legislature in enacting such provision, an order is passed by a Matrimonial Court asking a party to the proceeding (husband or wife) to remain personally present, it cannot successfully be contented that the court has no such power and in case a party to a proceeding does not remain present, at most, the court can proceed to decide the case *ex parte* against him/her. Upholding of such

argument would virtually make the benevolent provision nugatory, ineffective and unworkable, defeating the laudable object of reconciliation in matrimonial disputes. The contention of the learned counsel for the appellant therefore cannot be upheld."

Hence, the order of the Apex Indian Court upholding the directions of the High Court summoning the respondent – husband in the above case through non-bailable warrants clearly reflects the legislative intent of attempting mandatory reconciliation procedures. This judgment of the Supreme Court clearly confirms that settlement efforts in matrimonial matters are not an empty meaningless ritual to be performed by the matrimonial Court. The verdict clearly reflects the benevolent legislative purpose.

A novel question came up for decision before the High Court of Kerala in *Bini* v. *K.V. Sundaran,* AIR 2008 Ker 84, that is as to whether conciliation is mandatory after the introduction of the Family Courts Act, 1984, even on the excepted grounds of conversion to another religion, renunciation of the world, mental disorder, venereal diseases and leprosy. Calling the Family Courts Act, 1984 a special statute, and its provisions to make attempt at reconciliation mandatory at the first instance, the High Court held:

"The parties can disagree on matters of faith and still lead a happy marital life if they could be convinced that matters of faith should not stand in the way of union of hearts. Thus though under the Hindu Marriage Act, 1955, no endeavor for reconciliation need be made in a petition for divorce on the ground of conversion to another religion, or other grounds excepted under section 13(1) of the Hindu Marriage Act, 1955 or on similar or other grounds available under any other law also, after the introduction of the Family Courts Act, 1984, the Family Court is bound to make an endeavor for reconciliation and settlement. The requirement is mandatory. That is the conceptual change brought out by the Family Courts Act, 1984 which is a special statute."

The Court further says that "the primary object is to promote and preserve the sacred union of parties to marriage. Only if the attempts for reconciliation are not fruitful, the further attempt on agreement or disagreement be made by way of settlement."

Hence, from a reading of the above judgment it is clear that the beholden duty cast upon the matrimonial Courts to attempt mandatory reconciliation cannot be avoided and cannot be circumvented even when divorce is sought on certain exceptional grounds which under the HMA and SMA do not provide compulsory settlement action.

Still further, stressing on the need to treat the cases pertaining to family matters in a humanitarian way, the Supreme Court of India in the case *Balwinder Kaur* v. *Hardeep Singh,* AIR 1998 SC 764, laid down that "stress should always be on the preserving the institution of marriage. That is the requirement of law. One may refer to the Objects and Reasons which lead to setting up of Family Courts under the Family Courts Act, 1984. For the purpose of settlement of family disputes emphasis is "laid on conciliation and achieving socially desirable results" and elimination adherence to rigid rules of procedure and evidence."

The Supreme Court further lays down that "it is now obligatory on the part of the Family Court to endeavor, in the first instance to effect a reconciliation or settlement between the parties to a family dispute." "Even where the Family Courts are not functioning, the objects and principles underlying the constitution of these courts can be kept in view by the Civil Courts trying matrimonial causes." The Supreme Court held that the objectives and principles of section 23 of the Hindu Marriage Act, 1955 govern all Courts trying matrimonial matters.

Deciding on the importance of making an attempt at reconciliation at the first instance, a Division Bench of the Calcutta High Court in *Shiv Kumar Gupta* v. *Lakshmi Devi Gupta,* 2005 (1) HLR 483, felt that the compliance of section 23(2) of the Hindu Marriage Act, 1955 is a statutory duty of the Judge trying matrimonial cases. The Court in this case relied upon the decision of the Supreme Court in *Balwinder Kaur* v. *Hardeep Singh* (supra) and held in para 8 of the judgment that:

> "on a reading of section 23(2) of the Act and on the perusal of the judgment in Balwinder Kaur on the interpretation of section 23(2) this Court held that the decree, which was passed without complying with section 23(2) of the said Act, cannot be sustained."

In another perspective, in *Love Kumar* v. *Sunita Puri,* AIR 1997 P&H 189, it was held that the matrimonial Court had acted in haste to pass a decree of divorce against the husband for his non-appearance at the time of reconciliation proceedings. The High Court accordingly set aside the divorce decree and remanded the matter back to the matrimonial Court to be decided on merits. The object in purpose of section 23(2) of the HMA was explained in the following terms in paras 19 and 21 of this judgment as follows:

> "19. Under section 23(2) of the Act it is incumbent on the matrimonial Court, to endeavour to bring about reconciliation between the parties, a great responsibility is cast on the Court. A Hindu marriage is not contractual but sacrosanct, it is not easy to create such ties but more difficult to break them; once annulled, it cannot be restored. A Judge should actively stimulate rapprochement process. It is fundamental that reconciliation of a ruptured marriage is the first duty of the Judge. The sancity of marriage is the corner stone of civilization. The object and purpose of this provision is obvious. The State is interested in the security and preservation of the institution of marriage and for this the Court is required to make attempt to bring about a reconciliation between the parties. However, omission to make attempts at reconciliation will not take away the jurisdiction of the Court to pass any decree under the Act. This is not correct to say that in a divorce case reconciliation efforts have to be timed immediately preceding the grant of decree and not at any other stage of the proceedings of the trial. Such an attempt can be and should be made at any stage. The matrimonial Court is required to call parties and make a genuine effort for their reconciliation, there is not even a whisper in this provision that the matrimonial Court has the power to strike off the defence of that spouse, who after being given opportunities for reconciliation fails to appear.
>
> 21. But under section 23(2) of the Act neither such a liability is cast on the one spouse nor such a right is given to the other spouse. Reconciliation is

a mutual dialogue to burry their differences. A duty is cast on the Court to call the party at the initial stage for reconciliation. Even before delivering judgment and decree, the Court can make effort for reconciliation. Thus, the stage of trial for calling the parties for reconciliation is left to the discretion of the Court."

From a reading of the above judgments, it can clearly be spelt out that though reconciliation is a mandatory process but the timing and stage at which it is to be implemented may vary depending on the facts and circumstances of each case. At the same time causing prejudice to the rights of one party by striking off the defence or dismissing the petition may actually work injustice to the rights of such party. Therefore, the matrimonial Court in its wisdom may fashion and design the stage of attempting matrimonial reconciliation depending on the facts of each case without causing prejudice to the substantive rights of the parties. However, at the same time, the matrimonial Court ought not to give the mandatory settlement procedure a go by.

In another case, High Court of Allahabad called it the duty of the Family Court for making an attempt for conciliation before proceeding with the trial of the case. In a very recent case titled *Aviral Bhatla* v. *Bhavana Bhatla*, 2009 (3) SCC 448, the Supreme Court has upheld the settlement of the Delhi mediation centre, appreciating the effective manner in which the mediation centre of the Delhi High Court helped the parties to arrive at a settlement.

From a joint reading of the recent pronouncements of law discussed above, it can be apt to conclude that there is a growing emphasis on the need for attempting mandatory reconciliatory measures and wherever matrimonial Courts have been lacking in their duties to do so, superior Indian Courts have stepped in, to set the records straight. Therefore, there is a growing jurisprudence to adapt to out of Court settlement reconciliation rather than litigating in matrimonial Courts. However, the performance of this mandatory exercise ought not to be reduced to an empty ritual or a meaningless exercise. Otherwise, the utility of the beneficial provision will be lost.

## (VI) CONCLUSIONS: NEED FOR REFORM AND SOME SUGGESTIONS

The philosophy of Alternate Dispute Resolution systems is well made out by Abraham Lincoln's famous words: *"discourage litigation, persuade your neighbours to compromise whenever you can. Point out to them how the normal winner is often a loser in fees, expense, cost and time."* These words spell out grim realty and truth.

Litigation in respect of any matter concerning the family, whether divorce, maintenance and alimony or custody, trial of juvenile offenders or any other matrimonial cause should not be viewed in terms of failure or success of legal action but as a social therapeutic problem. It should not be viewed as a prestigious dispute in which parties and their counsels are engaged in winning or defeating, but as a societal problem needing resolution. The amicable settlement of family conflict requires special procedures-designed to help people in conflict and in trouble, to reconcile their differences, and where necessary to obtain professional assistance. Family disputes need to be seen with a humanitarian approach and hence, attempts should be made to reconcile the differences so as to not disrupt the family structure. Adjudication of family disputes is an entirely different matter other than conventional civil or criminal proceedings, it is a different culture and has a different jurisprudence altogether. The whole society feels the reverberations of a family dispute in society outside the home.

Whereas there already exist some provisions for conduct of arbitration, conciliation and Lok Adalat in different Statutes, the need for a framework to regulate the ADR process as a whole and mediation in particular has been sought to be fulfilled by the Supreme Court of India. It has done so by providing the final version of the Model Rules of ADR and the Model Rules of Mediation, both framed by the Law Commission of India, in its orders passed in the case of *Salem Bar Association* v. *Union of India*, 2003 (1) SCC 49 with a direction that all High Courts should adopt these with such modifications as they may consider necessary.

The Supreme Court has also made an observation regarding the disturbing phenomena of large number of cases flooding the courts pertaining to divorce or judicial separation. Very recently, in 2009, in *Gaurav Nagpal* v. *Sumedha Nagpal*, AIR 2009 SC 557, the Supreme Court observed as hereunder:

> "It is a very disturbing phenomenon that large numbers of cases are flooding the courts relating to divorce or judicial separation. An apprehension is gaining ground that the provisions relating to divorce in the Hindu Marriage Act, 1955 (in short the 'Marriage Act') has led to such a situation. In other words, the feeling is that the statute is facilitating breaking of homes rather than saving them, this may be too wide a view because actions are suspect. But that does not make the section invalid. Actions may be bad, but not the Section. The provisions relating to divorce categorise situations in which a decree for divorce can be sought for. Merely because such a course is available to be adopted, should not normally provide incentive to persons to seek divorce, unless the marriage has irretrievably broken. Efforts should be to bring about conciliation to bridge the communication gap which lead to such undesirable proceedings. People rushing to courts for breaking up of marriages should come as a last resort, and unless it has an inevitable result, courts should try to bring about conciliation. The emphasis should be on saving of marriage and not breaking it. As noted above it is more important in cases where the children bear the brunt of dissolution of marriage."

However, we cannot remain oblivious to the fact that India with its population of 1.1 Billion Indians has over 30 million Non-Resident Indians who live in 180 countries abroad. Some of these former Indian citizens are foreign nationals with overseas spouses. But, the fact remains that their personal family law still governs them due to extra territorial application. Resolution of marital disputes of such citizens of Indian origin creates conflicts since India does not have on its statute book irretrievable breakdown of marriage as a ground for divorce in India. Therefore, foreign divorce decrees on the break down ground with no prior mandatory reconciliation procedures do not find favour either in Indian Courts or in the domestic societal set up. How does one resolve such emerging dimensions of family law disputes where marriages solemnized in India are sought to be dissolved abroad in countries of foreign residence. The authors have advocated a solution [For more details see, "Acting for Non-Resident Indian clients" (Anil Malhotra and Ranjit Malhotra) (Jordans), London, 2004, at chapter 3, pages 76-77] penned down as follows:

> "The answer therefore is that the existing three-tier divorce structure in India under the HMA 1955 and the SMA 1954, that is faulty grounds, mutual consent principle and break-down theory, seems to provide sufficient options in the existing societal structure. Therefore, no major changes are called for. However, a civilized parting of spouses where a marriage has irretrievably broken down needs to be incorporated in the statute book as an additional ground for divorce, but only in cases where both the parties to the marriage jointly petition the court for such relief. This, in the opinion of the authors, will have an immediate two-fold benefit. First, where parties have irreconcilable differences and want to part amicably, an option will be available to them to part legally and logically without resorting to a protracted time-consuming legal battle on 'trumped-up' grounds. Secondly, recourse to divorce in foreign jurisdictions may decline once a proper legal option of irretrievable break-down is available on Indian soil. Irretrievable breakdown can thus serve as an additional ground for divorce in the HMA 1955 and the SMA 1954, and to prevent hasty divorces or misuse, sufficient statutory safeguards can be incorporated to arm the judiciary to prevent any abuse of the process of law. Keeping the Hindu ceremonial and sacramental concept of marriage intact is essential. Erosion of values in matrimonial life must be checked, and traditional marriage protected. The institutions of family, home and children of the marriage, as they exist today under Hindu law, need protection. Hindu law therefore, does not need any major overhaul. It is self-sufficient, but does need some immediate amendment."

The above views of the authors, clearly depict the inbuilt conciliatory settlement theory embedded in the Indian family law to save the marriage by in-house settlement. But, marriages solemnized in India according to personal laws of Non-Resident Indians who have permanently migrated abroad need to find resolution in the existing statutory family laws either by suitable amendments or a brand new legislation which will incorporate corresponding mandatory conciliatory procedures. For this problem, the authors have advocated their suggestions in this regard in the following words [for more details see, "India, NRIs and the Law" (Anil Malhotra) (Universal), New Delhi 2009 at pages 271-272]:

> "A reading in totality of the matters in the overseas family law jurisdiction gives an indication that in such affairs, it is the judicial precedents which provide the much available guidance and judicial legislation on the subject. With the large number of Non-Resident Indians now permanently living in overseas jurisdictions, it has now become important that some composite legislation is enacted to deal with the problems of Non-Resident Indians to avoid them from importing judgments from foreign Courts to India for implementation of their rights. The answer therefore, lies in giving them law

> applicable to them as Indians rather than letting them invade the Indian system with judgments of foreign jurisdictions which do not find applicability in the Indian system. Hence, it is the Indian legislature which now seriously needs to review this issue and come out with a composite legislation for Non-Resident Indians in family law matters. Till this is done, foreign Court judgments in domestic matters will keep cropping up and Courts in India will continue with their salutary efforts in interpreting them in harmony with the Indian laws and doing substantial justice to parties in the most fair and equitable way. However, in this process, the Indian judiciary has made one thing very clear that is the Indian Courts would not simply mechanically enforce judgments and decrees of foreign Courts in family matters. The Indian Courts have now started looking into the merits of the matters and deciding them on the considerations of Indian law and the best interest of the parties rather than simply implementing the orders without examining them. Fortunately, we can hail the Indian judiciary for these laudable efforts and till such time when the Indian Legislature comes to rescue with appropriate legislation, we seek solace with our unimpeachable and unstinted faith in the Indian judiciary, which is rendering a yeoman service."

Therefore, the dire pressing need of the day in the current social milieu where 30 million Indians now live outside India, is to create a law and infrastructural machinery for ADR mechanisms in resolving marriages solemnized in India but which have been fractured or broken abroad. For the lack of resolution, they lead to inter-parental child removal custody conflicts, disputes of maintenance and differences over settlement of matrimonial property. It is these limping marriages which need reconciliatory formulas in India to prevent them from being split abroad on grounds and reasons which do not find favour with the personal family laws of the parties in India. These cross-border marital conflicts should not stem into or branch out into other ancillary issues multiplying the problem. This, in the opinion of the authors ought to be the focus of the legislative intent today in creating, harmonizing and balancing the societal structure of Indians, Non-Resident Indians and all those who form relationships with them to build families abroad. ADR needs to be developed in a big way for resolving limping unions.

*Suggestions:*

Some suggestions can be mooted by the authors to improve the situation and to make ADR a reality in the structure of the current Indian family law.

- *Participation of citizens:*

Alternative Dispute Resolution cannot see the light of the day unless citizens also "participate" in that movement. The citizens can help in the achievements of these benign objectives by restraining themselves while invoking jurisdictions of the "traditional courts" where the matter in dispute can be conveniently and economically taken care of by ADR mechanisms. The right to speedy trial is not a fact or fiction but a "Constitutional reality" and it has to be given its due respect. The Courts and the legislature have already accepted it as one of the medium of reducing the increasing workloads on the Courts. The same is also gaining popularity among the masses due to its advantages. We need "private initiatives" for not only establishment of ADR facilities in India but equally a "liberal use" of the same by the citizens and netizens. This initiative needs awakening by self consciousness and not by implementation of laws. Spouses, parents and couples need to realise the advantages of reconcilation, mediation and Alternative Dispute Resolution methods in the family structure. Matrimonial reliefs carved out by settlement will serve better than results obtained by adversary litigation involving time, efforts, financies and above all by breaking a family.

- *More authority should be given to the Family Courts:*

Family matters should not be litigated in any Court unless it is of an extraordinary grave nature, it should be amicably resolved. Family disputes such as divorce, matrimonial property division, custody of children and maintenance should not come into the higher Courts and they should be resolved mutually and conclusively in the Family Court itself. It would save the time of the superior Courts where other matters could be resolved in the time which would have been consumed for settling matrimonial disputes. Family disputes are such disputes that can be resolved even in the home itself by a unanimous consensus. Mandatory reconciliatory procedures should assume finality so that matters can be put to rest conclusively without any further challenge.

- *Creation of more Family Courts:*

The necessity and urgency of creating more Family Courts under the Family Courts Act, 1984 in India is a very important factor which will contribute to the Resolution of family law disputes by ADR. The current handling of matrimonial litigation by conventional Courts in jurisdictions where there are no Family Courts is a poignant reminder of the situation created by lack of Family Courts in such jurisdictions. The availability of trained counselors, mediators, professionally trained persons and above all specialist family law Judges would all form part of a well organised team in a Family Court which in turn would itself create a mechanism and structure for alternative disputes resolution of family law disputes. This would therefore, give a new dimension to the existing matrimonial scenario in the Indian jurisdiction.

India has the laws to promote Alternative Dispute Resolution modes in the existing litigative setup but the infrastructure, professional assistance and the medium through which these beneficial reconciliatory mediation procedures are to be implemented are lacking within India. Therefore, creating the via media by which the beneficial ADR laws can be implemented in family law disputes is what is required today. Additionally, legislative changes are required for providing reconciliatory methods of marriages of Non-Resident Indians. The package is wholesome. The need is dire. The numbers are huge. The sooner we begin, the sooner reform will start.

# TO RETURN OR NOT TO RETURN: *HAGUE CONVENTION* V. *NON-CONVENTION COUNTRIES*

## 1. Introduction

Inter-continental abduction of children by parents is now a contemporary legal issue which baffles and mesmerizes different legal systems of nations whose *inter se* conflicting positions prevents return of children to the country of their habitual residence. Solace can be found *inter-se* between countries which are signatories to the Hague Convention on Civil Aspects of International Child Abduction, 1980. But what happens to those aggrieved parents who are not a part of this global conglomerate of like-minded nations who honour each other's laws? No global family law governs them. Defiant stands in different Courts of such jurisdictions create deadlocks. The sufferers are innocent children who are victimized by legal systems.

The world is a far smaller place now than it was a decade ago. Inter-country and inter-continental travel is easier and more affordable than it has ever been. The corollary to this is an increase in relationships between individuals of different ationalities and from different cultural backgrounds. Logically, the world in which we and our children live has grown immensely complex. It is filled with opportunities and risks. International mobility, opening up of borders, cross-border migration and dismantling of inter-cultural taboos have all the positive traits but are fraught with a new set of risks for children caught up in cross border situations. Caught in cross-fire of broken relationships with ensuing disputes over custody and relocation, the hazards of international abduction loom large over the chronic problems of maintaining access or contact internationally with the uphill struggle of securing cross-frontier child support. In a population of over 1.1 billion Indians, about 30 million are Non-Resident Indians living in 180 countries overseas, who by migrating to different jurisdictions have generated a new crop of spousal and family disputes.

### *1.1 Definition of child removal*

Families with connections to more than one country face unique problems if their relationship breaks down. The human reaction in this already difficult time is often to return to one's family and country of origin with the children of the relationship. If this is done without the approval of the other parent or permission from a Court, a parent taking children from one country to another may, whether inadvertently or not, be committing child removal or international child abduction. This concept is not clearly defined in any relevant legislation. As a matter of convention, it has come to mean the removal of a child from the care of the person with whom the child normally lives.

A broader definition encompasses the removal of a child from his/her environment, where the removal interferes with parental rights or right to contact. Removal in this context refers to removal by parents or members of the extended family. It does not include independent removal by strangers. The Convention on the Civil Aspects of International Child Abduction signed at the Hague on 25 October 1980 with 80 contracting countries today as parties from all regions of the globe, however defines removal or detention wrongful in the following words:

"Article 3: The removal or the retention of a child is to be considered wrongful where:

(a) it is in breach of rights of custody attributed to a person, an institution or any other body, either jointly or alone, under the law of the State in which the child was habitually resident immediately before the removal or retention; and

(b) at the time of removal or retention those rights were actually exercised, either jointly or alone, or would have been so exercised but for the removal or retention. The rights of custody mentioned in sub-paragraph (a) above, may arise in particular by operation of law or by reason of a judicial or administrative decision, or by reason of an agreement having legal effect under the law of that State."

Child removal does not find any specific definition in the Indian statute books and since India is not a signatory to the Hague Convention, there is no parallel Indian legislation enacted to give the force of law to the Hague Convention. Hence, in India all interpretations of the concept of child removal are based on judicial innovation in precedents of case-law decided by Indian Courts in disputes between litigating parents of Indian and/or foreign origin.

### *1.2 Global solutions and remedies*

The Hague Convention on Civil Aspects of International Child Abduction came into force on 1 December 1983 and now has 80 nations signed up to it. The objects of the Convention were:

(a) To secure the prompt return of children wrongfully removed to or retained in any Contracting State; and

(b) To ensure that rights of custody and of access under the law of one Contracting State are effectively respected in the other Contracting States.

It operates as an effective deterrent providing real and practical means of restoring the *status quo* prior to the abduction, prevents abductors from reaping the benefits of an act opposed to the interests of children, upholds the right of the child to maintain contact with both parents and introduces harmony where previously chaos prevailed. The Permanent Bureau of the Hague Conference on Private International Law at the Hague, Netherlands, renders a superb service by monitoring and helping the development of services to support effective implementation and consistent operation of the Hague Conventions and review their operations. Since, there is no centralised system of enforcement or interpretation, the Secretariat of the Hague Conferences guides nations in post convention services. In terms of the Hague Convention on Civil Aspects of

International Child Abduction, the Secretariat has published in three parts guides to good practice, namely Central Authority Practice, Implementing Measures and Preventing Measures which are all approved by Contracting States. The Secretariat thus helps to create an international medium of Consenting States who contract with each other to return children who are wrongfully removed.

***1.3 Why should India be interested in joining the Convention?***

The Hague Convention on the Civil Aspects of International Child Abduction is a remarkable document, which has had significant impact on child protection policies in much of the world. In a civilised society where globalisation and free interaction is part of a rapidly changing set-up, India is emerging as a major destination in the developing world. Non-Resident Indians have achieved laurels in all walks of life. But, back home, the problems on the family law front are largely unresolved. Times have changed but laws are still the same. Marriage, divorce, custody, maintenance and adoption laws in India need a makeover. Child removal is often treated as a custody dispute between parents for agitating and adjudicating rights of spouses while spontaneously extinguishing the rights of the child. Therefore, in an international perspective, four major reasons can be identified to establish and support the necessity of India's need to sign the Convention.

**Firstly,** India is no longer impervious to international child removal. In the absence of the Convention principles, the Indian Courts determine the child's best interest whereby any child removal is dealt with like any custody dispute. In this process, the litigation is a fight of superior rights of parties and the real issue of the welfare of the child becomes subservient and subordinate. Clash of parental interests and rights of spouses determine the question of custody. The most powerful parent succeeds in establishing his rights and the resultant determination of the best interest of the child is a misnomer and a misconception. Such a settlement is not truly in the best interest of the removed child.

**Secondly,** such a determination in India plays into the hands of the abducting parent and usurps the role of the Court which is best placed to determine the long-term interests of the child, namely the Court of the country where the child had his or her home before the wrongful removal or retention took place. By contrast, the advantage of the Hague Convention approach is that it quickly restores the position to what it was before the wrongful removal or retention took place and supports the proper role played by the Court in the country of the child's habitual residence. The correct law to be applied to the child would be of the country of the child's origin and so would be the Court of that country. In India, determination of rights as per Indian law of a foreign child removed to India by an offending parent may often be clouded and may not be in the best interest of the child and ought to be determined by the law and the Court of the child's origin.

**Thirdly**, the fact that India is not a party to the Hague Convention may have a negative influence on a foreign Judge who is deciding whether a child living with his/her parent in a foreign country should be permitted to spend time in India to enjoy contact with his/her Indian parent and extended family. Without the guarantee afforded by the Hague Convention to the effect that the child will be swiftly returned to the country of origin, the foreign Judge may be reluctant to give permission for the child to travel to India. As a logical corollary of this principle; membership of the Hague Convention will bring the prospect of achieving the return to India of children who have their homes in India but have been abducted to one of the 80 States that are parties to the Convention.

**Fourthly**, the Convention provides a structure for the resolution of issues of custody and contact which may arise when parents are separated and living in different countries. The Convention avoids the problems that may arise in Courts of different countries which are equally competent to decide such issues. The recognition and enforcement provisions of the Convention avoid the need for re-litigating custody and contact issues and ensure that decisions are taken by the authorities of the Country where the child was habitually resident before removal. It is thus hoped that India will give a serious consideration to joining the 1980 Hague Convention due to the convincing grounds cited above.

### *1.4 The UK judicial initiative*

In January 2005, the Right Honourable Lord Justice Thorpe at the Royal Courts of Justice, London was appointed Head of International Family Law for England and Wales. For the first time such a position has been created within the UK Judicial system. The appointment confirms the increasing importance attached to the development of international instruments and Conventions in a field of family law and to the value of international judicial collaboration, particularly in the extension of the Global network of liaison Judges specialising in family law. This may prompt some other jurisdictions in the world, whether or not they are signatories to the Hague Convention on Civil Aspects of International Child Abduction, 1980, to make similar appointments. In relation to wrongful removal or retention of children, as between UK and Pakistan, a protocol has been agreed between the President of the family division of the High Court of London and the Chief Justice of the Supreme Court of Pakistan for co-operation between the judicial authorities of the two countries and providing agreed procedures for dealing with such cases. India, however has not taken any steps in such regard.

## *2. Relevant legislation and forum for custody proceedings*

As far as the forum for securing the return of the children is concerned, it is important to take into account that India is not a signatory to the Hague Convention on the Civil Aspects of International Child Abduction 1980. Under article 226 of the Constitution of India, a parent whose child has been abducted can petition the State High Court to issue a Writ of *Habeas Corpus* against the abducting spouse for the return of the child. Alternatively, a *Habeas Corpus* petition seeking recovery of the abducted child can be directly filed in the Supreme Court of India under article 32 of the Constitution of India. Insofar as relating to the relevant legislation, the aggrieved parent could well seek recourse to the provisions of the Hindu Minority and Guardianship Act, 1956 (hereafter 'HMGA, 1956'), which is an Act to amend and codify certain parts of the law relating to minority and guardianship among Hindus. The provisions of the HMGA, 1956 are supplemental to the earlier Guardians and Wards Act 1890 (GWA). The HMGA, 1956, like the Hindu Marriage Act, 1955 (HMA), has extra-territorial application.

It extends to the whole of India except the State of Jammu and Kashmir. Under section 4(a) of the HMGA, 1956, 'minor' means a person who has not reached the age of 18 years and a 'guardian' in section 4(b) is defined as a person having the care of the person of the minor or of his property or both and includes a natural guardian, a guardian appointed by Will of his natural parents and a guardian appointed or declared by the Court and a person empowered to act as such under any enactment.

### *2.1 India and the Hague Convention on Civil Aspects of International Child Abduction 1980*

As of now, India is not a party to the Hague Convention on Civil Aspects of International Child Abduction, 1980. Other than the statutory provisions of law quoted above in which matters of child custody are agitated in different Courts in different proceedings, the principles of the Hague Convention cannot be enforced in Indian Courts. Different recent decisions indicate a trend that Indian Courts generally tend to decide the inter-parental child custody disputes on the paramount consideration of the welfare of the child and the best interest of the child. A foreign Court custody order is only one of the considerations in adjudicating any such child custody dispute between parents. Foreign Court orders of child custody are no longer mechanically enforced and normally the Courts go into the merits of the matter to decide the best interest of the child irrespective of any foreign Court custody order. Hence, the position of law in India varies from case-to-case basis and there is no uniform precedent which can be quoted or cited as a universal rule. India not being a signatory to the Hague Convention of 1980 on the Civil Aspects of International Child Abduction, questions regarding the custody of such children are now considered by the Indian Courts on the merits of each case bearing the welfare of the child to be of paramount importance while considering the order made by the foreign Court to be only one of the relevant factors in such decision.

### *2.2 The position of Indian law on child abduction*

Under article 214 of the Constitution of India, there shall be a High Court for each State in India and under article 124 there shall be a Supreme Court of India. Under article 141, the law declared by the Supreme Court shall be binding on all Courts within India. However, the Supreme Court may not be bound by its own earlier views and can render new decisions. Part III of the Constitution secures "Fundamental Rights" to citizens, which can be enforced directly in the respective High Courts of the States or directly in the Supreme Court of India by issue of prerogative Writs under articles 226 & 32 respectively of the Constitution of India. The High Courts and the Supreme Court in India entertain petitions for issuance of a Writ of *Habeas Corpus* for securing the custody of the minor at the behest of a parent who lands on Indian soil alleging violation of a foreign Court custody order or seeks the return of children to the country of their parent jurisdiction. Invoking of this judicial remedy provides the quickest and most effective speedy solution. Different High Courts within India have from time-to-time expressed different views in matters of inter-parental child custody petitions when their jurisdiction has been invoked by an aggrieved parent, seeking to enforce a foreign

Court custody order or implementation of their parental rights upon removal of the child to India without parental consent. The Supreme Court of India too has rendered different decisions with different viewpoints on the subject in the past three decades. A quick summary of Indian law laying down this position is as hereunder:

(i) In *Marggarate* v. *Chacko,* AIR 1970 Ker 1, in deciding if custody and care of a child could be entrusted to a parent who was living outside the country and outside the Court's jurisdiction, it was held that where the welfare of the child so demands, the Court can also permit the child to be taken out of the country by one of the parents, with proper safeguards laid down by the Court.

(ii) In *Marilynn Anita Dhillon Gilmore* v. *Margaret Nijjar*, 1984 (1) ILR 1 (P&H), in a *Habeas Corpus* petition, it was held that, respecting the order of the foreign Court, the custody of the children who were US nationals and who were brought to India from USA, should be returned to the mother as per the US Court order, subject to the safeguards of this Court.

(iii) In *Surinder Kaur* v. *Harbax Singh Sandhu*, 1984 HLR 780 SC, it was held that the provisions of the Hindu Minority and Guardianship Act, 1956 cannot supercede the paramount consideration as what is conducive to the welfare of the child while exercising summary jurisdiction in returning the minor children to the foreign country of their origin.

(iv) In *Elizabeth Dinshaw* v. *Arvand M. Dinshaw*, AIR 1987 SC 3, the Court again exercising summary return of a removed child upheld the right of a foreigner mother to directly invoke the jurisdiction of the Supreme Court to seek the custody of a minor child from his father on the principle that the matter is to be decided not on the considerations of the legal rights of the parties but on the sole and predominant criterion of the best interest of the minor child.

(v) In *Kuldeep Sidhu* v. *Chanan Singh*, AIR 1989 P&H 103, in a criminal writ petition exercising summary return, it was held that the welfare of the children who were Canadian citizens would override any consented custody arrangement and the children have a right to be brought up in the culture and environment of the country of their birth.

(vi) In *Amita Gautam* v. *Ramesh Gautam*, 1989 (2) HLR 385 (P&H), following the above decisions, it was held that the orders of the Canadian Court granting interim custody to the mother must be honoured by restoring forthwith the custody of the minor to the mother who had been removed from Canada to India by the father in an unauthorized manner not warranted by law.

(vii) In *Sarvajeet Kaur Mehmi* v. *State of Rajasthan*, 1987(2) HLR 607 (Raj), the custody of the minor child was given to the mother without hearing the father in view of the orders passed by the High Court of Justice (Family Division), UK requesting Courts in India to pass necessary orders and issue directions seeking the return of the minor back to UK from India.

(viii) In *Kala Aggarwal* v. *Suraj Prakash Aggarwal*, 1993 (1) HLR 145 (Del), despite the children having been brought to India from the USA in violation of US Court custody orders, the Court upholding the maintainability of the petition only granted access but declined to grant the custody to the mother by concluding that the children's welfare is with the father till they attain majority.

(ix) In *Jacqueline Kapoor* v. *Surinder Pal Kapoor*, 1994 (2) HLR 97 (P&H), following earlier precedents, the High Court upheld the mother's petition seeking custody of her minor female child in accordance with the orders of the Court of competent jurisdiction in Germany and directed that the child be handed over to the mother as the judgment of the German Court was binding on the father who had removed the child to India by deceitful means.

(x) In *Atya Shamim* v. *Deputy Commissioner/Collector, Delhi,* AIR 1999 J&K 140, in a *Habeas Corpus* petition by a person who was not a citizen of India, it was held to be maintainable to secure the custody of a minor.

(xi) In *Dhanwanti Joshi* v. *Madhav Unde*, 1998 (1) SCC 112, the Supreme Court observed that the order of the foreign Court will only be one of the facts which must be taken into consideration while dealing with child custody matters, and India being a country which is not a signatory to the Hague Convention, the law is that the Court within whose jurisdiction the child is removed will consider the question on the merits, the welfare of the child being of paramount importance. It is in this case that the Supreme Court changed the earlier view and did not exercise summary jurisdiction in returning removed children to their parent country by observing that the welfare and best interest of the child should be of paramount consideration.

(xii) The above observations by the Supreme Court of India was followed in its later decision in *Sarita Sharma* v. *Sushil Sharma*, JT 2000 (2) SC 258. Thereafter, in *Sahiba Ali* v. *State of Maharashtra*, 2004 (1) HLR 212, the Supreme Court declined to grant the custody of her children to the mother but at the same time issued directions for grant of visitation rights in the interest and welfare of the minor children.

(xiii) In *Paul Mohinder Gahum* v. *State of NCT of Delhi*, 2005 (1) HLR 428, upholding the maintainability of a *Habeas Corpus* petition, the High Court held that the orders passed by foreign Courts granting custody take a back seat in preference to what lies in the best interest of the minor rather than what a foreign Court has directed.

(xiv) In *Eugenia Archetti Abdullah* v. *State of Kerala*, 2005 (1) HLR 34 (Ker) upholding the right of the US citizen that is the petitioner mother before the Court in a *Habeas Corpus* Petition, the custody of the children was handed over to the mother after holding that the High Court can exercise such jurisdiction under article 226 of the Constitution of India.

(xv) In *Leeladhar Kachroo* v. *Umang Bhat Kachroo*, 2005 (2) HLR 449 (Del), upholding the order of a Canadian Court granting custody to the mother of her younger son and allowing him to go back to Canada, the Court upheld the contention and that it has the jurisdiction to order the minor child's leaving the country with one of the parents, and that the mere possibility of losing jurisdiction would not dissuade the Court from permitting the departure of the child with that parent if it is in the interests of the child. Hence, the Court held that it was empowered to entrust the custody of a child to a parent who resides outside its jurisdiction, if it is conducive to the welfare of the child.

(xvi) In *Paul Mohinder Gahun* v. *Selina Gahun*, 2007 (1) RCR (Civil), 129, it was held that where the wife, husband and the minor female child were all Canadian citizens, and where the wife had stealthily come to India with the minor daughter, the Indian Guardian Court at Delhi had no jurisdiction to try and decide the petition of the mother for a guardianship order as their matrimonial home was in Canada where the child was ordinarily resident.

(xvii) In a judgment dated 3 March, 2006 of the High Court of Bombay at Goa, reported as *Mandy Jane Collins* v. *James Michael Collins*, 2006 (2) HLR Bom 446, between a 62-year-old American father and 39-year-old British mother resident in Ireland who were litigating over the custody of their 8-year-old minor daughter said to be illegally detained in Goa by the father, the Court declined the issue of a Writ of *Habeas Corpus* and held that the parties could pursue their remedies in normal civil proceedings in Goa. The Court, dismissing the mother's plea for custody, concluded that the question of permitting the child to be taken to Ireland without first adjudicating upon the rival contentions of the parents in normal civil proceedings in Goa was not possible, and directed that the status quo be observed. This in effect means that the 8 year old minor female must continue to live in Goa without her mother or any other female family member in the father's house. In a challenge to this decision by the mother before the Supreme Court of India, the appeal was dismissed on 21 August 2006, leaving it open to the parties to move the appropriate forum for the custody of the child, which if done, was directed by the Supreme Court to be decided within a period of three months, with earlier visitation rights continuing to the mother.

(xviii) In another matter reported as *Ranbir Singh* v. *Satinder Kaur Mann*, 2006 (3) PLR 571, the Punjab and Haryana High Court declined to issue a Writ of *Habeas Corpus* to the petitioner father residing in Malaysia who was seeking release of his five year old son and three year old daughter from their mother's custody in India. The High Court of Malaya at Kuala Lumpur had held that the petitioner was entitled to the legal guardianship of the minor children. However, The High Court in India, declining to enforce the foreign judgment of the Malaysian High Court, held that the matter could be reactivated before the appropriate forum with regard to the custody of the children on the basis of evidence to be adduced by the parties. The *Habeas Corpus* Petition was dismissed with the observation that it would be open to either party to move for custody of the minor children under appropriate law before an appropriate forum.

(xix) In *Kulwinder Dhaliwal* v. *State of Punjab,* ILR 2008 (2) P&H 730, decided by the Punjab and Haryana High Court on 21 July 2008, on a Writ of *Habeas Corpus*, it was held that the orders of the foreign Court giving custody of the minors to the petitioner deserved to be respected, and the children were directed to be handed over to the petitioner with liberty to take them to Canada. The children were citizens of Canada and by an order passed by the Ontario Superior Court of Justice, the custody of the minors had been given to the petitioner.

(xx) In Criminal Writ Petition No. 1076 of 2008, *Paramjeet Kaur Toor* v. *Santosh Kaur*, decided by the Punjab and Haryana High Court on 19 November 2008, on a Writ of *Habeas Corpus* it was directed that the custody of the minor children, who were British nationals and who were detained by the grandparents in India, be handed over to the mother along with their passports to enable them to return to England, and that any contentions sought to be made can be thereafter agitated before the High Court of Justice, Family Division, London, which was at that point of time was already hearing the matter and had passed orders for the return of the children.

(xxi) In Criminal Writ Petition No. 608 of 2008, *Manjit Kaur* v. *State of Punjab*, decided by the Punjab and Haryana High Court on 14 August 2008, where a minor child of 9 months was taken away by his grandparents when their Non-Resident Indian daughter-in-law had come from abroad for a short period, the High Court held that the *Habeas Corpus* petition filed by her was maintainable as the child had been illegally snatched away from the mother. The custody of the minor child was given to the mother leaving the parties to avail other remedies in accordance with law.

(xxii) In Criminal Writ Petition No. 543 of 2008, *Gippy Arora* v. *State of Punjab*, decided by the Punjab and Haryana High Court on 25 November 2008, the Court, after examining the entire law on the subject, held in a case of domestic child abduction that a Writ of *Habeas Corpus* should not be dismissed merely because it is for the Court of the Guardian Judge to determine the question of welfare of the minor child in custody of another person. Consequently, the minor child was directed to be handed over to the mother till the matter was finally decided by the Family Court or the Court of the Guardian Judge.

(xxiii) In *Gurmeet Kaur Batth* v. *State of Punjab,* 2009 (2) PLR 250 (P&H), the High Court held that it can exercise jurisdiction vested in it under article 226 of the Constitution of India by issue of the Writ of *Habeas Corpus* when the custody of the child had been taken away by one of the natural guardians playing a trick upon the other. Relying on the Canadian Court Order in favour of the petitioner mother, the Court held that since the Court of competent jurisdiction in Canada had held that the mother was entitled to the custody of the child, she would be permitted to take the child to Canada.

(xxiv) In *Shilpa Aggarwal* v. *Aviral Mittal*, 2010 (1) SCC 591, a three-and-ahalf-year-old female child, who was a British citizen born in UK to Indian parents, was removed to India from UK by the mother in contravention of British Court orders. The mother was directed by the Supreme Court of India to return with the child to UK.

(xxv) In *Dr. V. Ravi Chandaran* v. *Union of India*, 2010 (1) SCC 174, a seven-year-old boy, who was a US citizen and was born in USA to Indian parents (who had become US citizens), was removed to India from the USA by the mother, contrary to US Court orders. The mother was directed by the Supreme Court of India to return to USA with the child failing which the father would be entitled to do so.

(xxvi) In *Vikramvir Vohra* v. *Shalini Bhalla*, JT 2010 (3) SC 213, it was held by the Supreme Court of India that child custody orders are interlocutory in nature and can be altered for the welfare of the child. Consequently, the Supreme Court permitted the mother to take her minor son, aged about ten years old, to Australia in accordance with the wishes of the child to stay with the mother, upholding the welfare of the child as a paramount consideration. The above is the consolidated case-law summary on the proposition of inter-parental child removal with regard to cases of removal of children from foreign jurisdiction to India and their decisions in different Courts in India as a non-convention country.

(xxvii) In a Supreme Court judgment in the case of *Ruchi Majoo v. Sanjeev Majoo*, JT 2011 (6) SC 167, the wife left her husband in the US and returned to India with her son. She moved a Delhi Guardian Court and got custody rights. In a suit filed by her estranged husband claiming that his wife had abducted the child, a US Court issued a red corner notice against the wife directing her return to USA. In an appeal before the Delhi High Court, it set aside the order of the Delhi Guardian Judge directing the couple to submit before a US Court as they were all US nationals ordinarily residing in USA. The Delhi High Court ruled that the Guardian Judge had no jurisdiction to entertain the wife's petition. The wife appealed to Supreme Court. Thereupon, the Apex Court has set aside the judgment of the Delhi High Court and directed that the proceedings shall go on before the Delhi Guardian Judge to be disposed off as expeditiously as possible. Till then, the interim custody will remain with the mother and the father will enjoy visitation rights only.

**Conclusion of case-law analysis**

An analysis of the Indian case-law reveals that until 1997, Indian Courts whenever approached by an aggrieved parent invariably exercised a power of summary return of a removed child to the country of habitual residence in compliance with a foreign Court order to restore parental rights. However, changing the precedent, in 1998, the Indian Supreme Court decided that a custody order of a foreign Court should be only one consideration while determining the matters on merits, in which the welfare of the child will be of paramount importance. Thereafter, child removal and custody matters now get decided on the merits in India, and every individual decision is based on the facts of the case and there is no set pattern of decisions consistently being followed. However, a different trend set by some of the recent decisions above indicates that aggrieved parents who invoke the jurisdiction of the High Court in a Writ of *Habeas Corpus* are not non-suited simply for the reason that the determination of the best interest of the child can be done only by an adjudicatory process in the Family Court or before the Guardian Judge. The *Habeas Corpus* remedy to enforce the child custody order of a foreign Court is proving to be effective and result oriented. These recent decisions also indicate a trend in respecting foreign Court orders wherein an aggrieved parent seeks return of the removed child on the strength of such foreign Court decisions. The position however varies on the facts and circumstances of each case.

***2.3 Position of foreign Court orders in India***

The principles governing the validity of foreign Court orders are laid down in section 13 of the Indian Code of Civil Procedure (CPC). The CPC is an Act to consolidate and amend the laws relating to the procedure of the Courts of Civil Judicature in India. The principles in section 13 CPC have been affirmed in relation to the guidelines laid down by the Supreme Court of India on recognition of foreign matrimonial judgments It is reiterated, as discussed above, that Indian Courts would not exercise summary jurisdiction to return the children to the country of habitual residence. The Courts consider the question on the merits of the matter, with the welfare of the children being of paramount importance. Section 14 of the CPC relates to presumption as to foreign judgments. It provides that the Court shall presume, upon the production of any document purporting to be a certified copy of a foreign judgment, that such judgment was pronounced by a Court of competent jurisdiction, unless the contrary appears on the record, but that such presumption may be displaced by proving want of jurisdiction.

***2.4 No provision for mirror orders in India***

In light of the prevailing child abduction law in India discussed above, it is not possible to obtain mirror orders, as this is a concept known to the English, but not to the Indian, legal system. Since foreign Court custody orders cannot now be mechanically enforced, it is suggested that, in the event of any litigation in the foreign country of habitual residence, a letter of request be obtained from the foreign Court in which litigation is pending for incorporating safeguards and conditions to ensure the return of the minor child to the country of normal residence.

This letter of request should be addressed by the foreign Court to the Registrar-General of the High Court within whose jurisdiction the estranged spouse is residing with the minor child. It should also be specifically mentioned that the passports of both the parent and the child should be deposited with the Registrar-General of the State High Court to ensure that the child is not taken away from the jurisdiction of the Court where he or she is confined.

### *3. A possible solution*

With the increasing number of Non-Resident Indians abroad and multiple problems arising leading to family conflicts, inter-parental child removal to India now needs to be resolved on an international platform. It is no longer a local problem. The phenomenon is global. Steps have to be taken by joining hands globally to resolve these conflicts through the medium of Courts interacting with each other. While India does not become a signatory to the Hague Convention, this may not be possible. A time has now come where it is not possible for the Indian Courts to stretch their limits to adapt to different foreign Court Orders arising in different jurisdictions. It is equally important that to create a uniform policy of law some clear, authentic and universal child custody law is enacted within India by adhering to the principles laid down in the Hague Convention. Divergent views emerging at different times may not be able to cope with the rising number of such cases, which come up from time-to-time for interpretation. We in India are thus hoping for an expeditious acceptance and implementation of the international principles of inter-parental child removal which are couched in the Hague Convention. Let us not delay the path to resolution of these disputes.

### *3.1 Law in the making: an aftermath Borders divide jurisdictions but families reunite them.*

The chain to this link is the global citizen. However, this inter-nation cross-flow has with the passage of time generated a new crop of legal issues in the realm of private international law comprising rules a Court would apply whenever there is a case involving a foreign element. Such legal dilemmas of the diaspora baffle systems of law but do not defy solutions if nations make sincere efforts for resolving such complications.

A fugitive Non-Resident Indian (NRI) parent declared a proclaimed offender in matrimonial proceedings in India cannot even see or talk to his children removed to India. A foreign Court refuses to permit NRI children to be taken to India and likewise local Courts decline to implement foreign Court orders directing return of NRI children. These occurrences find daily mention but no straightforward resolution for the NRI in any Indian law. International parental child abduction, defined as the removal or retention of a child across international borders by one parent which is either in contravention of Court orders or is without the consent of the other parent, is sadly an increasing phenomenon which causes acute emotional distress to the abducted child. Happily, now this acute problem of the 30 million Indian Diaspora (which is still growing) has precipitated the process of the Government acceding to the Hague Convention on Civil Aspects of International Child Abduction. However, before that is done, and India becomes a member of the group of 80 or so contracting convention nations, appropriate Indian legislation will have to be enacted for its implementation. In this way children removed to and from India will be re-united with their aggrieved parent and India will no longer be a sought after destination for parking removed NRI children from foreign jurisdictions. Also, foreign Courts will be encouraged to permit NRI children to freely visit India without fear of abduction. The draft of the Indian Civil Aspects of International Child Abduction Bill 2007, meant to secure the prompt return of children wrongfully retained or removed to India, proposes to ensure that the rights of custody and access under laws of Contracting States are respected by providing for prompt removal of wrongfully removed children. The salient and salutary features of this proposed law are as follows.

• The proposed law seeks to create a Central authority for performance of duties under the Hague Convention for securing the return of removed children by instituting judicial proceedings in the High Court concerned.

• The appropriate authority of a contracting country may apply to the Central authority for return of a removed child to the country of habitual residence.

• The High Court may order return of a removed child to the country of habitual residence but may refuse to make such an order if there is grave risk of harm or if it would put the child in an intolerable situation. Consent or acquiescence may also lead to refusal for return of a child by the Court.

• The High Court may refuse to return a child if the child objects to being returned upon the Court being satisfied that the child has attained an age and degree of maturity to take into account his views.

• The High Court, before making an order of return, may request the Central authority to obtain from the relevant authorities of the country of habitual residence, a decision or determination as to whether the removal or retention of the child in India is wrongful.

• The High Court upon making an order of return may direct that the person who has removed the child to India pay the expenses and costs incurred in returning the child to the country of habitual residence. The sacrosanct feature, in recognizing and retaining the jurisdiction of the High Court to protect the paramount consideration i.e the best interest and the welfare of the child, by carving out exceptions for grounds of refusal, has upheld the majesty of law vested in the Indian Courts. But at the same time, this welcome law will be a great relief to distraught children who have been removed from their parents. The temptation to remove wrongfully will also be deterred. The cruel abduction of NRI children for the purposes of forced marriages will also be checked.

### *3.2 Plugging the holes: suggestions for amendments*

Though the efforts to make the Civil Aspects of International Child Abduction Bill, 2007 are salutary, in view of certain beneficial provisions of the Hague Convention on Civil Aspects of International Child Abduction, the following suggestions could be advanced to improve the proposed Indian law which is based on the domestic Sri Lankan legislation. These suggestions are as follows:

(a) The preamble of the proposed bill must open with the words "That the interests of children are of paramount importance in matters relating to their custody" as is stated in the Hague Convention.

(b) Section 1 or any other introductory section must clarify about the applicability of the Act to state that it would be applicable to every child removed or retained in India within the meaning of the Act from his or her country of habitual residence irrespective of religion, nationality, residence, domicile or status in India. This is necessary because of children of foreign nationals and professing different religions are often brought to India in violation of foreign Court orders. Lest, any objection arise, the Act must clarify that it would be applicable to children of all religions or nationality who are removed to India. The terms High Court, appropriate authority and specify country will require to be defined in section 2 of the proposed Act.

(c) Section 4 of the proposed law, while considering the qualification for appointment of the chairperson and members of the Central Authority, should bear in mind that they will need to have adequate knowledge and experience in "International Child Abduction, access, custody and related issues. An effective Central Authority can be a solitary legally qualified director assisted by case workers rather than *ex-officio*/non official members. The composition of the Central Authority should be as minimal as possible and all such appointments should be left to the exclusive discretion of the Supreme Court.

(d) Article 11 of the Convention enjoins a period of six weeks for an expeditious disposal of the proceedings before the judicial or administrative authority of the Contracting State. Sections 9 and 10 of the proposed law do not contain any time frame for such expeditious disposal. This time period to be specified in proceedings before the Central authority/High Court is very essential, since these proceedings are intended to be of a summary and expedient nature and delay is inimical to a child's best interest.

(e) The exclusive use of specialist or designated Judges in every High Court of every state may be necessary since unlike U.K which has 18 specialist Judges of the Family Division to hear the Convention proceedings, India with neither a Family Division nor a specialist family law judiciary may find it difficult to cope with Convention proceedings. Likewise specialist practitioners in the field of International Child Abduction will be required for assistance. Similarly, training of judges by specialists in the field of International Child Abduction will be essential for an understanding of the Hague Convention and the new proposed Indian law.

(f) For effective operation, the Central authority must be able to communicate with at least two liaison Judges, as is the statutory precedent in the Netherlands. The UK has the benefit of a Judge in the Court of Appeal acting as Head of International Family Law, who assists in liaising with the Judges abroad. In India too, such an office will need to be created. Even the Chairperson of the Central Authority should ideally be a Judge who can communicate effectively with the High Courts, to secure a smooth resolution of overseas child abduction disputes.

(g) A provision should be added for providing interim powers to move the High Court concerned to give such interim directions as necessary for the purpose of securing the welfare of the child or for preventing changes in the circumstances relevant to the determination of the case. This is suggested because there is no provision for interim directions in this new law.

(h) Another effective provision that needs to be added relates to the power to order disclosure of a child's whereabouts. Owing to the size of India, which is spread over an area of 3.28 million sq. kms. in 28 States and 7 Union Territories, it may be necessary to secure information about the child's whereabouts, or removal and harm to the child can result. Disclosure orders may be necessary to elicit information about the child's location. Thus, a penal provision to effect this may be necessary, otherwise the proceedings may be frustrated. Further, to provide territorial limits, section 9 ought to specify that the Central authority may apply to the High Court within whose territorial jurisdiction the child is physically present after being removed from a foreign jurisdiction.

(i) A deterrent of providing an effective mode of recovering costs for the aggrieved spouse is necessary. Hence, a section needs to be incorporated in the proposed law to ensure the true spirit of the rule that "costs must follow the event." This will deter future child removals and provide actual monetary recompense.

(j) The necessity of a section to permit making of procedural rules is of extreme importance as they lend great assistance. Hence, rules of procedure regarding making of applications before the Central authority and/or other requirements must be made a part of the new proposed Indian law. Hopefully the law is still in the making and has not yet been codified. The discussion is still pending and the Bill has not achieved finality. May be with the passage of time, more suggestions and views may mature it fully.

**4. Some experiences with Hague Convention countries**

There are two instances of removal of children from India to a Hague Convention country. Experience of these cases indicate that in such matters when children are removed from India to a convention country, either against parental consent or by violating Indian Court custody orders, the convention country has sought not to send them back summarily. Rather, the convention country Courts have chosen to determine the best interest of the child, thereby abandoning the summary return principle of sending the child back to the country of habitual residence. Since these two matters are still in the process of final adjudication, they are being referred to in hypothetical terms.

In the first instance a minor child was removed from India by a relative to a convention country in violation of an Indian Court custody order and against the consent of both the parents. Upon the writer's assistance to the Court as an amicus curiae, it transpired that the travel documents used by the relative to travel to the convention country violated Indian laws, and there was a clear case of overstaying in the convention country in violation of visa regulations. Regardless of this, the Courts of the convention country initially continued to determine the child's best interests in an environment and conditions which are alien to the child. Initially, the orders of the Indian Court seeking return of the child to determine its welfare went unheeded. Ultimately, when the Court of the Convention Country directed the return of the removed child back to India, the child was mysteriously abducted again whilst at school in the convention country. As a result, the indulgence granted to a fugitive of Indian laws by a convention country, which was totally inconsistent with the principles of the Hague Convention, led the small child to be used as a pawn for asylum being claimed by the abducting relative. Ultimately, whenever the child returns to India, a long lapse of time may create new problems for the removed child. The untold suffering and the misery of the parents and the child is distressing. In the second instance of the writer's assisting the Court of a convention country as a joint expert on behalf of the parties, the minor children were taken by one of the parents from India to a convention country purportedly for a holiday, but did not return to India. In response to the other parent's claim for return of the children to India, alleged domestic violence and safety issues were voiced. The matter is currently under examination before the convention country's Court to decide whether or not the children and the parent should go back to the country of habitual residence. The larger issue again would be as to which country's Court is the best forum to decide or adjudicate upon the welfare of the minors. Is it the country where the children are now resident or is it the country where the children were habitually resident? Does the Hague Convention Country make a departure in dealing with non convention countries in such a situation? This is a poser which needs to be elaborated and dwelt upon at a forum looking at the practical issues and lessons learnt in the implementation of the Hague Convention. Non-convention countries could adapt the answers for their own guidance. Furthermore, what should be the procedure in dealing with child removal matters when children are removed from non-convention countries to convention countries? Does the convention provide a side window for dealing on separate principles? How would the Courts of convention countries make departures in this regard? What is the message that a non-convention country's Court gets in the adjudication of such disputes in a convention country's Court? Is the principle of reciprocity disturbed? Should it not revert to the best interest principle in totality? Can it be said that a child in a foreign country, uprooted from his or her habitual residence, is in a position to judge his welfare and best interest? Could a temporary residence in a convention country be apt for determination of the child's best interests? Would it be appropriate to determine the child's best interest in the country of habitual residence? Can the abducting parent or relative be given the advantage of his or her own wrong by providing residence in a convention country when clearly the laws of a non-convention country or parental rights have been violated? Is it fair to expect an aggrieved parent to travel to the convention country to contest legal proceedings at considerable expense, costs and time, to press his or her rightful claim over protracted legal proceedings in the convention country? What law will apply in such circumstances to the removed child i.e. the law of the convention country which is the temporary residence or the law of the non-convention country which is the country of habitual residence? Will such precedents retard the process of having more signatory countries to the Hague Convention? These are some issues which may arise for determination and different viewpoints may emerge on these perspectives.

**5. Conclusion**

With the increasing number of Non-Resident Indians abroad and multiple problems arising leading to family conflicts, inter-parental child removal to and from India now needs to be resolved on an international platform. It is no longer a local problem. The phenomenon is global. Steps have to be taken by joining hands globally to resolve these conflicts through the medium of Courts interacting with each other. While India does not become a signatory to the Hague Convention, this may not be possible. A time has now come where it is not possible for the Indian Courts to stretch their limits to adapt to different foreign Court orders arising in different jurisdictions. It is equally important that to create a uniform policy of law some clear, authentic and universal child custody law is enacted within India by adhering to the principles laid down in the Hague Convention. Divergent views emerging at different times may not be able to cope with the rising number of such cases. We in India are thus hoping for an expeditious acceptance and implementation of the international principles of inter-parental child removal which are couched in the Hague Convention. Let us not delay the path to resolution of these disputes. Removed children cannot be allowed to live in a no-man's island.

# KEY INBOUND BUSINESS IMMIGRATION AND EMPLOYMENT ISSUES: RELOCATION OF FOREIGN BUSINESS PERSONNEL IN INDIA

This chapter addresses several new issues of practical concern in view of the increase in immigration of multinational business executives into India. The focus of this chapter is to highlight key business immigration issues regarding foreign personnel sought to be relocated in India, conditions to be complied with for short-term engagement of foreign nationals by Indian firms/companies, taxation of foreign nationals in India, legal provisions prohibiting dual nationality, provisions relating to newly introduced overseas citizenship and the penal consequences, arising from violations by business personnel in the context of immigration law requirements. Also, there is reference to the newly carved out Persons of Indian origin and the Overseas Citizens of India schemes. Persons of Indian Origin resident overseas qualifying in these two categories can derive immense benefits if they are looking to work in India. Towards the conclusion of the chapter, a case has been made out for India, to have a new set of consolidated rules focusing exclusively on business immigration into India, and as also for the introduction of a work permit scheme in the changing market conditions.

India clearly remains an attractive destination for foreign investors the world over. The UK and the USA are among the top ten foreign investors in India and increasing numbers of their citizens are coming to India for business reasons. The massive recent liberalisation of the Indian economy has promoted innumerable joint venture investments which involve the movement of manpower, machinery and technology. This chapter seeks to update immigration practitioners advising business personnel on relocation to India. In addition, brief reference is made to extension and variation of business visas, foreign exchange regulations, citizenship in India and questions of dual nationality, which is relevant in the context of the theme of the chapter.

## FOREIGNERS LEGISLATION

The principal Indian legislation regarding foreigners is contained in the Foreigners Act, 1946, which also provides for framing of relevant rules regulating the registration of foreigners. The 1946 Act also stipulates strict formalities with regard to the presence and movement of foreigners in India and their subsequent departure. Section 3 of the 1946 Act details the objectives of this enactment and provides as follows:

> The provisions contained in the above-mentioned legislation, make it quite clear that unfettered powers have been conferred on the Indian Government for regulating and restricting the movement and presence of foreigners in

India. It appears that, historically, the prime concern has been to safeguard the interests of national security. Furthermore, rule 6 of the Registration of Foreigner's Rules, 1992 details relevant procedures for the registration of foreigners visiting India. Under rule 6, a foreigner entering India on a valid visa for a period of more than one hundred and eighty days should present the registration report, as specified by the registration officer at the port or other place of arrival.

Rule 7(2) of the 1992 Rules provides that this registration report shall be presented within two weeks of the foreigner's arrival in India. Under rule 7(3), every foreigner, besides presenting a registration report to the registration officer, is duty-bound to furnish any relevant information in his/her possession to satisfy the registration officer of the authenticity of the particulars provided. The foreigner is also required to sign the registration report and is then entitled to receive a certificate of registration from the relevant officer.

Under rule 9 of the 1992 Rules, every registered foreigner is legally obliged to produce his/her certificate of registration within 24 hours of a demand being made by any registration officer, magistrate or police officer for the purpose of inspection, although discretion is given to the concerned officer to extend the time. It is also incumbent on returning foreign visitors, under rule 15 of the 1992 Rules, to surrender their certificate of registration prior to departure. Visiting foreigners who contravene any of the directions incorporated in the certificate of registration render themselves liable to penalties prescribed under section 14 of the 1946 Act.

The rigour of the penal consequences under the 1946 Act was highlighted by the Supreme Court of India already in 1955 in the matter of *Hans Muller* v *Superintendent Presidency Jail, Calcutta,* AIR 1955 SC 367. It was held (at page 374):

> 'The Foreigners Act confers the power to expel foreigners from India. It vests the Central Government with absolute and unfettered discretion and, as there is no provision fettering this discretion in the Constitution, an unrestricted right to expel remains'.

The relevant law was subsequently discussed in an important case which reflects the particular security concerns of Indian officials when dealing with Pakistani citizens. It was held in *Khalil Ahmad* v. *State of Uttar Pradesh,* AIR 1962 All 383 (at page 390):

> "It is true that there is no specific rule for obtaining a "permit" by a foreigner from the Registration Officer, but it may be implied from the fact that every foreigner entering India is required to present in person to the Registration Officer a registration report of his arrival in India, on the basis of which he is granted a certificate of registration duly endorsed by the Registration Officer. This certificate of registration is nothing else than a "permit" issued to the foreigner indicating the date of his arrival and the period during which he is permitted to stay in the country."

The Supreme Court's position in *Hans Muller* v. *Superintendent, Presidency Jail, Calcutta,* (supra), was followed by the Calcutta High Court in *A.H. Magermans* v. *S.K. Ghose,* AIR 1966 Cal 552. In this case, the petitioner had failed to get himself registered any where in India in accordance with the 1939 Rules. He had also not filed any application for extension of his visa. Accordingly, it was held that the order of deportation did not suffer from any infirmity. The High Court of Himachal Pradesh, in *Fred Howard Haering* v. *State of Himachal Pradesh*, AIR 1996 HP 27, reiterated the above-mentioned three rulings.

## RESTRICTIONS ON THE EMPLOYMENT OF FOREIGNERS

The power to grant or refuse permission to foreigners to enter India and subsequent restrictions on employment has been provided in the Foreigners Order of 1948.

Further, under section 10 of the 1948 Order, restrictions on the employment of foreigners in public sector undertakings have been provided. This section states that no foreigner shall, without the written permission of the civil authority, engage in employment in any public sector undertaking supplying electricity, power, water and petroleum products. Here again, it will be noticed that protection of matters of national importance and security appear to be of paramount concern. Unlike Dubai, expatriates cannot possibly occupy key positions in public sector undertakings.

Section 10 of the 1948 Order has to be read in conjunction with the provisions of the newly introduced Foreign Exchange Management Act, 1999 (hereafter FEMA, 1999), which came into force on 1 June, 1999. The FEMA, 1999, consolidates and amends the law relating to: (i) foreign exchange with the objective of facilitating external trade and payments; and (ii) for promoting the orderly development and maintenance of foreign exchange market in India. The Act also applies to:

(a) all branches, offices and agencies outside India when owned or controlled by a person resident in India; and

(b) also to any contravention there under committed outside India by any person to whom the Act applies.

The requirements regarding business and employment visas as stipulated by the Government of India are discussed hereunder:

## WORK-RELATED VISAS: BUSINESS VISAS AND EMPLOYMENT VISAS

Business visas are designated as *'B'* visas. While employment visas designated are as *'E'* visas. The key issues regarding both these sets of visas are tabulated hereunder:—

**BUSINESS VISAS:** A Business visa may be granted to a foreigner for the following purposes:—

(i) Foreign nationals who wish to visit India to establish industrial/business venture or to explore possibilities to set up industrial/business venture in India;

(ii) Foreign nationals coming to India to purchase/sell industrial products or commercial products or consumer durables;

(iii) Foreign nationals coming to India for technical meetings/discussions, attending board meetings or general meetings for providing business services support;

(iv) Foreign nationals coming to India for recruitment of manpower;

(v) Foreign nationals who are partners in the business and/or functioning as Directors of the company;

(vi) Foreign nationals coming to India for consultations regarding exhibitions or for participation in exhibitions, trade fairs, business fairs etc;

(vii) Foreign buyers who come to transact business with suppliers/potential suppliers at locations in India, to evaluate or monitor quality, give specifications, place orders, negotiate further supplies etc., relating to goods or services procured from India;

(viii) Foreign experts/specialists on a visit of short duration in connection with an ongoing project with the objective of monitoring the progress of the work, conducting meetings with Indian customers and/or to provide technical guidance;

(ix) Foreign nationals coming to India for pre-sales or post-sales activity not amounting to actual execution of any contract or project;

(x) Foreign trainees of multinational companies/corporate houses coming for in-house training in the regional hubs of the concerned company located in India;

(xi) Foreign students sponsored by AIESEC for internship on project based work in companies/industries;

(xii) Foreign nationals coming as tour conductors and travel agents and / or conducting business tours of foreigners or business relating to it, etc.

**Duration of Business Visas:** A Business visa with multiple entry facility can be granted for a period up to five (5) years or for a shorter duration as per the requirement. A stay stipulation of a maximum period of six (6) months will be prescribed for each visit by the concerned Indian Mission keeping in view the nature of the business activity for which such Business visa is granted. In case Missions/Posts abroad, while issuing Business visa, decide to prescribe a stay stipulation of maximum 6 months for each visit, a clear endorsement should be made stating **"each stay not to exceed 6 months (*or the duration of stay stipulation*) and registration not required".** In case no such stay stipulation is being prescribed, a simple endorsement stating **"registration within 14 days"** should be made.

Indian Missions can grant Business visa with 10 years validity and multiple entry facility to the nationals of the United States of America. This visa should be issued with the stipulation that the stay in India during each visit shall not exceed six (6) months.

**Main supporting documentation**: The person applying for a Business visa is required to fulfill the following conditions before the visa is granted:

(i) The foreign national must have a valid travel document and a re-entry permit, if required under the law of the country of nationality of the applicant;

(ii) The foreign national should be a person of assured financial standing. The foreigner must submit proof of his/her financial standing and documentation in support of intended business visit to India. Proof of his financial standing and expertise in the field of intended business will be checked thoroughly by the Indian Missions while granting the visa;

(iii) The foreign national should not be visiting India for the business of money lending or for running a petty business or petty trade or for full time employment in India, etc;

(iv) The foreign national shall comply with all other requirements like payment of tax liabilities etc.

(v) The Business visa must be issued from the country of origin or from the country of habitual domicile of the foreigner provided the period of residence of that foreigner in that particular country is more than 2 years. If the period of permanent residence of the applicant in the particular country is less than two years, the Mission/Post concerned will issue Business visa only after personal interview, review of documentation and prior clearance from the Mission where the applicant has permanent residence. Such cases will be examined by the Missions/Posts on merits on case-to-case basis and, after issue of Business visa, intimation will be sent to the Indian Mission/Post in the applicant's country of origin;

(vi) The documents/papers pertaining to proposed business activity such as the registration of the company under the Companies Act, proof of registration of the firm with the State Industries Department or the Export Promotion Council concerned or any recognised promotional body in the relevant field of industry or trade etc. will be thoroughly checked to decide the category of visa applicable to the foreigner;

(vii) The grant of Business visa is subject to any instructions issued by the Government of India on the basis of reciprocity with other foreign countries from time to time.

**EMPLOYMENT VISAS:** The key features of an Employment visa are as follows:

(i) Employment visas are granted to foreigners desirous of coming to India for the purpose of employment;

(ii) Applicant should be skilled and qualified professionals or persons who are being engaged or appointed by a company, organisation, industry, or undertaking, etc. in India on contract or employment basis at a senior level, or alternatively in skilled positions such as technical experts, senior executives, or either in a managerial position, etc;

(iii) Employment visas are not granted for jobs for which large numbers of qualified Indians are available;

(iv) Employment visas are not granted for routine, ordinary or secretarial/ clerical jobs;

(v) Employment visas are issued from the country of origin, or from the country of domicile of the foreigner, provided the period of permanent residence of that applicant in that particular country is for more than 2 years;

(vi) Indian company/organization engaging foreign nationals for executing projects/contracts to be responsible for the conduct of the foreign national during their stay in India and also for the departure of such foreign national upon expiry of visa;

(vii) It is mandatory for the concerned foreign national to comply with all other statutory requirements like payment of tax liabilities, etc;

(viii) The documents/papers pertaining to the proposed employment, like the registration of the company under the Companies Act, proof of registration of the firm in the State Industries Department or the Export Promotion Council concerned, or any recognized promotional body in the field of industry and trade etc will be thoroughly checked to decide the category of visa that may be issued to the foreigner;

(ix) It is mandatory for the Employment visas holders to register with concerned Foreigners Registration Officer/Foreigners Regional Registration Officer within two weeks from the date of arrival. This is a very important requirement. Failure to register in this regard entails very serious consequences;

(x) The name of the sponsoring employer/organization shall be clearly stipulated in the visa sticker.

**Duration of Employment visas:** The duration of Employment visas of different kinds are as follows:

(i) A foreign technician/expert coming to India in pursuance of a bilateral agreement between the Government of India and the foreign Government, or in pursuance of a collaboration agreement that has been approved by the Government of India, can be granted an Employment visa for the duration of the agreement, or for a period of five years, whichever is less, with multiple entry facilities.

(ii) In the case of highly skilled foreign personnel being employed in the IT software and IT enabled sectors, the Missions/Posts can grant Employment visa with validity up to 3 years or the term of assignment, whichever is less, with multiple entry facility.

(iii) A foreigner coming to India for employment not covered in (i) or (ii) above can be granted Employment visa with validity up to two years or the term of assignment, whichever is less, with multiple entry facility.

(iv) The Employment visa may be extended by the State Governments/UTs/FRROs/FROs beyond the initial visa validity period, up to a total period of 5 years from the date of issue of the initial Employment visa, on an year to year basis, subject to good conduct, production of necessary documents in support of continued employment, filing of Income tax returns and no adverse security inputs about the foreigner. The period of extension shall not exceed five years from the date of issue of the initial Employment visa.

**Supporting documentation**: The foreign national must have a valid travel document, a re-entry permit, employment/engagement contract, documentary proof of his educational qualifications and professional expertise. Practical experience suggests that for both the categories of above-mentioned visas, the documentation should be as comprehensive as much as possible.

**Latest Government of India Guidelines for obtaining Employment visas:** As per the modified guidelines of the Ministry of Home Affairs, issued on 30 September 2010, a foreign national being sponsored for an Employment visa in any sector should draw a salary in excess of US$ 25,000 per annum. However, this condition is not applicable to ethnic cooks, language teachers (other than English language teachers), translators and staff working for the concerned Foreign Missions in India.

The salary threshold limit of US $ 25,000 per annum would be worked out taking into account salary and other allowances paid to the expatriate/foreign employees in India. This limit would be exclusive of perquisites like housing, telephone, transport, entertainment etc. which are received in kind.

Foreign nationals who have arrived in India on the basis of Employment visas issued **after 1 November 2010 and drawing salary of less than US $25,000** would be registered by the concerned FRRO/FRO but all such foreigners would be granted EXIT by giving a maximum period of three months. Technically, such foreign employees should have made an exit from their Indian employment, as of date.

Foreign nationals who have been issued Employment visas **prior to 1 November 2010 and drawing a salary of less than US $25,000** would be allowed to continue in their present employment till the expiry of their present visa period.

Foreign nationals undertaking modelling assignments, dance shows, advertisements, bollywood etc. with different companies would be allowed to register but would be granted three months time to submit documentary proof to the effect that they would be getting remuneration of at least US $25,000 per annum. If they are not able to produce documentary proof to this effect, they may be granted immediate exit after 3 months from the date of their initial registration.

## RECENT DEVELOPMENTS REGARDING POSITION OF CONVERSION OF BUSINESS VISAS INTO EMPLOYMENT VISAS: GOVERNMENT NOW GETS TOUGH ON BUSINESS VISAS FOR FOREIGN EMPLOYEES: THE RISKS OF USING A BUSINESS VISA INSTEAD OF A REGULAR WORK/ EMPLOYMENT VISA

In theory, the immigration rules stipulate Business visas shall be non-convertible and non extendable beyond 5 years from the date of issue. Extension beyond the five year period in actual practice are very difficult, but the variation of leave from a Business visa to an Employment visa is remotely possible, only case specific, depending on the discretion of the Ministry of Home Affairs, at New Delhi. The principal employer, whether in India or abroad, "should be extremely wary," about the fact that such a permission is highly unlikely to be granted. Speaking from experience, this option should be exercised when a lot is at stake in connection with the presence of the foreign employee. Couple of instances may warrant such a situation:

The presence of the employee is indispensable to the organisation as part of ongoing commitments. Secondly, the foreign employers fear that if such an employee is sent back to the parent country, there may be substantial delay in processing of his/her visa or the worst fear is that such a person may not get the visa at all. Also, there is fear of disruption of important ongoing commitments/ projects.

The consequences of undertaking employment on a Business visa can be serious. This is a very common practice, even among very senior level foreign managers from leading multinationals, especially software companies, who initially come to India to explore the market and then want to stay on for longer period of time on an employment basis. The real practical problem lies in conversion of the Business visa application into a work visa application. This process is carried out by the Ministry of Home Affairs at New Delhi. It is at this stage, the immigration officers, and the Deputy Home Secretary in charge of immigration issues, can raise a serious objection in granting permission in conversion of the application from a Business visa to an Employment visa. The primary objection is that the applicant cannot engage in employment on the strength of a Business visa. Also, serious objections are raised over violation of taxation provisions. Quite often, when foreign employees are visiting India on a Business visa, but are in fact in full-time regular employment of their parent company while looking after the Indian operations, they generally do not pay taxes in India. So, in effect this becomes an issue for the immigration officer at the Ministry of Home Affairs in New Delhi at the time of the conversion or extension of the visa application of the overseas employee already present in India. Although, the immigration officer may overlook this aspect of the matter, it cannot be guaranteed and neither can it be used as a precedent. Also, because of the plethora of legislation with regard to entry, movement and presence of foreigners in India, as is the case with tax evasion, there is a risk of criminal liability for engaging in employment on the strength of a Business visa. In summary, it is not advisable to engage employees while the foreign employee is actually present in India on a Business visa.

## DEPENDANT VISAS AND FORMALITIES

That under the rules and the conditions laid down by the Ministry of Home Affairs and the Ministry of External Affairs, only the spouse and the children upto 18 years of age qualify as dependants. It is very important to mention that the Indian immigration rules do not recognise same sex relationships and neither is their any provision in the immigration rules for unmarried cohabitees and unmarried relationships as well.

Indian Missions overseas have the discretion to grant a 'X' visa [i.e. a dependent visa] to the family members of a foreign national granted a Business visa. This is subject to the usual security checks provided the family members are otherwise eligible for grant of such a dependent visa. And, in respect of family members of a foreign national who are granted the 'Employment' visa, the Indian Missions overseas may grant an 'X' visa [i.e. dependent visa]. The validity of the 'X' visa could be co-terminus with the validity of the visa of the principal visa holder or for such shorter duration as may be considered necessary by the Indian Mission overseas. This is of course subject to the usual security checks provided the family members are otherwise eligible for grant of such a visa. That as per the prevailing rules by the Ministry of Home Affairs, the dependent holding the 'X' category visa can only undertake employment or business subject to the following conditions:

The applicant will have to fulfill all the conditions laid down for grant of the Employment visa with the prior approval of Ministry of Home Affairs.

## TAXATION OF FOREIGN NATIONALS IN INDIA

The liability of income-tax of all persons staying in India depends primarily upon their "residential status" as stipulated in the Indian Income Tax Act, 1961 (hereafter IT Act, 1961).

If a foreign citizen is resident in India, all incomes received, accrued or arisen to him in India and abroad, i.e. his total world income, shall be subject to tax in India. In case a foreign national is not resident in India, then only incomes that are received accrued or arisen to him in India, shall be taxable. Rigorous consequences follow in case of tax violations by foreign personnel, which can also create serious problems, when extensions of visas are sought either within India or at the Indian Mission overseas. Certain tax exemptions are available to foreign Diplomats/Consuls and in certain limited specific situations only.

## LEGAL PROVISIONS IN THE CONSTITUTION OF INDIA PROHIBITING DUAL NATIONALITY.

Article 9 of the Constitution of India lays the foundations for almost total refusal on the part of Indian law to accept dual nationality and provides that 'No person shall be a citizen of India by virtue of article 5, or be deemed to be a citizen of India by virtue of article 6 or article 8, if he has voluntarily acquired the citizenship of any foreign State'. This would appear to make exceptions only for such individuals who became citizens of another state by the operation of law rather than their own free will. The Indian judiciary has supported this position and the so far rather slender Indian immigration case-load reveals a firm reluctance on the part of Indian Judges to accept, let alone approve, the concept of dual nationality (see Malhotra, Ranjit, 'Dual nationality for Indians: The need for a fresh debate', in 10 I&NL&P,57-59).

## OVERSEAS CITIZENSHIP

The Government of India has recently introduced overseas citizenship by making additions to the existing section 7 of the Citizenship Act, 1955. The Citizenship (Amendment) Act, 2003 came into force on 7 January 2004.

Following the legislation formulated, dual/overseas citizenship will confer the following benefits to PIOs: The Indian diaspora practically enjoy every other benefit of being an Indian. They will have visa-free entry, which will be a boon since NRIs and PIOs spend a lot of time travelling. Their stay will not be limited to the short periods permitted under the visa regime. Also, they will have 10-year passports, renewable for a fee. They can buy and sell property, movable or immovable. Transfer of money will be governed only by the Reserve Bank of India (hereafter RBI) restrictions. The RBI is the principal regulating authority of the Indian banking system. They will be taxed only in the host country. It will not be offered automatically but on a voluntary basis to people who want to be reassured that India has not disowned them. These are excerpts from the report of late Dr. L.M. Singhvi, Chairman, Report of Indian Diaspora, released in September 2000.

The new above-mentioned dual citizenship scheme denies almost all political rights in India. But as per recent announcements made by the Government of India in the latter part of 2010, voting rights have been granted to NRIs.

It can be argued that the new scheme is a modification of dual nationality. Or, is it a glorified version of the PIO card scheme? But at first blush, for the time being, the Indian diaspora is content and satisfied on this issue. The main attraction of this scheme is that it will ensure the unrestricted entry of the PIOs and exercising of their economic rights while they are on the home soil.

**NEW ISSUES - PERSONS OF INDIAN ORIGIN (PIO) CARD SCHEME AND OVERSEAS CITIZENS OF INDIA (OCI):**

The Persons of Indian Origin Card Scheme was launched on 31 March 1999, which can be taken advantage by an estimated 15 million PIOs.

Persons of Indian Origin settled in countries other than Pakistan and Bangladesh will be issued PIO Cards that would exempt them from the requirements of a visa to visit India. The scheme will bring them on par with Non-Resident Indians (NRIs) in respect of facilities in the economic, cultural and financial and educational fields.

A PIO Card shall be valid for a period of 15 years subject to the validity of passport of the applicant. The fee for a PIO Card for an adult is 365 USD while it is 185 USD for a minor or its equivalent in local foreign currency of the country concerned, payable along with the application. Gratis PIO Cards may be issued to exceptionally eminent Persons of Indian Origin who demonstrate an important role in building bridges between India and the country of his/her adoption, if she/he expresses a desire to obtain the PIO Card.

The person eligible for issuance of PIO Cards would include:

- Who at any time held an Indian passport; or
- She/he or either of his/her parents, grand parents or great grandparents were born in and permanently resident in India; as defined in the Government of India Act, 1935; or
- Who is a spouse of a citizen of India or a PIO as mentioned above; or
- The PIO Scheme is broad based and covers up to four generations.

Pakistan and Bangladesh have been specifically excluded under the scheme. Previously, the PIO Card scheme had failed to evoke the expected response, mainly due to its initial exorbitant enrollment fee. Seeing the anguish of the NRI community, the Government has now scaled down the fees for obtaining the PIO Card.

## OVERSEAS CITIZENS OF INDIA

A foreign national who was eligible to become a citizen of India on 26 January, 1950, or was a citizen of India on or at any time after the said date or belonged to a territory that became part of India after 15 August, 1947 and, his/her children and grand children are eligible for registration as OCIs. They enjoy multiple entry multipurpose life long visa for visiting India, are exempted registration with FRO/ police authorities for any length of stay in India and are entitled to benefits notified under section 7 B of the Citizenship Act. An OCI registered for 5 years and residing in India for one year can be granted Indian citizenship but have no political rights.

Quite often in our day-to-day practice, we are contacted by software companies, banks and multinationals in the UK and US as also different parts of the world, wanting to relocate urgently senior personnel to India on key assignments. If it is people of Indian origin, we often advise the corporate clientele that such category of their senior level employees can possibly be relocated in a fast track manner. This avenue of course obviates the red tape visa controls.

VISAS – FOREIGN NATIONALS OF INDIAN ORIGIN

Foreign national of Indian origin can visit India on a multi-entry visa when they hold letter of intent/acknowledgement of industrial entrepreneurs memorandum/licence or provisional registration with the director of industries etc. Such persons can get an endorsement on their passport for single/multi-entry visa from the Consulate General/High Commissioner/Embassy of India. Their spouses can also be granted multi-entry visa upto 5 years.

Business visas can also be converted into Employment visas. But practically, it is not that easy, because prior permission has to be obtained from the Home Ministry in New Delhi. This is the mandatory requirement of obtaining permission from the Central Government, which cannot be waived off under any circumstances.

## CITIZENSHIP IN INDIA

(1) Foreign Nationals of Indian origin, after their settling in India may intend to acquire citizenship of India, for which provisions are contained in the Citizenship Act, 1955. Citizenship of India can be acquired by (a) birth; (b) descent; (c) registration; and (d) naturalisation.

(2) Foreigners of Indian origin, can apply for citizenship by registration after their residence for five years in India. Prior to 1 July 1987, this period was six months. Foreigners of Indian origin who are ordinarily resident in commonwealth countries may also apply for registration. Persons who are married to citizens of India and are resident in India for five years can also apply for registration. Minor children can be registered as citizens, when their parents apply for registration.

(3) Applications should be made in the prescribed form in triplicate, to the collector within whose jurisdiction the applicant is ordinarily resident. The oath of allegiance shall be affirmed before the registration.

(4) Foreign citizens of non-commonwealth countries, may be granted a certificate of naturalisation by the Central Government, where the person has rendered distinguished service in the field of science, philosophy, art, literature,

world peace and human progress. The person to whom this certificate is granted, on taking the oath of allegiance, becomes a citizen of India by naturalisation.

## RIGHTS OF FOREIGNERS IN INDIA

Faced with pressure to recognise the presence of foreign business interests and personnel, recent Indian Courts decisions have given a resoundingly negative message. The Supreme Court of India, in the matter of *Louis De Raedt* v. *Union of India,* AIR 1991 SC 1886 held (at page 1890).

'The fundamental right of the foreigner is confined to article 21 for life and liberty and does not include the right to reside and settle in this country, as mentioned in article 9(1)(e), which is applicable only to the citizens of this country'.

This Supreme Court ruling was also reiterated in the case of *Fred Howard Haering,* AIR 1996 HP 27. The High Court of Madras, in *David John Hopkins* v. *Union of India,* AIR 1997 Mad 367, held that the Government of India has unrestricted powers to refuse citizenship to foreign nationals without giving any reason whatsoever, and foreign nationals cannot claim equality before the law under article 14 of the Constitution of India, while this fundamental right is guaranteed to Indian nationals. The High Court, while affirming the earlier line of judicial thought in *Louis De Raedt,* (supra) and *Hans Muller,* (supra), sternly decided that foreign nationals do not have any fundamental right guaranteed for the granting of Indian citizenship.

## RECENT DEVELOPMENT: ABOLITION OF QUOTAS AS TO NUMBER OF FOREIGN EMPLOYEES WORKING IN AN INDIAN ORGANISATION

In 2010, a notification was initially issued by the Directorate-General of Employment and Training at the Ministry of Labour and Employment, which for all practical purposes was akin to the quota system recently introduced by the British Government. The upshot of these guidelines which now stand withdrawn was to curtail the issuance of Employment visas to 1 per cent of the total number of workers working in a company, with the minimum of five workers and a maximum of 20 workers, except in the case of the power and steel sector; in this particular case, the maximum limit was temporarily increased to 40 workers until June 2010. This ceiling on foreign workers was causing tremendous problems to foreign multinationals in India with a large number of expatriate senior level personnel heading their foreign direct investment operations throughout the territories of India. The notification had a caveat that also provided that all such foreign applicants would be entitled to apply for Employment visas beyond the stipulated limit of 20 foreign employees per organisation or establishment provided there was a *bona fide* business requirement. But, the difficulty was that such decision-making power did not lie with the Indian Embassy, Mission or Consulate Overseas. All such applications in excess of the quota were to be vetted by the Directorate General of Employment and Training before any such permissions were granted. This led to bureaucratic delay at the Governmental level in India. Given the huge number of requests that came from different jurisdictions worldwide, certainly the delay in clearing such applications did not have a positive impact on foreign companies and organisations wanting to conduct business in India.

Effective the week of 7 June, 2010, the Ministry of Home Affairs (hereafter, MHA) forwarded new instructions to Indian Consular Posts abolishing the 1% quota for applicants filing Employment visa applications that were sponsored by registered Information Technology (IT) and Information Technology Enabled Service (ITES) companies in India.

As of 7 June, 2010, Indian IT and ITES companies are now free to sponsor foreign workers based on actual need versus an imposed quota. There is a broad range of interpretation in India as to what qualifies as an IT/ITES company. Therefore, prior to submitting an Employment visa application under this new regulation, the sending company should confirm that the Indian host company has appropriate corporate registration (*e.g.*, Certificate of Incorporation from the Registrar of Companies), and that the host company is recognized in India as a bona fide IT/ITES company.

The new MHA instruction generally advises Indian Consular Posts of the following:

- There is now no "1% quota" on Employment visas issued to foreign workers assigned to a qualified IT/ITES Indian host company. (NOTE: The MHA may issue further clarification on what qualifies as an IT/ITES company, and it could include companies that are located in Software Technology Parks in India (STPI) or Special Economic Zones (SEZ) that are dedicated to IT development purposes); and
- Employment visas sponsored by IT/ITES companies can be issued for up to three years initially, with an additional two-year extension available for a maximum, total duration of stay of up to five years. This will avoid the traditional 12-month visa extension process.

The following general conditions are required of the Indian host company:

- The company must have a valid Certificate of Incorporation and declare in its sponsoring letter that it is an IT/ITES company;
- The company is either an Export Oriented Unit (EOU), or an STPI unit, or an IT unit delivering services located in an SEZ;
- Foreign workers must earn a minimum annual salary of US $25,000; and
- Foreign workers who *do not qualify* to apply for this new type of E visa are applicants submitting passports issued by Afghanistan, China [People's Republic of China (PRC)] and Sri Lanka as well as nationals of Pakistan and persons of Pakistani origin.

Hence, the quota was abolished only for the Information Technology (IT) and Information Technology Enabled Service (ITES) companies in India with effect from 7 June 2010.

However, the Indian Government has removed the cap on the number of foreigners any company may hire. The quota which was previously abolished only for Information Technology (IT) and Information Technology Enabled Service (ITES) companies in India, under the new guideline applies to all industry sectors. Companies and applicants must still meet all other remaining requirements for an Employment visa.

**2010 THE YEAR IN REVIEW: IMPORTANT JUDGEMENT OF THE BOMBAY HIGH COURT: NO JUDICIAL REVIEW APPLICATION MAINTAINABLE AGAINST REFUSAL OF EMPLOYMENT VISA TO A FOREIGN NATIONAL**

Much more recently in November 2010, in November 2010, in the case of *Appellants: Stelmakh Leonid Iuliia* v. *Respondent: Secretary to the Ministry of External Affairs, Government of India and Union of India, in writ petition number 1648 of 2010 and Chamber Summons number 334 of 2010, decided on 25 November 2010,* the High Court of Bombay refused to entertain a writ petition under the article 226 of the Constitution of India seeking judicial review of a refusal of an Employment visa application of an applicant based in Ukraine.

In the present case, the petitioner was a citizen of Ukraine. She had applied for an Employment visa on 3 June 2010 before the Indian Embassy in Kyiv, Ukraine. She was promised employment as an analyst by JP Morgan Services India Pvt. Ltd., Mumbai. In order to join the employment she was required to have Indian visa. She applied for the same. The said application was rejected by the Indian Embassy on 28 July, 2010 informing her that as per the existing guidelines of the Government for issuance of Employment Visa, her application is required to be rejected. The above petition was filed on 24 June 2010 i.e. before the communication about rejection of visa of the petitioner. In the petition, the prayer was regarding issuance of directions in the nature of *Mandamus* directing the respondents to issue Employment visa to the petitioner. It was the case of the petitioner that at the time when the petitioner applied for visa, she was orally told by the Embassy that since the minimum income criterion fixed by the Government of India was $ 25000 per year at the place where a person is employed, a person drawing a salary of less than the prescribed amount, cannot be given Employment visa. Subsequently, since the petitioner has been communicated about the rejection of her visa, Chamber Summons is filed for amending the petition on the ground that this criterion of income should not be made applicable to the petitioner. The petitioner submits that at the time when the petitioner applied for visa on 3 June 2010 the criterion of income of $25,000 per annum was applicable. In between it was changed and subsequently it was decided to give go-by to the income criterion altogether. She has relied upon the newspaper report in Times Nation dated 8 July, 2010. Basing the argument on the said report, it was submitted that the Government of India at the relevant time i.e. before the rejection of the petitioner's application had taken the decision to change the rule and removed the income criteria. It was further submitted that at the time when the application of the petitioner was rejected the income criterion was not in force and that now again it has been reintroduced somewhere on 7 August, 2010. Therefore, the petitioner submitted that in any case fixing such minimum salary criterion for the foreigners for getting employment was arbitrary.

It was contended on behalf of the Union of India that as per the policy framed by the Government of India, the petitioner is not entitled to an Employment visa. As per the existing policy, employment in India can be given only to those foreigners who have specialised education in a particular field and who can be appointed on a special post only in situations when Indian citizens are not available for appointment in such posts. And the minimum income criterion fixed by the Government of India for the grant of requirements of the Employment visas to foreign employees is $ 25000 per year at the place where a person is employed and a person who is going to draw a salary less than the prescribed amount, s/he cannot be given Employment visa. In the present case the salary requirements of the appellant did not match the prescribed requirements by the Government of India and so the visa was rejected.

The main question in dispute was that when the petitioner applied for visa on 3 June 2010 the criterion of income of $ 25,000 per annum was applicable. In between it was changed and subsequently it was decided to give go by to the income criterion altogether. And, at the time when the application of the petitioner was rejected the income criterion was not in force and that now again it has been reintroduced somewhere on 7 August, 2010. And so it was contented that since, at the time of rejection of visa the income criterion was not in existence, the rejection of visa was against the law.

The question regarding the validity of rejection of visa by the Immigration authorities was answered by the Hon'ble High Court in para 10 of the judgment in the following terms:

> "10. So far as the argument of the learned counsel for the petitioner that at the relevant time when the application was rejected the income criterion was given a goby is concerned, it is not in dispute that at the time when the petitioner applied for Visa, the said income criterion was applicable. It is also not in dispute that the petitioner has not fulfilled minimum income criterion prescribed for getting the employment Visa. Even assuming that for the time being, the said policy was given a goby, it is not in dispute that at the time when the petitioner applied for employment Visa, the said income criterion was in existence. There is nothing on record to show that when the application was rejected income criterion was totally taken away. But even otherwise the application is rejected on the ground that as per the policy framed by the government, the employment Visa cannot be granted for the jobs for which qualified Indians are available. In the instant case, it is pointed out that for the post in question, so many Indians are available. It is also pointed out that employment Visa cannot be granted for routine, ordinary or secretarial/clerical jobs."

Clearly, according to the Hon'ble High Court, the rejection of the Employment visa both on the ground of non fulfillment of the income criterion and on the policy of the Government regarding the restriction on giving employment to foreign employees where qualified Indians are available was correct in the present case.

Further, in relation to the maintainability of the Writ petition, the Court held that the real question requiring consideration is whether such petitions are maintainable in the instance of a foreign national and whether the issue in question can be said to be justiciable.

The upshot of this significant ruling is carved out in paras 7, 9 and 11 of the said judgment, which read as follows:

"7. It is pertinent to note that so far as foreign nationals are concerned, all the fundamental rights enshrined in the Constitution of India are not available to them except articles 21 and 14 of the Constitution of India. In our view, it is not a fundamental right of a foreign national to get employment to get employment visa in India. If the visa is rejected on the basis of a policy framed by the Government of India, this Court cannot sit in appeal over such decision in order to find out as to whether visa application should have been granted or not. In our view, asking for visa by a foreign national cannot be said to be a justiciable issue and this Court cannot issue any writ under article 226 of the Constitution of India in connection with the availability of fundamental rights where a foreign citizen is concerned. [...]

9. So far as right to get visa is concerned, in our view, it is not a fundamental right of a foreign national and, therefore, the petition under article 226 of the Constitution of India, violating such right is not maintainable. So far as article 14 and 16 are concerned, article 16 relates to equality in the matter of public employment and non-citizen cannot invoke article 16 in any manner as the said article is only applicable to the citizens of the country. It cannot be said that there is violation of article 21 of the Constitution in present case, nor any such argument is canvassed before this Court. Considering the said aspect, in our view, this petition cannot be entertained which challenges the decision of Indian Embassy rejecting employment visa to the petitioner. It is not for this Court to find out whether such restriction in the matter of granting visa to a foreigner is proper or not.

11. [...] In our view what should be the guidelines for giving visa is a matter which is solely in the discretion of the Government of India in its department of External Affairs. This Court cannot decide the issue as to what policy should be framed for granting employment visa or other visa. This Court cannot lay down any criterion in this behalf in any manner. Similarly this Court is not expected to decide as to whether the visa application should be allowed or not. Rejection of visa by the Consulate is not an issue which is justiciable one. If the Government of India in its wisdom has taken a decision by prescribing certain criterion this Court cannot take a judicial review in such a matter. It is always open to the State to restrict the entries of foreign nationals by imposing restrictions by framing certain policy and the said policy decision should not be interfered. As pointed out earlier only few fundamental rights like article 21 of the Constitution of India are available to the foreign nationals and article 16 cannot be said to be applicable to the foreign nationals for getting public employment in this country. In our view, in the instant case, no relief can be granted to the petitioner in view of what is stated hereinabove. It cannot be said that there is a violation of article 21 in the present case. The petitioner has no right to approach this Court and it cannot be said that income criterion prescribed by the Government of India is arbitrary in any manner, which issue cannot be decided at the instance of the Petitioner, who is not an Indian citizen. We accordingly do not find any substance in the petition [...]."

## CRIMINAL CONVICTIONS: A BARRIER TO OBTAINING IMMIGRATION PERMISSION

The power to grant or refuse permission to foreigners to enter India and subsequent restrictions on employment has been provided in section 3 of the Foreigners Order of 1948. Section 3(2)(d) and 3(2)(e) are most relevant in this regard and provide that leave to enter shall be refused if the civil authority is satisfied that the said foreigner has been sentenced in a foreign country for an extradition offence within the meaning of the Indian Extradition Act, 1903 (XV of 1903) and his entry is prohibited either under an order issued by a competent authority or under the specific orders of the Central Government.

## PENALTIES FOR NON COMPLIANCE WITH THE IMMIGRATION LAW

In India, foreigners visiting India for long-term (more than 180 days) Student visa, Research visa, Employment visa, Medical visa are required to get themselves registered with concerned FRRO/FRO within 14 days of his/her first arrival, irrespective of the duration of their stay. Although, there is no fee for registration, but, a penalty in Indian currency equivalent to US$ 30 (Rs.1395) is charged in case of late registration.

However, from the practical point of view it is very important to discuss the issue of full fledged employment by a foreign employee on the strength of a Business visa. The consequences of undertaking employment on a Business visa can be serious. The practical problem lies in conversion of the Business visa application into a work visa application. This process of conversion is carried out in the Ministry of Home Affairs at New Delhi. It is at this stage, the Immigration Officers, and the Deputy Home Secretary incharge of immigration issues, can take a serious objection in granting permission in conversion of the application from a Business visa to an Employment visa. The first and foremost objection is that the applicant cannot engage in employment on the strength of a Business visa. Also, serious objections are taken as to violation of taxation provisions. Quite often, when foreign employees are visiting India on a Business visa, but are in fact are in full time regular employment of their parent company while looking after the India operations, they generally do not pay taxes in India. So, in effect this becomes a major bone of contention for the Immigration Officer at the Ministry of Home Affairs in New Delhi at the time of the conversion or extension of the visa application of the overseas employee already present in India.

Although, the Immigration Officer at the Ministry of Home Affairs in New Delhi has the power to overlook this aspect, nonetheless, it cannot be guaranteed and neither can it be used as a precedent.

Also, because of the plethora of legislation with regard to entry, movement and presence of foreigners in India as also with regard to evasion of taxes, there is threat of inviting penal consequences for engaging in employment on the strength of a business visa.

In nutshell, it is against the immigration laws to engage into employment, while the foreign employee is actually present in India on a Business visa.

## OTHER SIGNIFICANT ISSUES

Foreign lawyers handling infrastructure and transactional work, are making vigorous efforts to break into the Indian legal market. This arena also needs deliberation as well, in so far relating to immigration requirements.

The contours of our immigration policy need to adapt fast to the present day situation. It is no longer the case that inbound immigration to India is not a major issue. Biometrics and electronic border controls is the need of the hour. It is indeed a major exercise, both in terms of time and expense. But, it is not even on our road map for the future. In this way, anybody with a multiple identity or a dubious identity cannot be granted a visa.

## IMMIGRATION LAW IN INDIA: NEGLECTED AREA OF LAW

We now want to focus on the backdrop of the existing position of business immigration law in India, which has also remained completely neglected. The point to demonstrate here is that if the Government of India can ignore updating and modifying the existing business immigration law in India, which can be a huge potential source of revenue. We now briefly advert to the existing scenario relating to entry, movement and presence of foreign personnel in India.

## TREND OF REVERSE MIGRATION: RECENT GROWING PHENOMENON

A fast moving economic hub, high profile software opportunities, IT Parks, private equity and IPO's, a property boom, Foreign Direct Investment, a global center for medicare, developing trade and opportunity, avenues for professionals created by globalisation, the return of the NRI to his roots and homeland with funds for investment in India: this seems to be the predicted future forecast for India in the forthcoming era. Opportunities are booming with reverse migration on the way. A large number of software professionals of high caliber and standing have returned to India from the USA, and continue to do so.

## BIOMETRICS: NEED OF THE DAY

As of now, we do not have the concept of electronic visas or fast track processing of visas. Neither, do we have anything similar to the points based system which has been introduced in the UK on a rolling basis in a phased manner. That if we had something analogous to the points based system, a certain amount of discretion would be required to run the same, given the geographical size of our country and as also to suit the local conditions, with a view to a successful working of such a system.

## CONSOLIDATED WORK PERMIT REGIME REQUIRED

The Government of India has taken great care in suitably updating or modifying and introducing rules and regulations with regard to foreign equity investment into India. However, the provisions for business immigration into India have been completely ignored in as much as outdated, impractical, obsolete and rigid provisions of law which have outlived their utility now need to be suitably amended, revamped and revised in the scenario of the changing world today. A Centralised work permit regime in India in the present economic scenario is the need of the hour. Also, provisions need to be made forthwith for medical tourism, electronic visas, fast track processing of visas for blue chip workers and corporate personnel, besides taking measures to cope up with the trends of reverse migration. The realisation has dawned but the implementation is lacking.

It can be asserted that the prime concern of the stringent legislation and judicial decisions pertaining to the entry, presence and movement of foreigners in India, including business visitors, remains to safeguard the interests of national security. At the same time, the Reserve Bank of India acts like a watchdog, keeping a serious check on the flow of funds to and from India, routed through business channels and foreigners.

There is now definitely a clear case for framing a new set of consolidated rules focusing exclusively especially on corporate business immigration into India. The present immigration requirements are certainly not conducive to the substantial foreign direct investment that is presently taking place in India. The 1948 Orders are obsolete and have outlived their utility and must be replaced by a work permit regime. Indian Government could also explore the possibility of having a limit on the number of work permit visas, like the H-1B cap imposed by the US Government.

The boom in the Indian technology industry has precipitated the return of the Non-Resident Indians to their motherland, as they are finding the same opportunities and working conditions on the home soil. For such a class of blue chip workers, more than the money, the attraction of coming back to their roots is a bigger motivating factor. A new trend is also now emanating, whereby highly skilled foreign manpower is employed on the Indian soil by the foreign parent companies, for running their businesses in India controlled abroad. This issue has been discussed in detail in the main body of the paper.

Likewise, foreign personnel of blue chip companies are coming in large numbers to India to set-up and manage offices on behalf of their parent foreign companies. Hence, this scenario, all the more warrants the introduction of a work permit scheme. Bangalore alone has reportedly 300,000 software professionals.

Additionally, on account of changing economic conditions and a world without borders, we need to keep pace with the times in the arena of immigration law. Over and above, we also need to think of fast track processing of visas which of course can entail a charge for premium processing, electronic visas which would be very beneficial for the software industry. Consolidated licensing or compliance system for employers qua foreign workers should be in place as well.

We also need a better useful website with public information about immigration and visa matters. As of now, there is no Indian website that of the Government or that of a private agency offering comprehensive consolidated information on immigration rules, and guidelines followed by the Ministry of Home Affairs are not adequately publicised or made available to the public readily. A great deal of running around is required at times, to get hold of the relevant information, even relating to penal consequences relating to immigration law, both as applicable to employees and employers.

**CONCLUSION:**

To conclude, it can be asserted that the prime concern of the traditional thinking in enacting stringent legislation and judicial decisions pertaining to the entry, presence and movement of foreigners in India, including business visitors, remains to safeguard the interests of national security. At the same time, the Reserve Bank of India closely monitors all inward and outward financial remittances undertaken by expatriate foreign personnel and cross border business transactions of foreign establishments operating from India.

But now, the contours of our immigration policy need to adapt fast to the present day situation. It is no longer the case that inbound immigration to India is not a major issue. Biometrics and electronic border controls is the need of the hour. It is indeed a major exercise, both in terms of time and expense. But, it is not even on our road map for the future. In this way, anybody with a multiple identity or a dubious identity cannot be granted a visa.

Trends move like a pendulum. At the Wilton Park conference on, "The Future of Migration," held in December 2008 in Wilton Park itself at Sussex in the UK attended by both the authors of this chapter, experts from all over the globe pondered on the impact of climate change on migration issues in the next couple of decades. How do we deal with HIV infected patients wanting to come to India for work, medical treatment or otherwise. For the US, HIV will no longer lead to inadmissibility. The Indian immigration rules are conspicuously silent on this aspect of the matter.

Foreign lawyers handling infrastructure and transactional work, are making sustained vigorous efforts to break into the Indian legal market. This arena also needs deliberation as well, in so far relating to immigration requirements. At the moment, "laptop lawyers," from foreign jurisdictions come to India to conduct regular professional work, of course minus court appearance. The point to be conveyed is that the Government should have some sort of immigration procedures and regulations in place for foreign lawyers, wanting to come to India to conduct transactional work or any sort of professional work.

There is of course a clear cut case now for framing a new set of consolidated rules focusing exclusively on business immigration into India, which should replace the existing outdated and rigid provisions. The present immigration requirements are certainly not conducive to the substantial foreign direct investment that is presently taking place in India. The Government of India has taken great care in suitably updating, modifying and introducing rules and regulations with regard to foreign equity investment into India, while the business immigration provisions have been completely ignored. As in the European Union, safeguarding freedom of movement for goods and capital is one thing, facilitating the free movement of business personnel is another.

Lastly, it is about time that the Government of India introduced a work permit regime for foreign nationals wanting to set up businesses in India and run offices on behalf of multinationals. All global giants now have a presence in India. They are tapping the cheap labour market. Sadly enough, their entry is unrestricted and without a price tag. More importantly, the fees for processing work permit applications could be a source of revenue to the exchequer.

# CHILD AND FAMILY LAW IN INDIA

## A. INTRODUCTION

Indian child and family law has undergone a sea-change over the last fifty years since most family laws were enacted by the Indian Parliament after 1955 upon India gaining .independence from British rule in 1947. The family system which developed from the Mitakshara school (law according to the ancient scriptures of the Hindus) which, in its essence, began as a extended family, has been transformed into one based on the nuclear system. The metamorphosis was an inevitable one because it was a result of the changing social conditions and attitudes multiplied by the various social revolutions through which Indian society has gone.

### Historical roots, sources and law reform

The Constitution of India, which forms the basis of family law and was enacted on 26 November 1949, and its Preamble resolved to constitute India as a Union of States and a Sovereign, Socialist, Secular Democratic Republic. Today, a population of over one billion Indians live in twenty-eight States and seven Union Territories within India besides about twenty five million Indians who reside in foreign jurisdictions and are known as 'Non-Resident Indians'. Within the territory of India spread over an area of 3.28 million square kilometres, the large Indian population comprising multicultural societies, professing and practicing different religions and speaking different local languages coexists in harmony in one of the largest democracies in the world.

The Indian Constitution established a High Court for each State and the Supreme Court of India (article 214). Under article 141 of the Constitution of India, the law declared by the Supreme Court shall be binding on all Courts within the territory of India. However, the Supreme Court may not be bound by its own earlier views, and can render new decisions.

Part III of the Constitution of India secures to its citizens 'fundamental rights' which can be enforced directly in the respective High Courts of the States or directly in the Supreme Court of India by issue of prerogative Writs under articles 226 and 32 respectively of the Constitution of India. Under the Constitutional scheme, freedom of religion and the right to freely profess, practice and propagate religion is sacrosanct and is thus enforceable by a Writ.

## EXISTING FAMILY LAW LEGISLATIONS PREVALENT IN INDIA

India is a land of diversities with several religions. The oldest part of Indian Legal System is the personal laws governing the Hindus and the Muslims. The Hindu personal law has undergone changes by a continuous process of codification. The process of change in society has brought changes in law reflecting the changed social conditions and attempts the solution of social problems by new methods in the light of experience of legislations in other countries of the world. The Muslim personal law has been comparatively left untouched by legislations

The Indian Legal system is basically a common law system. The Indian Parliament has enacted the following family laws which are applicable to the religious communities defined in the respective enactments themselves. A brief description of each of these separate enactments is given as hereunder.

â The main marriage law legislation in India applicable to the majority population constituted of Hindus is known as the Hindu Marriage Act, 1955, which is an Act to amend and codify the law relating to marriage among Hindus. Ceremonial marriage is essential under this Act and registration is optional. It applies to any person who is a Hindu, Buddhist, Jaina or Sikh by religion and to any other person who is not a Muslim, Christian, Parsi or Jew by religion. The Act also applies to Hindus resident outside the territory of India. Nothing contained in this Act shall be deemed to affect any right recognized by custom or conferred by any special enactment. Likewise, in other personal law matters, Hindus are governed by the Hindu Succession Act, 1956, which is an Act to amend and codify the law relating to intestate succession among Hindus. The Hindu Minority and Guardianship Act, 1956 is an Act to amend and codify certain parts of the law relating to minority and guardianship among Hindus and the Hindu Adoptions and Maintenance Act, 1956 is an Act to amend and codify the law relating to adoptions and maintenance among Hindus.

It may be pertinent to point out that the Indian Succession Act, 1925, is an Act to consolidate the law applicable to intestate and testamentary succession in India unless parties opt and choose to be governed by their respective codified law otherwise applicable to them. In respect of issues relating to guardianship, the Guardian and Wards Act, 1890 would apply to non-Hindus. Interestingly, section 125 of the Code of Criminal Procedure, 1973, provides that irrespective of religion, any person belonging to any religion can approach a Magistrate for being provided maintenance. Therefore, apart from personal family law legislations, both Hindus and non-Hindus have an independent right of maintenance under the general law of the land, if he or she is otherwise entitled to maintenance under this Code.

➢ The Indian Parliament also enacted the Special Marriage Act, 1954, as an Act to provide a special form of marriage in certain cases, for the registration of such and certain other marriages and for divorces under this Act. This enactment of solemnizing marriage by registration is resorted to by Hindus, non-Hindus and foreigners marrying in India who opt out of the ceremonial marriage under their respective personal laws. Registration is compulsory under this enactment. Divorce can also be obtained by non-Hindus under this Act. This legislation governs people of all religions and communities in India, irrespective of their personal faith. Likewise, under the Foreign Marriage Act, 1969, a person has only to be a citizen of India to have a marriage solemnized under this Act outside the territorial limits of India.

➢ The Parsi Marriage and Divorce Act, 1936 as amended in 1988, is an Act to amend the law relating to marriage and divorce among the Parsis in India.

➢ The Christian Marriage Act, 1872, was enacted as an Act to consolidate and amend the law relating to the solemnization of the marriages of Christians in India and the Divorce Act, 1869 as amended in 2001, is an Act to amend the law relating to divorce and matrimonial causes relating to Christians in India.

➢ The Muslim Personal Law (Shariat) Application Act, 1937, the Dissolution of Muslim Marriages Act, 1939, the Muslim Women ( Protection of Rights on Divorce) Act, 1986 and the Muslim Women ( Protection of Rights on Divorce) Rules, 1986, applies to Muslims living in India.

For enforcement and adjudication of all matrimonial and other related disputes of any person in any of the different religious or non-religious communities under the respective legislations mentioned above, the designated judicial forum or Court where such petition is to be lodged is prescribed in the respective enactments themselves. There is an organized system of designated civil and criminal judicial Courts within every State in India which works under the overall jurisdiction of the respective High Court in the State. It is in the hierarchy of these Courts that all family and matrimonial causes are lodged and decided by the aggrieved party. In addition, the Indian Parliament has enacted the Family Courts Act, 1984 to provide for the establishment of Family Courts with a view to promote conciliation in and to secure speedy settlement of disputes relating to marriage and family affairs. Despite the existence of an organized, well regulated and established hierarchy of judicial Courts in India, there are still unrecognized parallel community and religious Courts in existence whose interference has been deprecated by the judicial Courts since such unauthorized and unwarranted bodies work without the authority of law and are not parts of the judicial system.

Simultaneously, Part IV of the Indian Constitution lays down 'Directive Principles of State Policy' which are not enforceable by any Court but are, nevertheless, fundamental in the governance of the country and it is the duty of the State to apply these principles while making law. Under article 44 of the Constitution in this Part, the State shall endeavour to secure for the citizens a Uniform Civil Code throughout the territory of India. However, realistically speaking, a Uniform Civil Code remains an aspiration which India has yet to realise.

India has ratified both the UN Convention on the Elimination of Discrimination Against Women [(1979) 1249 UNTS 13] and the UN Convention on the Rights of the Child and, as we shall see, legislative changes, designed to ensure compliance with the convention, have followed [(1989) 1577 UNTS 3]. The enactment of the Juvenile Justice (Care and Protection of Children) Act, 2000, the Commissions for Protection of Child Rights Act, 2005, the Protection of Women from Domestic Violence Act, 2005 and the Right of Children to Free and Compulsory Education Act, 2009, now provide effective remedies for the protection, care and grant of effective remedial relief to women and children in need.

## Dispute resolution and access to legal services

### *India's legal system*

The development of the country can be understood from the capacity of its legal system to render effective justice. The practice of amicable resolution of disputes can be traced back to historic times, when village disputes were resolved between members of particular families or occupations, or between residents of a particular locality. In rural India, the 'panchayats' (assembly of elders and respected inhabitants of the village) decided almost all the disputes between the residents of the village, while disputes between the members of a clan continued to be decided by the elders of the clan. These methods of amicable dispute resolution were recognised methods of administration of justice and not just an 'alternative' to the formal justice system formed by the sovereigns, feudal lords or the adalat systems initiated by the British and the formal Court system. The two systems continued to function alongside each other.

India has a massive legal system comprising nearly 15,000 Courts across the country. It is the constitutional obligation of the judiciary to exercise its jurisdiction to reaffirm the faith of the people in the judicial system. Therefore, evolution of new juristic principles for dispute resolution is not only important but imperative. In India, the need to develop alternative mechanisms simultaneous with the revival and strengthening of traditional systems of dispute resolution has been reiterated in reports of expert bodies. [for more details see: Report of the Committee on Legal Aid, *Report of the Expert Committee on Legal Aid: Processual Justice to the People* (New Delhi, Government of India, 1971); Government of India, Ministry of Law, and Justice and Company Affairs, *Report on National Juridicare Equal Justice – Social Justice* (New Delhi, Government of India, 1978)]. Each of these reports saw the process of improving access to justice through legal aid mechanisms and Alternative Dispute Resolution (ADR) as a part of the systemic reform of the judiciary coupled with substantive reforms of laws and processes.

### Extra-judicial Courts

However, community practices in certain states in India amongst certain religious denominations have led to the creation of community or religious Courts which are not authorised by law and are not sanctioned by the official legal system. It is in the matter of inter-caste or inter-religious marriages and divorces that such self-styled extra-constitutional authorities take upon themselves the power of Courts to issue community mandates. Such religious edicts result from summary hearings often in violation of fundamental rights guaranteed by the Constitution of India. In this regard, in *Vishwa Lochan Madan* v. *Union of India*, [On 27 March, 2006, the Supreme Court of India had issued notices in this matter and The Supreme Court website does not give any citation as the matter is pending and still not concluded], the Supreme Court of India issued notices to the Central Government, State Governments, All India Muslim Personal Law Board (AIMPLB) and Darul Uloom (an Islamic seminary), in the matter of the existence of these parallel unconstitutional Courts, which pose a challenge to the Indian judicial system. The petitioner was seeking immediate dissolution of all Islamic and Shariat (also known as Sharia) Courts in India. He sought a ban on the establishment of such Islamic Courts, along with a declaration that fatwas have no legal sanctity, and requested the Court to direct the Central and the State Governments to take effective steps to dissolve all Darul Qazas and Shariat Courts in India. The petitioner further sought a direction from the Court to the AIMPLB and Darul Uloom, Deoband, other seminaries and Muslim organizations asking them to refrain from establishing a parallel Muslim Judicial System (Nizam-e-Qaza).

This no doubt raises a crucial issue as to whether there could be two parallel legal systems in operation; one secular and the other religious. In particular, it should be remembered that the Constitution of India prohibits discrimination on grounds of caste or religion. Furthermore, questions should be asked as to whether the right to freedom of religion could be extended to the establishment of a parallel judicial system. The matter is still pending final adjudication in the Supreme Court of India and no final judgment has been handed down.

On similar lines, there are the Caste Panchayats (village councils), especially in the State of Haryana in India. These Caste Panchayats become involved in disputes, often by declaring marriages invalid, and invariably their victims belong to the weakest sections of society. Traditionally, Caste Panchayats have also played a powerful role at village level in several other states in the country. However, Khap Panchayats (caste-based village councils) are not elected bodies and their decisions are not enforceable by law. As such, these extra-constitutional bodies have no sanctity or recognition in law but, rather, derive support from community recognition. Khap Panchayats are so powerful because of their ability to mobilise a large number of people. They appear to be democratic from outside, but they are not since they exclude women, the youth as well as the groups who are lower down in the caste hierarchy in the village.

The constructive decisions of the Courts are undoubtedly a setback to the Caste Panchayats of Haryana which have a powerful influence. While a positive step has been taken by the Court, there cannot be a positive outcome until society as a whole seeks to demolish this obsolete system. The authorities have done little to check the extra-judicial activities of these Courts, which are a blatant interference with the fundamental rights of the citizens. The responsibility of the State cannot be abdicated. The judiciary seems best-placed to provide relief in matters involving blatant violation of fundamental rights by community councils. Courts cannot legislate, but must vindicate human rights. Notwithstanding, the duty of the State to enforce the law of the land is the need of the day. The Courts unhesitatingly should strike down any mandates of any such extra-judicial bodies which have no legal sanctity in a civilized society.

**Access to legal services and Alternative Dispute Resolution**

Access to legal services is a major problem, rendering the use of ADR vital. Empowering individuals to resolve their own disputes and assisting them by promoting ADR can bring many benefits; not least in avoiding the acrimony, delay and cost often associated with litigation. The duty to enact or amend law lies with the legislature, but its development and interpretation in a manner designed to best serve the needs and circumstances of society, lies firmly with the judiciary. Accordingly, until the beneficial provisions of the matrimonial legislation promoting and advocating reconciliation in matrimonial disputes in India is favourably interpreted and strictly implemented by the Courts, the letter of law may be an illusion which remains on the statute book only. It is the solemn duty of the matrimonial Courts in India to ensure that the mandatory settlement efforts are actually put into practice and parties are encouraged to utilise them for out-of-Court settlements. Thus, there is a heavy burden on the Courts in discharging this solemn duty, failing which it will neither be possible nor useful to enforce reconciliatory measures in matrimonial disputes.

It is clear that the duty cast upon the matrimonial Courts to attempt mandatory reconciliation cannot be avoided or circumvented, even when divorce is sought on certain exceptional grounds which the Hindu Marriage Act 1955 and Special Marriage Act, 1954 do not provide compulsory settlement action.

Accordingly, the Supreme Court in *Balwinder Kaur* v. *Hardeep Singh*, AIR 1998 SC 764, laid down in para 9 of the judgment that,

'stress should always be on the preserving the institution of marriage. That is the requirement of law. For the purpose of settlement of family disputes emphasis is laid on conciliation and achieving socially desirable results and eliminating adherence to rigid rules of procedure and evidence.'

In light of this, the purpose of section 23(2) of the Hindu Marriage Act 1955 was explained in *Love Kumar* v. *Sunita Puri*, AIR 1997 P&H 189, in para 9 as follows:

> 'It is fundamental that reconciliation of a ruptured marriage is the first duty of the Judge. The sanctity of marriage is the cornerstone of civilization. The State is interested in the security and preservation of the institution of marriage and for this the Court is required to attempt reconciliation between the parties. Such an attempt can be and should be made at any stage. The matrimonial Court is required to call parties and make a genuine effort for their reconciliation; there is not even a whisper in this provision that the matrimonial Court has the power to strike off the defence of that spouse, who after being given opportunities for reconciliation, fails to appear.'

It is clear that reconciliation is a mandatory process. However, the timing and stage at which it is to be implemented may vary, depending on the facts and circumstances of each case. At the same time, causing prejudice to the rights of one party by striking off the defence or dismissing the petition may actually work injustice to the rights of such party. Therefore, the matrimonial Court may fashion and design the reconciliation process, depending on the facts of each case, without causing prejudice to the substantive rights of the parties.

## B. CHILDREN IN THE FAMILY SETTING AND STATE INTERVENTION

India has ratified the United Nations Convention on the Rights of the Child. Has this led to any changes in the law and is the legal system's approach to children consistent with the Convention?

### Defining and classifying children

Under setion 4(a) of the Hindu Minority and Guardianship Act, 1956 (hereafter 'HMGA 1956'), 'minor' means a person who has not reached the age of

18 years. Under section 2 of the Juvenile Justice (Care and Protection of Children) Act, 2000, a juvenile or child means a person who has not completed the eighteenth year of age. The Indian Contract Act, 1872 does not define the age of majority and under section 11 every person is competent to contract who is of the age of majority according to the law to which he is subject. The Hindu Marriage Act, 1955 and the Special Marriage Act, 1954, uses the words "minor children" but does not define as to who are minor children. Ordinarily, the definition contained in section 3 of Indian Majority Act, 1875 will apply and under which a person ordinarily remains a minor until he or she attains the age of 18 years. Regardless, section 16 of the Hindu Marriage Act, 1955 confers legitimacy to children born to both void and voidable marriages. Even under section 20 of the Hindu Adoptions and Maintenance Act, 1956, a legitimate or illegitimate child make claim maintenance from his or her father or mother so long as the child is a minor i.e. less than eighteen years of age.

**Recognising parentage and family ties**

A 'guardian' is defined under section 4(b) of the HMGA, 1956 as a person having the care of the person of the minor or of his property or both and includes a natural guardian, a guardian appointed by Will of his natural parents and a guardian appointed or declared by the Court and a person empowered to act as such under any enactment.

**Surrogacy – A new law in the making**

In a phenomenal exercise to legalise commercial surrogacy, the Assisted Reproductive Technology (Regulation) Bill & Rules – 2010, a draft bill prepared by a 12 members committee including experts from ICMR, medical specialists and other experts from the Ministry of Health and Family Welfare, Government of India has been posted online recently for feedback. This Bill, earlier also floated in 2008 for comment, is stated to be an Act to provide for a national frame work or the regulation and supervision of Assisted Reproductive Technology and matter connected therewith or incidental thereto as a unique proposed law to be put before the Indian Parliament. Abetting surrogacy, it legalizes commercial surrogacy stating that the surrogate mother may receive monetary compensation and will relinquish all parental rights. Single parents can also have children using a surrogate mother. Foreigners, upon registration with their Embassy can seek surrogate arrangements. It also legalizes commercial surrogacy for single persons, married or unmarried couples stating that the surrogate mother shall enter into a legally enforceable surrogacy agreement. The 2010 draft bill states that foreigners or NRIs coming to India to rent a womb shall have to submit documentation confirming that their country of residence recognizes surrogacy as legal and that it will give citizenship to the child born through the surrogacy agreement from an Indian mother. This bill has not yet been debated in the Indian Parliament and has accordingly no legislative sanction.

The Preamble of the said proposed Bill which is called an Act "to provide for a national framework for the regulation and supervision of Assisted Reproductive Technology and matters connected therewith or incidental thereto" provides the constitution of a National Advisory Board for Assisted Reproductive Technology, comprising of members not exceeding 21, whose functions are confined to promoting the cause of reproductive technology. The salient details of the aforementioned Surrogacy Bill are:

- The new Assisted Reproductive Technology (Regulation) Bill & Rules, 2010, legalises commercial surrogacy, stating that the surrogate mother may receive monetary compensation for carrying the child in addition to health-care and treatment expenses during pregnancy.
- Both the couple or individual seeking surrogacy through the use of Assisted Reproductive Technology, and the surrogate mother shall enter into a surrogacy agreement which shall be legally enforceable.
- The surrogate mother will relinquish all parental rights over the child once the amount is transferred and birth certificates will be in the name of commissioning parent/s.
- The prescribed age-limit for a surrogate mother is between 21- 35 years. The proposed Bill also states that no women shall act as a surrogate mother for more than five children including her own.
- Single persons, men or women or single parents, unmarried couples can also have children using a surrogate mother. In case of a single man or a woman, the baby will be his/her legitimate child. A child born to an unmarried couple using a surrogate mother and with the consent of both the parties shall be their legitimate child.
- All foreigners seeking infertility treatment in India will first have to register with their Embassy. Their notarised statement will then have to be handed over to the treating doctor. The foreign couple will also state whom the child should be entrusted to in case of an eventuality such as a genetic parent's death.
- A foreigner or foreign couple not resident in India or an NRI individual or couple seeking surrogacy in India shall appoint the local guardian legally responsible for taking care of the surrogate child during and after pregnancy.
- The party seeking surrogacy must ensure and establish to the ART clinic that the party would be able to take the child born through surrogacy outside India to the country of the party's origin or residence as the case may be.
- A child born out of surrogacy shall be the legitimate child of both the parties or of the single man or woman as the case may be. The birth certificate will contain the name or names of the genetic parent or parents (as the case may be) who sought such use. If parties get divorced or separated, the child shall be the legitimate child of the couple. The birth certificate of a child born through the use of Assisted Reproductive Technology shall contain the name or names of the parent or parents, as the case may be, who sought such use.
- If a foreigner or a foreign couple seeks sperm or egg donation, or surrogacy, in India, and a child is born as a consequence, the child, even though born in India, shall not be an Indian citizen.

- Foreigners or NRIs coming to India seeking surrogacy in India shall appoint a local guardian who will be legally responsible for taking care of the surrogate during and after pregnancy till the child is delivered to the foreigner or foreign couple or the local guardian. Further, the party seeking surrogacy must ensure and establish through proper documentation that the country of their origin permits surrogacy and that the child born through surrogacy in India will be permitted entry in the country of their origin as a biological child of the commissioning couple/individual. If the foreign party seeking surrogacy fails to take delivery of the child born to the surrogate mother, the local guardian will be legally obliged to take the child and be free to hand over the child to an adoption agency. In case of adoption or the legal guardian having to bring up the child in India, the child will be given Indian citizenship.
- Surrogacy be recommended for patients for whom it is medically impossible/undesirable to carry a baby to term.
- ART clinic must not advertise surrogacy arrangements. The responsibility should rest with the couple or a semen bank.
- ART clinic must ensure that the surrogate woman satisfies all the testable criteria (sexually transmitted or communicable disease that may endanger the pregnancy).
- A prospective surrogate mother must be tested for HIV and shown to be a seronegative for this virus just before embryo transfer.

However, the moot question which may arise for determination whether a judicial verdict for determination of rights of parties in a surrogacy arrangement is essential in respect of a foreign biological parent who wishes to take the surrogate child to his/her country of origin or permanent residence, it can be said that either a declaration from a civil Court and/or a guardianship order ought to be a must to conclusively establish the rights of all parties and to prevent any future discrepancies arising in respect of any claims thereto. Hence, much remains to be said about judicial safeguards in the Bill.

**Delivering parenting**

In *Gita Hariharan* v. *Reserve Bank of India*, 1999 (2) SCC 228, the Supreme Court interpreted section 6 of the Hindu Minority and Guardianship Act 1956 (HMGA) as meaning that a mother is also a natural guardian, and, irrespective of whether the father was unfit or not, the mother should also be given equal rights as a natural guardian. In this judgment in para 14, the Apex Court held that the message of international instruments – Convention on the Elimination of All Forms of Discrimination, 1979 (CEDAW) and the Beijing Declaration, which directs all State parties to take appropriate measures to prevent discrimination of all forms against women is quite clear. India is a signatory to CEDAW having accepted and ratified it in June 1993, the Court held that their interpretation gives effect to the principles contained in these instruments as domestic Courts are under an obligation to give due regard to international conventions. Consequently, natural guardians enjoy equal rights in respect of the welfare of their minor children.

In *Jajabhai* v. *Panthakhan*, 1970 (2) SCC 717, where the father and mother had fallen out and were living separately and the minor daughter was under the care and protection of her mother, the mother was considered to be the natural guardian of the minor girl. In *Rosy Jacob* v. *Jacob Chakramakkal*, 1973 (1) SCC 840, it was conclusively established that the controlling consideration governing the custody of the children is the welfare of the children and not the right of the parents. This settled position of law continues till date in respect of custody battles of natural parents. The wishes of the child weigh equally to assist the Court to take decisions on custody rights.

A Court appointed guardian has full responsibility and powers as a natural guardian subject to the limitations prescribed in section 8 of the HMGA. Under section 8(5) of the HMGA, the Guardian and Wards Act, 1890 (GWA) shall apply to and in respect of an application for obtaining permission of the Court for permission to take decisions regarding immovable property of the minor. All applications for appointment of a Court nominated guardian are made to the Guardian Judge under the GWA. If the child in question is a Hindu, this application is made under the HMGA read with the GWA since the powers of the Court to make an order as to guardianship is vested under section 7 of the GWA irrespective of the religion or nationality of the child. Under section 9 of the GWA, the application in respect of the guardianship of the minor is made to the District Court within whose jurisdiction the minor ordinarily resides. For taking this decision, under section 17 of the GWA, the Court shall have regard to the age, sex and religion of the minor, the character and capacity of the proposed guardian, and the preference of the minor if he is old enough to form an intelligent preference. Under section 17 of the GWA and under section 13 of the HMGA, the welfare of the minor will be the paramount consideration in appointment of a guardian. Under section 39 of the GWA, the Court upon application or of its own motion can remove a Court appointed guardian or a guardian appointed by Will or other instrument on grounds in this Section.

Happily enough India has signed and ratified the Hague Convention on Inter-Country Adoptions, 1993 and the UN Convention on Child Rights with a view to strengthening international cooperation and protection of Indian children placed for inter-country adoption. For the purpose of implementation of this convention, the Ministry of Social Justice and Empowerment of the Government of India is functioning as the administrative ministry and Central Adoption Resource Authority (CARA) is functioning as the Central authority under the said Conventions. CARA which is the nodal Central body in New Delhi for adoption measures is registered as a society and now functions as an autonomous body under the newly created Central Ministry of Women and Child Development in the Government of India. All inter-country adoptions are routed through CARA to prevent any violation of children rights and abuse of children abroad.

The Guardian and Wards Act, 1890 (GWA), an 116 years old Indian enactment plays spoil sport in the way of reported 12 million orphan children in India who need parents by not allowing Muslims, Christians, Jews and Parsis to become a Indian child's adoptive parents. They can be appointed as guardians only. The Hindu Adoption and Maintenance Act, 1956 (HAMA) does not allow non-Hindus to adopt a Hindu child. The result, non-Hindus and foreign nationals can at most become guardians under the GWA but cannot adopt children from India.

In order to facilitate the implementation of the norms, principles and procedures relating to adoption of children from India to foreign countries, the Supreme Court in three successive decisions under the same name i.e. *Laxmi Kant Pandey* v. *Union of India*, AIR 1984 SC 469: AIR 1986 SC 272 and 1988 (1) HLR 699, had directed the Government of India to issue guidelines for the above purposes. Accordingly, CARA from time to time, has issued guidelines for adoption of children from India to foreign jurisdictions besides in-country adoptions.

The recent announcement that new guidelines by CARA will mandate full and final "adoption" of children in India before they are sent abroad with prospective parents and that these fresh guidelines will mandate "final adoption of Indian children" under HAMA and the Juvenile Justice (Care and Protection of Children) Act, 2000 (JJ Act) seems attractive but illusory. This is because unless non-Hindu parents are statutorily permitted to "adopt" and not be merely guardians, any guidelines cannot overreach statutory law. Till such time, adoption is permitted only to Hindus, any foreigner who is a non-Hindu cannot adopt a child in India simply because no law permit so. In such event, the exercise of CARA to frame guidelines to allow foreign couples to adopt children in India may be flawed and defective. Any guidelines can supplement the law but not supplant it. Consequently, CARA cannot enact a law of its own.

The HAMA permits adoption to a male or a female Hindu through a process of adoption enacted by the Indian Parliament to codify the law relating to adoptions among Hindus. Even the JJ Act, permits adoption of orphaned, abandoned, neglected and abused children through institutional and non-institutional methods. The fact remains that there is no statutory law which permits non-Hindus who are foreign nationals or professing other religions to adopt children in India. For them, the limited recourse is to the GWA to become guardians which enables them to use the guardianship order obtained in India under the GWA to ultimately gain adoption in foreign jurisdictions. In this event, Indian statutory law does not permit adoption to foreign nationals and persons professing other religions to adopt in India.

HAMA gives a conclusive status to an adoption deed recording an adoption in compliance with its provisions. However, all foreign Embassies or High Commission in India still insist that the adoption deed is not enough. Rules of foreign jurisdiction stipulate that the adoptive parents have to thereafter obtain guardianship orders from a Guardian Judge under the Hindu Minority and Guardianship Act, 1956 (HMGA) for Hindus and a similar order under the GWA for non-Hindus. Genuine transfer of parental responsibility by a irrevocable adoption deed is rendered redundant. A paradox in law results. A valid adoption deed under HAMA is not acceptable to foreign jurisdictions for immigration purposes unless it is supported by a guardianship order under the GWA or HMGA. Strange but true, that is how the law is read by foreign Embassies and High Commissions in India.

In the above backdrop, what should CARA do. It should resolve the conflicts and not compound them. CARA could well send a recommendation that before it enacts any guidelines, they should confirm to statutory law. Any guidelines which differ from codified law will only add but not subtract to the current muddle of inter-country adoptions law.

Mechanics of inter-country adoptions, stringent adoption procedures, insurmountable technicalities, high refusal rates of visas for children in adoption matters and inordinate delay in Indian Court procedures have been a deterrent to adopt a child from India. What do we need. Where is the change desired. May be, a general law for adoption in India enabling any person, irrespective of his religion, race or caste to adopt a child from India will help. Further, keeping in view the repeated guidelines of the Supreme Court in adoption by foreign nationals to prevent trafficking of children and to protect their welfare, a uniform streamlined statutory procedure acceptable to foreign jurisdictions would also serve the purpose better to mitigate the plight of the adoptive child.

**Intra-family disputes**

As a general rule, Indian Courts decide the inter-parental child custody disputes on the basis that the welfare of the child is the paramount consideration, a position consistent with the UN Convention. For example, *Mandy Jane Collins* v. *James Michael Collins,* 2006 (2) HLR 446 (Bom), concerned an American father and a British mother, both resident in Ireland. The parties were litigating over the custody of their 8-year-old minor daughter, said to be illegally detained in Goa by the father. The Court, after taking into consideration the views of the child in chambers who clearly expressed to live with either parent, declined to issue a Writ of a *Habeas Corpus* (a Writ to secure the return of the child), holding that the parties could pursue their remedies in normal civil proceedings in Goa. Dismissing the mother's plea for custody, the Court concluded that the question of permitting the child to be taken to Ireland without first adjudicating upon the rival contentions of the parents in normal civil proceedings in Goa was not possible and directed that status quo be observed. This meant that the 8 years old minor girl continued to live in Goa without her mother or any other female family member being present in the father's house. In a challenge to this decision by the mother before the Supreme Court of India, the appeal was dismissed on 21 August, 2006. This meant it was left open to the parties to move the appropriate forum for the custody of the child, which was directed by the Supreme Court to be decided within a period of three months with earlier visitation rights continuing to the mother. This leads the discussion appropriately on to child protection and the intervention of the state in such matters.

The latest verdict of the Indian Apex Court in matters of child custody disputes has been rendered recently on 13 May 2011, in *Ruchi Majoo* v. *Sanjeev Majoo,* JT 2011 (6) SC 167. The matter arose in a US based NRI couple's case. The wife left her husband in the US and returned to India with her son. She moved a Delhi Guardian Court and got custody rights. In a suit filed by her estranged husband claiming that his wife had abducted the child, a US Court issued a red corner notice against the wife directing her return to USA. In an appeal before the Delhi High Court, it set aside the order of the Delhi Guardian Judge directing the couple to submit before a US Court as they were all US nationals ordinarily residing in USA. The Delhi High Court ruled that the Guardian Judge had no jurisdiction to entertain the wife's petition. The wife appealed to Supreme Court. Thereupon, the Apex Court has set aside the judgment of the Delhi High Court and directed that the proceedings shall go on before the Delhi Guardian Judge to be disposed off as expeditiously as possible. Till then, the interim custody will remain with the mother and the father will enjoy visitation rights only.

The 2011 Apex Court verdict is salutary and laudable. It has culled out three questions for determination. The first question relates to the jurisdiction of the Guardian Judge to entertain the petition for adjudicating custody issues. Interpreting the phrase "ordinarily resident", the Court held that the intention of parties would determine this important question. The fact that the child was studying and resident in Delhi for the past three years had clearly established that there was no coercion or duress for parties to do so as the father was a party to this arrangement. The conduct of parties led the Court to establish that the Guardian Judge was competent to decide the matter as the child was ordinarily resident in Delhi and not in USA.

The second issue urged with deft and ardent skill by the wife led the Court to hold that the jurisdiction of the Guardian Judge could not be declined on the principle of comity of Courts. Examining earlier precedent, the Court ruled that proceedings in *Habeas Corpus* matters are summary in nature which may lead to determination of custody issues when the child is within the jurisdiction of the High Court. Distinguishing and contrasting guardianship proceedings based on evidence, it has been held that if the removed child is not ordinarily resident within its jurisdiction, the Guardian Judge has no jurisdiction to entertain the proceedings even if it is an act of violation of a foreign Court custody order. Disapproving of the application of the "Comity of Courts" principle in the matter, the Supreme Court held that no foreign Court order had been violated by the wife, there was no final decision by any US Court, the minor was voluntarily in India and there was no intention of the wife and child to return to USA. Distinguishing earlier judgments, the Supreme Court held that the interest of the minor could be better served if the mother having custody continued which was a more acceptable option. Hence, the principle found no application in the facts of the case.

With all fairness to the husband, the Supreme Court in the third question also modified the order of the Guardian Judge and granted visitation rights to him during the pendency of the petition before the Court in Delhi. Holding that the "father's care and guidance" is necessary at the "formative and impressionable stage" of the child's life, the Court viewed that for the "child's healthy growth and to stay in touch and share moments of joy, learning and happiness with each other", the father be granted visitation rights through telephonic contact, video conferencing, visits during vacations as determined by the Guardian Judge. This was indeed a humane and a benevolent view of the whole situation despite the discussion with the child in an interactive session with the Court wanting to be left alone by the respondent father.

The well-settled and balanced verdict is a harmonious blend of legal principles, a positive interpretation of parental rights, a decisive pronouncement of jurisdictional issues and brings out a confluence of earlier precedents by distinguishing them on factual basis. It is a much needed decree of the Apex Court shedding light in the realm of the battles of child removal normally fought on uncertain grounds with no legislation on the subject. Thus, the dire need to enact a statutory law on inter-parental child removal to be uniformly followed in all such matters is the appropriate legislative solution in the larger interests of children. The yeoman effort by the Courts to carve out solutions on a case-to-case basis as a result of vibrant efforts can only be a time tiding exercise which cannot be stretched indefinitely.

With the increasing number of migratory Indians and Overseas Citizens of India status, inter-parental child removal needs to be resolved on an international platform. It is no longer a local problem. The phenomenon is global. Parallel Court proceedings in two jurisdictions by warring parents reduce the child to be won over as a trophy at the end of a legal war. Steps have to be taken by joining hands globally to resolve these conflicts by interaction of Courts and countries. Till India does not become a signatory to the Hague Convention on Civil Aspects of International Child Abduction, this cannot be achieved. It is equally important to create a domestic uniform law with clear authentic and universal child custody principles before India accedes to the Convention. The machinery to implement the convention must first be devised. Divergent views only divide children. Removed children cannot be allowed to live on a no man's island. The temptation to wrongfully remove children must be deterred. The cruel abduction of children must find a legislative solution forthwith.

## Child protection and State intervention

### *The law on child abduction generally*

The Hague Convention on Civil Aspects of International Child Abduction 1980 (HCCH No. 25) came into force on 1 December, 1983 and, at the time of settling there are 85 states contracting to it. The Convention secures the prompt return of children wrongfully removed to or retained in any contracting state and ensures the rights of custody and access under the laws of such contracting states. Unfortunately, India is not a signatory to the Hague Convention and, from practical experience, it can be stated that the principles laid down in the Convention are not applicable in India.

These unfortunate circumstances promote and encourage some parents to remove their children to India, thereby hindering the operation of the child's custody rights and diverting attention from the best interest of the child. Indian litigation is often a battle over the rights of the respective parents, with the real issue of the welfare of the child becoming subservient and subordinate. Furthermore, practical experience shows that foreign Courts now largely prohibit children from overseas jurisdictions being brought to India, apprehensive that those children will not be returned to the country of their residence.

Where a child has been abducted to India, article 226 of the Constitution of India, allows the parent seeking the child's return to petition the State High Court to issue a Writ of *Habeas Corpus* against the abducting spouse for the return of the child (*Eugenia Archetti Abdullah* v. *State of Kerala*, 2005 (1) HLR (Ker) 34). It has been held that the High Court can exercise jurisdiction vested in it under article 226 by issuance of the writ of *Habeas Corpus* when the custody of the child had been taken away by one of the natural guardians perpetrating a fraud upon the other (*Gurmeet Kaur Batth* v. *State of Punjab,* [2009] (2) PLR (P&H) 250). Alternatively, a *Habeas Corpus* petition seeking recovery of the abducted child can be filed directly in the Supreme Court of India under article 32 of the Constitution of India. The petitioner need not be a citizen of India (*Atya Shamim* v. *Deputy Commissioner*, ([1999] Del AIR (J&K) 140).

In addition, as another option, the aggrieved parent could have recourse to the provisions of the HMGA 1956, which is an Act to amend and codify certain parts of the law relating to minority and guardianship among Hindus. The provisions of the HMGA, 1956 are supplemental to the Guardians and Wards Act 1890. The HMGA, 1956, like the Hindu Marriage Act, 1955, has extra-territorial application. It extends to the whole of India except the State of Jammu and Kashmir (which is one State described together).

Twelve million orphan children in India need adoptive parents. Abandoned children find themselves in shelter homes, care centres and placement bureaus. The unfortunate ones grow up without care or shelter. The Guardian and Wards Act, 1890, permits guardianship but not adoption. The Hindu Adoption and Maintenance Act, 1956 does not permit non-Hindus to adopt a Hindu child. The plight in so far abandoned children is concerned is protracted by huge numbers and little infrastructural facilities to help them.

The constitutional mandate in Part IV of the Constitution of India containing the Directive Principles of State Policy being non-justiciable, the obligation of the State to secure a social order for the promotion of the welfare of the children remains unimplemented. The policy of the State under article 39 of the Constitution in respect of true and actual protection of children thus does not find a complete legislative voice. Additionally, there is till date no specific Indian legislation on child abuse though, there is a Bill contemplated on the subject but no such clear Statute law on child abuse exists as of now. However, in respect of care, protection, treatment, development and rehabilitation of neglected and delinquent juveniles, The Juvenile Justice (Care and Protection of Children) Act, 2000 exists with an implementing machinery in practice.

***Case law on child abduction***

A foreign Court custody order is only one of the considerations in adjudicating any such child custody dispute between parents. Foreign Court orders of child custody are no longer mechanically enforced, and normally the Courts go into the merits of the matter to decide the best interests of the child, irrespective of any foreign Court custody order. Hence, Indian position on the matter varies from case to case, and there is no uniform precedent which can be cited as a universal rule. Not being a signatory to the Hague Convention of 1980 on the Civil Aspects of International Child Abduction, questions regarding the custody of such children are now considered by the Indian Courts on the merits of each case. The welfare of the child is of paramount importance when considering the order made by the foreign Court.

The High Courts and the Supreme Court entertain petitions for issuance of a Writ of *Habeas Corpus*, which seek to secure the custody of the minor, (For practical application, see *Marilynn Anita Dhillon Gilmore* v. *Margaret Nijjar*, [1984] (1) ILR (P&H) 1) where the parent is in violation of a foreign Court custody order, (See, e.g. *Kala Aggarwal* v. *Suraj Prakash Aggarwal*, [1993] (1) HLR (Del) 145) or is attempting to return the child to the country of the parent's jurisdiction. Invoking this judicial remedy provides the quickest and most effective solution. Indian Courts have often given considerable respect to foreign custody orders, as has been seen in *Sarvajeet Kaur Mehmi* v. *State of Rajasthan*, 1987 (2) HLR 607 (Raj), *Jacqueline Kapoor* v. *Surinder Pal Kapoor*, 1994 (2) HLR 97 (P&H) and *Kulwinder Dhaliwal* v. *State of Punjab*, 2008 (2) ILR 730 (P&H), [for more details see, *Sahiba Ali v. State of Maharashtra*, 2004 (1) HLR 212, *Leeladhar Kachroo v. Umang Bhat Kachroo*, 2005 (2) HLR 449 (Del), *Shilpa Aggarwal v. Aviral Mittal*, 2010 (1) SCC 591, *Dr. V. Ravi Chandran v. Union of India*, 2010 (1) SCC 174]. These cases concerned English, German and Canadian orders, respectively.

Different High Courts have from time to time expressed different views in matters of inter-parental child custody petitions when their jurisdiction has been invoked by an aggrieved parent seeking to enforce a foreign Court custody order or implementation of their parental rights upon removal of the child to India without parental consent. The Supreme Court of India too has rendered different decisions with different viewpoints on the subject in the past three decades.

For example, in *Marggarate* v. *Chacko*, AIR 1970 Ker 1, the Court had to decide if the custody and care of a child could be entrusted to a parent who was living outside the country and outside the Court's jurisdiction. It was held that where the welfare of the child so demands, the Court can also permit the child to be taken out of the country by one of the parents, with proper safeguards laid down by the Court.

In *Dhanwanti Joshi* v. *Madhav Unde*, 1998 (1) SCC 112, the Supreme Court observed that the order of the foreign Court will only be *one* of the facts which must be taken into consideration while dealing with child custody matters. As India is not a signatory to the Hague Convention, the Court within whose jurisdiction the child is removed will consider the issue on its merits, whilst regarding the welfare of the child as its paramount consideration. In this particular case, the Supreme Court overturned the earlier view and did not exercise summary jurisdiction to return the removed children to his parental country. The Hon'ble Apex Court arrived at this decision by observing the best interests of the child. This follows on from *Elizabeth Dinshaw* v. *Arvand M. Dinshaw*, AIR 1987 SC 3, where the Court pronounced that the matter is to be decided not on the considerations of the legal rights of the parties, but on the sole and predominant criterion of the best interest of the minor child. Furthermore, it was held in *Kuldeep Sidhu* v. *Chanan Singh*, AIR 1989 P&H 103 that the welfare of the children would override any consensual custody arrangement, and the children had a right to be brought up in the culture and environment of the country of their birth (in this case, Canada) [*See* also *Amita Gautam* v. *Ramesh Gautam*, 1989 (2) HLR (P&H) 385. In procedural terms, it was held by the Supreme Court in *Vikramvir Vohra* v. *Shalini Bhalla*, JT 2010 (3) SC 213, that child custody orders are interlocutory in nature and can be altered for the welfare of the child. Consequently, the Supreme Court permitted the mother to take her minor son aged about ten years to Australia as per the wishes of the child to stay with the mother. In *Shilpa Aggarwal* v. *Aviral Mittal*, 2010 (1) SCC 591, a three and a half year old girl child, who was a British citizen born in UK to Indian parents was removed to India from UK by the mother in contravention of British Court orders. The mother was directed by the Supreme Court of India to return with the child to UK.

In *Dr. V. Ravi Chandaran* v. *Union of India*, 2010 (1) SCC 174, a seven year old boy, who was a US citizen and was born in USA to Indian Parents (who had become US citizens) was removed to India from USA by the mother contrary to US Court orders. The mother was directed by the Supreme Court of India to return to USA with the child failing which the father would be entitled to do so. Accordingly, the Supreme Court upheld the welfare of the child as a paramount consideration in deciding such custody issues.

An analysis of the case-law reveals that, until 1997, Indian Courts invariably exercised a power of summary return of a removed child to the country of habitual residence in compliance with a foreign Court order to restore parental rights. However, changing the precedent in 1998, the Indian Supreme Court decided that a custody order of a foreign Court shall be only *one* consideration while determining the matters on its merits, in which the welfare of the child will be of paramount importance. Though, in 2010, in *Shilpa Aggarwal* v. *Aviral Mittal*, (supra), and in *Dr. V. Ravi Chandaran* v. *Union of India*, (supra), children were returned to the countries from where they were removed but again on 13 May, 2011, the Apex Court in *Ruchi Majoo* v. *Sanjeev Majoo*, (supra), upheld the jurisdiction of the Guardian Judge to decide the matter by keeping the child in India in his best interest.

Child removal and custody matters now get decided on the merits of each individual case. The *Habeas Corpus* remedy to enforce the child custody order of a foreign Court is proving to be effective and result-oriented. Recent decisions also indicate a trend in respecting foreign Court orders, whereby an aggrieved parent seeks return of the removed child. The position, however, varies on the facts and circumstances of each case as has been demonstrated by cited and quoted precedent held over the years.

***Position of foreign Court orders in India***

The principles governing the validity of foreign Court orders are laid down in section 13 of the Indian Code of Civil Procedure (CPC). The CPC is an Act to consolidate and amend the laws relating to the procedure of the Courts of civil judicature in India. The principles in section 13 CPC have been affirmed in relation to the guidelines laid down by the Supreme Court of India on recognition of foreign matrimonial judgments.

It is reiterated, as discussed above, that Indian Courts would not exercise summary jurisdiction to return the children to the country of habitual residence. The Courts consider the question on the merits of the matter, with the welfare of the children being of paramount importance.

Section 14 of the CPC provides that the Court shall presume, upon the production of any document purporting to be a certified copy of a foreign judgment, that such judgment was pronounced by a Court of competent jurisdiction, unless the contrary appears on the record; but such presumption may be displaced by proving want of jurisdiction.

***No provision for mirror orders in India***

In light of the prevailing child abduction law in India discussed above, it is not possible to obtain mirror orders, as this is a concept known to the English, but not to the Indian legal system. Since foreign Court custody orders cannot now be mechanically enforced, it is suggested that, in the event of any litigation in the foreign country of habitual residence, a letter of request be obtained from the foreign Court in which litigation is pending for incorporating safeguards and conditions to ensure the return of the minor child to the country of normal residence. This letter of request should be addressed by the foreign Court to the Registrar-General of the High Court within whose jurisdiction the estranged spouse is residing with the minor child. It should also be specifically mentioned that the passports of both the parent and the child should be deposited with the Registrar-General of the State High Court to ensure that the child is not taken away from the jurisdiction of the Court where he or she is confined.

***A possible solution to inter-parental child removal***

With the increasing number of Non-Resident Indians abroad and multiple problems arising leading to family conflicts, inter-parental child removal to India now needs to be resolved on an international platform. It is no longer a local problem. The phenomenon is global. Steps have to be taken by joining hands globally to resolve these conflicts through the medium of Courts interacting with each other. Until India becomes a signatory to the Hague Convention, this may not be possible. The time has now come when it is not possible for the Indian Courts to stretch their limits to adapt to different foreign Court orders arising in different jurisdictions. It is equally important to adopt a uniform policy leading to a clear and universal child custody law, adhering to the principles laid down in the Hague Convention, and applying throughout India. Divergent views emerging at different times are inadequate to deal with the rising number of such cases. What is required is the expeditious acceptance and implementation, in India, of the international principles of inter-parental child removal which are provided in the Hague Convention.

***The Civil Aspects of International Child Abduction Bill 2007***

Before the Indian government can accede to the Hague Convention on Civil Aspects of International Child Abduction, appropriate domestic legislation will have to be passed and the Civil Aspects of International Child Abduction Bill, 2007 is designed to serve that purpose. The salient features of this proposed law are as follows. It will create a Central authority for performance of duties under the Hague Convention for securing the return of removed children by instituting judicial proceedings in the concerned High Court. The appropriate authority or a person of a contracting country will be able to apply to the Central authority for return of a removed child to the country of habitual residence. The High Court will be empowered to order the return of a removed child to the country of habitual residence although it may refuse to make such an order if there is grave risk of harm or if it would put the child in an intolerable situation. Consent or acquiescence may also lead to refusal for return of a child by the Court. In addition, The High Court will be able to refuse to return a child if the child objects to being returned, provided the Court is satisfied that the child has attained sufficient age and degree of understanding. Before making an order of return, the High Court will be able to request the Central authority to obtain from the relevant authorities of the country of habitual residence, a decision or determination as to whether the removal or retention of the child in India is wrongful. Finally, upon making an order of return, the High Court will be able to direct that the person who has removed the child to India pay the expenses and costs incurred in returning the child to the country of habitual residence.

This proposed law will be a welcome relief to distraught children who have been removed from their parents. The temptation to wrongfully remove will also be deterred. Moreover, the cruel abduction of NRI children for the purposes of forced marriages will be checked.

## C. ADULT RELATIONSHIPS

### *The relationships*

The Indian Parliament has enacted different family law legislations for different religious communities based on their personal laws. Article 44 of the Constitution of India requires the State to secure for the citizens of India a Uniform Civil Code throughout the territory of India. However, article 44 contained in Part IV of the Constitution dealing with the Directive Principles of State Policy are non justiciable and cannot be enforced. Accordingly, India is a unique blend and merger of codified personal laws of Hindus, Christians, Parsis and to some extend the laws of the Muslim community. In respect of persons who do not profess any particular religion or are foreigners, the Special Marriage Act, 1954 governs all matrimonial causes as according to the Preamble, it is an Act to provide a special form of marriage in certain cases, for the registration of such and certain other marriages and for divorce. Hence, any foreigner not professing any personal law can marry another foreigner or an Indian under the Special Marriage Act. The Foreign Marriage Act, 1969 makes provisions relating to marriages of citizens of India who are resident outside the territorial limits of India. There exists no uniform family related law in a single statutory book for all Indians which can be universally acceptable to all religious communities who co-exist in India. Polygamous relationships are not recognised except under Muslim law. Marrying again during the lifetime of husband or wife is punishable by the offence of bigamy under section 494 of the Indian Penal Code prescribing imprisonment and fine. Even though live in relationships are morally not accepted in traditional Indian society generally, they have now found legislative acceptance after the enactment of the Protection of Women from Domestic Violence Act, 2005. Section 2(f) of this Act recognises live in relationships between two persons in a shared household and under section 17 of this Act, every women in a domestic relationship shall have the right to reside in the shared household whether or not she has any right, title or beneficial interest in the same. Adultery committed by a man with the wife of another man without the consent or connivance of that man is punishable under section 497 of the Indian Penal Code with fine and imprisonment. The woman is not liable to be punished even as an abettor under section 497. Likewise, unnatural offences against the order of nature with any man, woman or animal is punishable under section 377 of the Indian Penal Code with imprisonment and fine. However, the Delhi High Court in *Naz Foundation* v. *Government of NCT of Delhi*, 160 (2009) DLT 277 declared section 377 of the Indian Penal Code, in so far it criminalises consensual sexual acts of persons of or above 18 years of age in private, as unconstitutional being violative of article 21 (Protection of Life and Personal Liberty), article 14 (Equality before Law) and article 15 (Prohibition of Discrimination). Nevertheless, the Court held that the provisions of section 377 will however continue to govern non-consensual homosexual acts involving minors.

***Entering an adult relationship***

*The changing nature of marriage*

Each statute on marriage in India stipulates conditions of a valid marriage. The main areas of contention relate to the legal age of marriage and the registration of marriages and, to some extent, the issues are inter-connected. While the principal family law statute in India, the Hindu Marriage Act 1955, sets the minimum age for marriage at 21 for men and 18 for women (the age of marriage is different for men and women), it does not render a marriage void or voidable in the event that one or both of the parties has not attained the requisite age. Child marriages are performed even though the Child Marriage Restraint Act, 1929 provides punishment for solemnising child marriages of boys below 20 years of age and girls below 18 years of age. To add to the problem, Indian law to date does not require the registration of marriages. Child marriages in practically all religious communities in India are accepted practices, which obviously cannot be registered due to non-fulfilment of minimum age of marriage. Therefore; the violation of the condition of minimum age of marriage does not entail nullity of marriage since registration is optional and not compulsory.

However, the lack of will on the part of the Indian legislature to enact a compulsory law for registration of marriages has not gone unnoticed by the Courts. The Supreme Court of India in *Seema* v. *Ashwani Kumar*, JT 2006 (2) SC 378, has directed all states in India to promulgate rules for compulsory registration of marriages irrespective of religion, in a time-bound period. This reform, which has been spearheaded by the National Commission for Women, has struck a progressive blow; it hinders child marriages, prevent marriages without consent of parties, checks bigamy/polygamy, enables women's rights of maintenance, inheritance and residence, and deters men from deserting women.

The orders of the Indian Apex Court may open a Pandora's Box. Besides Hindus, there are problems amongst other minority religious communities. Even among Muslims, mere non-registration of a marriage will not make it invalid. Codification of some personal laws among some religious communities in India is itself a very contentious issue. As a result of the non-registration of marriages there is a large number of abandoned spouses in India, deserted by Non-Resident Indians who habitually reside abroad. Times have changed but the law has not.

Education, economic prosperity, agricultural improvements, cross-border migration and western influences have changed practices and lifestyles in urban India, while rural arrangements are still struggling with adherence to customary practices in family law matters. Will society catch up with law or will the legislature enact a law on the asking of the Courts to change societal practices? This remains to be seen. Law lags behind social change. However, the fact remains that until the rural masses in India are educated and motivated to change for the better, any changes to the law may not really help. People must learn that child marriage is unacceptable and more needs to be done to avoid the exploitation of married women. Awareness must come from the people themselves and cannot be enforced by the law alone.

***Cross-border and inter-caste marriages***

The Constitution of India under article 14 of the Constitution guarantees the fundamental right to equality and article 21 of the Constitution guarantees protection of life and personal liberty. Equality of laws and equal protection of laws is the touchstone and the spirit of these rights. In addition, the Directive Principles of State Policy endeavour that ensure that the state strives to promote the welfare of the people in a sysytem in which justice and social, economic and political equality informs all the institutions of national life. However, the fact remains that, in India, when young men and women marry outside their caste or community, it sometimes evokes strong sentiments and even honour killings, even though there is no bar to inter-caste marriages under any codified marriage law. In *Lata Singh* v. *State of Uttar Pradesh*, JT 2006 (6) SC 173, it was held that the caste system is a curse on the nation and needs to be eradicated. Acts of violence and threats against inter-caste couples are wholly illegal and those who commit them should be severely punished. The Indian police authorities were directed by the Supreme Court to ensure that no inter-caste couple is harassed by anyone or subjected to any threat or acts of violence. The message of the Court is clear; India of the twenty first century cannot be built on the basis of a caste-oriented approach. To amalgamate as a nation, inter-caste and inter-religious marriages among communities in India must be accepted by society. The barbaric practice of honour killings must be obliterated. But how far can Court decisions achieve this? The Government must enforce the law of the land and uphold the citizen's fundamental rights. A heavy hand is required to check this menace. Therefore, law and society must act in tandem to root out such prejudicial practices.

**Consequences of relationships**

*Dowry and the law: A social menace*

The evil of dowry – any property or valuable security given or agreed to be given by parties to the marriage or to their parents, and given before or at any time after the marriage in connection with or in consideration of the marriage – is rampant in India. The Dowry Prohibition Act, 1961 was enacted to prohibit the giving and taking of dowry, but this social menace is a deep-rooted community practice which carries on despite stringent court verdicts. The practice by which dowry seekers attempt to justify it by quoting examples from Hindu scriptures has percolated to all religions in India, though it has no customary or religious sanctity attached to it. Both the Dowry Prohibition Act, 1961 and section 498A of the Indian Penal Code (IPC) deal with dowry-related harassment of a married woman. Unfortunately, sometimes dowry leads to violence and murder. Dowry deaths by burning or suicide have become a ponderous point. Decisions of the Supreme Court of India, [See *Vidhya Devi* v. *State of Haryana*, [2004] AIR (SC) 1757; *Surinder Kaur* v. *State of Haryana*, [2004] AIR (SC) 1747; *Kunhiabdulla* v. *State of Kerala*, [2004] AIR (SC) 1731], show that dowry deaths by suicide result in conviction of only one person whereas dowry deaths by burning result in convictions of all concerned. This anomaly of law does not mitigate the crime. In societal terms, the menace of dowry cannot be uprooted until the public is educated about the ills of this malpractice and awareness comes from within. At the same time, law must come down with a heavy hand on dowry seekers, and provide punishment a deterrent to others who follow it. Harsher and more stringent penalties in law must be further advocated.

This has been recognised by the Courts and appropriate judgments have been handed down in recent years. For example, in *Re: Enforcement and Implementation of Dowry Prohibition Act 1961*, [*See, Re: Enforcement and Implementation of Dowry Prohibition Act, 1961*, JT 2005 (5) SC 71], the Apex Court directed the Indian Government to implement all the interim directions issued by the Supreme Court earlier, and take effective measures to eradicate the social evil of dowry through the machinery of the Act. Moreover, in *Sushil Kumar Sharma* v. *Union of India*, JT 2005 (6) SC 266, the Apex Court, upholding the Constitutional validity of section 498A of the Indian Penal Code, held that the object of section 498A is the prevention of the menace of dowry. It further pronounced that its overarching purpose is to prevent cruelty to, and harassment of, women. Accordingly, the provision did not offend the Constitution of India.

***Termination of relationships***

*The law of divorce in India*

The two principal family law statutes in India are the Hindu Marriage Act 1955 and the Special Marriage Act, 1954, which contain three grounds in a three-tier divorce structure. These are the fault ground, the break-down ground on non-compliance with judicial separation and the ground of mutual consent. Irretrievable break-down of marriage *simplicitor* is not a ground of divorce under any Indian statute. The Parsi Marriage and Divorce Act, 1936 (as amended) and the Divorce Act, 1869 (as amended) follow suit. The Dissolution of Muslim Marriages Act, 1939 lays down the grounds for a decree for dissolution of marriage of Muslims.

***Customary divorces***

Section 29 of the Hindu Marriage Act 1955 gives statutory recognition to customary divorces. This in effect means that parties relying on a custom need not go to Court and obtain a decree for divorce. However, the onus on the party who relies on a custom is indeed weighty and the custom should be ancient, certain, reasonable and not opposed to public policy. Even though Courts take judicial notice of customs, the validity of a deed of dissolution of marriage under a customary practice has to be established by leading cogent evidence by the person propounding such custom. In *Subramani* v. *M. Chandralekha*, JT 2005 (11) SC 562, the Apex Court, following well-settled principles of law, held that since there was no custom prevalent in the community to which the parties belonged for dissolution of marriage by mutual consent, the alleged deed of dissolution marriage could not be executed.

It is common for parties in India to set up customary divorce practices as a shortcut to the statutory procedures, but with the vigilant judiciary, such abuse of the process of law does not succeed. Regardless, multiple marriages are often solemnized in contravention of codified law by taking advantage of non-existent customs. To this extent neither law nor the courts come to rescue of such parties. However, section 16 of the Hindu Marriage Act clearly provides that, notwithstanding that such marriage is null and void, any child of such marriage who would have been legitimate if the marriage had been valid, shall be legitimate. Consequently, even though spouses may not gain, the statute protects and provides property and other inheritance rights to children of such unions. Conferring such rights upon children has been recently reiterated by the Supreme Court of India in *Bhogadi* v. *Vuggina*, 2006 (5) SCC 532. The policy of the law is therefore clear to provide beneficial effects to the offspring without condoning the contravention and violation of marriage laws. Customs will not die but their misuse must be prevented and curtailed.

***Divorce by irretrievable breakdown of marriage***

Keeping in mind that the institution of marriage in Indian society is largely still a sacrament and not a contract, especially under the Hindu Marriage Act 1955, any major overhaul may be offensive to the very concept of Hindu marriage. The existing three-tier divorce structure in India, largely applicable to all communities, provides the codified and statutory grounds for divorce in Indian Courts. Two decisions of the High Court, *Yudhister Singh* v. *Sarita*, 2004 (1) HLR 228, and *Kakali Dass* v. *Dr. Asish Kumar*, 2004 (1) HLR 448, as well as a Supreme Court of India decision in *Sham Sunder* v. *Sushma*, JT 2004 (8) SC 166, give a clear indication that the ground of irretrievable break-down of marriage should be rarely used.

However, some recent decisions of the Supreme Court of India indicate that the Apex Court has recommended that "irretrievable break-down of marriage" should be added as a ground for divorce on the statute book. The case of *Naveen Kohli* v. *Neelu Kohli*, JT 2006 (3) SC 491, recommended to the Union of India to seriously consider bringing an amendment to the Hindu Marriage Act, so as to incorporate irretrievable break-down of marriage as a ground for divorce. It is not uncommon for the Apex Court to apply this principle in dissolving marriages, as was recently done in *Durga Prasanna* v. *Arundhati*, JT 2005 (7) SC 596.

In the case of *Anil Kumar Jain* v. *Maya Jain*, 2009 (10) SCC 415, it was held that the Supreme Court can grant relief to parties without waiting for the statutory period of six months to grant divorce by mutual consent to willing spouses. However, the Supreme Court clearly held that this doctrine of irretrievable breakdown of marriage is not available under statute to the High Courts or subordinate Courts, which do not have powers similar to those exercised by the Supreme Court under article 142 of the Constitution. In the case of *Manish Goel* v. *Rohini Goel*, 2010 (3) SCC 189, it was held that the Court will not use its powers under article 142 of the Indian Constitution to consider irretrievable breakdown of marriage as a valid ground for divorce.

In the opinion of the authors, a civilized parting of spouses where a marriage has irretrievably broken down must be incorporated into statute as an additional ground for divorce. However, this should only be in cases where both parties to the marriage jointly petition the Court for such relief. This will have an immediate two-fold benefit. First, where parties have irreconcilable differences and want to part amicably, an option will be available to them to part legally and logically without resorting to a protracted time-consuming legal battle on trumped-up grounds. Secondly, recourse to ex-parte divorce in foreign jurisdictions by Non-Resident Indians against hapless spouses on Indian soil may decline once a proper legal option of irretrievable break-down is available to spouses on Indian soil. However, to prevent hasty divorces or misuse, sufficient statutory safeguards can be incorporated to arm the judiciary to prevent any abuse of the process of law. Retaining the ceremonial and sacramental concept of marriage, irretrievable breakdown hedged with safeguards can be introduced where both parties consent to it. To harmonise and blend modern family requirements in urban areas with traditional Indian concepts of family law, the above middle path can be best advocated.

On 10 June, 2010 the Union Cabinet approved the introduction of a Bill, that is the Marriage Laws (Amendment ) Bill, 2010, to be tabled in the forthcoming winter session of Parliament. It seeks to amend the Hindu Marriage Act, 1955 and Special Marriage Act, 1954, to provide irretrievable breakdown of marriage as a ground for divorce. Till date, it has not become law in India.

The long awaited move comes more than a year after the Law Commission of India *suo moto* took up the study of the subject and in its 217th report in March 2009 had strongly made the above recommendation. The Commission examined the existing legislations as well as a number of judgments of the Supreme Court and High Courts on the subject and was of the view that "irretrievable break-down of marriage" should be incorporated as another ground for granting divorce under the provisions of the Hindu Marriage Act, 1955 (HMA) and the Special Marriage Act, 1954 (SMA). The commission also recommended that the Court before granting a decree for divorce on the ground that the marriage has irretrievably broken down, should also examine whether adequate financial arrangements have been made for the parties and children.

Although such a ground for divorce is currently not mentioned in HMA, the Apex Court has in appropriate cases granted a decree of divorce on grounds of "irretrievable breakdown of marriage" by virtue of powers vested in the Apex Court under article 142 of the Constitution of India to pass such orders for doing complete justice in any cause or matter pending before it. However, different Benches of The Supreme Court have taken separate stands over this issue.

In March, 2006, a three-Judge Bench of Supreme Court granted divorce in *Naveen Kohli* v. *Neelu Kohli,* 2006 (4) SCC 558. But in February, 2009, a two-Judge Bench of the Apex Court in *Vishnu Dutt Sharma* v. *Manju Dutt Sharma,* 2009 (6) SCC 379, refused to grant divorce on the ground of Irretrievable Breakdown of Marriage, as the Court observed that it could not add such a ground to section 13 of HMA as it would amount to amending the Act which is a function of the Legislature. In the most recent view in May, 2010, in *Neeti Malviya* v. *Rakesh Malviya,* 2010 (6) SCC 413, the Supreme Court while examining the question of waiving the six months waiting period for divorce by mutual consent by invoking its extraordinary powers under article 142 of the Constitution, has referred the question for consideration by a Bench of three-Hon'ble Judges. Clearly, the underlining note of invoking irretrievable breakdown of marriage as a ground for divorce did not find favour with the Bench. Thus, from the views in the judgment of the Supreme Court in *V. Bhagat* v. *D. Bhagat,* 1994 (1) SCC 337 allowing divorce on the ground of irretrievable breakdown of marriage to the pronouncement of the Apex Court in *Anil Kumar Jain* v. *Maya Jain,* 2009 (10) SCC 415, not allowing so, there has been a variant view on this controversial subject for fifteen years. The Apex Court, however, has been consistent in its view that neither the High Courts nor the subordinate Courts can exercise such power vested only in it.

Realistically speaking, a broken marriage limps to dissolution. Law cannot reunite parties if the matrimonial bond has severed. Consequently, a peaceful parting is necessary if parties cannot reconcile despite best efforts. Thus, adding of irretrievable breakdown of marriage as a ground for divorce by Parliament by amending marriage laws may be the best possible solution for the future for limping marriages. However, the power of the Court to grant divorce on the ground of irretrievable break-down of marriage should be exercised with extreme care and caution only in circumstances warranting so and when it is in the interest of both the parties. Due regard for maintenance of the dependent spouse, besides care and welfare of children must be safeguarded by an enabling legislation. Hence, simultaneous amendments to other provisions of marriage laws in this regard must follow forthwith whenever such a law is made.

A balance needs to be maintained wherein sanctity of the institution of marriage should be protected as well as individual interests of aggrieved spouses should be addressed. India is deeply embedded by moral and cultural values and thus, emulation of western principles in matrimonial matters is not appreciable and should not be adapted with ease. Hence, the ground of irretrievable breakdown of marriage should be introduced cautiously hedged with safeguards so that the provision is not subject of misuse.

Nevertheless, there is also an urgent need to set up Family Court in every district of the country for adjudicating all kinds of matrimonial disputes. It is really unfortunate that even after more than twenty-five years of enactment of the Family Courts Act, 1984, only a miniscule number of such Courts have been set up only in metropolitan cities of India. It may also be advocated that not only among Hindus, but also for Muslims, Christians, Parsis and other religious denominations, there must be marriage and divorce laws in line with contemporary practices of young generations who receive higher education and have more cosmopolitan thinking of the new world. Times have changed and people of India must move ahead without living in the past. Harmony at home and peace at work is the most important component and quality of successful Indians in the twenty first century. The stable family is an epitome of Indian society.

In domestic matrimonial disputes, settlement of maintenance, alimony and matrimonial property besides issues relating to custody of children are dealt with as ancillary relief in a matrimonial cause under the respective personal laws of all religious communities. Maintenance is decided on a need based basis and the earning capacity besides living standards of spouses. There is no standard 50 : 50 division rule regarding division of matrimonial property which is normally settled on a lump sum basis. Custody of children is generally awarded on the basis of the welfare of the child as a paramount consideration. All these issues are determined by respective judicial Courts of competent jurisdiction designated to hear matrimonial matters under the respective codified personal laws of the religious communities in India. All parties find due redressal and hearing in this regard under the adversary litigation system in India.

***Consequences of termination***

*Enforcement of foreign matrimonial judgments and orders in India*

Whilst there is an ever-increasing population of Indians migrating and settling in foreign jurisdictions, the link with their home country does not sever. Family links, connections to property and moveable assets, and other ties with India often lead to cross-border litigation in human relationship matters. Non-Resident Indians often use their domestic Courts to obtain favourable orders which can then be implemented in India.

Indian law reports contain a number of judgments on matters relating to marriage, divorce, maintenance, succession, settlement of matrimonial property, child custody, parental abduction of children from foreign jurisdictions in matrimonial disputes and cases relating to adoption. Attempts are made to enforce these foreign Court orders in India through the domestic Courts. Since there exists no separate provision for recognition of foreign matrimonial judgments in Indian law (as relates to family matters), the only recourse lies to section 13 of the Indian Code of Civil Procedure (CPC), which is the general provision of law relating to conclusiveness of judgments by foreign Courts. In such a situation, the precedents giving instances of such reported matters are therefore available only in the shape of judicial pronouncements of Indian Courts, which have from time-to-time rendered a laudable service in interpreting foreign Court orders in the best interests of human relationships rather than executing them *simplicitor* in letter and spirit. The Indian judiciary is extremely humane and considerate in family matters, implementing the foreign Court orders in a practical way, rather than engaging in a mechanical execution of the order or judgment of the overseas Court. Perhaps this openness and fluidity is possible since the Indian Courts are not strictly bound by a foreign Court order in family matters but when asked to implement or enforce the same, the Indian Courts apply principles of good conscience, natural justice, equity and fair play, thereby rendering substantial justice to parties in litigation. This can be best seen in decisions of some Indian Courts which have resulted in the Court being asked to implement or execute a Court order or judgment arising from a foreign jurisdiction.

A very commonly arising issue pertains to recognition and indirect implementation of divorce decrees of foreign Courts produced in India by spouses residing in foreign jurisdictions. In this regard, different views have been expressed by different Indian Courts at different points of time. Consequently, the Supreme Court, in 1991, laid down fresh comprehensive guidelines for the recognition of foreign matrimonial judgments by the Courts in India. It may be pertinent to point out that under article 141 of the Constitution of India, the law declared by the Supreme Court shall be binding on all Courts within the territory of India. The Apex Court in *Y Narasimha Rao* v. *Y. Venkata Lakshmi*, JT 1991 (3) SC 33, made it clear that Indian Courts would not recognise a foreign judgment if it had been obtained by fraud, which need not be only in relation to the merits of the matter but may also be in relation to jurisdictional facts. The Court accordingly declared a divorce decree, passed by a US Court, unenforceable in India. Interpreting section 13 of the Indian CPC the Court laid down broad principles to be followed by Indian Courts with special emphasis on matrimonial judgments.

It will be noted that the proposed guidelines in *Narasimha Rao* (supra) and *Neeraja Saraph v. Jayant Saraph*, JT 1994 (6) SC 488, are meaningful and, if implemented, can mitigate the plight of wives dumped in India by foreign husbands. The Apex Court has clearly stated the need for suitable legislation on the subject, as no Indian law has been enacted to protect the rights of deserted and abandoned spouses in India. In essence, the judgments of the judiciary are the only available law in India to come to the rescue of hapless Indian spouses, who protest against the uncontested foreign divorce decrees invariably obtained in default by spouses from overseas jurisdictions. Codification is now an absolute necessity.

In such affairs, it is judicial precedent which provides the much available guidance and judicial legislation on the subject. With a large number of Non-Resident Indians now permanently living in overseas jurisdictions, it has now become important that legislation be drafted to deal with the problems of Non-Resident Indians to avoid them from importing judgments from foreign Courts to India for implementation of their rights. The answer therefore lies in providing domestic, as opposed to foreign, remedies. Hence, it is the Indian legislature which now seriously needs to review this issue and provide statutory remedies for Non-Resident Indians in family law matters. Until this is done, foreign Court judgments in domestic matters will keep cropping up and Courts in India will continue with their salutary efforts in interpreting them in harmony with Indian law and doing substantial justice to parties in the most fair and equitable way. However, in this process, the Indian judiciary has made one thing very clear. It would not simply mechanically enforce judgments and decrees of foreign Courts in family matters. The Indian Courts have now started looking into the merits of the matters and deciding them on the considerations of Indian law and the best interest of the parties, rather than simply implementing the orders without examining them. Fortunately, we can applaud the Indian judiciary for these laudable efforts. Until suitable legislation is drafted, we must have faith in the Indian judiciary.

Hindu marriages made in heaven and solemnized in India are now wantonly dissolved abroad. Sad but true. A prelude follows. Over 30 million overseas Indian are domiciled in 180 countries abroad. The parallel adjudication of their matrimonial disputes in Courts simultaneously in India and abroad activates a new inter se martial discord. This clash of jurisdictional battles also germinates a conflict amongst authority of Courts. Foreign Courts often impose penal sanctions oblivious of prior directions of existing Indian Courts of superior hierarchy. Rules of private international law offer little resolution. Spouses, children and extended families bear the brunt of multi-faceted parallel directives of Courts of different overseas territories.

The Supreme Court in *Neerja Saraph* v. *Jayant Saraph,* (supra) proposed feasibility of enacting a legislation to ensure that no marriage between a NRI and an Indian which has taken place in India may be annulled by a foreign Court. Earlier in *Y. Narasimha Rao* v. *Y. Venkata Lakshmi,* (supra), the Apex Court spelt out guidelines for recognition of foreign Court matrimonial judgments to decide when Hindu marriages solemnized in India were said to be dissolved by unenforceable foreign decrees.

The Bombay High Court in *Sondur Rajani* v. *Sondur Gopal,* 2006 (2) HLR 475, ruled that a foreign domicile of parties will not take away the jurisdiction of Indian Courts to decide the annulment of their ceremonial Hindu marriage solemnized when they were domiciled in India. In *Navin Chander* v. *Leena,* 2005 (2) HLR 582, the matrimonial dispute of a ceremonial marriage of Hindus celebrated in USA, was held by the Bombay High Court to be amenable for adjudication by the Family Court, Pune. The Delhi High Court in *Veena Kalia* v. *Jatinder Kalia,* AIR 1996 Del 54, ruled that an ex-parte decree of divorce of a foreign Court being a nullity, would not bar a subsequent petition for divorce in India even though maintenance had been accepted under the foreign judgment. In *Harmeeta Singh* v. *Rajat Taneja,* 2003 (2) RCR (Civil) 197, the Delhi High Court temporarily restraining the foreign Court divorce proceedings held that even if the Hindu marriage is dissolved in USA, it would still have to be confirmed by an Indian Court. In *Moina* v. *Amardeep,* AIR 1986 Del 399, a foreign domicile was held by the Delhi High Court to be no deterrent to a divorce petition preferred in India to dissolve a Hindu marriage celebrated here. These authoritative and laudable verdicts clearly reflect that Indian Courts rightly have a prerogative to adjudicate matrimonial disputes falling in their domain.

In this backdrop, a new dimension of matrimonial litigation is coming in practice in the matrimonial arena in the shape of anti-injunction suits which is the remedy against filing of suits at different jurisdictions in respect of the same cause of action. A petition preferred in India for restraining an opposing spouse from pursuing or continuing with a complaint for matrimonial relief in a foreign Court would be such an anti-injunction suit in matrimonial matters. Lack of jurisdiction, both regarding the corpus of the Hindu marriage and the physical presence of an Indian spouse in the territory abroad, are the grounds of such suits in India. However, even the reverse application now finds popular practice.

An extreme view finds enunciation in a unreported judgment in *Singh* v. *Singh* rendered on 20 September, 2010 in an anti-injunction suit. The Federal Magistrates

Court of Australia at Canberra restrained the wife from taking any action, as also for causing, allowing or assisting any other person, to pursue a complaint in India against the husband under the Dowry Prohibition Act, 1961. Both parties were Australian citizens married according to Sikh rites in India. By Australian consent orders, settlement of maintenance, property and child custody were resolved. The Canberra Court found that on evidence presented, Ms. Singh had not established that a dowry was either requested or paid as alleged. Accordingly, the Court held "that the injunction acts in personam only in relation to Ms. Singh, and does not, either in terms or otherwise, purport to affect the administration of justice in India". The judgment was said to be based on considerations of equity and justice.

In the above backdrop, the thought proposed for conscious deliberation which reverberates in the minds of those who live on home soil is the dire need for evolving an Indian jurisprudence in matrimonial litigation to deal with anti-injunction suits in India. If an American Court imposes a fine of one lac US Dollars a day for not complying a US Court child custody order contrary to an Indian Court order or a divorce petition on grounds of irretrievable breakdown of marriage is proceeded with in USA despite a pending Indian divorce litigation, such oppressive litigation must be restrained by the dictates of equity, good conscience and comity of Courts. Such unconscionable acts are estoppel by conduct. If foreign Courts can evolve principles, similar thinking must develop at home too.

In the far-reaching repercussions which tend to shake the foundations of strong traditional Hindu marriages, a foreign Court matrimonial order may at times invade the privacy of the home and leave the hapless Indian spouse to abject surrender without a remedy. Surely, Law must come to rescue. The yeoman verdicts of Indian Courts are a big crutch. However, the need for a preventive remedy is stronger than a powerful cure at the end. What can be prevented must be stopped. What should not be suffered should not be endured. Anti suit injunctions in matrimonial matters in fit cases must deter oppressive foreign Court orders without technicalities. The majesty of Indian law must prevail.

***Self-regulation and custom-made relationships***

Today, the nuclear Indian family is plagued by new generation ills. Forced marriages, honour killings, live in relationships, parental child removal, inter-country adoptions, and surrogacy defy solutions in codified laws. Conventional family law framers never visualized these societal complexities which have mushroomed recently. Statutory law has not caught up with the maze of legal intricacies which dog these family law issues. Judicial verdicts render a yeoman service resolving these vexed questions daily.

Provisions for settlement of disputes outside the Court find a prominent place in the Civil Procedure Code, Codified Marriage laws and the Family Courts Act. However, settlement, reconciliation and mediation in family law matters are today largely unutilized. The Supreme Court in *Jagraj Singh* v. *Birpal Kaur,* (2007) 2 SCC 564 upholding the salutary provisions to endeavour reconciliation in the first instance clearly confirms that settlement efforts in matrimonial matters are not an empty meaningless ritual. It is this thought which needs strict practice. Matters of the family which can be repaired must be mediated and settled by sewing and patch work. Human relationships must be bonded by settlement and as far as possible not litigated in Court battles.

Litigation in respect of any matter concerning the family, whether divorce, maintenance, alimony, child custody or any other matrimonial cause should not be viewed in terms of failure or success of legal actions. The amicable settlement of family conflicts is a social therapeutic problem. Family disputes need to be seen with a humanitarian approach. They should be reconciled in the family fold so as not to disrupt the family structure. Adjudication of family disputes is entirely different from conventional civil or criminal proceedings. Reverberations of a family dispute are felt in society. Their effective resolution by mediation or conciliation may provide lasting solutions for overall good.

The Apex Court in *Gaurav Nagpal* v. *Sumedha Nagpal,* (2008) 2 HLR 584 emphasized that efforts should be made to bring about conciliation to bridge communication gaps to prevent people from rushing to Courts. This salutary verdict has both depth and meaning. Therefore, the dire pressing need of the day in the current social milieu, is to create an infrastructural machinery for Alternative Disputes Resolution (ADR) mechanisms. Particularly, marriages solemnized in India and fractured abroad in the 30 million NRI community can be mediated and settled. It is these limping unions which need reconciliatory formulas in India to prevent them from being split. Conflicts, arising locally or overseas should not stem into other ancillary issues multiplying the problem. ADR needs to be developed in a big way for resolving limping family unions.

The mediation cell of the Punjab and Haryana High Court which attempts to mediate matrimonial disputes is an extremely positive development. The culture of settlement needs propagation. The solutions of settlement permeate peace in extended families. ADR cannot see the light of the day unless citizens participate in the movement. The conventional Peoples Courts can be a means to this end. Individual initiatives need awakening by self-consciousness and not by implementation of laws. Spouses, parents and families need to realize the advantages of ADR in the family structure. Matrimonial relief carved out by settlement will serve better than results obtained by adversarial litigation involving time, effort, finances and above all by breaking up a family.

Family matters ought not to be litigated in any Court unless extraordinarily grave. Issues of marriages, divorces and children ought to be put before Family Courts. Trained counselors, mediators and advisors should resolve them mutually. superior Courts themselves too must inject the spirit of mediation in appellate jurisdictions. A unanimous consensus saves a home, a family and a societal foundation. Mandatory reconciliation procedures should be affirmed with the seal of the Court to put to rest conclusively without any challenge.

The necessity and urgency of creating more Family Courts under the Family Courts Act, will contribute to resolution of family law disputes by ADR. The current handling of matrimonial litigation by conventional Courts is a poignant reminder of what prevails today. The availability of trained counselors, professional mediators and above all specialist family law Judges could all form part of a well organized family disputes adjudication team. This would give a new dimension to ADR in family law.

Laws to promote ADR exist but the infrastructure, professional assistance and the medium through which these beneficial reconciliatory mediation procedures are to be implemented are lacking. The package is wholesome. The numbers are huge. The need is dire. The solution is inbuilt. An effective implementation machinery is required. The solution is with the people. The makers of law must aid, abet and implement ADR.

A recent judgment of the Bombay High Court setting aside the parallel proceedings for divorce of the Family Court, Pune and upholding a divorce decree passed by the Court of Oakland, State of Michigan, USA, dissolving a Hindu marriage on the principle of breakdown, has evoked a new stream of thought with which the author respectfully differs. The verdict, *Kashmira Kale* v. *Kishore Kumar Mohan Kale*, 2011 (1) HLR 333 lending sanctity to a US divorce decree in preference to proceedings under the Hindu Marriage Act between the same parties upsets the settled law.

The parties married in Mumbai in 2005 according to Hindu rites lived in USA and intermittently visited Mumbai and Pune. In September 2008, the wife filed divorce proceedings in the US whose jurisdiction was challenged by the husband in the US. Simultaneously, in October 2008, the husband filed a divorce petition in the Pune Family Court, claiming it to be the competent forum for adjudication of their dispute. The husband did not pursue the wife's divorce petition in the US any further and in January 2009, the US Court dissolved the marriage and divided the assets of the parties. However, the Family Court in Pune in September 2009 held that it still had the jurisdiction to try the husband's petition for divorce in India. In appeal, the Bombay High Court set aside the order of the Family Court, Pune, and upheld the US divorce decree dissolving the Hindu marriage.

The conclusions drawn by the Bombay High Court that the parties were domiciled in the US and hence the Hindu Marriage Act (HMA) cannot apply to them is *per se* erroneous. Furthermore, the non-application of the HMA to Hindus was misconstrued and the application of the breakdown principle without considering the written statement of the husband challenging the jurisdiction of the US Court were factors which did not lend a imprimatur to the foreign decree which did not take into consideration the provisions of the HMA under which the parties were married.

Noticing that section 1(2) of HMA applies only to Hindus in the territories to which the HMA applies but not considering that it also "applies to Hindus domiciled in the territories to which this Act extends who are outside the said territories" left the contention only half noticed. To add to it, section 2 of HMA prescribing application of the Act to Hindus, irrespective of domicile, nationality or citizenship, renders the decision of the Bombay High Court fallacious. Earlier precedents on the point enunciated by different High Courts stipulate that HMA applies to all Hindus irrespective of domicile or residence if they have married in India according to Hindu rites. Thus, it has been held that HMA has extra territorial application as a Hindu carries with him his personal law of marriage and Courts in India have jurisdiction to try their matrimonial disputes regardless of change of nationality or new domicile.

The Bombay High Court in *Sondur Rajini* v. *Sondur Gopal,* 2006(2) HLR 475, had held that the provisions of the HMA do not cease to apply on change of domicile which is determined when the parties tie the nuptial knot under the HMA and not on the date when an application is made for matrimonial reliefs. In *Naveen Chander Advani* v. *Leena Advani,* 2005 (2) HLR 582, the Bombay High Court held that the Family Court in Pune wrongly declined to entertain a matrimonial petition relating to a marriage where parties who last resided and married in USA according to Hindu rites and ceremonies as the Family Court has jurisdiction to deal with matters under the HMA/SMA. The Delhi High Court had earlier echoed similar views in *Harmita* v. *Rajat,* 2003 (2) RCR 197 holding that in consonance with principles of private international law, a US divorce decree would have to be confirmed by a Court in India. Even in *Moina* v. *Amardeep,* AIR 1986 Del 399, it had been held that under section 1(2) of HMA, the Canadian domicile of the husband could not be a ground to decline jurisdiction of Delhi Courts.

Equally flawed is the view of the Bombay High Court that since the parties last resided together in Michigan, USA, the U.S Court has territorial jurisdiction to decide their divorce dispute. This conclusion falls foul of the settled law laid down by the Supreme Court in *Jagir Kaur* v. *Jaswant Singh,* AIR 1963 SC 1521 that prescribing the limits of jurisdiction, speaking of last residence of a person with his wife, can only mean his last residence in the territories of India. It cannot obviously mean his residing with her in a foreign country for an Act cannot confer jurisdiction on a foreign Court. The Bombay High Court in *Meera* v. *Anil Kumar,* 1992 (2) HLR 284 also held that "last resided" in section 19 of HMA means last residence in India and the High Court in India within whose jurisdiction the parties last resided together can take cognizance of the matter. Flowing from the same stream of thought, the Punjab and Haryana High Court has held that any temporary residence would confer jurisdiction to try the matrimonial dispute. This settled view militates against the erred conclusion of the Bombay High Court that temporary stay at Pune or Mumbai could not mean last residence in India as parties last resided together in USA.

Above all, the view of the Bombay High Court disagrees with the celebrated view of the Apex Court in *Y. Narasimha Rao* v. *Y. Venkata Lakshmi,* (1991) 3 SCC 451 clearly holding the rule that the jurisdiction assumed by the foreign Court as well as the grounds on which the relief is granted must be in accordance with the matrimonial law under which the parties are married. Three exceptions were culled out to this rule by the Supreme Court. **Firstly**, permanent foreign residence and invoking of relief on a ground available in matrimonial law under which parties were married. **Secondly**, voluntary submission to foreign jurisdiction coupled with contest on merits abroad on grounds available under matrimonial law under which parties were married. **Thirdly**, parties unconditionally consent to grant of relief although jurisdiction of foreign Court is not in accordance with provisions of matrimonial law of parties. The Apex Court in *Neerja Saraph* v. *Jayant Saraph,* (supra), thereafter had even suggested feasibility of a legislation to hold that "no marriage between a NRI and an India women which has taken place in

India may be annulled by a foreign court". Not noticing the above precedents of the Apex Court, the recent view of the Bombay High Court *per se* appears to be disagreeable if not *per incuriam*.

With due deference, the verdict of the Bombay High Court neither agrees with precedent on the point, does not adapt to Hindu law of marriage of the parties, nor is it conclusive. Parties may be treated as divorced in USA and still married in India. Confusion confounded. In this breath, the line of action adopted in a number of matrimonial disputes in the Punjab and Haryana High Court is most useful to quote. Limping marriages are taken before the mediation and conciliation centre at the High Court premises where the hatchet is peacefully buried and matters are amicably compromised to convert the matrimonial feuds to divorce petitions by mutual consent. Matters thereafter rest without contest on written settlements. Warring claims are put to sleep harmoniously. This is the better path than allowing foreign Courts to decide Hindu marriage disputes without conflict of laws. Indian Courts are better suited to decide them without foreign interference. Domestic law must prevail.

## D. CONCLUSIONS

### *The need for a Uniform Civil Code in India*

Article 44 of the Constitution of India requires the State to secure for the citizens of India a Uniform Civil Code throughout the territory of India. As has been noted above, India is a unique blend of codified personal laws of Hindus, Christians, Parsis and to some extent of laws of Muslims. However, there is no single, uniform family law statute applicable to all Indians.

For the first time, in *Mohammad Ahmed Khan* v. *Shah Bano Begum*, AIR 1985 SC 945, in 1985, the Supreme Court of India directed the Indian Parliament to frame a Uniform Civil Code. There, a penurious Muslim woman claimed maintenance from her husband under section 125 of the Code of Criminal Procedure after her husband pronounced triple Talaq (divorce by announcing the word "Talaq" thrice). The Apex Court held that the Muslim woman had a right to maintenance under section 125 of the Code and also held that article 44 of the Constitution prescribing that the State shall endeavour to secure for its citizens a Uniform Civil Code in India had remained a dead letter. To undo the above decision, the Muslim Women (Right to Protection on Divorce) Act, 1986, which curtailed the right of a Muslim Woman for maintenance under section 125 of the Code, was enacted by the Indian Parliament. Article 44 of the Constitution prescribes that a Uniform Civil Code shall be enacted for its citizens. However, none exists till date.

Thereafter, in the case of *Sarla Mudgal* v. *Union of India*, AIR 1995 SC 1531, the question which arose was whether a Hindu husband, married under Hindu law, could, by embracing the Islamic religion, solemnise a second marriage. The Supreme Court held that a Hindu marriage solemnized under Hindu law can only be dissolved under the Hindu Marriage Act and conversion to Islam and marrying again would not, by itself, dissolve the Hindu marriage. Further, it was held that a second marriage solemnised after converting to Islam constituted the offence of bigamy under section 494 of the Indian Penal Code.

The Supreme Court reiterated the need for Parliament to frame a Common Civil Code which will help the cause of national integration by removing contradictions based on ideologies. Thus, the Directive Principle of enacting a Uniform Civil Code has been urged by the Apex Court repeatedly in a number of decisions as a matter of urgency. Unfortunately, in a subsequent decision, [*Lily Thomas* v. *Union of India*, 2000 (6) SCC 224], the Apex Court clarified that the Court had not issued any directions for the codification of a common civil code and that the Judges constituting the different Benches had only expressed their views in the facts and the circumstances of those cases. However, this ought not to deter the efforts of the Supreme Court in issuing mandatory directions to the Indian Government to draft a common civil code, applicable to all communities, irrespective of their religion and practices in a secular India. Hopefully, the Apex Court may review its findings in some other case and issue mandatory directions to the Central Government to bring a common civil code applicable to all communities irrespective of their religion.

***Secularism and a Uniform Civil Code***

The Preamble of the Indian Constitution resolves to constitute a "Secular" Democratic Republic. This means that there is no state religion and that the State shall not discriminate on the ground of religion. Articles 25 and 26 of the Constitution of India guarantee the fundamental rights of freedom of religion and freedom to manage one's religious affairs. At the same time, article 44 (which is not enforceable in a Court of law) provides that the State shall endeavour to secure a Uniform Civil Code in India. How are these different provision to be reconciled? What will be the ingredients of a Uniform Civil Code? Since the personal laws of each religion contain separate ingredients, the Uniform Civil Code will need to strike a balance between protection of fundamental rights and respecting the religious principles of different communities. Marriage, divorce, succession, inheritance, and maintenance can be matters of a secular nature and law can regulate them. India needs a codified law which will cover all religions in relation to the personal laws of different communities.

It is imperative in a multi-religious society that a Unified Code is promoted, for the sake of national unity and solidarity. Different streams of religion have to merge to a common destination and some unified principles must emerge in the true spirit of secularism. India needs a Unified Code of family law under an umbrella of all its constituent religions. Whether it is the endeavour of the State, the mandate of the Court or the Will of the people, it is an issue which only time will decide for a true Indian Secular Democratic Republic.

The views of the Indian Apex Court on matters such as the registration of marriages, inter-caste marriages, child marriages, the Dowry Prohibition Act, 1961, divorce, a Uniform Civil Code, and a secular approach have already been referred to earlier. A legislature which is slow to respond to societal changes and a proactive judiciary which is keen to motivate reforms in law is therefore clearly visible in India. Even in matters affecting the environment, pollution and health of people, the role of the judiciary in India has been very constructive. The vibrant, dynamic and open jurisprudential system in India is flexible and well-suited to meeting the changing needs of the people. We could therefore well have reform in family law through the decisions of the Court even if there is opposition from religious communities in respect of personal laws. If a Uniform Civil Code does not come as a result of legislation, judicial precedent will always suggest reforms to improve the plight of children and women who are affected the most. The Indian judiciary accordingly deserves to be hailed in this regard.

### *Concluding thoughts on child and family law in India*

While child and family law in India is advancing at a great pace, much still remains to be done to improve it. With the changing international atmosphere and interactive diplomatic relations, many new treaties and understandings are being concluded in the area of private international law. India was a part of that process and was successful in understanding the needs of both its resident and Non-Resident citizens. This dire need for India to recognise and resolve family law problems of its nearly thirty million Non-Resident Indians necessitates such steps.

Modern concepts and issues including commercial surrogacy, inter-country adoptions, inter-parental child removal, inter-continental matrimonial litigation and instances of global child abuse present new challenges. The law never anticipated or visualised these new generation legal complexities, and hence statutory law in India contains no provisions to define or rectify them.

Marriage, divorce, child custody, maintenance and ancillary relief is undergoing a sea change in terms of the concepts themselves and the goals they seek to achieve in India. One finds that laws passed decades ago are now in urgent need of reform. Times have changed, but law has not kept pace. The judiciary renders an indispensible service in providing relief on a case by case basis. But that is not enough. Often viewed as an example of judicial activism, a Court decision may provide relief in a particular case on the basis of a given set of facts and circumstances. However, no precedent is set. Thus, responsibility for finding the solution lies with the legislature which must enact legislation. Family laws – particularly those meant to protect and serve the interest of children – must be amended for a better future for India. The discussion herein is by no means exhaustive. It is merely an overview of a number of examples of law, which require change for a better future for children. The global effort in this direction prompts India to follow suit.

# BRIEF OVERVIEW OF THE LAW OF ARREST IN THE INDIAN JURISDICTION

## (I) INTRODUCTION TO THE CRIMINAL PROCEDURE, 1973

The Indian Code of Criminal Procedure, 1973 (hereafter CrPC 1973) tells you how to lodge a criminal complaint, how the case is to be started, investigated, pleaded and argued in the competent Court of first instance i.e. the trial Court. Further proceedings are maintainable in the High Court of the respective State or the Union Territory, as the case may be. And finally, the Apex Court is the Supreme Court of India at New Delhi. The Indian criminal system, is principally governed by uniform Central legislation, as applicable throughout the territories of India. The CrPC 1973, extends to the whole of India except the state of Jammu and Kashmir. Further, it is important to highlight, that the respective states and the Union Territories, are empowered to frame their own local legislation and rules, for specific purposes and offences, which will be applicable depending on the nature of local requirements, and any offence committed in that regard.

## (II) FUNDAMENTAL RIGHTS WITH RESPECT TO CRIMINAL LAW IN INDIA

- A person cannot be punished for any act except when it is recognized as an offence under existing law. The law must apply to the accused at the time the offence was actually committed. For example, cruelty by a husband or his relatives (as defined by section 498A, of the Indian Penal Code) was made punishable only in the year 1983. A person cannot be punished under the said provision for committing cruelty before this date.
- A person cannot be prosecuted and punished for the same offence more than once. If a person has been prosecuted and acquitted, s/he cannot be prosecuted again for the same offence.
- A person cannot be forced to incriminate himself/herself. This means that a person cannot be forced to confess to having committed any offence, nor is s/he under any obligation to say anything that would show that s/he is potentially or actually guilty of any offence, so committed. Even in a Court of law, a person cannot be forced or compelled to be a witness against himself/herself. However, the accused may be made to give blood samples, handwriting samples and produce documents that may point towards guilt.

It is important to mention that the foreigners are entitled to the protection of article 21 of the Constitution of the India as held in the case of *Louis De Raedt* v. *Union of India*, JT 1991 (3) SC 306, and several other judgments of the Supreme

Court of India in this regard. Article 21 of the Constitution of India provides that no person shall be deprived of his life or personal liberty according to the procedure established by law. This was also reiterated by the Supreme Court of India in the case of *National Human Rights Commission* v. *State of A.P.*, JT 1996 (1) SC 163.

That it is important to understand the concept of bailable and non bailable offences. Accordingly, the same are defined hereunder for ease of reference.

***Bailable offences***

Offences for which a person may obtain bail as a matter of right. Whether an offence is bailable or non-bailable may be found out by the classification of offences in the first schedules to the Indian Code of Criminal Procedure, 1973.

***Non-Bailable offences***

Offences for which bail may be granted or refused by the Court in the exercise of its discretionary power to do so. Non-bailable does not mean that a person cannot get bail, but simply, that getting bail is not the right of the accused. Whether an offence is bailable or non-bailable may be found out by the classification of offences in the first schedule to the Indian Code of Criminal Procedure, 1973.

## (III) STARTING A STATE CASE

Basically, there are two ways in which a case can be started under the Indian criminal legal system i.e. by starting a State case or by starting a private case on the basis of a private complaint. A State case is one in which the entire responsibilities of investigation, proving facts in the Court and arguing the case are vested with the Government pleader. In such a case, the aggrieved person's only responsibility is to make a complaint and get the First Information Report (hereafter FIR) registered with the police authorities in whose jurisdiction, has the alleged offence is said to have been committed.

At the same time, it is important to know that even in a State case, it is mandatory for the complainant to be present at every hearing. This is in your own interest, so that you remain aware of the proceedings.

A private complaint is one in which the aggrieved person will have to take all the responsibilities of prosecution. This includes actually litigating the case in Court as a person would in a civil case.

If an aggrieved person wants to start a state case s/he have two main choices. The first is to approach the police and the other is to make a complaint with the Magistrate. If these options do not work out, the aggrieved person has other choices as well.

## CRIMINAL OFFENCES AND PROCESS IN CRIMINAL MATTERS IN INDIA

1. The substantive Law of Crimes in India is contained in the Indian Penal Code (Act XLV of 1860) (hereinafter referred to as IPC) which is governed by the procedure enacted in the Code of Criminal Procedure, 1973 (hereinafter referred to as Cr.P.C). Both are federal laws and apply uniformly throughout the territory of India.

2. Section 2 (c) of the Cr.P.C defines a **'cognizable offence'** as an offence for which, and defines a **'cognizable case'** as a case in which, a police officer may

in accordance with the first schedule or under any other law for the time being in force, **arrest without warrant**.

Section 2 (l) of the Cr.P.C defines a '**non-cognizable offence**' as an offence for which, and defines a **'non-cognizable case'** as a case in which, a police officer has **no authority to arrest without warrant**.

3. An aggrieved person can approach a police station which falls in the jurisdiction of the area where the offence has been allegedly committed and can get his/her grievance recorded. The police are under a duty to record the complaint in the form of a Daily Diary Report (DDR).

(i) If upon inquiry, the police are of the opinion that **a cognizable offence** is made out in terms of the Indian Penal Code or any other law in force in India, then the DDR can be converted to a First Information Report (hereinafter referred to as F.I.R.) under section 154 of Cr.P.C.. An F.I.R. is recorded by the police officer on duty upon information given either by the aggrieved person or any other person about the commission of an alleged offence and is followed by an investigation into the offence.

(ii) If upon inquiry, the police are of the opinion that **a non-cognizable offence** is made out in terms of the Indian Penal Code or any other law in force in India, then according to section 155 of the Cr.P.C., the concerned police officer shall enter or cause to be entered the substance of the information in a book to be kept by such officer in such form as may be prescribed by the State Government from time to time (DDR). He shall then refer the informant to the Magistrate.

(iii) According to section 155(2) of the Cr.P.C, a Police Officer does not have the power to investigate a non-cognizable case without an order of a Magistrate having power to try such case or commit the case for trial.

4. Therefore, any person who is aggrieved on account of a criminal wrong having been committed against her/him on account of any offence having been made out in terms of the Indian Penal Code or any other law in force in India, has an option of making a grievance in **three possible ways** which are briefly explained as hereunder:

a. **Firstly**, the aggrieved person can give the information relating to the Commission of a cognizable/non-cognizable to an officer in charge of a police station as mentioned under sections 154/155 of the Cr.P.C.

Section 154 of the Cr.P.C. is reproduced hereunder for ready reference:

"**154. Information in cognizable cases.**—(1) Every information relating to the commission of a cognizable offence, if given orally to an officer in charge of a police station, shall be reduced to writing by him or under his direction, and be read over to the informant; and every such information, whether given in writing or reduced to writing as aforesaid, shall be signed by the person giving it, and the substance thereof shall be entered in a book to be kept by such officer in such form as the State Government may prescribe in this behalf.

(2) A copy of the information as recorded under sub-section (1) shall be given forthwith, free of cost, to the informant.

(3) Any person, aggrieved by a refusal on the part of an officer in charge of a police station to record the information referred to in sub-section (1) may send the substance of such information, in writing and by post, to the Superintendent of Police concerned who, if satisfied that such information discloses the commission of a cognizable offence, shall either investigate the case himself or direct an investigation to be made by any police officer subordinate to him, in the manner provided by this Code, and such officer shall have all the powers of an officer in charge of the police station in relation to that offence."

b. **Secondly**, If a person has a grievance that the police station is not registering his/her F.I.R. under section 154 Cr.P.C., then he/she can approach the Superintendent of Police under section 154(3), Cr.P.C. by an application in writing as stated above.

c. **Thirdly**, if the F.I.R. is not registered in any way as mentioned above, then it is open to the aggrieved person to file an application under section 156(3), Cr.P.C. before the learned Magistrate concerned. If such an application under section 156(3) is filed before the Magistrate, the Magistrate can direct the F.I.R. to be registered.

The Supreme Court of India in *Sakiri Vasu* v. *State of U.P.*, AIR 2008 Supreme Court 907 has ruled at page 908 in para 11 as hereunder:

"....if a person has a grievance that the police station is not registering his F.I.R. under section 154, Cr.P.C., then he can approach the Superintendent of Police under section 154(3), Cr.P.C., by an application in writing. Even if that does not yield any satisfactory result in the sense that either the F.I.R. is still not registered, or that even after registering it no proper investigation is held, it is open to the aggrieved person to file an application under section 156(3), Cr.P.C. before the learned Magistrate concerned. If such an application under section 156(3) is filed before the Magistrate, the Magistrate can direct the F.I.R. to be registered and also can direct a proper investigation to be made, in a case where, according to the aggrieved person, no proper investigation was made. The Magistrate can also under the same provision monitor the investigation to ensure a proper investigation."

That when a Magistrate directs the police to register a case and investigate it under section 156(3) of the CrPC 1973, the complaint is actually transformed into an FIR. Even if the direction made by the Magistrate does not ask the police to register the case, but only to investigate it, the police has the duty to treat the direction as an FIR. This was also the law laid down by the Hon'ble Supreme Court of India in the case of *Madhu Bala* v. *Suresh Kumar* (1997) 8 SCC 476.

If the police fails to register an FIR, the aggrieved person can also file a Writ petition in the High Court of the relevant jurisdiction under Article 226 of the Constitution of India, directing the police authorities to register an FIR. Generally, the High Courts in India are firm and emphatic in passing directions to the police authorities for registering FIRs, taking into account the police inaction, in genuine cases sought to be pursued without any motive.

The two above-mentioned judgments are cited in support of the submissions made above.

5. Once the F.I.R. has been registered, the investigation in the case commences. Investigation includes all the proceedings of the collection of evidence conducted by a police officer or by any person who is authorized by the Magistrate on his behalf.

Section 156 of the Cr.P.C. in this regard which gives the powers to the police to investigate the cognizable offences is reproduced as hereunder.

> "**156. Police officer's power to investigate cognizable cases.**—(1) Any officer in charge of a police station may, without the order of a Magistrate, investigate any cognizable case which a Court having jurisdiction over the local area within the limits of such station would have power to inquire into or try under the provisions of Chapter XIII.
>
> (2) No proceeding of a police officer in any such case shall at any stage be called in question on the ground that the case was one which such officer was not empowered under this section to investigate.
>
> (3) Any Magistrate empowered under section 190 may order such an investigation as above-mentioned."

According to the above-mentioned judgments of the Indian Supreme Court, even if after registering the F.I.R. no proper investigation is conducted, it is open to the aggrieved person to file an application under section 156(3) of the Cr.P.C. before the Magistrate concerned. If such an application under section 156(3) is filed before the Magistrate, the Magistrate can direct a proper investigation to be made. It may be added here that the Magistrate can also under the same provision monitor the investigation to ensure a proper investigation.

6. The police while conducting the investigation of the case records the statements of the witnesses under section 161 of the Cr.P.C. Section 157 of the Cr.P.C. casts a duty upon the investigating police officer to forthwith send the report of the cognizable offence, prepared under section 173 of the Cr.P.C., to the concerned Magistrate. The police officer is also under a duty to follow the procedure laid down in section 157 of the Cr.P.C. which is reproduced as hereunder:

> "**157.Procedure for investigation.**—(1) If, from information received or otherwise, an officer in charge of a police station has reason to suspect the commission of an offence which he is empowered under section 156 to investigate, he shall forthwith send a report of the same to a Magistrate empowered to take cognizance of such offence upon a police report and shall proceed in person, or shall depute one of his subordinate officers not being below such rank as the State Government may, by general or special order, prescribe in this behalf, to proceed, to the spot, to investigate the facts and circumstances of the case, and, if necessary, to take measures for the discovery and arrest of the offender:
>
> Provided that—
>
> (a) when information as to the commission of any such offence is given against any person by name and the case is not of a serious nature,

the officer in charge of a police station need not proceed in person or depute a subordinate officer to make an investigation on the spot;

(b) if it appears to the officer in charge of a police station that there is no sufficient ground for entering on an investigation, he shall not investigate the case.

(2) In each of the cases mentioned in clauses (a) and (b) of the proviso to sub-section (1), the officer in charge of the police station shall state in his report his reasons for not fully complying with the requirements to that sub-section, and, in the case mentioned in clause (b) of the said proviso, the officer shall also forthwith notify to the informant, if any, in such manner as may be prescribed by the State Government, the fact that he will not investigate the case or cause it to be investigated."

7. Thereupon, after all the evidence has been collected by the police, a report (called 'Challan') is filed in the Court before a competent Magistrate and thereafter, as prescribed in the Cr.P.C., charges are framed by the Court against the accused under section 211 of the Cr.P.C. The Court under section 211, Cr.P.C. has the power to alter the charges at any time during the trial but before the judgment.

8. It may also be added that, besides the procedural provisions quoted above, section 482 of the Cr.P.C may also be reproduced as hereunder for ready reference:

"**482. Saving of inherent power of High Court.**—Nothing in this Code shall be deemed to limit or affect the inherent powers of the High Court to make such orders as may be necessary to give effect to any order under this Code, or to prevent abuse of the process of any Court or otherwise to secure the ends of justice."

It may be commented that, if there is any lacunae in the criminal process or there is failure to comply with the provisions of law or there is any apprehension to any party in any criminal litigation of any threat to life or personal liberty, he/she can invoke the jurisdiction of the High Court directly in a petition under section 482 Cr.P.C. for seeking appropriate orders to secure the ends of justice.

From a reading of the above position of Indian law, it can be stated that for protection of life and personal liberty, any person including a foreign national can invoke the extraordinary Writ jurisdiction under articles 32 or 226 of the Constitution of India. Likewise, under the criminal law of India, there is a well established procedure for taking cognizance of complaints and dealing with them in Courts of competent jurisdiction. Additionally, the Cr.P.C. has an inherent saving provision to prevent the abuse of the process of any Court and to secure the ends of justice.

## (IV) REGISTERING A FIRST INFORMATION REPORT (FIR)

The complainant has a right to register an FIR. If the offence is cognisable, the Station House Officer is duty-bound to register the FIR, on the basis of the complaint made by the aggrieved person. But, experience suggests that in actual practice, it is quite a difficult and a cumbersome job to have the FIR registered, and it involves a lot of running around, before the FIR, is actually registered by the police authorities.

## GUIDELINES FOR REGISTERING A FIRST INFORMATION REPORT (FIR)

- **The complainant should write out a complaint.**
- **The complainant can make an oral complaint** that the police will reduce into writing. But, in actual practice it may not happen at all. In India, it is very difficult to get the police authorities to register an FIR on the basis of oral complaints alone.
- **This complaint will be converted into an FIR** by filling the information into a form. This will be done by the policeman. The police officer cannot refuse to register an FIR. The complainant must insist on the registration of the FIR. The complainant must also insist that a copy of the FIR be given to the complainant.
- **Entry in the Daily Diary:** Every police station has a register called the "Daily Diary". Also complaints that come to the police station every day are supposed to be entered into this diary. To ensure that action is taken on the basis of the complaint made by the aggrieved person, the complainant must make sure that his/her complaint is entered in the daily diary, maintained by the police authorities in the police station.
- **Registering the FIR correctly is very important**. The aggrieved person must make sure that all the facts are recorded correctly by the complainant in the written complaint, and by the policeman, both in the complaint and the FIR.
- **The complainant has a right to obtain a copy of the FIR free of cost.** In actual practice, it is not so easy for an aggrieved citizen or a foreigner to actually obtain a copy of the FIR, lodged by the police authorities. It is proclaimed that there is online registration of FIRs in sum major metropolitian cities. But, it cannot be said so as to how successful, it is in actual practice. By way of abundant caution, foreign nationals of Indian origin, should not expect online registration of FIRs. From experience this is a common query on behalf of foreign nationals of Sikh origin, who have enormous property title and possession disputes, with the regard to their holdings in their native villages in the State of Punjab and these land holdings are of enormous value.

## WHAT SHOULD BE WRITTEN IN THE FIR

- Whether the complainant writes the complaint himself or herself or it is made orally, it must be ensured that the FIR contains the following information:
- The name and address of the accused.
- The date, place and time at which the offence occurred.
- Details of what happened and what the complainant thinks is the motive behind the accused person's behaviour. If there is a property involved, the details of the property must be included.
- If there are witnesses to the incident, violence, theft, robbery or fraud, the complaint should include the name of these witnesses.
- If the complaint relates to an economic fraud or a white collar fraud or an online fraud, details of the entire fraudulent activity or the *modus operandi*

so deployed in committing the crime, should be described in complete detail.

- If there are marks or injuries on the body of the aggrieved person, the complainant must mention them in the complaint and the FIR. Any evidence of immediate medical treatment after injury has been inflicted on the body of the accused person, should also be recorded both in the complaint and the FIR.

## WHAT HAPPENS AFTER FIR OF THE COMPLAINANT HAS BEEN REGISTERED?

There are two direct effects of registration of the FIR. **First**, if it is a case of a cognisable offence, the police can arrest the accused person without going to court and asking for a warrant. **Secondly**, the police will have to start the process of investigation in the case.

## WHO CAN FILE A COMPLAINT

Anyone who knows that an offence has been committed can start the criminal procedure by making that information available to the police. However, there are some exceptions to this rule. Restrictions on who may file a complaint apply to some offences.

## STEPS YOU MAY HAVE TO GO THROUGH TO REGISTER YOUR FIR

- Firstly, the complainant should approach the SHO of the police station to lodge the FIR.
- **If the police officer refuses to lodge an FIR on the basis of the complaint, then the complainant should send a written complaint to the local Superintendent of Police** of the concerned jurisdiction by post, explaining the facts of the case. It is strongly advisible to send the complaint by registered post/speed post and the complainant should keep a record of the original receipt, which may be required as proof at a later stage. Also, a visit can be made to the office of the local Superintendent of Police. The complainant can also personally approach the Superintendent to lodge the complaint. If the Superintendent thinks that your case related to a cognisable offence, s/he will either investigate the case himself or herself, or direct some officer to investigate the matter.
- **If no action is taken in your case by the Superintendent of Police, the complainant should then make a complaint to the Magistrate** asking her/him to direct the police to register the FIR.
- **If still no action is taken in the said case, then the aggrieved person should file a Writ petition in the High Court** under article 226 of the Constitution of India, in the High Court of the appropriate jurisdiction pleading for the FIR to be registered.

## (V) CASELAW ANALYSIS ON THE POTENTIAL AVAILABLE REMEDIES WHERE THE PROCEDURE UNDER THE CrPC, 1973 IS NOT FOLLOWED BY THE POLICE AUTHORITIES IN CASE A COGNIZABLE OFFENCE IS COMMITTED

In cases where a cognizable offence has been committed the first step in order to start the proceedings will be informing the police regarding the commission of an offence. The information given to the police is to be compulsorily reduced in writing by the concerned police officers. Such information as to the details of the offence, written by the police is called a First Information Report (hereafter FIR). But, it has been seen that a common grievance of the persons informing about commission of a cognizable offence is non-registration of FIR by the police authorities and thereafter, not conducting any investigation regarding the same.

Remedies available where such grievances are faced with regard to non registration of FIR and the subsequent problems that arise from the non registration is discussed in the caselaw analysis below.

Before, talking about the potential remedies which a person can adhere to, it is important to discuss the provisions of the CrPC, 1973 which talk about the procedure followed when a cognizable offence is committed. The provisions of the CrPC, 1973 also provide for some solutions in cases where there is a breach on part of either of the parties under the provisions.

## FAILURE OF POLICE AUTHORITITES TO REGISTER THE FIR IN CASES OF COGNIZABLE OFFENCES

The provisions regarding the registering of FIR by a police officer is laid down under section 154 of the CrPC, 1973 respectively. The provisions are as follows:

> "154. Information in cognizable cases:
>
> (1) Every information relating to the commission of a cognizable offence, if given orally to an officer in charge of a police station, shall be reduced to writing by him or under his direction, and be read over to the informant; and every such information, whether given in writing or reduced to writing as aforesaid, shall be signed by the person giving it, and the substance thereof shall be entered in a book to be kept by such officer in such form as the State Government may prescribe in this behalf.
>
> (2) A copy of the information as recorded under sub-section (1) shall be given forthwith, free of cost, to the informant.
>
> (3) Any person, aggrieved by a refusal on the part of an officer in charge of a police station to record the information referred to in sub-section (1) may send the substance of such information, in writing and by post, to the Superintendent of Police concerned who, if satisfied that such information discloses the commission of a cognizable offence, shall either investigate the case himself or direct an investigation to be made by any police officer subordinate to him, in the manner provided by this Code, and such officer shall have all the powers of an officer in charge of the police station in relation to that offence."

In cases where the aggrieved persons do their duty in informing the police authorities about the commission of a cognizable offence, as also subsequently vigorously following up the matter, with a view to registration of the FIR, which is not registered on account of police inaction, interference and total non cooperation, no delay or laxity can be attributed to the aggrieved persons in this regard. It is believed that they have fully performed their duty diligently in informing the police authorities, and in fact it is a failure on part of the police authorities not to convert the information given by them into a FIR.

It is very clear from the above provisions that in cases where information relating to cognizable offences is received with the police authorities, the FIR should be registered under section 154(1) and in cases where police officials refuse to register the FIR a remedy is available for the same under section 154(3) of the CrPC, 1973.

The Supreme Court judgment in the case of *Aleque Padamsee* v. *Union of India*, 2007 (6) SCC 171, elaborates upon the modalities of the available legal recourse under the sections 154 and 156 of the CrPC, 1973, clarifying the legal position on the registration of FIR's by the police officials, and further recourse available where no action is taken by the police authorities.

Paras 7 (at page 175) of the judgment above provides the following analysis:

> "7. Whenever any information is received by the police about the alleged commission of offence which is a cognizable one there is a duty to register the FIR. There can be no dispute on that score. The only question is whether a writ can be issued to the police authorities to register the same. The basic question is as to what course is to be adopted if the police does not do it. As was held in *All India Institute of Medical Sciences's* case (supra) and re-iterated in *Gangadhar's* case (supra) the remedy available is as set out above by filing a complaint before the Magistrate. Though it was faintly suggested that there was conflict in the views in *All India Institute of Medical Sciences's* case (supra), *Gangadhar's* case (supra), *Hari Singh's* case (supra), *Minu Kumari's* case (supra) and *Ramesh Kumari's* case (supra), we find that the view expressed in *Ramesh Kumari's* case (supra) related to the action required to be taken by the police when any cognizable offence is brought to its notice. In *Ramesh Kumari's* case (supra) the basic issue did not relate to the methodology to be adopted which was expressly dealt with in *All India Institute of Medical Sciences's* case (supra), *Gangadhar's* case (supra), *Minu Kumari's* case (supra) and *Hari Singh's* case (supra). The view expressed in Ramesh Kumari's case (supra) was re-iterated in *Lallan Chaudhary* v. *State of Bihar*, AIR 2006 SC 3376. The course available, when the police does not carry out the statutory requirements under section 154 was directly in issue in *All India Institute of Medical Sciences's* case (supra), *Gangadhar's* case (supra), *Hari Singh's* case (supra) and *Minu Kumari's* case (supra). The correct position in law, therefore, is that the police officials ought to register the FIR whenever facts brought to its notice show that cognizable offence has been made out. In case the police officials fail to do so, the modalities to be adopted are as set out in sections 190 read with section 200 of the Code."

That from the analysis contained in para 7 of the above-mentioned judgment it will be noticed that the remedy of invoking the Writ jurisdiction of the High Court for registration of the FIR and therefore, directions to register the cases in accordance with section 196 of the CrPC, 1973, did not find favour with the Hon'ble Supreme Court of India.

In another case of *Sakiri Vasu* v. *State of U.P.*, AIR 2008 SC 907, the Hon'ble Supreme Court has elaborated the procedure by which an aggrieved person can approach the Courts in cases where his/her FIR has not been registered by the police officers. The provisions have been mentioned in paras 11 and 26 (at pages 908 and 910) respectively of the said judgment in the following terms:

"11. In this connection we would like to state that if a person has a grievance that the police station is not registering his FIR under section 154 Cr.P.C., then he can approach the Superintendent of Police under section 154(3) Cr.P.C. by an application in writing. Even if that does not yield any satisfactory result in the sense that either the FIR is still not registered, or that even after registering it no proper investigation is held, it is open to the aggrieved person to file an application under section 156(3) Cr.P.C. before the learned Magistrate concerned. If such an application under section 156(3) is filed before the Magistrate, the Magistrate can direct the FIR to be registered and also can direct a proper investigation to be made, in a case where, according to the aggrieved person, no proper investigation was made. The Magistrate can also under the same provision monitor the investigation to ensure a proper investigation.

26. If a person has a grievance that his FIR has not been registered by the police station his first remedy is to approach the Superintendent of Police under section 154(3) Cr.P.C. or other police officer referred to in section 36 Cr.P.C. If despite approaching the Superintendent of Police or the officer referred to in section 36 his grievance still persists, then he can approach a Magistrate under section 156(3) Cr.P.C. instead of rushing to the High Court by way of a writ petition or a petition under section 482 Cr.P.C. Moreover he has a further remedy of filing a criminal complaint under section 200 Cr.P.C. Why then should writ petitions or section 482 petitions be entertained when there are so many alternative remedies?"

Clearly, it will be noticed that the above mentioned judgment of *Sakiri Vasu* (supra), again provides a restrictive view similar to the law laid down in *Aleque Padamsee* (supra), with the net effect that both the judgments cumulatively put together frown upon availing the remedy of the Writ jurisdiction, in the event of non-registration of a FIR.

## FAILURE ON PART OF POLICE AUTHORITIES TO INVESTIGATE COGNIZABLE OFFENCES UNDER SECTION 156 OF THE CrPC, 1973

The provisions regarding the investigation of cognizable cases are laid down under section 156 of the CrPC, 1973 respectively. The provisions are as follows:

"156. Police officer's power to investigate cognizable cases:

(1) Any officer in charge of a police station may, without the order of a Magistrate, investigate any cognizable case which a Court having jurisdiction over the local area within the limits of such station would have power to inquire into or try under the provisions of Chapter XIII.

(2) No proceeding of a police officer in any such case shall at any stage be called in question on the ground that the case was one which such officer was not empowered under this section to investigate.

(3) Any Magistrate empowered under section 190 may order such an investigation as above-mentioned."

It is clear from the above mentioned provisions that under section 156 of the CrPC, 1973, police officers have been given the powers to investigate cases where cognizable offences have been committed without an order from the Magistrate.

The Supreme Court judgment in the case of *Aleque Padamsee* (supra) also elaborated the available legal recourse under the sections 156, 190 and 200 of the CrPC, 1973, clarifying the legal position with regard to the investigation of cases by the police officials, and further recourse which is available where no action is taken by the police authorities. Para 6 of the said judgment provides an analysis on the above issue in the following terms:

> "6. When the information is laid with the police, but no action in that behalf is taken, the complainant can under section 190 read with section 200 of the Code lay the complaint before the Magistrate having jurisdiction to take cognizance of the offence and the Magistrate is required to enquire into the complaint as provided in Chapter XV of the Code. In case the Magistrate, after recording evidence, finds a prima facie case, instead of issuing process to the accused, he is empowered to direct the police concerned to investigate into offence under Chapter XII of the Code and to submit a report. If he finds that the complaint does not disclose any offence to take further action, he is empowered to dismiss the complaint under section 203 of the Code. In case he finds that the complaint/evidence recorded prima facie discloses an offence, he is empowered to take cognizance of the offence and could issue process to the accused. These aspects have been highlighted by this Court in *All India Institute of Medical Sciences Employees' Union (Reg) through its President* v. *Union of India*, (1996) 11 SCC 582."

Clearly, the Supreme Court in its judgment has provided a solution in cases where an arrest can be made by the police officers without an order from the Magistrate but, no action has been taken by the authorities after repeated requests of the aggrieved persons in the case which is registered.

## PROPER PROCEDURE OF INVESTIGATION AND INQUIRY NOT FOLLOWED BY THE POLICE OFFICIALS UNDER SECTION 174 OF THE CrPC, 1973

In cases where police officers obtain information regarding a person who has committed suicide or had died under suspicious circumstances a strict procedure has to be followed by the designated police officer under section 174 of the CrPC, 1973, which mandates the following statutory directions to the investigating officers:

> "174. Police to inquire and report on suicide etc:
>
> (1) When the officer in charge of a police station or some other police officer specially empowered by the State Government in that behalf receives information that a person has committed suicide, or has been killed by another or by an animal or by machinery or by an accident, or has died under circumstances raising a reasonable suspicion that some other person has committed an offence, he shall immediately give intimation thereof to the nearest Executive Magistrate empowered to hold inquests, and, unless

otherwise directed by any rule prescribed by the State Government, or by any general or special order of the District or Sub-divisional Magistrate, shall proceed to the place where the body of such deceased person is, and there, in the presence of two or more respectable inhabitants of the neighborhood shall make an investigation, and draw up a report of the apparent cause of death, describing such wounds, fractures, bruises, and other marks of inquiry as may be found on the body, and stating in what manner, or by what weapon or instrument (if any), such marks appear to have been inflicted.

(2) The report shall be signed by such police officer and other persons, or by so many of them as concur and shall be forthwith forwarded to the District Magistrate or the Sub-divisional Magistrate.

(3) When

(i) The case involves suicide by a woman within seven years of her marriage: or

(ii) The case relates to the death of a woman within seven years of tier marriage in any circumstances raising a reasonable suspicion that some other person committed an offence in relation to such woman; or

(iii) The case relates to the death of a woman within seven years of her marriage and any case relative of the woman has made a request in this behalf, or

(iv) There is any doubt regarding the cause of death; or

(v) The police officer for any other reason considers it expedient so to do, he shall, subject to such rules as the State Government may prescribe in this behalf, forward the body, with a view to its being examined, to the nearest Civil Surgeon, or other qualified medical man appointed in this behalf by the State Government, if the state of the weather and the distance admit of its being so forwarded without risk of such putrefaction on the road as would render such examination useless.

(4) The following Magistrates are empowered to hold inquests, namely, any District Magistrate or Sub-divisional Magistrate and any other Executive Magistrate specially empowered in this behalf' by the State Government or the District Magistrate."

But, in a number of cases, there is almost total non-action on part of the concerned police authorities and no action is taken at all by the police authorities to refer the case to the local Executive Magistrate to hold an inquest with a view to probing the circumstances of the case.

Furthermore, no police report is sent to the office of the District Magistrate or the Sub Divisional Magistrate as mandated under section 174(2) of the CrPC, 1973.

Further, there are more than glaring defects in the so called investigation carried out by the police authorities in such cases and the gross misconduct of the police authorities and glaring omissions on their part in not complying with the statutory requirements as prescribed by procedure and law laid down in the CrPC, 1973, and the relevant provisions in the Constitution of India that have to be statutorily followed by the police officers in cases clearly, brings the cases in the category of defective investigations.

Accordingly, it is necessary to advert to the law in this area of law as laid down by the Hon'ble Supreme Court of India and various other High Courts in the country. It will be noticed that the tenor of the said case-laws is applicable in all cases where such problems *prima facie* appear.

Such cases where a defective investigation is a primary issue, could well be akin to the much publicised Best Bakery Case reported as *Zahira Habibullah H. Sheikh* v. *State of Gujarat*, AIR 2004 SC 3114, where the Supreme Court of India had ordered a re-trial to be conducted outside the State of Gujarat.

The Hon'ble Supreme Court has analysed the law regarding defective investigations in cases where cognizable offences have been committed in many of its decisions. The position regarding the same will be clear from the caselaw analysis hereunder:

The Apex Court in *Dhanaj Singh* v. *State of Punjab*, AIR 2004 SC 1920, has ruled that an accused should not be acquitted solely on the account of defect in investigation. A defective investigation can be non-fatal to prosecution where ocular testimony is found credible and cogent. Justifying this stand the Apex Court observed in para 5 (at page 1922) of the said judgment as follows:

> "5. In case of a defective investigation the court has to be circumspect in evaluating evidence. But it wouldn't be right in acquitting accused person solely on account of the defect, to do so would tantamount to playing into the hands of the investigating officer if the investigation is designedly defective."

From the above decision of the Supreme Court of India, it emerges that the accused person/s in cases where cognizable offence has been committed should not be allowed to evade the due process of law, simply because of a defective investigation.

In *Zahira Habibullah H Sheikh*, (supra), the Supreme Court of India not only reiterated this view but also advised the subordinate judiciary to adopt an active role in the process of collecting evidence and elicit all the relevant materials necessary for reaching the correct conclusion, with a view to find out the truth.

Para 38 (at page 3125) and paras 64 and 65 (at pages 3133 and 3134) of the above mentioned judgment reads as under:

> "38. This Court has often emphasised that in a criminal case the fate of the proceedings cannot always be left entirely in the hands of the parties, crimes being public wrongs in breach and violation of public rights and duties, which affect the whole community as a community and harmful to the society in general. The concept of fair trial entails familiar triangulation of interests of the accused, the victim and the society and it is the community that acts through the State and prosecuting agencies. Interests of society are not to be treated completely with disdain and as persona non

grata. Courts have always been considered to have an over-riding duty to maintain public confidence in the administration of justice - often referred to as the duty to vindicate and uphold the 'majesty of the law'. Due administration of justice has always been viewed as a continuous process, not confined to determination of the particular case, protecting its ability to function as a Court of law in the future as in the case before it. If a criminal Court is to be an effective instrument in dispensing justice, the Presiding Judge must cease to be a spectator and a mere recording machine by becoming a participant in the trial evincing intelligence, active interest and elicit all relevant materials necessary for reaching the correct conclusion, to find out the truth, and administer justice with fairness and impartiality both to the parties and to the community it serves. Courts administering criminal justice cannot turn a blind eye to vexatious or oppressive conduct that has occurred in relation to proceedings, even if a fair trial is still possible, except at the risk of undermining the fair name and standing of the judges as impartial and independent adjudicators.

64. In the case of a defective investigation the Court has to be circumspect in evaluating the evidence and may have to adopt an active and analytical role to ensure that truth is found by having recourse to section 311 or at a later stage also resorting to section 391 instead of throwing hands in the air in despair. It would not be right in acquitting an accused person solely on account of the defect; to do so would tantamount to playing into the hands of the investigating officer if the investigation is designedly defective. [See *Karnel Singh* v. *State of M.P.*, (1995) 5 SCC 518].

65. In *Paras Yadav* v. *State of Bihar*, (1999) 2 SCC 126 it was held that if the lapse or omission is committed by the investigating agency or because of negligence the prosecution evidence is required to be examined de hors such omissions to find out whether the said evidence is reliable or not. The contaminated conduct of officials should not stand on the way of Courts getting at the truth by having recourse to sections 311, 391 of the Code and section 165 of the Evidence Act at the appropriate and relevant stages and evaluating the entire evidence; otherwise the designed mischief would be perpetuated with a premium to the offenders and justice would not only be denied to the complainant party but also made an ultimate casualty."

That from reading of paras 38, 64 and 65, it emerges that the contaminated conduct of the officials should not stand in the way of getting to the bottom of the truth, and in this regard the Courts can seek recourse to sections 311 and 391 of the CrPC, 1973, as also section 165 of the Indian Evidence Act, 1872.

Sections 311 and 391 of the CrPC, 1973 provides as follows:

"Section 311 – Power to summon material witness, or examine person present:

Any court may, at any stage of any inquiry, trial or other proceeding under this Code, summon any person its a witness, or examine any person in attendance, though not summoned as a witness, or recall and re-examine any person already examined; and the court shall summon and examine or recall and re-examine any such person if his evidence appears to it to be essential to the just decision of the case.

Section 391 – Appellate court may take further evidence or direct it to be taken:

(1) In dealing with any appeal under this Chapter, the Appellate Court, if it thinks additional evidence to be necessary, shall record its reasons and may either take such evidence itself, or direct it to be taken by a Magistrate, or when the Appellate Court is a High Court, by a Court of Session or a Magistrate.

(2) When the additional evidence is taken by the Court of Session or the Magistrate, it or he shall certify such evidence to the Appellate Court, and such court shall thereupon proceed to dispose of the appeal.

(3) The accused or his pleader shall have the right to be present when the additional evidence is taken.

(4) The taking of evidence under this section shall be subject to the provisions of Chapter XXIII, as if it were an inquiry."

Section 165 of the Indian Evidence Act, 1872 reads as under:

"Section 165 – Judge's power to put questions or order production—

The Judge may, in order to discover or to obtain proper proof of relevant facts, ask any question he pleases, in any form at any time, of any witness, or of the parties about any fact relevant or irrelevant; and may order the production of any document or thing; and neither the parties nor their agents shall be entitled to make any objection to any such question or order, nor, without the leave of the Court, The Orient Tavern cross-examine any witness upon any answer given in reply to any such question.

Provided that the judgment must be based upon facts declared by this Act to be relevant, and duly proved.

Provided also that this section shall not authorize an Judge to compel any witness to answer any question or produce any document which such witness would be entitled to refuse to answer or produce under sections 121 to 131, both inclusive, if the questions were asked or the documents were called for by the adverse party; nor shall the Judge ask any question which it would be improper for any other person to ask under section 148 or 149; nor shall he dispense with primary evidence of any document, except in the cases herein before excepted."

Clearly, the provisions of law cited above and the Supreme Court judgments have in detail elaborated the powers of the Court in directing a further investigation in cases where it appears *prima facie* to the satisfaction of the Court that there have been glaring defects in the investigation.

## POWER OF MAGISTRATE TO ORDER FURTHER INVESTIGATION WHERE THE AGGRIEVED PERSON FEELS THAT THE INVESTIGATION IS NOT PROPER

However, recourse is available in such cases where even though investigation is carried out by the police officers but is not proper according to the aggrieved person. The Hon'ble Supreme Court judgment in the case of *Sakiri Vasu* v. *State of U.P.*, AIR 2008 SC 907, has provided an alternative available remedy in such cases in para 13 (at page 909) of the said judgment. Para 13 reads as follows:

> "The same view was taken by this Court in *Dilawar Singh* v. *State of Delhi*, JT 2007 (10) SC 585 (vide para 17). We would further clarify that even if an FIR has been registered and even if the police has made the investigation, or is actually making the investigation, which the aggrieved person feels is not proper, such a person can approach the Magistrate under section 156(3) Cr.P.C., and if the Magistrate is satisfied he can order a proper investigation and take other suitable steps and pass such order/s as he thinks necessary for ensuring a proper investigation. All these powers a Magistrate enjoys under section 156(3) Cr.P.C."

In the light of the above rulings, it is very clear that in cases where the aggrieved person is of the view that the investigation in a case of cognizable offence has not been carried out as per the provisions of the law, s/he can approach the Court of the local Magistrate under any of the above-mentioned provisions of the CrPC, 1973 with a view to obtaining orders for a proper investigation to be conducted by the police officers.

Therefore, the above stated provisions give a detail overview of the provisions under which a person can register a case where a cognizable offence has been committed. The cases in which such provisions are not followed are a breach of law under the CrPC, 1973. The provisions have also given the ways under which the aggrieved person may seek redressal in case there is a breach on any stage of the registration of the case.

However, apart from the legal remedies available under sections 154, 156, 174, 190 and 200 of the CrPC, 1973, the aggrieved persons have some other potential remedies available with him in order to seek a redressal for his grievances.

## POTENTIAL REMEDIES AVAILABLE TO THE COMPLAINANTS

### 1. COMPLAINT TO BE PREFERRED BEFORE THE STATE HUMAN RIGHTS COMMISSION OR BEFORE THE NATIONAL HUMAN RIGHTS COMMISSION AT NEW DELHI

The Constitution of India, the supreme guarantor of fundamental rights in the Indian jurisdiction entitles everyone living in India to protection of their basic human rights with dignity. One of the basic human rights made available to every person in the country is the registration of a FIR by the police authorities where a cognizable offence has been committed. But, the incidents of non registration of FIR are extremely common in the present day working of the Indian legal system. Indeed, it is one of the most common and widespread grievances of citizens, particularly from the underprivileged sections of the society, and where the disputes are of significance involving affluent and influential people as well.

The gross misconduct on part of the police authorities in performing their statutory duties, amounts to serious violation of human rights. The misconduct of the police authorities by not registering the FIR and not conducting the investigation under the provisions of the CrPC, 1973 is a clear example of the violation of the basic human rights of the aggrieved persons, for which a complaint or a petition may be instituted under section 12 read with section 29 of the Protection of Human Rights Act, 1993, to the State Human Rights Commission by the aggrieved persons for violation of human rights or abetment thereof.

But, there are other available options hereunder, which will possibly be more efficacious, than instituting proceedings in either of the above mentioned human rights bodies.

However, it is suggested that a petition under section 482 of the CrPC, 1973 or a civil Writ petition under article 226 of the Constitution is a much better available remedy with a view to seeking directions from the High Court for registration of a case and other connected reliefs as so applicable. Also, if the relief in the Writ Court in the High Court is granted, the jurisdiction of the Writ Court will be a much better exercise of legal option also with a view to have an expeditious trial. The reasons for the same are discussed in detail below.

## 2. PETITION UNDER SECTION 482 OF THE CrPC, 1973

Section 482 of the CrPC, 1973 provides inherent powers to the High Court to prevent the abuse of the process of court and to secure the ends of justice. Section 482 of the CrPC, 1973 mandates as under:

> "482. Saving of inherent power of High Court – Nothing in this code shall be deemed to limit or affect the inherent powers of the High Court to make such orders as may be necessary to give effect to any order under this code, or to prevent abuse of the process of any court or otherwise to secure the ends of justice."

The powers of the High courts under section 482 of the CrPC, 1973 have been elaborated in many judgments of the Supreme Court of India from time to time. One such recent judgment is the case of *Jeffery J. Diermeier* v. *State of West Bengal*, JT 2010 (5) SC 278.

The Supreme Court in para 16 (at page 285) of the judgment has analysed the scope and ambit of section 482 of the CrPC, 1973 in the following categoric terms:

> "16. Before addressing the contentions advanced on behalf of the parties, it will be useful to notice the scope and ambit of inherent powers of the High Court under section 482 of the Code. The section itself envisages three circumstances under which the inherent jurisdiction may be exercised, namely, (i) to give effect to an order under the Code; (ii) to prevent abuse of process of Court; and (iii) to otherwise secure the ends of justice. Nevertheless, it is neither possible nor desirable to lay down any inflexible rule which would govern the exercise of inherent jurisdiction of the Court. Undoubtedly, the power possessed by the High Court under the said provision is very wide but is not unlimited. It has to be exercised sparingly, carefully and cautiously, *ex debito* justitiae to do real and substantial justice for which alone the court exists. It needs little emphasis that the inherent jurisdiction does not confer an arbitrary power on the High Court to act according to whim or caprice. The power exists to prevent abuse of authority and not to produce injustice."

Clearly, the powers of High Courts under section 482 of the CrPC, 1973 are wide but limited to an extent. The power of the High Courts under section 482 of the CrPC, 1973 can be invoked only in the rarest of rare cases as laid down by the Supreme Court of India in its various prominent decisions.

The Supreme Court of India in *Pankaj Kumar* v. *State of Maharashtra,* AIR 2008 SC 3077 has discussed as also analysed at length the powers of High Court under section 482 of the CrPC, 1973 in relation to article 21 of the Constitution in paras 10 to 18 of the above judgment of Pankaj Kumar (2008). Paras 10 to 18 of the said judgment (at pages 3080 to 3083) sum-up the position of law in this regard as follows:

> "10. The scope and ambit of powers of the High Court under section 482, CrPC or Article 227 of the Constitution has been enunciated and reiterated by this Court in a series of decisions and several circumstances under which the High Court can exercise jurisdiction in quashing proceedings have been enumerated. Therefore, we consider it unnecessary to burden the judgment by making reference to all the decisions on the point. It would suffice to state that though the powers possessed by the High Courts under the said provisions are very wide but these should be exercised in appropriate cases, ex debito justitiae to do real and substantial justice for the administration of which alone the courts exist. The inherent powers do not confer an arbitrary jurisdiction on the High Court to act according to whim or caprice. The powers have to be exercised sparingly, with circumspection and in the rarest of rare cases, where the court is convinced, on the basis of material on record, that allowing the proceedings to continue would be an abuse of the process of the court or that the ends of justice require that the proceedings ought to be quashed. [See: *Janata Dal* v. *H.S. Chowdhary,* (1992) 4 SCC 305; *Kurukshetra University* v. *State of Haryana,* (1977) 4 SCC 451 and *State of Haryana* v. *Bhajan Lal,* AIR 1992 SC 604]
>
> 11. Although in *Bhajan Lal's* case (supra), the court by way of illustration, formulated as many as seven categories of cases, wherein the extra-ordinary power under the afore-stated provisions could be exercised by the High Court to prevent abuse of process of the court yet it was clarified that it was not possible to lay down precise and inflexible guidelines or any rigid formula or to give an exhaustive list of the circumstances in which such power could be exercised.
>
> 12. The purport of the expression "rarest of rare cases" has been explained very recently in *Som Mittal* (supra). Speaking for the three-Judge Bench, Hon'ble the Chief Justice has said thus:
>
> > "When the words 'rarest of rare cases' are used after the words 'sparingly and with circumspection' while describing the scope of section 482, those words merely emphasize and reiterate what is intended to be conveyed by the words 'sparingly and with circumspection'. They mean that the power under section 482 to quash proceedings should not be used mechanically or routinely, but with care and caution, only when a clear case for quashing is made out and failure to interfere would lead to a miscarriage of justice. The expression "rarest of rare cases" is not used in the sense in which it is used with reference to punishment for offences under section 302 IPC, but to emphasize that

the power under section 482 Cr.P.C. to quash the FIR or criminal proceedings should be used sparingly and with circumspection."

13. Bearing in mind the above legal position, we are of the opinion that, for the reasons stated hereafter, the ends of justice require that prosecution proceedings in the instant case be quashed.

14. Time and again this Court has emphasized the need for speedy investigations and trial as both are mandated by the letter and spirit of the provisions of the CrPC. (In particular, sections 197, 173, 309, 437(6) and 468 etc.) and the constitutional protection enshrined in Article 21 of the Constitution. Inspired by the broad sweep and content of Article 21 as interpreted by a seven-Judge Bench of this Court in *Maneka Gandhi* v. *Union of India*, (1978) 1 SCC 248, in *Hussainara Khatoon* v. *Home Secretary*, (1980) 1 SCC 81, State of Bihar, this Court had said that Article 21 confers a fundamental right on every person not to be deprived of his life or liberty except according to procedure established by law; that such procedure is not some semblance of a procedure but the procedure should be 'reasonable, fair and just'; and therefrom flows, without doubt, the right to speedy trial. It was also observed that no procedure which does not ensure a reasonably quick trial can be regarded as 'reasonable, fair or just' and it would fall foul of Article 21. The Court clarified that speedy trial means reasonably expeditious trial which is an integral and essential part of the fundamental right to life and liberty enshrined in Article 21.

15. The exposition of Article 21 in *Hussainara Khatoon's* case (supra) was exhaustively considered afresh by the Constitution Bench in *Abdul Rehman Antulay* v. *R.S. Nayak*, AIR 1992 SC 1701 Referring to a number of decisions of this Court and the American precedents on the Sixth Amendment of their Constitution, making the right to a speedy and public trial a constitutional guarantee, the Court formulated as many as eleven propositions with a note of caution that these were not exhaustive and were meant only to serve as guidelines. For the sake of brevity, we do not propose to reproduce all the said propositions and it would suffice to note the gist thereof. These are:

(i) fair, just and reasonable procedure implicit in Article 21 of the Constitution creates a right in the accused to be tried speedily;

(ii) right to speedy trial flowing from Article 21encompasses all the stages, namely the stage of investigation, inquiry, trial, appeal, revision and retrial;

(iii) in every case where the speedy trial is alleged to have been infringed, the first question to be put and answered is — who is responsible for the delay?;

(iv) while determining whether undue delay has occurred (resulting in violation of right to speedy trial) one must have regard to all the attendant circumstances, including nature of offence, number of accused and witnesses, the work-load of the court concerned, prevailing local conditions and so on— what is called, the systemic delays;

(v) each and every delay does not necessarily prejudice the accused. Some delays may indeed work to his advantage. However, inordinately long delay may be taken as presumptive proof of prejudice. In this context, the fact of incarceration of accused will also be a relevant fact. The prosecution should not be allowed to become a persecution. But when does the prosecution become persecution, again depends upon the facts of a given case;

(vi) ultimately, the court has to balance and weigh several relevant factors—'balancing test' or 'balancing process'—and determine in each case whether the right to speedy trial has been denied;

(vii) Ordinarily speaking, where the court comes to the conclusion that right to speedy trial of an accused has been infringed the charges or the conviction, as the case may be, shall be quashed. But this is not the only course open and having regard to the nature of offence and other circumstances when the court feels that quashing of proceedings cannot be in the interest of justice, it is open to the court to make appropriate orders, including fixing the period for completion of trial;

(viii) it is neither advisable nor feasible to prescribe any outer time-limit for conclusion of all criminal proceedings. In every case of complaint of denial of right to speedy trial, it is primarily for the prosecution to justify and explain the delay. At the same time, it is the duty of the court to weigh all the circumstances of a given case before pronouncing upon the complaint;

(ix) an objection based on denial of right to speedy trial and for relief on that account, should first be addressed to the High Court. Even if the High Court entertains such a plea, ordinarily it should not stay the proceedings, except in a case of grave and exceptional nature. Such proceedings in High Court must, however, be disposed of on a priority basis.

16. Notwithstanding elaborate enunciation of Article 21 of the Constitution in Abdul Rehman Antulay (supra), and rejection of the fervent plea of proponents of right to speedy trial for laying down time-limits as bar beyond which acriminal trial shall not proceed pronouncements of thisCourt in *"Common Cause" A Registered Society* v. *Union of India (UOI)*, (1996) 4 SCC 33; *"Common Cause", A Registered Society* v. *Union of India*, (1996) 6 SCC 775; *Raj Deo Sharma* v. *State of Bihar*, (1998) 7 SCC 507 and *Raj Deo Sharma II* v. *State of Bihar*, (1999) 7 SCC 604 gave rise to some confusion on the question whether an outer time limit for conclusion of criminal proceedings could be prescribed whereafter the trial court would be obliged to terminate the proceedings and necessarily acquit or discharge the accused.

The confusion on the issue was set at rest by a seven-Judge Bench of this court in *P. Ramachandra Rao* v. *State of Karnataka*, (2002) 4 SCC 578. Speaking for the majority, R.C. Lahoti, J. (as his Lordship then was) while affirming that the dictum in *A.R. Antulay's* case (supra) is correct and still holds the field and the propositions emerging from Article 21 of the Constitution and expounding the right to speedy trial laid down as guidelines in the said case adequately take care of right to speedy trial, it was held that guidelines laid down in the *A.R. Antulay's* case (supra) are not exhaustive but only illustrative. They are not intended to operate as hard and fast rules or to be applied like a strait-jacket formula. Their applicability would depend on the fact-situation of each case as it is difficult to foresee all situations and no generalization can be made. It has also been held that it is neither advisable, nor feasible, nor judicially permissible to draw or prescribe an outer limit for conclusion of all criminal proceedings. Nonetheless, the criminal courts should exercise their available powers such as those under sections 309, 311 and 258 of CrPC to effectuate the right to speedy trial. In appropriate cases, jurisdiction of the High Court under section 482 CrPC and Articles 226 and 227 of the Constitution can be invoked seeking appropriate relief or suitable directions. The outer limits or power of limitation expounded in the aforenoted judgments were held to be not in consonance with the legislative intent.

17. It is, therefore, well settled that the right to speedy trial in all criminal persecutions is an inalienable right under Article 21 of the Constitution. This right is applicable not only to the actual proceedings in court but also includes within its sweep the preceding police investigations as well. The right to speedy trial extends equally to all criminal persecutions and is not confined to any particular category of cases. In every case, where the right to speedy trial is alleged to have been infringed, the court has to perform the balancing act upon taking into consideration all the attendant circumstances, enumerated above, and determine in each case whether the right to speedy trial has been denied in a given case. Where the court comes to the conclusion that the right to speedy trial of an accused has been infringed, the charges or the conviction, as the case may be, may be quashed unless the court feels that having regard to the nature of offence and other relevant circumstances, quashing of proceedings may not be in the interest of justice. In such a situation, it is open to the court to make an appropriate order as it may deem just and equitable including fixation of time for conclusion of trial.

18. Tested on the touchstone of the broad principles, enumerated above, we are of the opinion that in the instant case, appellant's constitutional right recognised under Article 21 of the Constitution stands violated. It is common ground that the First Information Report was recorded on 12th May, 1987 for the offences allegedly committed in the year 1981, and after unwarranted prolonged investigations, involving afore-stated three financial irregularities; the chargesheet was submitted in Court on 22nd February, 1991. Nothing happened till April, 19, 1999, when the appellant and his deceased mother filed criminal writ petition seeking quashing of proceedings before the trial court.

Though, it is true that the plea with regard to inordinate delay in investigations and trial has been raised before us for the first time but we feel that at this distant point of time, it would be unfair to the appellant to remit the matter back to the High Court for examining the said plea of the appellant. Apart from the fact that it would further protract the already delayed trial, no fruitful purpose would be served as learned Counsel for the State very fairly stated before us that he had no explanation to offer for the delay in investigations and the reason why the trial did not commence for eight long years. Nothing, whatsoever, could be pointed out, far from being established, to show that the delay was in any way attributable to the appellant. Moreover, having regard to the nature of the accusations against the appellant, briefly referred to above, who was a young boy of about eighteen years of age in the year 1981, when the acts of omission and commission were allegedly committed by the concerns 20 managed by his parents, who have since died, we feel that the extreme mental stress and strain of prolonged investigation by the Anti Corruption Bureau and the sword of damocles hanging perilously over his head for over fifteen years must have wrecked his entire career.

Be that as it may, the prosecution has failed to show any exceptional circumstance, which could possibly be taken into consideration for condoning the prolongation of investigation and the trial. The lackadaisical manner of investigation spread over a period of four years in a case of this type and inordinate delay of over eight years (excluding the period when the record of the trial court was in the High Court), is manifestly clear. Thus, on facts in hand, we are convinced that the appellant has been denied his valuable constitutional right to a speedy investigation and trial and, therefore, criminal proceedings initiated against him in the year 1987 and pending in the court of Special Judge, Latur, deserve to be quashed on this short ground alone."

It was, therefore, well settled that the jurisdiction of the High court under section 482 of the CrPC, 1973 can be invoked only in rarest of rare cases. Regarding the right to speedy trial, the same is an inalienable right under article 21 of the Constitution of India, as also noticed in paras 16 and 17 (at page 3082) of the Supreme Court judgment in the case of *Pankaj Kumar* (supra). Also in para 17 of the said judgment it has been categorically held that article 21 of the Constitution of India also includes within its ambit the preceding police investigations as well.

Para 16 (at page 3082) of the said judgment in the case of *Pankaj Kumar* (supra) concludes that it is neither advisable, nor feasible, nor judicially permissible to prescribe an outer limit for conclusion of the criminal proceedings, but it has been held that criminal Courts should exercise their powers as provided under the CrPC, 1973 to effectuate the right of speedy trial. However, in appropriate cases jurisdiction of the High Court under section 482 of the CrPC, 1973 or article 226 and 227 of the Constitution of India can be invoked in order to seek appropriate reliefs.

The right to speedy trial even at the police investigation stage as in terms of the law laid down by the Hon'ble Supreme Court of India in the case of *Pankaj Kumar* (supra) if infringed, the aggrieved person in a case would well be justified within his/her rights in invoking the provisions of section 482 of the CrPC, 1973 in order to explore the possibility of getting a direction from the High Court at competent jurisdiction principally asking for the following reliefs:

(a) Forthwith registration of the FIR

(b) Speedy investigation with regard to the police investigation

(c) Entrustment of the investigation of the case to the Central Bureau of Intelligence, or any other police agency so thought to be appropriate in the wisdom of the Hon'ble High Court, other than the police.

(d) Request for day to day trial in the case proceedings before the subordinate court, pursuant to lodging of the FIR.

Now, coming to the option of filing the Writ petition under article 226 of the Constitution of India, with regard to the above-mentioned circumstances.

## 3. CIVIL WRIT PETITION UNDER ARTICLE 226 OF THE INDIAN CONSTITUTION

Article 226 of the Indian Constitution, provides powers to the High Court to issue Writs and orders as are necessary for administrative action and judicial or quasi judicial action. The said article provides as follows:

"226. Power of High Courts to issue certain writs:

(1) Notwithstanding anything in Article 32 every High Court shall have powers, throughout the territories in relation to which it exercise jurisdiction, to issue to any person or authority, including in appropriate cases, any Government, within those territories directions, orders or writs, including writs in the nature of habeas corpus, mandamus, prohibitions, quo warranto and certiorari, or any of them, for the enforcement of any of the rights conferred by Part III and for any other purpose

(2) The power conferred by clause (1) to issue directions, orders or writs to any Government, authority or person may also be exercised by any High Court exercising jurisdiction in relation to the territories within which the cause of action, wholly or in part, arises for the exercise of such power, notwithstanding that the seat of such Government or authority or the residence of such person is not within those territories

(3) Where any party against whom an interim order, whether by way of injunction or stay or in any other manner, is made on, or in any proceedings relating to, a petition under clause (1), without

(a) furnishing to such party copies of such petition and all documents in support of the plea for such interim order; and

(b) giving such party an opportunity of being heard, makes an application to the High Court for the vacation of such order and furnishes a copy of such application to the party in whose favour such order has been made or the counsel of such party, the High Court shall dispose of the application within a period of two weeks from the date on which it is received or from the date on which the copy of such application is so furnished, whichever is later, or where the High Court is closed on the last day of that period, before the expiry of the next day afterwards on which the High Court is open; and if the application is not so disposed of, the interim order shall, on the expiry of that period, or, as the case may be, the expiry of the aid next day, stand vacated

(4) The power conferred on a High Court by this article shall not be in derogation of the power conferred on the Supreme Court by clause (2) of Article 32."

High Courts have been given wide powers under article 226 of the Constitution of India to issue Writs in cases where fundamental rights of any person have been infringed. The High Courts can be approached directly under this provision by the person whose fundamental rights have been infringed.

In cases where the basic right of getting a FIR registered is infringed where a cognizable offence has been committed, the aggrieved person under article 226 can directly approach the High Court for the issuance of Writ of *Mandamus*.

## 4. CASE-LAW ANALYSIS OF JURISDICTION OF THE HIGH COURTS UNDER ARTICLE 226 OF THE CONSTITUTION OF INDIA IN RELATION TO CASES WHERE POLICE INVESTIGATIONS HAVE BEEN UNJUST, UNFAIR AND MALA FIDE

The Hon'ble Supreme Court of India in a number of recent judgments has upheld the right of an aggrieved person to approach the High Court for invoking the provisions of article 226 of the Constitution of India for issuance of a Writ of *mandamus* in cases where investigation by the police authorities has been conducted in a partial and unjust manner. Caselaw now abounds in this area of law.

In the case of *Rubabbudin Sheikh* v. *State of Gujarat*, 2010 (2) SCC 200, the Supreme Court has upheld the inherent powers of High Courts under article 226 of the Constitution of India to interfere in criminal investigations.

The Hon'ble Supreme Court in paras 52, 53 and 54 (at pages 214 and 215) of the above judgment has laid down a factual situation where the investigation of a case can be transferred to the CBI or any specialised agency. The cited paras state as follows:

"52. In *R.S. Sodhi* v. *State of U.P.*, AIR 1994 SC 38 on which reliance was placed by the learned senior counsel appearing for the writ petitioner, this Court observed: (SCC pp. 144-45, para 2)

"2. ....We have perused the events that have taken place since the incidents but we are refraining from entering upon the details thereof lest it may prejudice any party but we think that since the accusations are directed against the local police personnel it would be desirable to entrust the investigation to an independent agency like the Central Bureau of Investigation so that all concerned including the relatives of the deceased may feel assured that an independent agency is looking into the matter and that would lend the final outcome of the investigation credibility. However, faithfully the local police may carry out the investigation, the same will lack credibility since the allegations are against them. It is only with that in mind that we having thought it both advisable and desirable as well as in the interest of justice, to entrust the investigation to the Central Bureau of Investigation. (emphasis supplied)"

This decision clearly helps the writ petitioner for handing over the investigation to the CBI Authorities or any other independent agency.

53. It is an admitted position in the present case that the accusations are directed against the local police personnel in which High Police officials of the State of Gujarat have been made the accused. Therefore, it would be proper for the writ petitioner or even the public to come forward to say that if the investigation carried out by the police personnel of the State of Gujarat is done, the writ petitioner and their family members would be highly prejudiced and the investigation would also not come to an end with proper finding and if investigation is allowed to be carried out by the local police authorities, we feel that all concerned including the relatives of the deceased may feel that investigation was not proper and in that circumstances it would be fit and proper that the writ petitioner and the relatives of the deceased should be assured that an independent agency should look into the matter and that would lend the final outcome of the investigation credibility, however, faithfully the local police may carry out the investigation, particularly when the gross allegations have been made against the high police officials of the State of Gujarat and for which some high police officials have already been taken into custody.

54. It is also well known that when police officials of the State were involved in the crime and in fact they are investigating the case, it would be proper and interest of justice would be better served if the investigation is directed to be carried out by the CBI Authorities, in that case CBI authorities would be an appropriate authority to investigate the case."

Clearly, the Hon'ble Supreme Court has observed a situation where the police authorities of the state are involved in the crime, it would be just and proper in the interest of the justice if the CBI or any other specialised agency is directed to carry out the further investigations.

The Hon'ble Supreme Court further in Para 60 (at page 216) of the said judgment has extended the powers of the High Courts to transfer investigation to CBI even after the charge sheet is submitted to the Court. Para 60 in this regard elaborates as follows:

"60. Therefore, in view of our discussions made hereinabove, it is difficult to accept the contentions of Mr.Rohatgi learned senior counsel appearing for the state of Gujarat that after the charge sheet is submitted in Court in the criminal proceeding it was not open for this court or even for the High Court to direct investigation of the case to be handed over to the CBI or to any independent agency. Therefore, it can safely be concluded that in an appropriate case when the court feels that the investigation by the police authorities is not in the proper direction and in order to do complete justice in the case and as the high police officials are involved in the said crime,

> it was always open to the court to hand over the investigation to the independent agency like CBI. It cannot be said that after the charge sheet is submitted, the court is not empowered, in an appropriate case, to hand over the investigation to an independent agency like CBI."

Further, in paras 73 and 81 (at pages 219 and 221) respectively, the Hon'ble Court has concluded by elaborating upon the operational ambit of the directions for the purpose of investigation that can be passed by the High Courts in such cases in the following terms:

> "73. That apart, from the Action Taken Reports submitted by the State Police Authorities, we also find that the State Police Authorities of the Gujarat had to take help from the other police officials of other States, namely, Andhra Pradesh and Rajasthan. If the investigation is transferred to the CBI Authorities it would be fair and proper that the other State police officials should also help the CBI Authorities in coming to a final conclusion on the allegations made by the writ petitioner and also on the offences alleged to have committed by some of them.
>
> 81. In the present circumstances and in view of the involvement of the police officials of the State in this crime, we cannot shut our eyes and direct the State Police authorities to continue with the investigation and the charge sheet and for a proper and fair investigation, we also feel that the CBI should be requested to take up the investigation and submit a report in this Court within six months from the date of handing over a copy of this judgment and the records relating to this crime to them."

The Hon'ble Supreme Court in the above-mentioned paras has provided with the directions that need to be issued in such cases. That in order to draw benefit from the above judgment in *Rubabbudin Sheikh* (supra), it can be averred that in such cases the aggrieved parties can approach the High Courts pleading that the Hon'ble High Court may kindly order the police authorities to assist the CBI authorities in the investigation, so that the investigation can be carried out expeditiously. And further, it can be prayed in the Writ petition that the directions may be issued to the CBI for submitting a report in a fixed amount of time.

Furthermore, in another recent Supreme Court judgment in the case *State of West Bengal* v. *Committee for Protection of Democratic Rights, West Bengal*, (2010) 3 SCC 571, the powers of High Court under article 226 of the Constitution of India were reiterated in relation to upholding the fundamental rights of the citizens of India.

It is very important to refer to the facts and circumstances of the case, as a result of which the initial litigation in the Calcutta High Court, led to filing of an appeal in the Supreme Court of India. The Supreme Court bench at the initial stages of hearing was of the view that the question of law involved in the appeal was of great importance. And, being agitated before the Court quite frequently. Accordingly, the matter was referred to be settled by a larger bench. Ultimately, the issue in the case landed up before a Constitution bench of five Judges. Hence, the present judgment is the culmination of a judgment delivered by the Constitution Bench of the Supreme Court of India.

The background of the above-mentioned judgment is very clear from paras 4, 5 and 6 (at page 580) of the judgment and the same read as follows:

> "4. On 8 January, 2001, Director General of Police, West Bengal directed the C.I.D. to take over the investigations in the case. A writ petition under Article 226 of the Constitution was filed in the High Court of Judicature at Calcutta by the Committee for Protection of Democratic Rights, West Bengal, in public interest, inter alia, alleging that although in the said incident 11 persons had died on 4th January, 2001 and more than three months had elapsed since the incident had taken place yet except two persons, no other person named in the FIR, had been arrested; no serious attempt had been made to get the victims identified and so far the police had not been able to come to a definite conclusion whether missing persons were dead or alive. It was alleged that since the police administration in the State was under the influence of the ruling party which was trying to hide the incident to save its image, the investigations in the incident may be handed over to the CBI, an independent agency.
>
> 5. Upon consideration of the affidavit filed in opposition by the State Government, the High Court felt that in the background of the case it had strong reservations about the impartiality and fairness in the investigation by the State police because of the political fallout, therefore, no useful purpose would be served in continuing with the investigation by the State Investigating Agency. Moreover, even if the investigation was conducted fairly and truthfully by the State police, it would still be viewed with suspicion because of the allegation that all the assailants were members of the ruling party. Having regard to all these circumstances, the High Court deemed it appropriate to hand over the investigation into the said incident to the CBI.
>
> 6. Aggrieved by the order passed by the High Court, the State of West Bengal filed a petition for special leave to appeal before this Court. On 3rd September, 2001 leave was granted. When the matter came up for hearing before a two-Judge Bench on 8th November, 2006, taking note of the contentions urged by learned counsel for the parties and the orders passed by this Court in *The Management of Advance Insurance Co. Ltd.* v. *Shri Gurudasmal*, (1970) 1 SCC 633 and *Kazi Lhendup Dorji* v. *Central Bureau of Investigation*, 1994 Supp (2) SCC 116, the Bench was of the opinion that the question of law involved in the appeals was of great public importance and was coming before the courts frequently and, therefore, it was necessary that the issue be settled by a larger Bench. Accordingly, the Bench directed that the papers of the case be placed before the Hon'ble Chief Justice of India for passing appropriate orders for placing the matter before a larger Bench. When the matter came up before a three-Judge Bench, headed by the Hon'ble Chief Justice of India, on 29th August, 2008, this batch of cases was directed to be listed before a Constitution Bench. This is how these matters have been placed before us."

Clearly, the fact that no arrest was made even after 3 months of filing of FIR and no serious attempts were made by the police authorities in solving the case, the High Court doubted as to whether the said investigation was partial and just at all and found it to be a suitable case for transferring the investigation to the CBI.

The Supreme Court in para 68 (at pages 600 to 602) in the case of *State of West Bengal* (supra), has laid down conclusions elaborating upon article 21 of the Constitution of India and the Constitutional scheme and the jurisdiction conferred on the Supreme Court under article 32 of the Constitution of India and on the High Courts under article 226 of the Constitution, emphasising that the power of judicial review is an integral part of the basic structure of the Constitution. The said conclusions read as follows:

> "68. Thus, having examined the rival contentions in the context of the Constitutional Scheme, we conclude as follows:
>
> (i) The fundamental rights, enshrined in Part III of the Constitution, are inherent and cannot be extinguished by any Constitutional or Statutory provision. Any law that abrogates or abridges such rights would be violative of the basic structure doctrine. The actual effect and impact of the law on the rights guaranteed under Part III has to be taken into account in determining whether or not it destroys the basic structure.
>
> (ii) Article 21 of the Constitution in its broad perspective seeks to protect the persons of their lives and personal liberties except according to the procedure established by law.
>
> The said Article in its broad application not only takes within its fold enforcement of the rights of an accused but also the rights of the victim. The State has a duty to enforce the human rights of a citizen providing for fair and impartial investigation against any person accused of commission of a cognizable offence, which may include its own officers. In certain situations even a witness to the crime may seek for and shall be granted protection by the State.
>
> (iii) In view of the constitutional scheme and the jurisdiction conferred on this Court under Article 32 and on the High Courts under Article 226 of the Constitution the power of judicial review being an integral part of the basic structure of the Constitution, no Act of Parliament can exclude or curtail the powers of the Constitutional Courts with regard to the enforcement of fundamental rights. As a matter of fact, such a power is essential to give practicable content to the objectives of the Constitution embodied in Part III and other parts of the Constitution. Moreover, in a federal constitution, the distribution of legislative powers between the Parliament and the State Legislature involves limitation on legislative powers and, therefore, this requires an authority other than the Parliament to ascertain whether such limitations are transgressed. Judicial review acts the final arbiter not only to give effect to the distribution of legislative powers between the Parliament and the State Legislatures, it is also necessary to show any transgression by each entity. Therefore, to borrow the words of Lord Steyn, judicial review is justified by combination of "the principles of separation of powers, rule of law, and the principle of constitutionality and the reach of judicial review".

(iv) If the federal structure is violated by any legislative action, the Constitution takes care to protect the federal structure by ensuring that Courts act as guardians and interpreters of the Constitution and provide remedy under Articles 32 and 226, whenever there is an attempted violation. In the circumstances, any direction by the Supreme Court or the High Court in exercise of power under Article 32 or 226 to uphold the Constitution and maintain the rule of law cannot be termed as violating the federal structure.

(v) Restriction on the Parliament by the Constitution and restriction on the Executive by the Parliament under an enactment, do not amount to restriction on the power of the Judiciary under Article 32 and 226 of the Constitution.

(vi) If in terms of Entry 2 of List II of The Seventh Schedule on the one hand and Entry 2A and Entry 80 of List I on the other, an investigation by another agency is permissible subject to grant of consent by the State concerned, there is no reason as to why, in an exceptional situation, court would be precluded from exercising the same power which the Union could exercise in terms of the provisions of the Statute. In our opinion, exercise of such power by the constitutional courts would not violate the doctrine of separation of powers. In fact, if in such a situation the court fails to grant relief, it would be failing in its constitutional duty.

(vii) When the Special Police Act itself provides that subject to the consent by the State, the CBI can take up investigation in relation to the crime which was otherwise within the jurisdiction of the State Police, the court can also exercise its constitutional power of judicial review and direct the CBI to take up the investigation within the jurisdiction of the State. The power of the High Court under Article 226 of the Constitution cannot be taken away, curtailed or diluted by section 6 of the Special Police Act. Irrespective of there being any statutory provision acting as a restriction on the powers of the Courts, the restriction imposed by section 6 of the Special Police Act on the powers of the Union, cannot be read as restriction on the powers of the Constitutional Courts. Therefore, exercise of power of judicial review by the High Court, in our opinion, would not amount to infringement of either the doctrine of separation of power or the federal structure."

That the above mentioned conclusions laid down by a Constitution bench of the Supreme Court of India, has emphasised the power of judicial review of High Courts and the Supreme Court in India.

In paras 69, 70 and 71 (at page 602) of the above judgment in the *State of West Bengal* (supra), the Hon'ble Supreme Court has elaborated the power and jurisdiction of the High Courts under article 226 of the Constitution of India regarding the protection of fundamental rights of the citizens and the further powers of High Court to transfer the investigation to the CBI in order to protect the fundamental rights, in appropriate cases.

Penultimate paras 69 to 71 of the judgment above in the *State of West Bengal* (supra), conclude as follows:

> "69. In the final analysis, our answer to the question referred is that a direction by the High Court, in exercise of its jurisdiction under Article 226 of the Constitution, to the CBI to investigate a cognizable offence alleged to have been committed within the territory of a State without the consent of that State will neither impinge upon the federal structure of the Constitution nor violate the doctrine of separation of power and shall be valid in law. Being the protectors of civil liberties of the citizens, this Court and the High Courts have not only the power and jurisdiction but also an obligation to protect the fundamental rights, guaranteed by Part III in general and under Article 21 of the Constitution in particular, zealously and vigilantly.
>
> 70. Before parting with the case, we deem it necessary to emphasise that despite wide powers conferred by Articles 32 and 226 of the Constitution, while passing any order, the Courts must bear in mind certain self-imposed limitations on the exercise of these Constitutional powers. The very plenitude of the power under the said Articles requires great caution in its exercise. In so far as the question of issuing a direction to the CBI to conduct investigation in a case is concerned, although no inflexible guidelines can be laid down to decide whether or not such power should be exercised but time and again it has been reiterated that such an order is not to be passed as a matter of routine or merely because a party has levelled some allegations against the local police. This extra-ordinary power must be exercised sparingly, cautiously and in exceptional situations where it becomes necessary to provide credibility and instil confidence in investigations or where the incident may have national and international ramifications or where such an order may be necessary for doing complete justice and enforcing the fundamental rights. Otherwise the CBI would be flooded with a large number of cases and with limited resources, may find it difficult to properly investigate even serious cases and in the process lose its credibility and purpose with unsatisfactory investigations.
>
> 71. In *Secretary, Minor Irrigation & Rural Engineering Services, U.P.* v. *Sahngoo Ram Arya*, this Court had said that an order directing an enquiry by the CBI should be passed only when the High Court, after considering the material on record, comes to a conclusion that such material does disclose a prima facie case calling for an investigation by the CBI or any other similar agency. We respectfully concur with these observations."

Clearly, the Constitution bench of the Supreme Court of India in the above case of *State of West Bengal* (supra), has also upheld the power and jurisdiction of the High Court, upon consideration of material on record in appropriate cases and circumstances to refer an enquiry by a specialised agency like the CBI.

In another case of *Babubhai Jamnadas Patel* v. *State of Gujarat*, (2009) 9 SCC 610, a criminal appeal was filed in the Apex Court directed against the judgment passed by the Gujarat High Court interfering with a criminal investigation under article 226 of the Constitution of India. The Supreme Court in paras 41 and 42 of the said judgment has laid down the exceptional circumstances in which the inherent powers of the High Courts may be invoked necessitating interference in the investigations.

Paras 41 and 42 (at page 618) of the judgment read as under:

> "41. There is little doubt that normally investigation of offences is the function of the investigating agencies and the Courts do not ordinarily interfere with the same. But, at the same time the High Court is vested with such powers, though the same are invoked only in cases where extraordinary facts are involved, necessitating such monitoring by the Courts. In the circumstances, we are only required to see whether such an extraordinary fact situation exists in this case which warranted such a course of action to be adopted by the High Court.
>
> 42. Though Mr. Nariman has in unequivocal terms denied that such extraordinary circumstances exist in this case, which requires monitoring by the High Court, it cannot be denied that the progress of the investigation has been tardy and slow. It is in such circumstances that the investigation had to be handed over to the Assistant Commissioner of Police, `C' Division, Ahmedabad City, with a further direction upon the said Assistant Commissioner of Police to file a progress report of the investigation undertaken in respect of the First Information Report dated 24th December, 2008."

In cases where the progress of investigation has been very slow and tardy to the effect that even after a long lapse of time nothing has been done, it is an extraordinary situation in which the powers of High Court can be invoked under article 226 of the Constitution of India.

Paras 46, 47 and 49 (at page 619) of the said judgment further, dwell on the extraordinary powers of judicial review both of the Hon'ble Supreme Court and the High Courts as hereunder:

> "46. The Courts, and in particular the High Courts and the Supreme Court, are the sentinels of justice and have been vested with extraordinary powers of judicial review and supervision to ensure that the rights of the citizens are duly protected. The Courts have to maintain a constant vigil against the inaction of the authorities in discharging their duties and obligations in the interest of the citizens for whom they exist. This Court, as also the High Courts, have had to issue appropriate writs and directions from time to time to ensure that the authorities performed at least such duties as they were required to perform under the various statutes and orders passed by the administration.
>
> 47. As for example, in the instant case, the High Court had to repeatedly intervene and pass orders to ensure that the investigation was being conducted diligently. Periodical status reports were required in that regard. In fact, the High Court had to direct the Additional Public Prosecutor to ask the Investigating Officer to incorporate the details of the action taken by him from the date of receipt of the letter dated 5th December, 2008. There is little doubt that only after the High Court began monitoring the progress of the

investigation that the Investigating Authorities began to deal with the matter with some amount of seriousness.

49. The various decisions cited by Mr. Dave endorse the view that when required not only could the High Court or this Court direct the Investigating Agencies to conduct the investigation in a fair and unbiased manner, but that in exercise of its powers under Article 142 of the Constitution, the Supreme Court could also issue directions for enforcement of fundamental rights and to ensure that complete justice was done to the parties."

Certainly, the Supreme Court is of the view that where the investigations carried on by the investigating agencies are not conducted in an unbiased, impartial and a fair manner the High Courts as well as the Supreme Court has the power to direct a fair and just investigation.

The Hon'ble Supreme Court in paras 50 and 51 (at page 620) of the judgment above held that in cases where the investigation is believed to have been conducted in a partial, tainted and unjust manner, the Courts can not only direct the agencies to conduct a proper investigation but can also pass orders for monitoring the investigations. Paras 50 and 51 provide as follows:

"50. In fact, in *Kashmere Devi's* case, 1988 SCC 864, this Court had directed the Magistrate to exercise powers under section 173(8) Cr.P.C. to direct the C.B.I. to make a proper and thorough investigation in an independent and objective manner and to submit an additional charge-sheet, if circumstances so required, in accordance with law.

51. There is, therefore, no doubt that in appropriate cases, the Courts may monitor an investigation into an offence when it is satisfied that either the investigation is not being proceeded with or is being influenced by interested persons."

In light of the above Supreme Court judgment, the aggrieved parties in cases can not only pray for an impartial and just investigation, but in addition to the same, they can also pray for monitoring of the investigation by the High Courts, on a rolling basis.

In the case of *Smt. Rajni Vishram Patil* v. *CBI* and others bearing Criminal Petition number 1278 of 2007 decided on 18 July, 2009, the Bombay High Court has elaborated the powers of High courts to issue a Writ of *Mandamus* in cases where investigations have been unjust and unfair. The judgment has been traced from the official website of the Bombay High Court. The Hon'ble Court in paras 20, 22, 35, 39 and 40 have discussed various aspects under consideration with respect to the Writ issued by the High Court under article 226 of the Constitution. The paras read as follows:

"20. The power of judicial review and supervisory control is implicit in the Constitution and there is no express provision excluding this power. Judicial intervention and judicial review in consonance with stated principles is the heart and soul of the constitutional scheme. The right of the police to investigate into a cognizable offence is statutory in nature. But, the plenary power of the police to investigate cases is not unlimited. The power is subject to recognized limitations. The power of the High Court to direct investigation by CBI wherever the investigating agency does not proceed with the case properly is implicit and the High Court can direct investigation by a special investigating agency.

22. Questions (b) and (c) can conveniently be dealt with together as they have a common basis. The petitioner contends that the investigation is tainted, unjust and unfair primarily with the object of protecting influential persons, (Dr.G.N. Patil and Dr. Ulhas Patil). It is also urged that the investigating agency has ignored material evidence or had not made complete and full efforts to detect the true culprits or to unravel the conspiracy in regard to the commission of the offence. In order to bring home this submission, Counsel appearing for the Petitioner, placed stress on the following material irregularities or unfairness apparent on the face of the record in the investigation conducted by CBI:

(c) The Narco Analysis test of the witnesses/accused points towards the fact that there are other persons involved in the commission of the crime which has also been ignored by the investigating agency;

(d) The death of accused Raju Mali while in custody is a suspicious circumstance which demonstrates the unfairness of the investigation....

35. During the course of argument, reliance was also placed on behalf of the Petitioner upon the judgment of the Supreme Court in *M.C. Mehta* v. *Union of India*, AIR 2007 SC 1025 to contend that there has to be a fair investigation and the jurisdiction of the Court to have control over the investigation is beyond any controversy. This proposition of law cannot be disputed and in fact this principle has been followed in this proceeding. But on facts, in that case, the investigation had shown involvement of suspects and all authorities except the Director of Prosecution and Senior Prosecutor had come to the conclusion that the chargesheet as contemplated under the law should be filed. The Supreme Court while referring to various facets of investigation in that case finally directed the CBI to place material evidence collected by the Investigating Team along with the report of the Superintendent of Police before the concerned Special Court Judge, who would decide the matter in accordance with law.

39. We have to keep in mind the caution spelt out by the Supreme Court in *State of Bihar* v. *P.P. Sharma*, 1992 Supp (1) SCC 222, where the Supreme Court said that the inherent jurisdiction of the High Court should not be used for appreciating documents and evidence placed before it as it may amount to a "pretrial" of disputed questions. The appreciation of evidence is the function of the trial court and should normally be left to that court. The Court observed as under:

"68. Another crucial question is whether the High Court, in exercise of its extraordinary jurisdiction under Article 226 of the Constitution, would interfere and quash the chargesheet.

The High Court found that the documents relied on by the respondents/accused were not denied by the State by filing the counter affidavit.

> Therefore, they must be deemed to have been admitted. On that premise the High Court found that no prima facie case was made out on merits and chances of ultimate conviction is "bleak". The court is not passive spectator in the drama of illegalities and injustice. The inherent power of the court under Article 226 of the Constitution of India is permitted to be resorted to. When the documents relied on by the respondents "demonstrate that no prima facie offence is made out on the face value of those materials, then the criminal prosecution should not be allowed to continue and so it should be quashed", and "in such a situation and circumstances the petitioners who had got a right under the Constitution for the protection of their liberty have rightly approached this Court and this Court in these circumstances has no option but to grant the relief by quashing the FIR and both the chargesheets".

Accordingly it quashed them. If this decision is upheld, in my considered view startling and disastrous consequence would ensue. Quashing the chargesheet even before cognizance is taken by a criminal court amounts to "killing a stillborn child". Till the criminal court takes cognizance of the offence there is no criminal proceedings pending. I am not allowing the appeals on the ground that alternative remedies provided by the Code as a bar. It may be relevant in an appropriate case. My view is that entertaining the writ petitions against chargesheet and considering the matter on merit in the guise of prima facie evidence to stand an accused for trial amounts to pretrial of a criminal trial under Article 226 and 227 even before the competent Magistrate or the Sessions Court takes cognizance of the offence. Once the proceedings are entertained the further proceedings get stayed. Expeditious trial of a criminal case is the cardinal rule. Delay feeds injustice to social order and entertaining writ petitions would encourage to delay the trial by diverse tricks. It is not to suggest that under no circumstances a writ petition should be entertained. As was rightly done by Rajasthan High Court in this case at the instance of the directors of the company, wisdom lies to keep the hands back and relegate the accused to pursue the remedy under the Code. In several cases this Court quashed the criminal proceedings on the sole ground of delay. In a case FIR filed in 1954 for violation of the provisions of the Customs Act and Foreign Exchange Regulation Act was challenged in the Allahabad High Court. It was deliberately kept pending in the High Court and in this Court till 1990. The accusation was violation of law by named persons in the name of nonexisting firm. The FIR was quashed in the year 1990 by another Bench of which I was a member solely on the ground of delay. He achieved his object of avoiding punishment. This would show that an accused with a view to delay the trial, resorts to writ proceedings, raises several contentions including one on merit as vehemently persisted by Sri Jain to consider this case on merits and have the proceedings kept pending. The result would be that the people would lose faith in the efficacy of rule of law. Documents relied on by the respondents are subject to proof at the trial and relevancy. If proved to be true and relevant then they may serve as a defence for the respondents at the trial. The State quite legitimately and in my view rightly did not choose to file the counter affidavit denying or contradicting the version of the respondents, in those documents. The commission of offence cannot be decided on affidavit evidence. The High Court has taken short course "in annihilating the still born prosecution" by going into the merits on the plea of proof of prima facie case and adverted to those facts and gave findings on merits. Grossest error of law has been committed by the High Court in making pretrial of a criminal case in exercising its extraordinary jurisdiction under Article 226. After the chargesheet and the evidence placed in support thereof form the base to take or refuse to take cognizance by the competent court. It is not the case that no offence has been made out in the chargesheetsand the first information report. It is, therefore, not necessary to consider all the decisions dealing with the scope of the power of the High Court either under section 482 CrPC or Article 226 of the Constitution to quash the first information report."

40. A similar view was also expressed by the Supreme Court in *Assistant Collector of Central Excise* v. *Jainson Hosiery Industries*, (1979) 4 SCC 22 where the court held that "it is right to point out that the High Courts will be careful to be extremely circumspect in granting these reliefs especially during the pendency of criminal investigation".

The Supreme Court observed that "investigation of a criminal offence is a very sensitive phase". The law has undoubtedly developed thereafter but the jurisdiction under Article 226 has not been so expanded to the extent that the court in exercise of its discretionary power would assume functions which squarely fall within the domain of the court dealing with the trial, unless rare and exceptional circumstances are made out which exfacie show that the investigation is so unfair, unjust or malafide that it could have the effect of completely prejudicing the trial to the disadvantage of the affected parties. There are certain matters which need to be explained by CBI particularly in regard to the statement of accused. Thus, it would be obligatory for CBI to place before the Trial court the entire material which would have effect on a just and fair decision of the case in bringing out the truth."

In essence, the above Bombay High Court ruling in the case of *Smt. Rajni Vishram Patil* (supra) clearly lays down that the Court cannot be a passive spectator to the illegalities and the injustice so perpetrated, which warrant exercise of inherent power of the Court under article 226 of the Constitution of India. The Bombay High Court in the larger interests of the criminal justice system also held in para 45 sub para 1 of the judgment that the exercise of monitoring the investigation and the power vested in the High Court to issue a Writ of continuing *mandamus* would depend on the facts and circumstances of each case. This very para concludes that where the investigation is so very unjust, unfair and is in unlawful exercise of statutory discretion, the Court could interfere and monitor the investigation even after a report under section 173 of the Criminal Procedure Code, 1973 has been filed before the Court of competent jurisdiction.

## 5. WIDER JURISDICTION OF HIGH COURTS UNDER ARTICLE 226 OF THE CONSTITUTION OF INDIA, IN CONTRAST TO JURISDICTION OF THE SUPREME COURT UNDER ARTICLE 32 OF THE CONSTITUTION OF INDIA

Para 57 (at page 595) in the judgment handed down by the Constitution bench of the Supreme Court of India in the case of *State of West Bengal* (supra), amplifies the magnitude of the wider jurisdiction of the High Courts under article 226 in contrast to jurisdiction of the Supreme Court of India under article 32 of the Constitution of India in the following eloquent terms:

> "57. The power of judicial review conferred on the High Court, undoubtedly they are, in a way, wider in scope. The High Courts are authorised under Article 226 of the Constitution, to issue directions, orders or writs to any person or authority, including any government to enforce fundamental rights and, "for any other purpose". It is manifest from the difference in the phraseology of Articles 32 and 226 of the Constitution that there is a marked difference in the nature and purpose of the right conferred by these two Articles. Whereas the right guaranteed by Article 32 can be exercised only for the enforcement of fundamental rights conferred by Part III of the Constitution, the right conferred by Article 226 can be exercised not only for the enforcement of fundamental rights, but "for any other purpose" as well, i.e. for enforcement of any legal right conferred by a Statute etc."

**6. MERITS OF PREFERING A WRIT PETITION UNDER ARTICLE 226 OF THE CONSTITUTION OF INDIA**

Clearly, the above case-law analysis gives a clear position of law and the powers of the High Court under article 226 of the Constitution of India. It is implicit that the powers of police with regard to maintenance of law and order and investigation of cases are wide and should be conducted in an impartial, fair and transparent manner. But, in cases where a crime is committed against the life and liberty of a person and proper investigation is not done by the concerned police officers, it is clearly a violation of a human right recognised under the Constitution of India to seek and implement effective redressal in law.

Article 226 provides wide powers to the High Court in cases where rights under Chapter III of the Constitution of India are infringed and violated. The person approaching the High Court can seek the transfer of investigation by the High Court to a specialised agency with the aim of having a fair and an expeditious trial and investigation in the case.

A complaint or a petition may be presented in such cases alternatively to the State Human Rights Commission as mentioned above but since the High Courts are vested with wider jurisdiction and powers under article 226 of the Constitution of India, it is strongly recommended that the jurisdiction of the High Court is invoked under article 226 of the Constitution of India directly by filing a civil Writ petition in the High Court. Consequently, in addition to the investigation being conducted in a fair and impartial manner under the orders and directions of the High Courts, a fair and expeditious trial is most likely to follow under the directions of the High Court.

**7. REGISTRATION OF FIR IN INDIA AMOUNTS TO ABUSE OF PROCESSOF CRIMINAL LAW WHEN LARGER PART OF THE OFFENCE HAS TAKEN PLACE IN A FOREIGN COUNTRY AND MARRIGE DISSOLVED ABROAD AS WELL. DOWRY AND CRUELTY COMPLAINT LODGED IN INDIA IN SUCH CIRCUMSTANCES TO BE QUASHED.**

**In failed cross-border marriages, especially from the State of Punjab, allegations and counter allegations are common practice to settle scores against the immediate as also extended family members of the warring spouses. Such disputes often culminate even into criminal complaints, even whilst either of the spouses may not be residing in India at all.**

The Punjab and Haryana High Court in the matter of *Bahadur Singh* v. *State of Punjab,* 2010 (2) HLR 411, laid down the law in the following categoric terms. Para 6 (at page 413) of the said judgment provides as follows:

> "Learned counsel for the petitioners has brought into my notice Clause 30 of the divorce petition which states that the parties have entered into the domestic contract and other written or oral financial arrangements. In the written statement filed by respondent No.2/complainant, through her attorney Balbir Singh, it has been admitted that the couple had left for Canada after their marriage on 4.3.2000. It is further stated that ever after the registration of the case, husband and wife are residing in Canada. Two peculiar features of this case cannot be ignored that the demand of dowry was made through phone calls received by the complainant at Canada and that the demand was also made through the husband of complainant who was also residing there. It is stated that once demand was made, the husband used to beat the complainant at Canada. Thus, in the present case, the larger part of offence has taken place in Canada. The marriage between Ajmer Singh and the complainant has already been dissolved at Canada. Thus the impugned FIR is nothing but an abuse of process of criminal law as the complainant through her attorney intends to satisfy her feeling of revenge and vengeance. To arrive at a conclusion that the FIR can be quashed, this Court place reliance upon the judgment rendered in ***Harmanpreet Singh Ahluwalia v. State of Punjab 2009(2) Recent Criminal Reports 956. [2009(3) All India Criminal LR (S.C.) 609].***"

Certainly, the above-mentioned crystallised position of law in such circumstances will be of immense help to relatives and elderly parents of spouses who are trapped for no fault of theirs, in legal wrangles arising out of matrimonial litigation, simply because sometimes it is so pliable to abuse the process of criminal law for settling scores between the families of two estranged/divorced spouses.

## (VI) PROCEDURE AS TO THE LAW OF ARREST

Chapter five of the Code of Criminal Procedure, 1973 deals with the arrest of persons. Section 41 is the main section providing for situations when Police may arrest without warrant. It reads as follows:

> "**When police may arrest without warrant.**—(1) Any police officer may without an order from a Magistrate and without a warrant, arrest any person—
>
> (a) who has been concerned in any cognizable offence, or against whom a reasonable complaint has been made or credible information has been received, or a reasonable suspicion exists, of his having been so concerned; or

(b) who has in his possession without lawful excuse, the burden of proving which excuse shall lie on such person, any implement of house-breaking; or

(c) who has been proclaimed as an offender either under this Code or by order of the State Government; or

(d) in whose possession anything is found which may reasonably be suspected to be stolen property and who may reasonably be suspected of having committed an offence with reference to such thing; or

(e) who obstructs a police officer while in the execution of his duty, or who has escaped, or attempts to escape, from lawful custody; or

(f) who is reasonably suspected of being a deserter from any of the Armed Forces of the Union; or

(g) who has been concerned in, or against whom a reasonable complaint has been made, or credible information has been received, or a reasonable suspicion exists, of his having been concerned in, any act committed at any place out of India which, if committed in India, would have been punishable as an offence, and for which he is, under any law relating to extradition, or otherwise, liable to be apprehended or detained in custody in India; or

(h) who, being a released convict, commits a breach of any rule made under sub-section (5) of section 356; or

(i) for whose arrest any requisition, whether written or oral, has been received from another police officer, provided that the requisition specified the person to be arrested and the offence or other cause for which the arrest is to be made and it appears therefrom that the person might lawfully be arrested without a warrant by the officer who issued the requisition.

(2) any officer in charge of a police station may, in like manner, arrest or cause to be arrested any person, belonging to one or more of the categories of persons specified in section 109 or section 110."

**(VII) OTHER PROVISIONS RELATING TO THE LAW OF ARREST**

Section 42 of the CrPC 1973 specifies yet another situation where a police officer can an arrest a person. According to this section if a person commits an offence in the presence of a police officer or where he has been accused to committing a non-cognizable offence and refuses, on demand being made by a police officer to give his name and residence or gives false name or residence, such person may be arrested but such arrest shall be made only for the limited purpose of ascertaining his name and residence. After such ascertaining, he shall be released on executing a bond with or without sureties, to appear before a magistrate if so required. In case the name and residence of such person cannot be ascertained within 24 hours from the date of arrest or if such person fails to execute a bond as required, he shall be forwarded to the nearest magistrate having jurisdiction.

Section 43 of the CrPC 1973 speaks of a situation where an arrest can be made by a private person and the procedure to be followed on such arrest. Section 44 deals with arrest by a magistrate. Section 45 of the CrPC 1973 protects the members of the Armed Forces from being arrested under section 41 to 44 of the CrPC 1973.

Section 46 of the CrPC 1973 sets out the manner in which the arrest should be made and section 47 of the CrPC 1973 enables the police officer to enter a place if he has reason to believe that the person to be arrested has entered into that place or is within that place.

Section 48 of the CrPC 1973 empowers the police officers to persue the offenders into any place in India beyond their local jurisdiction. Section 49 of the CrPC 1973 however provides that "the person arrested shall not be subjected to more restraint than is necessary to prevent his escape".

Section 50 of the CrPC 1973 (which corresponds to clause (1) of Article 22 of the Constitution) creates an obligation upon the police officer to communicate to the person arrested full particulars of the offence for which he is arrested or other grounds for such arrest forthwith. It also provides that where a person is arrested for a bailable offence without a warrant, the police officer shall inform the person arrested that he is entitled to be released on bail and that he may arrange for sureties on his behalf.

Section 51 of the CrPC 1973 provides for search of arrested person while section 52 of the CrPC 1973 empowers the police officer to seize offensive weapons from the arrested person. Sections 53 and 54 of the CrPC 1973 provide for medical examination of the arrested person at the request of the police officer or at the request of the arrested person, as the case may be.

Section 55 of the CrPC 1973 prescribes the procedure to be followed when a police officer deputes his subordinate to arrest a person without warrant. Section 56 of the CrPC 1973 (which corresponds to clause (2) of Article 22) of the Constitution, provides that the person arrested shall not be kept in the custody of a police officer for a long period than is reasonable and that in any event such period shall not exceed 24 hours exclusive of the time necessary for the journey from the place of arrest to the Magistrate's Court. Of course if the Magistrate permits the police officer to keep such person in his custody, he can do so beyond the period of 24 hours.

Section 58 of the CrPC 1973 casts an obligation upon the officers in charge of police station to report to the specified authorities i.e. the District Magistrate of arrests made without warrant within their jurisdiction and of the fact whether such persons have been admitted to bail or not.

Section 59 of the CrPC 1973 says that no person arrested by a police officer shall be discharged except on his own born or bail or under the special order of the magistrate. Section 60 of the CrPC 1973 which is the last section in the chapter, empowers the person having a lawful custody to pursue and retake the arrested person if he escapes or is rescued from his custody.

## PREVENTIVE ACTION OF THE POLICE: WIDER POWERS OF ARREST UNDER SECTION 151, CRPC 1973

Added to these provisions are the preventive provisions in the Code of Criminal Procedure which empower the police to arrest persons. Section 151 of the

CrPC 1973 empowers a police officer to arrest any person, without orders from a Magistrate and without a warrant, "if it appears to such officer," that such a person is designing to commit a cognisable offence and that the commission of the said offence cannot be prevented otherwise.

**RIGHTS ON ARREST**

- The police officer making the arrest must communicate to the accused person the full particulars of the offence for which the arrest is being made.
- That if the accused person is being arrested for a bailable offence, the accused person has a right to be released on bail by the police authorities itself. It is the duty of the arresting officer to inform the accused person that s/he has a right to be released on bail and that the accused person has the right to arrange sureties for himself/herself.
- The police have the duty to inform at least, one relative or friend of the accused person that s/he has been arrested, and as to where is the said person being kept in custody. That since the accused person is vested with the right of the police authorities having to inform at least one relative/ friend, that s/he has been arrested, in such a situation the arrested person/ foreigner should also vigorously assert before the police authorities, that the various High Commissions at New Delhi or the Consulate of the competent jurisdiction, as they case may be, should well be informed about the arrest of the arrested foreigne national, as they case may be. That if still, the police authorities do not establish contact with the respective High Commission at New Delhi or the Consulate, then the lawyer representing the arrested foreigner before the Magistrate or the Court of competent jurisdiction, should bring the same plea/situation to the attention of the Court, and preferably attempt to seek specific directions in this regard from the Court.
- The accused person has a right to be produced before a Magistrate within 24 hours of being arrested.
- The accused person has a right to obtain legal aid, but it is does not happen that easily in actual practice.
- The accused person has a right to be represented by an advocate in Court.
- The accused person has a right to apply to the Magistrate for bail if the arrested person has been accused of a non-bailable offence. For this purpose, the arrested person should get in touch with someone who will bring him/her an advocate for representation in Court. If the arrested person cannot do so at all, s/he can tell the Magistrate that s/he requires legal aid and or legal assistance.
    - The arrested person has a right to have an advocate present when the police are interrogating the arrested person. This was the law laid down by the Hon'ble Supreme Court of India in the matter of *Nandini Satpathy* v *P.L. Dani*, 1978 (2) SCC 424. But, in actual practice it is very difficult to keep a track of interrogation of arrested persons. Generally, counsels obtain permission or manage to be present at the time of interrogation in certain high profile cases.

- That if an arrested person is made to sign a statement or a confession before the police authorities, s/he can well retract from the said statement or confession by stating that the same was signed/tendered involuntarily under duress and/or coercion. This can well be done before the Magistrate seized of the matter or by a written complaint by the arrested person or his counsel to the higher police authorities.

## RIGHTS PROVIDED SPECIFICALLY FOR ARREST OF WOMEN

- Women and children cannot be arrested after sunset and before sunrise.
- The police officer arresting women has the right to search your person and take into custody any articles that may be found on you. The CrPC 1973 specifically provides that only a woman police officer can search a woman who is being arrested.
- That any medical examination that is conducted will have to be done by a woman medical practitioner, or under her supervision.
- The arrested women have a right to free legal aid. If she cannot afford to engaged an advocate, the Court has the duty to appoint an advocate to defend any such arrested lady.
- Any such arrested lady has to right to be kept in a cell that is meant specifically for women only. The arrested lady cannot be put into a cell where there are male accused as well in custody.

## MISUSE OF POWER OF ARREST

Notwithstanding the safeguards contained in the Code of Criminal Procedure, 1973 and the Constitution of India referred to above, the fact remains that the power of arrest is wrongly and illegally exercised in a large number of cases all over the country. Very often this power is utilised to extort monies and other valuable property or at the instance of an enemy of the person arrested. Even in case of civil disputes, this power is being resorted to on the basis of a false allegation against a party to a civil dispute at the instance of his/her opponent. The vast discretion given by the CrPC 1973 to arrest a person even in the case of a bailable offence (not only where the bailable offence is cognizable but also where it is non-cognizable) and the further power to make preventive arrests (e.g. under section 151 of the CrPC 1973 and the several city police enactments), clothe the police with extraordinary power which can easily be abused.

The most important decision which may be usefully referred to in this regard is the Supreme Court of India decision in the famous case of *D.K. Basu* v. *State of West Bengal,* AIR 1997 SC 610.

Para 36 of the said judgment (at pages 623 and 624) issued the following directions, the same are reproduced hereunder:

"We, therefore, consider it appropriate to issue the following requirements to be followed in all cases of arrest or detention, till legal provisions are made in that behalf, as preventive measures:

1. The police personnel carrying out the arrest and handling the interrogation of the arrestee should bear accurate, visible and clear identification and name tags with their designations. The particulars of

all such police personnel who handle interrogation of the arrestee must be recorded in a register.

2. That the police officer carrying out the arrest of the arrestee shall prepare a memo of arrest at the time of arrest and such memo shall be attested by at least one witness, who may be either a member of the family of the arrestee or a respectable person of the locality from where the arrest is made. It shall also be countersigned by the arrestee and shall contain the time and date of arrest.
3. A person who has been arrested or detained and is being held in custody in a police station or interrogation center or other lock-up, shall be entitled to have one friend or relative or other person known to him or having interest in his welfare being informed, as soon as practicable, that he has been arrested and is being detained at the particular place unless the attesting witness of the memo of arrest is himself such a friend or a relative of the arrestee.
4. The time, place of arrest and venue of custody of an arrestee must be notified by the police where the next friend or relative of the arrestee lives outside the district or town through the Legal Aid Organisation in the District and the police station of the area concerned telegraphically within a period of 8 to 12 hours after the arrest.
5. The person arrested must be made aware of this right to have someone informed of his arrest or detention as soon as he is put under arrest or is detained.
6. An entry must be made in the diary at the place of detention regarding the arrest of the person which shall also disclose the name of the next friend of the person who has been informed of the arrest and the names and particulars of the police officials in whose custody the arrestee is.
7. The arrestee should, where he so requests, be also examined at the time of his arrest and major and minor injuries, if any, present on his/her body, must be recorded at that time. The "Inspection Memo" must be signed both by the arrestee and the police officer effecting the arrest and its copy provided to the arrestee.
8. The arrestee should be subjected to medical examination by a trained doctor every 48 hours during his detention in custody by a doctor on the panel of approved doctors appointed by Director, Health Services of the concerned State or Union Territory, Director, Health Services should prepare such a panel for all Tehsils and Districts as well.
9. Copies of all the documents including the memo of arrest, referred to above, should be sent to the Ilaqa Magistrate for his record.
10. The arrestee may be permitted to meet his lawyer during interrogation, though not throughout the interrogation.
11. A police control room should be provided at all district and State headquarters, where information regarding the arrest and the place of custody of the arrestee shall be communicated by the officer causing the arrest, within

12 hours of effecting the arrest and at the police control room it should be displayed on a conspicuous police board."

That if the arrested person is subjected to torture in police custody, clearly it is a gross violation of basic human rights, and the directions laid down by the Supreme Court of India in the above-mentioned case of *D.K. Basu,* (supra). The issue of torture of the arrested person in police custody should be brought to the notice of the Magistrate or the Court of competent jurisdiction. This should be done by the lawyer representing the arrested foreign national.

There are a large number of significant cases decided by the Supreme Court of India and the various High Courts in India, where compensation has been awarded by the Courts for illegal detention, and deaths of detenues, which have taken in police custody.

**ARREST OF FUGITIVE CRIMINAL NOT MECHANICAL AND AUTOMATIC IN THE INDIAN JURISDICTION WHERE A RED CORNER NOTICE HAS BEEN ISSUED BY INTERPOL: POINT OF LAW - INTERPOL NOTICES DO NOT CONSTITUTE AUTOMATIC INTERNATIONAL ARREST WARRANTS AND MATRIMONIAL DISPUTES DO NOT CONSTITUTE AN EXTRADITABLE OFFENCE**

The Hon'ble Supreme Court judgment in the case of *Bhavesh Jayanti Lakhani* v. *State of Maharashtra,* 2009 (9) SCC 551, has laid down the guidelines for arrest of a fugitive criminal where a red corner notice has been issued against him by the Interpol. The present case is a criminal appeal against the order of the Bombay High Court, which was of the opinion that in cases where a red corner notice has been issued against a criminal having directions for his arrest it should not be interfered with in any circumstances.

The three issues that came up for consideration before the Apex Court in the above-mentioned case have been summed-up in para 31 (at page 568) of the judgment as follows:

> "31. In view of the rival contentions of the parties, the following questions which arise for our consideration are:
>
> (i) Whether having regard to the concept of sovereignty the Executive Government of India can enforce a warrant passed by the Probate and Family Court, Massachusetts?
>
> (ii) Having regard to the provisions contained in sections 44A and 13 of the Code of Civil Procedure, is the foreign judgment enforceable in India?
>
> (iii) Whether the CBI established under the DPSE Act has the authority to deal with Interpol notices?"

In the above-mentioned case, the appellant married the respondent no. 6 on 6 April, 2002 at Mumbai. They moved to California on 19 April, 2002 and stayed there till 2005. Out of the said wedlock, a daughter Eesha was born on 26 April, 2003. Marital life of the appellant and the respondent no. 6 was however not happy. On or about 9 May, 2005 an application before the Probate and Family Court of Massachusetts for grant of divorce was filed by respondent no. 6. In the said proceeding, she also sought for orders of custody of her daughter. The Probate and Family Court, Massachusetts passed an order of temporary custody of the child, restraint and abuse prevention *ex parte* in favour of the respondent No.6 and against the appellant on 10 May, 2005. Service of the said order is said to have been effected on the appellant on 20 May, 2005. Admittedly, the appellant came to India with the child on 15 April, 2006 in violation of the Court custody orders. The contention of the appellant is that despite the initial marital discord, the parties started living together. It was decided that he should return to India with the child wherefor even a written consent was given by the respondent no. 6.

After, the appellant came to India with his daughter, the Interpol issued a yellow or watch notice on 13 June, 2007 in respect of Eesha, minor daughter of the respondent no. 6. It, however, issued a red or detain and arrest notice on 21 June, 2007 to locate and arrest the appellant. Pursuant thereto or in furtherance thereof, the Assistant Director, National Crimes Bureau (NCB) forwarded a letter dated 4 January, 2008 received from the U.S. Embassy (Department of Justice) to the Mumbai Police to locate the appellant and his daughter on 14 January, 2008. Appellant was located by Mumbai Police on 3 May, 2008 and the said information was passed on to the U.S. Embassy on 9 May, 2008.

Before, dealing with the procedure that has to be followed by the police authorities and the Courts in the requested state, the Apex Court has highlighted the consequences that follow the issuance of a red corner notice. The Hon'ble Supreme Court in the above mentioned judgment in paras 35 and 36 (on page 569) has elaborated the consequences of a red corner notice in the following terms:

> "35. A Red Corner Notice has large number of consequences, some of which are:
>
> (i) The requesting country may make a deportation request.
>
> (ii) The law enforcement agency in India is required to "take follow up action with regard to the arrest of a fugitive criminal".
>
> (iii) The information emanating from the red corner notice is required to be distributed all over the Interpol website.
>
> (iv) The requesting Embassy would instruct the CBI to carry out its instructions for surveillance, arrest and detention.
>
> (v) The requesting Embassy can even contact the Indian police directly.
>
> (vi) Thereafter extradition proceedings may follow.
>
> Indisputably, therefore, when a proceeding under the Act is initiated, the civil liberty of a person would be directly affected. The provisions of the Act, therefore, should be strictly construed. Any request for extradition therefore must undergo the strict scrutiny test. Extradition offence keeping in view its definition in section 2(c) of the Act in relation to a treaty State must be one provided for the extradition treaty therewith. Application of the provisions of the Act, thus, in a case of this nature must be held to be imperative in character.
>
> 36. We have noticed hereinbefore that for the purpose of applying the provisions of the Act, existence of a treaty between the requesting State and the requested State plays an important role. It makes a distinction between

an extraditable offence and other offences including political offences subject of course to the condition that offences relating to illegal tax are not to be treated to be a political offence. Sections 4-18 provides for the mode and manner in which a request for extradition of a person is required to be made by the concerned country. The requirements are specific in nature and are required to be accompanied by a large number of documents."

Further, the Supreme Court in paras 39 to 42 (at pages 570 and 571) of the said judgment, has analysed the provisions of law of arrest of a person, against whom a red corner notice has been issued, the conditions which should necessarily be fulfilled before making such an arrest and the procedure to be followed in cases where an arrest is to be made. Paras 39 to 42 of the said judgment in this regard read as under:

> "39. It is beyond any doubt or dispute that no request for extradition has been received by the Government of India. It could act only when a request is received. It is accepted at the Bar that Red Corner Notice by itself cannot be a basis of arrest or transfer of an Indian citizen to a foreign jurisdiction. There is furthermore no dispute that the Act cannot be bypassed in red corner cases concerning Indian citizens. Hence the Extradition Treaty is subject to the provisions of the Act.
>
> 40. It also stands admitted that appellant being an Indian citizen is entitled to enforcement of his fundamental rights.
>
> 41. The legal position that a person cannot be arrested without any authority of law again is not denied or disputed. Thus, the arrest of a person must be effected in terms of the provisions of the Act. A person wanted for an offence in a foreign jurisdiction may be arrested on fulfillment of the following conditions:
>
> (i) That the offence should be counted as one by Indian Law as well, and
>
> (ii) The person must be liable to be arrested in India - either under any law relating to extradition, or otherwise.
>
> Such an arrest can be effected only pursuant to a warrant issued by the Magistrate in view of sections 6, 16 and 34B of the Act or an arrest warrant issued by a foreign country and endorsed by the Central Government under section 15 of the Act. It is also not in doubt or dispute that in a case where there is no treaty, it is only the Magistrate who issues the warrant for arrest subject of course to the condition that the Central Government had ordered a Magisterial Inquiry in terms of section 5 of the Act. Such an order of arrest, emanating from a Treaty-State, is also permissible under a 'Provisional Warrant' issued by a Magistrate in exercise of its power under section 16 of the Act, upon information that the fugitive should be apprehended subject to the condition that the detention thereunder may continue only for the time requisite for obtaining an endorsed warrant from the Central Government.
>
> 42. All arrested persons are required to be immediately produced before a Magistrate whereupon it would have power to grant bail. Section 34B

provides that the person so arrested would have to be released on bail after a period of 60 days. If actual request for extradition is required within the said period having regard to section 41(g) of the Code of Criminal Procedure, the Central Government cannot direct or effect an urgent arrest in anticipation of an extradition request without obtaining a warrant issued by a Magistrate. Article 12 provides that provisions of provisional arrest according to which in a case of urgency, the Contracting State may request the provisional arrest of the person sought pending presentation of the request for extradition. It also provides that the facilities of International Criminal Police Organization (Interpol) may be used to transmit such a request. However, when a request for provisional arrest in terms of Article 12 is communicated, it must satisfy the requirement of section 34B of the Act. Such request from a foreign country must be accompanied by the requisite documents and not a communication from Interpol alone."

Certainly, the provisions in the above-mentioned paras indicate that the Supreme Court of India in its judgment has categorically held that in the absence of a specific request for extradition, no criminal extraditable offence can be made out in cases where a red corner notice has been issued by Interpol.

The Court has further in paras 46 and 47 (at page 571) of the said judgment, has put on a pedestal the supremacy of domestic law over treaty arrangements between member-states. Paras 46 and 47 of the judgment read as follows:

> "46. The Act as also the treaties entered into by and between India and foreign countries are admittedly subject to our municipal law. Enforcement of a treaty is in the hands of the Executive. But such enforcement must conform to the domestic law of the country. Whenever, it is well known, a conflict arises between a treaty and the domestic law or a municipal law, the latter shall prevail.
>
> 47. It furthermore stands admitted that matrimonial dispute as such does not constitute an extraditable offence and, thus, no effect could be given thereto. However, whether this case concerns an extraditable offence or not has to be determined by the Magistrate under the Act."

Clearly, the treaties are subject to the municipal laws of a country and the State in taking decisions with regard to such notices issued by the Interpol, should take into consideration the supremacy of municipal law.

Paras 58 and 59 (at page 574) have very clearly summed-up the organizational structure of Interpol notices in the following terms:

> "58. The organizational system of issuing International notices forms the backbone of its functioning. The Member countries in terms of notices share critical crime related information. They concern individuals wanted for serious crimes, missing persons, unidentified bodies etc. Such notices contain comprehensive identity particulars of the individuals concerned including the physical description, fingerprinting, occupation and all other relevant information including the offence with which the person has been charged, reference to the law under which the charge was made or the conviction was obtained etc. The notices issued by the Interpol are of six

types - Red Notice ; Yellow Notice ; Blue Notice; Green Notice ; Black Notice and Orange Notice. It also contemplates Interpol-United Nations Special Notice. We are concerned herein only with Red and Yellow Notices.

59. A red corner notice is issued to seek the provisional arrest of a wanted person. However, it by itself does not have the effect of warrant of arrest. It is issued for persons, against whom a national or international court has issued a warrant of arrest. It is solely a request of the issuing entity to provisionally or finally arrest the wanted person for extradition. A Yellow notice, however, is issued for finding a missing person or to identify people who are not capable of identifying themselves. It is an "International Missing Person Notice". It is issued specially to locate minors."

Further, the Supreme Court has emphasised upon the purpose and the binding nature of a red corner notice issued by the Interpol in order to have a clear answer to the facts and circumstances of the case in hand. The Hon'ble Court "in paras 63 and 64 (at page 575)" of the judgment has discussed the binding nature of the Interpol notices in the following terms:

"63. The notices issued by Interpol are not considered as administrative decisions on individual cases with transnational effect. They are not construed as an "international administrative act." They lack a character of regulation. They do not constitute an international arrest warrant and they are not in any other form binding the individuals concerned legally. They, however, gain de facto with special relevance to the Human Rights through multiplication of its recipients.

64. In fact Interpol's "red notices" often function as de facto international arrest warrants and countries issue warrants immediately upon receipt of such a notice. However, they do so with the understanding that a request for extradition with supporting evidence will follow the red notice, without delay. The suspect must then go through the standard extradition process. The bottom line is that "warrants to arrest suspects must have legal authority in the jurisdiction where the suspect is found" and Interpol red notices do not have such authority. They are primarily a means of facilitating communication between police agencies and the success of the Interpol system still depends entirely upon voluntary cooperation. They, however, do not entirely lack external effects."

As elaborated in the above-mentioned paras, it can be clearly seen that an Interpol notice for arrest of a fugitive criminal, only when followed by a request for extradition has a legal binding on the criminal and the requested State. However, the issuance of a red corner notice if not supported by a demand for extradition then in such cases the notice is not binding on the accused or any other person concerned.

The Hon'ble Supreme Court has very lucidly and eloquently in paras 112 to 114 (at pages 587 and 588)% of the judgment, has summed up the position of law regarding enforcement of Interpol notices in the Indian jurisdiction, whilst holding the supremacy of Indian domestic law in the following terms:

"112. We have already held above that the Municipal Laws of a country reign supreme in matters of Extradition. It is thus for the State concerned to take a decision in regard to such Notices, keeping in view the Municipal Laws of the country. The High Court was, therefore, in our opinion, clearly wrong in holding that a Red Corner Notice should not be tinkered with. When a person complains of a violation of his Fundamental Right and/or otherwise of his fundamental right he is entitled to the right of judicial review. It ought not to be forgotten here that the dispute between the Appellant and the Respondent No. 6, being essentially a Matrimonial dispute, is a private dispute and no criminal extraditable offence can be made out of the same, in the absence of a specific request for extradition. The High Court, thus, in our opinion, committed a serious error in so far as it failed to take into consideration the provisions of the Act, in the absence of any request having being made by the Govt. of USA to the Executive Government of the Union of India or any authorization made by the latter on its behalf.

113. A fundamental Right of a citizen whenever infringes, the High Courts having regard to their extraordinary power under Article 226 of the Constitution of India as also keeping in view that access to justice is a human right would not turn them away only because a Red Corner Notice was issued. The Superior Courts in criminal cases, thus are entitled to go into the manner in which such Red Corner Notice, if any, is sought to be enforced and/or whether the local police is threatening a citizen of India with arrest although they are not entitled to do so except in terms of the provisions Act as and when applicable.

114. Furthermore, if a violation of any order passed by a civil court is made the ground for issuance of a Red Corner Notice, indisputably, the court will enquire as to whether the same has undergone the tests laid down under sections 13 and 44A of the Code of Civil Procedure."

It is clear from the above analysis given by the Hon'ble Supreme Court of India that simply because a red corner notice has been issued by the Interpol, it will not have any binding effect on the fugitive criminal till the time it is followed by a demand of extradition of the said criminal by the requesting state to the requested state.

The Hon'ble Apex Court has also taken into account compliance of the necessary provisions of the Indian Code of Civil Procedure, 1908 pertaining to enforcement of foreign Court orders and judgment in the Indian jurisdiction.

Finally, the Hon'ble Apex Court granted relief to the appellant father in para 115 of the judgment in the following terms:

"115. As regards the question of custody, we have, however noticed, hereinabove that although the family court at Bombay for all intent and purposes relying on or on the basis of the order passed by the Massachusetts Court directed custody of the girl in favour of her mother, the Bombay High Court has stayed the operation thereof. The Appellant therefore, must be held to be in lawful custody of his daughter unless any other or further order is passed by a court of competent jurisdiction."

## LARGE PERCENTAGE OF UNDER TRIAL PRISONERS IN JAILS

The percentage of under-trial prisoners in jails is unusually large. The reasons for this may be the delays in concluding the trials in criminal Courts, the rigidity of the present law of bail and in some cases, the inability of the accused to furnish bail. The Supreme Court of India directed in two cases *'Common Cause, A Registered Society'* v. *UOI*, (1996) 4 SCC 33 and *'Common Cause, A Registered Society'* v. *UOI*, (1996) 6 SCC 775 that under-trial prisoners whose cases have been pending beyond a particular period should be enlarged on bail or on personal bond. These directions applied not only to cases pending on the dates of those orders but were also effective prospectively.

Many of the under-trial prisoners who were granted bail are unable to avail of the said facility because of their inability to furnish sureties or to comply with the conditions for release.

The number of arrests for petty offences is substantial, if not more than the arrests made for serious offences.

## (VIII) LAW AND PROCEDURE RELATING TO GRANT OF BAIL

When the accused is arrested, the police will keep him in police custody for investigation. The police is duty bound by the law to produce the accused before the Magistrate within twenty-four hours of his arrest. If the investigation has not been completed within twenty-four hours, the police officer is supposed to present the accused before the Court and ask the Court to extend the detention of the said accused person. That usually at this point of time , the accused person will ask to be released on bail. It is important to oppose the bail application and ask the Magistrate to remand the accused to police custody if the investigation is not complete.

## WHAT WILL THE COURT CONSIDER ON A BAIL APPLICATION

That under section 437 of the CrPC 1973, the Court shall consider the following grounds:—

- **The nature of the accusation:** if the offence is serious, there are less chances of the accused being granted bail.
- **The quality and quantity of the evidence gathered against the accused**. If the evidence shows that the offence has been committed, there are less chances of the accused being granted bail.
- The **likelihood of the accused fleeing from justice or s/he is likely to abscond from India,** if s/he is released at all.
- If the **offence is one that has a punishment of death penalty or life imprisonment**, the Court cannot release the accused on bail, except if the accused is below the age of 16, is sick, infirm, or a woman, depending on the facts and circumstances of the case.
- If the **accused is likely to manipulate, threaten or intimidate witnesses or destroy evidence** while out on bail, the prosecution should provide details of how s/he may do so to the Magistrate adjudicating upon the said bail application.

## WHAT HAPPENS AFTER AN APPLICATION FOR BAIL IS MADE

That after an application for bail has been made, the Magistrate may release the accused person on certain conditions and ask for financial security from the accused person to ensure that s/he co-operates in the investigation or reject the bail application and remand the accused to either police custody or judicial custody.

The Magistrate can also reject the bail application and the remand the accused person either to police or judicial custody.

In very serious cases where evidence is still to be collected, the Magistrate will remand the accused to police custody.

If the Magistrate decides to release the accused on a bail bond, the accused person can ask for the inclusion of various conditions. This is called conditional bail. If the accused does not obey the stipulated conditions in the bail order, the bail will be automatically stand cancelled and a warrant of arrest will be passed against him/her, for violating the conditions stipulated in the bail bond.

The Conditional bail may be restricted to certain period of time. For example, the Magistrate may say that the bail will last for three months, after which the accused and the complainant will be asked to appear before the Court and explain the present situation, for example, in case of domestic violence whether the accused has stopped the violence against the complainant, etc. At this point, the Magistrate will reconsider the bail application and may cancel, extend, confirm or modify the bail.

## (IX) ANTICIPATORY BAIL

## HOW DO YOU OPPOSE AN APPLICATION FOR ANTICIPATORY BAIL

The application for anticipatory bail is usually made in the morning session of the Court and is heard in the afternoon session. The relevant provision is section 438 of the CrPC 1973.

The affected person of party can either explain the facts of his/her case to the Public Prosecutor in charge of that Court and ask her/him to oppose the application, or the affected/aggrieved person should appear before the Court himself/herself and explain the facts of the case. Anticipatory bail is usually awarded for a limited period of time; and the affected/aggrieved person can always oppose its extension.

When the affected/aggrieved person appears before the Court, s/he may contest that if anticipatory bail is granted,

- There is a threat to the safety of the affected/aggrieved person.
- The accused may tamper with evidence or intimidate witnesses.
- The accused will interfere or try to evade the investigation.

That the anticipatory bail is usually awarded for a limited period of time, and the affected/aggrieved person can always oppose the extension of the same.

That if the Court decides to grant anticipatory bail, it can include in the order certain conditions to ensure that

- The accused makes himself available for investigation of the offence.
- The accused will not try and influence any of the potential witnesses.
- The accused does not leave the country.

The affected/aggrieved person can ask the Court to include other conditions that are necessary to the safety of the affected/aggrieved person.

## (X) CONCLUSION

Since, issues regarding the law of arrest affect the freedom and human rights of any individual, the same have added significance for a person whether he is resident in India or abroad. The legal issues in this area of law which are of significant concern to the NRI community have been highlighted in the present chapter.

# SUBJECT INDEX

• • •

"The vibrant NRI community worldwide will welcome this timely survey of legal issues concerning non-resident Indians. This is the third volume that the Authors have devoted to this subject. They deserve to be commended for their efforts and for the wide range of research that they offer to the general public and to the specialised reader alike."

***Giacomo Sanfelice***

*Ambassador of Italy in India*